Philosophy of Law

Works of John Finnis available from
Oxford University Press

Reason in Action
Collected Essays: Volume I

Intention and Identity
Collected Essays: Volume II

Human Rights and Common Good
Collected Essays: Volume III

Philosophy of Law
Collected Essays: Volume IV

Religion and Public Reasons
Collected Essays: Volume V

Natural Law and Natural Rights
Second Edition

Aquinas
Moral, Political, and Legal Theory

Nuclear Deterrence, Morality and Realism
with Joseph Boyle and Germain Grisez

PHILOSOPHY OF LAW

Collected Essays: Volume IV

John Finnis

OXFORD
UNIVERSITY PRESS

OXFORD
UNIVERSITY PRESS

Great Clarendon Street, Oxford OX2 6DP

Oxford University Press is a department of the University of Oxford.
It furthers the University's objective of excellence in research, scholarship,
and education by publishing worldwide in

Oxford New York

Auckland Cape Town Dar es Salaam Hong Kong Karachi
Kuala Lumpur Madrid Melbourne Mexico City Nairobi
New Delhi Shanghai Taipei Toronto

With offices in

Argentina Austria Brazil Chile Czech Republic France Greece
Guatemala Hungary Italy Japan Poland Portugal Singapore
South Korea Switzerland Thailand Turkey Ukraine Vietnam

Oxford is a registered trade mark of Oxford University Press
in the UK and in certain other countries

Published in the United States
by Oxford University Press Inc., New York

First published 2011

British Library Cataloguing in Publication Data
Data available

Library of Congress Cataloging in Publication Data
Data available

Typeset by Newgen Imaging Systems (P) Ltd, Chennai, India
Printed in Great Britain
on acid-free paper by
CPI Antony Rowe

ISBN 978-0-19-958008-8

1 3 5 7 9 10 8 6 4 2

PREFACE

The earliest of the essays collected in these five volumes dates from 1967, the latest from 2010. The chronological Bibliography of my publications, near the end of each volume, shows how the collected essays are distributed across the volumes. But each volume also contains some essays previously unpublished.

Many of the essays appear with new titles. When the change is substantial, the original published title is noted at the beginning of the essay; the original can of course always also be found in the Bibliography.

Revision of previously published work has been restricted to clarification. Where there seems need for substantive qualification or retractation, I have said so in an endnote to the essay or, occasionally, in a bracketed footnote. Unless the context otherwise indicates, square brackets signify an insertion made for this Collection. Endnotes to particular essays have also been used for some updating, especially of relevant law. In general, each essay speaks from the time of its writing, though the dates given in the Table of Contents are dates of publication (where applicable) not composition—which sometimes was one or two years earlier.

I have tried to group the selected essays by theme, both across and within the volumes. But there is a good deal of overlapping, and something of each volume's theme will be found in each of the other volumes. The Index, which like the Bibliography (but not the 'Other Works Cited') is common to all volumes, gives some further indication of this, though it aspires to completeness only as to names of persons. Each volume's own Introduction serves to amplify and explain that volume's title, and the bearing of its essays on that theme.

CONTENTS

LIST OF ABBREVIATIONS

AJJ	American Journal of Jurisprudence
AL	Joseph Raz, *The Authority of Law: Essays on Law and Morality* (OUP, 1979)
Aquinas	1998d: John Finnis, *Aquinas: Moral, Political and Legal Theory* (OUP)
CL	H.L.A. Hart, *The Concept of Law* (1961; 2nd edn, OUP, 1994)
CLR	Commonwealth Law Reports (of decisions of the High Court of Australia)
CLS	Joseph Raz, *The Concept of a Legal System* (1970; 2nd edn with a new Postscript, OUP, 1980)
CUP	Cambridge: Cambridge University Press
FoE	1983b: John Finnis, *Fundamentals of Ethics* (OUP; Washington, DC: Georgetown University Press)
GTLS	Hans Kelsen, *General Theory of Law and State* (1945)
HUP	Cambridge, Mass.: Harvard University Press
In Eth.	Aquinas, *Sententia Libri Ethicorum* [Commentary on *NE*] (ed. Gauthier) (1969)
In Pol.	Aquinas, *Sententia Libri Politicorum* [Commentary on *Pol.* I to III.5] (ed. Gauthier) (1971)
LJ	Adam Smith, *Lectures on Jurisprudence* (eds R. Meek, D.D. Raphael, and P. Stein) (OUP, 1978)
LQR	Law Quarterly Review
LSLR	Julius Stone, *Legal System and Lawyers' Reasonings* (1964)
MA	1991c: John Finnis, *Moral Absolutes: Tradition, Revision, and Truth* (Catholic University of America Press)
NDMR	1987g: John Finnis, Joseph Boyle, and Germain Grisez, *Nuclear Deterrence, Morality and Realism* (OUP)
NE	Aristotle, *Nicomachean Ethics*
NLNR	1980a: John Finnis, *Natural Law and Natural Rights* (2nd edn, OUP, 2011)
OUP	Oxford: Oxford University Press (including Clarendon Press)

PFL	Julius Stone, *Province and Function of Law* (1946)
Pol.	Aristotle, *Politics*
Sent.	Aquinas, *Scriptum super Libros Sententiarum Petri Lombardiensis* [Commentary on the Sentences [Opinions or Positions of the Church Fathers] of Peter Lombard] (c. 1255)
ST	Aquinas, *Summa Theologiae* [A Summary of Theology] (c. 1265–73)
TMS	Adam Smith, *The Theory of Moral Sentiments* [1759] (eds D.D. Raphael and A.L. Macfie) (OUP, 1976)
TRS	Ronald Dworkin, *Taking Rights Seriously* (1977 rev edn with Reply to Critics) (HUP; London: Duckworth, 1978)

THE COVER PICTURE

Government Hut, Adelaide; painted by Martha Berkeley in Adelaide c. 1839.†

Built in 1837 for the first Governor, Government Hut was made of earth, wood, and thatch, and burned down by a deranged colonist in 1841. Soon after this picture was painted, however, construction of the substantial Government House which stands to this day had begun, a few score yards from the left-hand (eastern) end of the Hut as Berkeley depicted it from a spot near the northern end of the present Parliament House of South Australia. She shows us the Hut from the rear, and above it the flag denoting imperial royal authority. The flagpole was at the Hut's front entrance, which faced Adelaide's newly surveyed and then largely forested square mile from the mid-point of its northern edge.

In the Note overleaf are the operative provisions of the Act of Parliament authorizing the colony's establishment and governance, and of the royal Letters Patent defining the province of South Australia and stipulating what would be its government's duties in relation to the peoples already living there. The new administration's first legislative acts, promulgated six days after disembarkation near Adelaide on 28 December 1836, established magistrates' courts and defined the qualifications of jurors; on the same January day, in London, Letters Patent provided for a Supreme Court of South Australia, endowed with all the common law and probate jurisdiction of the courts of Westminster. This began sitting in May 1837, under the provisions of a new ordinance of the Governor in Council mirroring those Letters Patent.

The first governorship lasted only about eighteen months. London had divided executive power in the colony between the Governor and the Resident Commissioner of Public Lands. But these public officers quarrelled so fiercely that in February 1837 the Resident Magistrates' Court ordered them to keep the peace towards each other. By the time Government Hut was fully completed and the picture painted, the first Governor had been dismissed and a new Governor was in place, vested with all the formerly divided executive powers.

NOTE

† *Instituting a new political community by law*...The South Australia Act 1834, a statute of the United Kingdom Parliament, authorized the British Government (His Majesty in Council) to

> empower any one or more persons resident...to make ordain and establish all such laws institutions or ordinances and to constitute such courts, and appoint such officers...and to impose and levy such rates, duties, and taxes as may be necessary for the peace order and good government of His Majesty's subjects and others within the said province...

(subject to annulment by the authorities in London). The statute presupposes the constitutional doctrine, first clearly enunciated by Coke CJ in *The Case of Proclamations* (1610), that legal rights cannot be adversely affected, or taxes imposed, except by or under the authority of Parliament. The authority conferred by the above provision was first exercised by Letters Patent of 19 February 1836, whose two operative provisions (i) defined the colony's geographical limits and (ii) provided that 'nothing in these our Letters Patent contained shall affect or be construed to affect the rights of any Aboriginal Natives of the said Province to the actual occupation or enjoyment in their own Persons or in the Persons of their Descendants of any Lands therein now actually occupied or enjoyed by such Natives'. When the first Governor landed near the site of Adelaide on 28 December 1836, he read out a proclamation largely devoted to emphasizing his government's responsibility and determination to use law and practice to protect the existing, native population as subjects of His Majesty like the colonists themselves, and as objects of 'His Majesty's most gracious and benevolent intentions toward them'. These good intentions were not as resolutely, fairly, and carefully pursued and funded, or as unanimously shared, as was needed to fulfil them really well: see the unsparing critique in Eyre, *Journals of Expeditions* (1845) ii 147–204, 412–507; cf. Bull, *Early Experiences of Life in South Australia* (1884) 63–75, 239–43. Nor did the objects of the benevolence respond with the measure of aptitude and energy needed to care for and manage land, stock, and other property as part of a division of labour capable of sustaining civil society and the institutions of the Rule of Law: see the four reports by the Protector of Aborigines which are printed with the Colonization Commissioners' report of July 1842 to the Secretary of State: Parl. Pap. (1843) 320–38; also Eyre, *Journals of Expeditions* ii/2 chs I, IV, VI, VIII.

INTRODUCTION

Making, acknowledging, and complying with law involves acts of rational judgment. The reasonableness and justification of these acts cannot be assessed without premises about true human goods, the nature of persons and their acts, and the contours of the common good and human rights. So a volume on the philosophy of law fittingly comes *fourth*. Issues of legal doctrine and interpretation resolvable by technique usually have some intellectual appeal. But legal studies are really attractive and worthwhile because law, and juristic argumentation, is an arena where themes and theses in ethics, political theory, and related philosophical domains all come to bear on—and crystallize out in—legislating and adjudicating to make a difference to human persons.

I. FOUNDATIONS OF LAW'S AUTHORITY

Very many legal theorists, some moved by one concern, some by another or other concerns, have thought that law is essentially a (kind of) social fact, and that the accounts of it appropriate to legal theory are purely descriptive. The social facts to be described will, of course, include countless evaluations (by law-makers, -finders, and -enforcers), especially ideas about how members of the relevant society should (according to law) behave. But the descriptive accounts themselves, it is usually supposed, can and should be value-free.

One concern motivating these meta-theoretical thoughts was political: Bentham's belief that, absent a social fact as transparent as statutory enactment, law-finding is corrupted by the class prejudices and partisanship of judicial cabals ('Judge and Co.'). Another concern was philosophical: Bentham's empiricist belief that if what we or judges refer to lacks the tangibility of sounds, marks, and mental images, it can be no more than a fiction. A more recent concern is that, given plurality of values and beliefs ('the fact of pluralism'), no method of settling social conflicts can be as reliably efficient as the legal: reliance exclusively on relatively uncontroversial historical facts ('social-fact sources') such as enactment or the judge's articulation of a *ratio decidendi* and an order of the court. Some of the theorists who hold that law is exclusively social-fact source-based also find an independent, logically indirect support for that thesis in their concern that social science itself be value-free. This concern, in its turn, is fed by emulation of the impressively successful sciences we call natural, and by the sceptical thesis (about which natural science knows nothing) that evaluations all lack objectivity and truth. Theories animated by one or more of these concerns usually describe themselves as 'positivist',[1] and are widely treated as the default position in jurisprudence or philosophy of law.

The modern concerns just mentioned partly overlap with, and partly diverge sharply from, the perennial concern identified and promoted by the mediaeval theorists who first articulated the concept of *positive law* (see essay 7). Countless arrangements needed for a just, peaceful, and prosperous political community could reasonably take more or less different forms, and so can be put in place and maintained only by *decision* between incompatible acceptable alternatives. Such a *determinatio*,[2] once made, can only yield its benefits if it is adhered to with substantial unanimity even absent a persisting consensus about its superiority to the alternatives rejected, ignored, or hitherto unenvisaged. A legal system responsive to human need largely consists, therefore, of rules, principles, standards, and institutions adopted by such past decisions—decisions now treated as binding by reason of their pedigree as validly made by persons with authority to so decide. That is, the law consists largely of rules, standards, and institutions resting on and derived from social-fact sources.

Accounts of law's positivity offered by leading positivists were examined in several of my essays around 1970. Kelsen's main-period thesis that a legal system's norms must not or cannot contradict each other was a

[1] See what I say in essay 1, at the beginning of its sec. IV, about how desirable it is not to talk at all of *positivism*, as if there is such a position (even when qualified as *legal positivism*). At the most, as Joseph Raz says,

> we should think of legal positivism as a historical tradition containing writings some of which bear greater similarity in their central tenets to writings outside it (e.g. to Finnis, and to Aquinas as he understands him) than to each other, a tradition which cannot be characterized by adherence to any central tenet or tenets.... [T]here is little value, other than historical, in using the classification of writings into positivist and non-positivist when considering various accounts of the nature of law (if it has a nature). ('Comments and Responses', 253.)

Still, for all its confused variegations, there is a loose historical tradition, and it is one in which most of my contemporaries, notably Raz, have been very willing to be counted. (Raz's hesitation, here, about whether law 'has a nature' is warranted by that tradition's unclarities about what it was trying to do.)

[2] See e.g. essay 13 at nn. 5–6; essay 7, secs II, III.

starting point.[3] Another focus of investigation was his theses, explicit and implicit, defended and assumed, about the persistence of legal norms after their creation and about their termination by revolutions (even by *coups d'état* intended to preserve them).[4] Appeals to Kelsen's accounts, by courts in the aftermath of *coups d'état* which left the judiciary unchanged, afforded further matter for reflection in the same period.[5] These investigations all converged on the conclusion that treating something as a source of rules (or other standards), like treating rules as derived from a *source*, and as persistingly valid by reason of that derivation, is a form of thought whose premises refer not only to social facts (few or many, stark or subtle) but also to social *needs*. Such needs include the good of flexibility and clarity in social regulation in changing circumstances, the good of fairness across time between those who benefit others by conforming to rules and those who have been so benefited and now are summoned to comply with the same or other rules of the system, and the good of a stability sufficient to merit the expectations needed to make venturesome investments rational.[6]

To bring such needs into the light of social theory, and to show how, in themselves and in their juristic effects, they are needs not peculiar to the societies that have responded to them juridically, is to breach the confines of a value-free social science. But these are confines that, as the first chapter of *Natural Law and Natural Rights* argued, any *general* theory of human affairs must break. In no general theory of human institutions could such bounds be maintained without self-imposed arbitrariness in selecting the terms and concepts in which it is articulated, and an unreflective inattention to the explanations and theses actually deployed in every descriptive theory that succeeds in being more than a juxtapositing of local histories and vocabularies. An example (besides those given in that chapter): Weber's decision to call the central type of governmental *Herrschaft* 'legal-rational authority', when put alongside his accounts of ways of legitimating authority, shows that this type gets clear of mere rule fetishism (and of rule by fear and favour) just insofar as it rests on acknowledging intrinsic intelligible human goods in a way that (as he knew) only natural-law theories of law systematically articulate and defend.[7] What is that way? It surely is the way traced, doubtless imperfectly, in Part II of *Natural Law and Natural Rights* and recalled in many of the programmatic essays in this volume: identifying the forms of human flourishing, the interdependencies of persons, the need for authority to preserve and promote

[3] See essay I.6 (1970a), sec. I. On Kelsen's abandonment of that thesis in his last period, see essay 5, sec. III.

[4] See essay 21.

[5] See at n. 30 below.

[6] See e.g. essay 2, sec. III; essay 3, sec. III.

[7] See essay 9, sec. III.

common good, and the desirability of regulating authority by the Rule of Law, that is, of positive law judicially interpreted and enforced. Weber, like his philosophical masters Hume and Kant, never (when philosophizing) clearly and reflectively understood, even to reject, the basic principles of practical reason that pick out the forms of flourishing with which the whole 'way' just recalled begins. In rejecting what he rightly took to be the only eligible explanation of the rationality of 'legal-rational' authority, Weber was rejecting only the distorted images presented to him by his era's philosophical culture.

But we do not need to concern ourselves with these historical and philosophical issues to be able to see how problematic is the modern 'sources thesis' (or 'social-fact sources thesis') that:

> *All* law is source based. A law is source-based if its existence and content can be identified by reference to social facts *alone*, without resort to any evaluative argument.[8]

To this 'exclusive' legal positivism, the most closely relevant reply is not the 'inclusive' positivist's, that the sources in some legal systems may make and/or authorize reference to moral or other evaluative considerations and thereby include them in (incorporate them into) the law. Rather, it is that the easygoing phrase 'identified by reference to social facts alone', offered as a translation of 'source-based', is doubly problematic.

For, first, no one ever can rationally treat a *fact alone* as giving reason for anything, let alone something as demanding and choice-restricting as a law. There must always be some 'evaluative argument' for treating any fact or combination of facts as a 'basis' for identifying a proposition as obligation-imposing or in some other way directive or normative. What reason have I as citizen or judge for identifying certain utterances as now legally directive (for me or for anyone else), utterances made on some past occasion by an assembly styling itself constituent or legislative or a tribunal styling itself a superior court of record? The answer must, to make sense, refer to some good or goods (human need or needs) that will be promoted if I make the identification or prejudiced if I do not.[9]

[8] Raz, *Ethics in the Public Domain*, 211 (emphasis added); likewise *AL* 39, 47; Raz, *Between Authority and Interpretation*, 386.

[9] Of course, once a community has, with sufficient stable consensus, treated a set of laws as sufficient reasons for action, historians, sociologists, and other observers (including its own members) can refer to that fact by stating that those laws exist as laws of that community. But as is plainly acknowledged in Raz, *Practical Reason and Norms*, 171–7 esp. 172 and Raz, 'Promises and Obligations' at 225 (see *NLNR* 234–6), such statements are altogether parasitic upon the basic and primary thoughts and statements about the existence, validity, and obligatoriness of laws, viz. the thoughts and statements of those subjects and officials who thereby express their judgment that, in the factual situation they presuppose or identify, these are laws giving them sufficient legal and

And second, in no legal system responsive to human needs do citizens, judges, or other officials look to the bare social fact of a past legislative act or act of adjudication. Always the reference is to such acts in their intra-systemic context. And that context is, first and foremost, a set of propositions identifying necessary and sufficient conditions of validity both of legislative and adjudicative acts and of the legal rules identifiable by reference (directly but in part!) to those acts. And such validity conditions pertain not only to the circumstances and form of those acts but also to the consequent rules' persistence through time as members of a set of propositions whose membership changes constantly by addition, subtraction, amendment, clarification, explanation, and so forth. Contributing both rationale and countless details of content to this complex of propositions and intellectual acts (juristic interpretation), will be found 'references'—often silent but detectable by inference—to the desirability of coherence here and now, of stability across time, of fidelity to undertakings, respect for legitimate expectations, avoidance of tyranny, preservation of the community whose laws these are (and of its capacity for self-government), protection of the vulnerable, incentives for investment, maintenance of that condition of communal life we call the Rule of Law, and many other 'evaluative arguments'. Of course, these references, whether tacit or expressed, are themselves social facts, which like all other social facts could, instance by instance, be given a value-free, descriptive report. But their pervasiveness witnesses to the rational *need* for them. Only by looking to such desirabilities can there be a sensible response to the plain questions to which a consistent, rigorous positivism[10] is so unresponsive: Why treat past acts or social facts as sources of guidance in deliberation and reasonable decision-making today? How can any social fact validate? Or bind? And why *these* facts, not those?

However, as sec. III of this Introduction will reiterate and refine, those wholly evaluative desirability considerations can contribute to answering these fundamental questions about even 'easy cases', and to resolving a 'hard case' juristically, only when taken in combination with another, further range of factual considerations. These concern not past acts of legislation or adjudication but past conflicts and compact-like settlements of them,

moral *reason(s) to act* in the way they validly direct (reasons over and above avoidance of immediate sanctions).

[10] Positivists themselves are another matter: see at nn. 19, 20 below. On this incoherence of a consistent, rigorous legal positivism *with the explanatory task it sets itself*, see secs III, IV, and VII of essay 5, or 2000d, which begins:

> Legal positivism is an incoherent intellectual enterprise. It sets itself an explanatory task which it makes itself incapable of carrying through. In the result it offers its students purported and invalid derivations of *ought* from *is*.

present circumstances of various kinds, and future likely outcomes and consequences, threats, risks, and opportunities as estimated against wide ranges of background scientific and historical knowledge and belief.

Essay 4 reaches similar conclusions about how to understand authority. It shows that 'conceptual analysis' of authority cannot yield anything worth counting as a jurisprudential achievement unless it proceeds with attention to the intelligible human goods at stake, and to means of attaining them which are both effective and respectful of other such goods that the pursuit of them may affect. One can discern an 'analytically' possible concept or concepts of governmental authority entailing only that its possessors are entitled not to be usurped or impeded, and not that anyone has any obligation to attend to their directives. But any such concept will be simply inferior, to the point of irrelevance, compared with a concept of authority—just as analytical and even more clearly discernible—in which its exercise standardly results (and is intended and taken to result) in obligation. That obligation will be 'legal obligation' in two senses, or of two kinds: an intra-systemic legal obligation[11] extending as far as the scope of the authority supports and the juristically sound interpretation of its directive or other act determines; and a moral obligation, of presumptively the same extent, the force and effect of which, however, varies according to a number of morally relevant considerations about the justice of the law and the other moral obligations of its subject(s). Joseph Raz's ambivalent efforts to detach legal authority from presumptive (generic, prima facie, defeasible) moral obligatoriness[12] fail analytically, by failing to concede that between the extremes to which he exclusively attends—either a mere prima facie reason for action or an unqualified moral obligation to act just as the law requires[13]—there stands the desirable and coherent middle position: legal

[11] See *NLNR* 308–20, esp. 309–10, on the invariant strength or force of legal obligation 'in contemplation of law', i.e. intra-systemically.

[12] *AL* 234–7; Raz, *Between Authority and Interpretation*, 169–75. One of the several aspects of this ambivalence is that Raz (e.g. at 188; cf. 331, 332 at n. 4) also maintains that legal authorizations and obligations, since they authorize or require important interferences in other people's lives, *are* moral claims. (Contrast *AL* 158.) Another aspect: contrary to *AL* 236, Raz *ibid.*, 379 maintains that judges consider themselves entitled to break ('flout') the law.

[13] Raz *ibid.* 169–71 retains essentially the same false contrast (contrast between non-exhaustive, implausible alternatives). Similarly: Gardner, 'How Law Claims, What Law Claims', argues for the (Razian) thesis that, in asserting or stipulating obligations, 'the law claims' that what these are is moral obligations. This argument fails most importantly by assuming the very point in issue, viz. that morality and self-interested prudence exhaust the realm of reasons and that there cannot be normativity (and thus obligation) which is *legal* (and so far forth not moral). *NLNR* 308–18 argues that there can be and is, even though its independence from the general flow of practical reasoning is incomplete and provisional. And of course, as the book also argues, a sound morality holds that obligation-stipulating laws, not on their face immoral, should be presumed, defeasibly, to create a moral obligation the strength of which is not invariant in face of competing moral responsibilities; and morally decent law-makers and law-appliers (who instantiate the central case of law-making and -applying) will try to ensure that the law they make or apply is fit to impose moral obligations

obligation in the moral sense, and with the qualified force and extent,[14] just summarized as *presumptive.*

Reflections such as these yield a general result. A disciplined *normative* legal theory can do all that a would-be value-free general theory can, and can do it with much greater power, not only as justification or critique but also as explanation. The normative foundations of such a legal theory are vindicated against some main forms of scepticism in essays I.1, I.2, and I.5. The theory's many-levelled normative structure is outlined and applied to legal issues in essay I.14, and the importance to it of a sound, non-fictitious understanding of the person and of political community in essays II.1 and II.6–7 respectively. How to consider law's proper scope and limits is thematic in essays III.1 and III.5. Essay 1 in this volume expounds and illustrates the fundamental method and some main theses of a normative theory of law's positivity, in direct debate with the leading contemporary positivist theories and theorists.

But that same last-mentioned essay, like the rest of my work hitherto,[15] fails to convey clearly enough the sheer oddity of the 'debate' that still dominates the construction of textbooks and distracts the attention of students. It is said to be a debate about *whether there is any necessary connection between law and morality.* It is supposed that until positivism cleared the air by its robust denial that there is such a connection, legal philosophy was entangled with moralizing and obfuscated by misplaced idealism. This supposition rests on simple inattention to the idiom of classic western philosophy, in which the propositions 'An invalid argument is no argument', 'A tyrannical constitution is no constitution', 'A false friend is no friend', and 'An unjust law is no law' *presuppose and entail* that arguments are not necessarily valid, constitutions are sometimes tyrannical, friends are not necessarily faithful, and law is not necessarily moral. But besides the inattention or ignorance, there is—and this is more interesting—the odd illogicality of supposing that the question whether there is 'any necessary connection' could be answered without conducting a *moral* inquiry.

What does morality say about whether law needs to be moral? Obviously, the morality (moral belief) handed down in our civilization vigorously asserted the moral necessity (requirement, stringent moral need, and duty)

that could only be overridden by moral responsibilities applicable in particular kinds of circumstance not provided for by law: see n. 14 below.

[14] Qualified, that is to say, by moral considerations (relating to the justice of the rule in general and/or the competing moral responsibilities of particular subjects in their circumstances) *going beyond* whatever moral considerations have been built into the legal meaning and content of the rule itself by the design of the law-maker and/or by other rules and principles of the legal system that bear upon the rule in question and modify its tenor.

[15] Even essay 10 n. 66, and *NLNR* 364–5.

that law be morally upright, and the viciousness of rulers (tyrants) who defy or ignore this necessity. More interestingly, the justified, true morality, as I have argued out in *Natural Law and Natural Rights*, takes the same position. It is morally necessary for responsible persons in community to arrange the community's affairs by introducing laws and adhering to the Rule of Law. It is morally necessary for citizens to treat their community's law as presumptively obligatory. And sound morality says something more about each of those morally necessary connections between law and morality. It says that the presumptive obligation of subjects is defeated (a) by countervailing moral responsibilities serious enough to make non-compliance just, and (b) by serious and relevant injustice in the formation or content of the law.[16] And it says that, whether similarly or by entailment, the moral necessity that rulers rule according to law is a necessity qualified by the moral necessity to take steps to preserve the community and its members against threats which the community has not forfeited its right to be defended from, including steps contrary to the law and even the constitution.[17]

In short, in the sense that self-styled positivists intend when defining positivism as the denial that there is any necessary connection between law and morality, no significant thinker has ever asserted or implied or assumed any such connection, and the positivists merely beat the air.[18] And

[16] *NLNR* 360–1.

[17] Thus the Colonization Commissioners for South Australia wrote to the Secretary of State for the Colonies in December 1837, demanding the recall of the province's first governor for illegal conduct:

> Exigencies may arise requiring vigour beyond the law. Cases may occur in which the magnitude of the evil to be prevented, or of the good to be obtained, may justify the exercise of unconstitutional and illegal power. The colonization commissioners, however,... are of opinion that the objects for which their regulations and instructions were set aside were not beneficial but injurious. (Parl. Pap., *Correspondence relative to Settlement of South Australia*, 56–7.)

[18] The fashion for summoning up such phantasms has not passed. Raz, *Between Authority and Interpretation*, 1 says that:

> theories of law tend to divide into those which think that, by its very nature, the law successfully reconciles the duality of morality and power, and those which think that its success in doing so is contingent, depending on the political realities of the societies whose law is in question. Belonging with the second tendency, I have suggested that it is essential to the law that it recognizes that its use of power is answerable to moral standards....

No instance of the first tendency is or could be identified. At 167, Raz says that Aquinas and Finnis (*NLNR* chs 1 and 10) 'regard the law as good in its very nature'; but actually Aquinas and I belong, from beginning to end, with the second tendency. Indeed, we recognize, more frankly and steadily than Raz, that the political realities of power sometimes occasion a law or legal system so amorally devised and imposed that nothing in its content or its context suggests that it claims to reconcile power with morality or recognizes its answerability to moral standards (cf. e.g. Raz *ibid.* 180: 'Necessarily the law claims to have legitimate moral authority over its subjects'). Certainly, no conceptual necessity rules out such a possibility, though any sound general theory of law will treat it as a non-central (deviant) instance of law, and legal theory specifically oriented to justification and moral guidance will treat it as not at all a law (that counts as law in conscience).

the only connection between law and morality that any classic philosopher or jurist had the slightest interest in asserting is a connection which cannot be denied without taking a moral position, on moral grounds—that is, without making legal theory a part of moral theory. Need one add that the moral position supporting such a denial will have all the moral plausibility of anarchism, egoism, and tyranny?

Arriving at a position too sophisticated and perhaps too unstable for the textbooks, today's leading positivists have come to agree with much if not all that is outlined in the last two paragraphs. They hold, for example,[19] that:

> a theory of law is... among other things, a theory of the conditions, if any, under which the law is morally legitimate and of the consequences that follow from the assumption that it is morally legitimate.... our interest in legal authority lies in how it establishes the moral authority of the law, or of parts of it. We are interested in the authority of the law, if any, in order to establish whether we have an obligation to respect and obey it.[20]

Thus, over the period in which these essays were written, there has been a very marked and welcome development in their discourse context, a development particularly about what is accepted as legal-philosophical inquiry into the nature and foundations of law's authority.

II. THEORIES AND THEORISTS OF LAW

As at other points in this Collection, the essays under this heading do not exhaust the set that might fittingly have been put here rather than elsewhere. So, for example, Posner and Economic Analysis of Law,

[19] See also Gardner, 'Legal Positivism: 5½ Myths', as discussed in essay 1, sec. IV, p. 43 points (1), (2) and (4). Similarly Green, 'Legal Positivism'. Contrast the account of legal positivism in the passage of 2007c discussed in the following footnote.

[20] Raz, *Between Authority and Interpretation*, 331–2. Accordingly, the summary in the opening paragraphs of 2007c needs amendment. I said:

> *Contemporary 'positivist' theories are, it seems, natural law theories*, distinguished from the main body of natural law theory (a) by their denial that the theory *of law* (as distinct from the theory or theories of adjudication, judicial duty, citizens' allegiance, etc.) necessarily or most appropriately tackles the related matters just listed, and accordingly (b) by the incompleteness of their theories of law, that is, the absence from them (and usually, though not always, from their accounts of those related matters) of systematic critical attention to the foundations of the moral and other normative claims that they make or presuppose.

Though the first (and main) proposition (here italicized) is correct, the rest of the passage should report that among those who label their theories about law 'positivist' there is fundamental disagreement about what is or is not included within a theory *of law*. And one may add to the passage the reflection that the classificatory meltdown and philosophical disorder it discusses still seem to have as their main cause an Enlightenment or Enlightenment-style *haste* to repudiate—before understanding—the mainstream way of thinking about society, morality, and law that runs from Plato through Aristotle, Cicero, Augustine, Aquinas, down to today. See again essay 7, especially its last section.

doubtless as deserving of a place here as Unger and Critical Legal Studies, are considered in essay 16, at the head of the essays on legal reasoning. Kant's legal theory is a primary topic of essay III.2. The whole set of essays on punishment, essays III.10–12, might properly have been placed among the present volume's first part, or essay III.10 put alongside the present volume's other essays on Hart.

The whole Collection's longest essay, essay 5, undertakes both some history of normative legal theories, and some detailed though summary illustrations of results I think sounder than well-known theories past and present. A little more history of legal theory is offered in essay 6. Essays 7–13 are detailed studies of specific theorists of law from Aquinas through to Unger, with Hart in central position. The study of Dworkin's legal theory in essay 12 can be put alongside the critiques of his politico-constitutional theory in essay II.6 and, earlier, in essays III.1–2, and of his account of the good of human life in essays III.17–18.

Should a normative theory of law have the enviably wide and substantive sweep of Adam Smith's *Lectures on Jurisprudence* of 1762–66, collated and published in 1978? Can it emulate the late pre-Benthamite *Essay on the Law of Bailments* by my predecessor at University College Oxford, William Jones?[21] Adam Smith was drawn, whether by his method or his interests, into more or less speculative theses about economic causality that go beyond what can plausibly be called a theory of *law*. And legal theory, subalternated as it is to normative ethics and political theory (each taken broadly enough to comprehend at least the outlines of an account such as Smith's of marriage, family, and domestic and civil economics), must certainly be more careful and precise than were Smith or his master Hume to distinguish clearly between the *ought* of intelligible goods and norms of practical reasonableness and the *is* of common or typical human tendencies of feeling and action.

A theme in early sections of essay 5 is that theory regresses as well as progresses. To be sure, the 'modern natural law' theorists Locke, Pufendorf, Blackstone, and Smith were to some extent easygoing and confused about method; here there was already regression from the 'classical natural law' theories of Plato, Aristotle, and Aquinas. But the neo-Hobbesian remedy prescribed and administered by Bentham and Austin, and with neo-Kantian sceptical themes by Kelsen, was devastatingly crude. Hart's grand work was one of strategic recovery from nearly two centuries of accelerated regression. At the core of the recovery was the internal viewpoint's openness to normativity, that is, to reasons for action considered precisely as such.

[21] See *NLNR* 289, 296.

It was an incomplete recovery, work in progress, as is stated, somewhat floridly, in the first section of essay 4, a paper for the Hart conference in Jerusalem. The measure of the advance made by Hart is explored further in essay 10 for the Hart centenary conference in Cambridge, and in sec. II of essay 11, where I show the extent to which he broke with the idea, fashionable for twenty years after the Second War, that philosophy is a matter of conceptual analysis. Normative legal theory is the proper extension of his strategic recovery of practical reasons as law's foundation and method, an extension freed from his serious mistakes about normative legal theory's incapacity (he claimed) to handle the study of vicious or other defective instances of law and legal system. Essay 11, in its later sections, considers some of the strategic mistakes in Hart's grasp of basic practical reasons, mistakes liable to subvert the very achievements in civilization that his method made legal philosophy cognisant of once again.

III. LEGAL REASONING

Legal reasoning's connections with the sources and modalities of other kinds of practical reason are surveyed in essay I.14 (1992a); critical comments on an earlier version of this (1992c) elicited the response that is essay 17. Essay 16, written for the same colloquium, takes up the legal significance of intention, especially in tort (studied on a broader canvas in essay II.11). Clarifying the elementary logic of the juridical relations that are a primary element in legal reasoning—rights, duties, liberties, powers, and so forth—was the very explicit purpose and topic of Hohfeld's analysis, vindicated against its learned misinterpreters in essay 18. Essay 19 brings out the role of insight ('abduction') in that discernment of principle which is the heart of analogical reasoning in properly legal reasoning. And Dworkin's account of legal reasoning, criticized for its 'one right answer' thesis in essay 12, is taken up in essay 20 as the helpful clarification it is, in relation to judicial developments of doctrine.

Still, Dworkin (like many others) over-emphasizes the judicial, at the expense of the legislative, in law. And quite generally it is a mistake to treat legal reasoning and judicial reasoning as identical. Certainly, judicial reasoning should be legal reasoning, of the best kind appropriate to the judicial context and responsibilities. But it is law-makers who have the first responsibility to think legally. For legislating ought to be done in full consciousness of the existing law, so that the changes that the enactment will make in the existing set of propositions of law can be made with precision—with the minimum, that is, of unintended and unexpected side effects on that set. If the judiciary faithfully carry out their duty to do justice according to law, the principles of interpretation they use to identify the extent of the change will be the same principles as the legislators, guided by their legal advisers, had in mind in crafting the terms of their enactment. Neither organ of governance then is fully in charge; each contributes to an ongoing interaction between them, for the sake of common good and the Rule of Law, an interaction in which the reasoning of the one should track the reasoning of the other, with the initiative (and corresponding duties of justice) always properly with the legislator. (Of course, in some societies, the judiciary has been a primary law-maker in many fields, and in our society it has been primary in some, and still today, though now not without the odour of usurpation, it is perhaps still so.) Law is a kind of ongoing plan for common good, and to take seriously the moral reality that the bulk of the law consists of *determinationes*—because true moral principles under-determine what individuals and societies should choose and do—is to accept that a law's initial and presumptively decisive existence is as an adopted plan in the mind, the expressed intention, of the law-maker. The primary law-makers, properly, are those with conferred or attributed authority ('constituent' authority) to make a constitution, under which, and subject to which, certain sets of persons will have ongoing legislative authority: to make the laws to be carried out by persons with executive authority and applied by persons with judicial authority.

My doctoral thesis was on the idea of judicial power, studied first in theories of governance from Aristotle through Montesquieu, Locke, Bentham, Kelsen, and others, and then in the constitution-making and -interpreting of the founders and judicial interpreters of the Australian federal Constitution of 1900. The investigation of theories turned up little surprising, and little to challenge the conventional view articulated at the end of the preceding paragraph. Along the way, it did confirm (to me freshly) the extreme fragility and basic arbitrariness of the naïve empiricism that dominated Bentham's 'analysis'. And of the helpless determinism and egoism against which he struggled to make sense of his utilitarianism and constitutional code-making and -vending. It confirmed, too, the self-imposed incapacity of Kelsen to make any sense of so elemental an aspect of legal systems as judicial power. More interesting, in the end, was the detailed Australian history: how the statesmen who debated and drafted the Constitution distributed legislative, executive, and judicial powers; how they deliberately, against a vocal but small minority, established a constitutional institution—the Inter-State Commission to regulate aspects of trade among the federation's states—which combined some administrative, legislative, and judicial powers; and how that same two-man minority, as soon as they, now judges, were able (in 1915) to constitute a majority in the supreme constitutional court, declared that the Constitution embodies a strict separation of powers, or at least of judicial from legislative or executive power, and that the Inter-State Commission therefore was constitutionally disqualified from exercising the powers that the Constitution's text and their own vivid knowledge of its founders' intention plainly conferred upon it. This rather shocking (and by 1960 long-forgotten) episode of judicial wilfulness[22] initiated a separation of powers doctrine strenuously and repeatedly enforced to invalidate federal legislation and institutions. In its unseemly origin and its subsequent judicial development alike, all this opened my eyes to the intellectual, juridical, and moral fragility of much of the legal or judicial reasoning of even the most widely admired and would-be austerely legalist (non-political) judges of the 1940s, 1950s, and early 1960s.

If we reject, as we should, the thesis that there is always or virtually always, even in hard cases, a uniquely correct legal answer available to be discovered and judicially enforced, we need to confront two issues: (1) what are the legal implications of a judgment which changes settled judicial and/or professional opinion about what the law is, in particular the implications for the question whether transactions entered into in reliance on that former opinion were made under a mistake of law; (2) how to explain the fact that virtually all judgments, even in hard cases where the tribunal is deeply divided, will be found to be constructed so as to give warrant to an affirmation that there is only one correct legal-judicial resolution of the points of law in issue.

(1) This issue is taken up in essay 20, in the context of English common law doctrine about rights to restitution of moneys paid under a mistake. Should we say that a payment made in reliance on a settled opinion (formed with or without professional advice) that it is legally required was caused by a mistake of law if that settled opinion is subsequently declared by authoritative judicial decision to have been legally erroneous? Essay 20 supports the recent judicial opinion that that question should be answered: Yes. But that answer obliges us to accept—as the essay does not get around to noticing—that, as a matter of momentary legal dogma (so to speak), an 'only one right answer' thesis is correct. (I hesitate to say that it is Dworkin's thesis, for so far as I know he has not himself deployed the

[22] Discussed, and related to the elementary typologies of governmental-power analysis that were the fruit of my thesis's theoretical part, in 1968c. *New South Wales v The Commonwealth* (*Wheat Case*) (1915) 20 CLR 54 remains authoritative today, as in 1960 and 1920. It is its historical background that was and largely remains forgotten.

argument I trace, and whose implications I consider, in this paragraph.) That is to say, the judgment that prevails in such a case (and in any hard case, as in any easy case) includes as part of its legal content or entailment the proposition that, just as the losing party's appeal to legal rules or principles is (to the relevant extent) legally erroneous and the losing party's liberty, property, or other relevant interests are accordingly (to the relevant extent) simply negated, so too the dissenting judgments and any earlier judgments or settled opinions contrary to the here and now prevailing judgment are and were mistaken. That proposition is included in the *res judicata*. So far forth, we can say that Dworkin's prolongation of Hart's salutary flight from legal 'Realism' (Hart's adopting or reproducing the internal point of view, paradigmatically the view of the law-abiding judge), insofar as that prolongation involves treating jurisprudence as a replication of judicial judgment, correctly identifies the legal-logical content of that judgment. But (as Dworkin's jurisprudence vividly stresses) the law is not a momentary system. Its rules about *res judicata* commonly and appropriately ensure that (once appeals and collateral challenges are exhausted) the law applicable to the adjudicated dispute between the parties is simply what it was declared to be in the relevant final judgment, right or wrong. But the status of that same judgment's statement of the law is not settled, for any other courts, advisers, or subjects of the law, by the rules of *res judicata*, but rather by the general flow of legal doctrine and argumentation—rules and principles understood as a whole to be treated so far as possible as both coherent and just, both here and now and across time. (That indeed is what Dworkin calls law's 'integrity'.) So: that judgment's status as a precedent, an authority, a source may sometimes be appropriately regarded as questionable, slight, perhaps nugatory, even while it is being enforced *inter partes*. Hence, the correctness of 'one right answer' as an exegesis of the judgment *inter partes* does not entail its correctness as a jurisprudential thesis at large. Nor do the reasonable dogmatic implications of the judgment for the application of rules about transactions made under mistake of law suffice to settle the jurisprudential issue about hard cases having only one right answer.

(2) Essay 12 argues in sec. IV that, *pace* Dworkin, judges need not expect to find or reach a uniquely correct legal answer in hard cases. The argument has nothing in common with the objection of naïve critics of Dworkin who think he has overlooked the fact that judges quite often disagree in such cases. Rather, it points to Dworkin's failure to specify, even in principle, *how well* an account or interpretation of the law must fit the legal materials (statutes, precedents, etc.). The failure's cause is the lack of commensuration between fit (stability) and moral soundness, compounded by the

under-determinacy of affirmative[23] moral principles and norms, particularly in face of pervasive uncertainty about past, present, and, above all, future facts. That judges nonetheless—even in or in face of dissent—construct their judgments in hard cases as if, even in such a case, there were a uniquely correct answer (which the judgment argues towards and articulates) cannot be explained simply by the dogmatic facts about every judicial judgment's legal meaning, recalled in (1) above. We need to add to the explanation this: judges each bring to their task the personal schedule of preferences and predictions with which they each, in their individual deliberating and choosing (in many contexts, legal and non-legal), drastically reduce the otherwise pervasive moral under-determinacy and factual uncertainty just mentioned. Neither the preferences nor the estimates of likelihood are legally controlled, or within range of reasonable legal control. They often differ widely from judge to judge. To attempt completely to free one's judicial assessment (of the law's bearing on the issues in hard cases) from the guidance afforded by one's sober beliefs about the desirable and the likely would be unreasonable. Beliefs about, say, the benefits of local as opposed to national or international governance (or vice versa), about the likelihood (or unlikelihood) of political control of a reforming judiciary, about the bearing of the Golden Rule[24] on proposals to upset legitimate expectations in the interests of other aspects of the common good—these are only a few of the many kinds of beliefs that, as a judge, one can with integrity employ to guide one to a definite, non-arbitrary resolution of hard cases. The reasons afforded by *these* beliefs break the stalemate between the competing fit and moral-soundness rankings. They justify one in reaching the decision one does, even when one's fellow judges are reaching opposite conclusions about that resolution and are doing so by express or tacit appeal to beliefs which one can acknowledge are morally and legally open to them to use in the way they do.

But, of course, one should not in one's adjudication employ these extra-legal beliefs to convert easy cases into hard cases that one then resolves contrary to what respect for law requires. That is lawless judging. Most of the plainly erroneous decisions of great courts, such as the High Court of Australia's already mentioned decision in the *Wheat Case* (1915), or the House of Lords' decision in the *Belmarsh Prisoners' Case* (2003),[25] or

[23] On the distinction between affirmative and negative moral principles, and its significance, see e.g. essay 17 at nn. 34–6, sec. III *passim*, and at n. 45; essay I.15 (1997b), sec. VI.

[24] The operation of the Golden Rule is always affected by what one would oneself be willing to undergo at the hands of others, and this willingness is affected by (not only reasons but also by) emotions, which vary somewhat between persons, and between groups.

[25] *A v Secretary of State for the Home Department* [2004] UKHL 56. For the background, see essay III.9 and for the errors see 2007a at 429–42: the Law Lords entirely ignored the provision

the US Supreme Court's decisions in *Dred Scott* (1856),[26] and *Roe v Wade* (1973),[27] and *Romer v Evans* (1996),[28] turned on the majority judges' extra-legal beliefs about likelihood and/or desirability, employed to set aside laws that presupposed more or less contrary beliefs which nothing in the constitutional framework disentitled the law-makers to presuppose and act on in the way they did.

IV. THE TWO SENSES OF 'LEGAL SYSTEM'

Not without the spur of Brian Simpson's comments, given as editor of the volume for which it was written and as someone whose scholarly legal-historical and jurisprudential learning was then and there being enhanced by vivid experiences of the struggling legal-political order of Ghana, essay 21 became clear, in its sec. IV, about the two main senses of 'legal system'. There is the system of rules and other norms or standards which as a set can guide the jurist and the citizen. And there is the system as a set of interacting persons, groups, and institutions, with their dispositions to interact both in compliance with, and in defiance or ignorance of, the system of rules etc. In the second sense, the legal system is the society to which the legal system in the first sense belongs, the society which *has* those rules and other standards. The way in which that society subsists and persists through time is part of what it is for the rules and standards themselves to last, to have the temporal dimension they do, a dimension very hard to explain without reference to the lasting identity of the society (political community) and of the persons who are that society's members.[29] Yet the lasting of the society as a distinct society with a history of its own is not independent of the formal question what rules and standards are treated by its members as their society's own legal system, for them to follow and to amend.

of the Human Rights Act 1998 (a provision on which they frequently act) requiring them to seek a rights-compatible interpretation of the statutory provisions in question, and such an interpretation was readily available. Precisely what result-orienting desire motivated this averting of the eyes (see 2007a at 433) from plain legal duty remains a matter for speculation irrelevant to legal analysis.

[26] *Scott v Sandford* 60 US 393. See essay II.1 (2000a) at nn. 40–3.

[27] 410 US 113. See 2000c at nn. 53–6; essay I.16 final endnote; essay II.1 (2000a) at n. 46.

[28] 517 US 620, based on the professed belief, ungrounded in evidence, that the law-makers had been motivated by 'animus', 'animosity', and 'bare...desire to harm a politically unpopular group'. Behind this very implausible assertion may lie something of that attitude towards 'majorities' which Dworkin had been promoting for more than two decades: see the discussion of it in essay III.1, sec. II.

[29] The lasting identity of persons is discussed in essay II.2 (2005c). But regrettably the lasting identity of political communities, with its cultural and other conditions, does not really become a theme again (after 1971) in my legal theory until essays II.6 (2008b) and II.7 (2008a).

That essay, 'Revolutions and Continuity of Law', was preceded and prepared for by annual essays of mine in the *Annual Survey of Commonwealth Law* on the judicial aftermath and discussion of revolutions or *coups d'état* in Pakistan, Uganda, Rhodesia, Cyprus, and Ghana.[30] The philosophical reflections in those essays, which reasons of space preclude including in this Collection, largely concerned the incoherence of using professedly value-free, 'pure', 'positivist' legal theories such as Kelsen's as a guide to judicial duty in the assessment of a revolution's impact on the country's law and legal system. That issue was presented in its purest form in Pakistan in the late 1960s. Around the same time it was presented in a more complex (and in that way more illuminating) form in and in relation to (Southern) Rhodesia. For in the latter context, the fundamental issue was whether there was indeed one country (the undivided realm of the United Kingdom and its colonies including Southern Rhodesia) or two (the United Kingdom and the already distinct country the lawful government of which had unlawfully declared its independence from the United Kingdom). That issue was considered, very amply, first by two courts in Rhodesia and then by the supreme court of the British imperial system, the Judicial Committee of the Privy Council. The essay was written before the judgments in the last of these tribunals; an endnote to the present version of the essay summarizes my *Annual Survey* commentary on those judgments.

In the 1980s, as the adviser to a committee of the House of Commons concerned with Parliament's residual powers in respect of Canada, and to two State governments in Australia, I had occasion to articulate and document in detail the ways in which it is conceptually possible, and can be juridically appropriate, to judge that one or more constitutional organs of an independent state have constitutional functions in and under the constitutional order (the legal system) of another, independent state.[31] Here the distinction and relation between the two senses of legal system becomes very important. Equipped with the distinctions worked out and applied in relation to Canada and Australia, it is easier to see and say how, for example, (a) the organs of the European Union can follow and in part generate a set of norms and doctrines according to which those organs and that set constitute a legal system which has juridical supremacy over the legal systems of the Union's member states, and (b) the norms and organs of a member state accord legal effect to the Union's norms and doctrines, including its doctrine of supremacy, while at the same time,

[30] See 1968b at 82–3; 1969a at 73–5, 89–95, 108–13; 1970d at 71–81.

[31] See 1981a, c, and d; 1983a.

(c) the people and the organs of the same member state consider themselves a distinct people and political community (sovereign state) which can, according to its own law (and in pursuance of its own distinct common good), revoke in whole *or* (despite Union doctrine) *in part* the supremacy of the Union's norms, doctrines, and organs. This is not a matter that has arisen for decision in the United Kingdom.[32] A matter that has arisen, involving at bottom the same kind of issue—*which* is the relevant community whose common good is rightly served as the ultimate object of and framework for the acts of constitutional organs—is the subject of my paper 2008e, on the lawfulness and probable justness of requiring the inhabitants of (part of) a dependency (technically and unknown to them just reconstituted as a separate dependency) to move to another (part of the same) dependency in the defence interests of the United Kingdom and its dependencies considered as a whole. Of the willingness of the House of Lords' majority to follow this analysis in *Bancoult (No. 2)*,[33] it can at least be said that it certainly does not have the jurisprudential incoherence involved in following a positivist analysis of the effects of revolution on a people's legal system.

Essay 22, finally, sums up a controversy that enabled me to become clear about precisely what are the components of a legal system as a 'set of rules and other standards'. These rules must be understood not as the statements found in the texts of constitutions, statutes, and judgments or judicial orders, but as the *propositions* which are true, as a matter of law, by reason (a) of the authoritative utterance of those statements taken with (b) the bearing on those utterances and statements (and on the propositions those utterances were intended to make valid law) of the legal system's other, already valid propositions. To say that is simply to make explicit what implicitly engages law students from the outset of their studies—the search for what (proposition) the legal sources and authorities, taken all together, *establish*. But there is no embarrassment to philosophy when it articulates with precision, and confirms, what was already known to common sense, any more than it is an embarrassment when philosophical

[32] *Pace* much legal-academic opinion, it was in no way raised in *Factortame (No. 2)* [1990] UKHL 7, [1991] 1 AC 603.

[33] [2008] UKHL 61, [2009] 1 AC 453. This follows 2008d in treating the undivided realm of the United Kingdom and its overseas territories as the community whose common good is at stake in assessing the justice and legality of requiring a few hundred tenants in one part of those territories to move to another territory (the judges assume that it is an expulsion from one dependency to another). The majority fail, however, to accept the essay's showing that in 1865 a Parliament guided by Liberal ministers sensibly decided to remove such issues from the supervision of the courts, not least the English courts (not to mention the court in Adelaide that had provoked the enacting of the Colonial Laws Validity Act 1865).

reflection issues in affirmations which, when tested reflectively and reflexively, turn out to be consistent with the worth of pursuing truth in discourse and philosophy.[34] All too many philosophical doctrines that have influenced and distracted the philosophy of law in recent centuries fail that important test.

[34] On self-referential inconsistency and resultant self-refutation, see essay I.3 (1977a), which in sec. III also discusses some puzzles about legal sovereignty, and essay I.4 (2005b).

Part One

Foundations of Law's Authority

1

DESCRIBING LAW NORMATIVELY*

I

Suppose we tried to think about law without trying first to describe it or to work out what the concept of it is. Suppose we asked instead whether, and if so why, and when, we—or more precisely each one of us—should favour introducing, having, endorsing, maintaining, complying with, and enforcing it. We would be trying to think about law, about something not limited to our own time and town, but as something that people of any time and place of which we are aware would, as we can understand, have the same or similar need for and reasons to comply with as we have. But this subject-matter we would be calling law from the outset because we would be beginning these reflections with an awareness, linguistic, experiential, and by report, of *the* law of our own time and town or country. Of that we could give some description, because we have some understanding of the sorts of things referred to in our neighbourhood as parts of or related to the law (of our time and town, our law), and thus a conception or concept of that law, a conception which we could, if asked (or if reflecting), sketch out as a set of beliefs about an aspect of what's going on around us, beliefs which we are quite prepared to amend in the light of new information or of our own reflections about the consistency of these beliefs with each other and with other things we believe.

Structurally our inquiry would be running parallel to the course of inquiry recommended by Aristotle. Take a very different context, a subject-matter of the kind that exist and are what they are whether we consider them or not. For example, eclipses of the moon. People talk about eclipses of the moon, and so one can ask what an eclipse is, not because one's trying either to record or even to attain clarity about their speech, or their ideas (concepts), but because one's interested in the sort of thing or things they

* 2003b ('Law and What I Truly Should Decide').

are referring to. They talk about eclipses, referring to a black patch moving over the face of the moon, not nightly or monthly but regularly though quite rarely. Aristotle's counsel[1] is: translate the What? into a Why? Why does a black patch move across the bright face of the moon? I'll skip now to the end of the inquiry. The black patch is the shadow of the earth, that is, it appears *because* the earth is blocking the light from the sun, and so an eclipse of the moon *is* the visible result of the earth coming between the sun and the moon, which can happen not nightly or monthly but only—because of the differing but correlated cycles of the earth and the moon around the sun—more rarely but regularly. That's what a lunar eclipse is. Or take a subject-matter of the kind that are what they are because we have decided to exercise control over natural matter. What is a clock? Perhaps the only ones I'm aware of are worked by chains and pulleys. But why have these chains and pulleys, and a face and hands (or a dial and numbers, or whatever) connected up to each other like this? As an *instrument for* measuring the passing of time relative to some unit or units marked by some perceptible marker such as a hand on or passing, or a frame around, a visible numeral. Or take a subject-matter of the kind that involve our putting our own thoughts in order. What is an argument? I hear the word used in relation to statements, or connected series of statements, asserting reasons for accepting some proposition; I learn soon enough that some such statements or sets of statements really do give reason for their purported conclusion, while others, intended and perhaps appearing to do so, fail, on reflection, to do so. Why link these statements in a series, or juxtapose the one statement (premise) with the other (conclusion)? In order to compel or justify or warrant accepting the latter. So I come to understand that not everything proposed and spoken of and considerable as a reason is a reason, and that not every argument is really any argument at all for what it is proposed as arguing for. That is, part of coming to understand what argument really is consists in coming to understand that, and why, not all arguments are really arguments at all, even though these non-arguments, failed, fallacious, invalid arguments *are* still, in a secondary or watered down sense, arguments, as eclipses and clocks and people and most of the other subject-matters in this or any imaginable universe are simply not.

So the inquiry we are hypothesizing, the inquiry about law, starts humbly enough as: Why *have* the sort of thing or things that get called the law and

[1] *Posterior Analytics* II.2: 90a5–20:

> ...in all our searches we seek either whether there is an explanation or what the explanation is.... For in all these cases it is evident that *what* something is and *why* it is are the same. What is an eclipse? Privation of light from the moon by the earth's screening. Why is there an eclipse? or Why is the moon eclipsed? Because the light leaves it when the earth screens it.

legal system, legal institutions, and processes and arrangements that we call the law of our time and town? 'Why have it?' is of course elliptical for 'Why, if at all, should we have it?' The inquiry is nakedly about whether and if so why I, the reflecting person doing the inquiring, should want there to be this sort of thing, and be willing to do what I can and should to support and comply with it (if I should). It arises in the course of reflection, *deliberative* reflection, on what I should really do, here and now, and with my life as far as I can envisage it.

This sort of radically practical question first arises, Aquinas suggests,[2] when I am young enough to be in the junior school playground, aged about 7—about as far back as my adult memory of deliberation goes. Someone is teasing or punching or pinching someone else to make them cry. Should I join in? Or try to help the victim? Or call the teacher? Or just hope that the teacher will come and restore order? Or hope that no one will intervene to spoil this fun? Or be completely indifferent to all this and just get on with my sandwiches? If the teacher does come and break things up, should I be glad if she gives both the bully and the victim impartially a slap or detention or expulsion? Or should I hope she'll try to establish what happened, and deal differently with the two, restraining the wilfulness of the one, requiring also some restitution and apology, while comforting and reasserting the dignity of the other? In such primal incidents, at the dawn of the age of deliberative reason, Aquinas suggests we find the child—you or me—confronted with the need to choose whether to be the sort of person who joins the bully, or instead the sort of person who does what they can to help the victim and the teacher if and when that teacher acts to police the scene, judge the guilty, and make clear to all what will and will not be treated as acceptable conduct in the playground, the classroom, the bus stop outside the school, or anywhere else where one school child can interact with another. The child brings to this primal moment of choice many years of emotional formation, but now for the first time can envisage the choice as one between options which truly are *instances* of benefits which can be found in countless other instances, so that the immediate issue or practical problem of what to do in this situation invites deliberation which, however rapidly it takes place, is open to thoughts of the kind: What if I were the victim in a similar situation of disparate strength and aggressiveness? What if many people were free to do this to others? And so forth.

In such childhood situations one enters what I shall call the moral domain or, fully synonymously, the ethical domain or domain of morality. In that domain, which we never leave save through unconsciousness or a

[2] See the texts cited and summarized in *Aquinas* 41 n. 68. [Also essay I.11 at 184–5.]

supervening incapacity to understand options as instances of intelligible benefits realizable in indefinitely many situations, the question is always: What should I decide? 'Decide' straddles two distinguishable aspects of the existential issue: Which of the alternative incompatible courses of conduct (action or inaction) of mine should I think a reasonable option for me here and now? And do I here and now choose and at the relevant time carry out one of those reasonable options, or the one and only reasonable one among the options available, or do I choose and carry out one of the options which I judge attractive even though unreasonable (because cruel, disruptive, or in some other way unfair, and/or because a waste of my opportunities for pursuing and doing good)? *Decision*, then, includes both the practical *judgment* (a judgment of the kind we call judgments of conscience) and the self-directing, self-determining, self-shaping *choice*. In as much as it is obvious to me that I can be mistaken in my judgments about what is and is not reasonable, the issue presents itself more precisely as about *what I truly should decide*. The primary meaning of 'morality'—that is, morality's primary reality—is as the set of considerations that I understand as bearing upon the making of such decisions, and as available criteria for assessing my decisions as good or bad precisely as decisions, that is, as right—because choosing and putting into practice judgments which are true—or wrong because not doing do.

In, and in relation to, such childhood situations as the one I recalled from my playground, we did then and we do now as adults understand the need for a pattern of relationships between ourselves and other persons such that force is not used to inflict pain or other harm but only to preserve or restore a proper pattern of relationships. Among the aspects of this pattern are (a) that what one person reasonably possesses cannot be taken from that person without showing that another person has a better reason—to be sharply distinguished from a stronger desire or stronger capability to impose desire—to have that possession; and (b) that some persons have special responsibility for deciding on behalf of, or in relation to, all persons involved what pattern of relationships will be treated as acceptable, what to do about violations of it, whether or not to change it in light of new circumstances or of new or newly represented arguments, and so forth.

Part of a school's teaching, then, will concern the school's own rules about times of classes, conduct within classes, acceptance of the authority of teachers and perhaps of designated pupils and a headteacher, misconduct in the playground, dress and demeanour on and off the premises of the school on schooldays, and so forth. Another part, small in bulk perhaps but weighty, will be concerned to inform the children that shoplifting, playing truant, vandalism, and such like are offences against the law of the land and therefore also against the school's requirements of its pupils (even though not part of the school's rules as such), and that they will be enforced not, in the first instance, by the school's teachers but by the police and courts and custodial authorities of the state. To a child who understands the case for not joining the bully in the playground or the cheat in the schoolroom, the need for this Law is obvious, too. And the case for not joining the bully was never merely that I might be hurt by the bully or outranked by the cheat, but primarily that it is unfair for anyone to be. The injustice of the bully and the cheat is what cries out for prevention and restitution and penalty—and for rules written or otherwise posited (put in place) to make this clear in advance to all. The child who thinks that (to put it as H.L.A. Hart did),[3] we need rules (of school, town, and country) promulgated to restrict the free use of violence, theft, and fraud *means* that we need them *for the sake above all of justice.* The primary need or necessity here is precisely a moral one. And any sensible adult clear-headedly thinking practically—that is, in the context of the question what I truly ought to do—likewise means just that. (Influenced by considerations[4] which most of us here know operate, or have operated, in our own thinking, Hart did *not,* alas, *mean* that.) Thus, law is rightly conceived of as *by its nature morally valuable*—not in the sense that Joseph Raz attributes to that phrase,[5] according to which the thesis would be making a claim about 'the way [law or the law] is actually implemented in history', the obviously false claim that 'law in its historical manifestations through the ages has always, or generally, been a morally

[3] See *CL* 91, 193–200.

[4] These are hinted at in Hart, *Essays on Bentham*, 266–7:

> Of course, if it were the case, as a cognitive account of duty would hold it to be, that the statement that the subject has a legal duty to act in a way contrary to his interests and inclinations entails the statement that there exist reasons which are 'external' or objective, in the sense that they exist independently of his subjective motivation, it would be difficult to deny that legal duty is a form of moral duty. At least this would be so if it is assumed that ordinary non-legal moral judgments of duty are also statements of such objective reasons for action. For in that case, to hold that legal and moral duties were conceptually independent would involve the extravagant hypothesis that there were two independent 'worlds' or sets of objective reasons, one legal and the other moral.

For all its caution, it is reasonable to infer from this that a meta-ethical scepticism played a significant albeit largely unadmitted role in Hart's legal philosophy, and in his conclusion on p. 267 that 'judicial statements of the subject's legal duties need have nothing directly to do with the subject's reasons for action', a conclusion of which he says 'I am vividly aware that to many it will seem paradoxical, or even a sign of confusion', coming as it does 'at the end of a chapter, a central theme of which is the great importance for the understanding of law of the idea of authoritative reasons for action...' See also *CL* 191 and comments on this in my *NLNR* 30–1. [For a correction of the inference I articulate in this footnote, see essay 11 n. 72.]

[5] Or rather to the phrase which he treats as equivalent: '*the* law is a morally valuable institution'.

valuable institution'.[6] Rather, the sense of the thesis is like the sense in which, as Raz accepts, promising is a morally valuable institution. Or the sense in which the doctor says 'You need medicine', meaning something which by its nature is curative, without for a moment claiming or imagining that what has been served up as medicine 'through the ages' has always, or generally, or even usually been curative.

No need to labour this line of thought much further. It is obvious—as obvious, at least virtually and in rough outlines, to a child as it fully is to any reflective and reasonable adult—that, for the sake of justice and a flourishing community of people in good shape and doing as well as extrinsic circumstances permit, we need a set of rules, arrangements, processes, institutions, and persons with responsibility and thus authority, the set that is commonly called law, legal, legal system, and so forth. For the sake of justice, we need the rules to be public, clear, general, stable, capable of being complied with, and explicable to any fair-minded person; and we need them, again for justice's sake, to be complied with (save where there is an overriding moral obligation not to) by those whose responsibility it is to announce and/or enforce them and/or to resolve disputes about their application. Some finer points about what it is for a society to have its need for law adequately met are elaborated by Timothy Endicott.[7] His discussion proceeds by repudiating any concept of the rule of law that '*we should not want*'. That is a sound way of proceeding in legal philosophy, though I am inclined to carp that just as it would be odd to use the phrase 'moral ideal' to describe the thought that one should not side with the bully or the cheat and that the teacher should urgently sort things out, so there is something equivocal about the common saying that the rule of law is an 'ideal'.[8] The principles of the rule of law are, at least in their main lines, moral *requirements*, strong even though not unconditional, unqualifiable, or indefeasible.

The life of the law, more precisely its primary reality, is not in the *logic* of conceptual coherence or of understanding what other people have thought or said or stipulated or commanded or enacted, nor in the *experience* of cause and effect and patterns of recurrence. Those are part of its matrix

[6] Raz, 'About Morality and the Nature of Law' at 13 (= Raz, *Between Authority and Interpretation*, 179).

[7] Endicott, 'The Reason of the Law' at 85.

[8] There is a sense in which the idea of having a society regulated by justice and responsible government and the rule of law is an ideal (or three interrelated ideals). But there is another sense in which the rule of law, like responsible (answerable) government, and justice (all of which are described by Endicott as ideals), is a set of moral *requirements* which in many situations are here and now mandatory, rather than an ideal. (Endicott recognizes this, too, e.g. when he says that what he calls a responsible form of government is a 'requirement'.)

of necessary preconditions. The primary reality of the law is rather in its claim, as itself a moral requirement, on my deliberating about what to decide—that is, what to judge about the options available to me, and what to choose and do once I have made my judgment. This mode of *our positive law*'s existence—as a morally legitimate and compelling, albeit conditionally and only defeasibly compelling, *claim on my action when I am thinking what to do* as a plain citizen (child or adult), a judge, a police officer, a tax inspector, and executor, and so forth—is the primary reality of *law*. It is primary because the rational force of this claim is fully intelligible even before one knows anything much about the content of the law and certainly before one has been taught anything about law in general or 'the concept of law'.

That rational force, like all rational force, is at bottom the attractiveness of truth. Because I judge it to be true that, say, the victim's bodily and emotional well-being is as much an instantiation of intelligible human good as the well-being of the bully or of myself, and true that this or any bully's infliction of pain for the pleasure of it is a violation of the master moral principle/requirement that one's choices should always be open to the fulfilment of every human person, and a violation of that master principle's specification in the Golden Rule of fairness, and true that offenders against justice should not be left to enjoy the fruits of their wrongdoing, I should, at the moment of decision, treat as authoritative the positive legal norms empowering somebody to appoint somebody else to the responsibility and authority of adjudicating complaints of bullying and punishing them to an extent specified not only by norms of fairness but also by positive rules adopted 'optionally' for the sake of consistency across wider spans of time and social context. Indeed, if child, I should take the risk of reporting the bully to the teacher, and if teacher, I should exercise the adjudicative and punitive role according to the rules of the school, the law of the land, and the requirements of fairness when the school rules and the law leave something to be decided. And so forth, in reference to any more or less reasonable legally posited rule or principle you like to consider: at the moment of decision on an issue on which that rule bears, any obligation it expressly or impliedly purports to impose, or to authorize the imposition of, is fit to be acknowledged by me as truly what it purports to be, viz. the decisive regulator of my action here and now—so decisive that it could be overridden only by some competing *moral* obligation bearing on me here and now with such weight that anyone with the community's common good in mind would acknowledge the justice of my treating the latter as overriding the law and its legal-moral obligation.

But, of course, these purely moral thoughts about *our* law certainly warrant a theory of *law*, a general account of what—because it is so obviously needed—one should anticipate finding in existence, to one degree or another, in any human community and of what, as historical studies confirm, has indeed existed (with many and various imperfections and reasonable and unreasonable adaptations and approximations) in virtually every human community of which we are aware, and has been and is manifested in the translatable language, that is, the self-understanding and thus the concepts, of every such community.

But whatever the case about other peoples and their concepts, it is clear to us why we need such rules, institutions, processes, and so forth. Thus it is clear to us *what* law—positive law—is, at least so far as we need it and find we, by and large, have it. Nor is this core of clarity impaired by the fact that *some* elements of what has been posited in our community in response to our shared moral need are, in my judgment or yours, so unreasonable that the presumptive moral claim on us of these elements is, in my judgment or yours, defeated in whole or part. Posited (enacted or judicially pronounced) rules of the latter kind are analogous to contracts which have been made in full compliance with every formality and other procedural condition specified by the law of contract but are void for illegality. Or, to take two perhaps closer analogies, they are like medicines which prove futile or lethal and are thus *not medicinal* at all, or like *arguments* the formal elegance of which only masks their invalidity: *no argument.* Unjust laws are not laws, though they may still count in reasonable conscientious deliberations, and certainly warrant attention and description. So, too, invalid arguments may win a place both in manuals of rhetoric as the art of persuasion, and in guides to fallacies for young logicians, quack and lethal medicines are sold as medicines and listed in histories of medicine and on warning notices, and contracts void for illegality earn a place both in books on the law of contract and, more interestingly, in books on restitution where their apparent validity, or their widespread acceptance as valid, may affect the success or quantum of a restitutionary claim. It should go without saying that some people are persuaded by fallacies, that parties may for years consider themselves legally bound by a contract in fact void for illegality, and that the police and the hangman may act against me in accordance with unjust laws. The excitement and hostility aroused by the old saying that unjust laws are not laws is quite needless.[9]

[9] On the presentation of this essay as a lecture, Raz asked why law should be thought to be like argument, medicine, or contracts, rather than like novels or paintings or people, that are still novels or paintings or people, even if they are bad. The answer is that, like argument, medicines, and contracts, law has a focused and normative point to which everything else about it is properly to

The course of practical moral deliberation and reflection which concludes by acknowledging the need for and presumptive obligatoriness of posited law is obvious and obviously reasonable. So there is nothing surprising about the plain historical fact that the first articulation of *positive law* as a category or a technical term, and the first adequate explanations of that term's referent, were by moralists.[10] These theorists had little or no interest in either undertaking or adopting any general descriptive theory of human affairs, except insofar as understanding representative patterns of human behaviour and misbehaviour is and was one element in a general reflection which from beginning to end focused upon the question what should I—first of all the very person doing the reflecting—truly decide and do.

The work of moral reflection, whether it is contemplatively and anticipatorily general-practical or here and now deliberatively practical, always—as I have said—takes the world as we know it, and shuns utopianism and Rawlsian hypotheses of a world of 'full compliance' with justice. So it is also no surprise that the moralist Thomas Aquinas, as Lon Fuller says, identified[11] each of the eight elements pulled together by Lon Fuller as the components of the Rule of Law, considered as structural requirements of justice which bear on the institutional and procedural implementation of the justice-required response to the need to have law rather than either mere anarchy or the masked anarchy and oppressive unfairness of tyrannical or arbitrary government or government which treats its subjects as mere pawns, mere instruments in some game or managerial project of the governors. (And it is no surprise that the Thomist account of law includes 'success conditions' of the kind desired[*] by Joseph Raz: law must be directed to the *common* good, must not go outside the domain of justice, which is *external* acts affecting *other* people,[12] is subject to equitable override, and so forth.)

In short, a complete and fully realistic theory of law can be and in all essentials has been worked out from the starting point of the 100 per cent normative question, what should I decide to do and, equivalently, what kind of person should I resolve or allow myself to be. I can think of no interesting project of inquiry left over for a philosophical theory

be regarded as subordinate. Novels and paintings, on the other hand, can have incompatible points, e.g. to entertain or arouse (like kitsch or porn) or to tell a truth with artistry. People exist in the natural order as living substances even if they are not functioning adequately or at all in the orders of logic and thought, deliberation, and/or exercises of skill.

[10] [And canonists]: see essay 7. [11] For the texts, see *Aquinas* 257.

[*] Raz, 'About Morality and the Nature of Law' at 8–9, 13 (= Raz, *Between Authority and Interpretation*, 173–4, 178).

[12] See *Aquinas* 222–45.

of law with any different starting point. Perhaps someone will be able to suggest one.[13]

II

Some people have thought there is room for a theory with a different starting point, a theory which is not even a tiny bit normative (directive of my decisions) but instead enjoys what Brian Leiter, appropriating a phrase of John Gardner's, praises as 'comprehensive normative inertness'.[14] This theory does not, Leiter says, endorse what law-abiding and just judges or officials or citizens do, or criticize what lawless and unjust judges, officials, or citizens do. Instead it identifies all or at least some of the 'necessary features' of what judges, other lawyers, and I suppose officials and law-abiding citizens do in making and/or abiding by the law.[15] It aims *merely* to state—describe—what features 'all legal guidance necessarily has'.[16]

My argument in sec. I was that such an enterprise is redundant: everything you could want as an accurate and factual description of what judges, officials, and law-abiding citizens do, and why they need to do it, is supplied by the theory which is as robustly normative in its starting point and conclusions as anything could be, though taking in, along the way, all that the world offers in the way of variegated implementations, improvements, distortions, abuses, and so forth. But there is, as Leiter reminds us, another question: Is a purely descriptive, normatively 100 per cent inert theory of law even possible? Can such a theory identify what features all legal guidance *necessarily* has? He argues that it is possible, and that it can identify these necessities while remaining normatively entirely inert.

His argument brings him to conclude that 'the defense of descriptive jurisprudence turn[s] on a rather uncritical invocation of the claim that we [are] describing "our" concept, where the first person plural possessive [is] to be cashed out in terms of statistical frequency',[17] a procedure capable of delivering, as he says, 'no more than ethnographically relative results'.[18] Such results, I think he hints, are scarcely worthy of the name of *philosophy* or *general theory*. And certainly they fall far short of warranting, or even making sense of, the initial claim—sponsored, curiously, by Leiter himself—to have identified what features law *necessarily* has. Whatever

[13] For whatever reason, at the time no such suggestion was offered.

[14] Leiter, 'Beyond the Hart/Dworkin Debate: The Methodology Problem in Jurisprudence' at 29, quoting Gardner, 'Legal Positivism: 5½ Myths' at 203.

[15] Leiter *ibid.*, quoting Gardner *ibid.* [16] Leiter at 30, quoting Gardner at 203.

[17] Leiter at 50. [18] *Ibid.* at 51.

Leiter's final position, in his paper, about this question of necessities,[19] I myself fully agree with these conclusions about the project of a normatively 100 per cent inert descriptive philosophy or theory of law.

Unhappily, Leiter is not in agreement with my own argument for those conclusions. He does think I have an argument; showing why my argument is wrong will go a long way, he says, to resolving some main issues in the present debates about method in legal theory. His demonstration that my argument is wrong consists of a quotation from *Natural Law and Natural Rights* and the brisk observation that at its core there is a non sequitur. Here's how he puts it:

> The non-sequitur occurs in the slide from... the 'Banal Truth' that 'evaluations... are an indispensable and decisive component in the selection or formation of any concepts for use in description of such aspects of human affairs as law or legal order' to the claim that the evaluation in question involves 'decid[ing] what the requirements of practical reasonableness really are.' I take the Banal Truth to be the uncontested legacy of post-Kuhnian and post-Quinean philosophy of science: there is no such thing as a presuppositionless inquiry, of facts that are 'theory-free,' and so on. But that goes no distance at all to establishing that the presuppositions of the descriptive enterprise require judgments about what Finnis calls 'practical reasonableness' or that the viewpoint from which 'importance' and 'significance' are to be assessed is the 'practical viewpoint'.[20]

And with that last sentence I fully agree: the Banal Truth of post-Kuhnian and post-Quinean philosophy of science certainly goes no distance at all in establishing my conclusion, and I've never imagined or suggested it does.

Part of the trouble here is that the passage Leiter has quoted contains none of my argument, but only its conclusions. The sentence which begins his key quotation from me begins, not where he starts, but like this:

> Thus by a long march through the working or implicit methodology of contemporary analytical jurisprudence, we arrive at the conclusion reached more rapidly (though on the basis of a much wider social science) by Max Weber:[21] namely, that [and

[19] His Quinean dismissal of the distinction between necessary and contingent truth cannot be accepted, since the supposed distinction cannot be satisfactorily assessed if the discussion flips, like Leiter's, into an external point of view, as when he says:

> there is simply the socio-historical fact that, at any given point in the history of inquiry, there are some statements we are unlikely to give up in the face of recalcitrant empirical evidence, and others that we are quite willing to give up when empirical evidence conflicts. (Leiter at 44.)

The question is whether, when we adopt an internal point of view (i.e. consider the data, evidence, subject-matter on its merits), we have grounds for being unwilling to give up what we consider necessary—and what these grounds are.

[20] Leiter at 34, quoting *NLNR* 16.

[21] *Pace* Leiter (at 34 n. 61), what I was invoking here was *not* (as I put it on the page he cites from an earlier section of my chapter) 'Max Weber's not too clearly explained methodological device, the *ideal-type*', but rather (as I put it in the endnote to the passage Leiter quotes from me) Weber's specific

here Leiter begins quoting] the evaluations of the theorist are an indispensable and decisive component in the selection or formation of any concepts for use in description of such aspects of human affairs as law or legal order.

My argument and its conclusion has nothing to do with a general philosophy of science or of theory-construction, post-Kuhn, Quine, or anybody, and nothing to do with the fact that if you are to undertake some research or reflection you must think there is something valuable in doing so and something important about the subject-matter. My argument is, as the sentence says, about *social* science and 'such aspects of *human affairs as law and legal order*'. What differentiates subject-matter of this broad kind from anything in the sciences of nature or mathematics and logic is stated on pp. 1 and 2 of *Natural Law and Natural Rights*: unlike what I there call 'natural sciences including a part of the science of psychology', human actions, practices, dispositions, and the discourse partially constitutive of some such practices, cannot be understood without understanding their point, objective, significance, or importance '*as conceived by the people who performed them, engaged in them, etc.*' I here took for granted and implied, but treated as too obvious to need stating, that those conceptions of point, objective, and so forth, the conceptions concrete people have actually had, can be well described without being shared and, indeed, can be well described without any sharing in the practice of evaluation at all. That is what biographers, military historians, and others do all the time. And it is precisely this that gives rise to the problem that set my chapter off on the 'long march through the working or implicit methodology of contemporary analytical jurisprudence'.

The problem is that biography and history are one thing and a *general* social theory or a *philosophy* of society or power or authority or coordination or law is (or are) something purportedly quite different. There is only one italicized sentence in Chapter I, and it is right here at the top of p. 2: '*How, then, is there to be a general descriptive theory of these varying particulars?*' There is no problem of principle or method in describing with complete value-freedom, purity, and complete normative inertness the concerns, self-interpretation, conduct, institutions, vocabulary, and discourse of as

thesis about 'the necessity of the theorist using his own evaluations in order to assess significance for descriptive theory', for which I cited (*NLNR* 21) Weber's arguments in Shils and Finch, *Max Weber on the Methodology of the Social Sciences*, 58, 76–82, 21, as well as Freund, *The Sociology of Max Weber*, 51–61. My endnote proceeded with some cautions about some of Weber's argumentation for his thesis. The passages that Leiter quotes from Gerth and Mills, *From Max Weber* in an effort to explicate the Weberian ideal-type reveal how unexplained are the key terms 'construction [in what sense?] of certain [which?] elements of reality' as 'theoretically illuminating [why? how?] features of varied situations'. My discussion in Chapter I of *NLNR* endeavours to explain and justify a much higher level of methodological specificity than anything Leiter has found in Gerth and Mills's Weber.

many people as you like. But can you finish up with anything more than what I called, on the same page, 'a conjunction of lexicography with local history, or... a juxtaposition of all lexicographies conjoined with all local histories'—a mere list or heap? My concern had much in common with Leiter's: the concern that conceptual analysis and appeals to intuition can deliver no more than 'ethnographically relative results',[22] a lexicography or 'glorified lexicography'[23] or 'pop lexicography'[24] the results of which are 'strictly ethnographic and local',[25] a 'banal descriptive sociology of the Gallup-poll variety'.[26] What the long march through contemporary jurisprudence (as it extended from Bentham to the late 1970s) made manifest can be summarized in two propositions: (1) any plausible theory that results from an effort to describe law, a subject-matter considered as something transcending any local history, has not been and will not be normatively inert; (2) this is in large part because, given that any general theory of law, however merely descriptive its ambition, necessarily prefers one concept of law over countless others—given (that is to say) that the theorist's is always a more or less new concept, one that the theorist considers an improved concept, better fitted to answer the questions people have about how law relates to other things and why its various elements hang together as they do—explanations of why this concept is an improved one, to be preferred to other concepts, are designed to show that this concept, this theory, makes better sense of the complex idea that law is something there is reason to have.

If there is a worthwhile general theory, or philosophy, of human cities or the human city, as Leiter imagines but I rather doubt, it will have much the same character: neither human laws nor human cities exist in any interesting way unless human persons, who could think and choose otherwise, understand the set of interlocking good reasons there are for trying to create them and maintain them. They (the laws and cities) are not part of the world of the naturally given, though the reasons for wanting to create and maintain laws, if not cities, are so important for the well-being of creatures whose life and capacities are part of the naturally given, but whose flourishing is not, that those reasons have reasonably—though at the hazard of countless misunderstandings—been called elements of natural law (in a sense of which natural scientists, as such, are entirely innocent).

Back to that long march through contemporary jurisprudence. No question, however, of repeating it here. And no question of repeating my own direct dialectical argument[27] for the conclusions Leiter quoted: that

[22] Leiter at 51. [23] *Ibid.* at 46. [24] *Ibid.* at 45 n. 89. [25] *Ibid.* at 46.
[26] *Ibid.* at 45. [27] *NLNR* 13–16.

there must be and is a central case of that so-called internal point of view which plays so structural a role in every contemporary jurisprudence. A reminder or two must suffice. Hart argues, against Kelsen and (in a different way) Bentham and Austin, that rules conferring private power on individuals (for example to make a contract) should not be described as mere fragments of obligation-imposing rules. His argument adduces or describes no fact that Bentham, Austin, and Kelsen had failed to describe, other than the truth that there is reason to want and value private powers, a kind of reason different from the reasons to want and respect rules making certain kinds of act or forbearance obligatory. About this truth Hart was not normatively inert. Precisely in order to argue for his theory as against Kelsen's, Bentham's, and Austin's, Hart called the kind of private powers resultant from power-conferring rules 'a huge and distinctive amenity',[28] 'at least as valuable to society as duty'.[29] Of course, he begins by saying that, to understand these rules (and their distinctness from obligation-imposing rules), we must look at them 'from the point of view of those who exercise them'.[30] But this point of view proves to be simply (or at least primarily) his, yours, and mine, not because they are his, yours, or mine, but because it seems true to him, you, and me, that there is *value* in having the rules at stake, *reason* for having them (which is not in the least incompatible with our also understanding that there might be circumstances where countervailing reasons might give sufficient reason not to have them).

Further on in *The Concept of Law*, Hart argued that law should be understood as, centrally, a union of primary with secondary rules. The former are, he said, to impose obligations to abstain from violence, theft, and fraud, and other obligations. The latter are, he said, to remedy the defects of a set-up in which rules of the primary kind were unaccompanied by rules conferring powers to change them and adjudicate about their application—rules which although logically secondary are so important to a society that their introduction 'is a step forward' comparable to the invention of the wheel.[31] Talk about valuable amenities and steps forward cannot reasonably be described as normatively inert.

Hart's discussion is particularly illuminating when he takes up the precise question whether there are, as Leiter and Gardner propose, some 'necessary' features of law or legal systems or what lawyers do. Hart does so in relation to 'the traditional question whether every legal system *must* [his italics] provide for sanctions'.[32] There are, he says:

> two unsuitable alternatives which are often taken as exhaustive: on the one hand that of saying that this is required by 'the' meaning of the words 'law' or 'legal

[28] *CL* 41. [29] *Ibid.*, 41. [30] *Ibid.* [31] *Ibid.*, 42. [32] *Ibid.*, 199.

system', and on the other hand of saying that it is 'just a fact' that most legal systems do provide for sanctions.[33]

(So here he is also taking up, in order to set aside, the statistical typicality criterion that Leiter's paper seemed for a time to be proposing.)

Neither of these alternatives is satisfactory. There are no settled principles forbidding the use of the word 'law' of systems where there are no centrally organized sanctions, and there is good reason (though no compulsion) for using the expression 'international law' of a system which has none. On the other hand, we do need to distinguish the place that sanctions must have within a municipal system, if it is to serve the purposes of beings constituted as men are. We can say, given the setting of natural facts and aims which make sanctions both possible and necessary in a municipal system, that this is a natural necessity; and some such phrase is needed also to convey the status of the minimum forms of protection for persons, property, and promises which are indispensable features of municipal law.

Six pages earlier he had given this form of necessity a description more illuminating than the opaque term 'natural'; he had called it 'rational': 'It is important to stress the distinctively rational connexion between natural facts and legal or moral rules',[34] and again 'the facts mentioned [about vulnerability and so forth] afford a *reason* [Hart's italics] why, given survival as an aim, law and morals should include a specific content'.[35] This content must—that is, there is a strong rational requirement that it—include sanctions. Why? Because:

submission to the system of restraints would be folly if there were no organization for the coercion of those who would then try to obtain the advantages of the system without submitting to its obligations. 'Sanctions' are therefore required [necessary, Leiter and Gardner might say] not as the normal motive for obedience, but as a *guarantee* that those who would voluntarily obey shall not be sacrificed to those who would not. To obey, without this, would be to risk going to the wall. Given this standing danger what reason demands is *voluntary* co-operation in a *coercive* system.[36]

Nothing normatively inert about all or any of this.

But, of course, Hart wanted to keep to a minimum the normative virility of his explanatory-descriptive account. Only the minimum of purpose or purposes (conception(s) of value) is meant to get into the account, and in this minimum the only identified component is the purpose or good of survival. Concern for survival might indeed explain well enough why a legal system *must* contain rules against the free use of violence and sanctions against violation of *those* rules. Concern for survival does not seem a plausibly

[33] *Ibid.* [34] *Ibid.*, 193. [35] *Ibid.* [36] *Ibid.*, 198.

sufficient explanation for the alleged necessity of rules providing even 'minimum forms of protection for...property, and promises which are similarly indispensable [necessary] features of municipal law'.[37] And it has virtually no explanatory power in relation to the other great feature of law which Hart's whole book argues is necessary: the set of secondary rules of change, adjudication, and recognition which together move us from the pre-legal (or the non-paradigmatically 'legal' like international law) to the paradigmatically or centrally legal instantiated by mature systems of municipal law. The defects which these rules are needed [necessary] to remedy have little to do with survival. One cannot speak of defects and remedies without presupposing some good diminished or damaged by the defect; if the good is merely a supposed good, the defect will be merely a supposed defect. But Hart speaks of defects, not supposed defects. Still, he does not identify the goods harmed by these defects, beyond glancing references to uncertainty, waste, vendettas, and the absence of that earlier-mentioned amenity and great step forward of being able to change and shift and vary the obligations imposed upon one by general rules.[38] What matters, however, is that he has here, at the heart of his theory, quite left behind the concern for *minimum* purposes.

According to Leiter:

> Finnis admits...that positivism—understood either in Hart's or Raz's version—gives an adequate account of 'what any competent lawyer...would say are (or are not) intra-systemically valid laws, imposing "legal requirements"'.[39]

And then he intimates surprise that I do not treat this 'concession' of mine as an admission of 'natural law theory's demise'. Even if I had made this admission or concession, Leiter's surprise would be misplaced because, as I have argued above, natural law theory can do, did, and does all that is needed to describe law's positivity—to describe, that is to say, the kind of law that has among the necessary conditions for its existence the sheer fact that it has been made or adopted by some person or persons at some identifiable place and period. But I made no admission about the 'adequacy' of anyone's account. Here is the passage containing the sentence that Leiter has, I'm afraid, misunderstood. It makes no reference to Hart or Raz or their accounts, and neither asserts nor presupposes that their accounts have the normative inertness to which paradigmatic positivism aspires.[40] It is, as the sentence and paragraphs preceding it make explicit, a sentence

[37] *Ibid.*, 199. [38] *Ibid.*, 93. [39] Leiter at 28–9.

[40] Hart conceived his account of the necessity of sanctions and primary rules as a '*reply to* the positivist thesis that "law may have any content"': *CL* 199.

concerned with laws that, though widely treated as valid, and rigorously enforced, are very unjust:

Positivism never coherently reaches beyond reporting attitudes and convergent behaviour (perhaps the sophisticated and articulate attitudes that constitute a set of rules of recognition, change and adjudication). It has nothing to say to officials or private citizens who want to judge whether, when, and why the authority and obligatoriness *claimed* and *enforced* by those who are *acting as* officials of a legal system, and by their directives, are indeed *authoritative reasons* for their own conscientious action. Positivism, at this point, does no more than repeat (i) what any competent lawyer—including every legally competent adherent of natural law theory—would say are (or are not) intra-systemically valid laws, imposing 'legal requirements' and (ii) what any street-wise observer would warn are the likely consequences of non-compliance.... Positivism is... redundant.[41]

So far from admitting that a normatively inert description of law gives an adequate account of anything, I was saying there, and—subject to an important qualification that I shall come to later—I am happy to repeat, that positivism in Leiter's sense gives no *account*, no theory or what Hart would call *elucidation* or explanation, at all, let alone an adequate one. The aspiration to be normatively inert makes it impossible to provide any explanation of the kind Hart was seeking throughout his work.

Leiter says my objections 'seem to reflect, at bottom, misunderstanding of... the "comprehensive normative inertness" of legal positivism.'[*] I don't doubt that I may misunderstand it from top to bottom. But if so, it will not have been for want of attention to this aspiration to normative inertness, and to the travails of theorists who struggle to reconcile that aspiration with their other aspirations: to identify what is and is not necessary in law and legal systems, and to add some explanatory or elucidatory content to what every competent lawyer or citizen already knows. My first published essay on general practical philosophy, nearly thirty-five years ago, began with a study[42] of Kelsen's efforts to determine whether positivism's comprehensive normative inertness (called by him purity) requires or permits legal theory to say that legal systems make sense, that

[41] 2000d at 1611; also in essay 5 at 115. The ellipses are filled as follows:

It cannot explain the authoritativeness, for an official's or a private citizen's conscience (ultimate rational judgment), of these alleged and imposed requirements, nor their lack of such authority when radically unjust. Positivism is not only incoherent. It is also redundant.

The incoherence is explained earlier as 'its inherent and self-imposed incapacity to succeed in the explanatory task it sets itself'. In the terminology of the present essay, it is the incoherence of complete normative inertness *with* the ambition to explain law (even descriptively). There is no confusion in my essay between incoherence and mere failure to seek a moral justification.

[*] Leiter at 29. [42] Essay I.6 at 105–6 (1970a at 103).

is, whether it is a necessary feature of legal systems that they exclude the juristic finding that completely contradictory legal rules (norms) coexist, each equally valid. In the end, Kelsen came to the same conclusion as I did in that paper: that a theory does not have comprehensive normative inertness unless it holds that contradictory legal norms can coexist, each equally valid. To treat non-contradiction as a necessary feature of law is to surrender to natural law methods of theorizing, he judged.[43]

Most other people who wish to think of themselves as normatively inert when doing legal theory have denied that their aspiration requires of them this late-Kelsenian austerity. They think a purpose of giving *coherent* guidance should be included among the 'minimum purposes' of any legal system and is thus a necessary feature of law. I cannot think of any good reason, compatible with normative inertness, for their thinking this. As I argued thirty-five years ago: Why should not some régime wish to use the law's norm-creating capacities to keep the population at its mercy by confronting them with contradictory legal requirements, so that the régime's judges and other officials can enforce against selected persons whichever of a pair of contradictory legal norms those officials choose: either, or both, or neither?[*] And I would now go on to add: Why should it not do so in accordance with some further secret rule of law? How can one justify the legal-theoretical (or so-called conceptual) claim that law must be promulgated? How can Austin justify his legal-theoretical claim that one type of particular command of a sovereign is a law but another is necessarily not? How can Hart justify his claim that a rule of recognition is a necessary feature of legal systems? Or power-conferring laws, distinct from obligation-imposing laws? Or rules of change? How can Joseph Raz justify his claim that it is a necessary feature of laws that they claim legitimate moral authority? Why should not some regime set up a legal system which has every feature of, say, Hart's concept of law but expressly asserts that morality is for sissies, and that its authority as a system of law is nothing more, and nothing less, than its willingness and ability to impose sanctions, damages awards, injunctions, requisitions, etc., for non-compliance?

[43] Kelsen, *General Theory of Norms*, 214, 217, 224, 391, 394–5. He also (*ibid.* at 226–41) judged it a fatal breach of comprehensive normative inertness for legal theory to hold that if [P1] a valid legal norm of a jurisdiction specifies that thieves ought to be imprisoned for ten years, and [P2] Smith a subject in that jurisdiction has committed theft, then [P3] it is legally required that Smith ought to be imprisoned for ten years. For legal theory to hold that P3 is legally required by P1 and P2 would be for legal theory to participate in practical reasoning; the time for legal theory to assert P3 is after someone with legal authority to do so decides that P3; only then can legal theory include P3 in its inert description of that legal system. [Kelsen adopted these positions in writings later than those I was considering in essay I.6 (1970a).]

[*] Essay I.6 at 106 (1970a at 103).

In all such cases, it seems to me, there is no necessity to be had save necessity of the kind that good practical reasons pick out for us when we are deliberating about what to want and choose to try to have, necessities that thus earn a place in a normatively virile theory or philosophy of law.

III

A word about 'earning a place in the theory or philosophy of law'. Like Leiter, Jules Coleman argues that the norms for evaluating theories 'are pragmatic, theoretical, epistemic, and most importantly, discursive'.[44] Unlike Leiter, Coleman thinks that theories of law are theories of the concept of law, and he says:

> We are choosing a theory of the concept—the best theory of the concept—as part of a construction of a general theory of the world and the concepts we employ to structure it. Different theories of the concept allow us to nest law and the concept of it differently: some emphasizing its centrality to the guidance of conduct; others to the theory of political obligation; others to an ideal of the person that can be realized only given certain social forms and institutions.

For my part, I think theories of law are concepts of law, not theories of concepts.[45] I think no good theory is ever chosen; it is a matter of judgment, not choice: the subject-matter is in command, and our only choice is whether to pursue the questions that occur to us about it, and to respect the disciplines of truth: evidence, coherence, and the like. We don't, strictly speaking, *construct* a general theory of the world, we develop one. And I cannot imagine why a theory of law could not and should not say what is true about law's 'centrality to the guidance of conduct' *and* to political obligation *and* to the reality of persons and the way in which their flourishing 'can be realized only given certain social forms and institutions'. No need at all for 'different theories'. A page or two earlier, Coleman had been speaking more realistically, about what is and is not 'inherent in the nature of law'.[46] Indeed, he said that 'the morally attractive property of law is its inherent potential to realize or to manifest an ideal of governance'.

[44] Coleman, *The Practice of Principle*, 196.

[45] So I agree with much in Leiter's critique of 'conceptual analysis'. But if the 'naturalistic turn', with which he associates that critique, is well represented, as he suggests (Leiter nn. 77 and 101), by Quine's essay 'Natural Kinds', in Quine, *Ontological Relativity and Other Essays*, 114–38, it seems likely to be a turn for the even worse: Quine's essay is a striking example of (multiple) self-refutation, relying again and again on distinctions between natural kinds of e.g. arguments, disciplines, stages in 'the [human] race's progress', etc., etc., to argue that 'it is a mark of maturity of a branch [sc. kind] of science that the notion of similarity or kind finally dissolves, so far as is relevant to that branch of science' (121), that 'induction itself is essentially only... animal expectation or habit formation' (125), and so on.

[46] Coleman, *The Practice of Principle* at 192.

But then Coleman went on to argue for what we can call the paperweight theory of law. It goes like this. Law is a thing that, by its nature,[47] has the inherent capacity to realize certain moral ideals. Because that is indeed an inherent capacity, an analysis of law 'should help us to understand what we find morally attractive about it, and an analysis that failed to do so would be lacking'.[48] But though hammers have the inherent capacity to be paperweights, being a paperweight or suitable for service as a paperweight is no part of the concept of a hammer. So, too (the argument goes), being morally attractive is no part of the concept or proper analysis or theory of law:

> autonomy, dignity, welfare do not enter at any point into the analysis... nor do any other moral properties. These ideals are external to the concept of law; law [just] happens to be the kind of thing that can serve them well.[49]

Justice, like human rights, dignity, and welfare, is as external to the concept or nature of law as the hammer's capacity to serve as a paperweight, or as the backbone of a garden gnome, is external to the concept and nature of a hammer.

This confident and unargued slicing between what is internal and what external to the nature of law overlooks the truth for which I have been arguing throughout this essay. One can reasonably spend a lifetime of using hammers without ever noticing that they would be good as paperweights or the backbones of garden gnomes. But one cannot begin to understand what law is about without noticing, not merely that it shares much of the same action-guiding vocabulary as morality, but—overwhelmingly more important—that it does so because it purports to occupy *the same place in the world* as morality: the decisive framing of the options for choice at the point where deliberation is ending in decision about what I should do and what kind of person I should be. To hold that the 'morally attractive' virtue of justice stands to judicial responsibilities for adjudicating disputes according to law as loosely and extrinsically as paperweights and garden gnomes stand to hammers is, I suggest, a plain *reductio ad absurdum*.[50]

IV

As I mentioned earlier, I should qualify an assertion I made in the essay from which Leiter quoted: that, given its desire for normative inertness,

[47] *Ibid.* at 194. [48] *Ibid.* at 195. [49] *Ibid.*

[50] As [or rather: to the extent loosely indicated in the last two sentences, one can concur with what] Raz says, in *The Authority of Law*, 159, 158: 'positivists can and should adopt' the thesis 'that normative terms like "a right", "a duty", "ought" are used in the same sense in legal, moral, and other normative statements'.

positivism cannot do more than replicate what every lawyer already says. The qualification: it is a mistake to talk about positivism at all. I have been trying for decades not to do this sort of thing, and repent of having done it. (My excuse for having done it is not worth exploring here.) Better to think: there's no such thing as positivism.

Take, for example, the talk of 'normative inertness' which I have been pursuing through much of this essay. Here is Leiter's phrase: 'what John Gardner has aptly called the "comprehensive normative inertness" of legal positivism'.[51] But in Gardner's essay, the subject of which 'comprehensive normative inertness' is predicated is a *proposition*, labelled by Gardner (LP*):

> In any legal system, whether a given norm is legally valid, and hence whether it forms part of the law of that system, depends on its sources, not its merits (where its merits, in the relevant senses, include the merits of its sources).[52]

Thus Gardner's full phrase is: 'the comprehensive normative inertness in (LP*)'.[53] And then Gardner, unlike Leiter, goes on to make the following points about (LP*):

(1) It[54] 'is not a whole theory of law's nature, after all. It is a thesis about legal validity, which is compatible with any number of further theses about law's nature, including the thesis that all valid law is *by its nature* subject to special moral objectives and imperatives *of its own*'.[55]

(2) (LP*) relates to the question 'Is this really a law' and not to the 'more abstract' question 'What is law?' And 'once one has tackled the question whether a certain law is valid there remain many relatively independent questions to address concerning its meaning, its fidelity to law's purposes, its role in sound legal reasoning, its legal effects, and its social functions... To study the nature of law one needs to turn one's mind to the philosophical aspects of these further questions too. To these further questions there is no distinctively "legal positivist" answer, because legal positivism is a thesis only about the conditions of legal validity.'[56]

(3) *Natural Law and Natural Rights* 'tak[es] (LP*) for granted although remaining studiously unexcited about it'.[57]

(4) Legal positivists 'need not deny that in some contexts "legality"... names a moral value, such that... laws may be more

[51] Leiter at 29. [52] Gardner, 'Legal Positivism: 5½ Myths' at 201. [53] *Ibid.* at 203.

[54] *Ibid.* at 210: the subject of his sentence is 'Legal positivism' but the whole context shows that this is here understood as or stipulated to be a theory the entire content of which is (LP*).

[55] *Id.* (emphases added). [56] *Ibid.* at 224. [57] *Ibid.* at 227.

> or less valid depending on ... their merits. Nor need they deny that one must capture this moral value of legality ... in order to tell the whole story of law's nature.'[58]

So: the normative inertness endorsed by Gardner is vastly narrower than that endorsed by Leiter or by Kelsen in their envisaged positivist accounts of 'law's essential properties'[59] or nature.

And here is Gardner on the thesis which Coleman and Leiter (writing in 1996) take to be one of the 'two central beliefs' shared by 'all [legal] positivists'—that 'there is no necessary connection between law and morality':[60] writing in 2001 and using the identical words to articulate the thesis, Gardner says it is an absurd thesis. That legal positivists hold this thesis is, he surprisingly adds, a mere myth.[61]

To cut a very long story short, the question whether any truth is conveyed 'by legal positivism', like the question what is to be understood by 'legal positivism', is a gloomy jungle into which it is best never to stray.

As Gardner remarked, I see little to object to in (LP*). The sense it gives the terms 'legally valid' and 'law' is *precisely* the sense needed to give sense to the well-known slogan, recalled in sec. I and not usually associated with legal positivism, 'an unjust *law* [something *legally valid* in its making but seriously unjust]—is *not a law* [lacks something essential to law's central purpose of determining what I truly should do].' (Recall: a bad argument is no argument—and all the other analogous sayings.) Once one acknowledges that there is strong (moral) reason to recognize some persons as having the responsibility and thus the authority of changing the answer to the question 'What truly should I do?'—changing it by their sheer say-so, their law-making or law-determining *act*—one is bound to acknowledge the utility of a concept of intra-systemic legal validity responsive to no questions other than this question: Was such-and-such indeed what it appears to have been, a law-making or law-determining act of the kind those persons were authorized to make, and done in the manner and form required for it and its normative juridical product to be authentic, that is, legally valid? Answering *that* question, and deploying the corresponding concept of legal validity, can be a matter simply of social-fact sources, and involve no inspection of merits.

[58] *Ibid.* at 226. [59] Leiter at 51.

[60] Coleman and Leiter, 'Legal Positivism', in Dennis Patterson (ed.), *A Companion to Philosophy of Law and Legal Theory*, at 241.

[61] Gardner at 223. But Coleman and Leiter are in very good company: e.g. Hart, *Essays on Bentham*, 262–3: 'positivist jurisprudence, ... like Bentham's and my own work[,] denies that there is any conceptual or necessary connection between law and morality ...'

As Gardner also said, that question does not settle what a judge should do, and more generally leaves entirely untouched the question whether and when and why any of us should ever bother to have or to follow any valid legal norms.[62] The positivist interest in the (LP*) sense of law and legal validity, as Gardner went on to say, 'does not distinguish law from a game'.[63] 'But', as he rightly adds 'law is not a game. It purports to bind us morally, i.e. in a way that binds even those of us who do not fancy playing.'[64] And one cannot tell whether it succeeds or fails in its endeavour to do so, unless one tells 'the whole story of law's nature' and why 'legality' in certain contexts has a much richer meaning than 'legal validity' in the (LP*) sense.

So John Gardner faced up to the problem that does indeed confront him:

> Why begin [the necessary inquiry into law's whole nature] by asking about [law's] legal validity in the thin, practically noncommittal [normatively inert] sense found in (LP*)?[65]

His response was that this is the right place to begin because the question (LP*) tries to answer is 'a logically prior question. What is the field of human endeavor, to which the natural lawyer's proposed criteria [of legality and the nature of law] apply?'[66] And so we come back to the point I took up on p. 1 of *Natural Law and Natural Rights* and have taken up again in this essay: the assumption that in relation to human things constituted by human choices, like law, you can answer the question 'What is it?' before you tackle the question 'Why choose to have it, create it, maintain it, and comply with it?' That assumption, I have been arguing, is a philosophical mistake, induced or at least made apparently plausible by the surface grammar of the latter question. I think that this mistake sets many of my friends and colleagues off on the wrong foot.

Even so, most of us end up on the same road and indeed at much the same point on the road.† *Their* (official) route to that point has, I admit, the attraction of making it seem possible to build a legal-philosophical dwelling place without first spending time on the foundations.

NOTE

† *Convergence in contemporary legal philosophy*...See also the end of sec. I of the Introduction to this volume (p. 9).

[62] Gardner, 'Legal Positivism: 5½ Myths' at 225.
[63] *Ibid.* at 227. [64] *Ibid.* at 226. [65] *Ibid.* at 227. [66] *Ibid.* at 226.

2

LAW'S AUTHORITY AND SOCIAL THEORY'S PREDICAMENT*

Legal theory is only a part of social theory. The shape of a methodologically critical social theory is determined by moral and political theory.[1] The effort of moral and political theory is to discern principles for solving practical problems of behaviour and distribution in human community—principles that are reasonable (fair, efficiently beneficial ...), and preferable or even best. The effort of legal theory, when specifically focused, is different. It is to explain why, and on what conditions, principles and solutions once settled upon are to be given effect even when there is no consensus that the settlement was or is still correct, or that correct principles for arriving at such solutions were followed or are even available.

Because legal theory must assume that those subject to the law disagree about what the content of particular laws should be, it must walk a narrow path, from which many legal theorists stray. On the one side, legal theory must not ignore the lack of consensus about solutions to practical problems. On the other side, it must not assume that there really are no correct principles for solving practical problems; or that one can do legal theory well without having a correct moral and political theory; or that the correct principles conform to the model of techniques in themselves amoral and sub-political, such as cooking, bridge-building, or competitive games.

This essay explores one of the central enterprises of legal theory: the explanation and justification, in principle, of the law's moral authority. Section I shows how one influential contemporary rejection of that authority rests on an unwarranted assumption of social consensus. Section II has much wider horizons. It surveys, partly historically and partly systematically (though not, of course, exhaustively), some main aspects of the predicament

* 1984b ('The Authority of Law in the Predicament of Contemporary Social Theory'). The argument of this essay is defended in essay 3.

[1] For the dependence of even purely descriptive social theory on an implicit or explicit ethics and political theory, see *NLNR* 3–22.

of contemporary social theories as they struggle to make do with *emaciated conceptions of practical reasonableness.* The critique of these struggles hints at richer conceptions which I have recently expounded and defended more fully.[2] Finally, sec. III resumes the problem of legal authority, to show how legal theory can and should appeal to a full conception of fairness to explain why a law can be judged morally binding even by those who reasonably regard it as unwise.

I

In the 1970s, legal theorists began to argue that law, even good law, creates no moral reason to obey it just because it is law.[3] There is, they have argued, no generic moral obligation, not even prima facie or presumptive or defeasible, to obey the law. And this contention about obligation is equally a contention about authority. For to show that subjects have some moral obligation to obey the law is, by entailment, to show that the law has moral authority.[4]

I offer here no point-by-point refutation of the arguments of these theorists.[5] Instead, I identify one structural weakness in their case. Reflection on this weakness will bring to light the materials needed to construct a positive case affirming the moral obligation to obey the law.

[2] See *NLNR* 59–197; *FoE*. These works argue that being practically reasonable is one of the basic opportunities or basic human goods or basic aspects of human flourishing, along with other basic goods such as bodily life, knowledge, play, aesthetic experience, friendship.... They further argue that practical reasonableness involves a number of basic requirements, structuring the pursuit of all the basic human goods; requirements such as call for a coherent plan of life, detachment, commitment, no arbitrary preferences amongst basic goods, no arbitrary discrimination amongst persons, attention to consequences and efficiency, no attack on any basic human good in any act.... This footnote, of course, gives only hints of that account; the text below, without attempting to repeat or even summarize the books, introduces some of these conceptions in a way that is, I hope, sufficiently self-explanatory.

[3] See Smith, 'Is There a Prima Facie Obligation to Obey the Law?'; Raz, *The Authority of Law*, 233–49; Sartorius, 'Political Authority and Political Obligation'.

[4] It is possible to conceive of a form of moral authority of rulers which does not entail any moral obligation of their subjects to comply with the rules; Rolf Sartorius contends that this form of moral authority is not merely conceivable but is actually worth considering: Sartorius *ibid.* But he does not deny that any generic moral obligation to obey the law entails that the law and its authors have moral authority. He fails to show that arguments capable of justifying a claim to moral authority to make and enforce the law would not equally (or by addition of only uncontroversial premises) justify the claim that there is a generic moral obligation to obey that law. Since this is not disputed by Joseph Raz, I will treat the questions of authority and obligation without further differentiation. On the tight interrelationship between the concepts of authority and obligation, see *NLNR* 233–4, 255, 314–20, 335–7, 345; Hart, *Essays on Bentham*, 253–9. [On all this, see essay 4.]

[5] For a brief refutation of the central argument of Smith, 'Is There a Prima Facie Obligation to Obey the Law?', see *NLNR* 345.

The weakness comes to light when we observe how Joseph Raz's influential denial of the law's moral authority[6] goes along with two ungrudging admissions: that everyone has moral reason to cooperate in securing certain social goals, and that law is instrumental in securing those goals. These admissions expose Raz's case to an obvious objection: what is instrumental in securing a morally obligatory goal must itself be morally obligatory, unless there is some other instrumentality, equally or more serviceable. Raz responds unsuccessfully to that objection, and the failure of his response clarifies the way in which law serves the goods attainable by cooperation.

Raz begins by granting that law indeed has, as one of its two principal functions, the role of securing morally desirable cooperation. As he points out, schemes of social cooperation are of various kinds. One of the most typical and pervasive schemes concerns acts which are useful if a sufficiently large number of people behave in appropriate ways but are without any value if nobody does or if only few people do. Polluting the rivers is an example. If a sufficiently large number of people refrain from polluting the rivers, they will be clean, and each person has a moral reason to contribute to keeping them clean.[7] The law, continues Raz, is indeed

> instrumental in setting up and maintaining schemes of social co-operation, and this not only by providing sanctions to motivate those who would not otherwise contribute their shares... but also through designating in an open and public way what the scheme is and what each has to do as his contribution to it..., thus enabling those who are motivated by the appropriate reasons to take part in the cooperative enterprise.[8]

But, he concludes, the fact that law thus 'enables' us to do what we have moral reason to do does not create for us a moral reason to comply with the law. For, he says,

> the moral reasons affecting such cases derive *entirely* from the factual existence of the social practice of cooperation and *not at all* from the fact that the law is instrumental in its institution or maintenance. Consider the example of river pollution mentioned above. It matters *not at all* to one's moral reasoning whether the practice of keeping the rivers clean is sanctioned by law, is maintained by exhortations and propaganda undertaken by enthusiastic individuals, or whether it grew up entirely spontaneously.[9]

[6] *AL* 233: 'there is no [moral] obligation to obey the law even in a good society whose legal system is just'.

[7] *AL* 247–8. Note that by 'a moral reason to ...', Raz means a moral obligation: see 12, 235–6, 248.

[8] *Ibid.*, 248–9. [9] *Ibid.*, 249 (emphases added).

In short, the moral authority of the scheme of cooperation derives entirely from the practice of cooperation and not at all from the fact that the practice is legally stipulated. The goal, cooperation, is morally obligatory, but the law is not necessary for attaining it; other available means will do.

In affirming that law has moral authority, one is contradicting Raz's claim that it 'matters not at all to one's moral reasoning' whether a scheme of social cooperation is sanctioned by law, or maintained merely by the alternative means of exhortations and propaganda or spontaneous social practices. And the ground for contradicting Raz's claim is essentially that human good is complex, and conceptions of human goods are even more so. To speak to the case discussed by Raz: the benefit of having clean rivers neither is, nor is universally regarded as, the only relevant good.

It is perfectly possible for farmers or manufacturers on the banks of the river to judge that there is no sufficient reason for a national policy of eliminating river pollution. Such a view may equally be held by persons with no special personal interest, concerned only for the well-being of the national economy. They may rest their view on the heavy economic costs of the anti-pollution policy: the cost of compensating riparian owners, and the cost of providing alternative means of waste disposal, at a time of economic stringency in export industries competing with foreigners unhampered by anti-pollution laws. And so forth.

Confronted with an anti-pollution propaganda campaign, whether by pressure groups or even by government, the farmer or manufacturer has, therefore, no sufficient reason to comply. He may well think the policy misguided; and it will damage him personally while yielding him nothing which he counts a significant benefit. Similarly, with a practice of not polluting rivers, the farmer has no reason to treat the incipient or prevailing trend as morally compelling. For, once again, he may well think the practice misguided; and, again his own immediate interests also suggest that he should have no part in it.

But if and when a *law* is passed, things are changed for the farmer's practical reasoning. Now he can reason thus:

I should comply with this law, even though this law is neither in the national interest nor in my own. I should comply because I get many benefits from 'the law', from the legal system within which I live. My farm is protected from damage; my sales of farm produce are enforceable against the purchaser for the purchase price; those prices are supported by a government policy based on the laws of taxation and of market regulation; and so forth. Getting these benefits from the law, I should accept its burdens. Even though I might be able to 'benefit' even more by my secret non-compliance, I want to be a fair and upright citizen, just as I want others to be fair and upright in their dealings with me, whether they be my employees, fellow tradesmen, bankers and insurers, or the local police and courts. Moreover, I think the votes of elected representatives a useful and fair method of resolving national issues; in this instance my view has not prevailed in that political process; but sometimes the view I favour is in the majority, and when that happens I expect the law to be obeyed; so I should go along with it when I'm on the losing side in the vote.

Still, it may be asked, why does the law, and not the propaganda campaign or the spontaneous social practice, gain the benefit of these considerations of fairness? An answer must begin by pointing to the *wide range* of benefits which the subject derives from others' compliance with law. This particular law, just because it is the law, lays on him the burden of avoiding river-polluting methods of farming or manufacturing. But the law (not this particular law, but the same 'law of the land'), just as law, enforces against his neighbours the obligation not to burn down his buildings, and not to build new premises in defiance of zoning regulations, and the obligation to pay the purchase price of goods bought from him. Equally, the law, just as law, imposes on countless other people the obligation to pay the taxes which make possible a farm price support policy rather beneficial to the farmer.

The law presents itself as a seamless web. Its subjects are not permitted to pick and choose among the law's prescriptions and stipulations. It links together, in a privileged way, all the persons, and all the transactions, bearing on the farmer's present and immediate future situation. It also links all the people and transactions which have borne on the farmer's well-being or interests in the past. And finally, it links, too, all the people and transactions that may bear on his future interests and well-being as he moves into other occupations, into retirement, old-age, illness, and death. The metaphors, 'web' and 'links', here stand for the fact that in all these differing times and situations, a common reason for action—the law—was available and peremptory.[10]

Not all aspects of the common good are identified and protected or advanced, even purportedly, by the law. Not all the requirements of fairness or of appropriate community-mindedness are brought into play by the law's requirements. But to trace out the seamless web of the law is to gain a singularly adequate view of the breadth and *complexity* of the common good, of fairness, and of what may be involved in an appropriate *philia politikē* ('friendship within the polity', good neighbourliness towards the whole of society).[11]

[10] On the notion of peremptory reasons for action, see *AL* 235; Hart, *Essays on Bentham*, 261; cf. *NLNR* 234.

[11] On *philia politikē*, see Voegelin, *Order and History*, vol. 3, *Plato and Aristotle*, 320–1.

The law has a further significance. Apart from the law, the farmer could reasonably be relatively indifferent to the concerns and interests of persons whose activities, apart from the law, do not affect him or at least do not benefit him. To take only the most obvious example, the farmer could, apart from the law, be indifferent to the concerns and interests of all the environment-conscious enthusiasts who campaign for anti-pollution laws. But when the law forbids pollution, he cannot but recognize that those who pressed on him this burden are themselves subject to burdens which, while they have no intrinsic relation to his burden, do share with him the quality of being peremptory and imposed for the supposed common good of this same community.

These, then, are some reasons for denying Raz's claim that 'it matters not at all to one's moral reasoning whether the practice of keeping rivers clean is sanctioned by law [or] is maintained by enthusiastic pressure groups'.[12] These reasons do not yet adequately express the case for affirming that such a law is morally authoritative. I return to that case in sec. III. But first I explore some of the main reasons why contemporary legal theories lack, or distort, the conceptual materials needed for making out that case.

II

Legal theory gets off to a shaky start with the Platonic discussion in the *Minos*.[13] Socrates is shown making two moves. The right move is the explanation of legal authority and obligation in terms of what is needed for securing human good. The wrong move (presented by the author as right) is to treat the hoped-for human good, the end, as if it were a producible, that can be *made* and *completed* like the omelette that can be made by following a recipe, or the bridge that can be built by following a blueprint. In this conception, the end is external to the process required to produce it; the processes have only instrumental value. Practical reasonableness, individual or political, is conceived in emaciated fashion as a craft, only more extensive in its ambition and perhaps more demanding in its skills than other crafts.[14]

Western social theory has frequently reverted to some such emaciated conception of practical reasonableness. Aristotle teetered on the brink of instrumentalizing all human practical reasonableness and virtue to

[12] *AL* 249. I should make it clear that Raz's own social theory is scarcely open to the charge of employing an emaciated concept of practical reason.

[13] Plato (or pseudo-Plato), *Minos* 316e–317a (trans. R. Hathaway, in 14 AJJ 116, 120).

[14] On the craft analogy in the early works of Plato, see Irwin, *Plato's Moral Theory: The Early and Middle Dialogues*, 71–86, 90–101, 109, 127–31, 174–81, 196–7.

the attaining of opportunity for contemplation.[15] Aquinas often spoke in similar fashion,[16] but in fact makes the essential corrective move. There is, he says,[17] not one first principle of practical reasoning, rather there are many, all equally fundamental and equally substantive. Thus, there is no determinate one natural last end or determinate unifying purpose of individual or social life. But Aquinas's texts were sufficiently Aristotelian to be widely misread; many, thinking to follow him, treated contemplation of theoretical truth as a determinate natural last end, and avoided instrumentalizing moral life only by declaring that the first principles of which Aquinas spoke are not human goods to be done and pursued, but negative moral principles in the same logical form as the Ten Commandments.[18] Others instrumentalized the human virtues to the pursuit of a supernatural end conceived *simply* as a vision of God.[19] This simplified account had two unfortunate consequences. The point of the virtues, and even of ordinary good actions, was made obscure (for *how* do they tend to fit one for a future contemplative vision?). And the lives of those who did indeed stand in the way of the divine project were liable to be treated instrumentally in the fashion of mere obstacles.

The theological inadequacy of such conceptions of human good was recently explained by the Second Vatican Council, which identifies the ultimate end of mankind, not simply as a vision of truth, nor even as a participation in holiness and grace, but as a participation by a multiplicity of persons in a manifold of goods. The goods are specified, in outline, as: human dignity, brotherhood, and freedom and thus 'all the good fruits of our nature and of our effort'. The envisaged participation in these goods is called 'a kingdom of truth and life, holiness and grace, justice, love and peace'. On this account, ordinary good deeds and virtues of every kind can go to building up here and now that supernatural kingdom. And when that kingdom is hereafter completed, there 'will be found again', as intrinsic to its heavenly constitution and life, those good works and virtues themselves (which thus are revealed to faith to have more than merely instrumental value).[20]

[15] *NE* X.7: 1177a12–1178a9.

[16] *ST* I–II q.3 a.6c; q.57 a.1 ad 2; q.66 a.4 ad 1.

[17] *ST* I–II q.58 a.4c; q.63 a.1c; q.94 aa.2c, 3c, 4c; II–II q.47 a.6c and ad 1 and ad 3. For a brief exposition of these texts, see *FoE* 68–9.

[18] See e.g. Bourke, *Ethics: A Textbook in Moral Philosophy*. For the historical background in Cajetan, Medina, Suarez, and other theologians of the sixteenth and seventeenth centuries, see de Lubac, *The Mystery of the Supernatural*, 25–67, 181–201. A brief and penetrating survey is Grisez, 'Man, the Natural End of', 134–7.

[19] See almost any neo-scholastic manual of moral theology; for a brief survey and critique, see Grisez, *Christian Moral Principles*, 12–13, 103–6, 112.

[20] Second Vatican Council, Pastoral Constitution on the Church in the Modern World (*Gaudium et Spes*), no. 39, reprinted in Abbott, *The Documents of Vatican II*, 199, 237.

While Aquinas affirmed the plurality of basic and intrinsic human goods and first principles of practical reasoning, modern legal theory has followed another path. It is the inheritor of the Enlightenment, which repudiated both the (ill-conceived) heavenly last end, and the crystallized negative moral principles prematurely declared by theologians and rationalist philosophers to be truly first principles of practical reason. While Kant tried to resurrect the moral principles by giving them the rational force of the principle of non-contradiction,[21] Bentham wanted to instrumentalize all principles, virtues, and social arrangements to the pursuit of an attainable worldly end: the maximum net pleasure, or minimum net pain, of the maximum number of human beings.[22] Contemporary social theory rightly treats as absurd each of Bentham's key notions: (a) that pleasure is the maximand, (b) that pain and pleasure are simply higher and lower points on a single scale, and (c) that sense can be made of an injunction conjoining two superlatives, whether 'the most words in the shortest time' or 'the greatest good of the greatest number'.[23] Nothing of Bentham's project for guiding social choice remains for serious consideration; it was not merely impracticable, but radically incoherent and senseless, in many different respects. Bentham himself was uneasily aware of one further incoherence that I have not mentioned. He could not decide whether his injunctions were offered to each individual as guides to maximizing his own happiness, or rather to an entire society (and thus to each of its members) as guides to maximizing the happiness of 'the greatest number'.[24] He could not make up his mind in fifty years what his recipe was for, a boiled egg or an omelette.

Perhaps the only successor to Bentham in contemporary legal theory goes by the name of Economic Analysis of Law.[25] For this school proposes as the criterion of just social choice the aggregative maximization of the wealth of society. The wealth of a society is in turn defined as the sum of all goods and services in the society, weighted by their values, while what one values is defined as what he is willing and able to pay for, and the measure

[21] Kant, *Grundlegung zur Metaphysik der Sitten* 424 (1785; ed. Prussian Academy, vol. IV (1911)), 424 (trans. Beck, *Foundations of the Metaphysics of Morals*, 47–8). For a balanced account of the place of non-contradiction in Kant's ethics, see Ward, *The Development of Kant's View of Ethics*, 99–130.

[22] Bentham, *The Principles of Morals and Legislation*, 11 note d (note added in 1822).

[23] On the implausibility of pleasure as the point of everything, see Nozick, *Anarchy, State and Utopia*, 42–5; *NLNR* 95–6. For reasons why pain and pleasure are not to be treated as points on a scale, see Grover, 'The Ranking Assumption'. For the logical problems caused by conjoined superlatives, see Geach, *The Virtues*, 91–4.

[24] See e.g. Bentham (1843) 9 at 5–8. For a brief account of the modern exegesis of Bentham on this problem, see Hart's 'Introduction' in Bentham, *The Principles of Morals and Legislation* at xlix–lii.

[25] See Posner, *The Economics of Justice*, 48–115. In his Preface to the 1983 edition, Judge Posner seems virtually to abandon any claim that his normative theory is justified or correct, and points to the 'rather bizarre results that its unflinching application could produce'.

of that value is defined as how much he is willing and able to pay. But this maximand, wealth as thus defined, is quite implausible. It incompletely represents the basic forms of human well-being and lacks any account of the intrinsic relations between resources and those basic goods. Moreover, the injunction to maximize wealth without regard to either prior or resulting patterns of distribution is even less plausible. Economic Analysis of Law, as a normative theory, grotesquely lacks any account of the limits on what is up for distribution (hearts of live donors?, children for torture?, anybody for slavery?, ...). Equally lacking is a coherent account of why what counts as payment should be distinguished from duress, fraud, or theft.

There remains a substantial body of theory seeking with pertinacity and some success to explore the resources and limits of instrumental rationality in the context of social life. *Game theory* concerns individual decision-making in a social context. *Social choice theory* focuses instead on decisions to be made on behalf of a society, decisions to be chosen on the basis of an aggregation of individual preferences. These two branches of the theory of instrumental rationality are analogous to the two projects between which Bentham could not make up his mind.

The principal result of the vast and rigorous effort of social choice theory over the last forty years has become rather well known under the label 'Arrow's theorem':[26] under any non-arbitrary, fair, or non-perverse method of amalgamating the preferences of individuals, instances of *intransitive* or cyclical outcomes occur. Outcomes are intransitive or cyclical when outcome A beats outcome B, and outcome B beats outcome C, but outcome C beats outcome A. In such a situation, the amalgamation of individual preferences fails to provide a rational, consistent, or meaningful identification of the preferred 'social choice'. To Arrow's inconvenient theorem we can add other assured results of social theory. There is, for example, Elizabeth Anscombe's demonstration that even when all issues are decided by majority vote, the majority of voters can be in the minority on the majority of issues and the person or persons directly affected by the vote can always be in the minority.[27] Indeed, as William Riker has shown, for *any* method of amalgamation which involves the summation of revealed preferences (that is, a system of voting), the possibility of strategic voting *guarantees* that, where more than two possible outcomes were available for choice, we cannot know whether the result of the amalgamation is

[26] Arrow, *Social Choice and Individual Values*, 51–9. For a simple exposition of the General Possibility Theorem in a context of political theory, see Riker, *Liberalism against Populism*, 115–36.

[27] Anscombe, 'On Frustration of the Majority by Fulfilment of the Majority's Will'. Anscombe is not, of course, a professed 'social choice theorist'.

meaningful or is rather the result of manipulation of the voting process by the strategic voting of perhaps a small minority.[28]

The upshot of social choice theorizing is to this extent clear. Legal theory must make its way in a world in which we know that fair procedures cannot guarantee outcomes which are fair in the sense of accurately representing, say, majority preferences.

The problems of intransitivity which undermine the project of aggregating individual preferences into a 'social choice' are, in fact, not restricted to *social* choice. In arriving at his or her own determinate preferences, an individual must choose, and in this choosing will encounter the same paradoxes of intransitivity as have been demonstrated in the context of social choice. Whenever one has several interests or desires or standards of evaluation or criteria of choice, and is choosing between more than two alternatives, one can find that alternative A is preferable to B and C in respect of value v1 (say, having unpolluted river water), while alternative B is preferable to C and A in respect of value v2 (say, minimization of transaction costs), and alternative C is preferable to A and B in respect of value v3 (say, likelihood of fair and uncorrupt administration).[29]

This problem of intransitivity has serious consequences for every form of utilitarianism, consequentialism, or proportionalism[30] in ethics. But intransitivity also generates logically necessary and severe limitations on the usefulness of social choice theory's partner in the theory of instrumental rationality: game theory.

Game theory offers to guide the choices of players, each of whom knows his own interests or preferences, and the interests or preferences of the other participants, and each of whom seeks to maximize the satisfaction of his own interests and preferences by choices made in circumstances where the outcome for him will or may be affected by the choices of the other participants but where the choices must be made in ignorance of the other participants' actual choices. Since the theory predicts the outcomes for all players, its results are considered guides to social decision-making, too. Some theorists, such as Hobbes, have thought to explain the point of legal regulation in terms of one of the paradigm games in game theory: the Prisoners' Dilemma.

This paradigm, like Hobbes's state of nature, posits a situation with two significant features: (1) the effort by each player to maximize his gains, or

[28] Riker, *Liberalism against Populism*, 115–36. Note Arrow's remark that 'in a generalized sense all methods of social choice are of the type of voting'. Arrow, *Social Choice and Individual Values*, 27–8.

[29] See Grisez, 'Against Consequentialism', 21, 37–8.

[30] For the meaning of these three terms, see *FoE* 80–6; see also n. 43 and endnote below, and text between nn. 43 and 44.

to minimize his possible losses, yields an equilibrium in which for each player the outcome is much inferior to what each could have attained by cooperation; (2) all cooperative arrangements are radically unstable because each has the incentive to renege on the arrangement, both for the sake of further gain and for the avoidance of very serious loss in the event of the other player's reneging.[31] Many discussions of the Prisoners' Dilemma focus on the 'paradoxical' character of the first feature. But legal theory has a special interest in the second. For the introduction of enforceable norms requiring cooperation could enable the players to reach the higher and, for each, more desirable of the two equilibria, the one attained by stable cooperation. Yet on the postulates of game theory, each player has only the following incentive: to support the introduction of enforceable norms but then to break the equilibrium by deviating secretly from those norms.

The postulates of game theory in fact render unintelligible any judgment *by the players* that the higher level equilibrium is *preferable* to any alternative outcome *just because* it is an outcome in which each is doing equally well and no one is suffering very serious loss. Such a judgment is unreasonable on the postulates of game theory because on those postulates there is another outcome which is more in each player's interests: the outcome in which he gains the highest possible individual payoff by secretly deviating from the collaboration equilibrium.

Expositions of game theory often skate over this problem by labelling the units in the calculus 'preferences' rather than 'units of self-interest'.[32] But, as authoritative exponents such as Arrow[33] and Sen[34] have indicated, in the real world no one's preferences and choices need be determined by the emaciated rationality of self-interest. Participants in the real world may prefer fairness to a marginal or even to a substantial increment in the advancement of their own interests; and if each participant is willing to guide his choice by considerations of fairness, the dilemma can be resolved and the higher equilibrium attained. Players with a preference for a fair outcome to the game do have the incentive to introduce laws or other norms, not as a mere ruse for secret personal advancement, but as a

[31] The eponymous Prisoners' Dilemma concerns the pre-trial interrogation of two (guilty) prisoners. Each is interrogated separately, and knows the following: (a) if neither confesses they will each receive a short sentence; (b) if one confesses but the other doesn't, the one will be released and the other will receive a heavy sentence; and (c) if both confess each receives a moderate sentence. On game-theoretical postulates, (a) would be higher 'equilibrium' but is unstable, and the actual outcome will be the lower but stable equilibrium, (c). A standard exposition is Luce and Raiffa, *Games and Decisions*, 94–102. For an accessible presentation of many problems sharing the generalized structure of the Prisoners' Dilemma, with particular reference to the relevance of norms in attaining the higher equilibrium, see Ullmann-Margalit, *The Emergence of Norms*, 18–73, esp. 18–29.

[32] See e.g. Green, 'Law, Co-ordination and the Common Good'.

[33] Arrow, *Social Choice and Individual Values*, 114–15.

[34] Sen, 'Rational Fools: A Critique of the Behavioral Foundations of Economic Theory'.

path to an equilibrium the fundamental attractiveness of which is a good uncountable in the calculus of game theory: fairness in the playing and outcome of the game itself.

Notice that the resolution of the dilemma is attained not by substituting altruism for egoistic self-interest, but by two factors in conjunction. First, the concern (fundamental to game theory) to maximize one's own pre-established preferences is to be replaced by a concern for a fair and desirable outcome to the game. Secondly, there must be a procedure (in game theory usually given with the structure of the problem) for coordinating the individual choices so as to attain the desirable fair outcome. An altruistic desire to advance the interests of other persons is not generally an adequate substitute for either of the two factors just mentioned. For there is a game-theoretical Altruists' Dilemma, analogous to the Prisoners'. That is to say, there are situations in which the shared preferences for increasing the other player's payoff yields (on game-theoretical postulates) an outcome worse for both than the outcome yielded by selfish choices.[35]

John Rawls has pointed out how the Prisoners' Dilemma is resolvable by mutual adherence to principles of fairness.[36] But his *A Theory of Justice* is the great monument to game theory's emaciated conception of reasonableness. For the book's absolutely fundamental strategy is to explain and justify fairness by reference to what would be chosen by persons on postulates which are, in fact, the postulates of game theory: that each of the choosers is out to maximize his own interests, selfish or altruistic, and has no concern for the fate of the other participants *as such*. Those postulates and certain conditions of ignorance together constitute the model that Rawls calls the Original Position. The central claim of his theory is that the principles of 'justice as fairness' are those that would, in the Original Position, be unanimously chosen as principles to regulate social life in the real world outside the Original Position. The rational attraction of this argument is that the conditions of ignorance in the Original Position do indeed guarantee that the principles there selected would be free from any taint of bias, and would thus be fair.

But this strategy has an irremediable weakness. It assumes that a principle which would go unchosen in the Original Position cannot be a fair principle. The assumption is gratuitous; Rawls offers no defence of it (though he defends the conclusions it entails). But a defence of the

[35] See Ullmann-Margalit, *The Emergence of Norms*, 48n, citing Schelling, 'Some Thoughts on the Relevance of Game Theory to the Analysis of Ethical Systems', in Ira Buchler and Hugo Nutini (eds), *Game Theory in the Behavioral Sciences.* On the important difference between friendship in the classical sense (*amicitia*, *philia*) and altruism (a concept invented in the nineteenth century, by Auguste Comte, with intent to supersede friendship), see *NLNR* 142–4, 158.

[36] Rawls, *A Theory of Justice*, 269 n. 9.

assumption is required. For there are many principles for ordering social life that would not be selected by the self-interested persons in the Original Position. Principles which give priority, for example, to truth and beauty over error and trash, or which give support to interpersonal fidelity over the whims of self-interest, would go unchosen, as Rawls explains, because each of those choosers, not knowing what beliefs and values they will have in the world outside the Original Position, would be afraid to disadvantage error or infidelity in case he might turn out to be a person with beliefs deemed erroneous, or one who prefers 'liberation' to fidelity.[37] The Rawlsian theory of fairness thus rests on nothing more adequate than an appeal to individual 'prudence', in the sense of cautious self-interest. Once this has been identified as its basis, its very claim to be a theory of *fairness* is seen to be unfounded.

Indeed, the entire construction of Rawlsian justice proceeds on the emaciated conception of practical reason, in which there is no acknowledgement of the intelligible good, the attractive beauty or worth for its own sake, of truth and knowledge, friendship and authenticity, beauty, devotion, skill, and even fairness itself. The whole construction is a device for guaranteeing that each shall get what he wants whatever that may be, so far as is consistent with every other getting what he wants consistent with…and so on. Here we have the characteristic modern modelling of practical life and reason on techniques of making or getting what happens to be wanted, rather than on the doing of, or participation in, substantive human goods. The goods and the virtues are carefully reconstructed or reinterpreted as in themselves neutral instruments of self-protection and the advancement of self-interest. To repeat: the concept of self-interest in these emaciated theories of practical reason is not necessarily one of selfishness. But it is a concept in which friendship or fairness are not intrinsic intelligible goods to be cherished and advanced for their own sake. Rather they have the status of something which someone happens to want, but which others perhaps just don't want, and which therefore have no *structural* role.

One might suppose that the other well-known game-theoretical paradigm, the Coordination Problem,[38] could help to explain the human

[37] *Ibid.* at 207–9, 327–8.

[38] See Ullmann-Margalit, *The Emergence of Norms*, 74–133. Confusion has arisen because there is a game-theoretical model of 'coordination problem' and there is a conception going under the same name but unconstrained by the emaciated and instrumental rationality of game-theoretical postulates. For the latter, see e.g. Raz, *Practical Reason and Norms*, 64, 159; Gans, 'The Normativity of Law and Its Coordinative Function'; *NLNR* 232–3, 244–9, 306 (the note at 255 implicitly distinguishes between the two conceptions, but ought to have done so much more explicitly). Failure to notice the distinction renders irrelevant the critique in Green, 'Law, Co-ordination and the Common Good'.

good of coordination and cooperation. Several recent social theorists have tried to use this paradigm as an explanatory model of law and legal system.[39] But it will not provide what we are seeking.

In the game-theoretical Coordination Problem, the players have a shared interest in some objective attainable only by cooperation, but there are more than one incompatible alternative ways of coordinating their actions. The players wish, for example, to meet, and they could meet at places P1, P2, or P3. In the purest version of the Coordination Problem, the players are entirely indifferent as between the possible meeting places (equilibria). In less pure instances of the paradigm, player A most prefers P1, player B most prefers P2, but each player regards all three places as acceptable and any of them as preferable to not meeting at all. Clearly, some rule of thumb, or legal rule like the rule of the road, or a system of traffic lights, will enable the players to identify a salient[40] solution, say P2. The salient solution, once chosen, is stable because preferred by all to the absence of a solution, for all the players prefer meeting to missing (while in the traffic situation all prefer missing to meeting).

Obviously, the game-theoretical Coordination Problem is no adequate model for explaining the emergence and the feature of law. In the game-theoretical Coordination Problems, once a solution is identified, there is no possibility of deviation from it. The sole point of the game is that the players shall 'meet', and no player has any rational motive, whether selfish or altruistic, for choosing an action which will disrupt the equilibrium.[41] For the postulate of the game-theoretical Coordination Problem, as of other game-theoretical models, is that each player can and does rank the possible outcomes in a preference ranking which is complete and transitive[42] (and then seeks to do the best he can in terms to secure those outcomes, as ranked). In the Coordination Problem, the alternatives to the chosen salient equilibrium rank higher on no one's preference ranking, and since that ranking is presupposed to be complete and transitive, deviance would be

[39] See Gans, 'The Normativity of Law and Its Coordinative Function', and the reply by Ullmann-Margalit, 'Is Law a Co-ordinative Authority?'.

[40] As Schelling and Lewis have shown, coordination problems are, very generally, solved through *salience*: one of the co-ordination equilibria might appear conspicuous to the people involved, owing to some specific feature it possesses, and might hence serve as a focal point for the convergence of their choice of actions. The salience of the co-ordination equilibrium need not be, and in general is not, a result of its being in any obvious sense better than the other co-ordination equilibria.... Precedent and agreement also solve recurrent co-ordination problems. They can, however, be viewed as special cases—albeit important ones—of salience. (Ullmann-Margalit, *The Emergence of Norms*, 83–4 (original emphasis).)

[41] See Green, 'Law, Co-ordination and the Common Good' at 317, 319.

[42] As is implied in my use of 'intransitivity', in the text after n. 28, a relationship R between choices or outcomes x, y, z... is transitive if for all x, y, z ..., xRy and yRz implies xRz.

not so much wrong as irrational. Indeed, it would be so irrational that deviation is not an intelligible choice.[43]

In the real life of practical reasonableness, alternatives do not present themselves for choice in transitive orderings. Choice A will be better than choice B in respect of its friendliness or fairness or of its increasing my long-term security, but choice B will be better than choice A in respect of its increasing my here-and-now satisfactions or short-term security. These different types of goods are not commensurable apart from particular scales of assessment which one *chooses* to employ. And the reasons for one's most fundamental choices of scales of assessment cannot be that they identify *quantities* of the good to be assessed or even transitive *ordinal relations* between outcomes in terms only of that assessable good.[44]

In short, the Coordination Problem model, as understood in game theory, takes things too easily to be of assistance in legal theory. By assuming that the players have complete and transitive preference rankings, and that these coincide to support the choice of a salient solution preferred by each to no solution, the model shares the weakness I identified in Raz's denial that law is needed to secure morally desirable schemes of cooperation. Within the confines of the river pollution game, many players prefer no solution to any of the salient solutions. The game of coordination in society can only be played if it is extended to a field of choice which is, in terms of time and subject-matter, a *wide* field, so that burdens in one part of the field can be envisaged as related to benefits in others. But widening the field of choice has a further result: all individual and social decision procedures will yield conspicuous intransitivities. The resulting dilemmas can be overcome, as they in practice are overcome, by acknowledging a certain sort of good or 'benefit', the good of fairness and the related good

[43] This impossibility of deviance is the counterpart of the impossibility of morally significant choice in the utilitarian, consequentialist, or proportionalist model of rational choice, as argued in *FoE* 89–90 [see endnote].

[44] Thus Duncan Luce and Howard Raiffa, in their standard work on game and decision theory, make the appropriate caveat about the axiom of transitivity, the first and decisive axiom in the theory:

> No matter how intransitivities arise, we must recognize that they exist, and we can take only little comfort in the thought that they are an anathema to most of what constitutes theory in the behavioral sciences today. We may say that we are only concerned with behavior which is transitive, adding hopefully that we believe this need not always be a vacuous study. (Luce and Raiffa, *Games and Decisions*, 25.)

The authors are aware, too, that intransitivities often emerge because a subject (i.e. a topic or situation)

> forces choices between inherently incomparable alternatives. The idea is that each alternative invokes 'responses' on several different 'attribute' scales and that, although each scale may itself be transitive, their amalgamation need not be. (*Ibid.*)

On the reasonable choice of the basic commitments in terms of which we can subsequently rank, transitively, a good many alternatives, see *FoE* 87–8, 90–2; *NLNR* 115–18.

of social or political friendship or good neighbourliness. These are goods which certainly multiply the intransitivities. But they enable the individual to acknowledge the moral authority of decision-procedures which cannot pretend to *maximize* the satisfaction of his own or others' preferences. There is, in short, an intelligent concern for the structure and outcome of whole systems of personal interactions which is not a concern either for maximized aggregations of preferences or for maximizing one's own individual payoffs (whether selfish or altruistic).

III

Law is one of the paradigms of political authority. Political authority has its most thorough explanation as the source of solutions to coordination problems. But now 'coordination problems' must be understood without the restrictions of game theory's postulates. The term now extends to any situation where, if there were a coordination of action, significantly beneficial payoffs otherwise practically unattainable would be attained by significant numbers of persons, where there is sufficient shared interest to make some such coordination attractive, and where the problem is to select some appropriate pattern of coordination in such a way that coordination will actually occur.

In a general theory of law, the principal object of concern is the last-mentioned aspect of the problem. The focal question is not: What is the right decision in such circumstances? (There is good reason, as we have seen, to think that most often no uniquely correct solution could be found.) The focal question for legal theory is rather: How is action to be coordinated? How, first, is a solution to be selected? Why, once selected, is it to count as *the* solution? And then, what is involved in maintaining it as the solution all through its implementation?

In the final analysis, there are only two ways of coordinating action in a group. There must be either unanimity or authority. Whichever method is employed, it must handle two distinguishable problems: (1) the selection of a pattern of coordination, and (2) the implementing of that pattern in actual cooperation to the degree required to attain desired benefits. The selection may, for example, be by exchange of promises, which requires unanimity between the promising parties at the time of the promise. Or it may be by some legislative body which in the extreme but possible case might comprise every member of the community and make decisions only by unanimity. But in either case, if the desired result is to be attained by cooperation, the unanimity about the selected pattern must either continue all the way through the period of implementation or must, during that period and for its duration, be replaced by authority. Such authority may take one or other of the following forms: either the authoritativeness of the selection process (promise or enactment) must be quasi-unanimously acknowledged, or some authoritative person or body of persons must hold the parties to the selected pattern.

The invocation of political authority to settle coordination problems can be illustrated by returning to the problem of river pollution, the case used by Raz in denying the moral authority of law. The problem arises because people, even people of purest goodwill, can discern a variety of practical possibilities. We can have:

S1: a river of really pure running water. The benefits will be that it looks and smells good and so is apt for human aesthetic enjoyment and play, that it sustains natural plants and fish for conservation, science, or sport, that its waters are drinkable without expensive processing and cause no infections or injuries... and many other potential payoffs. Alternatively, we can have:

S2: a river that is freely available as a sewer. The benefits of such a régime will be that it allows producers to dispose of their waste far more cheaply than by any available alternative means, and saves the community the costs of policing the river. Or we can have:

S3: a river that is available for unlimited waste disposal by those willing to pay a waste-disposal fee to defray the costs of alternative drinking water supplies and additional health services, and perhaps to finance other public services whether or not made necessary by the policy of permissive disposal. The benefits of this will be some, but not all, of those available under scheme S2, supplemented by additional payoffs to taxpayers because the scheme provides an additional source of public revenue. Or, finally (in a list that could in fact be extended), we can have:

S4: a river that is available for limited waste disposal, the quantity and quality of pollutants being policed so as to be compatible with some plant and fish life, some aesthetic enjoyment, a low level of infection, and other benefits such as those in scheme S1, but at a level lower than in S1 though at a much higher level than in S2 or S3.

Obviously, each of these schemes (even, to a limited extent, the practice of unlimited waste disposal, S2), involves coordination if it is to attain the payoffs envisaged. Each potential solution involves a pattern of actions and abstentions by a (large) number of agents and potential agents, such that the benefits of any individual action or abstention depend on the actions and abstentions of the other parties. Moreover, selecting and moving to one scheme in preference to its predecessor involves a more or less distinct 'framework' coordination problem: How shall *such* questions of selection of schemes be decided? For this river is only one of many, and pollution of rivers is only one form of pollution, and pollution is only one of countless forms of socially relevant phenomena involving costs and benefits, human goods and harms.

There is a sense in which this 'framework' coordination problem is only ephemeral in character, at least by comparison with the day-in day-out character of coordinating the operation of the selected scheme. Once the appropriate persons have coordinated the processes of selection and the polity has adopted the scheme, the framework problem seems to be solved. But there is also a sense in which the framework problem and its procedural solution subsist as standing features of the polity. Those who participate in the life of the polity must go on, day-in and day-out, acknowledging that what was done by way of selecting a scheme did settle that question not only for then but also for now. In other words, the selection, whether it was by a process of custom-formation or by enactment, judgment, or other authoritative decree, must be treated as *authoritative.*

The necessity ('must') just mentioned is to be understood as follows. Schemes S1, S3, and S4 do not yield their payoffs unless the relevant population displays a high level of conformity with the selected scheme. It may well be that 25 per cent of the population favour S1, while 25 per cent favour S2, 25 per cent S3, and 25 per cent S4. What is certain is that none of the schemes will yield any significant benefits if there is only 25 per cent compliance. The required level of compliance is quasi-uniformity, a kind of unanimity in action. But since there is no unanimity at all about the intrinsic desirability of the respective schemes, such unanimity in action must result from quasi-unanimity about the desirability of conforming to the authoritatively selected scheme. The uniformity of action must result from quasi-unanimous acknowledgement of the authority of that selection, of the process which settled upon one scheme rather than the others.

The farmer confronting the anti-pollution policy confronts concretely the essential questions about political and legal authority. Why should he treat a law against river pollution as authoritative, while treating propaganda, appeals to community spirit, and developed or developing practice as of no consequence? And what is his 'shared interest' in a scheme which he thinks is mistaken, and which he knows may be damaging to him?

The answer to the first question lies in the *quality* of the legal system as a device for solving coordination problems. The quality of a legal system that makes it authoritative is its general salience. By holding itself out as a public and privileged identification of a solution for the case of every coordination problem, and by offering grounds for acknowledging that privileged status, the law achieves the salience it seeks in particular coordination problems. The grounds for acknowledging that privileged status are several. The law, if accorded that status, offers the prospect of combining speed with clarity in generating practical solutions to constantly emerging and changing coordination problems, and in suggesting devices by which such solutions can be generated. Its institutions for devising and maintaining solutions secure fairness by the stability, the practicability, and the generality or non-discriminatory character of the solutions, and by the imposition of those solutions on free-riders and other deviants by processes which minimize arbitrariness and self-interested or partisan deviance in the very processes themselves. In short, it is the values of the Rule of Law[45] that give the legal system its distinctive entitlement to be treated as the source of authoritative solutions.

These valuable features of a legal system are important precisely because, in the real world, recalcitrance is always possible, even on the part of one for whom cooperation would bring benefits. The variety and complexity of basic human goods, and of reasonable ways of pursuing and realizing human good, make actual 'preferences' radically unstable. For 'payoffs' are ambivalent and 'orderings' always remain incomplete and actually or potentially intransitive. Friendship, and fairness, are amongst the causes of that ambivalence, intransitivity, and instability; they are interests and goods that unsettle any individual preference ranking by demanding, attractively, the sacrifice of some of one's 'own' goods and interests for the sake of a shared interest.

There remains the question whether and how the farmer has a shared interest in complying with the anti-pollution law. There is a shared interest, or sharing of aim, which makes a community possible and lasting despite lack of consensus on almost every practical problem. This sharing of aim has as its most directly significant component the shared willingness to treat friendship and fairness for what they are: aspects of human flourishing which provide a counter-attraction to, and *critique* of, many alternative, vividly attractive, but diminished conceptions of that well-being. Concretely, then, the farmer can judge that the regular, impartial maintenance of the legal order itself is a good which gives him sufficient shared interest in, and reason for, cooperation by compliance with the anti-pollution law. The good he thus discerns and seeks to realize is a good indiscernible in the emaciated models of practical

[45] On the Rule of Law, see Raz, *The Authority of Law: Essays on Law and Morality*, 210–29; *NLNR* 270–6, 292–3. Both these treatments profited greatly from Fuller, *The Morality of Law*.

reasonableness: the good of a fair method of relating burdens to benefits, and persons to persons, over an immensely complex and lasting but shifting set of persons and their aspirations and transactions. Nothing other than legal order can promise such a method.

NOTES

Impossibility of morally significant choice in the utilitarian, consequentialist or proportionalist model of rational choice...(at n. 43). The passage from *FoE* 89–90 is:

> One can choose only what appears to one to be good; but if, as proportionalists claim, (i) 'wrong' entails 'yielding (or promising) less good', and (ii) [one is in a situation in which some] choices can be identified as yielding (or promising) less good than some alternative choice(s), then it becomes inconceivable that a *morally* wrong (as distinct from a merely mistaken) choice could ever be made [in that situation]. How could anyone *choose* an act which he can see yields less good than some alternative open to him? Morally wrong choices are, of course, unreasonable. But unreasonable choices are possible precisely because the goods apparently realizable by choices are *not* commensurable as yielding (or promising) greater or lesser good; they retain their attractiveness as yielding (or promising) some real good, an attractiveness which would be destroyed if that could be seen to embody less good, all things considered, than some available alternative. The unreasonableness of morally wrong choices is not the incomprehensibility of choosing a lesser good [i.e. a good that is simply lower on the (supposed) one rational measure]. Rather it is the unreasonableness of pursuing goods arbitrarily, or unfairly, or fanatically, or inconstantly, or by means of a direct attack on some basic good, or in some other way contrary to a principle of practical reasonableness.

This kind of argument against consequentialism etc. is defended in 1990f.

3

LAW AS COORDINATION*

I

Recent writings by, for example, Raz, Postema, Gans, and myself offer to explain law's authority by law's function as providing solutions to coordination problems.[1] This venture has met with a confused response, because the term 'coordination problem' had earlier become a technical term in a body of social theory generated by economists and strategists known as game theory. The game-theoretical concept of a coordination problem, and hence of a solution to a coordination problem, is inappropriate for use in legal theory, or indeed in any social theory which wishes to give realistic attention to the shaping of human action and society by 'ideals' such as friendship and fairness.

Game theory offers to predict, explain, and guide the choices of players, each of whom knows his own interests or preferences, and the interests or preferences of the other participants in a structured situation, predicament, or game. Each player is presupposed to be seeking to maximize the satisfaction of his own interests or preferences. The choices of each are made in circumstances such that the outcome for each will be affected by the choices of the other participants; but the choices must be made in ignorance of the actual choices being made by the other participants. By predicting the choices of the other players, game theory can guide a player's choice.

Game theory generates a number of paradigm games, of which two have proved powerfully attractive in social theory: the Prisoners' Dilemma and

* 1989b.

[1] See Raz, *Practical Reason and Norms*, 64, 159; Postema, 'Coordination and Convention at the Foundations of Law'; Gans, 'The Normativity of Law and Its Coordinative Function'; and *NLNR* 147–50, 231–3, 238–56, 276, 334–5.

the Coordination Problem. I shall say nothing here about the Prisoners' Dilemma situation and its analysis.[2]

In the game-theoretical Coordination Problem, the players have a shared interest in some objective attainable only by coordination, but there is more than one incompatible alternative way of coordinating their actions. The players wish, for example, to meet, and could meet at places P1, P2, or P3. In the purest version of the Coordination Problem, they are all indifferent about the possible meeting places (equilibria, solutions). In less pure instances of the paradigm, one player prefers P1, another P2, and so on, but each regards all three places as acceptable and any of them as preferable to not meeting at all. Coordination problems are solved through the *salience* of one solution: one of the coordination equilibria appears conspicuous to the people involved, and so can serve as the focal point for the convergence of their choices. The salience of this equilibrium will typically have little or nothing to do with its merits as a solution: meeting at noon at Grand Central Station is salient for people who must meet in New York at an unspecified hour on a certain day but who know little about that city; yet noon may be unpleasantly hot, and Grand Central Station both dangerous and less accessible than some other New York venues.

But in recurrent coordination problems, such as which side of the road to drive on or what currency to use in markets, the salient solution, once identified, is relatively stable. For it is preferred by all to the absence of a solution. Past behaviour (precedent), convention, agreement, decree—these are all ways in which one solution can become salient without any consensus as to its superiority over other solutions. Ullmann-Margalit gives a clear account of the way in which the utility of discernible regularities of behaviour as sources of solutions to coordination problems is likely to be enhanced by the emergence of social norms, the salience of which is secured by teaching them to the young, telling them to newcomers, and supporting them by the pressure of disapproval on non-conformity.[3]

Yet it is clear that the game-theoretical Coordination Problem is not an adequate model for explaining the emergence and features of law. In a game-theoretical Coordination Problem, there is no practical likelihood of deviation from a solution once identified. For the options of each and every player are bounded by the 'game', the sole point of which is that the players shall 'meet'. Thus, no player has any rational motive, whether

[2] A rich introduction to Prisoners' Dilemma situations as a context for the emergence of norms is Edna Ullmann-Margalit, *The Emergence of Norms*, 18–73. See also essay 2 at 55–8.

[3] Ullmann-Margalit, *The Emergence of Norms*, 76–87; cf. Lewis, *Convention: A Philosophical Study*, 42.

selfish or altruistic, for choosing an action which he knows will disrupt the equilibrium. The game-theoretical Coordination Problem, like other game-theoretical models, postulates that each player can and does rank the possible outcomes in a preference ranking which is complete and transitive[4]—and that he seeks to do the best he can to secure those outcomes, as ranked. Since, in the game-theoretical Coordination Problem, the alternatives to the chosen salient equilibrium rank higher on no one's preference ranking, and since that ranking is presupposed to be complete and transitive, deviance would be not so much wrong as irrational-unintelligible (Green, 'Law, Co-ordination and the Common Good', 317, 319). But this postulate or presupposition is not verified in the real life of practical reasonableness.

For in real life, alternatives do not present themselves for choice in fully bounded situations or in transitive rankings. Choice P will be better than choice Q in respect of its friendliness or fairness, or by increasing one's long-term security, but choice Q will be better than choice P in respect of one's here-and-now satisfactions, or short-term security. These different types of goods are not commensurable apart from particular scales of assessment which one *chooses* to adopt and employ. And the reasons for one's most fundamental choices of scales of assessment cannot be that they identify quantities of the good to be assessed, or even that they identify transitive ordinal relations between outcomes in terms only of that assessable good.[5]

II

In short, the Coordination Problem model, as understood in game theory, takes things too easily to be of assistance in legal theory. By assuming that the players have complete and transitive preference rankings, and that these coincide to support the choice of a salient solution preferred by each to no solution, the model departs widely from the reality that many participants in the life of any complex community would, in relation to many particular 'problems', prefer 'no solution' to any of the proposed solutions. Indeed, there is often quite wide disagreement about what circumstances are and

[4] A relationship R between choices or outcomes x, y, z... is transitive if for all x, y, z ..., xRy and yRz implies xRz.

[5] *NLNR* 111–18; *FoE* 86–94; Grisez, 'Against Consequentialism' at 37–8. The standard work on game and decision theory recognizes the problem confronting the theory's very first axiom, the axiom of transitivity:

> No matter how intransitivities arise, we must recognize that they exist, and we can take only little comfort in the thought that they are an anathema to most of what constitutes theory in the behavioral sciences today. We may say that we are only concerned with behavior which is transitive, adding hopefully that we believe this need not always be a vacuous study. (Luce and Raiffa, *Games and Decisions*, 25.)

are not a 'problem', and what are the bounds of 'relevant circumstances' and of the set of 'players'.

As Ullmann-Margalit pointed out: the specific difference of coordination problems within the class of situations in which the outcomes of one's choices depend upon the actions chosen by others is that in coordination problems the interests of the parties coincide.[6] She rightly used the central-case or focal-meaning analysis so indispensable to social theory:

> When the coincidence of interests is perfect we speak of a *pure* co-ordination problem. In the non-pure co-ordination problems the convergence of the parties' interests is less than perfect, but still outweighs any possible clash of interests.[7]

The first difference, then, between the concept of coordination problem used in game theory and the concept appropriate for political or legal philosophy is that the latter must extend to include situations where, *in relation to the 'situation' itself and the interests of the parties in that situation as such*, there is no convergence or sharing of interests. And the second difference will be that political and legal theory must take into consideration a type of 'interest' systematically excluded from game theory (and the exclusion of which is particularly evident in the game-theoretical handling of Prisoners' Dilemma problems), viz. interest in the fairness of the game's play and outcome, which any player *can* prefer to an increment in the advancement or protection of his 'own' interests. This interest is very closely related to the interest that a person has in the well-being of his friend (or of someone towards whom he has friendly dispositions)—an interest not to be confused with the flat nineteenth-century concept of altruism.[8]

Thus, the term 'coordination problem' extends, in political and legal theory, to any situation where, if there were coordination of action, significantly beneficial payoffs, otherwise unattainable, could be attained by significant numbers of persons *in a way which other persons, even if harmed or at least not benefited by that option in that situation, could count as 'a good thing'*. Thus understood, coordination problems are neither more nor less than the 'problems of united action' (that is, 'common action' for the 'common good'), identified and powerfully handled by Yves Simon in his restatement of the (rather implicit) Aristotelian and Thomist account of authority.[9] And it is this richer conception of coordination problems which is used by Raz, Gans, and myself, amongst other contemporaries.[10]

[6] Ullmann-Margalit, *The Emergence of Norms*, 78. [7] *Ibid.*

[8] *Ibid.*, 48n; *NLNR* 142–4, 158.

[9] Simon, *The Philosophy of Democratic Government*, ch. 1; Simon, *A General Theory of Authority*, ch. 2; *NLNR* 231–2.

[10] These writers also appear to me to share the very wide conception of coordination problem, which I explicitly use, viz., one which includes all problems constituted by the collision of one

The bearing of coordination on legal theory can now be conveniently explored by sketching a recent controversy between Raz and myself about the authority of law.

Raz accepts that a principal function of the law is to secure morally desirable coordination (usually called by him 'cooperation'), that is, coordination which everyone has moral reason to further, or at least to refrain from frustrating. He accepts, too, that law can be instrumental in securing desirable sorts of coordination, for example, in securing the inception or maintenance of schemes (such as anti-pollution schemes) which depend for their value on general if not universal support. But even when the law is thus instrumental in securing schemes of coordination with which everyone has moral reason to collaborate, it lacks moral authority. For the morally relevant reasons for complying with the scheme of coordination derive, he says, entirely from the practice of coordination, and not at all from the law; the moral situation is the same whether the practice exists by virtue of legal sanctions, government exhortations, pressure-group propaganda, or spontaneously emergent custom.[11]

Raz, it seems to me, here overlooks the diversity of views about social 'problems'. Some people think pollution no problem, some think it a lesser evil than the expense of avoiding it; some envisage one scheme for overcoming it, and others imagine different and incompatible schemes. Exhortations, propaganda, or even custom favouring one anti-pollution scheme over others (and over a polluters' free-for-all) give those who favour another solution (or none) no sufficient reason to comply, even though the non-compliance of even a few of these dissenters will, foreseeably, render the scheme nugatory. But a *law* against pollution does create a sufficient moral reason for even these dissenters to comply; that is to say, the law is (morally as well as legally) authoritative.[12] But why?

III

I retain but redeploy the game-theoretical concept of salience. The law, I suggest, makes itself salient in identifying and solving particular

person's interests or desires with another's. Be that as it may, this is perhaps the place to note again that failure to distinguish between the game-theoretical concept of a Coordination Problem and the richer concept sketched above renders irrelevant the critique in Green, 'Law, Co-ordination and the Common Good'.

[11] *AL* 233–49.

[12] Essay 2 at 49–50, 63–4

coordination problems, not by the merits of its particular solutions, but by having the features which are characteristic of 'the law', notably:

(a) The law presents itself as a seamless web by forbidding its subjects to pick and choose. To say this is not (as Raz thought)[13] to beg the question of law's moral authority; it is merely to point to the fact that, by virtue of this empirical feature of a healthy legal system, all the subjects of the law are, in at least one significant respect, put in like case, and indeed are actually, in many more than one respect, linked to each other by that network of protections and other benefits which the law secures for each by imposing restraints and exactions upon all. Where burdened by a legally enforced coordination scheme he thinks misguided, each can reflect that he has been or at some time will be benefited by the burdens which the law has in other respects (other ways, other contexts) imposed and will impose on others, including those misguided individuals whose exhortations, propaganda, or customs have inspired this new and unmeritorious law.[14]

(b) The 'procedural' features of law give reason for regarding it as authoritative in identifying and solving coordination problems. By comparison with propaganda, exhortation, and custom, the law's legislative capacities hold out the prospect of generating relatively prompt but also relatively clear and subtle solutions to coordination problems as they emerge and change. Its forms and its modes of application and enforcement, too, tend to ensure that its solutions will be relatively discriminating but non-discriminatory, and will be imposed on free-riders and other deviants so that the willing collaborator in the legally required coordination solution can have some assurance that he is not a mere sucker or fall-guy. And the legal process of detecting and penalizing free-riders and deviants is so structured as to minimize the unfairnesses perpetuated by enthusiasts who demand conformity to their exhortations, propaganda, or customs, and would press these demands in ways ill-adapted to finding and acting on the truth.

For these two (related) sorts of reasons, I argue, the existence of the legal order creates a shared interest which gives everyone moral reason to collaborate with the law's coordination solutions, that is, moral reason to regard the law as (morally) authoritative. Most specifically, that shared interest is in the regular, impartial upholding of the law itself. More generically, the shared interest is in the good of there being and continuing to be (and not merely patchily) a fair method of relating benefits to burdens, and persons to persons, over an immensely wide, complex, and lasting,

[13] 'For [Finnis], if this is how the law presents itself, then this is how we ought to take it.... a most vicious circle indeed': Raz, 'The Obligation to Obey: Revision and Tradition' at 150.

[14] Essay 2 at 51.

though shifting, set of persons and transactions—a method which nothing other than law plausibly offers.[15]

Raz replies that laws striving to achieve coordination, having to address masses of people and be adapted for judicial and administrative enforcement, will sometimes oversimplify. Those individuals who understand the situation will then, on occasion, have 'no reason' to conform to legal requirements which are simplifications ill-suited, in those circumstances, to the goal of the coordination. And this non-conformity does not threaten the effectiveness of government and the law; for some offences never become known, and many torts and breaches of contract violate the interests of one individual only.[16]

My rejoinder: 'effectiveness' for what? The point of law is not merely to ensure the survival of government or the future conformity of the potentially recalcitrant. Part of the law's point is to maintain real (not merely apparent) fairness between the members of a community; and this aspect of law's point is unaffected by the detection or covertness of breaches of law. The institution of law gains much of its value, as a contribution to the common good, precisely from the fact that the obligations it imposes hold good even when breach seems likely to be undetectable.[17]

Of course, for Raz undetectability was not a licence for non-conformity but one of the pre-conditions for a justified breach motivated and licensed by the violator's superior understanding of what is needed for the particular goal of a law's coordinative scheme. And it would be foolish to deny that in some circumstances an individual can serve fairness or other aspects of the common good better by breach than by conformity. But Raz's claim that in those situations the law gives 'no reason' for doing what it commands, this is, has *no* moral authority at all, seems extravagant. The thesis which Raz and others deny[18] is that law creates a prima facie generic moral obligation and thus has prima facie and generic moral authority. Although on this thesis a prima facie reason and authority of this sort can be *overridden* by countervailing reasons, there is no reason to say that, morally speaking, the law (and its authority) never extended at all to the situations in which it is overridden.

The reason (I suggested) for taking the law seriously to the full extent of its tenor and intended reach—and never regarding it as giving *no* reason

[15] Essay 2 at 64.

[16] Raz, 'The Obligation to Obey: Revision and Tradition' at 149.

[17] *NLNR* 303–5, 319.

[18] Smith, 'Is There a Prima Facie Obligation to Obey the Law?'; Woozley, *Law and Obedience: The Arguments of Plato's Crito*; Simmons, *Moral Principles and Political Obligation*; Lyons, 'Need, Necessity and Political Obligation'; Sartorius, 'Political Authority and Political Obligation'; Postema, 'Coordination and Convention at the Foundations of Law'.

for doing what it commands—is a reason connected with that irreducible multiformity of human goods (and that plurality of human persons) which imposes intrinsic limitations on human practical reasoning and makes nonsense (and injustice) of totalitarian projects. Generally speaking, an individual acts most appropriately for the common good not by trying to estimate the needs of the community 'at large' nor by second-guessing the judgments of those who *are* directly responsible for the common good, but by performing his particular undertakings and fulfilling his other responsibilities to the ascertained individuals who have contractual or other rights correlative to his duties. For the common good simply *is* the good of individuals living together and depending upon one another in ways that tend to favour the well-being of each.[19]

Correspondingly, those who do have legislative or other constitutional responsibility for the common good as such, do well to regard it as quite other than a goal which could be defined and attained by skilful disposition of efficient means, such as a bridge or an omelette. Attempts to absorb the individual or particular groups into a vast overall coordination 'solution', so as to eliminate all *private* purposes and all enterprises launched for reasons other than the advancement of the public coordinative scheme, confuse the idea of a national common good with the idea of a national common enterprise or scheme of coordination. Such attempts, indeed, thereby do grave damage to the common good. Their injustice *is* a reason for regarding laws made pursuant to them as morally *ultra vires* and devoid of law's generic moral authority—though not of the possible 'collateral' moral significance which both Raz and I admit.[20]

NOTE

† *Hart saw that the moral obligation to obey the law is owed to fellow-subjects, rather than to the rulers*...(in n. 19). See Hart, 'Are There Any Natural Rights?' at 185, quoted in the first endnote to essay 5.

[19] If one must locate a party to whom the obligation to obey the law is owed, it should be one's fellow-subjects rather than the rulers (legislators, judges, administrators, police, et al.). Hart saw this.† But certain writings denying the generic prima facie obligation to obey the law are shipwrecked by their authors' supposition that such an obligation would have to be (or is commonly supposed to be) *to officials*: see e.g. Postema, 'Coordination and Convention at the Foundations of Law', 196.

[20] Raz, 'The Obligation to Obey: Revision and Tradition' at 146–7n; *NLNR* 361–2.

4

POSITIVISM AND 'AUTHORITY'*

Rolf Sartorius's paper has two main theses with which I can concur. But I think that Sartorius fails to pursue consistently the implications of his own, and Hart's, methodology.

The first thesis guides Part I of Sartorius's paper. Explanations of law, social rules, and the like had better proceed, he says, not 'by way of the specification of a set of conditions which are individually necessary and jointly sufficient for [the] correct application' of the relevant term or concept, but rather by identification of 'central features' of legal or other forms of social order and social ordering, and by consideration of the 'important differences made in our lives...by the presence or absence of [those] central features...'.

The second theme runs through Part II of his paper. The question which 'ultimately interest[s]' Sartorius—'By what moral right may some people exercise coercion over others?'—is to be answered not by 'logical analysis' but by identifying, first, the 'ends' which give 'reasons' for undertaking tasks or 'responsibilities', and then by identifying 'what is required to get on with the task' in view of 'certain contingent but virtually universal features of human beings and their natural environment'.

As Sartorius rightly says, those two methodological theses were a principal source of 'the great richness of illumination offered by *The Concept of Law*'. I would go further. Those theses, subtly explored in the context of a comprehensive and precise understanding of mature legal systems, enabled Hart to restore his discipline ('jurisprudence') to the *philosophy of human affairs*[1] with all the *descriptive richness and critical openness to practical questions of good, less good, and evil* of Aristotle's original

* 1987d, a Comment on Sartorius, was a contribution to the conference in Jerusalem in March 1984 on Hart's work, which resulted in Gavison, *Issues in Contemporary Legal Philosophy: The Influence of H.L.A. Hart*, where it is entitled 'Positivism and the Foundations of Legal Authority'. In Gavison, the footnotes run on from lead papers through their respective commentaries; so the first footnote in 1987d is numbered 47.

[1] *NE* X.9: 1181b15: *he peri ta anthrōpina philosophia.*

enterprise. That enterprise has long needed, of course, to be reworked, to overcome the serious limitations in Aristotle's empirical knowledge of human culture, and in his understanding of human nature (of free choice for example). Attempts to undertake this reworking have foundered on diversions such as Hegel's or Comte's *gnosis* about the meaning of history, Bentham's hedonist determinism, Weber's value-demonism...and many others. Hart has distanced himself from such diversions and shown how one can get on with the job of overcoming both the complacent eclecticism of the legal practitioner and academic, and the arbitrary scepticisms of empiricists such as Bentham and, at a remove, Austin, of neo-Kantians such as Kelsen, and of behaviourists such as the Scandinavian and American Realists.

One sign of Hart's openness to reality has gone unnoticed by Sartorius. In *The Concept of Law*, the end or 'aim' which is the basis for the 'natural' or, better, 'rational necessity' of the central features of law is said to be 'survival'. Sartorius rightly suggests that 'surely room must be made for loftier human pursuits than mere survival'. But Hart got there before him; in his 1967 essay 'Problems of the Philosophy of Law', Hart proposes as the final point of law not mere survival, but rather that:

> whatever other purposes laws may serve, they must, to be acceptable to any rational person, enable men to live and organize their lives *for the more efficient pursuit of their aims*...certain rules [are] necessary *if fundamental human needs are to be satisfied*....[2]

No doubt the faithful and cautious interpreter of Hart's works might see in this shift no more than a new stratagem in the unaltered grand strategy of declining to participate (or at least to involve jurisprudence) in the great 'dispute'[3] about the point of human existence, the basic forms of human flourishing, and the basic requirements of practical reasonableness; the new stratagem is that so amply developed in Rawls's 'thin theory of the good'—of saying (no more than): *if anything* is wanted, these [primary goods] will be needed. But one who speaks at all of human needs and human rationality cannot prevent his hearers reflecting that human intelligence can also understand some 'ultimate' wants as really no more than worthless means to self-gratification while other objects of desire are really desirable or worthwhile. Human rationality can also reflect that the arbitrariness involved in unrestricted self-preference is itself a deviation from 'rationality' and something one *needs to avoid* whatever else one's wants.... As Sartorius's whole paper hints, Hart's method points out a land which is left to his readers and hearers to hazard to enter.

[2] Hart, *Essays in Jurisprudence and Philosophy*, 113 (emphases added). [3] Cf. *CL* 187–8.

I

That the analysis of legal authority yielded by Part I of Sartorius's paper would be 'positivistic' was pre-determined by the restricted nature of his question in that part, 'just what is being claimed when it is said that a particular social norm exists in, *or is accepted by* the members of, a community?'[4] If one's interest in the 'existence' of social (for instance, legal) norms is restricted to the question, 'When are they accepted?', one will be a positivist simply by the narrowness of theoretical concern.

Every competent 'natural law theorist' (Plato, Aristotle, Aquinas) can produce a 'positivist' analysis of what is involved in people accepting a rule, that is, of what is involved in the pragmatic 'existence' of such a rule (for example, of the 'existing law' of a corrupt and tyrannical democracy such as executed or judicially/legally murdered Socrates). What would strike these theorists as odd, and in need of explanation, is that some 'social scientists and ethical theorists' apparently consider such an 'analysis' somehow an interesting and complete topic in its own right. After all, law's existence in this pragmatic sense will be evident enough to anyone who strolls into the marketplace and attends to the goings-on of courts, hangmen, secret and not-so-secret police, barrackroom lawyers in the legislature... Such an observer might, I suppose, become interested in what is involved in *acceptance*, as part of, say, a Thucydidean inquiry into the likelihood of breakdown, revolution, and civil war or counter-revolutionary suppression; or as part of a Weberian inquiry into the fate of bureaucratic mass democracy. But he will hardly turn to a philosopher's 'analysis' to help him.

Sartorius ignores the claim made by Joseph Raz and other students of Hart that, in the world of social life and common speech which lies open to our 'analysis', we find statements about the existence of norms—that is, statements of the form 'N [a law or other social norm] still exists as part of English law', 'N is a valid law', 'There is in England a law, N', 'By virtue of N, X has power to...'—statements which may be understood in three ways, one of which is *basic* or *primary*, the other two being secondary and derivative or even parasitic;[5] and that the basic or primary form of such statements is that in which the statement asserts that N gives *good reason* for acting in a certain way. I am not going to explore this claim here; for Sartorius does not confront it. I shall simply observe that legal theorists

[4] Emphasis added. The next sentence begins 'This question...', thus establishing that the 'or' in the sentence quoted signifies synonymity, not alternatives. That the question is indeed restricted to 'acceptance' is made clear by the phrasing in other places.

[5] Raz, *Practical Reason and Norms*, 172. See *NL* 234–6. Likewise MacCormick, *H.L.A. Hart*, 39–40.

who are not determined a priori to restrict their theoretical inquiries after the manner of Sartorius's 'positivistic' Part I can undertake an inquiry which I suggest is more enticing: What sort of good *reasons* are there for thinking that laws or other social norms can and sometimes do *give good reasons for acting*?

What is the attraction of such an inquiry? Well, it permits *all* the hard-headed, undeluded, undistracted attention to social facts which a 'positivist' (or an Aristotle!) could desire; for social facts both affect one's choice or approval of means in one's practical reasoning, and serve as a stock of reminders of reasons which other people have considered to be good reasons and which may thus be plausible. And at the same time it opens up a line of thought to which a philosopher could hope to contribute much, namely the analysis of reasons *as reasons*.

The attractive power of such more-than-positivist inquiry is indicated, perhaps, by the way in which Sartorius strays across his own self-imposed boundaries. Consider the following:

> Whether or not one has in mind the acceptance of social rules in general, or the acceptance of constitutional rules by officials in particular, the existence of social rules is simply *too complex an affair to permit* of any interesting claims about what in the nature of their existence generates moral obligations on the part of either those who apply them or those to whom they apply. (Emphasis added.)

This seems to suggest that if the facts involved in acceptance were less 'complex', one might be able to say that something about 'the nature of their existence' (*scilicet* about that acceptance) 'generates moral obligations'. But how do facts, simple or complex, 'generate' moral obligations? How does the question of generating moral obligations arise in the course of a 'positivistic' discussion of what counts as acceptance of social rules? Sartorius seems, similarly, to have confused MacCormick's claim—that rules cannot be said to be accepted unless people have a certain set of preferences and beliefs including a belief that the rule is [morally] binding—with the quite distinct claim that where the rule is thus accepted it does indeed 'generate' moral obligations. We shall see, in our discussion of Part II of his paper, that Sartorius really does speak as if an 'analysis' of terms or 'phenomena' might, in principle, yield a moral conclusion. I must say that the main stream of natural law theorizing never falls into this sort of confusion, which is by no means peculiar to Sartorius.

Following Aristotle, Aquinas, and Hart, I agree with Sartorius that any useful theoretical concept of *legal system*, or of *acceptance*, had better be a 'cluster concept'. So I may be excused from dwelling on Sartorius's interesting discussion of the 153 conditions which might, he thinks, have to be acknowledged by someone who misguidedly sought a set of necessary and sufficient conditions for the existence/acceptance of a legal system;[6] or on his argument that none of the 153 is in fact a strictly necessary condition.[7]

Nor do I wish to dwell on the fact that Sartorius himself seems to engage in a bit of 'essentialism' when he opines that 'constitutional rules... are juristic constructs, the correct description of which *must* fit the facts with respect to the relevant behaviour of officials and norm subjects'. The truth is that the concepts of *juristic construct* and *correct description of juristic constructs* are each concepts which had better be treated as cluster concepts. One may readily see this, in precisely the context of constitutional rules, if one reflects on the rival 'correct juristic descriptions' which can intelligibly and reasonably be given of the constitutional situation in a civil war, or during an enemy occupation and 'government in exile', or in circumstances such as prevailed in and in relation to Rhodesia in the years after its Unilateral Declaration of Independence from the United Kingdom in 1965. In such circumstances, one can of course *adopt* a particular viewpoint from which one and only one description of the constitutional rules will be 'correct'. But to assert that only one such particular viewpoint can be correct is to distort both common opinion and practice, and the legal and moral complexities of the situation.

The most substantial point I want to make about Part I is that Sartorius has not followed through the implications of his recognition that the analysis had better be by way of cluster concepts. For, as he acknowledges from time to time, a cluster concept is not a shapeless sprawl of features. It is a set of criteria or features all of which are satisfied in 'standard or normal' cases, and some of which, with due (extreme) caution, can be recognized to be 'central' or 'crucial'. But what makes a feature 'crucial' or (better) 'central'? And what makes an instantiation of the concept 'standard or normal'? As to the latter question, it is perhaps significant that Sartorius

[6] [Sartorius, 'Positivism and the Foundations of Legal Authority' at 49–51.] I am not to be taken to agree that the generation of most of the 153 conditions is sound; one wonders whether it takes sufficient account of the point made by the classical natural law theorists: doing justice (in whatever capacity) is a matter not of having the right attitudes but of the right *practice* regardless of attitude: e.g. *ST* II–II q.57 a.1c [and on this important point, see essay 7 at n. 21]. Why should people bother to have all, or even any, of these preferences (or even of these beliefs) about other people's preferences or beliefs, so long as the others are *complying*?

[7] I think his argument [at 51] about adultery in contemporary American sexual mores is weak; the fact that most people commit adultery at least once would not nearly show that the rule had no 'external aspect'; the proper question (relative to this so-called external aspect [Sartorius's condition 1 for the existence of social rule/norm N]) is whether most people *usually* abstain from adultery when occasion offers. (Perhaps they do not, but Sartorius does not tell us about that.) But I do not want to question his point that condition 1 ['Most members of community C conform to N on most occasions when N applies to them, and the occasions on which N is applicable to them are relatively frequent': *ibid.* at 49] may not be necessary [to the existence of a social rule N].

spends time on 'insist[ing]', against Hart, that 'mindless passive obedience is not *the norm*' (emphasis added). Why should Sartorius want to insist on his purely empirical question of what 'obtains in most modern states'? I fear it may be because he lacks any clear conception of what should count as the central case or cases (instantiations) of a theoretical concept such as *legal system* or *internal attitude*, and equally of what should count as the central or crucial features of that concept.

Weber was right, I believe, to insist that social science advances understanding by identifying not the universal, or the common, or the average (or, one might say, the Sartorian 'norm'), but rather the characteristic, the culturally significant, the intelligible, and meaningful.[8] And certainly, when it is a question of developing a theoretical concept encapsulating a clarified and improved understanding of a range of social phenomena (such as the concept of law developed by Hart in the book of that name), one should share Hart's assumption that 'the extension of the general terms of any serious discipline is never without its principle or rationale'.[9] The project of identifying such a principle or rationale should be particularly easy to distinguish from the question of their universality or even frequency of instantiation, when the relevant term and concept signify a range of social phenomena constituted principally by *reasons*, good and/or purportedly good, for action. For the coherence and mutual supportiveness of reasons is certainly distinct from the question of how frequently those reasons, or any subset of them, are actually adopted and acted upon. Thus, for example, Hart's critique of Kelsenian reductionism ('distortion as the price of uniformity')[10] does not depend on demonstrating that the law-abiding man's attitude to law is more *common* than the 'bad man's' perspective. Nor does his critique of 'realism'[11] depend on showing that judges never or rarely fail to use the law as a reason for their judgments; rather, it suffices that the whole idea of having rules which courts are to apply to the litigants who were subject to those rules—an idea central to any plausible project of distinguishing law from other forms of coercive social ordering[12]—would be unintelligible if rules were not reasons for judgment but mere predictions.

I quite agree with Sartorius that it is possible to envisage a legal system in which every official in his heart rejected the system's values and wished for its downfall and continued to play along largely or 'basically' out of

[8] Shils and Finch, *Max Weber on the Methodology of the Social Sciences*, 43, 90; Hekman, *Max Weber and Contemporary Social Theory*, 22, 25, 48.

[9] *CL* 15, 210; also 234; also Hart, *Essays in Jurisprudence and Philosophy*, 22, 30n, 43 ff.

[10] *CL* 38–41.

[11] *CL* 81–2; 'Scandinavian Realism', in Hart, *Essays in Jurisprudence and Philosophy*, 165.

[12] See Raz, *Practical Reason and Norms*, 136, 137, 139.

fear. Equally, I agree with Hart that 'allegiance to the system may be based on many different considerations', such as 'calculations of long-term interest...an unreflecting inherited or traditional attitude; or the mere wish to do as others do'.[13] But I would like to suggest again what I have argued elsewhere:

> All these considerations and attitudes ... are manifestly deviant, diluted or watered-down instances of the practical viewpoint that brings law into being as a significantly differentiated type of social order and maintains it as such. Indeed, they are parasitic upon that viewpoint.[14]

For, unreflecting traditionalism or sheer conformism, while capable (up to a point) of maintaining a legal system in being if it already exists, are blind or practically indifferent to the need to remedy the defects of a pre-legal (or post-legal!) social order; that is, they do not share the concern which Hart himself treats as the explanatory source of legal order. Likewise, the man motivated dominantly by calculations of long-term self-interest will dilute his allegiance to law and his adherence to legal processes with doses of that very self-interest which, on everybody's view, it is an elementary function of law to subordinate to social needs.

I will not here repeat the whole argument in favour of identifying, as the central case of allegiance to law (the 'internal viewpoint'), the attitudes of one who considers that morality and a rationally imperative impartiality of concern for others require him to cooperate in establishing and/or maintaining legal order, as distinct not only from anarchy but also from discretionary or statically conventional forms of social ordering. I have argued elsewhere that this is the set of attitudes that should be taken as the standard of reference by the theorist seeking to describe the features of legal order. A principal attraction of this method, for me as for Plato[15] and Aristotle and Aquinas, is this: the mature person of practical reasonableness (whose relevant attitudes I have just sketched) can understand and appreciate the concerns and the reasons for action of the merely self-interested, the mere conformist, the mere careerist, *but the converse does not hold.* So, adoption of this person's practical concerns as the criterion for discerning what features really do 'cluster together' as a coherent, meaningful, and important social institution will make possible not only the most intelligible account of legal reasons for action (including reasons for having law and the rule of law at all) but also the best *empirical* account of this aspect of human affairs.

[13] *CL* 198; also 111, 226. [14] *NLNR* 13–15.

[15] *Republic* IX, 582a–e; III, 408d–409e; *NLNR* 15n.

But since Sartorius's paper does not advert to this type of objection to Hart's refusal to identify a central case of the internal point of view, I shall not labour the matter further here.

II

Why should someone who is 'ultimately interested...in considering by what moral right some people may exercise coercive authority over others' *want* a 'positivistic' account of the existence of a legal system? Why should he want an account which treats some rather indeterminate (we may not talk of 'necessary and sufficient conditions') cluster of facts about practices and attitudes as amounting to the acceptance (by a community) of a legal system?

I suspect that the reason is a fear that the moral inquiry will somehow be *prejudiced* unless the object of that inquiry has first been identified in morally neutral terms.

As a reason for sponsoring a 'positivistic' general theory of law or legal system, this would be, I suggest, a muddle. For, as Hart reminded us many years ago,[16] we begin our inquiry—*any* theoretical inquiry—about law with a wide knowledge of the facts about law and legal systems. We already know, before we start either 'positivistic' description or moral argument, that in our own society as well as in others, there are existing institutions of courts, legislature, police and bailiffs, lawyers, enactments, valid and invalid instruments, and so forth. This knowledge is not going to be lost during the development of a descriptive general theory, and is perfectly sufficient to permit us to raise, without any prejudgment, the question whether these institutions have any moral justification and make any morally obligatory claims upon us.

What, then, is the point of a descriptive general theory? It is, as Hart also taught us, by word and example, to *explain* the *function*, the practical point, of the various aspects and components of law and legal systems, so as to show *why* there is *good practical reason* for these aspects and components to cluster together as a distinct social enterprise.[17]

And that is why a fruitful, descriptive general theory of law cannot proceed at all without adopting and seeking, as Hart would say, to 'reproduce' a particular practical viewpoint.[18] Hart identified that viewpoint as 'the internal attitude'. He characterized that viewpoint more closely than Sartorius, for he treated merely fearful compliance as not 'internal'.[19] In this, his view is to be preferred to Sartorius's. It matters not that one

[16] *CL* 4–5. [17] *NLNR* 6–7. [18] See *CL* 88; also *NLNR* 12. [19] *CL* 88.

can imagine a society in which every single person complies only out of fear. For such a society, as Sartorius himself points out, would have to be founded on a vast series of factually mistaken beliefs (about the attitudes of everyone else). And no illumination *about law* is to be gained by reflecting on this grossly pathological[20] social condition.

I have argued, above, that the practical viewpoint from which to explain the point of a legal ordering would be better characterized even more closely than Hart does, by treating as insufficiently illuminating those explanations which would satisfy the mere conformist or careerist or traditionalist, and by looking further, for explanations which would satisfy someone with a sound morality, that is, a fully reasonable person.

You will say that descriptive jurisprudence cannot, on this view, be safely carried out until one has completed a moral inquiry into the foundations of the moral authority of law. I reply that the moral inquiry cannot be safely carried out until one has an exact knowledge of the functions of legal ordering and of the institutions and devices which have been devised to serve those functions. The truth is, then, that *explanatory descriptive general theory* of law and *the moral justification and critique of law for the guidance of one's own conscience* are radically inter-dependent intellectual enterprises.[21]

III

The question addressed in Part II of Sartorius's paper is: 'When may those who correctly claim to act with legal authority be said to have a moral right to rule?'

Sartorius's first move is to explain 'what [he understands] this claim to mean'. I want to raise two sorts of doubts about the explanation he offers: the first, about the content of his analysis of the claim to a moral right to rule; the second, about what he thinks, or seems to think, *might* be established by any such analysis.

Sartorius's analysis of the claim to a moral right to rule identifies it as a compound of two elements: (1) a claim to a 'justification-right', viz. a claim that A (the bearer of legal authority) is morally justified, by virtue of his authority, in using coercion against S (his legal subject); (2) a claim to a claim-right against usurpers, who thus are said to have a correlative obligation not to usurp (say, by kangaroo courts or lynchings) the processes of, for example, trial and punishment.[22]

[20] By which I do not *mean* 'rare' (though I think it is).

[21] *NLNR* 16–19.

[22] In one place, Sartorius loosely expresses this obligation or duty to abstain from usurpation as a mere 'no right'. In another, he correctly identifies the correlative of the claim-right as a '[positive] obligation'.

The point that Sartorius seems to want to make is that this claim to a right to rule does not include a claim that S has a moral obligation to obey the law.[23]

The effort to keep S out of the picture of A's moral right to rule leads to some oddities. It is odd to think of the obligation not to usurp being owed (as Sartorius insists) not to S (the victim of the usurping kangaroo court or lynch mob) but to A. I would be prepared to grant that A does have some rather secondary and not very interesting Sartorian claim-right not to be usurped; but, in relation to usurpation, I should say that A's primary right is his justification-right (and responsibility) to take coercive steps to deter, resist, and punish usurpers. And I can see no ground, either in common opinion or sound political philosophy, to doubt that it is S who has the primary and interesting claim-rights (a) against usurpers, that authority over him shall not be usurped, and (b) against A, that A shall resist usurpers.[24]

Much more odd is the following implication of Sartorius's analysis: to claim that A has a moral right to rule is to claim that A is morally justified in coercing S, by trial and punishment, for an action *that S had and has no moral obligation to abstain from.* For this is the implication of Sartorius's assertion that A's justification-right has no correlative obligation. I do not say that this defies 'logic'. On the contrary, there has been for centuries an important and influential strand of western political philosophizing which contends that many laws are 'purely penal', that is, that the enactment of the laws is morally justified, but that the laws themselves impose no moral obligation to comply with their legal-obligation-imposing content, but only a moral obligation to submit to the legal penalty for non-compliance, or alternatively and more popularly, a disjunctive moral obligation to either comply or submit to penalty.[25] Those who have defended this interpretation have occasionally visualized the logical possibility that S has no moral obligation even to submit to the penalty. But this logical possibility seems to have almost no moral plausibility. For if the structure of the situation is such that A really is morally entitled not only to enact the law but also to impose really coercive penalties on S, what could be the features of that

[23] It is hard to be sure about Sartorius's point here, because neither he nor the quoted passages from Ladenson, 'In Defense of a Hobbesian Conception of Law', distinguish between deriving the *existence of an obligation* from an *(existing) (moral) right to rule*, and deriving *the existence of an obligation* from *a (mere) claim to have a (moral) right to rule.*

[24] I do not say that Sartorius denies these rights of S; but neither does he mention them; secondary takes the place of primary, and primary is not mentioned, in his analysis.

[25] For an account of these theories, and of the reason for the label 'purely penal law', see *NLNR* 325–7, 346–7.

structure that would relieve S of the moral obligation to cooperate with A, if not by complying with his law at least by submitting to the penalty?

It would have been helpful if Sartorius had indicated where he stands in these debates about 'purely penal laws'. I cannot discern from his paper whether or not he thinks that S, whom he envisages as having no moral obligation to *comply*, has any moral obligation to submit to the penalties which A, on Sartorius's own analysis, has the moral justification-right to impose on him.

And I confess that I am simply defeated by his discussion of the legitimate exercise of coercive force. I cannot be sure how it is supposed to stand in relation to the principal thesis that a moral right to rule does not entail a moral obligation to comply. For at one point the picture is that 'authority is associated with' [oddly weak phrase] 'the legitimate [*scilicet* justified] exercise of coercive force *because* compliance with the norms which are enforced by those in authority is taken to be *required* for the successful completion of a necessary task', and then the next sentence 'suggests' that where 'co-operation (*in the form of obedience*)' [no 'purely penal law' here!] 'is *not required*' then the exercise of the heavy hand of coercive authority would not be legitimate (emphases added).

But the important thing to establish is not whether Sartorius is wholly consistent, but how he can suppose (as he seems to) that *what is being claimed* by those who claim a moral right to rule is that the imposition of coercive measures (by those with that right) is morally justified, even though those on whom the morally justified penalty/punishment is imposed had no moral obligation to abstain from the conduct for which they are being penalized/punished (and [?] have no moral obligation to submit to, that is, not obstruct the imposition of, that penalty/punishment). In the hazy area of 'regulation', where language, institutional practice, and common attitudes neglect or smudge the distinction between tax and fine, and where 'penalty' does not necessarily connote punishable desert or culpability, there is both logical space for and some arguable moral/political ground for this supposition. But as a general analysis of authority to impose the *serious* penalties/punishments involved in any serious exercise of governmental authority in the modern state, it has, I think, no claim to represent common opinion, and no intrinsic moral plausibility.

Now for my second doubt about Sartorius's procedures in Part II of his paper. A theme of Part II is that, to justify a claim that S has a moral obligation to obey A, one must supply more than a 'mere analysis of the notion of [A's] moral right to rule'. I quite agree; it is fundamental to clear thinking that the mere analysis of *what a* [*moral*] *claim comes to* can never suffice to establish that the claim *is* morally justified, whether generically or in a particular case. What is so surprising is that Sartorius seems to think, at least some of the time, that the need for a *moral argument* (to show that S has a moral obligation to obey), an argument supplementing the analysis of the moral claim, arises only because the *claim* in question does not, on analysis, *include* or [*analytically*] *entail* the claim that S has such an obligation. The truth, I suggest, is that even if the analysis of the claim to a moral right to rule did disclose or include or entail a claim that S has a correlative duty to obey, *nothing would follow, morally*, about whether anyone really has a moral right to rule or a moral duty to obey.

What is the function of an analysis of the sort supplied by Sartorius? Perhaps it is intended to be an exploration of the meaning (or one meaning) of the term 'authority'. But it is also called an 'analysis of the nature of authority', and Sartorius declares himself more or less indifferent to the question whether his use of the term (and presumably also of correlative phrases such as 'right to rule') amounts to stipulating for it a new sense which it does not ordinarily possess. Then he says that his analysis 'isolated an important legal-moral-political phenomenon of considerable interest'. But what is the 'phenomenon'? If Sartorius is not here making an assertion about common speech, is he asserting that, in some actual communities known to us, people (A) *are considered* to have a moral right to rule coercively while their subjects (S) are considered not to have a moral duty to obey but only a moral duty not to usurp? No reason is given for supposing that this assertion is true. And even if it were true, Sartorius would still have to show why that sort of social order is 'important' and 'interesting' and more worthy of our attention than the alternative social order envisaged by Anscombe† (and, I venture to think, much more familiar in thought and in social life to all of us), in which the needs and facts which are considered to form a basis for a moral right to rule are equally considered to be the basis for a moral duty/obligation to comply with the rules of the rulers.

The one thing certain is that no moral argumentation was supplied as Sartorius's analysis unfolded. And there was no argumentation there, to show the importance and interest of the perhaps rather novel conjunction: moral-right-to-rule-with-no-duty-to-obey-but-duty-not-to-usurp.

But is some moral argumentation supplied by Sartorius later, to justify his claim that it is important to acknowledge that this strange (to me) conjunction has some kind of priority in a discussion of the moral relationship between A and S? There is only the passage which dismisses as 'too quick' Anscombe's premise that authorities have a right to what is necessary for the successful performance of their tasks; 'too quick', he says, because 'independent argument is required to establish a moral obligation to obey the law'. But 'independent' of what? Certainly, any conclusion like

Anscombe's needs argument which is 'independent' of the fact that A has *legal* authority; that such independent argument is needed is a central claim of the whole natural law tradition, at least. But Sartorius is asserting that 'independent' argument is required over and above (a) the *fact* (Anscombe's unchallenged second premise) that authority's tasks cannot be successfully performed without obedience, and (b) the *evaluative* [*moral*] *assessment* that authority's tasks are simply 'required' that is, necessary for the necessary end(s) of protecting moral rights and conferring fundamental benefits. He does not even hint at what such an independent argument might be.

For my part, I do not see how any argument that is independent in this last sense is either possible or needed. Nor do I see that Anscombe's argument for a moral obligation to obey is any 'quicker' than Sartorius's own argument for a moral right to rule and impose coercion and resist and punish usurpation.

Is it not the case, *pace* Sartorius, that the human needs to which he refers bring in the whole set of rights and obligations, or bring in none of them? If they bring in the fearsome right to rule coercively, they bring in, equally, the obligation to obey.

This assertion of mine does not rely on any 'analysis' of authority, nor on any 'logical' inference about the 'correlatives' or 'entailments' of a right to rule. It relies (like Anscombe's) on a moral assessment of what is humanly appropriate in face of the needs for cooperation in its many forms. *After* one has made that moral assessment, and has drawn the moral conclusion in the way I have just (very summarily) drawn it, one is equipped with a (morally justified) concept of authority, and within the conceptual framework thereby established it will be possible to say that right to rule entails obligation to obey. If, as I believe is the case, this morally justified concept coheres quite nicely with standard English usage and common political thought, that is a bonus. But all the work for the moral conclusion must be done by one's assessment of human good and what, in the human situation, is needed to attain it.

I have just said that in the morally justified, political-philosophical concept of authority, right to rule entails obligation to obey. But this must not be misunderstood as the relationship of claim-right to duty, in which S's duty would be an obligation owed *to* A, the holder of the claim-right. On the contrary, I think that in *that* (quasi-Hohfeldian) sense of 'right', rulers have no right to be obeyed.[26] Rather, rulers have the right (Hohfeldian power-right) to make laws which, once made, impose on their subjects an obligation (presumptively or defeasibly a moral as well as a legal obligation)

[26] *NLNR* 359; see also 332–7. See also Weber, *Economy and Society*, 218.

to do or abstain from certain acts. If one had to locate a party to whom the obligation is owed, would it not be one's fellow-subjects, particularly the law-abiding, rather than the rulers (legislators, judges, administrators, police)?[27] Some of the recent crop of arguments against the existence of a generic prima facie moral obligation to obey the law are shipwrecked because their authors suppose that such an obligation would have to be (and/or is commonly supposed to be) *to officials*.[28] This supposition, I suggest, falsifies both common opinion and critical moral plausibility.

NOTE

† *Anscombe on 'the source of the authority of the state'*...(at p. 85). Sartorius's contribution to the conference discusses Anscombe, 'On the Source of the Authority of the State' (= Anscombe, *The Collected Philosophical Papers of G.E.M. Anscombe*, 130–55.)

[27] See Hart, 'Are There Any Natural Rights?' at 185, quoted by Sartorius, 'Political Authority and Political Obligation' at 14 [and on p.155 below].

[28] See e.g. Postema, 'Coordination and Convention at the Foundations of Law' at 196.

Part Two

Theories and Theorists of Law

5

A GRAND TOUR OF LEGAL THEORY*

INTRODUCTION

We can speak of law wherever we can speak of obligation. Indeed, we can use the word more broadly still, and speak of law(s) wherever we can speak of normativity, that is of general directions considered as counting, or entitled to count, in one's deliberations about what to do. So, though it certainly has other meanings, 'law' can be used to refer to any criteria of right judgment in matters of practice (conduct, action), any standards for assessing options for human conduct as good or bad, right or wrong, desirable or undesirable, decent or unworthy. That is how the word is used in the term 'natural law'.

Though it, too, has a range of meanings, 'natural' can be used to signify that some of those criteria or standards[1] are somehow normative prior to any human choices. On this conception, these prior standards are not the product of either individual or collective choosing or positing, and cannot be repealed, however much they may be violated, defied, or ignored. The idea is that acknowledging these standards in one's deliberations is part of what it is to be *reasonable*—as much part of reasonableness as acknowledging basic natural realities (the world's longevity, or time's one-way flow, etc.), or the requirements of logic, or the aptness or inaptness of means to clear-cut ends (recipes for cakes, remedies for deflation, strategies for battle, circuitry for chips, etc.). Persons or cultures which fail to acknowledge these standards are in that respect unreasonable, even if in many respects rational (see secs X and XVIII below).

* 2002a: 'Natural Law: The Classical Tradition', Chapter 1 of Coleman and Shapiro, *The Oxford Handbook of Jurisprudence and Philosophy of Law.* The twenty-eight enumerated sections were written to track the book's twenty-seven other commissioned chapters, which were subsequently, however, rearranged and reduced to twenty-four in number.

[1] For economy, this essay uses 'standards' to refer to any principles, rules, or norms which give or purport to give direction (to motivate and to sort and rank motivations) in the deliberations of someone considering what to do. So the word covers not only the 'general directions' mentioned in the preceding paragraph, and the 'criteria' mentioned in the present text sentence, but also principles and rules of positive law, and so forth.

Unreasonableness of this kind is, as the saying goes, 'human, all too human'. But to speak more precisely, it is a way of being less than fully what a human person can be. And this is not the only reason for calling it 'unnatural'. Poor thinking and choosing not only fails to actualize to the full one's capacities to be intelligent and reasonable, but also results in actions and omissions which fail to respect and promote the humanity, the nature, of everyone they affect. A community in which the standards by which we identify such failure are violated is not flourishing as it might. Its members, whether they are those acting (and forbearing) or those who should have been benefited not harmed, do not fulfil their capacities. However typical of human affairs, such a condition is unnatural so far as it is disrespectful of human persons. It is unnatural *because* unreasonable, and unreasonable *because* neglectful of the good of persons, the good which is the subject-matter of practical reason's standards.

'Classic(al)' can be taken normatively or merely descriptively. Descriptively it can signify mere chronology; so 'classical natural law theory' might mean no more than the theory that emerged in 'classical times'; for us, ancient Greece. Or the description may be of conventional assessment; so 'classical natural law theory' might mean no more than the theory that is commonly taken to be the version or subclass of such theories which is typical or most commonly under discussion. Or one can use the phrase normatively, to signal one's judgment that this theory or set of ideas, however popular or unpopular, neglected or well known, is actually sound and entitled to acceptance as a guide to personal and communal life. In this essay, I normally use the term in all three senses at once; the weight of my interest is, of course, in the normative sense and claim.

Natural law theory claims to be the *adequate* or *sound* jurisprudence (or legal philosophy), and the sound ethics and political theory. So I shall explore the theory not only in the brief section which follows but also under a further twenty-seven headings. What sorts of things does the theory say—or would it say if consistently developed—about each of the central questions of contemporary legal philosophy? Sketching a response to that question, I followed the order of the *Handbook* in which this essay first appeared, at the expense of some repetition, and some departure from a more natural (more coherent, illuminating, fruitful) sequence of ideas and issues.

I. CLASSICAL NATURAL LAW THEORY

The thesis that, despite the variety of opinions and practices, there are indeed some true and valid standards of right conduct was philosophically (reflectively and critically) articulated by Plato. In his dialectic with sceptics Plato also found it appropriate to recapture from them the words 'nature' and 'natural'. For sceptics contended that by nature, naturally, the strong and selfish prevail over those who are weak or who weaken themselves by care for other persons, or for promises, or for their other 'responsibilities'. With resourceful brilliance Plato responded that trying to live 'naturally' or 'in line with the law of nature' by ruthless pursuit of one's desires for power or other satisfactions is self-stultifying, incoherent, and unreasonable. By nature one's desires, whether intelligent (say for knowledge and friendship), or primarily emotional (say for tasty food, sex, power, reputation, and so forth) are in need of being governed and moderated by the standards of reason. These standards extend beyond setting one's own psyche in order, and include the establishment and maintenance of a good order with, and among, one's fellows. Justice in the soul, indeed in the whole make-up of the particular individual, is the source of, and mirrors and is reflected by, justice in society. The nature of the political community is the nature of a human individual 'writ large'—and vice versa. The standards by which we judge the lustful tyrant a bad human being, a failure (as well as, and because, wicked), are *natural right, natural law*. The sceptics' 'law of nature', despite appearances (the glamour of evil), is unnatural because unreasonable. Such is the theme of Plato's *Gorgias*, his *Republic*, his *Laws*, and others of his works.[2]

The dialectic undertaken by Plato with scepticism, and with the prototypes of modern utilitarianism and pragmatism, is a dialectic carried forward more or less continuously to this day. His conceptual apparatus and argumentative strategies are employed by Aristotle, Cicero, Augustine, and Aquinas, not to mention the works of Shakespeare and many others. Indeed, some main elements of the tradition are present in Locke, Kant, and Hegel, though with such heavy concessions to scepticism about practical reason that their theories can no longer be called classical but 'modern'. This modernity was in some respects an advance on the classic understanding and on the political and legal orders sustained by theories more or less classical in kind. But in important and fundamental ways, the 'modern' conceptions are a regression from Plato's insights, back toward the pre-Socratic philosophers and sophists. Moreover, it is a modernity already passing away.

Three introductory points about the tradition of natural law theory are as follows:

(1) Its guiding purpose is to answer the parallel questions of a conscientious individual or a group or a group's responsible officers

[2] See essay I.2 (1999a).

(for example a judge): 'What should I do?' 'What should we decide, enact, require, promote?' True, these normative questions cannot be answered well without a sound and unblinkered knowledge of the facts about the way the world works. So good descriptions, general and specific, are needed. But descriptions remain of secondary, derivative interest. The dominant concern is with *judging for oneself* what reasons are good reasons for adopting or rejecting specific kinds of option. Societies and their laws and institutions are therefore to be understood as they would be understood by a participant in deliberations about whether or not to make the choices (of actions, dispositions, institutions, practices, etc.) which shape and largely constitute that society's reality and determine its worth or worthlessness. This 'internal' point of view is dominant, and standards and norms of conduct are never constituted by the facts of convention, custom, or consensus. (Nor by the *fact* that the deliberating person accepts them.) 'Ought' is never derivable from 'is', save by virtue of some higher, more ultimate ought-premise. Positivism, as we shall see, fails to meet this demand of logic coherently. But everything that positivism reasonably wishes to insist upon is clearly, and coherently, accommodated in classical natural law theory.

(2) The reason why classical natural law theory does not reduce ought to is (whether by 'deduction' or otherwise) is that in its debates with pre-scientific superstition and with sophistic reductions of right to might, it got clear about the irreducibility to each other of four kinds of order, to which correspond four kinds of theory: (i) orders which are what they are, independently of our thinking, that is, nature, laws of nature, and correspondingly the natural sciences and metaphysics; (ii) the order which we can bring into our thinking, and correspondingly the standards and discipline of logic; (iii) the order which we can bring into our deliberating, choosing, and acting in the open horizon of our whole life, and correspondingly the standards of morality and the reflective discipline of ethics; (iv) the order which we can bring into matter (including our own bodies) subject to our power, as means to relatively specific purposes, and correspondingly the countless techniques, crafts, and technologies.[3] Morality, and natural law (in the relevant sense

[3] On the four kinds of knowledge/science/discipline considered in this paragraph, and their irreducibility, see e.g. *Aquinas*, ch. 2; essay I.14 at 217–8 (1992a at 139–40).

of that term), cannot be reduced to, or deduced from, the principles of natural science or metaphysics, logic, or any craft.

(3) Nonetheless, the tradition has a clear understanding that one cannot reasonably affirm the equality of human beings, or the universality and binding force of human rights, unless one acknowledges that there is something about persons which distinguishes them radically from sub-rational creatures, and which, prior to any acknowledgement of 'status', is intrinsic to the factual reality of every human being, adult or immature, healthy or disabled.

II. THE MODERN NATURAL LAW TRADITION

'Modern' might here mean 'contemporary'. But virtually all who today are willing to call their own work 'natural law theory' regard themselves as re-presenting and developing the classical tradition. Moreover, they reject the characteristic tenets of that 'modern' tradition which emerges in the 1600s and which self-consciously set aside some of the very elements of the classical tradition that today's 'new classical' theorists esteem most highly.

So I shall follow a conventional scholarly view: the modern tradition of natural law theory emerges clearly by 1660, when Samuel Pufendorf published in The Hague his *Elements of Universal Jurisprudence*.[4] Characteristic features of this kind of natural law theory can be studied there, or in Pufendorf's fuller treatise *On the Law of Nature and of Nations*,[5] or in John Locke's long-unpublished *Questions concerning the Law of Nature*[6] dating apparently from around 1660 to 1664. Both writers are clearly derivative in some ways from Hugo Grotius and in other ways from Thomas Hobbes. Very tellingly, Pufendorf prominently describes Hobbes's *De Cive* (1642) (on being a citizen), which anticipates the moral and jurisprudential substance of Hobbes's more famous *Leviathan* (1651), as 'for the most part extremely acute and sound'.[7]

From Grotius's massively influential *On the Law of War and Peace* (1625), Locke and Pufendorf take the well-sounding but quite opaque idea that morality and the law's basic principles are a matter of 'conformity to rational nature'. How this nature is known, and why it is normative for anyone, these writers never carefully consider. Such fundamental questions were confronted and answered by Hobbes. But his answers treat our practical

[4] (1660). [5] (1672). [6] (1990). [7] Preface, p. xxx.

reasoning as all in the service of sub-rational passions such as fear of death, and desire to surpass others—motivations of the very kind identified by the classical tradition as in need of direction by our reason's grasp of more ultimate and better ends, of true and intrinsic goods, of really intelligent reasons for action. Hobbes proclaims his contempt for the classical search for ultimate ends or intrinsic reasons for action. Accordingly there can be for him no question of finding the source of obligation and law in the kind of necessity which we identify when we notice that some specific means is *required* by and for the sake of some end which it would be unreasonable not to judge desirable and pursuit-worthy.[8] Rather, obligation and law are defined, by Hobbes and then by Locke and Pufendorf, as matters of superior *will.*

'No law without a legislator.'[9] No obligation without subjection to the 'will of a superior power'.[10] 'Law's formal definition is: the declaration of a superior will.'[11] 'The rule of our actions is the will of a superior power.'[12] These definitions and axioms are meant by these founders of modern natural law theory to be as applicable to natural law, the very principles of morality, as to the positive law of states.[13] So obligation is being openly 'deduced' from fact, the fact that such-and-such has been willed by a superior. To be sure, when natural law (morality) is in issue, the superior, God, is assumed to be wise. But the idea of divine wisdom is given no positive role in explaining why God's commands create obligations for a rational conscience. God's *right* to legislate is explained instead by the analogy of sheer power: 'For who will deny that clay is subject to the potter's will and that the pot can be destroyed by the same hand that shaped it?'[14]

Locke, like Hobbes, is uneasily though dimly aware that 'ought' cannot be inferred from 'is' without some further 'ought'. That is to say, he is uneasily aware that the fact that conduct *was* willed by a superior, or

[8] What this obligation-explaining end is, in the last analysis, is considered in sec. X below.

[9] *John Locke: Questions concerning the Law of Nature*, 192–3. [10] *Ibid.*, 158–9, 166–7.

[11] See *ibid.*, 102–3. [12] See *ibid.*, 204–5.

[13] See e.g. Pufendorf, *Elementorum Jurisprudentiae Universalis* i, def. 12, sect. 17:

For, if you have removed God from the function of administering justice, all the efficacy of... pacts, to the observance of which one of the contracting parties is not able to compel the other by force, will immediately expire, and everyone will measure justice by his own particular advantage. And assuredly, if we are willing to confess the truth, once the fear of divine vengeance has been removed, there appears no sufficient reason why I should be at all obligated, after the conditions governing my advantage have once changed, to furnish that thing, for the furnishing to the second party I had bound myself while my interests led in that direction; that is, of course, if I have to fear no real evil, at least from any man, in consequence of that act.

[14] *John Locke: Questions concerning the Law of Nature*, 165–6:

patet... posse homines a rebus sensibilibus colligere *superiorem esse aliquem potentem sapientemque* qui in homines ipsos *jus habet et imperium*. Quis *enim* negabit lutum figuli *voluntati esse subjectum*, testamque eadem manu qua formata est. (Emphasis added, here as elsewhere.)

indeed by a party to a contract, does not explain why that conduct is *now* obligatory, or indeed can ever be *obligatory*. So he sometimes thinks of supplementing his naked voluntarism (oughts are explained by acts of will) by the rationality of logical coherence: fundamental moral principles are tautologies, norms which it would be *self-contradictory* to deny.[15] Hobbes had ventured a similar account of the obligatoriness of his fundamental social contract, of subjection to the sovereign. His official and prominent explanation was of the form, 'clubs are trumps' (superior will and power/force). But, for anyone unimpressed by the naked assimilation of right with might and ought with is, he offers another explanation: it is *self-contradictory* not to keep a promise one has made.[16]

The strategy of assimilating the norms of natural law (morality) with those of logic finds its principal exponent in Kant, whose *Metaphysics of Morals* (1797) is in some ways the most sophisticated exposition of modern natural law theory. Officially rejecting any reduction of *ought* to the *is* of will, Kant holds that reason alone holds sway in conscientious deliberation and action. The rational necessity decisive for this sway is the logical necessity of non-contradiction, and all Kant's efforts to explain particular kinds of obligation (promissory, proprietary, political, marital, etc.) are claims that to proceed on any other 'maxim of action' would entail (self-) contradiction.[17]

Kant's reductions of moral rationality to logic all fail. They were bound to, because his basic theory lacks the concept of a substantive reason for action—a reason which is not a true judgment about natural facts, or a logical requirement, or a technical necessity of efficient means to a definite and realizable end. His theoretical and practical purpose is to save the content of civilization from the ravages of utilitarianism and scepticism. He articulates with novel power the radically anti-utilitarian principle that one must always treat humanity, in oneself as in others, as an end and never as a mere means. But his own official definition of 'humanity' would rob this categorical imperative of its significance. For if our humanity is, as he says, our rationality, and that rationality has no directive content save that one be consistent, we are left with neither rational motivation nor intelligent direction that could count in deliberation.

In the end, like Locke and Hume, Kant remains firmly in the grip of the assumption that what motivates us towards one purpose rather than

[15] See *ibid.*, 178–9 (passage deleted by Locke in 1664).

[16] See Hobbes, *De Corpore Politico*, Part I, ch. 3; *Leviathan*, ch. 14; *NLNR* 348–9 (quoting and analysing the relevant passages, and pointing to the fallacies of temporal equivocation and unexplained chronological preference inherent in the strategy).

[17] See *NLNR* 349.

another is our sub-rational passions. He lacks almost all the building blocks of classical natural law theory, the substantive first principles—basic reasons for action—that direct us towards bodily life and health, marriage, friendship, knowledge, and so forth,[18] as the intrinsic human goods which give us reasons (intelligent, not merely passionate motives) for action, and which, as aspects of our humanity as flesh-and-blood persons, are to be treated always as ends and never as mere means. He cannot account for the obligations and institutions which he does try to justify, let alone others which he overlooks, such as the obligation in justice to employ much of one's wealth for the relief of the needs of others. Kant's official rejection of reductions of *ought* to the *is* of will is subverted by the ambiguities of his claim that the moral law is a matter of one's legislation for oneself, ambiguities made inevitable by the absence of any substantive *ends* (*reasons for* action) in his conception of what practical reason understands.[19]

In the mid-twentieth century it became popular to distinguish classical from modern natural law theory by saying that the former works with the idea of natural *right* but, unlike the latter, has no concept of natural or human *rights*. Some scholars added that the concept of natural rights is inextricably bound up with the individualist voluntarism of theories which try—of course in vain, like Hobbes—to ground political obligation in a contract of self-imposed political allegiance, and which often fail to integrate rights to freedom with obligations both of self-restraint and of service to others. And so the shift from classical to modern was judged by some a mere corruption of thought. But further reflection and investigation has shown that the concept, if not the idiom, of natural or human rights is certainly present in the classical theory, and deserves a central place in any sound moral and political theory (see further sec. VIII below).

So the break between 'modern' and 'classical' natural law theories should be located, fundamentally, in the loss of the classical theorists' insight that one comes to understand human nature only by understanding human capacities, and these capacities in turn only by understanding the acts which actualize them, and those acts only by understanding their 'objects', that is, the goods they intend to attain.[20] Those goods are the *reasons* we have for action, and nothing in moral, political, or legal theory is well understood save by attending to those goods with full attention to their intrinsic worth, the ways they fulfil and perfect human persons, and their directiveness or normativity for all thinking about what is to be done.

[18] For a list of basic goods, see e.g. essay III.5 at 88 (1996a at 4); more fully, *Aquinas* 79–86; earlier, *NLNR* 59–99.

[19] See essay III.2 at 55–7, 69–70 (1987c at 443–5, 454–6).

[20] See *Aquinas* 29–34, 90–1.

III. EXCLUSIVE LEGAL POSITIVISM

The notion that there are no standards of action save those created—put in place, posited—by conventions, commands, or other such social facts was well known to Plato and Aristotle.[21] Developing a sustained critique of any such notion was a primary objective of these philosophers and of successors of theirs such as Cicero. Today the promoters of this radical type of 'exclusive positivism' are the followers, conscious or unconscious, of Nietzsche or of others who, like him, reduce ethics and normative political or legal theory to a search for the 'genealogy', the immediate and deeper historical (perhaps partly or wholly physiological) sources, of ethical, political, or legal standards. These standards have their immediate sources in exercises of the will of charismatic individuals or power-seeking groups, and their deeper sources in the supposedly will-like sub-rational drives and compulsions of domination, submission, resentment, and so forth. Such ideas about the 'genealogy of morals' are also found among those who today promote 'pragmatism' in legal theory.

Legal positivism is in principle a more modest proposal: that state law is, or should systematically be studied as if it were, a set of standards originated exclusively by conventions, commands, or other such social facts. As developed by Bentham, Austin, and Kelsen, legal positivism was officially neutral on the question whether, outside the law, there are moral standards whose directiveness (normativity, authority, obligatoriness) is not to be explained entirely by any social fact. Bentham and Austin certainly did not think that their utilitarian morality depended for its obligatoriness upon the say-so of any person or group, even though Austin held that the whole content of utilitarian moral requirements is also commanded by God. Until near the end of his life, Kelsen's official theory—at least when he was doing legal philosophy—was that there may be moral truths, but if so they are completely outside the field of vision of legal science or philosophy. His final position, however, was one of either complete moral scepticism or undiluted moral voluntarism: moral norms could not be other than commands of God, if God there were. Such a position was the consummation, not only of the voluntarism that ran through all Kelsen's theorizing about positive law, but also of every earlier theory which took for granted (see sec. II above) that law and its obligatoriness are and must be a resultant of the will and coercive power of a superior. As Kelsen argues, this position ultimately leaves no room for a requirement of logical consistency in the law, or for any attempt to reason that a general rule ('murder is to be punished'), taken with a relevant factual proposition

[21] See e.g. *NE* I.3: 1094b15–16.

('Smith murdered Jones last week'), can require a normative conclusion ('Smith is to be punished'). The only source of normativity, and therefore of the normativity of a particular norm, is positivity, that is, the actual willing of that norm by a superior; reason, even the rationality of logic and uncontroversial legal reasoning by subsumption of facts under rules, can never substitute for will.[22]

Kelsen's final positions cannot be written off as eccentricities, of merely biographical interest. Still, the exclusive legal positivism defended today by legal philosophers such as Joseph Raz, is very different.[23] While affirming that all *law* is based upon and validated by social-fact sources—the affirmation which makes it exclusive legal positivism—it accepts also that judges can and not rarely do have a legal and moral obligation to include in their judicial reasoning principles and norms which are applicable because, although not legally valid (because not hitherto posited by any social-fact source), they are, or are taken by the judge in question to be, *morally true.* Perhaps some enacted rule is directing the judge to decide certain cases according to what is fair and equitable. Or perhaps the judge considers that where substantive justice is sufficiently urgently at stake, judges are entitled to import the moral rule of justice where it is not explicitly excluded by any legally posited rule.

Classical natural law theory does not reject the theses that what has been posited is positive, and what has not been posited is not positive. (Indeed, the very term 'positive law' is one imported into philosophy by Aquinas, who was also the first to propose that the whole law of a political community may be considered philosophically as *positive* law.)[24] But the theses need much clarification. What does it mean to say that a rule, principle, or other standard 'has been posited by a social-fact source'? Does it mean what Kelsen finally took it to mean, that nothing short of express articulation of the very norm in all its specificity—and no kind of mere derivation (inference) or derivability—will suffice? Virtually no other positivist can be found to follow Kelsen here. But if not, which kinds of consistency-with-what-has-been-specifically-articulated by a social-fact source are necessary and sufficient to entitle a standard to be counted as 'posited'? By what criteria is one to answer that last theoretical question? Clearly, legal theorists have little reason to be content with any notion that legal theory should merely report the social facts about what has and has not been expressly posited, by actual acts of deliberate articulation, in this or that community. Raz himself goes well beyond so confined a project

22 Kelsen, *General Theory of Norms* (1st pub. 1979), chs 57–8.
23 See e.g. 'A postscript', in Cohen, *Ronald Dworkin and Contemporary Jurisprudence*, 81–7.
24 See essay 7.

when he affirms that courts characteristically have the legal and/or moral duty to apply non-legal standards.

Now consider the judicial or juristic process of identifying a moral standard as one which anyone adjudicating a given case has the duty to apply even though it has not (yet) been posited by the social facts of custom, enactment, or prior adjudication. This specific moral standard will usually be a specification of some very general principle such as fairness, of rejecting favourable or unfavourable treatment which is arbitrary when measured by the principle (the Golden Rule) that like cases are to be treated alike, unlike cases differently, and one should do for others what one would have them do for oneself or for those one already favours... (see sec. X below). But such a specification—a making more specific—of a general moral principle cannot reasonably proceed without close attention to the way classes of persons, things, and activities are already treated by the indubitably posited law. Without such attention one cannot settle which cases are alike and which different, and cannot know what classes of persons, acts, or things are already favoured, or disfavoured, by the existing positive law. The selection of the morally right standard, the morally right resolution of the case in hand, can therefore be done properly only by those who know the posited (positive) law well enough to know which new dispute-resolving standard really fits it better than any alternative standard. This selection, when thus made judicially, is in a sense 'making' new law. But this judicial responsibility, as judges regularly remind themselves (and counsel, and their readers), is significantly different from the authority of legislatures to enact wide measures of repeal, make novel classifications of persons, things, and acts, and draw bright lines of distinction which could reasonably have been drawn in other ways. This significant difference can reasonably be signalled by saying that the 'new' judicially adopted standard, being so narrowly controlled by the contingencies of the existing posited law, was in an important sense *already part* of the law.[25] (See further sec. XIV below.) Exclusive legal positivism's refusal to countenance such a way of speaking is inadequately grounded.

The law has a double life, for a judge or a lawyer trying to track judicial reasoning. It exists as the sheer fact that certain people have done such-and-such in the past, and that certain people here and now have such-and-such dispositions to decide and act. These facts provide exclusive legal positivism with its account of a community's law.[26] But the law also exists

[25] See essay 20 at 402 (1999c at 174–5).

[26] Raz rightly begins to leave behind the view that legal theory should attend only to what is posited in social-fact sources, when he affirms that law is systemic, so that the content of what counts as 'expressly posited' is settled by the content of *other* norms and principles of the system. For this

as standards directive for the conscientious deliberations of those whose responsibility is to decide (do justice) according to law. From this 'internal' viewpoint, the social facts of positing yield both too little and too much. Too little, because in cases of legal *development* of the kind just sketched, those facts, while never irrelevant, must be supplemented by moral standards to be applied because true. And too much, because sometimes the social-fact sources yield standards so morally flawed that even judges sworn to follow the law should set them aside in favour of alternative norms more consistent both with moral principle (full practical reasonableness) and with all those other parts of the posited law which are consistent with moral principle.

On positivism's incoherence and redundancy, see sec. VII below.

IV. INCLUSIVE LEGAL POSITIVISM

Inclusive legal positivists are unwilling to sever the question 'What is the law governing this case?' from the question 'What, according to our law, is my duty as judge in this case?' If a state's law, taken as a whole, explicitly or implicitly authorizes or requires the judges, in certain kinds of case, to ask themselves what morality requires in circumstances of this kind, then the moral standard(s) answering that question—or at least the moral conclusions applicable in such circumstances—have legal as well as moral authority. The moral standard(s) are to that extent, and for that reason, to be counted as part of our law. They are, as some say, 'included' within or 'incorporated' into the community's law. The exclusive legal positivist (to recall) insists that such standards, even if controlling the judges' duty in such a case, remain outside the law, excluded from it by their lack (at least hitherto) of social-fact pedigree.

Those who work in the classical natural law tradition suspect that the disputes between exclusive and inclusive legal positivists are a fruitless demarcation dispute, little more than a squabble about the word 'law' or 'legal system'. As was stated at the end of sec. III, law in general, and the law of a particular community past or present, can be profitably considered in one or other of two basic ways. It can be considered as a complex fact about the opinions and practices of a set of persons at some time, prioritizing (usually) the beliefs and practices of those members of the community who are professionally concerned with law as judges, legal advisers, bailiffs, police, and so forth. In describing this complex fact, one will observe that

entails that, even if these other standards are each posited by social facts, no law-makers, judicial or otherwise, do or can settle by themselves the legal content and effect of their act (social fact) of positing.

these people treat the law as a reason for action, and one will perhaps describe the law as they do, as a set of reasons (some authorizing, some obligating, some both) which are systematized by interrelationships of derivation, interpretative constraint, or other kinds of interdependence, and which purport to give coherent guidance. But since one is ultimately concerned with the facts about this set of people's belief and practice, one will not need to make judgments about whether the system's standards are indeed coherent, or whether its most basic rules of validation, authorization, origination, or recognition satisfyingly account for the system's other standards or give anyone a truly reasonable, rationally sufficient reason for acting in a specific way, whether as judge, citizen, or otherwise.

Alternatively, law and the law of a particular community can be considered precisely as good reasons for action. But, when deliberation runs its course, the really good and only truly sufficient *reasons* we have for action (and forbearance from action) are moral reasons: that is what it is for a reason to be moral, in the eyes of anyone who intends to think and act with the autonomy, the self-determination and conscientiousness, that the classical tradition makes central.[27] And it is obvious that, *for the purposes of this kind of consideration*, nothing will count as law unless it is in line with morality's requirements, both positive and negative. Morality, for reasons to be indicated (see sec. VII below), requires that we concern ourselves with making, executing, complying with, and maintaining positive, social-fact source-based and pedigreed laws, and that we keep them coherent with each other. These positive laws add something, indeed much, to morality's inherent directives. What is added is specific to the community, time, and place in question, even if it is, as it doubtless often should be, the same in content as other specific communities' positive-law standards on the relevant matters.

Classical natural law theory is primarily concerned with this second kind of inquiry. But it has respect for descriptive, historical, 'sociological' considerations of the first kind, and seeks to benefit from them. Classical natural law theory also, as we shall see (sec. V below), offers reason for considering *general* descriptions of law fruitful only if their basic conceptual structure is, self-consciously and critically, derived from that understanding of *good reasons* which inquiries of the second kind make it their business to reach by open debate and critical assessment.

Anyone who makes and adheres steadily to this basic distinction between inquiries about what *is* (or *was*, or *is likely*) and inquiries about what *ought* to be will notice that much of the debate among

[27] See Plato, *Gorgias*; *ST* I–II, prol.; *Aquinas* 20, 124–5.

legal positivists arises from, or at least involves, an inattention to the distinction. Indeed, much of the contemporary jurisprudential literature swings back and forth between the rigorously descriptive ('external' to conscience) and the rigorously normative ('internal' to conscience), offering various but always incoherent mixes of the two. A rigorously descriptive understanding of Ruritania's law can do no more than report that it is widely or in some other way *accepted* in Ruritania that in certain circumstances the judges should settle cases by applying standards which they judge morally true even though unpedigreed—that is, not hitherto certified by any social-fact source of law.

Suppose that the rule of recognition so reported includes in its own terms the statement that any unpedigreed standard which the judges are required or authorized by this rule of recognition to apply (because considered by them to be morally true) shall be taken and declared by the judges to be *an integral part of the community's law*. What reason have exclusive positivists to say that such a rule of recognition is somehow false to the nature of law? Suppose, on the other hand, that Ruritania's rule of recognition stipulates (a) that under certain conditions its judges are *required* to apply an unpedigreed standard because they consider it *morally true*, but also (b) that in doing so they shall treat that standard *not* as an *integral part* of Ruritanian law, but rather as analogous to those rules of foreign states which are applicable in Ruritanian courts by virtue of the choice-of-law rules in Ruritania's law of Conflicts of Laws. (Stipulation (b) could well have legal consequences, for example in cases concerning the retrospective applicability of the standard, or its use in assessing whether there has been a 'mistake of law' for the purposes of rules of limitation of action, or restitution.) What reason have inclusive legal positivists to say that part (b) of such a rule of recognition is somehow false to the nature of law?

Can a dispute between rival 'isms' in legal philosophy have serious theoretical content if it could be affected by what a particular community declares to be its law? No truth about law seems to be systematically at stake in contemporary disputes between exclusive and inclusive legal positivists. The central dispute seems not worth pursuing. Provided one makes oneself clear and unambiguous to one's readers, it matters not at all whether one defines positive law as (a) all and only the pedigreed standards or as (b) all and only the standards applicable by judges acting as such. Either definition has its advantages and inconveniences. Counting as law only (a) what has been pedigreed has the inconveniences already mentioned: the relationship between legal duty and the duty of courts seems to fall outside the 'science' or 'philosophy' *of law*, and there seems no way of specifying precisely what counts as 'pedigreed' ('derived', 'derivable', etc.) short of the late-Kelsenian amputation of most of juristic thought and method (that is, all reasoning from one standard to another, or from systematic consistency) by virtue of the demand that there be a specific act of will to pedigree each and every proposition of law. Counting as law (b) whatever standards the courts have a judicial duty to enforce has the inconvenience that it cannot be done well—critically and sufficiently—without undertaking precisely the task, and following substantially the route, of classical natural law theory.

Law's 'positivity' was first articulated, embraced, and explained by the classical natural law theorists.[28] Legal positivism identifies itself as a challenge to natural law theories. It has had, say, 225 years[29] to make its challenge intelligible. The best its contemporary exponents can offer as a statement of its challenge seems to be: 'There is no necessary connection between law and morality.'[30] But classical natural law theory has always enthusiastically affirmed that statement. Some *laws* are utterly unjust, utterly immoral; the fact that something is declared or enacted as law by the social sources authorized or recognized as sources of valid law in no way entails that it is (or is even regarded by anyone as) morally acceptable or is even relevant to a consideration of someone's moral responsibilities (whether in truth, or according to some conventional or idiosyncratic understanding). There is no necessary connection between law and morality or moral responsibility. The claim that natural law theories overlook some of the social facts relevant to law is simply, and demonstrably, false.

So the statement meant to define legal positivism is badly in need of clarification. (See further sec. VII below.) More fundamentally still, no genuine clarification is possible without considering *both* terms of the alleged disjunction: law *and* morality. That there is *no* necessary connection, in any relevant sense of 'connection' and 'necessity', could not be rationally affirmed without steady, critical attention to *what morality has to say* about

[28] See sec. III at n. 24 above; essay 7.

[29] ie since Bentham, *A Fragment on Government* (1776).

[30] Thus Coleman and Leiter, 'Legal Positivism' at 241. They add one other 'central belief' and one further 'commitment'. (1) The central belief is that 'what counts as law in any particular society is fundamentally a matter of social fact or convention ("the social thesis")'. On this the classical natural law theorist will comment that it is equivocal between (a) the tautologous proposition that what is counted as law in a particular society is counted as law in that society, and (b) the false proposition that what counts as law for fully reasonable persons (e.g. fully reasonable judges) deliberating about their responsibilities is all and only what is counted as law by others in that society—false because *ought* (e.g. the ought of reasonable responsibility) is not entailed by *is* (and see sec. VII below). (2) The further commitment is 'a commitment to the idea that the phenomena comprising the domain at issue (for example, law ...) must be accessible to the human mind'. This commitment is fully shared by classical natural law theory, which defines natural law as principles accessible to the human mind, and positive law as rules devised by human minds (either reasserting those principles and/or supplementing them by 'specification').

law, either in general or as the law of particular communities. What basis is there for asserting, or implying, or allowing it to be thought, that lawyers, judges, and other citizens or subjects of the law should not, or need not, be concerned—precisely when considering how the law bears on their responsibilities as lawyers and so forth—with the question what *morality* has to say about law, and about what is *entitled* to count as law? And where is a student of law going to find such a steady, critical attention to morality as it bears on law, and on the very idea of law, and on particular laws, other than in an inquiry which, whatever its label, extends as ambitiously far as classical natural law theory does?

If you want to be 'positivist', 'rigorously descriptive' about law as a kind of social fact, you had better be positivist, rigorously descriptive, about morality, too. It is careless of 'inclusive legal positivists' to assume that any legal system whose pedigreed sources refer its judges to 'morality' ('justice', etc.) is a legal system that includes *morality*. What that legal system, descriptively regarded, includes is: what that community or those judges think moral, a set of beliefs which, morally regarded, may well be radically immoral. There is no halfway house, as inclusive legal positivists seem to suppose, between considering law and morality as social facts (as *beliefs about* reasons for action, and practices corresponding to such beliefs) and considering them as reasons for action (genuine reasons).[31] Considered precisely as genuine *reasons* for action, positive laws are social facts which count as reasons—as positive law—just insofar as morality makes their social sources and their social-fact content count.

V. METHODOLOGY

There is much uncertainty in contemporary jurisprudence about whether its subject-matter is (a) the *concept* of law, or rather (b) law as a social reality and/or as a kind of reason for action, of which people including theorists have more and less adequate concepts.[32] Late twentieth-century legal theory's paradigm text is called *The Concept of Law*.[33] But despite

[31] There is a third or 'halfway house' way of *articulating* law or morality, the 'detached' or 'professional' statement in which one speaks *as if* one were articulating standards as genuine reasons for action, while in fact reserving one's opinion. And indeed there are many other ways of speaking, including lying, play-acting, and so forth. None of this affects the position stated in the text.

[32] See e.g. Raz, 'Two Views of the Nature of the Theory of Law: A Partial Comparison' at 280: 'legal philosophy...merely explains the concept that exists independently of it'; 256: 'having a concept can fall well short of a thorough knowledge of *the nature of the thing* it is a concept of...a philosophical explanation...aims at improving [people's] understanding *of the concept* in one respect or another' (emphases added; Raz's italicizing of the first three words removed). But see also n. 35 below.

[33] Hart, *The Concept of Law*.

the definite article ('the'), Hart's book takes it as obvious that there exist many concepts of law, and even of the law of sophisticated nation-states. The book does not for a moment try to establish that there exists in some communities, large or small, a concept of law which is entitled to be called 'the' concept of law. Instead it attends to the reality of law, both as a 'social phenomenon' and as a characteristic kind of 'reason for action', and—with notable if incomplete success—seeks by doing so to arrive at an 'improved understanding', a *better concept*, of law. Hart might more accurately, if less elegantly, have called his book *A New and Improved Concept of Law*.

Such an uncertainty about subject-matter is an uncertainty about method. One cause of the uncertainty is that, as was said in sec. III above, law has a double life. More precisely, there is the law that exists as reportable facts about the ideas and practices of a community. And there is the law that is a set of reasons for action which count in the deliberations of someone who, in the circumstances of a particular community, is deliberating with full reasonableness about what to do. For such a person, a purported reason is a *reason* only if it is a reason which is *good* precisely as a reason. Somewhat similarly, for logicians an invalid argument towards a conclusion is *no* argument, no reason for affirming the conclusion. To be sure, the reasons which we call our law are profoundly and in almost every detail shaped by our community's present and past ideas and practices. But what makes a reason a good reason for action can, in the last analysis, never be a fact, such as facts about what a certain community does or thinks. No *ought* from a mere *is*. So, once again (see secs III and IV) there are two distinct kinds of worthwhile inquiry about law, not one. There is inquiry about law *as* a matter of fact, that is, about what is in fact, reasonably or unreasonably, counted as law in particular communities and sub-communities. And there is inquiry about the laws *as* giving reasons (= good reasons) for acting as, say, a judge.

It is, of course, possible to understand and describe a person's or a people's reasons for action without oneself regarding them as sound reasons. One can 'adopt' another's viewpoint without 'endorsing' it, describe evaluations without evaluating, and so on. But if one aspires to say something *general* about human affairs, and to reach beyond an endless newsreel, a listing and reproduction of other people's ideas in their conceptual idiom, one must judge which concepts better illuminate the human situation, and which purported reasons for action are more important for understanding human conduct and opportunities. Does *any* idea of law earn its place in general accounts of human affairs, or should it be replaced, in such accounts, with a concept such as domination, or socialization, or relationships of production and consumption? And if it earns its place, why so, and in what form? Command of superiors? Rules for efficient survival? Or for dispute resolution? Or for common good? And so on.

Classical natural law theory, as Aristotle's work makes plain, considers that the proper method in social sciences, including the political theory of which legal theory is a part (see sec. VI), requires that the selection of concepts for use in general descriptions and explanations be guided by the very same criteria that the theorist employs when judging what is *good* for a society (and therefore also what is *bad* for it), that is, when judging what are good reasons for actions in the kinds of situation encountered by and in the theorist's own society. There is thus an inherent, if often unrecognized, dependence of descriptive general social theory (such as Hart's *The Concept of Law*) upon the conscientious evaluations of the person who is now not deliberating but rather theorizing (describing, explaining, analysing).

Notwithstanding Hart's claims to descriptive neutrality or value-freedom, his actual method abundantly verifies what classical theory asserts. *General* description and explanation are necessarily dependent on evaluations presumed to be shared between writer and reader. Rightly Hart proceeds at every point by identifying social functions, benefits, amenities, defects and their remedies, and so forth. Without these appeals to value, to good reasons for action, his arguments against rival descriptive and explanatory theories of law could hardly begin let alone succeed. There are no grounds for thinking that it could be otherwise. The history of legal theories which, like Bentham's or Kelsen's, attempted to base themselves on bare fact is a history of definitions which manage to combine arbitrariness with lack of explanatory power.[34] And we need not accept Raz's claim[35] that we can come to know the 'essential nature' or 'essential properties' of law without considering what kind of other rule(s), institution(s), or, in general, social arrangement(s) and corresponding reason(s) for action, it would be valuable to have to overcome or alleviate the evils of anarchy, tyranny, and

[34] There is a moment in Bentham's thought when he half sees the intrinsic connection between understanding law and evaluating it: see Bentham, *An Introduction to the Principles of Morals and Legislation*, 401 (ch. 16, para. 57); likewise paras 48–57 of Bentham, *A Fragment on Government*, 23–5. But his official and stable view of general descriptive jurisprudence is the raw, barren, and reality-obscuring empiricism of his *Of Laws in General*.

[35] Raz, 'Postema on Law's Autonomy and Public Practical Reasons' at 16. But cf. Raz, 'Two Views of the Nature of the Theory of Law' at 267:

> Hart...denied that the explanation of the nature of law is evaluative. For him it was a 'descriptive' enterprise. For reasons explained by John Finnis [*NLNR* ch. 1], I believe that Hart is mistaken here, and Dworkin is right that the explanation of the nature of law involves evaluative considerations.

Still Raz, like other contemporary positivists who acknowledge the necessity of such 'evaluation', insists that it need not and should not or does not extend to *moral* evaluation. Like Hart's insistence that the evaluation which is intrinsic to the concept of law can and should be limited to 'survival', all such attempts to truncate practical reason (evaluation) seem arbitrary.

the 'rule of men'. Nor his equivalent claim that 'law has' its essential nature or properties otherwise than in virtue of requirements of practical reason, that is, of the reasons there are for action: human goods.

The classical concepts of analogy and focal meaning, used extensively by Plato and articulated by Aristotle and Aquinas, enable theory to proceed in the way indicated in the last paragraph but one, and to do so without suppressing or even obscuring any of the evils, deviations, perversions, and vicious practices or institutions which disfigure human affairs. The immature, the decayed, the parasitic, and the morally corrupted instances of constitutions, or friendship, or legal system, are not allowed to force a thinning down of the account of the good kinds of constitution, friendship, law, etc., but appear in the account, nonetheless, as what they are: as not *fully* constitutions, law, and so on—not central cases of those kinds of human reality and human purposefulness, and not within the focal meaning of those terms.[36]

This method is used throughout my *Natural Law and Natural Rights*: see especially the definition of law, and my explanation of the ways in which reaching such a definition differs from 'describing a concept'. The classical method is vindicated in general terms in Chapter 1 of that book, and its bearing on the remarkable mistakes of interpretation made by positivists when they glance at classical texts is explained in the penultimate chapter (on unjust laws).

VI. ON THE RELATIONSHIP BETWEEN LEGAL AND POLITICAL PHILOSOPHY

Aristotle's treatment of law appears in both parts of his 'philosophy of human affairs': in Book V of his *Ethics*, in Book III and other parts of his *Politics*, and as the subject-matter of his careful bridging passage between the two treatises (the final pages of *Ethics*, Book X). Aquinas's main treatment appears in two prominent parts of his vast treatise on human self-determination (Part II of his *Summa Theologiae*): a treatment dedicated to over forty issues about law as a type of guide to coordination (qq. 90–7 of Part I–II), and a treatment of rights, adjudication, and many related aspects of justice (in the midst of Part II–II, esp. qq. 57–71).

[36] There is no suggestion here that to understand *any* term, one must identify one instance (or type of instance) as central or paradigmatic, and one meaning as focal. On the contrary, the identification of meanings as 'focal' and instances or types as 'central' is always *relative* to some viewpoint or specific line of inquiry or focus of interest, and so has a particular importance in the social sciences, insofar as their subject-matter is constituted by what people have chosen to do: essay I.6 at 104–5 (1970a at 101); *NLNR* 11; *Aquinas* 45–6: '*Judged by the standards appropriate for evaluating human actions as reasonable or unreasonable*, some constitutions are central ...'.

As these analyses and syntheses suggest, both legal philosophy and political philosophy are parts of aspects of a wider enterprise, no part of which can safely be pursued without some attention to the others and to the character of the whole. That wider enterprise could be characterized as Aristotle does: 'philosophy of human affairs'. Or, more pointedly, as Aquinas does: the study of human action as self-determined and self-determining. Neither characterization in any way excludes the analysis of those aspects of human make-up, motivation, and behaviour that are biological, physiological, and in many respects similar to the life of other animals and organisms. But in focusing specifically upon the implications of human *freedom of choice*, Aquinas is putting squarely on the table, for critical analysis and appropriation, that feature of human reality which makes sense of practical philosophy's distinctive concern with understanding action from 'the internal point of view', that is, precisely as action is understood by the acting person who deliberates, identifies intelligent options, chooses, and successfully or unsuccessfully carries out the intention(s) so adopted.

Those who thus deliberate with intelligence, honesty, and care about what to do find good reasons to respect and promote the well-being not only of themselves but of the members of their family, of their neighbourhood, and of their economic associates and associations. The critical reflective analysis of those reasons is what Aristotle called ethics. In the first instance this is the ethics which focuses on the core of an individual's self-determination, virtue, or viciousness, and so forth. This focus tends to abstract somewhat from the full range of *inter-personal* associations whose flourishing is intrinsic, not merely instrumental, to any individual's well-being. So the study of the ethical ideas of, for example, justice, or marriage, broadens out into the practical philosophy of households, their 'economy', and its relationship to the wider network of economic relations which we follow Aristotle in calling economics. But the reasoning about what to do—about what anyone should regard as a responsibility—cannot rest there. Problems of justice between contracting parties (including spouses), between injurer and injured (including parent and child), between property-holder and trespasser, and so forth, and similarly problems of coordinating action—be it for defence of the whole network of neighbourhoods and associations, or to facilitate exchange, productive enterprise, and fair distribution of wealth—all call for the institution and maintenance of an all-embracing association of the kind we call political community or state. Ethical philosophy, without any essential shift in its normative, good-reason-seeking purpose and method, extends into political philosophy. And since the problems of administering justice, and of coordination for defence and economic welfare, cannot reasonably be resolved without new norms of conduct, new procedures for enforcing morality's perennial requirements, and new procedures for introducing and maintaining those new norms and procedures appropriately, political philosophy must include a theory of law.

Insofar as it is a matter of acknowledging genuinely good reasons for action, the philosophy of politics and law cannot but be as normative as ethics itself, of which it is a specialized extension. Insofar, however, as ethics is a matter of reasonable ways of thinking, both ethics in general and political and legal philosophy in particular draw upon logic, a distinct because wider discipline. Similarly, insofar as ethics and the rest of practical philosophy guide the conduct of flesh-and-blood people, they draw also upon the understanding of nature which we call science and Aristotelians used to call natural philosophy. And finally, insofar as law's ethically warranted response to the problems of social life mentioned in the previous paragraph involves the *creation* of new norms and institutions by the manipulation of language and of other conventional devices such as voting systems, jurisdictional boundaries, and so forth, legal philosophy has the character of other non-ethical 'arts'—techniques and technologies for attaining goals far more limited than ethics' unbounded horizon of human good. So, just as technologies cannot be reduced to ethics (nor technologies and ethics to logic or natural science), so legal theory cannot be reduced without remainder to ethics or to political philosophy in general.

'Legal realism' tends to reduce its subject-matter and method to natural science. Kantian legal theory tends to reduce its subject-matter, and its method, to logic. Positivisms of various kinds, to the extent that they are not simply incoherent (see secs IV above and VII below), reduce legal theory to a kind of technology. Natural law theory seeks to avoid all these kinds of reductionism. And its centrepiece is its explanation of why, and how law, though dependent on its ethical reasonableness for its worth and its normativity or authority, *cannot be reduced to ethics*, or any deduction from ethics, but is in large part genuinely created, fully positive. That strategy of explanation is sketched in the following section.

VII. AUTHORITY

Now we can see the problem with the natural lawyer's account of authority. For in order to be law, a norm must be required by morality. Morality has authority, in the sense that the fact that a norm is a requirement of morality gives agents a (perhaps overriding) reason to comply with it. If morality has authority, and legal norms are necessarily moral, then law has authority too.

> This argument for the authority of law, however, is actually fatal to it, because it makes law's authority redundant on morality's.... [I]f all legal requirements are also moral requirements (as the natural lawyer would have it) then the fact that a norm is a norm of law does not provide citizens with an additional reason for acting. Natural law theory, then, fails to account for the authority of law.[37]

The criticism entirely fails. No natural law theory of law has ever claimed that 'in order to be law, a norm must be required by morality', or that 'all legal requirements are also'—independently of being validly posited as law—'moral requirements'. Natural law theorists hold that the contents of a just and validly enacted rule of law such as 'Do not exceed 35 mph in city streets' are *not* required by morality until validly posited by the legal authority with jurisdiction (legal authority) to make such a rule. The centrepiece of natural law theory of law is its explanation of how the making of 'purely positive' law can create moral obligations which did *not* exist until the moment of enactment. Unfortunately, Coleman and Leiter's error, thorough as it is, has many precedents. Kelsen, particularly, used to claim that, according to natural law theory, positive law is a mere 'copy' of natural law and 'merely reproduces the true law which is already somehow in existence'; the claim has been shown to be mere travesty.[38] Like Coleman and Leiter, Kelsen cited no text to support his claims about what natural law theory says, because (as he had every opportunity to know) none could be cited.

As the fifty-five years of Kelsen's jurisprudence abundantly illustrate, positivism's efforts to explain the law's authority are doomed to fail. For, as Coleman and Leiter rightly say, 'A practical authority is a person or institution whose directives provide individuals with *a reason for* acting (in compliance with those dictates)';[39] and they might have added, a reason that is not merely a replica, for each individual, of that individual's self-interested 'prudential reasons' for so acting. But, as they ought (but fail) to acknowledge, no facts, however complex, can by themselves provide a *reason for* acting, let alone an *ought* of the kind that could speak with authority against an individual's self-interest. (To repeat, 'authority' that does no more than track the 'I want' of self-interest is redundant for the individual addressed, and futile for the community.) No *ought* from a mere *is*. So, since positivism prides itself on dealing only in facts, it deprives itself of the only conceivable *source* of reasons for action (oughts), namely true and intrinsic values (basic human goods, and the propositional first principles

[37] Coleman and Leiter, 'Legal Positivism' at 244.

[38] Kelsen, *General Theory of Law and State*, 416; *NLNR* 28.

[39] Coleman and Leiter, 'Legal Positivism' at 243 (emphasis added). For 'dictate' read directive or prescription (e.g. enactment, judicial judgment, etc.).

of practical reason that direct us to those goods as to-be-pursued, and point to what damages them as to-be-shunned).

The incoherence of positivism—its inherent and self-imposed incapacity to succeed in the explanatory task it sets itself—is nicely illustrated by Coleman and Leiter's effort to explain 'the authority of the rule of recognition'.[40] They preface this explanation with the remark that 'we all recognize cases of binding laws that are morally reprehensible (for example, the laws that supported apartheid in South Africa)'.[41] So we can conveniently test their explanations of this bindingness, this authoritativeness, by asking how such explanations could figure in the deliberations of an official (say Nelson Mandela when practising as an advocate of the Supreme Court) in South Africa in those days. Mandela (let us imagine) asks Coleman and Leiter *why* (and whether) the South African rule of recognition, which he knows is the propositional content of the attitudes accompanying and supporting the massive fact of convergent official behaviour in South Africa, gives him a reason for action of a kind that he could reasonably judge authoritative. How does this fact of convergent official behaviour, he asks, make the law not merely *accepted as* legally authoritative but actually *authoritative as law* for him or anyone else who recognizes its injustice? Coleman and Leiter's explanation goes like this: (a) often your self-interest requires you to coordinate your behaviour with that of these officials or of other people who are in fact acting in line with those officials (but Mandela is inquiring about authoritative directions, not guides to self-interest—self-interest requires cooperation with local gangsters, but their directions are not authoritative), (b) moreover, if you think that those officials are trying to do what morality requires, you have reason to follow their lead (Mandela will not think so, and will be right); (c) you may 'believe that the rule of recognition provides something like the right standards for evaluating the validity of norms subordinate to it'[42] (he rightly does not); (d) '... quite apart from [your] views about the substantive merits of the rule of recognition itself... [t]he avoidance of confusion and mayhem, as well as the conditions of liberal stability require coordination among officials.' Here at last Coleman and Leiter offer a reason of the relevant kind, a reason which could be rationally debated by being confronted with reasons of the same kind. The requirement asserted in the quoted sentence goes far beyond the 'fact of convergent behaviour'; it acknowledges strong evaluations of order, peace, and justice ('liberalism'); it is indeed nothing if not a moral requirement. It is *available* to explain the law's authoritativeness only if the

[40] *Ibid.*, 248. [41] *Ibid.*, 243. [42] *Ibid.*, 248.

'separability thesis'[43] is recognized as an equivocation between defensible and indefensible theses, and Coleman and Leiter's favoured, 'positivist' interpretation of it is abandoned as the mistake it is. In jurisprudence, there is a name for a theory of law that undertakes to identify and debate, openly and critically, the moral principles and requirements which respond to *deliberating persons'* requests to be shown why a legal rule, validly enacted, is binding and authoritative *for them*, precisely as law. That name, for good and ill, is 'natural law theory'.

Coleman and Leiter might reply that I am confusing legal with moral authority. But this reply depends upon the mistaken view—one which, as we have seen, they starkly hold—that positive law as understood in natural law theory adds nothing to pre-existing moral requirements. Once we acknowledge that very many (not all!) legal requirements would not be moral requirements unless legally created in accordance with the law's own criteria of legal validity, we can readily see the sense in saying that the law's authoritativeness, in the focal sense of 'authoritative', is nothing other than its moral authoritativeness. To repeat, most of our laws would have no moral authority unless they were legally valid, positive laws. So their moral authority is also truly *legal* authority. Laws that, because of their injustice, are without moral authoritativeness, are not legally authoritative in the focal sense of 'authoritative'. Their 'authority' is in the end no more than the 'authority' of the Syndicate, of powerful people who can *oblige* you to comply with their will on pain of unpleasant consequences, but who cannot create what any self-respecting person would count as a genuine obligation. (See also sec. XIII below.)

Natural law theory's central strategy for explaining the law's authority points to the under-determinacy (far short of sheer indeterminacy) of most if not all of practical reason's requirements in the field of open-ended (not merely technological) self-determination by individuals and societies. Indeed, the more benevolent and intelligent people are, the more they will come up with good but incompatible (non-compossible) schemes of social coordination (including always the 'negative' coordination of mutual forbearances) at the political level—property, currency, defence, legal procedure, and so forth. Unanimity on the merits of particular schemes being thus practically unavailable, but coordination around *some* scheme(s) being required for common good (justice, peace, welfare), these good people have sufficient reason to acknowledge authority, that is, an accepted and acceptable procedure for selecting particular schemes of coordination with which, once they are so selected, each reasonable member of the

[43] See sec. IV at n. 30 above.

community is morally obligated to cooperate *precisely because they have been selected*—that is, precisely as *legally* obligatory for the morally decent conscience.

This is the source of the content-independence and peremptoriness that Hart, in his late work, rightly acknowledged as characteristic of legal reasons for action, and as the essence of their authoritativeness. And as the explanation shows, this content-independence and peremptoriness is neither unconditional nor exceptionless. A sufficient degree of injustice in content will negate the peremptoriness-for-conscience. *Pace* Coleman and Leiter, the laws of South Africa, or some of them, were not binding, albeit widely *regarded and treated and enforced as* binding. Positivism never coherently reaches beyond reporting attitudes and convergent behaviour (perhaps the sophisticated and articulate attitudes that constitute a set of rules of recognition, change, and adjudication). It has nothing to say to officials or private citizens who want to judge whether, when, and why the authority and obligatoriness *claimed* and *enforced* by those who are *acting as* officials of a legal system, and by their directives, are indeed *authoritative reasons* for their own conscientious action. Positivism, at this point, does no more than repeat (a) what any competent lawyer—including every legally competent adherent of natural law theory—would say are (or are not) intra-systemically valid laws, imposing 'legal requirements' and (b) what any streetwise observer would warn are the likely consequences of non-compliance. It cannot explain the authoritativeness, for an official's or a private citizen's conscience (ultimate rational judgment), of these alleged and imposed requirements, nor their lack of such authority when radically unjust. Positivism is not only incoherent; it is also redundant.

For all their sophistication, contemporary legal positivisms are essentially in the position adopted by Austin in his brutal, *and irrelevant*, account of the authoritativeness of wicked laws: if I say that laws gravely contrary to morality are not binding, 'the Court of Justice will demonstrate the inconclusiveness of my reasoning by hanging me up, in pursuance of the law of which I have impugned the validity'.[44]

VIII. RIGHTS

Jurisprudence progresses as well as regresses. The late nineteenth-century analysis of rights which Hohfeld brought to completion makes a notable advance in clarity. But rights of each of the four Hohfeldian types

[44] Austin, *The Province of Jurisprudence Determined*, 185; see *NLNR* 354–5.

are spoken of by Aquinas,[45] as well as by the civilian lawyers of his age (and indeed of earlier ages). The word 'right' translates the Latin *ius* or *jus*, the root of the words 'justice', 'jurist', 'juridical', and 'jurisprudence'. Though Aquinas does not use the plural forms of the word *ius* as often as we use the plural 'rights', it is a sheer mistake to claim, as some have, that he lacked or repudiated the concept of rights in the modern sense, in which a right is 'subjective' in the sense of belonging to someone (the subject of the right). When he defines justice as the steady willingness to give to others *what is theirs*, Aquinas immediately goes on to treat that phrase as synonymous with *their right* (*ius suum*); hence he treats a right/rights (*ius/iura*) as subjective. (He also uses the word to speak of 'objective' right, that is, what interpersonal action or relationship is *right*—morally or legally, depending upon the context.)[46]

Hobbes, who inspired much in Benthamite and Austinian positivism, spurned the classical juristic tradition and defined 'right' as liberty in the sense of sheer absence of duty. So people have most rights in the state of nature where they have no duties. This move exemplifies regression in legal and, more generally, in political and moral philosophy. Fortunately, the mistake is quite obvious. If no one has any duties to or in respect of others, it will be more accurate to say that no one has any rights at all. For everyone, in such a state of affairs, is subject to being destroyed or abused by everyone and anyone else, and everyone's actions can be impeded as much as any person or group cares, and is able, to arrange. The truth is that the concept of a right makes little sense save as (the Hohfeldian claim-right) a correlative of someone else's duty, or as a Hohfeldian liberty protected by someone else's duty of non-interference, or (the Hohfeldian power) as promoted by the duty of officials and others to recognize and effectuate one's acts-in-the-law (or their ethical counterparts), or (the Hohfeldian immunity) as protected by a similar duty of officials and others not to recognize another's juridical act as it purportedly bears on my position.

It does not follow, as some have supposed, that in the classical view duty is conceptually or otherwise prior to right(s). Duties to others are (by definition) duties in justice, and justice is (by definition) the willingness to give to others their *right(s)*. So duties, at least to others, and rights are interdefined; neither is prior to the other. One does not really understand the relevant concept of duty unless one has an understanding of that factual and normative equality of human beings which is the foundation of justice; the concept of right(s) gives normative recognition to that equality. To

[45] See *Aquinas* 133 n. 10, 134 n. 12.

[46] See *NLNR* 206, 228; *Aquinas* 132–8; 2002c.

the extent that the school of 'modern natural law' defined rights rather unilaterally in terms of liberty and/or power, conceived as properties of the subject, it ran the risk of obscuring rights' essential correlativity, or interdependence, with duties and, in general, with right relationships between persons.

Though the phrase 'human rights' is rather recent, and he never happens to use the exactly equivalent phrase 'natural rights' (plural), Aquinas clearly has the concept of human rights. For he articulates a series of precepts or norms of justice which concern, he says, what is owed to *everyone* alike.[47]

More fundamental than either rights or duties, and also indispensable for rationally determining what rights people have, are the first principles of practical reason which identify the basic reasons for action, directing us towards the basic human goods. No theory of rights is grounded or, even in outline, complete unless it attends to the question of the basic aspects of human well-being. No theory of human rights can be satisfactory unless it attends to the question what real features of human reality make us each, in the relevant sense(s), the equal of other human beings, and make it the case that other creatures in this world are not our equals and lack the rights we have. Contemporary legal philosophy (and legal theory: see sec. XXVII below) is marred by its inattention to the human person,[48] an inattention exemplified (one may think) by the selection of topics in the *Handbook* for which this essay was written, and reparable only by taking up again the systematically complex and ambitious enterprise pursued by classical natural law theory.

IX. INSTITUTIONALITY

The clustered meanings of our word 'institution', as of its Latin root *institutio*, point to salient features of laws, and of many things that law concerns: they are *made*, originated, established, instituted; they establish a pattern, arrangement, *order*, system, constitution, and/or organization; they *last* while persons and/or their actions come and go. For those are the salient features of the quite various kinds of reality we call institutions: slavery, contract, property, banking, this bank (undertaking or building), the courts, jury trial, ritual suicide, Friday dressing-down, and so forth. Roman jurists such as Gaius and Tribonian did much to transmit the word to the modern world by calling their books of foundational instruction *Institut*[*ion*]*es*: books to initiate the student in the *principles* (the rational origins or foundations) and the *established* ideas and practices

[47] See *Aquinas* 136 ('*indifferenter omnibus debitum*'). [48] See essay II.1 (2000a).

which give a legal system its shape both as something distinct from other kinds of social arrangement and as something different from other legal systems.

Thus an exploration of the many facets of law's institutionality will be an exploration of the twin roles of reasonableness and rationally under-determined choice in the positing and maintaining of even a thoroughly decent legal system. It will also be an exploration of the ways in which law is both secondary or even subordinate to, while regulating, other social institutions which it does not institute, whether they be reasonable and good (like proper forms of marriage and family, or less ambitious kinds of promising, not to mention religious communities and practices), or unreasonable, vicious, and harmful (like prostitution, slavery, or the vendetta). We should not imagine that market institutions or marriages or corporations await the emergence of 'power-conferring' rules of law. Legal rules are often ratificatory and regulative rather than truly constitutive, whatever their legal form and their role in creating the law's versions of the social practices and institutions upon which it, so to speak, supervenes. This ratificatory and regulatory role is often highly desirable as a means of preserving peace and fairness. But, for all their originality and variability, the law's institutions—to the extent that they are reasonable and give rise to claims on conscience—remain dependent upon foundational moral principles which pick out the requirements of a reasonableness attentive to the basic human goods and the human characteristics of freedom of choice within constraints of bodiliness and emotionality, maturation, mortality, the shape and dynamics of the environment, and so forth.

Time and positivity: the law's institutional character is an emblem of law's aspiration to bring into the present and the foreseeable future an order rooted in the past, the past of some originating event (such as conception or birth) or act, usually but not always a juridical act—an act intended precisely to change legal relationships—such as accepting a contractual offer, incorporating a company or acquiring shares in it, settling a trust, and so forth. As the events of revolution and *coup d'état* remind constitutional theorists, judges, and practitioners from time to time, not even the most self-referentially elaborate and complete set of constitutional provisions can make provision adequate for all contingencies in the life of that ongoing institution, the state (the political community as a whole).[49]

[49] See *NLNR* 275–6 and citations in 275 n. 7.

X. REASONS

Hart set jurisprudence firmly on the road back—or rather, forward—to the point where it will rejoin the classical tradition. For his central message is that law and all its constitutive elements and concepts must be understood, in jurisprudence as in life, from the internal point of view (see sec. I). And what is the internal point of view? It is the way of thinking of someone who treats a rule as a *reason for* action (and not simply as a prediction or basis for prediction). Hart's neglected but important later works, notably some of his *Essays on Bentham*,[50] recast his entire theory of law even more firmly as a theory of a particular kind of reason for action—reasons that are peremptorily normative by virtue not of their content but of their relationship to other, authoritative rules (of change, adjudication, and above all recognition).

Hart goes further. He offers an account of the *reasons* people have to introduce these authorizing rules (of change, adjudication, and recognition) and treat them as authoritative. The reasons are, in short, that social life without them is very defective—dispute-ridden, unadaptable to change, and so forth. These 'secondary' rules are reasonable precisely as remedies for such defects. But he goes yet further, and offers reasons for the 'primary' rules whose contribution to desirable social life is so enhanced by the secondary rules. The primary rules, he says, are rationally required for the sake of 'survival'. We should note, however, that besides his official categories of primary, obligation-imposing rules against violence, theft, and fraud, and secondary rules of legislation, adjudication, and law-recognition, Hart gives prominence to another vast category of rules: those that confer more or less *private* powers of changing one's normative position by contracting, conveying, and so forth. There is *reason* to introduce these and acknowledge their authority, for the sake of their immense 'amenity'—they are a 'step forward' as important as the wheel, he says.

All this brings Hart well within the territory of classical natural law theory.[51] But he declines to settle down as a citizen there: (a) basic goods and reasons for acting besides 'survival' he declares 'controversial', and he declines to enter the classical dialectic showing how unreasonable and unrealistic it is to treat survival as the sole basic reason for acting; (b) the good reasons there are for benefiting society by having law (secondary as well as primary rules, etc.) he treats as entitled to no priority in accounting for the internal attitude of allegiance to the society and its law; people,

[50] Hart, *Essays on Bentham*, esp. the final essay and essay VII.

[51] For these purposes it does not matter that, as indicated in sec. IX, natural law theorists would rightly have reservations about the inference which some might draw from Hart, that people did not have the capacity to, say, marry until there were 'power-conferring' legal rules about marriage.

including judges, 'can' conform for other 'reasons' such as careerism, blind conformism, uncritical traditionalism, and so forth. He never responds to the classical objection that, though these alternative motivations can and do indeed exist, and may be widespread, they can never have the justificatory or even the descriptive-explanatory power of the good reasons there are for introducing and upholding law *against* the pull of careerism or other forms of selfish self-interest, and *against* conformism to old ways and traditions. When thinking of the variety of law-like social institutions, he firmly and most beneficially employs the distinction between central and secondary cases, and between focal and analogous meanings. But he never recognizes how the facts of varied motivation can, likewise, be best accommodated if one acknowledges central and secondary cases *of the internal attitude*.

Thus Hart sets us on the road of understanding law as a kind of good reason for action, but balks at a full-blooded, open, critical consideration of what kinds of reason for action are really reasonable, really good as reasons. The whole ambition of natural law theory is to be precisely such a consideration.

The road lies open once one notices the error in Hume's claim that reason can only be the slave of—cannot motivate save as directing means to satisfy or respond to—the passions.[52] Emotions are involved in human action but *need not* be the exclusive or even primary ultimate motivating factor. Far better fitted for that role are the basic intelligible human goods, the intelligent opportunities of real improvement and flourishing as a person with other persons. These intrinsic goods were introduced in sec. II above.[53] Their intelligibility, as benefiting and perfective of human persons, is the source of their directiveness, their counting as *reasons for* action. It is also the source of the further question: What is one to do, and what are the requirements of practical reasonableness,[54] given the multiplicity of basic human goods and of persons who could actualize them in their lives? The nub of the answer to that question is that one must not cut back on the directiveness of the basic reasons for action. Their combined or integral directiveness, while it is not another good or additional reason to add to the list, can be articulated as this principle: in all one's deliberating and acting, one ought to choose and in other ways will those and only those possibilities the willing of which is compatible with integral human fulfilment—that is,

[52] See e.g. George, *In Defence of Natural Law*, ch. 1. For Hume's own violations of the logical truth (often called, with some naïvety, Hume's law) that *ought* cannot be deduced from *is*, see *NLNR* 36–8, 41–2.

[53] See n. 18 above.

[54] In *NLNR* ch. 5 the requirements of practical reasonableness are presented as if they were each self-evident, but they should rather be understood as specifications of the unifying master principle of openness to integral human fulfilment: see *Aquinas* ch. 4.

the fulfilment of all human beings and their communities, in all the basic human goods.[55] This is the master principle of morality, and it can also be formulated as the primary principle of human rights: other persons, so far as satisfying their needs is dependent on one's choosing and other willing, have a right that one's choosing and other willing remain open to integral human fulfilment.

All other moral principles are specifications of this master moral principle. The Kantian imperative that in every act one regard oneself as legislating for 'a kingdom of ends' ('a whole of ends in systematic conjunction') is an intimation of it; so, too, is Christianity's first principle, love of neighbour as oneself for the sake of the Kingdom; the Aristotelian conception of *eudaimonia* as ultimate end, and the utilitarian injunction to seek 'the greatest good/happiness of the greatest number' are other, less happy attempts to articulate it. *Integral human fulfilment* can be thought of as a kind of ultimate point (end) of human life and action, but only in the sense that it is at the heart of the master principle.

How is the first principle of morality specified into less abstract moral standards? How is its rational prescription shaped into definite responsibilities? Integral human fulfilment is not a vast state of affairs which might be projected as the goal (end) of a worldwide billion-year plan. Rather, what the master principle prescribes is that one not voluntarily narrow the range of people and goods one cares about by following non-rational motives, that is, motives not grounded in intelligible requirements of the basic reasons for action. One type of non-rational motive is hostile feelings such as anger and hatred towards oneself or others. A person or group motivated by feelings of, for example, revenge does not have a will open to integral human fulfilment. So a first specification of the master principle is: do not answer injury with injury. This principle is treated as foundational in all decent legal systems and is quite compatible with standards of just compensation (even by self-help), and of retributive punishment to restore the balance of fairness between wrongdoers and the law-abiding (see secs XX–XXII and XXVI below).

A second strategic specification of morality's master principle is the principle which every form of consequentialist, proportionalist, utilitarian, or other purportedly aggregative moral theory is tailor-made to reject: do not do evil—choose to destroy, damage, or impede some instance of a basic human good—that good may come.[56] This is the foundation of truly inviolable human rights and is the backbone of decent

[55] On this 'master principle of morality', see e.g. *NDMR* 281–8.

[56] For some explanation and defence of this principle, see essay I.15 at 246 (1997b at 226); more extensively, *NDMR* chs 9 and 10.

legal systems, for these legal systems exclude unconditionally the killing or harming of innocent human persons as a means to any end, public or private; and on the basis of analogous specifications of the master moral principle exclude unconditionally the use of perjured testimony, the choice to render false judgment or other judicial or official support of fraud, rape even for the sake of national security, and chattel slavery. A necessary part of the defence of every such specification of morality's primary principle is the critique of aggregative ethical methods, which all claim to identify greater goods which outweigh the evil done, and all fail by overlooking the incommensurability of persons, of the basic goods of persons, and of the transitive with the intransitive effects of choosing.[57]

A third principle giving relative specificity to morality's master principle is the Golden Rule, the core principle of fairness: 'Do to others as you would have them do to you; do not impose on others what you would not want to be obliged by them to accept.' For a will marked by egoism or other partiality cannot be open to integral human fulfilment. This rational principle of impartiality[58] by no means excludes all forms and corresponding feelings of preference for oneself and those who are near and dear (for example parents' responsibility for, and consequent prioritizing of, their children); it excludes preferences motivated by desires, aversions, or hostilities that do not correspond to intelligible aspects of the real *reasons* for action, the basic human goods instantiated in the lives of other human beings as in the lives of oneself or those close to one's heart.

XI. FORMALISM

Law cannot fulfil its coordinating and other directive functions unless it is promulgated. Even if it could, it would normally be unfair to some if not all of the law's subjects for it to remain unpublished. Moreover, it is normally unfair for officials, including courts, not to apply the rules that were published to and taken by the law's subjects as applicable to circumstances of the kind now before the court or other official. That the law have a public 'form' is, in both these ways, at the heart of the idea of a rule of rules ('... of law') and not of personal discretion ('... of men'). And that the products of law-making be treated as valid, as law, only if made in accordance with a determinate 'manner and form' is equally essential

[57] See e.g. essay I.15 at 237–43 (1997b at 218–23); *FoE* 109–42.

[58] See further essay I.15 at 247–9 (1997b at 227–9), showing, inter alia, how the content of this rational standard is usually supplied, in specific cases, by sub-rational factors (taste for risk, conventions, etc.).

to the law's desirable positivity and the desirable limitation of political rulers and their officials by law. One should be able to know much if not all of the law by attending, and in large measure only by attending, to its form—rather than to the unpublished intentions of its makers, or to its or their purposes, or to its justice or other value. If all this were not so, positive law would be redundant; but it is not redundant (see secs III, VI, VII above); so form and formalities come as part of the very idea of having law.

Very occasionally a theory of law will describe itself as 'formalist'. Thus Ernest Weinrib offers, under that label, an account of certain institutions, such as the Law of Tort, which he considers can be understood only if one sets aside all questions about their point, their value, or social utility. Their intelligibility and ideal reality is independent of any value they may have, and is trans-historical in the sense that it is independent also of the purposes of particular communities. But both the metaphysics and the illuminating power of this thesis are highly questionable. Apart from the existence of laws and legal institutions in the minds and dispositions of particular persons and communities, the only reality of laws and legal institutions—but this is also their *primary* reality—is *as reasons for action* which are good because intelligibly related to (albeit usually not deducible from!) the basic reasons for action, the basic goods, the intrinsic values at stake in human action, and to their integral unfolding in moral standards.

Usually 'formalist' is an epithet applied with hostile intent by those who consider someone's actual or recommended adjudicative method insufficiently attentive to the unexpressed intentions or further purposes of law-makers, or to the considerations of justice, mercy, and/or some other aspect of human welfare.[59] Since much (though not all) of the law exists by virtue of a *determinatio* which cannot rightly claim to be the uniquely reasonable (morally required) resolution of a social problem (see sec. VII above), the question how much is 'too much' or 'too little' judicial attention to evaluations not expressed in the form of the *determinatio* (the legislation or prior judgment(s) or practices) is itself a question largely for *determinatio*, not deduction or insight into the self-evident nor any other intellectual process capable of yielding a uniquely correct answer. It is, in short, a question about which very little can usefully be said in abstraction from particular legal systems and particular kinds of issues arising within them.

[59] On Roberto Unger's accusations of formalism in our law, see essay 13, 302–4.

XII. PRAGMATISM

The term 'pragmatism' was introduced into the discourse of philosophers by Charles Sanders Peirce in 1878, to express a complex of ideas about logic (good thinking) which he had developed since 1867. In 1903 at Harvard he gave a series of seven lectures on 'Pragmatism as a Principle and Method of Right Thinking'.[60] These lectures enable their readers to see that a pragmatism which is true to the insights and arguments of its founder is compatible with, indeed a kind of continuation of, key philosophical methods and findings of Plato, Aristotle, and other proponents of classical natural law theory.

For there Peirce explains that 'the question of Pragmatism is the Question of Abduction'. Abduction he distinguishes from induction and deduction, as one of the three modes of inference, of moving soundly in one's thinking. Peirce's explains abduction as insight into data, into 'a mass of facts before us', which we find 'a confused snarl, an impenetrable jungle', until 'it occurs to us that if we were to assume something to be true that we do not know to be true, these facts would arrange themselves luminously. That is *abduction*.'[61] The core of Peirce's 'abduction' is (we can say) what Aristotle called *nous* and Aquinas *intellectus*: insight, understanding that is neither deduction nor induction in the modern senses of that term, but is into data of experience, not a mere data-less 'intuition'.

Peirce understands logic as properly normative, as directed and directing towards and by the good of truth, as the object(ive) of the human activity of thinking:

> Every man is fully satisfied that there is such a thing as truth, or he would not ask any question. *That* truth consists in a conformity to something *independent of his thinking it to be so*, or of any man's opinion on that subject.[62]

Since logic is a human activity guided by and towards a good to be attained (the logical goodness of enabling attainment of the cognitive good of truth), logic is subordinated to (though not a mere instrument of!) another, wider knowledge of normativity: ethics. And ethics, considered as norms of human action, is in turn based upon what Peirce (eccentrically) calls aesthetics—a knowledge of what is 'admirable *per se*'.[63] Truth and knowledge of it is, therefore, one of these per se, intrinsic goods.

[60] Peirce, *Pragmatism as a Principle and Method of Right Thinking*. William James invited Peirce, and suggested the title.

[61] *Ibid.*, 282. [62] *Ibid.*, 255 (emphasis in original).

[63] *Ibid.*, 118–19. The classical theorists are less willing to subordinate *any* of the four kinds of 'science' to the other three (e.g. logic to ethics).

True pragmatism is thus worlds removed from the 'pragmatism' of those, such as Richard Rorty or Richard Posner, on whose lips the term signifies a (self-refuting) scepticism about truth, and a wilful embrace of logical incoherence and other forms of overt arbitrariness in assertion. Such 'pragmatism', since it openly reduces assertion to an instrument of want-satisfaction or other drives, is no part of philosophy. (Of course, just as an unjust law is part of the law, and bad science is part of science, so base pragmatism *is* part of philosophy!) What needs to be said about it, for philosophical purposes, has been said in Plato's analysis of base rhetoric, in the first of his primary discussions of natural law, the *Gorgias*.[64] True pragmatism, recalled albeit incompletely by Jürgen Habermas, understands that there is a fruitful investigation of the presuppositions and preconditions of the human actions (freely chosen) of thinking reasonably (accurately, logically, responsibly) and discoursing authentically. And among the first of those preconditions is that one understand, by an unmediated *insight* into one's experience of inclination and possibility, that understanding, reasonableness, and knowledge are not merely possibilities but also an opportunity of participating in a basic human good, and thus a true *reason* for action. The occurrence of such insights and their consolidation and unfolding in practical reason is a child's reaching the age of reason.

XIII. LAW AND OBLIGATION

Once it is understood that the positivity of law is a reality (and a concept, and an ideal) vigorously promoted, if not also invented, by adherents of 'natural law' (objective morality), it will be readily understood that the disjunction 'legal obligation' versus 'moral obligation' is far too crude. There is, rather, a unique kind of moral obligation which obtains only as a property of, or resultant from, *positive* laws. This can be called 'legal-moral obligation', or 'legal obligation in the moral sense'. It is to be distinguished from, though normally it tracks, the 'intra-systemic legal obligation' which particular rules of law declare themselves (or are declared by other legal rules) to create, and which legal institutions also declare and take as a ground for punishments and penalties.

In recent years some jurists have argued that it is logically or conceptually possible to uncouple the concepts of authority and obligation. Rulers and their officials might be acknowledged as having authority, including moral authority to make and enforce law, and the right not to be

[64] For a consideration of the *Gorgias* and the ethics of discourse (as distinct from base rhetoric), in dialogue with Jürgen Habermas (not a pragmatist in the base sense), see essay I.2 (1999a).

usurped, while at the same time none of their laws, not even those imposing intra-systemic legal obligations, would create any legal obligation in the moral sense (though some of them might, of course, coincide in content with moral norms obligatory even in the absence of the law). It should be conceded that this is conceptually possible. But it should be denied that the resulting conceptions of authority and legal obligation correspond to any historical community attitudes or practices available for description. More importantly, the proposed new concepts do not pick out any reasonable kind of option, any kind of social arrangement or set of dispositions that might serve the goods for the sake of which law exists and is worth instituting, maintaining, or restoring.[65]

The discussion of authority in sec. VII above underlined the impotence of positivism to provide any account of it that could rationally satisfy those whom law most concerns—those who (for example, as judges) have the realistic opportunity to evade what the law seeks authoritatively to require of them. No *ought* from mere *is*, however complex. The same must therefore be true, even more obviously, of obligation. As Hart became vividly aware,[66] his own account of the law's obligatoriness—even of its intra-systemic obligation—was deeply unsatisfying. His own critique of Austin had pivoted on the radical difference between *being obliged* (the *is* of 'I am threatened' plus the fact or sub-rational motivation of fear) and being *under an obligation* (an *ought*). But his own explanation of legal obligation in terms of insistent social pressure motivated by *other people's* beliefs about importance yielded no more plausible bridge to the *ought* in need of explanation. Similarly, his account of the rule of recognition as a sheer fact about convergent official dispositions and practices 'worked' by abandoning the internal attitude—the reasonable concern with reasons for action—at its decisive moment. Hart's reasons for suspending all the legal system's *oughts* from the sheer *is* of official practice are weak. Undoubtedly, some or even many officials and others can abandon the search for good reasons for allegiance to law, and make do with sub-rational motivations such as conformism, traditionalism, or careerism. But such attitudes fail to make full sense of the law's demands. The central case of reasons is not what are commonly accepted as reasons but reasons good *as reasons*. The central case of the internal attitude is the rationally warranted acceptance of law as obligatory in conscience, as speaking with true authority at the moment of choice. Only a natural law theory traces the rational warrant for such an acceptance.

[65] For the suggestion and response discussed in this paragraph, see Sartorius, 'Positivism and the Foundations of Legal Authority', which essay 4 discusses.

[66] See e.g. Hart, *Essays on Bentham*, 266–7.

Nor is it true that classical natural law theory merely puts off the evil day by suspending all reasons and obligations from an ultimate *fact*, God's will. That may, as we saw, be true of some 'modern' natural law theories (sec. II above). But when Aquinas, following Augustine, says that the natural moral law (and thus all just human, positive law) has its obligatoriness 'from the eternal law' he is referring not to a divine command but rather to the intelligibility, goodness, and beauty, the rational attractiveness, of the great scheme of things chosen, in creating, by divine *wisdom*.[67] The normativity of the obligatory is the normativity of the first principle of practical reason or natural law: good is to be pursued and done, and bad avoided—the referents of this 'good' being given by practical reason's other first principles, the basic reasons for action (secs II, X above). The reason why a particular option for action or forbearance is obligatory is always, ultimately: if I do not choose this option I do not coherently, reasonably, respect the integral human fulfilment—the good of all human persons and communities—to which I am directed by the ensemble of the only *reasons* I or others have for choosing anything.[†]

XIV. ADJUDICATION

The primary responsibility of courts is to apply the law. The ethics of this process of adjudication were of intense concern to classical natural law theorists such as Aquinas. Judges must be concerned to establish the truth about what was done by the parties. But this responsibility, while never detachable from its goal—correspondence with the reality of past acts and facts—is to be carried out in accordance with rules of evidence and proof. These rules have a number of purposes. One is to give effect to the presumption of innocence, which is itself a specific form of the general principle of reason that one should love one's neighbour as oneself. Another purpose of the rules of evidence is to preserve the fundamental equality of the parties by lessening the risk that one party will gain an advantage over the other by surprise, rhetorical superiority, or other such means. A further purpose is to lessen the risk that the trier of fact, whether judge or jury, will be distracted by emotional or other non-rational responsiveness to features of the case not truly relevant to the goal of doing justice by applying the positive law on the basis of true facts. The classical theorists were impressed by the risk that persons adjudicating in the emotionally engaging circumstances of particular facts and parties will be deflected from that goal.

[67] See *ST* I–II q.96 a.4; *Aquinas* 307–12.

Some pessimism, or realism, about the balanced impartiality of judges/jurors inclined the classical theorists to favour legislation—if you like, codification—over common law methods of making the *determinationes* by which natural law is non-deductively specified into rules and institutions of a particular community's positive law. Here we reach the secondary responsibility and function of judges: the interpretation and development of our law. As the discussion of 'exclusive legal positivism' shows (sec. III above), this will involve considerations which somehow go beyond what is already fully specified and determined in the social-fact sources (prior legislation and precedent). But the aspiration that there be a rule, a governance, of *law* and not 'of men' (particular judges) demands that every reference back to, and reasoning forward from, morality's permanent standards be tempered by, and filtered through coherent maintenance of, the community's existing law 'as a whole' including its many sheer *determinationes* (secs VII and XI above).

The moral backbone of the law is a small number of strict and exceptionless rules against intentional harm, and lying (sec. X above). Much of the rest of the frame and flesh of the law involves giving specificity to broad affirmative responsibilities of care and fairness. This specificity results in particular systems of transactional, procedural, and property law. The reasonableness of these particular standards and institutions is not of the form 'inevitably required by reason (morality)' but rather of the form 'adopted by our law by choice from among the range of reasonable options'. But once *these* options have been chosen, the rational requirements of coherence strongly limit the range of reasonable options for further specification and development. (See further sec. XXV below.)

Short of a radical refashioning of a whole area of law, such as a legislature can undertake, legal development should proceed by what Coke called that 'artificial reason of the law'[68] which is peculiarly the responsibility of judges. For judges are simply persons dedicated to, and intellectually and morally equipped for, deciding as, so to speak, voices of the law and thus of the community rather than of themselves as individuals. Their responsibility to do justice between the parties—to make a morally *sound* and justified resolution of the case—is always to be harmonized with the responsibility to make that resolution also *fit*—at least, not contradict—the community's existing law, considered as a whole and to the extent that it is morally tolerable. One traditional way of pointing towards this requirement of fit was the principle that in resolving interpretative uncertainties, judges must ask what those who made the law in its existing forms and

[68] *Prohibitions del Roy* (1608), 12 Co Rep 64.

expressions *would have* enacted (within the limits of reasonableness) *if* they had attended to the circumstances in question.

While we should thus broadly accept some main elements of Ronald Dworkin's account of adjudication, we should reject his thesis that even in hard cases there is presumed to be a single legally right answer. That thesis exaggerates both the specificity of morality's own standards and the linguistic and purposive determinacy of most posited rules. The requirements of moral soundness and fit with the posited law and its social-fact sources are requirements which eliminate countless logically possible resolutions of the case, and yield a uniquely correct legal resolution of all easy cases. But in a hard case they will leave more than one answer which is morally and legally right, that is, *not wrong*. Dworkin is right to observe that as a judge one will usually, even in a hard case on a divided bench, consider that one of the answers presents itself as compelling. But this results from the fact that each judge adds to the fully posited set of laws a set of presumptions about matters which are or involve guesses about the future, for example about the consequences of adhering to 'states' rights' in an era of international economic interdependence or national economic dislocation, or of joining a speculative political venture such as the European Union, or of the supreme court's defying the desires and expectations of the national executive, and so on. Presumptions of this kind[‡] should be and usually are fairly stable in the mind of an individual judge, and lend that judge's own deliberations a specificity and inevitability which in some degree outrun the law's specificity.

Each of these two broad purposes and aspects of adjudication—application to facts, and interpretative development—requires some submerging of the judge's own mind, including moral preferences and factual beliefs, in favour of the community's. In the tradition this was dramatized in the moral and legal rule, defended by Aquinas and many but not all others, that judges must adjudicate in line with the legally admissible evidence, and without regard to facts which the law does not permit to be put in evidence even if they happen to be known to be true by the judge, as an individual.[69]

Much judicial reasoning takes the form of deciding that the relevant facts in new case B are analogous to those in previously decided case A and so should be treated in the same way. Such 'reasoning by analogy' has been found puzzling by theorists who observe that as reasoning it seems to have the pattern of a well-known fallacy. The puzzle is resolved by noticing that what warrants warranted appeals to analogy is not a pattern of reasoning,

[69] *Aquinas* 250; *ST* II–II q.67 a.2; q.64 a.6 ad 3[; cf. p. 370 n 41 and pp. 373–4 below].

but an *insight*[70] into some standard—perhaps never noticed or articulated before—which justifies *both* the earlier decision in A and the corresponding decision in B, and is appropriately coherent with the rest of the law and with sound practical judgment at large.

XV. LAW AND EPISTEMOLOGY

The law's positivity allows wide scope for 'deeming'. Some such deeming is morally and legally inevitable: for example, facts once determined by proper process must thereafter be taken to be true, and unchallengeably true after time for appeals or collateral challenges has passed. Some deeming is not inevitable but may be reasonable: for example, a court, to get jurisdiction and do justice otherwise unattainable, may deem that events occurred at a place where, in truth, they did not. But examples of fictions only serve to highlight the law's general epistemology. Events really occur and can be truly judged to have occurred. Some beliefs about events, and about good and evil, right and wrong, are false. Some accounts of events are lies because the persons giving them know, or can be known to believe, that they do not correspond to the realities they purport to describe. Some beliefs about what is choiceworthy are so contrary to the truth, so wrong and unreasonable, that anyone who acts upon one of them can and should be blamed and, where appropriate, penalized for doing so. Our law's epistemology is the commonsense realism about facts and values that, with reflective critical refinements, characterizes the classic tradition of natural law theory.

As we have seen (sec. I above), the tradition distinguishes forcefully between truths about the order of nature, truths about logic, truths about the reasonable order of human action (principles of ethics, politics, law), and truths about the technically or artistically effective. Truths of the third (moral) order cannot be reduced to truths of any other kind, not even truths of nature. For the nature of human beings is such that fulfilment is a matter of self-determination by free choices (and accompanying judgments of worth) in the open horizon of the human goods; so the full measure and character of human fulfilment, and the full meaning and implications of practical reason's first principles, cannot be fully known in advance of those choices and judgments and their carrying out in action by individuals and communities. But the nature of a being that can be fulfilled cannot be adequately known otherwise than by knowing what is that kind of being's

[70] This kind of insight is an instance of what Peirce called abduction: sec. XII above. [See further essay 19 on legal reasoning by analogy.]

fulfilment. So philosophical anthropology, knowledge of human nature in the first order, requires for its completion the practical, third-order knowledge we call ethics and political theory.

Hume's and Kant's writings amply display their authors' insightfulness. So it is very significant that the epistemological cause of their critiques of, and departures from, the classical theory of reality and value is their denial or neglect of *insight*, by which one adds to the data of experience and inclination an *understanding* of some fact or value. Such understanding is nonetheless authentic in those instances—which are of fundamental importance—when it can and must be attained without benefit of reasoning (but rather makes reasoning possible). Rejection of all *self-evidence* as arbitrary, spooky, fishy, or tautological, formal, and empty is self-refuting, as the epistemologies stemming from Hume and Kant all ultimately are.

XVI. LAW AND LANGUAGE

Since one can fail to express what one means, and can struggle to find words to convey what one has in mind, and since language expands closely in the wake of advancing knowledge and (real or apparent) understanding, it is clear that language is never truly fundamental. Still, our intellectual endeavours make little progress without the assistance of language and the shared and shareable insights, beliefs, and judgments it conveys. Among our intellectual endeavours are, of course, our law, and our discourses *de lege lata*, and *de lege ferenda*, and *de lege reformanda*—about what the law is, what law there should be, and on improving the laws we have.

Language, the transmission of meaning from mind to mind by material (audible, visible, tactile) symbols, manifests in its own way our remarkable nature as beings who are, at once and in a radically *unitary* way, both spiritual and material. This duality without dualism is the source not only of opportunities, such as play, the creative arts, and marriage, but also of limitations. Among those limitations is the indeterminacy, better the under-determinacy, the vagueness inherent both in our purposes and in the language by which we may try to articulate and promote them. By the language of legislation and precedent-forming judicial arguments, we make the countless *determinationes* morally required to give effect to our moral responsibility to love (respect and promote the well-being of) our neighbour as ourselves. But those acts of specification never altogether eliminate vagueness, or the need for further determinations which must seek an appropriate fit not only with the *determinatio* being interpreted, but also with the relevant remainder of our law, and the continuing or perhaps new requirements and implications of relevant moral truths. As was said in sec. XIV above, the classic theory of *determinatio* acknowledges plainly that in a good many cases there is no *one* right answer, but rather a number of right (not-wrong) answers, one of which must, for purposes of legislating or judging, be selected by a process designed both to be fair in its process of choosing between alternative reasonable (not-wrong) answers, and to minimize the risk that one of the countless *wrong* answers will be adopted. Semantic vagueness is one, but only one, of the causes of this pervasive under-determinacy of law.

More basic than the meanings 'of words' are the meanings, the intentions, of speakers and other users of words. Interpretation of legal language is in the service of cooperation and justice amongst the persons who are now or will be members of the community whose law it is. The special, 'legal' instrument of that cooperation is the making and maintaining of legal rules by law's 'social sources'—persons acting with certain kinds of intention. So the intentions of the founders, 'original intent', is always relevant. But it was their responsibility to use language in a way that would be understood reliably and in line with any conventional and professional expectations about and modes of interpretation. So the language of texts has a certain independence—not absolute or unconditional—from the minds of the law-makers. And both those aspects of legal interpretation remain within the framework of law's overriding purpose to promote common good by respecting rights and legitimate interests. This theme is pursued a little further in the remarks in sec. XXVII on constitutional and statutory interpretation.

XVII. LAW AND OBJECTIVITY

As bodily beings we have a bias in favour of understanding objectivity on the model of bodily objects and seeing (or otherwise sensing) them. Empiricist philosophy of every kind—not to be confused with empirical natural science and empirical common sense—trades on this bias. And empiricism was a very important assumption and premise in the work of contemporary legal positivism's main founder, Jeremy Bentham. In less naïve forms it remains an important under-tow in contemporary jurisprudence.

Objectivity is not properly understood on the model of a cat's seeing or anticipating a saucer of milk. Already the objectivity of meaning, and of successful transmission and understanding of meaning, is beyond empiricism's explanatory resources (and renders empiricist philosophizing self-refuting). Objectivity, rather, is a matter of openness to the data, and willingness to entertain all relevant questions, and to subject every insight to the critique of further questions. It is a matter of our intellectual operations being free from all biases that would make the attainment of truth—the goal of inquiry—less likely. To the extent that we as subjects (acting persons) have this openness and this freedom from truth-obscuring biases, we are being objective, our inquiries and judgments are objective, not merely subjective, and, subject to occasional error and deception, the realities we affirm and the goods we judge to be truly pursuit-worthy and beneficial are objectively what we judge them to be.

There are no sound reasons for thinking that judgments about goods, 'value-judgments', are doomed to be merely subjective. Philosophical efforts, such as John Mackie's, to treat them as 'too queer' to be objective fail because they overlook the 'queerness'—relative to the animal norm of clearly seeing a material object—of many other kinds of judgment, for example, about logical validity, or truth in natural scientific theory and in historical investigation, or about intersubjective meaning.[71]

XVIII. LAW AND RATIONAL CHOICE

There are at least three important and distinct senses of the ambiguous term 'rational choice': (a) choice is rational when it is fully reasonable, that is, complies with all the requirements of practical reasonableness and so is morally upright; (b) choice is rational in a thinner sense of 'rational' when it is rationally motivated in the sense that its object has been envisaged by practical intelligence and has rational appeal even if it is in some respect(s) motivated ultimately by feeling or emotion rather than by reason, the feelings or emotions having to some extent fettered and instrumentalized reason; (c) choices are 'rational' in a special sense invented by 'game' or 'decision' theorists in the mid-twentieth century, to signify decision and action which is technically or technologically right, by the standards of some art or technique for assessing the most cost-effective way of attaining a relevant technical objective; such a decision typically will be one for which, within the game, the technique 'rationally chosen' is a 'dominant' reason, one which, being commensurable with the reasons for alternative options, includes all the benefit they offer and some more.[72]

This complexity of senses causes much misunderstanding. Sense (c) is the only sense in which economics and game or decision theory, as such, employ the phrase. But common sense often uses it in sense (b). And the philosophers of the great tradition use it in sense (a), arguing

[71] See *FoE* 57–66.

[72] On 'rationality' in game theory and social-choice theory, see essay 2 at 54–60 (1984b at 129–33); essay I.14 (1992a).

that choices of the other two kinds are less than fully, or even adequately, rational. The classical argument is Plato's *Republic*, in which Socrates' young interlocutors most forcefully challenge him to show that justice and the other virtues opposed to egoism—opposed by egoism!—make sense even when one's justice and virtue puts one at the mercy of unscrupulous egoists and their emotion-driven supporters. The whole sweep of the dialogue is concerned, not to propose 'ideal states', but to meet the young men's challenge by showing that egoism is self-defeating, and self-defeating because it overthrows the constitutional rule (sway) of reason over the other forces in the egoist's soul, leaving egoists—tyrants—at the mercy of anarchic inner drives, lusts, and terrors, their psyches at once swollen and starved. Reason, when not subordinated by less intelligent powers, aligns one with the truths overlooked or defied by egoism. The basic human goods which give one all the reasons one can have for intelligent choices are goods for everyone, not just for me. And one of the basic human goods is the friendship that consistent egoism renders impossible.

The essence of friendship is this: A is interested in B's well-being for B's sake, and B in A's for A's sake; and so A has reason to be interested in A's own well-being not only for its own sake but also for B's; and B likewise. So the interest of neither person comes to rest solely on that person's own well-being, nor solely on the other person's well-being. Thus the relationship of interest (will, choice, action, affection) is, and is directed towards, a truly common good. This common good gives their relationship its self-sufficient point. Egoistic self-love is transcended. Or rather, it becomes clear that egoism is a form of self-mutilation, a dead-end deviation from the way to integral human fulfilment.[73]

There is a natural friendship, affectively thin but real and intelligent, of every person with every other person. Thus friendship and justice meet, or share a common intelligibility. The Prisoners' Dilemma or Hobbesian player who regards as satisfactory or 'rationally preferable' the outcome in which he himself gets off scot-free and the other player is imprisoned for life is unreasonable. Conversely, game-theoretical or economistic models of rational choice yield no determinate strategy or outcome when the players' preferences include a concern for the fairness and decency of the outcome—a concern for *common* good. So, though they have their utility as highlighting risks and unwanted side effects, they cannot substitute for the comprehensive theory of rational choice: natural law theory.

[73] See *Aquinas* 111–17.

XIX. LAW AND SEXUALITY

State law and government are morally limited; they have no proper jurisdiction beyond the maintenance of justice and peace. That is the position reached by natural law theory when Aquinas[74] left behind the Platonic–Aristotelian thesis[75] that the role of state law is to do everything needed to improve citizens' well-being, including their good character. When the compulsory jurisdiction of the state is no longer conceived on the model of parenting young children, it becomes clear that the law should not punish sexually corrupt adults for acts they do alone or together in complete privacy and with full consent.

Since some ethical theories and ideas popular today deny that there is an ethics of sexuality as such, it is necessary to indicate why some kinds of choice to engage in sex acts alone or between consenting adults can be corrupt. Indeed, without such an explanation, it will prove impossible to explain why sex acts between adults and willing children are child abuse rather than an agreeable form of play or (as some ancient Greeks maintained) of loving and educating.

There is a form of life—call it marriage—in which a male and a female, each of the age of reason and sexual maturity, agree to live together permanently, coordinating the whole of their lives by reference to the needs and true interests of each other and of any offspring of their union, and actualizing, experiencing, and expressing this mutual commitment by marital intercourse. A sex act is any act intended to lead to one's own or another's sexual satisfaction, and *marital* intercourse is a sex act which in its intentions and kind is apt to actualize, express, and allow the spouses to experience their friendship, commitment, and openness to procreation of offspring. Since willingness to accept and nurture children if they are conceived by marital intercourse is an integral aspect of the rationale of marriage—is what makes sense of its commitment to exclusiveness and permanence—no sex act can be marital unless it not only expresses the spouses' commitment in friendship but also is of a generative kind. For only a consensual act of the generative kind can express the couple's openness to procreation.[76] And even an act of the generative kind will be non-marital if either of the spouses is willing, even conditionally, to engage

[74] See the texts and analysis in *ibid.*, 222–54.

[75] e.g. Aristotle, *Pol.* III: 1280a31–1281a; VII: 1332a28–b12; *NE* V: 1130b23–6; X: 1179b32–1180a5.

[76] Such intercourse—a sex act which includes the man's depositing and the woman's taking his semen into her generative tract—can be of the generative kind even if the persons know or believe that they happen to be sterile: see Aquinas, *Quodlibet* XI q.9 a.2 ad 1 and other texts cited and explained in essay III.22 at 382–3 (1997d at 126–9); *Aquinas* 150, 181. See also George, *In Defense of Natural Law*, 139–83, esp. 140–7, 156.

in the same performances with someone outside marriage.[77] For if one has such a willingness, one *cannot* make—though, as many do, one can *hope* in vain to make—one's intercourse with one's spouse an expressing and experiencing of one's communion with and commitment to one's partner in *our marriage*. One's will being thus divided, one's sex act is one of the many kinds of sex act that lack the integrity of a truly marital act, the integrity of a union in which the uniting of organs is a uniting of bodies, emotions, senses, intelligence, and willed commitment. That lack of integrity is what is meant by 'sexually corrupt'.

Marriage is a basic form of human good.[78] It is a friendship, a relationship which is not a mere means to generating and nurturing children, as some inadequate natural law theories have taken it to be. And the procreativeness which, if children come, will be the relationship's completion is not a mere means to the satisfaction of the couple, as many today take it to be. So it is a relationship which is an *intrinsic* good, with two constitutive and mutually supportive aspects, friendship and procreation. Spouses' agreement to sharing of life includes agreement to engage together in marital intercourse whenever it is mutually agreeable and not unreasonable; this is a matter of mutual right. Kant grossly confused this right with dominion—a person's property relationship to a subpersonal thing—over one's spouse's body. (Much modern thought shares Locke's and Kant's erroneous assumption that one's living body is not oneself but something that belongs to the self/person.)

Integral to the good of marriage is this committed willingness[79] to actualize together, and enable each other to experience, the good of our marriage, in the intended joy[80] of authentically marital acts. Where the couple's sex acts are not authentically marital, the intelligibility of their marriage is disintegrated: their sex acts are unhinged from their mutual commitment. This unhinging and disintegration runs contrary to both of the goods constitutive of the complex basic good of marriage: not only the good of marital friendship but also the good of the children whose whole formation as persons is so deeply benefited by the context of a good marriage, and so vulnerable to everything that harms the marriage.

[77] For much fuller versions and discussions of the argument sketched in this sentence, and in the next paragraph, and of the argument's roots in Aquinas, see *Aquinas* 148–54; 1997d at 118–26.

[78] See *Aquinas* 82, 146 n. 58; [and essay III.20 (2008c)].

[79] This *positive* willingness, together with resolve *not* to engage in sex acts outside marriage (adultery), is what the tradition meant by *fides*, which is thus much richer than the modern 'fidelity': see *Aquinas* 144–7; essay III.22 at 360–5 (1997d at 106–11).

[80] See Aquinas, *In 1 Cor.*, 7.1 ad v.5 [325], and the discussion of pleasure as motive for and good aspect of marital intercourse in essay III.22 357–65 (1997d at 102–11); *Aquinas* 143–7.

Therefore, the conscience of any spouse who really understands the good(s) of marriage must reject, among other things, any kind of willingness, however conditional, to engage in non-marital sex acts. And since even *approving* (regarding as morally reasonable) the sex acts of the unmarried entails a willingness, albeit conditional, to engage in non-marital sex acts, every clear-headed spouse must disapprove all such acts. Moreover, since such disapproval is required by the good of marriage, and the good of marriage is truly a basic human good and an essential component of the common good, respect for the good of marriage requires even the unmarried, and those who for some good reason will never marry, to reject non-marital sex acts and judge them a wrong kind of choice.

It follows that a very important part of the education of children is fitting them, emotionally and intellectually, for authentic marriage or, if their vocational choices or other circumstances of their life prevent them from marrying, for respect for the good of marriage by withholding their consent or approval from non-marital sex acts. Wilfully allowing children in one's care to become sexually corrupt—to develop a disposition to approve of sex acts disintegrated from the good of marriage—is a great injustice to them, since it blocks their genuine participation in a basic human good. Parents and others responsible for the education of children are entitled to assistance in fulfilling their responsibilities in justice. It is a fundamental responsibility of the state's government and law—here Aristotle was correct[81]—to afford them its assistance, by coercively prohibiting, for example, every kind of paedophilia, any kind of publication or distribution of pornography to children, any teaching by public employees or agencies that non-marital (for example, homosexual)[82] sex can be reasonable, and any maintenance of places of resort arranged for non-marital sex, places whose public and deliberate availability for that purpose would suggest to children that such activities are approvable. A government and legal system which, having the resources to undertake these responsibilities, deliberately turns aside from them in the name of choice or pluralism or freedom of expression is mistaken about what the relevant human rights truly are, and is seriously unjust.

Similar considerations of justice to children require strenuous state support for the contract of marriage, and for mothers who devote their time to maintaining a home in preference to taking employment which will in

[81] See also *NLNR* 216–17, 222–3, on public morality and paternalism that is legitimate because for the sake of children.

[82] On the rejection of homosexual sex acts by Plato, Aristotle, Plutarch, and other masters of the classical natural law theory, see 1994b; a revised and shortened version, with replies to some objections, is essay III.21 (1997c). See also 1994d at 19–41.

most cases be less significant and worthwhile for the common good. The state's opposition to abuses such as polygamy is warranted by the other aspect of the good of marriage, the friendship which calls for a genuine and far-reaching *equality* between the spouses. It is of great importance for the common good that the intelligibility and worth of marriage be preserved in the minds of children and adults alike by prohibiting the appropriation of the title of marriages, and of any privileges commensurate to the heavy burdens of marriage, by relationships which, like so-called 'same-sex marriage', lack an essential part of marriage's rationale and are entered upon by people who almost universally[83] reject the constant exclusivity which is essential to marital fidelity and integrity (and so to justice to children). As Aristotle rightly said, 'human beings are by nature more conjugal than political'.[84] This centrality of the good of marriage to reasonable forms of life and community, and so to human fulfilment, is the reason why so many aspects of what promotes it, like what undermines or assaults it, are within the jurisdiction of state law and government despite that jurisdiction's limitation to peace and justice.

XX. PHILOSOPHY OF TORT LAW

Many contemporary legal theorists seem to value only one part of classical legal theory, a part that is among its weakest: Aristotle's account of corrective justice. True, Aristotle is right to say that the restoration of a wrongfully disturbed equality between one person and another is the principle requiring tortfeasors to compensate those whom they have wrongfully subjected to harm or loss, and that that principle is an essentially true principle of justice even though its concern to restore equality differs from the concern to maintain equality in distributing some shared stock of benefits or burdens among a set of persons.[85] But he has little or nothing helpful to say by way of response to the decisive and difficult questions: are persons drastically unequal in, say, wealth to be treated as having been *equals* immediately prior to the tort? How is a tortious to be distinguished from an inculpable or non-tortious causing of loss? What measure of compensation restores the hypothesized pre-existing equality when both the fault and (independently) the resources of defendants differ so greatly relative to any given scale of loss?

Tort law's distinctive project of compensation is clearly dependent upon a prior set of judgments about what forms of interaction between persons are

[83] See essay III.22 384–8 (1997d at 130–4).
[84] *NE* VIII: 1162a17–18.
[85] *NE* V: 1131b25–1132b20.

acceptable within a given community. But the priority of those judgments may be more logical than chronological: to some extent, a community should and does form its judgments of acceptability *in* the context of tort claims. Still, prior to such communal judgments are, in many contexts, judgments made in individual or other private deliberations about what is worthwhile and what threatens the worthwhile, and about what levels of risk of loss of the worthwhile are acceptable in different contexts. The backbone of tort is a set of moral—natural law—principles identifying as wrongful all choices precisely to harm or to deceive. But the flesh-and-blood of tort is a set of standards embodying both 'natural law' elements and 'positive elements'. The former reflect a more or less adequate understanding of the basic and intrinsic aspects of human well-being and the main social structures conducive to that well-being. (These aspects and structures are what tort theorists often call 'interests'.) The 'positive' elements in tort reflect more or less conventional—could-reasonably-be different—choices of ways of pursuing the basic human goods, choices among alternative designs for the social structures and interactions promotive of well-being, and choices among differing kinds and levels of risk of undesirable side effects of those alternative kinds of structure and ways of acting.

A sound tort law identifies as tortious every act *intended* precisely to cause harm to another person: the American doctrine that malice makes tortious is sound, the English rejection of it unsound (and half-hearted).[86] But an accurate understanding of *intention* identifies as an unintended *side effect* many fully foreseeable and foreseen consequences of a choice. The law-school doctrine that what is foreseen is intended is an undesirable fiction, as is the similar doctrine that the intended includes whatever is reasonably foreseeable as certain or highly probable. Responsibility for one's actions' side effects—foreseen or foreseeable—is morally and humanly different in kind from responsibility for what one intends, and therefore ought to be regarded as a distinct kind of basis for tortious liability. In principle, our law does treat it as distinct, first by dividing torts into the intentional and the negligent, and then by analysing the latter with the primarily normative apparatus of duties and standards of care and remoteness of causation.

The norms appropriately at work in those phases of tort's analysis of loss-causing incidents are, then, partly the permanently valid principles and norms of true morality, and partly the norms a community adopts by its choices of forms of life.[87] The principles and norms of natural law

[86] See essay II.11 (1995a).

[87] See Kelley, 'Who Decides? Community Safety Conventions at the Heart of Tort Liability'.

neither require nor exclude choices such as our community's choice to allow heavy vehicles to be propelled along the highways at speeds greatly exceeding walking pace. Nor choices such as a hypothetical community's choice to set the speed limit for motor vehicles at 4 mph. But such rationally under-determined choices once made—as they inevitably are by practice and usage if not by legislation or by courts adjudicating claims in trespass or negligence—provide a rationally determinate measure (at least presumptively or defeasibly applicable) for identifying many of tort law's duties and standards of care, and many of tort's demarcations between actionable and remote losses. All this is a paradigm of the interplay of morality and *determinatio*—of 'natural' and 'positive'—which is classical natural law theory's central theme (see sec. XIV above).

On the whole, the developed common law of tort, like the developed civil law of delict, embodies a true understanding of persons, of their worth, of their efficacious freedom to choose well or badly, and of the common good promoted by individual initiative and enterprise in community with and partly for the sake of other persons. The classic name for that true practical understanding of principles is natural law. It does not follow, however, that all the main features of our tort law are fully in line with the requirements of reasonableness—with natural law. How, for example, can it be just to require defendants to compensate to a measure that takes no account whatever of either the defendant's or the plaintiff's means to compensate or bear the loss, and no account whatever of the innocence or viciousness of the parties' conduct in respects not causally relevant to the actionable harm or loss? Should not tort law, without abandoning its central structure, incorporate some modifying principles of the kind which elsewhere in our law, as in natural law theory, are called equity?

XXI. PHILOSOPHY OF CONTRACT LAW

The distinction between the duties of care and compensation specified, regulated, and enforced by tort law and the duties of performance and compensation specified, regulated, and enforced by contract is not a complete separation. Quite reasonably there are torts such as interfering in certain ways with contractual relationships. Still, the distinction is clear, sound, and should not be expected to wither away. The 'death of contract', heralded a generation ago, was rightly ignored by those whom it most concerned: businesspeople willing to sue and expecting to be sued on even purely executory (wholly unperformed) contracts. For there is good reason to treat certain kinds of agreement voluntarily entered into as creating, from the moment of agreement (or other agreed commencement), a set of obligations, and of correlative rights which pertain, from that moment, to the legally protected holdings (wealth) of the right-holder.

Historically, legal systems have been cautious about undertaking the responsibility of regulating and enforcing informal, let alone purely executory informal agreements. This is neither surprising nor a sign of stupidity or superstition. Legal systems have many prior, more urgent responsibilities and, as lawyers in advanced legal systems easily forget, the existence of a clearly identifiable moral obligation does not entail that the state's legal organs have a moral responsibility to concern themselves with it. Affirmative responsibilities are always subject to circumstances. Nevertheless, the moral obligations creatable by agreement are obligations of justice, upholding justice is what the state's organs are essentially for, and the underlying moral obligations created by voluntary agreements are the rational basis for the legal obligations which are the heart of what we call contract. The moral obligations created by trustees' voluntary assumptions of responsibility are analogous to those central to contract, and are similarly the rational basis for much of the law of trusts. When the common law's old doctrines of privity and consideration are relaxed, it becomes obvious that contract and trusts are more deeply similar and interrelated than their usual doctrinal, institutional, and pedagogical separation would suggest.

So, too, contract and property are deeply interconnected at the level of principle. The 'chose in action' constituted by breach of even a purely executory contract is positive law's witness to the moral truth that one's freedom, dignity, and power as a person includes one's capacity to enrich other specific persons here and now by choosing to confer on them the present rights correlative to (entailed by) one's assuming (undertaking) the responsibility of doing them some future specific service. Still, persons are radically superior to all subpersonal realities, and property law is rightly distinct insofar as its paradigmatic subject-matter is subpersonal realities, not obligations of service, obligations which should never be treated as a kind of subpersonal thing. This insight rightly informs much of the remedial part of the law of contract, most obviously its aversion to ordering specific performance of *stricto sensu* personal service.

Essential to an account of the morally binding force of voluntarily assuming responsibility by promising or agreeing is some account of the benefits reasonably foreseeable from division of labour and cooperation. It is this benefit of cooperation between people who are *not* in *stricto sensu* partnership that gives to voluntary assumptions of responsibility (within limits) the normative significance they purport to have, and makes them reasonable kinds of act, neither mumbo-jumbo nor self-enslavement. The type of benefit at stake is essentially a kind of control over the future, a kind of security which is not so much warding off anticipated harms as positively improving the well-being of all the parties. Hobbesian, Lockeian, and Kantian efforts to explain promissory obligation by appeals to extrinsic sanctions, the supposed logic of self-consistency, and/or the metaphysics of personhood, all look the wrong way. They all fail for want of the key idea of a common good in which the parties attain individual benefits by the service of a cooperation which can be asynchronous and reliably extend well beyond the present, while not being committed to a common project such as *stricto sensu* partners share in.[88] The same key idea gives us reason to say that Oliver Wendell Holmes's conception of contracts as creating no more than the disjunctive legal obligation to either-perform-or-pay-damages is, while not incoherent or incapable of being adopted by a legal system, nonetheless neither accurate as an account of common, civil, or international law, nor at all desirable as an alternative.

Just as tort law presupposes certain truths about human action and intentionality which are often denied by theoretical sceptics, so contract presupposes all these and also some further, related truths about the intelligibility of language and the accessibility of other people's meanings, beliefs, and intentions. Even the so-called 'objective' test employed in analysing offers or acceptances takes as decisive what a reasonable person, in the context, would have judged to be the speaker's actual ('subjective') meaning and intent.

XXII. PHILOSOPHY OF THE CRIMINAL LAW

A just law of crimes cannot be adequately understood and justified without understanding some main elements in (a) political theory, (b) moral theory, (c) the metaphysics of persons and their acts, and (d) a commonsense awareness of the culture and dispositions of a given community's triers of fact (judges or juries). Classical natural law theory, in its contemporary forms, addresses these issues explicitly, and justifies the sharp distinction between criminal and civil law which is characteristic of modern legal systems but not of ancient or even mediaeval practice and theory.

That the state's law and government 'monopolize force' (as Kelsen puts it), or alone have the right to authorize and administer the irrevocably and deliberately harmful measures we call punishment (as Aquinas more

[88] Such a project need not be, and typically is not, entered upon out of motives of generosity (*liberalitas*), but once agreed upon by promise or contract is a matter of the virtue of strict justice and the vice of injustice, not generosity or meanness. Contrast Gordley, *The Philosophical Origins of Modern Contract Doctrine*.

accurately holds), is a decisive element in political theory, descriptive or normative. Legal theory must be regarded as incorporating and extending this element when it seeks to give an account of (a) the proper limits of the criminal law's prohibitive and affirmative requirements, and (b) the point and justice of imposing punishment when those requirements are violated. The criminal law's first function, of identifying what subjects *must* refrain from (or, in a few cases, do), is justified only by the premise that none of the other persons exercising legitimate, for example, parental or corporate directorial, authority, and no other legitimate kinds of measure save this, are likely to be either effective or fair in identifying, and seeking to avert or reduce, the prospect that some subjects will otherwise be treated *unjustly* by others.[89]

The criminal law's second function, of authorizing and requiring the imposition of punitive measures against those judicially found to have violated its requirements, is best understood as an element in the state's wider function of upholding, and where necessary making and re-making, a just distribution of benefits and burdens. The burden of complying with the law's just requirements falls, in fairness, on all the law's subjects, indeed all persons within its territorial jurisdiction. Whenever crimes which could justly be punished are committed, the offenders are helping themselves to the advantage of, at their own arbitrary will, renouncing that burden. The advantage they thereby illicitly and unfairly gain is precisely the advantage of a kind of freedom to do as they please, to follow their own preferences and choices in preference to the way laid down for all by the law. Pursuant to the state's function of maintaining distributive justice, the state's authorities can therefore be justified in coercively depriving offenders of this kind of advantage, so that the balance of advantage and disadvantage, between them and the law-abiding—a balance disturbed by the voluntary criminal act—is restored and rectified. This balance-restoring deprivation is of precisely the kind of advantage the offenders took: of excessive freedom. Just punishment is not essentially a matter of inflicting pain, but rather of repressing the will, the freedom, of offenders. (Nothing other than this line of thought can make sense of the opaque notion that crimes or criminals *deserve* punishment.)

Retribution, therefore, is the general justifying aim of punishment.[90] The opportunity to use retributively justified punishments to deter and reform is only a bonus side effect, and measures intended to deter and/or reform cannot rightly be more deleterious to the convicted offenders' interests than can be justified by retributive considerations. And retribution's intrinsic

[89] *Aquinas* 239–52. [90] See *ibid.*, 210–15; *NLNR* 262–4 [; essay III.12 (1999b)].

relation to the state's unique function and authority to uphold a fair pattern of relevant advantages and disadvantages explains why criminal law is so distinct from civil. In civil or private law, the victim of wrongdoing seeks redress from the wrongdoer, as a rectification of a pre-existing relationship between them presupposed to be fair. But in criminal proceedings, the wrongdoer's victim has no proper standing save as a witness, for here it is the interests of the law-abiding (normally including the victim) that are to be vindicated as a matter of restoring justice *to them*.

The criminal law's main general doctrines, about voluntariness, acts, and *mens rea*, are tightly connected with the retributive theory's understanding of what it is in offences that warrants punishment. Of course, the theory in turn, like the doctrines, rests on an understanding of what is involved in persons *acting* (rather than just behaving, as in sleepwalking). It rests particularly on an understanding that the paradigm of action is the *carrying out* of a *choice*, a specific *intention* adopted as an envisaged means to some envisaged end, some wider intention. That carrying out is typically—and in all cases that are within the proper scope of the criminal law—by bodily movements (though there are certainly acts, such as prayer or mental calculation, where there is no movement of the acting person). Many of the conundrums of criminal law theory concern the question of demarcating items of behaviour from *the act*,[91] and demarcating the act from what it causes, its *consequences*. Many offences, though by no means all, are legally defined in terms not only of kinds of intention and of bodily movement, but also of kinds of effect. The criminal law thereby creates for itself—and for good reason—problems that do not arise in purely moral reflection, in which what is intended, generally (as end) and specifically (as means), is decisive for judgment more or less independently of what in fact happens or fails to happen as a result.

In criminal law doctrine and practice, much confusion arises from the reluctance of those who administer it to differentiate clearly between *behaviour* and *action* (behaviour precisely *as* the execution of a choice), and between action and *consequences*, particularly when readily foreseeable but unintended consequences are impressively harmful and the intentions and other motivations of the accused are opaque to observers.

XXIII. PHILOSOPHY OF PROPERTY LAW

Property in all the forms known to legal doctrine is a defined set of normative relationships between people considered precisely insofar

[91] See essay I.10 (1991b).

as one or more of them is or might be concerned with some part of the world—some resource—which can be put to human use. The relevant kinds of concern with a resource (a *res* or thing) may, of course, be quite indirect and contingent, as in the case of money, shares, futures, patents, and the like. But always the ultimate source of the value of such intangibles is their potential to confer control over resources and the use of these resources to promote some (real or supposed) intrinsic good of a human person.

Although legal doctrine, for good technical reasons, contrasts *rights between persons* with *rights over things*, rights of the latter kind are always reducible to combinations of rights between persons, and always have as their primary point the regulating of relationships between persons (for example the exclusion of non-owners from the thing and its use). The entire law of property, every property right and relationship, and every item of property, is wholly in the service of human persons and just relationships between persons. No kind of physical relationship between particular persons and particular things—original and/or long-standing 'occupation', creation by personal labour working on other things, invention—constitutes by itself a normatively sufficient reason to acknowledge or rule that those persons have property in those things, still less that they rightly have 'absolute' ownership such as Roman *dominium* or common law fee simple in possession. The world's resources pre-exist all of us, and since we are all fundamentally each other's equals as persons the only reasonable normative baseline is that all those resources are to be treated at all times as for the benefit of everyone.

So property rights in all their forms (a) give particular persons rights to the use and/or fruits of resources in priority to all other persons (who are so far forth excluded from such enjoyment of the thing), but (b) at the same time are morally subject to a kind of inchoate trust, mortgage, lien, or usufruct in favour of *all other persons*. This moral burden on property holdings is given legal *specificatio* by the various norms of private and public law—varying, like the forms of property right themselves, from system to system—which qualify owners' priority of enjoyment and control: nuisance, prescriptive easements, taxation, eminent domain, 'antitrust' (anti-monopoly law), and so forth.

Hence the classical natural law tradition accepts the position articulated in Aristotle's apparently paradoxical slogan: property is to be private in possession but common (shared) in use.[92] This sounds paradoxical,

[92] *Pol.* II: 1263a25, a38.

since the point of possession is use, and the point of making possession private—the point of *appropriating* resources and rights to resources to particular people to the exclusion of others—is (as Aristotle's and Aquinas's famous discussions[93] make clear and the sad experience of two generations of Bolshevism super-abundantly confirms) to provide incentives to careful, prudent, but dynamic and forward-looking management and exploitation of those resources. Such incentives lie in the owners' priority of use and enjoyment. How then can use rightly be called common? How can it be said that non-owners, who have contributed nothing to the creation or cultivation and management of the thing, have some right to participate in its enjoyment? The answer lies in the idea already mentioned, that the owners' rights of enjoyment, though conferring sufficient priority and benefit to incentivize owners to care and cultivation, are qualified by a residuary quasi-trust for the benefit of all whose needs might reasonably be served by some share in the resource's use or fruits. The institutions of redistributive taxation are the devices perhaps most characteristic of modern legal systems' recognition of this moral burden on private property. Provided that the point of the institution of property—the well-being of persons—is kept always in view, the Aristotelian dictum escapes paradox and prescribes an appropriate balance between naïve communism and raw capitalism. The fact that no such balance can be expected to be simply optimal, or permanently even appropriate, does not entail that the search for appropriate balance is pointless.

Just as various technical contours of a legal system's institutions of property are delineated not in the treatise on property but under the heading of tort (conversion, trespass...) and contract (passing of title in sale...), so the rules enforcing the orderly subjection of all owners' rights to the interests and moral rights of the needy are found in many corners of the law. Many legal systems contain no explicit qualification of the laws of theft to accommodate the starving—a qualification prominent in the writings of moralists in the tradition ('in necessity, all things are common'[94]). Such a lack can be justified, if at all, only by robust countervailing practices of prosecutorial and sentencing discretion. Forgetfulness of the tradition seems to contribute to the heavy weather recent jurists have made of *Vincent v Lake Erie Transportation.*[95]

[93] *Pol.* II: 1262b36–1263b26; *ST* II–II q.66 a.2; *Aquinas* 188–90.

[94] *Aquinas* 190–6; Grotius, *De Jure Belli ac Pacis*, II. ii. 6; Pufendorf, *De Jure Naturae et Gentium*, II. vi. 5–8 (pp. 301–9).

[95] 124 NW 221 (Minn. 1910): saving one's life in a storm by attaching one's ship to another's wharf is no trespass, even if it creates an obligation to compensate for damage thereby done to the wharf.

XXIV. PHILOSOPHY OF INTERNATIONAL LAW

Whether or not coined for English by Bentham, the term 'international law' translates the term *Jus inter gentes* which emerges in the sixteenth-century renovation of natural law theory after the breakdown of a unitary secular-ecclesiastical Christendom. Articulated in succeeding centuries as a law between *states* rather than nations or peoples as such, international law manifests in its contemporary development both the underlying complexity of human community—a complexity far exceeding the multiplicity of states—and the inaccuracy of the thought that a state is, without qualification, a *perfecta communitas*, a complete community entitled to constitute the ultimate and unconditional horizon of a just person's allegiance. Has an individual person, or a group which is not a state, standing to move international organs as a subject of international law with substantive and procedural rights derived from international law? Has an international organization such as the United Nations an international personality comparable to that of a state, and are its rights in international law limited to those conceded to it by the states party to its establishment? Can the same be said of a non-governmental organization such as the International Red Cross? If 'persons' other than states can be subjects of international law rights, can they also be creators of international law rules, as states can?

These issues have driven many of the developments in international law during the past fifty years. They all emerge from a developing understanding that new interdependencies, economic, environmental, and cultural, are bringing into being a worldwide human community that might in principle become a *perfecta communitas* equipped to supervise the doing of justice everywhere. On occasion, as at Nuremberg in 1945–6, such issues have laid bare the natural law foundations which alone could justify holding that some conduct can be, and concretely was, a 'crime against humanity', triable internationally.

Why is state law and government, with jurisdiction over the families, neighbourhoods, and other associations within a distinct and economically viable territory, needed and justified? Most fundamentally by the need for an authority that can be expected to administer coercive and irreparable punishments with the justice of impartiality and care for truth.[96] Historically, it seems that states and their governments have very often been constituted by a sheer taking of authority unauthorized by any pre-existing legal title or any other moral claim other than the prospect of being, de facto, likely to succeed in securing a degree of coordination and

[96] *Aquinas* 247–52.

cooperation sufficient to allow justice to be not merely desired and ordered but actually done.[97] There is today no central-case type of international legislative, executive, or judicial authority because no person or group is capable of taking power, in the above sense, and because states tacitly concur in judging that no existing or envisageable authority could be relied upon to act with an effective justice sufficient to merit a general transfer or subordination of state jurisdiction to it.

Hence agreements (treaties) and to a lesser extent customary practice (especially of states) remain the primary sources of international law, which remains both descriptively and morally a relatively undeveloped, non-central case of law. Still, it should not be called simply a primitive legal system; so far as they go, international legal processes are sophisticated applications of 'the general principles of law recognized by civilized nations'[98] and of those techniques for stabilizing practical thought, and for rendering it an instrument of commonality and cooperation, which we call legal doctrine, as evidenced in the 'judicial decisions and the teachings of the most highly qualified publicists of the various nations'.[99] In these formulae, the terms 'recognized' and 'civilized', if not also 'qualified', point towards the assumption—fully justified—that there are true principles—traditionally called natural law—underlying this and every other legal order, principle, and doctrine.

XXV. PHILOSOPHY OF THE COMMON LAW

The term 'common law' is found in Euripides and Plato, and is well known (as *ius commune*) in legal and political thought in mediaeval civil (Roman law) and ecclesiastical law, in a meaning substantially the same as one aspect of its meaning in English legal and political thought: the general law of the realm, as distinct from local and personal customs pertaining to a family, or calling, or district. But another aspect of the common law is perhaps more significant: its distinction from statutes or other enactments—from law made by a body the authority and primary function of which is precisely to change the law of the realm.

Lawyers in the tradition called common law in distinction from Roman or civil law have reflected for nearly a thousand years on the common law's nature. The history of their reflections shows that there has never been a stable, articulate, coherent, and generally accepted account of the place or roles in its make-up of sources such as reason (moral principle),

[97] *NLNR* 245–52. [98] Statute of the International Court of Justice, Art. 38(1)(d).
[99] *Ibid.*, Art. 38(1)(e).

antiquity (permanence), popular custom, judicial precedent, or professional experience, opinion, and practice.[100] Nevertheless, two dimensions of the common law are identified, in one way or another, by everyone. The common law which it is the responsibility of the superior courts of justice to administer is a law which is inherently related to, indeed in some sense drawn from, *reason*, and it is somehow a matter of *usage*.

Each of these dimensions is complex. *Reason* signifies the principles of reasonable choice and action which have been called natural law or (with the same meaning and reference) law of reason, or morality, or human rights and human decency, or equity, fairness, and justice. But the 'reason' of the common law has often been taken to include the 'artificial reason' of a learned profession, leaving unclarified the question how far this is a matter of moral wisdom based on more than ordinary experience, and how far it is a matter of technical doctrines, institutions, and practices *posited* by choices of professional lawyers who could reasonably have chosen differently. In the latter sense, the common law's 'reason' merges with the second main dimension, usage, but retains the special sense that the doctrines and so forth posited by the legal profession's practices are subject to a requirement of internal consistency and coherence with each other. (See also secs III and XIV above.)

Most of the old common lawyers' confused and shifting discussions of common law's nature could have been clarified by a firm grasp of the Thomistic idea that practical reason's principles need to be extended and applied by *determinatio*.[101] As was noted towards the end of sec. III and in sec. XIV above, one of the unchanging principles that underlie any justifiable *determinatio* is the principle that like cases are to be decided alike. That grounds the common law's acceptance of norms of *stare decisis* (judicial precedent), an acceptance which crystallized almost as soon as the preconditions (especially printed law reports) were in place. For judges confronted by an issue not settled by the plain meaning of a constitution or statute ought to try to settle it in the way that it would be settled by any other judges hearing the case on the same day in the same realm. (That is part of what is involved in administering *common* law, and common law judges often think of their realm as, for some purposes, as wide as 'the common law world'.) But such synchronic (counterfactual) consistency

[100] This is amply demonstrated for the period 1150–1630 by Tubbs, *The Common Law Mind: Medieval and Early Modern Conceptions*.

[101] Chief Justice Sir John Fortescue's discussion of maxims, in his *De Laudibus Legum Angliae* (c. 1469), appeals to Aristotle's conception of self-evident principles; Fortescue's discussion of political community in *The Governance of England* (1475) appeals to Aquinas's conception of limited government (see essay III.5 (1996a)), but he fails to advert to Aquinas's development of Aristotle on law's derivation from principle by *determinatio*.

of decisions requires that there be some standard of decision besides the statutes and any given judge's moral response to the issue. The standard needs to be *salient*—identifiable by all and more easily identifiable than the answer to the question in issue. The fact that the issue has in the past been resolved in a particular way by judge(s) in the same general legal context is salient and so provides a standard presumptively and defeasibly appropriate for resolving the issue here and now.

XXVI. PRIVATE WRONGS AND RECOURSE

The law of private wrongs and remedies, of which tort law is one of the central types, certainly cannot be justified or well described by theories which overlook its fundamental structure as a set of primary and correlative rights and duties (for example not to be defamed and not to defame) whose violation ('breach') is taken to *warrant* the recognition that P, whose primary right was violated, thereby acquires a remedial right of action at law for compensation, and that D, having been in breach of a primary duty, correlatively becomes liable, at P's suit, to make such compensation to P. Breach of duty is violation of right and '*cause* of action'.

Any account which explains remedial rights, not as consequences of violation of primary rights but as means to maximizing social wealth or some other value (for example by reducing wasteful precautions and/or transaction costs incurred in attempted exchanges of rights), will fail to make sense of the pervasive rules and doctrines of our law of tort which deny P a remedial right where D's breach of duty to T foreseeably caused harm to P but involved no breach of any primary duty to P. So economistic analyses of tort, though helpfully drawing attention to certain side effects of legal rules and proceedings, will not do. But equally, theories which put on the mantle of Aristotelian 'corrective justice' have failed to fill the gaps in Aristotle's account: its insufficient attention to the *primary* rights and duties which make wrongs identifiable as wrongs, and its neglect to explain just how breach of primary right *warrants* tort's normal judicial order of fully compensatory damages.

The account[102] of tort as founded on a 'principle of civil recourse' was offered as descriptive and 'conceptual', and disclaimed any 'normative' or justificatory purpose. Its critique of rival accounts powerfully demonstrated that economistic, utilitarian, and (in different ways) Aristotelian corrective justice theories do not make sense of tort's structure and many of its rules. And the account's middle-level analysis of that structure rightly pointed to

[102] Zipursky, 'Rights, Wrongs and Recourse in the Law of Torts'.

the way in which social conventions and other norms of fairness give some determinacy to tort's primary rights and duties.[103] But at its deepest level, this theory of civil recourse fails by overlooking the radical dependence of descriptive or conceptual analysis on unrestricted critical engagement with issues of evaluation—with the normative truths which are the sole rational source of justifications (or condemnations). For a theory or account aspiring to any interesting level of generality cannot sufficiently 'make sense of' any rules or institutional structures without showing them to be warranted—if they are—by principles which the theorist not only can 'suggest' have 'certain appealing normative justifications'[104] but can reasonably judge to *be justified* in the rich sense of justification sought by a conscientious judge deliberating about changing the whole life of D, or P, or both by making or refusing an award of damages. In the absence of such full-blooded normative justification the defeated rivals can reclaim the field of battle by denouncing as anachronisms those features of the law unaccounted for—not shown to be justified, or shown to be unjustifiable—by their rival accounts.

As a justification for tort's structure, the theory of recourse would be rejected by the classical theory of natural law. At its root the theory of recourse treats as worthy the emotional impulse of a victim of wrongdoing to '*get even*',[105] by '*act*[*ing*] *against*—having recourse against—the rights-violator'.[106] This impulse is in most if not all respects contrary to the true principle, do not answer injury with injury (sec. X above). The recourse theory fails to explain why P's impulse should be allowed for when it is a desire to seize the wrongdoer's goods but not when it is a desire to impose on D a hurt or harm such as that which P has suffered. It leaves unexplained why the remedial right of action granted by the law in recognition of and substitution for P's emotional impulse should extend, as it does in tort, to full compensation for all foreseeable losses. But at the same time, though treating P's remedial rights as independent of any supposed moral duty of D to *volunteer* full compensation, the theory provides no support for the thought (see sec. XX above) that our law is simplistic, unbalanced, and to some extent unjust and unjustifiable in maintaining a quasi-universal rule of *full* compensation for foreseeable losses caused by D's breach of duty to P, however minor that breach and whatever the relative resources of P and D.

[103] Zipursky, 'Legal Malpractice and the Structure of Negligence Law' at 679–80.

[104] Zipursky, 'Rights, Wrongs and Recourse' at 97.

[105] What Zipursky calls a desire for retribution has nothing to do with the retribution argued for in the account of crime and punishment proposed in sec. XXII above, a theory in which the desires of the victim, and even the *desires* of the law-abiding, have no normative significance.

[106] *Ibid.* at 85.

Moreover, the recourse theory questionably offers to justify the institution of punitive damages, a part of the law of tort which, in its American forms, seems unjustifiably to commingle private with public (especially but not only criminal) law; even the more restrained forms of the institution of punitive damages, elsewhere in the common law world, can be justified only to the extent that the institution amounts (if it does) to awarding damages for a distinct though hitherto implicit wrong of contempt for P's personality, much like the Roman law delict (tort) of *Injuria*.

The recourse theory rightly identifies central features of our law of tort which have long been misunderstood or undervalued, and central issues of explanation or justification of those features. But it leaves those issues scarcely resolved. The needed resolution will have to recognize that not every feature of tort can be justified; some of the features in need of reform are of very long standing, but others are recent importations under the influence of economistic and other 'policy-oriented' approaches. Resolution will come from recognition that, like other parts of the law but in its own distinctive way, tort law's foundations are judgments about what kinds of relationship between people are fair and reasonable, both generically and in particular kinds of context. These judgments are the main basis for recognizing primary rights and duties. The remedial right to compensation in the event of D's violation of P's right invokes a further judgment about fairness and reasonableness in re-establishing the fair relationship between them that D's conduct ruptured. Very often—but by no means always—remedial fairness calls for that restoration of equality which is the rationale for what tort law (and in many cases only tort law) provides: D so far as possible restoring P to the position P would have enjoyed had D's breach of duty to P not occurred.

XXVII. CONSTITUTIONAL AND STATUTORY INTERPRETATION

Interpretation of texts and other statements is sometimes simply historical: What did a given author or set of authors intend to communicate in their text or other statement? That question, even when it concerns a text with multiple authorship, often has a determinate answer in whose accuracy one can reasonably have high confidence. (If you think this claim is over-optimistic, you have understood it and done your bit to verify it.) Often, however, the question cannot be given so determinate and reliable an answer, other than: we do not know and have no means of knowing what the author(s) intended to communicate on such and such a matter, to which their text seems more or less closely relevant. Often this uncertainty has its source in the limitations which make human beings unable to foresee all relevant issues or to address exhaustively even those issues they do foresee.

In adjudication and the practice of law, interpretation of constitutional and statutory texts and statements can never reasonably be exclusively historical. Constitutions and statutes arise for consideration—indeed, exist as *law*—only in a context of the interpreter's intention to serve persons and their well-being, the common good, for example, by doing justice according to law as a judge. Constitutions and statutes call for historically accurate understanding, so far as it is possible. To say otherwise is to deny their authority to *settle* any of the questions of social life which need to be settled by law. But constitutions and statutes—and what those who enacted them wrote, said, and intended to communicate and to bring about—also need to be interpreted as parts of a whole of immense complexity and scope: the community's constituent settlements and compromises amongst its constituent peoples, its past investments of every kind, its present needs including the overcoming of present sources of conflict, the wisdom and craftsmanship, and narrow-mindedness and selfishness, of its legal organs and other elites, and many other aspects of its common good. It is only as parts of this whole, conceived of as oriented to the present and future common good, that constitutions and enactments have any legal authority whatsoever, or any claim, legal or moral, to guide anyone's present deliberations.

Since law and legal thought are entitled to little respect or consideration unless they serve, or can be brought to serve, every person whom they could benefit, all the basic human rights should be regarded as controlling every otherwise open question of interpretation. The basic error of the US Supreme Court in *Dred Scott v Sandford*[107] was to approach the interpretation of the Constitution's provision, for example, in relation to the congressional power of naturalization, without a strong presumption that, whatever the assumptions and expectations of its makers, every constitutional provision must, if possible, be understood as consistent with such basic human rights as to recognition as a legal person. An essentially identical error is made by those judges, such as Justice Scalia, who interpret the Fourteenth Amendment's unelaborated references to 'persons' as permitting states to treat as non-persons and to authorize the killing, or the enslavement (in embryo banks), of the unborn, whom these same judges know to be in reality human persons.[108]

[107] (1857) 60 US 693; essay II.1 at 26–7 (2000a at 7–8).
[108] See essay I.16 at 268 (1998a at 373–4).

When unequivocal violations of fundamental human rights are not in issue, very little of wide generality can be said to resolve determinately the many issues of interpretation which call for a proper balance to be made between fidelity to the text, fidelity to the intentions of its makers, fidelity to the historic law, consistency with other parts of the law, respect for the division of constitutional responsibilities between legislatures, courts, and administrative agencies, the needs of present and foreseeable future persons, and the judge's own hunches about the likely consequences of alternative decisions and alternative developments of the law.

XXVIII. RESPONSIBILITY

The abstract noun 'responsibility' emerges only towards the end of the eighteenth century; its first user recorded in the *Oxford English Dictionary* is Hamilton, followed by Burke. But this word from the Enlightenment richly conveys a cluster of insights each of which the enlightened philosophies of Hume, Kant, Bentham sought to banish, or rendered needlessly obscure. They are insights familiar to common sense, today as much as with Plato and his interlocutors. They are essential to making sense of the idea of obligation, with which this essay began.

A first insight is that one can really bring about, *cause*, effects in the world, including benefits and harms to one's fellows, one's neighbour, and any or all other human persons. None of this is well explained in terms of observed constant conjunctions.

One's causal power, not least one's mind's power over matter, is a reality one both experiences and understands (albeit not in a fully explanatory way) in every act by which one carries out what one intended, for example, to say to one's class the audible words 'Hume and Mill refuted classical natural law theories'.

A second insight is that when A's conduct has harmed B, it is sometimes true (albeit sometimes not) that A is answerable, *liable*, to B, that is to say, ought to do something to rectify the present relationship between them and to restore a former, more appropriate relationship. Sometimes this ought is entailed by some rule of a legal system under which A can be required to answer—*respond*... in Latin and then modern languages—to B's complaint, both by denying or acknowledging his causal responsibility for B's harm, and by repudiating or accepting his duty to compensate B in some measure.

Liability-responsibility thus has at its core an instance of a wider insight: one may, and often or in some respects always does, stand in such a relationship to other human persons that one has the *role*, function, obligation to render them some service, perhaps only of taking care not to harm them, perhaps of positively caring for them in some way, as the person responsible for the advancement of their well-being in some or all respects. This is associated with the important practical truth that government, properly understood and carried on, is not a matter of lording it over others but of doing them some service, so that—speaking always of the central case, from conscience's internal point of view—*authority over* is a consequence of *responsibility for*. Authority ('power'), like law itself, is a means to an end which those in authority are responsible for promoting: the common good of (all who pertain to) the community in and over which they have whatever authority they do have.

A fourth insight is that what one does, and thereby what one causes, is peculiarly one's own if and only if one had the *capacity* to choose to do otherwise. One is, then, a responsible agent if one has this capacity of free choice between open alternatives—that is, if there are occasions when one envisages alternative options and nothing (whether inside or outside oneself), save one's choice of one option in preference to others, settles what one does. This status of capacity responsibility is, not etymologically but really (ontologically, metaphysically), at the core of the cluster of realities understood in the insights articulated in the fourfold analogy of responsibility.

All this leaves, of course, much to be said to explain the cluster's interrelationships and implications. But here this essay reaches the limit of its transgression of limits. The classical theory of natural law is open to development and new insights in every dimension. So one can expect other theoretical work, even in the *Handbook* for which this essay was written, to add much of value to the essay, and to correct it in various respects without overturning any of the main classical theses it has rearticulated.

NOTES

† *Law and Obligation*... (sec. XIII). This section of the essay is defective in at least two ways. (1) Although the central case of the internal attitude is indeed 'the rationally warranted acceptance of law as obligatory in conscience', that acceptance is also an acknowledgement of the legal system's character as a technical object (see I.14 (1992a), sec. IV) deliberately isolated, in part, from practical reasoning's general flow, and so of legal obligation in the intra-systemic legal sense. The relation between the two senses of 'legally obligatory' is that, from the internal viewpoint, a legal obligation in the intra-systemic sense entails, albeit only presumptively and defeasibly, a corresponding legal obligation in the moral sense. (2) An adequate account of the justification for acknowledging this generic prima facie moral obligatoriness of obligation-imposing legal rules will include a reference to a specific implication of openness to integral human fulfilment: fairness. This element in the justification, and ground for moral obligatoriness, was well brought out by early writings of Hart and Rawls. Thus Hart, 'Are There Any Natural Rights?' at 185:

> [W]hen a number of persons conduct any joint enterprise according to rules and thus restrict their liberty, those who have submitted to these restrictions when required have a right to a

> similar submission from those who have benefitted by their submission. The rules may provide that officials have authority to enforce obedience... but *the moral obligation to obey* the rules in such circumstances *is due to the co-operating members of the society*, and they have the correlative moral right to obedience. (Emphasis added.)

The thesis is encapsulated in the title of Rawls 'Legal Obligation and the Duty of Fair Play', in Sidney Hook (ed.), *Law and Philosophy: A Symposium* and formulated there at 9–10; see also Rawls, *A Theory of Justice*, secs 18 and 53. This is essentially the thesis deployed in essays 2 and 3 above.

‡ *Presumptions affecting the adjudication of individual judges...* (sec. XIV p. 129). These include not only presumptions about matters of fact of the types mentioned, by way of example, in the text, but also about moral matters, especially conceptions of fairness (which, for reasons explained at n. 58, contain not only the rational standard of impartiality but also psychologically and culturally influenced dispositions). A little more is said about this aspect of adjudication in hard cases in this volume's Introduction, sec. III at 15–16, and in essay III.1 (1985a).

6

LEGAL PHILOSOPHY: ROOTS AND RECENT THEMES*

Law is a means of introducing and maintaining the rule (governance) of reason in a community of many families and neighbourhoods, in place of the dominance of private violence or fraud, or the force of dominant groups directing the community's affairs for the profit of some but not all its members. That, at any rate, is the conception of law which has gained increasing acceptance in contemporary British and American philosophy. During the century from about 1850 to about 1950, the prevalent view understood law as a manifestation of power, dominance, and command, whereby sovereign persons or bodies of persons expressed their will about how members of political communities must behave, and reinforced those imperatives by the threat and execution of sanctions. The view now more prevalent in no way overlooks the need for forcibly imposed sanctions for recalcitrance, but emphasizes the opportunity and responsibility of rulers to govern for the sake of common, not private or partisan, advantage and to do so by means which tend to ensure that all relevant decisions are made in line with truth about facts and with transparency and fairness in legislative, executive, and judicial proceedings.

The newer view thus re-joins the tradition established in the classical reflections on law to be found in the works of Plato, Aristotle, Cicero, and, in the thirteenth century, Thomas Aquinas. Within contemporary philosophy of law, opposition to this understanding of law as a rational means of securing just social order comes not so much from proponents of a revived 'will' theory emphasizing commands and force, as from proponents of views sceptical that there is any truth for 'reason' to discover and apply or any determinably just outcome to be reached by judicial reasoning or legislative deliberation. The present essay is written by a philosopher and lawyer who judges that these sceptical objections

* 2005d, written and sent to the Chinese editors for translation in 1998; see also its earlier versions, 1995c, 1996e.

are generally unfounded, and that the recent 'return' of western legal philosophy to its classical roots—reconceptualized and critically appropriated—is well justified.

The view dominant from c. 1850 to c. 1950 is commonly called 'positivism' or 'legal positivism'. The classical view, revived in recent decades, is commonly called 'natural law theory'. These are confusing labels, because each is a theory precisely of *positive* law, that is, of the law made by or adopted—posited—for a specific community by identifiable persons claiming to have the authority to make or apply rules the validity of which derives immediately (if not ultimately) from the fact that those persons have authoritatively made or at least determined them. Moreover, the 'nature' referred to in the title 'natural law' is not the nature studied by 'natural sciences'. Rather, it is understood by the proponents of natural law theory as human well-being—human flourishing, human nature in good shape—in all its basic aspects and in all human persons and communities, *as* implicitly or explicitly favoured and respected by a set of principles directing human choices towards right and away from wrongful actions including the actions of persons who make (posit) laws (as legislators or as judges) or enforce them (executively or judicially).

It is thus, in effect, agreed that law—positive law—is to be distinguished from the laws of nature (discussed by physics, chemistry, biology, cosmology, etc.), from laws of thought (discussed by logicians), and from the moral law (discussed by ethical theorists and moralists). Indeed, throughout its history legal philosophy has sought to differentiate positive law (hereafter simply 'law' or 'the law') from all such other standards. But such differentiation can have more than one theoretical purpose. It can aim to clarify terminology and conceptual boundaries. Or equally it can seek to inquire whether the analogies or other relations between (positive) law and these standards or norms of other ontological and epistemological orders or domains are analogies and relationships that help to explain what is most puzzling about law. And what western legal theory has characteristically found most puzzling about law are perhaps these four features: (a) that law can 'necessitate' (make obligatory, indeed morally obligatory) actions which, until its enactment, were not so necessitated; (b) that legal rules and other 'institutions' somehow 'exist' by virtue of, but also long after, their positing by enactment or other 'act in the law', or by judicial precedent or custom; (c) that many of the law's rules have a normative form, and a social function, distinct from its obligation-imposing rules; and (d) that the law resorts to punitive and rectificatory coercion to outlaw force (as well as dishonesty and carelessness) in interpersonal relations.

The link between contemporary and classical legal theory or philosophy can be traced back as far as the Greek world in the sixth and fifth centuries BC; the surviving fragments of the Pre-Socratics suggest a vigorous debate which today cannot, however, be securely reconstructed. The accessible conversation of western legal philosophy really begins with two brief dialogues reflecting the debates in Socratic circles: a witty conversation put on the lips of the Athenian politicians Alcibiades and Pericles by Xenophon (*Memorabilia* I.2), and a 'Socratic' dialogue insecurely ascribed to Plato (the *Minos*). Each portrays the embarrassments awaiting philosophers who define law as whatever is decreed by rulers, and neglect or decline to refer to issues of (moral) right such as whether the law's subjects have in any way consented to it (Xenophon) or whether what it decrees is good, true, and in conformity with 'what really is' (*Minos* 313b–317d). Both dialogues suggest that, although everyone understands the sense in which a law's (in)justice is irrelevant to its empirical reality as enforced, there is nevertheless good reason to say that, in a more adequate understanding of law, unjust laws are 'more a matter of force than of law' and are 'not without qualification law' (*Minos* 314e).

So by the early fourth century BC two positions emerge, each of which is still defended in contemporary English-speaking philosophy. Modern legal positivism asserts that, to be described with realism and clarity, law must be considered without regard to any moral predicates which it attracts in discourse (for example in moral-political evaluation) outside the philosophy of law. Natural law theory asserts that such a description misses the point of law; legal systems get their sense and shape (which a good descriptive account of law will identify) from their point, and a rational evaluation of particular laws or legal systems (or political communities) will use that (perhaps complex) point as a criterion for measuring their conformity to or deviation from the very idea of law. Plato articulated this second position: 'Enactments, to the extent that they are not for the common interest of the whole community, are not truly laws' (*Laws* 715b; also 712e–713a; *Statesman* 293d–e). Cicero summed up the view that was and until the nineteenth century remained the philosophical mainstream: 'In the very definition of the term "law" there inheres the idea and principle of choosing what is just and true' (*De Legibus* II 11).

On this issue of definition, Plato warned that ordinary talk of 'law' is one thing, explanatory definition of law another, and the two coexist:

> *Socrates*: 'When would-be law-makers miss the good, they have missed law and legality. What do you say?'
> *Hippias*: 'Speaking precisely, that is so; but people don't usually put it that way.' (*Hippias Major* 284d).

Aristotle worked out the appropriate account of definition in social, including legal, theory: see, for example, *Politics* III 1275a–b. In this account, pure description or reportage ('this and this purport to be, and are commonly called, friendships, political communities, constitutions, ... laws') can coexist with explanatory definition within a theory which treats justification (and, where appropriate, critical delegitimation) as the primary mode of explanation. Thus, the humanly good type of, say, friendship, community, constitution ... or law is the paradigm, central case picked out by the explanatory definition, and by a corresponding word ('friendship' ... 'law') in its focal meaning; specimens of this good type are in this sense truly, properly, or unqualifiedly (Greek: *haplos*; Latin: *simpliciter*) friendship, law, etc. But instances of a type that is humanly deficient remain within the discipline's philosophical account, precisely as analogous to the central case. The philosophy of human affairs, as it bears on law, reflects on decent laws and legal systems, with due attention to what makes laws bad and how bad laws matter (*NLNR* chs X, XII).

Until Jeremy Bentham (foreshadowed in the fourteenth century by William of Ockham and Marsilius of Padua, and in the seventeenth century by Francis Bacon, Thomas Hobbes, and Baruch Spinoza), there is little or no specifically legal philosophy which could be called positivist. Yet from Plato to Bentham legal philosophy was substantially a philosophy of positive law, a subject-matter regarded as distinct from the other subjects of moral and political philosophy, but as adequately intelligible only on the basis of the moral principles and political purposes identified, explicated, and defended within moral and political philosophy. Legal philosophy's self-interpretation precisely as a philosophy of positive law can be traced back to the *Summa Theologiae* of Thomas Aquinas (c. 1270). His treatment of the concept, and types, of law is still read by many contemporary English-speaking legal philosophers, and for some has been highly influential.

The term 'positive law' had emerged in France c. 1135, and soon became popular among theoretically minded jurists. But the new terminology did not immediately modify the ancient accounts of the precise subject of philosophical reflection on law(s). Aristotle (*NE* V:1134b) had divided political right/just(ice) into the natural and the legal; the latter he also described as conventional and human. Late twelfth- and thirteenth-century jurists divided *ius* (law/right) into natural (the moral law) and positive, subdividing the latter into the Roman law categories of *ius gentium* (laws common to all peoples) and civil law (peculiar to a given community). Eventually Aquinas (*ST* I–II q.95 a.2) treats the distinction between natural and civil law as a distinction within positive law (that is, within law humanly laid down). Some parts of positive law are *conclusiones* (entailments) of the principles and norms of natural moral law; for these he appropriates the name *ius gentium*. The other parts are purely positive, though related to moral principles by an intelligible, non-deductive relationship which he names *determinatio* (concretization).

Thus human positive law in both its parts is at last differentiated as an integral object of philosophical reflection. The 'natural law theorist' Aquinas will be followed by the mid-nineteenth century 'positivist' John Austin in holding that it is by analogy with this central analogate that we understand as law (a) the eternal law of God's creative providence (including all the laws investigated by the natural sciences), (b) the natural law, or rational principles of good and right human deliberation and action, and (c) the 'divine law', that is, norms of positive law specially promulgated by divine revelation (for example as commandments) and including, like human positive law (ecclesiastical or secular), elements both of natural (moral) law and of purely positive law.

Aquinas describes human positive law as made by will (that is, by a choice to adopt one reasonable scheme in preference to another or others). But when speaking precisely, he contends that law is a matter of reason rather than will; obligation is a matter of means required for serving and respecting practical reason's ends and principles; the *imperium* by which, in executing one's choices, one directs oneself (or, analogously, as ruler directs one's community) belongs to reason rather than will. All this soon met with opposition, and for the next 500 years the philosophy of law was dominated by efforts to explain law's source and obligatoriness by reference to will, whether of superiors or of consenting parties to a social contract.

Bentham's *A Fragment of Government* (1776) initiated modern English-speaking legal philosophy by proposing a radical distinction between the 'provinces' of expositors, who by attending to facts explain what the law is, and 'censors', who by attending to reasons consider what it ought to be. Bentham's expository jurisprudence included a treatise, *Of Laws in General*, not published until 1945 but very like his pupil Austin's less ingenious account, *The Province of Jurisprudence Determined* (1832): all laws properly and strictly so-called are commands, expressions of wish (accompanied by threat of sanction) by the sovereign in an independent political community; however influential in courts, rules not made or adopted by sovereign command are not laws properly so-called; having a legal obligation is being the subject of a command and susceptible to its accompanying sanction; legal rights including powers are all to be explained in terms of commands and more or less complex permissions or negations of obligation.

English-speaking philosophy of law remained largely within the orbit of Bentham and Austin for more than a hundred years (though historico-comparative jurisprudence ranged widely). Even when American and other 'legal realists', in the second quarter of the twentieth century, denied that the substance of the law is rules or any other standard posited by commands or any other past acts, they retained and reinforced the conception of law as an instrument, in itself morally neutral, of 'social control' for the purposes of those in power (most directly courts and other officials).

Hans Kelsen (1881–1973), whose ideas became influential in Britain and America from the 1930s and who lived in the United States from 1940 on, attempted a union of Kantian with neo-Hobbesian and neo-Humean themes. This attempt resulted in a radically will-centred—ultimately an imperativist, that is, command-centred—account of law and legal system. Legal philosophy ('pure theory of legal science') must be free from every value, and from any reference to fact such as might suggest that law's normativity derives from or is reducible to its efficacy or other empirical reality (Kelsen, *General Theory of Law and State* and *The Pure Theory of Law*). Kelsen sought in effect a 'third theory', sharing with natural law theory the attempt to reproduce and explain non-reductively law's normativity, and with legal positivism the rejection of every norm or value not posited and made effective by contingent human acts and facts. The quest's failure is manifested in Kelsen's many shifts to and fro between contradictory views about the source and coherence of legal norms, the content of normativity, and the meaning of propositions of legal science, and in his final open reliance upon 'fictitious acts of will' (Kelsen, *The Pure Theory of Law*, 2nd edn, and his posthumous *General Theory of Norms*).

That explanations of law and legal obligation must point to commanding or consenting acts of will was denied in the most influential English-speaking work of legal philosophy in the second half of the twentieth century, H.L.A. Hart's *The Concept of Law*. Here and in his later *Essays on Bentham*, legal rules are described and explained as 'content-independent peremptory reasons for actions'; their sources may be commands but may equally be any fact having the normative significance attributed to it by a 'rule (or set of rules) of recognition' accepted by judges and officials (for any reason other than fear of immediate sanction). Not all laws are obligation-imposing; many rather confer power (authority), and an account which (like Austin's or Kelsen's) reduces these power-conferring or facultative rules to conditions or *protases* of obligation disguises the variety of law's *normative* forms and functions by overlooking the variety of its *social functions.* A descriptive legal philosophy can and should (Hart held) be free from moral presuppositions; intending to criticize Aquinas, he maintained that law is not 'necessarily or conceptually' connected to morality. But legal philosophy should (he argued) understand and 'reproduce' the viewpoint or 'internal attitude' of those participants in a legal system for whom law is a genuine reason for action and something of (not necessarily moral) value. So: legal philosophy cannot rightly maintain that law may have just any content.

Hart's many-sided resistance to reductive accounts of legal realities, and his strategy of understanding law as a type of reason created, maintained, and recognized for distinctive reasons, have encouraged many lines of inquiry into the point and function-related structure not only of law and legal system as a general type of social reality, but also of legal reasoning or judicial deliberation (for example, MacCormick, *Legal Reasoning and Legal Theory*; Schauer, *Playing by the Rules*), of the Rule of Law as a distinctive ideal for politico-legal order (for example, Raz, *The Authority of Law: Essays on Law and Morality*), and of the shaping moral point and justification(s) of particular legal institutions such as Contract, Tort (Delict), Property and Punishment (for example, Weinrib, *The Idea of Private Law*). Attention to Hart's neo-Aristotelian method of explanation by central and secondary cases has suggested that, despite his insistence on the opposition between the legal positivism he defended and every natural law theory, such opposition is needless unless positivism is taken (like Kelsen's but not Hart's) to deny that valuation and moral judgment have any philosophical warrant or truth.

Many positivist theories before Hart had been modelled on the natural (including mathematical and psychological) sciences. Hart's *The Concept of Law* opened English-speaking legal philosophy to issues of method in descriptive social theory earlier discussed by Max Weber (*Max Weber on Law in Economy and Society*), and showed, as Hart more or less clearly intended, the fruitlessness of seeking a value-free general social science. Interest has since shifted towards bringing legal theory into a clear relationship with ethics and an ethically grounded theory of politics (for example, Raz, *The Morality of Freedom*) or modelling it on the interpretation of cultural forms such as literature (for example, Dworkin, *Law's Empire*).

For instance: Ronald Dworkin's critique of 'positivism' seemed at first intended to establish that Hart had misdescribed the types of standard used in judicial deliberation (Dworkin, 'The Model of Rules' in *Taking Rights Seriously* (1977)). But Dworkin's real theses were not that legal principles differ from rules, but that they are authoritative not because validated by enactment or usage but because morally true (and irreducibly distinct from utilitarian or other collective-goal-based policies); and that legal theory, as adjudication's prologue, is a practical enterprise of 'creative interpretation', participating in developing a 'liberal' legal system which, without violating integrity by repudiating too many of its 'materials' (constitution, enactments, and precedents), will treat citizens with equality of concern and respect. The debate about these theses asks whether Dworkin's rather unarticulated moral theory is sound, whether the analogy with creative literary interpretation is not a new form of reductive explanation, and whether the claim that the law, even in hard cases, can always be identified by moral reasoning about the legal materials is not, likewise, a reductive oversight of law's dependence on a rationally under-determined authoritative *choice* (act of will) between two or more *reasonable* alternatives still legally open.

Mainstream work in contemporary English-speaking philosophy of law (legal theory) resists classification as either strictly positivism or natural law theory. Where work is self-described as positivist (for example, Raz, *The Authority of Law*; Waluchow, *Inclusive Legal Positivism*) or natural law (for example, *Natural Law and Natural Rights*), it in fact draws extensively on themes emphasized in the 'opposing' school. It is widely agreed that work in legal philosophy is distinct from, yet must draw upon, ethics, political philosophy, and a general social theory which builds on social anthropology and comparative history.

For: ethics inquires into standards of right judgment in deliberation towards choice and action, while philosophy of law investigates the ways in which those standards are related to the directives which are laid down, by usage or authoritative decision, to guide people's actions in political community and thereby, purportedly, protect basic interests or rights, distribute burdens and advantages fairly, and restore the position of persons wronged. Thus legal philosophy goes beyond but cannot elude the main problems in ethics—problems such as: whether moral propositions can be known as true; whether moral truths include intrinsic goods and reasons for action richer than Kantian conformity-with-reason's-universalizing-abstractness; whether right judgment is by maximizing values consequent on choice; and how far choice is free and intention morally decisive.

Again: political philosophy investigates the grounds on which persons may (and do) claim authority to shape a community's actions by directing individual conduct, while legal philosophy investigates reasons for and ways of making such authority and its exercise conditional on criteria of form (source, scope or vires, procedure, promulgation and publicity, adjudicative integrity, etc.). Thus legal philosophy adds to but is enmeshed in political philosophy's main issues—issues such as: whether authority is justified by consent or intent to benefit; whether interests are rights and rights secure equality, liberty, or other benefits; and whether political action is well understood on the model of decisions in economics or competitive games.

Again: social theory generalizes from knowledge of particular societies and events in their history, while legal philosophy investigates how such societies can be implicit subjects or bearers of 'legal systems', and treats some such events as sources of legal systems' elements. It, thus, confronts a main problem of general social theory: how to identify a subject-matter which can subsist as regimes and constitutions change and disappear; and how to select and justify descriptive and analytical concepts and terms, given the variety of social self-interpretations and competing vocabularies disclosed by ethnography and comparative historical and cross-cultural studies.

In line with Bentham's distinction between expository and censorial jurisprudence, legal philosophy is often divided into analytical and critical. Analytical jurisprudence proposes to consider the definition of law, the theory of legal system, the analysis of legal concepts such as duty, transaction, and intention, and the theory of legal reasoning especially in adjudication. Critical philosophy of law proposes to evaluate law and legal obligation, the minimum substantive content of legal systems, those interlocking procedural virtues in law-making and law-applying which are called the Rule of Law, etc. But against such a division, some have argued (for example, *NLNR*) that since creating and maintaining legal systems is for reasons, and like every reason for action presupposes and/or proposes evaluation(s), any general account of legal systems (or: of the concept of law and legal system) must identify those shaping evaluations.

Hart and Raz would respond that descriptive analysis of law's character as instrument can proceed without evaluating the diverse purposes and uses to which the instrument is put. But this response seems insufficient. For law's characteristic purport as obligatory and authoritative, like its purport as stipulating appropriate procedures and requiring fair trials and judgments based on truth, itself proposes an evaluation and critique of alternative social conditions (anarchy, arbitrary domination). There cannot be an adequately inward understanding or analysis of what characterizes *diverse* legal systems—an account showing why law deserves a place in any truly *general* account of human social life—without an understanding of the ways law's characteristic features themselves (even when being unjustly manipulated) manifest a critical evaluation of, and value-affirming constructive response to, the sorts of injustice or other lesion of human good which are inherent in lawlessness of every kind. (Analogously, one may understand and describe an argument without accepting or approving it; but one cannot well understand and describe *argument* in general unless one accepts some arguments as good and adopts as normative for one's general description/explanation the criteria by which their soundness is recognizable.)

More and more firmly, contemporary American and British legal philosophy acknowledges that law is somehow an institution or product of human reasoning, and addressed to human reasoning. Insofar as philosophers of law strive to avoid 'reductivism'—the restriction of strategies of inquiry and reflection to inappropriate models—they more or less explicitly acknowledge that laws and legal systems, like their human makers and subjects, somehow belong to all the four 'orders' with which (as Aquinas argued) human reason is concerned—roughly, nature, logic, morality, and culture (Finnis, *Aquinas: Moral, Political and Legal Theory*). Using the conventional symbols of an ordinary language, and supplementing them with new conventions and techniques, legal rules articulate conceptions of the natural order (which reason does not make but only considers), of logical consistency and implication, and above all of rightness and wrongness in official and unofficial deliberation and action. This articulation by legal rules is highly reflexive: Kelsen's slogan, 'the law regulates its own creation', captures some of this reflexivity. Indeed, even philosophical reflections on law (and nature, logic, morality, and non-legal techniques) are quite often to be found among the concepts and terms manipulated in making, interpreting, and using legal rules, institutions, and processes. Legal philosophers are always tempted—but today increasingly strive to resist the temptation—to resolve the resulting complexity into the relative simplicity of just one paradigm of order.

The 'ordinary-language philosophy' practised in Oxford in the 1950s (with roots in Wittgenstein) encouraged the opposition to reductivist methods. Among the most substantial fruits of that style of doing philosophy—hardly a 'school' of philosophical doctrine—is Hart and Honoré's *Causation in the Law.* Some legal-philosophical accounts of causation, particularly German accounts since Kant, have proposed that

it is by physical movements, and is unaffected by actors' purposes or other states of mind (which are relevant only to imputing culpability or legal liability). Such accounts of human causality are modelled on natural-scientific accounts of causality as regularities, or probabilities, or some inherent property of objects or events. Some other legal theories of causation, particularly American, have reduced 'cause in fact' to the minimal *conditio sine qua non* ('but for C, E would not have occurred'), and contended that 'cause in law' is merely a construct of social (that is, moral and/or cultural) *policies* about who is now to take the blame and/or pay. Against these reductions stands Hart and Honoré's account: judicial findings that someone's act or omission caused some event and/or loss are justified by considerations substantially independent of moral conclusions or other policies about liability, and are similar to scientific, historical, and commonsense conceptions in distinguishing the causally relevant as a *subclass* within the category of conditions *sine qua non*. On this account, the central causal concept, of deviation from *normal* conditions, itself extends to include conditions culturally established as conventional expectations or legal duties; attributions of causal-responsibility are nested in, but are not reducible to, conceptions of role-responsibility and liability-responsibility, distributions of burden of proof, criteria and methods of proof, and other non-causal considerations. The complexity of such a non-reductive account mirrors the irreducible complexity of the life of beings who live in the natural world as reasoning, choosing agents, artificers and creators, and for whom 'normality' is measured by diverse measures drawn from each of the four orders mentioned above.

Again, take legal personality. Some have said that because the only proper subjects of legal relations are members of the natural species, human beings, lawyers' talk of other juridical subjects (corporations, unincorporated associations, ships, idols, etc.) must be of mere fictions. Others (for example Kelsen) have said that the status of *legal person* is simply a creation of the law, which freely bestows or withholds it, and that the logic of legal rules leaves no room for attributing to human beings a legally cognizable priority. But a non-reductivist account can (a) deny that human associations are mere fictions, (b) acknowledge the convenience of attributing to associations and even non-human entities the status of subject of legal rules and processes, (c) accept that in a merely logical analysis of legal rules and relationships the human subject has no priority, but (d) maintain that since the very point of guiding deliberation by law is to protect and promote the good of human beings, and since that class of subjects is naturally constituted prior to any human decision, laws are radically disordered precisely as laws when they deny to any human being (slaves, embryos...) the 'equal protection of the law' (minimally, equality of fundamental legal status and immunity).

As the foregoing seeks to make evident, the vexed problem of defining law cannot be resolved by any purely 'analytical' technique aspiring to be neutral and conceptually prior to the taking of substantive positions on disputed questions about, for example, the natural and the moral orders. Of course, stipulative definitions and/or lexicographical clarifications assist inquiry and should avoid begging disputed questions. But explanatory definitions summarize the results of philosophical reflection; they are not sets or accounts of linguistic data or regulations for philosophical reflection. In legal philosophy it is particularly easy to see the value of the already-mentioned classical technique, announced by Aristotle, practised by his mediaeval followers, and revived if not fully consistently deployed by Hart: take as the subject of an explanatory definition the *central case* of the explanandum (and correspondingly the *focal meaning* of the term signifying that reality), and treat as secondary and relatively peripheral, but by no means unimportant or irrelevant, the many realities which instantiate the central case in a watered-down, immature, or defective way (and correspondingly the secondary uses of the term).

On that basis, one can (and should) say that a legal system which denies the legal personality and/or fails to protect the fundamental rights of some of its human subjects is not merely unjust and immoral but also a poor specimen of a legal system. But note: such a thesis depends on the further, widely disputed premise that what counts as the central case or fine specimen of a subject-matter of social, for example legal, philosophy is settled by reference to the evaluative concerns not of 'bad citizens' concerned only to avoid sanctions (as American legal realists proposed), nor of morally unconcerned judges or other officials as such (as Hart proposed), but rather of people who understand, accept, and promote law as a morally motivated and justified response to the evils and injustices of legally unregulated human relationships.

Such issues of definition and explanatory methodology are issues within the order of logic, that is, of the rational order we introduce into our own thinking. Some of the problems peculiar to legal philosophy arise primarily within this order. How does the propositional character of legal rules differ from that of legal principles or other legal standards (see Dworkin, *Taking Rights Seriously*)? What are the types of logical opposition between rules, and to what extent is contradiction between rules possible in a legal system (contrast Kelsen's *The Pure Theory of Law* with his *General Theory of Norms*)? Are all rules of, or at least reducible to, one logical type such as the imposing of obligation on pain of sanction or the hypothetical authorization of sanctions (see Hart, *CL*; Raz, *CLS*)? If so, are the logical types correlated with the social functions or point of different sorts of rules (see Raz, *AL*)? What are the irreducibly distinct types of right (perhaps claim, liberty, power, immunity)? Are rights mere logical constructs from, or shadows of, a logically or explanatorily prior concept of duty? Is a liberty (permission) the mere absence of a contrary duty, or does it entail a prohibition of some (or all) types of interference by A in the exercise of B's liberty and, if so, would it always or ever entail that B has a liberty-right to do what he ought not to?

Such issues have an irreducibly logical core. But progress in resolving them requires close attention to the special meaning and use of terms such as 'rule', 'obligation', 'right', and 'liberty' within the specific cultural and technical construct called the law. That construct, in turn, characteristically serves certain human purposes, and does so by guiding deliberation. A truly general account of it cannot be limited to recording the purposes, aims, and techniques of one people, or limited to reproducing in a 'detached' mode their 'committed' discourse. It must, therefore, engage to some extent in reflection on the moral order (which we bring by reason into our deliberations toward choice and action), by asking when action is intelligently related to basic human purposes and reasons for action. In short, all the questions listed in the preceding paragraph require the taking of some position on the *point* of law. Is law most illuminatingly regarded as an instrument of social control, whatever the controllers' purposes? Or does such an interpretation render much of the law's vocabulary and logic unintelligible? Is law to serve above all liberty, or is the liberty it serves (if it does) only one among many fundamental benefits? Such questions may seem remote from a strictly logical analysis, but answers to them have proved to be necessary (though not sufficient) for analysis of the structure of legal systems as interrelated propositions or quasi-propositional meaning contents.

Efforts to reduce problems of legal philosophy to the logical order have issued in striking failures: for example Hobbes's attempt to explain contractual obligation by equating breach with logical absurdity (see *NLNR*); or Kant's claim that since B's wrong contradicts A's rightful use of freedom, A's (or C's) use of coercion 'to hinder' B's wrong must, 'by virtue of the law of non-contradiction', be compatible with rightful freedom. As such failures powerfully suggest, the normativity of practical reasoning and legal norms is not reducible to logic's normativity, but rests on the necessity of means to or respect for basic ends (basic human goods, basic reasons for action).

Some have handled law-related moral problems and concepts by declaring them foreign to legal philosophy, or redefining them as cultural-technical not moral. Does the injustice of a law affect its authority, validity, or obligatoriness? Is equity a matter simply of interpretation or does it correct (for the sake of justice) the intentions of the law-makers? Do laws (and contracts) creating obligations entail no more than an obligation to pay the penalty (or damages) for 'non-fulfilment'? Problems such as these have been said to be matter merely for individual conscience, morality, or ethics. But in the proper (conscientious) performance of their judicial office as such, judges cannot avoid such questions. And there are other questions even more essentially concerned with the adjudicative role. Is it right for a judge to change the law at the cost of defeating the legitimate expectations of the unsuccessful litigant? Or to override the deliberately adopted policies of a democratic majority? Can judges rely upon their own personal knowledge unsupported or even opposed by the evidence admissibly tendered in the case? And then there are the responsibilities summarized in the ideal of a 'Rule of Law' (in German: *Rechtsstaat*): to ensure that the law is clear, coherent, stable, public, practicable, non-retroactive, general, and above all respected in official (including judicial) action. Is this set of purposes and features of legal ordering morally neutral (like the sharpness of a knife for cutting), as Raz in *The Authority of Law* contends? Or must the set, taken as a whole, have the moral purpose of securing a relationship of fair reciprocity between rulers and ruled, in recognition of the dignity and rights of the ruled (see Fuller, *The Morality of Law*)?

To conclude that such questions are properly part of legal philosophy is not to take sides in the perennial debate about whether to define the law as whatever standards are cognizable from social-factual sources (legislation, custom, judicial precedent) (Raz, *AL*), or rather as whatever standards a judge should take into account in giving judgment (Dworkin, *TRS*).

It remains that laws are manifestly in the cultural-technical order (order which by reasoning we bring into matter subject to our power); they are objects created by human decision as an instrument of social coordination. This aspect of law's positivity seems to be put in question, without sufficient reason, both by theories ('legal realism') which reduce the law to a prediction of judicial action, and by theories (for example, 'law as integrity' in Dworkin, *Law's Empire*) which locate the law not in any existing rules and standards (considered to be merely 'legal materials') but only in the moment of decision by a judge who, in a 'creative interpretation' subjects the 'legal materials' to ultimately individual moral assessment.

Law's many and varied artefacts include first the rules of law themselves. Even those rules which give legal expression to a moral norm are truly positive laws and usually of an artificial form: the law does not formally forbid murder, but rather defines murder as an offence, attaches penalties, disqualifications, and other legal consequences to offences, and posits that 'offences' are not to be committed. Still, *most* legal rules are no mere repromulgations of moral norms, but products of an irreducibly creative social decision. Their authenticity is a matter not immediately of moral truth, but rather of the considerations of form, source, and procedure encapsulated in the characteristically legal concept of validity.

Most other legal artefacts can be classed under another characteristically legal term: institutions. Legal institutions include not only public bodies such as courts and legislatures, but also types of legal arrangement involving clusters of rules (Contract, Sale, Property, Corporations, Crime, Delict...) and specific instances of such types, deliberately instituted for the sake of their legal effect (thus a particular constitution, contract, or corporation, but not a particular delict or crime). And these artefacts are to be distinguished from any documents used to create or record them. Obviously, then, the description and explanation of such artefacts would be complex even if the cultural-technical order could be sealed off from the orders of nature, logic, and morality. But it cannot, and some of the most intense debates in contemporary legal philosophy concern the moral and other (for example, causation) foundations of the legal institutions of Crime, Tort (Delict), Contract, and Property (for example, Fried, *Contract as Promise*).

Other legal artefacts include definitions. Whereas the purpose of definition in legal philosophy is to summarize an understanding and explanation of central (and non-central) cases and focal (and secondary) meanings, the purpose of definition in law is rather to assign objects and topics of human social life to *univocal* classes for the purposes of a given rule (for example, taxing 'ships'). Another legal artefact is the set of inference rules establishing presumptions for legal judgment on facts. Definitions and inference rules meet in the peculiarly legal practice of 'deeming' X to be an instance of Y, whether or not it would be considered a Y in ordinary logic or in, say, scientific, historical, or moral discourse.

Many issues discussed in contemporary legal philosophy arise in debate about the interpretation of constitutions, statutes, judgments, and other legal instruments (documents) and arrangements. Should legal interpreters find and follow the commitments originally made in the morally significant choices and intentions of the makers? Or should they give the language used—a set of conventional objects deployed to make a new and free-standing cultural object (the Constitution, the Act of…, etc.)—a new meaning and effect in accordance with new conventional understandings of the language? Are not both the act of legislation and the act of judicial interpretation (though immediately and directly exercises of a cultural technique) limited in their plasticity or malleability not only by other conventions but also by the natural givenness of human acts, by the requirements of logical coherence, and by the moral significance of every human act?

During the 1980s and 1990s some theorists, especially in the United States, proposed that all legal rules—not only those embodied in authoritative text such as a constitution or statute but also those transmitted by the quasi-customary forms of 'Common Law' adjudication—are essentially indeterminate, and thus are merely cloaks for the exercise of discretionary and elite power. This thesis of the 'Critical Legal Studies Movement' (Unger, *The Critical Legal Studies Movement*) has been extended into 'postmodern' and 'deconstructionist' theses which in analogous ways offer to deny the stable intelligibility of legal texts and standards. But theses of the latter kind are plainly self-refuting, since their own assertion and defence requires that the statements made by their proponents have a stable and determinate intelligibility. And the original 'critical' theses about indeterminacy depended for most of their plausibility on an equivocation about 'indeterminacy', that is, a failure to distinguish 'indeterminate' from 'under-determined' or 'not *fully* determinate'. It is characteristic of legal rules that they settle some (perhaps very many) issues for the practical purpose of coordinate, peaceful, and just life in political community, while leaving some other issues without any clear answer. After all, the issues thus left unsettled need not arise in practice, or if they do at some time arise may be resolved, even justly resolved, without resort to legal standards or procedures.

The dependence of law and judicial reasoning on morality (as well as nature, logic, and technique), coupled with the moral or ethical scepticism widely professed in contemporary English-speaking culture, inclines certain theorists to a form of 'pragmatism' which treats the main questions in legal philosophy as questions beyond *reason's* capacity to answer, and contents itself with a more or less ungrounded and unprincipled eclecticism (see, for example, Posner, *The Problems of Jurisprudence*). Such scepticism was also, it seems, one source of legal positivism's popularity in the early and mid-twentieth century. To the extent that that is so, it is left to the so-called 'natural law theorists' to assert, explain, and defend the rationality of the whole legal enterprise. In so doing, these theorists need not, and today commonly do not, repeat the kind of claim characteristic of 'rationalists' of the seventeenth and eighteenth centuries who optimistically and somewhat uncritically exaggerated the range of issues which have a rationally determinate right answer independently of the law-making choices of particular communities and their representatives. It is one thing to recognize such exaggeration when it occurs, and quite another thing to deny that there are definite and even exceptionless human rights, articulated in legal rules, standards, and institutions which are the backbone of every legal system appropriately called, without qualification, 'the law of this community'.

Every thesis in the philosophy of law, as in every other branch of philosophy, must satisfy the precondition that the proposition it asserts be fully consistent with the philosopher's reasonably choosing to investigate, assert, and argumentatively defend it, and with the natural, rational, cultural, moral, familial, and political conditions which make possible, and facilitate rather than obstruct, such investigation, rational assertion, and honest intellectual defence.

7

THE TRUTH IN LEGAL POSITIVISM*

I

Positivity was first articulated, as a concept organizing reflection on law, legal right(s), and legal justice, in about 1130, among the theological humanists of Paris* and Chartres,** nearly a thousand years after the term 'positive' was reported to be a tool for philosophical reflections on grammar.*** Positivity became an established classificatory concept among French and French-trained jurists of the mid-twelfth century,[1] crossing the Channel by about 1200[2] and the Alps to Bologna in the following decade.[3] Its first appearance in the still-extant literature in English is precisely in relation to law, in the unexpected context of a

* 1996c, whose first three footnotes are here the three asterisked endnotes.

[1] *Positivum*, like its cognates, is unknown to Gratian's *Decretum* (1140–1). But in the first generation (c. 1150–60) of glosses on it is a widely diffused *Introductio* which begins: 'In the first part he [Gratian] deals with natural and positive justice—justice both *constituta* and *inconstituta*.' See Kuttner, *Repertorium der Kanonistik (1140–1234)*, 455. In the *Summa Elegantius in Iure Divino* or *Summa Coloniensis* of 1169, a Rhineland decretist says:

> *Ius* is partly divine, partly human.... Human *ius* is either [i] natural...e.g. conjunction of man and woman, succession by children, free acquisition of things which belong to no-one, steady and moderate repelling of violence by force, restitution of things deposited or lent. Or it is [ii] positive, and then, if it belongs to a political community [*civitatis*], it is called civil...while if it belongs to various nations it is called *ius gentium*....

See Lottin, *Le Droit naturel chez Saint Thomas d'Aquin et ses predecesseurs*, 104. The *Summa* of the Belgian decretist Odo of Dour (c. 1170) begins: 'From the foregoing words of Gratian ["The human race is ruled by two things, natural *ius* and *mores*"] one can infer the division of law. For all *ius* is either natural or positive' (Kuttner, *Repertorium der Kanonistik (1140–1234)*, 173; 'Sur les origines du terme "droit positif"' at 731). Thereafter Odo uses *ius humanum* as a synonym for *ius positivum*. The decretist *Summa Reverentia Sacrorum Canonum* (c. 1183–92), commenting on Gratian's opening distinction between natural *ius* and *mores*, says that Plato in the *Timaeus* calls the latter [mores] 'positive'—clearly an allusion to Chalcidius's commentary (see endnote * below). See Kuttner, *Repertorium der Kanonistik (1140–1234)*, 176 n. 2, 195 n. 1; 'Sur les origines du terme "droit positif"' at 733. See also Aubert, *Le Droit romain dans l'oeuvre de saint Thomas*, 106.

[2] See Latham, *Revised Medieval Latin Word List, s.v. (ius) positivum*.

[3] Not before 1210, according to Kuttner, *Repertorium der Kanonistik (1140–1234)*, 175; 'Sur les origines du terme "droit positif"' at 733–4.

Yorkshire cosmological poem of about 1300.[4] But by then the concept had been extensively deployed in three major works by Thomas Aquinas, the first in about 1255, the other two in the years around 1270.

In these deployments, Aquinas asserts and illustrates positive law's variability and relativity to time, place, and polity, its admixture of human error and immorality, its radical dependence on human creativity, its concern with what its subjects do rather than their motives for doing it. And, by the end, he has worked up to a systematic position quite fresh and new. *Positive law* is put forward as a properly distinct category and subject of study in its own right; even those parts of it which reproduce the requirements of morality are conceived of, and can be studied, as parts of a genuine whole which in its entirety and in each of its parts, most of which neither reproduce nor are deducible from morality's requirements, can be studied as the product of human deliberation and choice. From 1270, then, positive law is taken to be in those ways autonomous.

There are, then, some important truths in legal positivism. Their mediaeval articulation is the first to state them precisely and with a purpose-built terminology, including but not only the very term 'positive'. The essentials sketched out in Aquinas's account have been significantly amplified and refined by subsequent experiences of and reflections on constitutional government, the rule of law, and the inner structure of legal system and legal reasoning. Here I shall simply recount Aquinas's essays in stating the truth in legal positivism, and shall then very briefly reframe some positions which modern positivists have often supposed were the whole truth of the matter.

II

The discussions of law's positivity in Aquinas's first major work, *Commentary on Peter Lombard's 'Positions' (Scriptum in Libros Sententiarum)* (c. 1255), arise more or less incidentally and, unlike his major subsequent discussions, concern particularly religious or ecclesiastical matters. As it happens, there is no occasion for him to consider unjust or immoral or otherwise unreasonable laws. The positive laws of which he speaks are always presupposed to be sufficiently reasonable ones. Even with the simplification of issues which this presupposition permits, these early discussions do not achieve the clarity of Aquinas's later efforts.

[4] Anon, *Cursor Mundi*, II. 9433, 9449, quoted in *Oxford English Dictionary*, *s.v.* Positive (usage A.l); in modern orthography: 'The first law was called "of kind [i.e. of nature]"... the other has "positive" to name.... The laws both be then forlete [forsaken], Both natural and positive.'

A first discussion[5] occurs in a treatment of the Decalogue, and responds to the question whether all legal precepts are somehow derived from[6] the precepts of the Decalogue. Aquinas's answer divides laws into three types. (1) There are laws which are called natural law (*ius naturale*); being intrinsic to reason, they are never inapplicable. (2) There are laws the relation of which to natural law is intrinsic, direct, and immediate, but which are inapplicable in some non-standard circumstances. For example, the standard rule that what you have borrowed you should return is inapplicable when the thing borrowed is a deadly weapon and the lender has turned into a maniac.[7] (3) There are laws called positive laws (*positiva iura*). When one considers these in themselves, one says 'there seems no reason (*nullam rationem*) to comply with them'. But circumstances can give one good and sufficient reason for compliance with them. There being such a reason, even these laws are to be understood as having an intrinsic relation back to the law of nature (*reducuntur ad legem naturae*)—not absolutely and in themselves, but rather in all the particular circumstances. (And, while the natural precepts of type (1) are the same for all peoples, it is the variety of circumstances that causes the readily observable variety among positive laws.[8])

Thus all legal precepts have, in one or other way, an intrinsic relation back to moral principles.[9] Aquinas ventures an ambitious comparison: laws of type (2) are like things which normally (*frequenter*) happen in nature, while positive laws are similar to the naturally abnormal (*raro*), that is, to things which can be explained (traced back to their natural causes) only by observation of the whole concatenation (*concursus*) of factors which make this relatively rare event occur.[10]

[5] *Sent.* III d.37 a.3c.

[6] *reducuntur*...one of Aquinas's most common and flexible philosophical terms; literally 'may be brought back to'; here the meaning is 'may be traced back to' or, reversing the metaphor, 'may be derived/are derivable from'—a matter of justification rather than of historical causation. See n. 16 below.

[7] This stock example is first put in Plato, *Republic* I. 331c. In *In Eth.* V. 12 (ad 1134b33) Aquinas will make something clear which he usually leaves unsaid when using, as he often does, the example of the duty to return something entrusted to one's care being overridden in exceptional cases (*ut in paucioribus*) by the duty not to arm a madman or a traitor. What he makes clear in this part of his commentary on Aristotle is that, while many *naturalia iusta*, like the returning of borrowed goods to their lender, are subject to exceptions, some *naturalia iusta*, like the wrongfulness of theft, are subject to no exception, since they are of the very *ratio* of justice.

[8] *Sent.* III d.37 a.3 ad 5.

[9] And indeed to the moral precepts of the Decalogue, whose status as the groundwork of all law was the subject of the discussion in III d.37 a.3.

[10] *Ibid.* A similar thought (distinguishing two sorts of natural *justum* from each other, and perhaps from a third sort, according as there is what is *justum* always and everywhere, what is *iustum* in most cases, and what is *iustum* in the minority of cases) seems to be expressed in III d.37 a.4 ad 2, an early wrestle with both Aristotle's treatment of natural, and mutable right (in *NE* V: 1134b34) and Cicero's account of natural *ius* and what comes from it (in *De Inv.* II. xxii. 65, see n. 15 below).

All this might suggest that, at least ideally, the content of any (any just and decent) positive law should be deducible from moral principles by anyone who can grasp the circumstances and their moral implications in all their complexity. On this view the legislator should be looking for *the* right law, in the sense of the prescription which is uniquely correct in all the circumstances, rather as a scientist of Laplacean cast of mind may think there is a determinate and complete explanation of everything that has happened and will happen, however unusual. But Aquinas does not go so far. Indeed, in a reply to the objection that (as the Roman tag says[11]) one ought not to seek a reason for everything laid down by law, he states that sometimes there is indeed no reason (again, *nulla ratio*) why a law's obligatory content should be X rather than Y. And he explicitly claims that this is what he meant in the earlier part of his discussion of positive laws.[12] So he may indeed have had in mind that the circumstances which make it proper to comply with a positive law (and so make that law, like every (decent) positive law, traceable to the natural law, somewhat as every natural event is traceable to natural causes) must include the circumstance—the sheer extrinsic fact—that the legislator has chosen to require X rather than Y. But Aquinas leaves the matter hanging.

Notice finally that in this initial discussion, only laws of class (3) are said to be 'positive'. Class (2) remains innominate, being neither 'natural' law nor 'positive'.

A second discussion in this early work of Aquinas occurs in connection with the question whether fasting is required by church law (that is, whether the church's rules about fasting impose a moral obligation).[13] Aquinas's answer begins with some general remarks. Precepts are of two sorts—of natural law and positive law (*iuris positivi*). Natural law precepts prohibit things evil in themselves, positive law precepts either prohibit things which can occasion evils, or require things which contribute to enhancing the good dispositions which the law-maker (*legis positor*) intends.[14] And that is why (says Aquinas) positive law, according to Cicero, is derived from natural. Aquinas's purported quotation imposes on Cicero both the word 'positive'[15] and the word 'derived'.[16] He proceeds immediately to

[11] *Digest* I. 3. 20–1. [12] *Sent.* III d.37 a.3 ad 3. [13] *Ibid.*, IV d.15 q.3 a.1 qa.4.

[14] Similarly, IV d.15 q.3 a.2c.

[15] In his youthful *De Inventione* (c. 87 BC) II. xxii. 65 and parallel passage in II. liii–liv. 160–2, Cicero distinguishes the *ius a naturae ductum* from *consuetudo* (custom) and *lex* (statute). He never uses any of the cognates of *positivus*. In II. liv. 162 he comes close to the idea of derivation when he says that customary law (*consuetudine ius*) is drawn only slightly from nature and is fed and strengthened by usage (*leviter a natura tractum aluit et maius fecit usus*).

[16] And, equipped with the more precise word 'derived', Aquinas can henceforth retire the term 'reduced/reducible to' in this context.

read the word 'positive' into another quotation, this time from Aristotle's argument[17] that law is needed to educate the young. His conclusion is that in fasting there is something which pertains to natural law (since it is a matter of natural law that one should live according to the mean between excess and excess, and abstinence helps discipline one's rebellious spirit). But 'the determination of such abstinence, in terms of determinate times and determinate rations, is a matter of positive law'.[18]

In this passage, Aquinas has taken it that law-makers are concerned with the dispositions (*virtus*) of their community's members.[19] But this must not be misunderstood. A few pages earlier he had restated a position which many have thought to be distinctively Kantian, liberal, positivist:

> a positive law enactment is not concerned with the intentions with which those who comply with it comply, but only with their actions themselves; so virtuous motives are not what a precept of positive law prescribes...[20]

It is, in fact, a constant but now little-noticed theme of classical political theory that the law's requirements extend only to the stipulated conduct (action or restraint), and not to the motives with which those subject to the law conform to it (though good law-makers hope that good conduct will inculcate good character).[21]

[17] *NE* X: 1179b35.

[18] *Sent.* IV d.15 q.3 a.1 qa.4c; in reply to a specific point (ad 3) he says:

> the precepts of positive law are binding more as regards the legislator's intention than as regards the law's own words themselves.... A. is not to be regarded as a law-breaker if he departs from the law's ordinance in a case where it can with real plausibility [*probabiliter*] be believed that, if the legislator were present, he would not wish to treat A. as under an obligation.

[19] See also e.g. IV d.15 q.3 a.2c and ad 1.

[20] 'but only a purpose [*finis*] of the prescription; and good or bad intentions can be a matter of merit or demerit).' IV d.15 q.3 a, 4 qa 1 ad 3:

> statutum positivae legis non attendit intentionem observantis, sed ipsum actum; eo quod motus virtutis non cadit in praecepto, sed est finis praecepti; sed ex intentione potest aliquis mereri vel demereri.

See also III d.37 a.4c:

> As the made law is the measure of subjects in their acts, so what pertains to the legislator, viz. the law's intention and purpose [*finis*], is the measure of positive law. So: just as the acts of subjects are wrongful if they are inconsistent with the positive law, so a law itself would not be right [*rectitudinem non haberet*] if it departed from the intention of the legislator, which is to establish and preserve rightness [*rectitudo*].

Note that the word *finis* is so protean that Aquinas's overall account of legislative intention remains unclear; thus, later in *Sent.* IV, he says that the precepts of positive law do not extend beyond that intention of the preceptor which is the precept's purpose [*finis*]: IV d.17 q.3 a.3 qa.4 ad 5. In this last passage the law-maker's *finis* is within the scope of the rule, not outside it.

[21] See *ST* I–II q.100 a.9. See also II–II q.58 aa.8–10: justice and legal relations (*ius*) are concerned not with the rectification of emotions, as other virtues are, but with external acts, dealings with things, and interpersonal coordination (*prout scilicet secundum eas* [*exteriores actiones et res*] *unus homo alteri coordinatur.* q.58 a.8c); the mean of justice is not the mean of reasonableness relative to the psychology of the acting person but is a *medium rei*, a mean or due measure of one thing (e.g. action, or share, or recompense) to another thing, concretely an *exterior operatio, secundum quod ipsa vel res cuius*

A third set of discussions, treating questions about the marriages of slaves and children, elaborate Aquinas's account of *determinatio*, the 'determination', specification, or concretization[22] which will be a conceptual centrepiece of his mature treatise on law. In his earlier discussion of fasting, the general lines of his account had already been firmly traced: 'positive law (*ius*) is said to proceed from natural law inasmuch as the way in which the natural law is to be respected is determined by positive law . . .'.[23] Now this is taken a little further. (1) Slavery is a particular kind of punishment. Natural law (*ius*) prescribes that punishment be imposed for fault, and that no one be punished without fault. But determining the punishment for particular classes of offender and fault is a matter of positive law (*iuris*);[24] so slavery, being a form of penal servitude, is a matter of positive law and arises from natural law as the determinate from the indeterminate.[25] (2) All contracts, says Aquinas, are subject to the arrangements of positive law (*legis positivae*), and the conditions for entering into a particular type of contract are determined—made determinate—by patterns of law (*secundum iura*).

But there is a qualification; the precepts of positive law (*juris positivi*) themselves deal only with standard cases—that is, with what happens usually (*ut in pluribus*).[26] Is this inconsistent with Aquinas's position in the first passage summarized above, maintaining that positive law is like rare events? No: the question whether general provisions in positive-law rules are intended by their makers to handle special cases is not the same as the question whether positive-law rules are related to underlying moral principles as the laws of physics are related to unusual physical events (that is, by a very complex relationship involving many contingencies).

To recapitulate: by 1256 Aquinas is an enthusiastic exponent of the bipartite classification of law: natural or positive. Positive law (when just) is always somehow derived from the basic moral principles he calls natural

est usus debitam proportionem habet ad aliam personam: a.10c. Aquinas is already clear about all this in *Sent.* II d.28 a.3c and ad 3; III d.33 q.1 a.3 qa.2; IV d.15 q.3 a.4 qa.1 ad 3.

[22] See essay 15 at 301–3; *NLNR* 281–90, 294–6.

[23] *Sent.* IV d.15 q.3 a.2 qa.1 ad 1. Later, in IV d.39 q.1 a.2 ad 3: 'those things which pertain to natural law [*legem naturae*] are determinable through positive law [*ius positivum*]'.

[24] Similarly, IV d.26 q.2 a.2 ad 1, and IV d.34 q.1 a.2 ad 4, noting that determinations will vary according to the varying circumstances of people in various times.

[25] *Ibid.* IV d.36 a.1 ad 3 and a.5c. Article 2c makes the point, explicit in these discussions of positive law and right, that positive law/right, based as it is on natural law/right, cannot prevail against [*praeiudicare*] it. In his *Quaestiones Quodlibetales* IX q.7 a.2c (probably c. 1258–9), Aquinas says that, since the bonds of positive law/right are established by men, they can be dispensed from (made subject to exceptions) by men.

[26] *Sent.* IV d.36 a.5c. So, he says, if a couple contract marriage before puberty and have intercourse while still legally under-age but physically and mentally mature, their marriage is valid, notwithstanding the general law about age as a condition of validity of marriage. (He is explaining an ecclesiastical ruling, not engaging in independent moral reasoning *ex iure naturae*.)

law. But in the limiting case, such a law may be enacted requiring X where there is 'no reason' for requiring X rather than for requiring Y, and 'no reason' for complying other than that it is right and obligatory to do so in all the circumstances, including, it seems, the fact that the legislator has chosen to prefer requiring X to requiring Y or other alternatives. Positive laws give determinacy to unchanging principles of natural law. But positive law does not stand in a direct and immediate relationship to those principles; it is to be distinguished from a somehow intermediate set of principles, to which he gives no name and which, though not positive, are not part of the natural law proper.

In this early phase of his work, then, Aquinas was working with a bipartite classification which had a tendency to slide into a tripartite. This tendency was reinforced by his interest in lining up his analysis of law with another threefold distinction, between (1) what holds always and everywhere, (2) what holds usually, and (3) what obtains only in rare cases. All in all, a good deal remained to be clarified by his later reflections.

III

In the theologian's commentary on Aristotle's *Ethics*,[27] the fruits of juristic reflection on legal positivity are reviewed and compared with those of philosophical reflection. Aristotle had divided *to politikon dikaion*, *political just(ice)*[28] into the *natural* and the *legal*; the latter he also described as conventional and human. With this analysis Aquinas juxtaposes the analysis common among 'jurists' (by whom he must here mean mediaeval, not Roman jurists). They divide *ius* into *natural* and *positive*, and what Aristotle had treated as the subject-matter to be divided up—political, this is, civil just(ice)—they treat as one division of positive law. He might have added that what Aristotle treated as a division (human just(ice)) some of the jurists treat as the subject-matter to be divided.[29] Aquinas is more concerned to show that the two analyses or terminologies are reconcilable. Aristotle, he says, calls just(ice) 'political' or 'civil' *ex usu*, that is, because

[27] Aquinas, *In Eth.* V. 12 (ad 1134b18–1135a15), Gauthier (ed.), *Sententia Libri Ethicorum*, 304–7. Gauthier dates the commentary to late 1271 or early 1272, after the writing of *ST* I–II. But there is still good reason to think that much of the work may have been done about five years earlier: see e.g. Weisheipl, *Friar Thomas D'Aquino*, 380; Tugwell, *Albert and Thomas*, 245, 256.

[28] I shall use 'just(ice)' here to translate *iustum* (and thus also the Greek words *to dikaion*), literally the just, i.e. the just action, thing, or arrangement. Aquinas will define *ius* as 'that which is *iustum*': see *ST* II–II q.57 a.1; *NLNR* 206, 228.

[29] Thus the *Summa Coloniensis* (1169), exemplifying the juristic analysis reported by Aquinas, says '*ius humanum* is either natural...or positive, and where the latter is peculiar to a *civitas* it is called *civil*...whereas where it pertains to various nations it is called *ius gentium*'. See Gauthier's annotation to lines 21–2 on p. 304 of *In Eth.*; also Lottin, *Le Droit naturel*, 105.

it is what citizens (*cives*) use; the jurists call one branch of positive just(ice) 'civil' *ex causa*, that is, because it is what is constituted or instituted *by* a political community (*civitas*). And the grand division between natural and legal or positive is common to Aristotle and the jurists; what they call 'positive' he calls 'legal', that is, posited by law; and both analyses recognize what Aquinas sees as the main point—namely, that the just(ice) used by citizens is partly natural to the human mind and partly posited by law.[30]

In tandem with Aristotle's text, Aquinas proceeds to emphasize various aspects of positivity. Where just(ice) results from being posited by some *civitas* or ruler, it settles what is virtuous among those, but only those, who are subject to the jurisdiction of that *civitas* or ruler. In states of affairs before this just(ice) is posited by law, it does not matter (*nihil differt*) whether people act this way or that. Moreover, the legal/positive is the product of human opinion and creative ingenuity (*industria*). It can establish a legal right or obligation peculiar to one individual (as in a particular law, that is, a *privilegium* or *lex privata*), and/or peculiar to one special topic; and it is often established by judicial decisions, that is, the application of legal just(nesses) to particular facts.[31]

But then Aquinas ventures beyond Aristotle to note that, for all its positivity, the legal or positive always arises from the natural. And this 'arising from' is in two distinct ways (*modi*). One way is like a conclusion from principles or premises; and positive or legal just(ice) cannot arise from natural just(ice) in this way; for when premises are in place, conclusions follow by necessity,[32] but natural just(ice) holds good always and everywhere, and that is simply not true of the legal/positive. The legal/positive arises from natural just(ice) by way of *determinatio*. Aquinas does not explain this second way, save by an example: that thieves be punished is a matter of natural justice, but the precise form of penalty is posited by law.

Instead of amplifying this, Aquinas hastens to make a different point. There are two ways in which *determinatio* takes place: (i) with and (ii) without admixture of human error. One of Aristotle's examples (though Aristotle did not realize this) is an instance of such erroneous, immoral *determinatio*—namely, the law requiring that divine honour be accorded to the Spartan war hero, Brasidas. In the context of a commentary on Aristotle, Aquinas does not add what he has very recently written, or is soon to write,

[30] *In Eth.* V. 12 (ad 1134b18) (p. 304). [31] *Ibid.*, 305, 306.

[32] Aquinas here does not say that such conclusions are called *ius gentium*, but a page or two earlier, ad 1134b19, he had remarked that included under the category of *iustum naturale* in Aristotle's sense is the (Roman) jurists' *ius gentium* (so-called because all peoples use it), i.e. the norms (such as that agreements are to be kept and diplomats left unharmed) which follow from human rationality (p. 305).

in his *Summa Theologiae*, about such laws inciting to idolatry (or anything else against divine law), laws which Aquinas treats as an extreme case of *lex iniusta*: 'such laws [*tales leges*] may in no way be obeyed'.[33]

IV

It is in the *Summa Theologiae* that Aquinas most decisively affirms law's positivity. What is new here is his break with all previous philosophical and juristic analyses which, in dividing natural or *ius gentium* from positive or 'legal' or 'civil', had taken the subject-matter of such divisions to be something other than positive law: for example, *ius* (Roman jurists), *to politikon dikaion* (Aristotle), or *ius humanum* (mediaeval jurists as in the *Summa coloniensis*). In his own writings reviewed above, Aquinas left these traditional characterizations of the subject-matter undisturbed.[34] In the *Summa* he treats the division between natural and civil as a distinction *within positive law* (literally, within *lex humanitus posita*, the law not simply human *ex usu*, that is, in its subjects and application, but human precisely *ex causa*, that is, 'humanly laid down').[35] Positive law is at last, in its own right, a complete subject or object of study.

Every human positive law, unless it is a mere *corruptio*,[36] is derived from that set of rational standards traditionally called the *lex naturae*. But the derivation can be in one or other of the two ways traced also in the commentary on Aristotle's *Ethics* (1) by conclusion from principles,[37] and (2) by *determinatio* or concretization of generalities—the latter being comparable to the way in which an architect or master-builder gives shape to the general (*communis*) idea of a house, by his decisions to build this or that house. The point to stress is the point underlined by Aquinas himself (and it is a clear shift from the terminology of the commentary on the

[33] I–II q.96 a.4c, one of the many texts which falsify *CL* 205–6; see also *NLNR* 364–5.

[34] But note that in his commentary on *NE* VI. 7:1141b23–9 (Marietti n. 1198) Aquinas deftly converts the Latin translation of Aristotle's word *nomothetikē*—namely, *legis positiva* (the positing *of* law)—into a reference to *lex positiva* (positive law), and proceeds to equate positive law with 'right reason' and 'architectonic practical wisdom' (*prudentia*), namely, the right reason by which rulers make right positive law.

[35] In *ST* I–II q.95 a.2 Aquinas treats his here-favoured phrase *lex humanitus posita* as synonymous with *lex humana posita* and with *ius positivum* (see obj. 2) and *lex positiva* (see ad 3); the very next article (a.3) settles down to talking of *lex positiva* as synonymous with *lex humana*.

[36] *corruptio* and *perversitas* are no mere terms of rhetorical abuse; the perverse or corrupt forms of regime (*parekbaseis*) are a topic of particular attention in an Aristotelian social/political science, and are discussed by Aquinas in *In Eth*. III. 10–11 (ad 1160a31–1161b10) and *In Pol*. III. 6 (ad 1279a22–1280a6).

[37] Laws so derived make up the *ius gentium*, said Aquinas (see nn. 40 and 41 below) by a *tour de force* of interpretation which preserves the elusive character of the Roman jurists' category as being both natural/rational and (as we can now say) positive.

Ethics).[38] This distinction between types of derivation is a distinction *within* the category of positive laws. Some humanly posited laws owe their moral import partly to the fact that they pertain to the natural law (because deducible from its highest principles); others owe their moral import as just (morally decent) laws 'solely' to the fact that they have been posited.[39] A page or two later, Aquinas summarizes his analysis. 'Positive law is divided into two, the *ius gentium* and the *ius civile*, according as there are two ways in which something can be derived from natural law.'[40] The two traditional organizing categories of the Roman and mediaeval jurists are preserved as labels for the products of a new analysis, a fresh synthesis.

The novelty, to repeat, consists in taking as the relevant subject-matter the whole of positive law—that is (in this context), the *whole* of human law—and showing by philosophical analysis of practical reasoning and decision how the affirmation of the positivity of all human laws is consistent with acknowledging the (various) ways in which each such law is morally justifiable (if it is!). Some positive laws are also norms of the natural moral law—that is, are requirements of practical reasonableness.[41] But to say this is not to detract in the least from the positivity of those laws—that is, from the fact (where it is the fact) that they have been posited humanly,[42] by human will,[43] and can be studied *as positive.*

In the same key passage, the patent and multiple diversity of positive laws at different times and places is affirmed and accounted for as resulting from the great variety of human affairs and, implicitly, the inherent freedom of *determinatio* as a choice between *reasonable* (as well as unreasonable) alternatives.[44] In nearby passages, however, Aquinas speaks also of the

[38] In reflecting on the possible chronological and other relationships between the commentary on the *Ethics* and the *ST* I–II, it should not be forgotten that the passage in Aristotle's *Ethics* which gave occasion for a treatment of positivity was not concerned with law, as such, but with just(ice).

[39] The latter '*ex* sola *lege humana vigorem habent*' (I–II q.95 a.2c). For illustrations, refinements, and amplifications of Aquinas's account, see *NLNR* 281–90, 294–6.

[40] '*dividitur ius positivum in ius gentium et ius civile, secundum duos modos quibus aliquid derivari a lege naturae*' (I–II q.95 a.4c). In II–II q.57 aa.2 and 3, where Aquinas is discussing *ius* not so much in the sense of 'law' as of 'right' (what is just), he restates the distinctions between *ius naturale*, *ius gentium*, and *ius positivum* in a manner designed primarily to reconcile the differing Roman juristic treatments (Ulpian v Gaius) of natural right with each other and with Aristotle.

[41] These are the parts of the positive law that Aquinas calls *ius gentium*. But when he is not feeling constrained to assimilate the old Roman juristic categories and labels, he will simply call these very same rules precepts of natural law: see e.g. I–II q.100 a.1c. His stock examples are: it is wrong to steal (*In Eth.* V. 12 ad 1134b20); it is wrong to kill the innocent (*ST* I–II q.95 a.2c), and both these precepts of the *ius gentium* reappear as precepts of natural law in I–II q.100 a.1c. In *Quaestiones Quodlibetales* II (c. 1270/1) q.4 a.3c the precepts against killing and stealing are called *moralia*.

[42] *ST* I–II q.95 a.2.

[43] I–II q.97 a.3c (*a ratione et voluntate legislatoris* or *a voluntate hominis ratione regulata*); II–II q.57 a.2 ad 2.

[44] I–II q.95 a.3 obj. 2 and ad 2.

diversity which results from unreasonableness, paradigmatically the unreasonableness of tyrannical regimes.

Such regimes may or may not be atrocious; what inevitably makes them unjust in the particular way labelled 'tyrannical' is that they use the law to promote the well-being of the ruler(s),[45] in preference to the common good.[46] (This is not the only source and form of injustice and unreasonableness in law.[47]) Being thus unreasonable, laws enacted for the advantage of such rulers are not unqualifiedly law (*non simpliciter lex*), but rather a kind of perversion of law (*sed magis quaedam perversitas*[48] *legis*). Still, Aquinas adds, such laws do have the character of law (*ratio legis*) in at least two important respects: (1) they are directives from the ruling authority to subordinates, and (2) they are not socially pointless but, like any law, intend to make their subjects good (though in this case the good is only the qualified or relative good of general compliance; the obedient subjects of such a régime are indeed 'good subjects', that is, good relative to that régime).[49] In short, the analysis does not ignore bad, unjust, wicked laws, but traces the ways in which they resemble, indeed imitate, laws which have more than the emaciated rationality of servicing the projects of those in power, laws which are really reasonable. As Joseph Raz has lately observed, 'the fact that the law ought to be just is relevant to the way the law, even when it is less than just, is understood'.[50]

V

'There is no necessary or conceptual connection between positive law and morality.' True, for there are immoral positive laws; 'there are two broad categories (with many sub-classes) of unjust laws...'.[51] And a conceptual

[45] In a narrow sense, 'tyrant' denotes the corruption of one-man rule; in a broader sense it denotes any régime in which the ruling group, big or small, rules in its own interest rather than for the common good.

[46] *In Eth.* VIII. 12 (ad 1160b1); *ST* II–II q.42 a.2 ad 3.

[47] See I–II q.96 a.4c; *NLNR* 352–62. [48] See n. 30 above.

[49] I–II q.92 a.1 ad 4:

> lex tyrannica, cum non sit secundum rationem, non est simpliciter lex, sed magis est quaedam perversitas legis. Et tamen inquantum habet aliquid de ratione legis intendit ad hoc quod cives sint boni; non enim habet de ratione legis nisi secundum hoc quod est dictamen alicuius praesidentis in subditis; et ad hoc tendit ut subditi legis sint bene obedientes; quod est eos esse bonos, non simpliciter sed in ordine ad tale regimen.

Or again, even a wicked law retains something of the similitude of law, because it is a product of the legislator's power structure: 'in ipsa lege iniqua servatur aliquid de similitudine legis, propter ordinem potestatis eius qui legem fecit...' (I–II q.93 a.3 ad 3).

[50] Raz, 'Formalism and the Rule of Law' at 339. The whole matter is argued out in detail in *NLNR* 3–22, 276–81, 363–8.

[51] *ST* I–II q.96 a.4c: *iniustae sunt leges dupliciter.*

distinction or disconnection is effortlessly established by the move made in the *Summa*, of taking human positive law as a subject for consideration in its own right (and its own name), a topic readily identifiable and identified *prior* to any question about its relation to morality.

'There is a necessary or conceptual connection between law and morality.' True, for the reasons people have for establishing systems of positive law (with power to override immemorial custom), and for maintaining them (against the pull of strong passions and individual self-interest), and for reforming and restoring them when they decay or collapse, include certain moral reasons, on which many of those people often act. And only those moral reasons suffice to explain why such people's undertaking takes the shape it does, giving legal systems the many defining features they have—features which a careful descriptive account such as H.L.A. Hart's identifies as characteristic of the central case of positive law and the focal meaning of 'law', and which therefore have a place in an adequate concept (understanding and account) of positive law.[52]

'The identification of the existence and content of law does not require resort to any moral argument.'[53] True, for how else could one identify wicked laws such as Israel's prophet denounced in words so often quoted by Aquinas: 'Woe to those who make unfair laws [*leges iniquas*], who draw up instruments imposing injustice [*iniustitiam*], and who give judgments oppressing the poor'?[54] And since the whole of a human community's existing law, however completely just and decent, is positive, somehow humanly posited, why deny that the facts which are referred to as 'human positing'—custom, legislation, judgments—can all be identified by lawyerly historical methods, without 'moral argument'?

'The identification of one's legal duty as a judge or other subject of the law sometimes requires resort to moral argument, and is always a matter of moral responsibility (both as to the identifying and as to the carrying out) which derives, in one way or another, from the bearing of moral principles and norms on the positive law of one's community.' True, for constitution-makers have a moral responsibility to establish sources of law which can be identified without resort to moral argument, and judges and other subjects have a moral responsibility to defer (within limits) to such sources. When the sources yield no determinate solution, all concerned

[52] *NLNR* 11–17.

[53] Raz, *The Morality of Freedom* at 81–2; this is the 'sources thesis' and the third of 'three major theses... traditionally associated with legal positivism' (*ibid.*).

[54] Isa. 10:1–2, quoted in *ST* I–II q.93 a.3; q.96 a.4; II–II q.57 a.2 ad 2; q.60 a.5.

have the responsibility[55] of supplementing the sources to fill the gap[†] by a choice guided by standards of fairness and other morally true principles and norms, where possible by standards which already have currency in the community and lend moral force to those parts of its positive law which are morally acceptable.

The dialectic which I have illustrated with the foregoing two pairs of apparently, but only apparently, incompatible assertions is one that could be extended. But its import should by now be sufficiently clear. Though human law is artefact and artifice, and not a conclusion from moral premises, both its positing and the recognition of its positivity (by judges, professionals, citizens, and thence by descriptive and critical scholars) cannot be understood without reference to the moral principles that ground and confirm its authority or challenge its pretention.

Maintaining the reflective balance indicated in the preceding sentence requires a use of theoretical terms which is more supple and nuanced than the usages of nineteenth- and twentieth-century 'legal positivists'. These latter-day thinkers, moreover, all failed to grasp steadily that 'ought' cannot be derived from 'is'. As the débâcle of Kelsen's late jurisprudence so powerfully illustrates, the fact of positivity, without the support of some prior normative principle, can yield neither a rational claim on the deliberations of judge or citizen nor a ground for construing the law as a *system*. Conversely, the truths of human moral responsibility in political community which are articulated in sound moral principles afford the basis for an unclouded affirmation of law's positivity, and indeed of all that is true in legal positivism.

NOTES

[*] *Positivity among Parisian humanists*...Hugh of [the Parisian abbey] St Victor, in his *Didascalicon* (c. 1127), distinguishes (Bk VI c. 5) between the *naturalis iustitia* which lies in the meaning of things and the *iustitia positiva* out of which arises the *disciplina morum nostrorum*, the discipline of our own (i.e. human) morals, customs, and usages. This perhaps surprising way of speaking clarifies and is clarified by his remark, in Bk III c. 2, that Socrates was the originator of ethics and wrote twenty-four books on it [!] from the point of view of positive justice, while his disciple Plato then wrote the many books of the *Republic* from the point of view of both kinds of justice, natural and positive (*iustitiam naturalem scilicet et positivam*). See Taylor, *The Didascalicon of Hugh of St Victor*, 84, 144. Behind this lies, if not the perhaps slightly earlier commentary by the Chartrean scholar (and later tutor to the English royal family), William of Conches, on Chalcidius' probably fourth-century commentary on

[55] Does this violate the bounds of positivism? If so, there are few positivists indeed who fail to go beyond those 'bounds'. See e.g. Hart, 'Introduction', in Hart, *Essays in Jurisprudence and Philosophy*, 7:

> in any hard case different principles supporting competing analogies may present themselves and the judge will *have to* choose between them, relying like a *conscientious* legislator on his *sense of what is best* and not on any established order of priorities among principles already prescribed for him by the law. (Emphasis added.)[‡]

Plato's *Timaeus*, then certainly (directly or indirectly) the statement in that commentary itself (I. vi) that the *Timaeus* is a contemplation and consideration of

> not *positive*, but rather that *natural* justice and equity which when inscribed in the making of laws and the articulation of forms of action gives them substance by way of authentic moderation.

(See Waszink, *Timaeus a Calcidio Translatus*, 59.) In William of Conches's commentary on Chalcidius, this becomes an extended theme:

> [Socrates dealt in his [supposed] treatise] with part of that justice [which had been debated between Socrates and Thrasymachus], namely with positive justice. For justice is partly positive, partly natural. The positive is that which is invented by men, like the hanging of thieves; the natural is that which is not invented by man, like love of parents, and suchlike. But because positive justice is manifested most in relation to the institutions of the political community [*instituta reipublicae*], in dealing with positive justice he gave his attention to the political community, so as to explain what is justice in relation to that [community].... Then Plato... when he had composed ten books *de Republica*, and desiring to perfect what his master had left undone, composed this work [*Timaeus*] concerning natural justice. But because natural justice is manifested most in relation to the creation [or conservation] of the world, he gave his attention to that. So we can say that the subject matter of this book is natural justice or the creation [or conservation] of the world.... In setting out to deal with natural justice, Plato recapitulates what he had said concerning positive justice, so that it might be one continuous treatment of justice.

(Migne, *Patrologiae Latinae*, 172, 246, 250; slightly different text in Delhaye, 'L'Enseignement de la Philosophie morale au XIIe siècle' at 95–6.)

** *Positivity among humanists of Chartres*... At some time in the 1130s, Thierry of Chartres, commenting on the vague remarks in Cicero's *De Inventione* (see n. 15 above) and the pseudo-Ciceronian *Rhetoric ad Herennium* concerning the natural, customary, and statutory (*lege*) sources of law, breaks free from the unclear and certainly non-jurisprudential grounds for distinguishing between natural and positive justice which had been suggested by Hugh of St Victor and William of Conches (see endnote * above). After repeating the long-conventional wisdom (e.g. Isidore, *Etymologiae* (c. 620) 5.3) that *ius* (right; law) is so named from *iustitia* and that the latter is either natural or positive (on *De Inv.* II. xxii. 65 and II. liii. 160), he finally draws the conceptual and terminological threads together in his commentary on the *Rhetoric ad Herennium* III. ii. 3, going far beyond the text before him and reaching back to the opening page of Justinian's *Institutes* to give it a new classificatory vocabulary:

> *Ius*, said Ulpian [*Dig.* I. i. 1 pr.], is the *ars aequi et boni. Aequum* refers to equity, *bonum* to utility and the decent [*honesti*]. *Ars* is the establishing of the useful and decent. Now sometimes this establishing is by nature, and is called natural law, or natural right, or justice.... The establishing is also by human institution, and is called positive right [*ius positivum*], or law. *Ius positivum* is called respectively *ius gentium* and *ius civile. Ius gentium* is the law/right common to all peoples, like the *ius* of wars, the *ius* of freeing slaves, of sale and purchase. Civil law [*ius*] is the law of one political community [*civitatis*], like the law of Athens and so forth.

For the text see Fredborg, *The Latin Rhetorical Commentaries by Thierry of Chartres*, 275–6; for the earlier passages mentioned, see 188–9, 209–10. On p. 276, before summarizing the whole scheme under the massive division between *ius naturale* and *ius positivum*, he subdivides *ius civile*, in Ciceronian manner (see n. 15 above), into *legale* (i.e. written, statutory) and customary, the latter including equity, agreement, and decisions. It all changes as times change and as the mores of the people change (*mutatur secundum tempus, secundum mores gentis*). The priority which Lottin, *Le Droit naturel*, Kuttner, *Repertorium der Kanonistik (1140–1234)*, and Aubert, *Le Droit romain dans l'oeuvre de saint Thomas* accorded to Peter Abelard, in relation to the *ius naturale—ius positivum* distinction, must now, it seems, be accorded to Thierry, writing probably several years before Abelard's *Dialogus inter Philosophum, Iudaeum et Christianum* (c. 1141).

*** *Positivity and early grammarians*... Aulus Gellius, *Noctes Atticae* (c. AD 160–70) X. 4 says:

> P. Nigidius very acutely taught that names are not positive [*positiva*], but natural. In his grammatical commentaries, Nigidius teaches that names and words were made not by chance positing but by a kind of force and rationale of nature.... For the [Greek] philosophers often raised the question whether words [*ta onomata*] are by nature [*physei*], not by positing [*thesei*].

(For example, Proclus reports the debate between Pythagoras and Democritus on whether words are *physei* or *thesei*: Diels, *Die Fragmente der Vorsokratiker*, 55 B 26. The semantics of the related Greek words *thesis*, *thesmios*, and *thesmos* are fairly closely tracked by the English words *positing/position*, *lawful*, and *positive law*.) Gellius was an author appreciated in the early Middle Ages and known to French decretists of the period 1150–1200: see e.g. Kuttner, 'Sur les origines du terme "droit positif"' at 739. But I know of no other evidence that in adopting the 'positive-natural' distinction, the jurists were influenced by Gellius, rather than by Chalcidius, though the grammarian's distinction reported by Gellius is far closer in substance to the jurisprudential distinction than is Chalcidius's Neoplatonizing distinction between a cosmological natural law and the whole set of human laws and morals. Probably the jurists took their cue from their theological contemporaries.

† *'When the sources yield no determinate solution, all concerned have the responsibility of supplementing the sources to fill the gap ...'* (at p. 186). This is not a satisfactory account of the range of situations in which interpretation and decision (especially but not only judicial decision) should draw upon moral considerations to supplement the social-fact sources and where appropriate modify the law they had established. The oversimplification begins in the preceding sentence's talk of 'sources of law which can be identified without resort to moral argument'. In the ways suggested in sec. I of the Introduction to this volume (in the main paragraph on p. 10), the bearing of social-fact sources (e.g. statutory provisions) on the law—i.e. on the whole set of propositions of law that are true in (and of) the relevant legal system at the relevant time (see essay 22)—is a resultant of many considerations, including not only systemic and *principled* coherence but also moral soundness (justice and other elements of the common good). Most hard cases involve neither gaps nor contradictions in the law, in any sense of 'gap' or 'contradiction' that could be fruitfully employed by reference to the social-fact sources alone. See also essay 20; also essay 19.

‡ *Positivist legal theory's concern with considerations other than social-fact sources*...(n. 55). To the quotation from Hart, add e.g. the quotations from Gardner in sec. IV of essay 1 and from Raz at n. 20 of the Introduction to this volume; and Raz, *Between Authority and Interpretation*, 379:

> by and large, all judicial reasoning is legal reasoning—i.e. reasoning according to law, *reasoning that imports moral and other premises in accordance with the role they have by law, or at any rate consistently with the law.* The exceptions are those cases where judges feel that the law does not allow enough scope for moral reasoning, that following it compels them to endorse immoral results, and that in the circumstances it would be right to flout the law and do the morally right thing. (Emphasis added.)

See also the whole paragraph at nn. 14 and 15, *ibid.*, 378.

8

BLACKSTONE'S THEORETICAL INTENTIONS*

If a definition of municipal law contains no reference to moral values or natural law, must its author be a legal positivist? If a natural law theorist's definition of positive law contains a reference to 'right' and 'wrong,' must this reference be to moral or natural standards? The answer to these questions is commonly affirmative, because it is widely assumed that the main business of natural law theorists is to affirm, and of legal positivists to deny, the thesis: *lex iniusta* by definition *non est lex*.

Some such assumptions have muddled the interpretation of Blackstone's introductory theoretical discourse on law.[1] To elucidate that discourse, by reference to Blackstone's structural and systematic preoccupations in constructing the *Commentaries*, is the object of this essay. The methodology of the *Commentaries* has been ignored in recent discussion. But reflection on it establishes, contrary to received interpretations,[2] *both* that Blackstone's interest in natural law was real and sustained, *and* that his definition of municipal law was free from any reference to natural law. To establish these limited exegetical points may help in dispelling a most widespread and obstructive misunderstanding of the natural law tradition in jurisprudence.

* 1967b.

[1] William Blackstone, *Commentaries on the Laws of England* I intro. § 2 (1778); hereinafter cited by volume and page of the eighth edition (the last in Blackstone's lifetime), published by Clarendon Press, Oxford, 1778: thus, I, 38–62. (The pagination of this edition is almost the same as that of the first edition of 1765–9, save that because of additions in vol. I the pages after p. 98 in that volume have numbers up to twelve higher than for the corresponding material in the first edition: e.g. I, 473 in the first edition is equivalent to I, 485 in the eighth.)

[2] See McKnight, 'Blackstone, Quasi-Jurisprudent'; Rinck, 'Blackstone and the Law of Nature'; Hart, 'Blackstone's Use of the Law of Nature'; Boorstin, *The Mysterious Science of Law*, 32–61. See also Bodenheimer, *Jurisprudence* 56–7; Friedmann, *Legal Theory*, 84; H.D. Hazeltine, 'Blackstone', Encyclopaedia of the Social Sciences 2: 580; Jones, *Historical Introduction to the Theory of Law*, 90; Paton, *Jurisprudence*, 114; Pound, *Jurisprudence* 2, 52–4, and cf. vol. 5 at 62; Barker, *Essays in Government*, 120–53. Cf. Lucas, 'Ex parte Sir William Blackstone, "Plagiarist"', proposing the extreme contrary view of Blackstone as a Hobbesian positivist.

I

Very commonly it is supposed that Blackstone's introductory chapter on 'The Nature of Laws in General' is ornamental, a mere concession to the stylistic or pedagogical conventions of the age, and without substantial intrinsic relation to the structure or content of the *Commentaries*.[3] On the basis of this supposition, scholars feel free to attribute to Blackstone the most lax and conflicting intentions concerning, for example, the definition of positive law, the relation of natural law to sovereignty, and the like. Now as will be shown, the content of Blackstone's theory of natural law and the precision of his exposition leave much to be desired. But what is in question at the moment is the scope and integration of the project he set himself. It is fortunate that Blackstone himself has provided an analysis of his work which sufficiently indicates the architectural purpose of his introductory discourse.

Recent scholarship largely ignores Blackstone's *Analysis of the Laws of England*, first published in 1756, and revised in 1771 to provide, in its author's view, an *exact* 'outline or abstract' of the *Commentaries*.[4] The 'first endeavour' of the *Commentaries* is stated in Blackstone's preface to his *Analysis*. It is

> to mark out a plan of the laws of England, so comprehensive as that every title might be reduced under some or other of its general heads, which the student might afterwards pursue to any degree of minuteness; and at the same time so contracted, that the gentleman might with tolerable application contemplate and understand the whole.[5]

This, if successful, would in Blackstone's view advance him in

> the remainder of his design; in deducing the history and antiquities of the principal branches of law, in selecting and illustrating their fundamental principles and leading rules, in explaining their utility and reason, and in comparing this with the laws of nature and other nations.[6]

No clause of the foregoing passages is redundant, hyperbolical, or misleading; the description of the preoccupations of the *Commentaries* is

[3] See the references in n. 2 above to works of Barker, McKnight, Hart, Bodenheimer, Friedmann, and Hazeltine. Bentham, *A Fragment on Government*, 96 (Montague ed., asserted for controversial purposes that the introductory discourse was 'the most characteristic part' of Blackstone's work and 'that which was most his own'.

[4] Blackstone, *An Analysis of the Laws of England* (hereinafter *Analysis*), vii (preface) (6th edn, 1771). The work, apart from its preface, appears as the contents pages of various later editions (e.g. Hovenden's [1836], Hargrave's [1844], Sharswood's [1894], et al.).

[5] *Analysis* iv (preface).

[6] *Ibid.* See also I, 35–6. The programme set out by Blackstone in these passages closely follows that commended in Locke, *Some Thoughts Concerning Education*, secs 186, 187.

exact. But our immediate concern is with the succeeding paragraphs, which make up the bulk of the preface to the *Analysis*. These enforce Blackstone's concern with method, since 'in pursuit of these his endeavours, he found himself obliged to adopt a method in many respects totally new'.[7] There follows a review of the leading English publicists, from Glanvil and Bracton to Wood and Finch, remarking on the deficiencies of their respective methods of 'reducing our laws to a system'. This review concludes with Hale, whose *Analysis of the Law* is praised as 'the most natural and scientifical of any'.[8] So Hale's 'distribution hath therefore been principally followed',[9] but with variations sufficient to entitle Blackstone to claim that his own method is 'in many respects totally new'. Blackstone stresses (without specifying) the variations and recommends that students study how he differs from Hale.[10]

May we not follow Blackstone's advice? In the preface to his *Analysis of the Law*, Hale had said:[11]

> The laws of this kingdom do respect either,
> Civil rights; or
> Crimes and misdemeanours.
>
> . . .
>
> I shall therefore divide the laws of this kingdom, in relation to their matter, into two kinds:
>
> 1. The civil part, which concerns civil rights, and their remedies.
> 2. The criminal part, which concerns crimes and misdemeanours.

However, it soon becomes evident that Hale's description of his own analysis was not quite exact. For in 'the civil part' of his analysis there was indeed a section on 'civil rights' (secs II–XXXVIII) and a section on 'their remedies' (secs XLV–LIV); but in between there was an equally demarcated section, equipped like the others with its own general introduction: 'of wrongs or injuries' (secs XXXIX–XLIV). Moreover, it is evident enough that remedies are appurtenant to wrongs; indeed, Hale's sections on remedies 'only give some *General Rules* relating to the manner of the application of those remedies; leaving every particular remedial writ' to the preceding sections in which he had 'considered of the various kinds of wrongs or injuries and under these distributions [had] already mentioned their ordinary remedies'.[12] Hence, the essential concepts in the 'civil part' were 'rights' and 'wrongs'; while 'the criminal part' (which Hale never actually analysed as such) evidently concerned 'wrongs' of some sort.

[7] *Analysis* iv (preface). [8] *Ibid.* at v. [9] *Ibid.* [10] *Ibid.* at vi.

[11] Matthew Hale, *Analysis of the Law*, preface (first published 1713).

[12] *Ibid.*, intro. to sec. 45.

Hale's analysis therefore ran into (at least) verbal difficulties and asymmetries. If the basal distinction was between 'civil' and 'criminal', what was the force of the adjective 'civil' in the phrase 'civil rights'? Were there 'criminal rights'? Evidently not; the phrase seems a solecism at least. But neither adjective could be omitted if the term 'wrongs' appeared, or ought to have appeared, in the description of both 'parts'. Might it not, therefore, be better to drop the terms 'civil' and 'criminal', retaining the terms 'rights' and 'wrongs', with an option to distinguish between types of rights and wrongs by terms corresponding to, but more perspicuous and symmetrically applicable than, 'civil' and 'criminal'?

Such, at any rate, was the course Blackstone took. The considerations advanced above are merely eligible conjectures; the outcome in the *Commentaries* is a plain fact. On the contents page of the *Analysis*, the four books of the *Commentaries* are designated as follows:

The objects of the laws of England; viz.

I	The rights of persons	Book I
II	The rights of things	Book II
III	Private wrongs	Book III
IV	Public wrongs	Book IV

And the first proposition of the analysis of Book I is: 'The objects of the laws of England are, 1. Rights. 2. Wrongs.'[13] Obviously, it is necessary to have an exact understanding of the term 'objects'. Above all, it is necessary to grasp that in this usage it is a formal juridical concept. It does not signify 'objectives' or 'values' or any moral, natural, or other pre-existing rule or relationship. It prescinds entirely from all such issues, and signifies nothing more than that, as a matter of juridical logic, the content of any legal rule can be expressed in terms of rights and their infringement.[14]

Correspondingly, Blackstone repeatedly stresses that, in this definition of the 'objects of the laws of England', the term 'rights' is to be taken as signifying something defined and enforced by human law.[15] Some of these rights also happen to be 'founded on nature and reason';[16] but in the same breath it must be insisted that 'their establishment (excellent as it is) [is] still human'.[17] Similarly, he opines that 'the principal view of human laws is, or ought to be, to explain, protect, and enforce such rights':[18] but in this sentence the term 'view' manifestly does not correspond to the term 'object'; its synonyms in the same paragraph are 'principal aim' and 'primary end',

[13] *Analysis* bk I, c. 1, § 1.

[14] See I, 122. Contrast Eser, 'The Principle of "Harm" in the Concept of Crime' at 352.

[15] See I, 124. [16] I, 127. [17] *Ibid.* [18] I, 124.

but never 'objects'. Moreover, natural rights are 'immutable',[19] but the same rights in their municipal juridical form are 'subject at times to fluctuate and change'.[20] Again, most rights and wrongs are not immediately founded in nature, but are wholly or partly things naturally indifferent where 'the very essence of right and wrong depends upon the direction of the laws to do or to omit it'.[21] By far the greater part of the *Commentaries* is expressly devoted to such rights and wrongs '*juris positivi*'.[22]

In short, the 'method' which Blackstone was seeking above all was to catalogue the laws of England in terms of the rights of persons and the rights of things, and private and public wrongs. Would it be surprising that a man preoccupied with 'method' should state the logic of his method in his definition of law?[23]

Blackstone's definition of municipal law is designed to justify his 'totally new' method of arranging English law. The definition is this:

> Municipal, or civil, law is the rule of civil conduct, prescribed by the supreme power in a state, commanding what is right, and prohibiting what is wrong.[24]

Our present concern is with the last clause. When Blackstone turns to justify it, he immediately remarks:

> ... in order to do this completely, it is first of all necessary that the boundaries of right and wrong be established[25] and ascertained by law. And when this is once done, it will follow of course that it is likewise the business of the law, considered as a rule of civil conduct, to enforce these rights and to restrain or redress these wrongs.[26]

This passage establishes the conceptual linkage between the definition of law and the structure of the *Commentaries*. It is quite clear that the thread of the discussion has nothing to do with 'natural law' or 'positivism'. That Blackstone's concern is with the juridical logic of his whole construction[27]

[19] *Ibid.* [20] I, 126. [21] I, 55. See also text at n. 66 below.

[22] II, 211. See also I, 125.

[23] On the general question of Blackstone's lifelong obsession with method, order, and architectural system, see Holdsworth, *History of English Law*, xii 718–20.

[24] *Analysis* intro. § 2. Also I, 44, 58.

[25] The force of the term 'established' may be gathered from the following:

> The absolute rights of every Englishman ... as they are founded on nature and reason ... though subject at times to fluctuate and change: their establishment (excellent as it is) being still human. (I, 127.)

[26] I, 53.

[27] This concern is made explicit on the first page of Book I (I, 121) and of Book III (III, 1); the latter passage is quoted here since this relegates to footnotes the decorative references to Cicero and Bracton which have bedevilled interpretation of the former, otherwise identical passage:

> At the opening of these commentaries municipal law was in general defined to be, 'a rule of civil conduct, prescribed by the supreme power in a state, commanding what is right, and prohibiting what is wrong.' From hence therefore it followed, that the primary objects of the law are the

is emphasized by the next paragraph beginning, 'For this purpose every law may be said to consist of several parts ...'[28] I quote the remainder in the shorter form of the *Analysis*.

1. The declaratory; which defines what is right, and wrong. 2. the directory; which consists in commanding the observation of right, or prohibiting the commission of wrong. 3. the remedial; or method of recovering private rights, or redressing private wrongs. 4. the vindicatory sanction of punishments for public wrongs; wherein consists the most forcible obligation of human laws.[29]

It is of the utmost significance that among the ten paragraphs which constitute Blackstone's own analysis of his introductory chapter on the nature of laws in general, there is no hint that the *definition* of municipal law canvassed any issue about the relations of natural and positive law.[30] However, 'in the explication' of his definition, Blackstone 'endeavoured to

establishment of rights, and the prohibition of wrongs. And this occasioned the distribution of these collections into two general heads; under the former of which we have already considered the *rights* that were defined and established, and under the latter are now to consider the *wrongs* that are forbidden and redressed, by the laws of England. (III, 1.)

Blackstone's first editor, Christian, was the first of many who have complained that the second portion of the definition of municipal law must either be superfluous and tautologous or else a false claim to actual or conceptual identity or correspondence of positive with natural law. See note to I, 44 in Christian's editions, also Hovenden's and Sharswood's editions. Other supporters of this view, or of the view that Blackstone's definition is a hybrid of positive and natural law elements, include Cohen, 'Transcendental Nonsense and the Functional Approach' at 838; McKnight, 'Blackstone, Quasi-Jurisprudent' at 402. See also the absurd exegesis in Jeremy Bentham, *A Comment on the Commentaries*, 70–2 (ed. Everett, 1928). In fact the definition has nothing to do with natural law, and is not superfluous since it seeks to reveal the juridical logic on which the *Commentaries* are based. Likewise, it is not *opposed* to natural law, as Lucas, 'Ex parte Sir William Blackstone, "Plagiarist"' represents.

[28] I, 53. [29] *Analysis* intro. §§ 2, 8.

[30] Blackstone's analysis of his introductory discourse is as follows:

Of the nature of laws in general.

1. Law is a rule of action, prescribed by a superior power.
2. Natural Law is the rule of human action, prescribed by the creator, and discoverable by the light of reason.
3. The divine, or revealed, law (considered as a rule of action) is also the law of nature, imparted by God himself.
4. The law of nations is that which regulates the conduct and mutual intercourse of independent states with each other, by reason and natural justice.
5. Municipal, or civil law, is the rule of civil conduct, prescribed by the supreme power in a state, commanding what is right, and prohibiting what is wrong.
6. Society is formed for the protection of individuals; and states, or government, for the preservation of society.
7. In all states, there is an absolute supreme power, to which the right of legislation belongs; and which, by the singular constitution of these kingdoms, is vested in the king, lords, and commons.
8. The parts of a law are [quoted in text at n. 29 above].
9. To interpret a law, we must enquire after the will of the maker: which may be collected either from the words, the context, the subject-matter, the effects and consequence, or the spirit and reason of the Law.
10. From the latter method of interpretation arises equity, or the correction of that, wherein the law (by reason of its universality) is deficient.

weave a few useful principles, concerning the nature of civil government, and the obligation of human laws'.[31] People who do not discern the central themes of the discourse, viz. the themes set out in the *Analysis*, often suppose that these interwoven passages are the main substance of the chapter; hence the chaos of interpretations.

It is true that, in discussing the 'declaratory part' of municipal laws, Blackstone offers a theory of natural rights and duties which do not in his view 'receive any additional strength when declared by the municipal laws to be inviolable'.[32] But this paragraph begins with the clear assertion that the declaratory part 'depends not so much upon the law of revelation or of nature, as upon the wisdom and will of the legislator'.[33] It is followed by a paragraph stressing the purely positive origin of most laws, and the discussion culminates, in the succeeding paragraph, with the remark that 'The law that says, "thou shalt not steal," implies a declaration that stealing is a crime'; and 'the principal obligation of human laws' (whatever their origin) 'consists in the penalty annexed'.[34] Blackstone is simply showing that his theory of the parts of a law, necessary to explain just 'how law commands what is right and prohibits what is wrong', is unaffected by the theory of natural laws and rights expounded earlier in the chapter.

Likewise, the famous discussion of 'purely penal laws', which occurs at the end of the justification of the definition, is merely an appendage or 'interweaving' of 'a few useful principles' about 'the obligation of human laws'.[35] It detracts nothing from the insistence that 'the main strength and force of a law consist in the penalty annexed to it'.[36] The obligation of laws 'upon men's consciences' is worth a paragraph; but this must be prefaced by insisting that 'if that were the only, or most forcible obligation, the good only would regard the laws, and the bad would set them at defiance'.[37]

Finally, it should be noticed how the 'parts of a law', adduced to explain the last clause of the definition of municipal law, correspond to the parts of the *Commentaries*. For the declaratory and directory parts should be taken together (since the directory 'virtually includes the former, the declaration being usually collected from the direction'),[38] and together they define rights (Books I and II) and the wrongs relative to them; while the remedial part indicates the 'method of recovering private rights, and redressing private wrongs'[39] (Book III) and the vindicatory concerns 'public wrongs' (Book IV).

In short, the introductory definition of law is, thus far, intimately related to the structure of the *Commentaries* as a whole. Moreover, the definition

[31] I, 59. [32] I, 54. [33] *Ibid.*
[34] I, 55, 57. Theft is by natural law *malum in se*. I, 54. [35] I, 59. [36] I, 57.
[37] *Ibid.* [38] I, 55. [39] *Analysis* intro. §§ 2, 8.

of municipal law is shown to be concerned with structural and methodical questions, not problems of political or moral theory.

II

Still, not a few pages of the introductory discourse are concerned with natural and divine laws, and with the origins of society as canvassed by political philosophers. Does it follow, from what has just been established, that these pages are mere ornamental interweavings, substantially unrelated to the rest of the *Commentaries*? Three main arguments are advanced and repeated in the literature on Blackstone, to establish the merely decorative character of these pages.

(1) First, there is said to be a contradiction between Blackstone's theory of natural law and his theory of parliamentary sovereignty; hence one of the theories must be sacrificed as inconsequential, and it is the natural law theory.[40]

More than one hundred pages separate the main discussion of parliamentary sovereignty[41] from the discourse on natural law. Can Blackstone by then have forgotten his introductory assertion that 'no human laws are of any validity, if contrary to' the law of nature?[42]

It seems not. The principle of parliamentary sovereignty is upheld within five pages of the assertion just quoted from page 41. On page 46, legislature is defined as 'the greatest act of superiority that can be exercised by one being over another',[43] and 'sovereignty' and 'legislature' are said to be convertible terms. On page 49, it is said that 'there is and must be in all [governments] a supreme, irresistible, absolute, uncontrolled authority, in which the *jura summi imperii*, or the rights of sovereignty, reside'. On page 51, it is said of Parliament: 'Here then is lodged the sovereignty of the British constitution'; 'the British parliament ... has the supreme disposal of everything'. And on page 54, it is again said of natural rights that 'no human legislature has power to abridge or destroy them'.

Blackstone's meaning is simply that no human law has any moral validity or force against a natural law, and that no human law can affect the content of a natural right as such. On the other hand, the significance of Parliament's 'irresistible, uncontrolled authority' is simply that stated on the very same page: 'all the other powers of the state must obey the legislative power in the execution of their several functions, or else the

[40] See the references in n. 2 above to works of Bodenheimer, Paton, Rinck, Barker, and Friedmann. Compare Gough, *Fundamental Law in English Constitutional History*, 188–90.
[41] I, 160. [42] I, 41. [43] i.e. legislation.

constitution is at an end'.[44] Again, in a little-noticed passage later in the Introduction, Blackstone specifies his meaning:

> if the parliament will positively enact a thing to be done which is unreasonable, I know of no power that can control it... for that were to set the judicial power above that of the legislature, which would be subversive of all government.[45]

Opinions may differ about the truth of the last clause. But only someone who mistakenly supposed that the doctrine of judicial review in *Marbury v Madison*[46] is an absolute juridical necessity[47] could suppose that there is any contradiction between the sovereignty of Parliament and a doctrine of a higher law critique of the exercise of that sovereignty. As Blackstone might have said, the courts may bow to Parliament rather than to the higher law, but it does not follow that individual conscience should similarly be subject; and vice versa.[48]

Hence, the alleged contradiction does not exist, and the natural law doctrine need not be sacrificed as inconsequential.

(2) Secondly, it commonly is suggested that Blackstone's introductory discourse on law in general was so extraneous to his central preoccupations that he merely transcribed (without acknowledgement) passages on natural law from the Swiss publicist Burlamaqui, whose work *The Principles of Natural and Politic Law* had then recently been translated.[49] Against this, it has recently been alleged that no such transcription occurred.[50]

The truth of the matter can readily be ascertained by anyone willing to read the two works; so there is no point in discussing the question at length. Suffice it to say that Burlamaqui's book, in Nugent's translation, obviously lay before Blackstone when he was writing his introductory discourse. Thus Burlamaqui's passage:

> ...the subjection in which he finds himself, does not permit him to entertain the least reasonable hopes of acquiring any solid happiness, independent of the will of his superior, and of the views he may propose in relation to him. Besides, this has more or less extent and effect, in proportion as the superiority of the one and the dependence of the other, is greater or less, absolute or limited.[51]

in Blackstone appears as:

> This principle therefore has more or less extent and effect, in proportion as the superiority of the one and the dependence of the other is greater or less, absolute or limited.[52]

[44] I, 49. [45] I, 91. [46] 1 Cranch 137 (1803).

[47] Compare *Eakin v Raub* 12 S & R 330, 344–58 (Pa. 1838) (Gibson J dissenting).

[48] Thus Blackstone can assert both that where a human law is contrary to natural law, 'we are bound to transgress that human law' (I, 43; also IV, 28), and that 'however that may be, obedience to the laws in being is undoubtedly a sufficient extenuation of civil guilt before the municipal tribunal' (IV, 28).

[49] See the many references assembled in Lucas (1963) at 143 n. 2. [50] *Ibid.* at 144.

[51] Burlamaqui, *The Principles of Natural and Political Law*, 77. [52] I, 39.

Similarly, Blackstone substantially reproduces Burlamaqui's categorization of God's attributes as 'power, wisdom and goodness',[53] his discussion of promulgation,[54] his concept of a 'rule',[55] and his strictures against Clarke's 'fitness' theory of natural law.[56] But Blackstone's definition of law in general[57] owes nothing to Burlamaqui's,[58] nor does his definition of municipal law.[59] Blackstone's idea of a state of nature contradicts Burlamaqui's,[60] and after transcribing the sentence last quoted above, Blackstone ignores Burlamaqui's repeated and emphatic insistence that the mere power and supremacy of God could not create an obligation.[61] Indeed, simply to read in each text the six sentences following the respective passages quoted above is to see the radical independence of Blackstone from Burlamaqui on matters of theoretical substance.

Our present purpose is not to trace the intellectual provenance of Blackstone's discourse, but to insist that the charge of lazily adopting any other man's theory for decorative purposes is unfounded.

(3) Finally, there is H.L.A. Hart's interesting suggestion that Blackstone's theory of natural law performs not a genuinely theoretical function, but rather the practical purpose of stifling criticism of existing law:

> his exploitation of the law of nature in defence of the existing law very largely consists in the assertion that the institution which he is defending is just one of such 'matters in themselves indifferent,' and that since the law of nature has nothing to say *against* the institution or is not 'contradicted' by it, there is no ground for criticism.[62]

Thus Blackstone's law of nature is said to dissolve into a series of gaps, leaving Blackstone with 'no tool of social criticism at all'.[63]

This suggestion, as will be shown in the concluding section, is not without point. But on the whole it cannot be admitted. In the first place, it is misleading to say, as Hart does, that the theory of 'things naturally indifferent' (that is, matters to which no natural law rule directly applies) is 'distinctive', or peculiar to Blackstone.[64] It is in principle a scholastic

[53] I, 40, 49, 51. Burlamaqui 89. [54] I, 45. Burlamaqui 79. [55] I, 44. Burlamaqui 78.
[56] I, 41. Burlamaqui 63. [57] I, 38. [58] Burlamaqui 45.
[59] I, 44. Burlamaqui 78. [60] I, 123. Burlamaqui 42–3.
[61] I, 39–40. Burlamaqui 88, 69, 77.
[62] Hart, 'Blackstone's Use of the Law of Nature' at 169, 171. Shuman, *Legal Positivism*, 186 follows Hart, and describes Blackstone's purpose as 'malicious'. See also Lucas, 'Ex parte Sir William Blackstone, "Plagiarist"' and McKnight, 'Blackstone, Quasi-Jurisprudent'.
[63] Hart, 'Blackstone's Use of the Law of Nature' at 172.
[64] *Ibid.* at 171. The phrase 'things *naturally* indifferent' (I, 55) (emphasis added) is used in the text to emphasize the variety of meanings attached by Blackstone to the term 'indifferent'. Note that by additions to his text after the 6th edn, Blackstone makes it clear that he is expressly postulating at least three categories of law, including laws about at least two categories of 'things indifferent'. See I, 58. First, there are laws about *mala in se*. Secondly, there are laws about things which are naturally indifferent, but which in given circumstances involve 'any degree of public mischief or private

commonplace, handed down in English law by St German, whose very examples are similar to Blackstone's.[65] But what is distinctive of Blackstone is the variety of senses in which he uses the term 'indifferent'—a variety which Hart seems to have overlooked. The fact is that the category of 'things indifferent in themselves' shifts its meaning uneasily between (a) matters so 'indifferent' that legislation on them is unjustified; (b) matters so 'indifferent' that a legislator should be content with either performance or payment of penalty; (c) matters 'indifferent' in that, though of great moment to a given society, they are not of moment to all conceivable societies; and (d) matters only 'indifferent' in that, though of great moment to social living, they would not be of great moment in a state of nature.[66] Moreover, the matters in categories (c) and (d) include matters, the regulation of which is of great moment, but which could be regulated in a variety of alternative but more or less equally reasonable ways.[67] With these cautions in mind, the three examples adduced by Hart should be given a closer interpretation.

The first concerns the rule that estates should escheat to the Crown rather than pass by succession to a brother of the half-blood. Hart cites only the discussion in the Introduction, where Blackstone is concerned merely to establish that those who devised rules of common law should not be presumed to have acted without reason, and that precedent must be followed by judges.[68] But Blackstone refers to the rule very elaborately in Book II. He defends it against the criticisms (not utilitarian!) of Craig,[69] establishes its feudal rationale, demonstrates the unlikelihood that it often causes hardship, admits that it is 'a very fine-spun and subtle nicety' that has

injury' (I, 58, added in 7th edn). Thirdly, there are laws about things 'wholly a matter of indifference', non-compliance with which laws will cause at most a compensable 'civil inconvenience': such a law is *lex pure poenalis*, whereas a law of the second category is *lex poenalis mixta*. (I, 58 note m, added in 7th edn. But notice that this defensive appeal to Sanderson is misleading, since Sanderson's wholly voluntarist theory of penal law has only terminology in common with Blackstone's.) Note also that none of the three examples adduced by Hart fall into any of these categories of *mala*, since all these examples concern laws conferring powers or rights. But as '*mala prohibita*' is for Blackstone a complex category, so is his category of 'things indifferent' complex in ways not noticed by Hart. Curiously, Austin misinterpreted Blackstone's remarks about the rights of the half-blood in the same way. John Austin, *Lectures on Jurisprudence*, 2: 913 (3rd edn, 1869).

[65] See Christopher St German, *Doctor and Student*, bk I, c. 5. Cf. Blackstone's discussion of distress at I, 55. Of course, Blackstone's notion of matters *wholly* indifferent (I, 58; see n. 64 above) is not shared by all scholastics nor by St German insofar as it relates to the theory of *mala* merely *prohibita* and purely penal laws importing an obligation only to pay the penalty. But it is shared insofar as it amounts to the theory that there are many cases in which alternative rules on the same matter could have been adopted with equal propriety (e.g. drive on the left rather than the right; property to descend to eldest rather than youngest son; etc.), and that in such cases no more than disputable and changeable balances of convenience are at stake. (See text below at nn. 68–79.) Hart's discussion of *mala prohibita* can obscure the fact that it is the latter, not the former, theory that is at stake in the three examples that he cites.

[66] See (a) I, 126; (b) I, 58; (c) I, 299; (d) I, 55. [67] See n. 65 above.

[68] I, 70–1. [69] II, 232. Cf. Thomas Craig, *De jure feudale* II, c. 15, § 14.

been pushed too far,[70] and concludes that the question whether legislative intervention is to be preferred to shaking a long-established rule 'is not for me to determine'.[71] Later he remarks that the 'artificial reason' of the rule, 'arising from feudal principles, has long ago entirely ceased', and that the rule is 'hard'.[72] So it does not seem right to say that his rebuttal of Craig's criticisms on Craig's own ground amounts to a general attempt to stifle all criticisms of the rule.

The other two passages concern rules of testamentary disposition and intestate succession.[73] Craig and Locke had raised natural law objections to the English rules,[74] and once again Blackstone meets them on their own ground. His arguments here are not ad hoc, but are strict deductions from his general theory of property and the state of nature.[75] But it is simply not the case that for Blackstone these natural law arguments close the matter or exhaust all criticisms. Besides the passages cited by Hart, there are important passages in which Blackstone sets out political and social justifications for these English rules,[76] and emphasizes that other rules have been adopted for other polities.[77] He defends the power to disinherit children as based on 'a principle of liberty',[78] but remarks that 'perhaps it had not been amiss, if the parent had been bound to leave them at the least a necessary subsistence'.[79]

Finally, we must notice a passage that stands Hart's interpretation on its head. This is the passage in which Blackstone repudiates the view that there is any '*natural* injustice' in the game and forest laws 'as some have weakly enough supposed'.[80] For this does not hamper him from levelling the most insistent and mordant criticisms at those laws on social grounds.[81] It must be concluded that Hart was misled by the variety of senses in which Blackstone uses the term 'indifferent'. All the examples advanced by Hart are of matters 'in which both the divine law and the natural leave a man at his own liberty; *but which are found necessary for the benefit of society to be restrained within certain limits*'. Hart quoted this description of 'indifferent points', but omitted the portion here emphasized.[82] The plain fact is that

[70] II, 228–31 [71] II, 233. [72] III, 430.

[73] Hart, 'Blackstone's Use of the Law of Nature' cites II, 2–3, 8–12, 208–12.

[74] II, 210, n. w. See Craig, *De jure feudale*, II, c. 13, § 15; Locke, *First treatise of civil government*, sec. 90.

[75] Cf. the very similar arguments in St German, op. cit. n. 65 above, at bk II, c. 10.

[76] II, 373–4. [77] II, 490–1. [78] I, 450. [79] *Ibid.* [80] II, 412.

[81] II, 412–16. IV, 173–4, 416.

[82] Hart, 'Blackstone's Use of the Law of Nature' at 171. (The passage from Blackstone is at I, 42.) Later on the same page, Hart notes, parenthetically, one of Blackstone's references to 'promoting the welfare of society' by regulating 'matters in themselves indifferent'. But Hart seems to give these phrases no weight in interpreting Blackstone. Cf. I, 126: '... laws...if they regulate and constrain our conduct in matters of mere indifference, without any good end in view, are laws destructive of liberty....'

considerations of 'the benefit of society' are in principle and in fact admitted by Blackstone.

III

With these standard obstacles to understanding Blackstone removed, it is possible to discern the role of the introductory discourse in the architecture of the *Commentaries*. Once again, since Blackstone is his best interpreter, we should look to his *Analysis* to establish what are the central notions of the introductory discourse (they are set out in footnote 30 above).

(1) First, there is the definition of law in general as a rule of action prescribed by a superior power. This stipulative (but also lexical) definition *per genus et differentiam* provides a characterization of the genus within which natural, divine, international, and municipal laws form differentiated species (secs 2, 3, 4, 5 of the analysis of Chapter I). The notions of command or prescription and of superior authority are introduced *ab initio*, and reappear in secs 6, 7, 8, and 9 of the analysis. Section 10 adverts to the defects of generality implicit in the idea of a 'rule'. Hence the interrelationship between sec. 1 and the remainder of the chapter is complete.

Of course, in the discourse itself, Blackstone predicates on this general definition a number of remarks about laws of nature in the physical sense, as patterns of action imposed by the Creator on creation. Hart has criticized this as a blurring of distinctions.[83] I do not wish to defend Blackstone against all charges of this sort; but it is worth pointing out that he is not the only jurist who has felt called upon to notice the similarities and connections as well as the differences and distinctions between physical 'laws' and moral or human laws. Hart himself has devoted some valuable pages to the ways in which even social, moral, and legal rules can be regarded from an 'external viewpoint' as simple 'regularities of observable behaviour' such as a scientific observer might record,[84] and some equally valuable pages on some of the constant human 'wants and fears'[85] that provide a stable function for law and thus a 'minimal natural law'.[86] Blackstone's distinction between what he calls laws of 'action in general' and laws of '*human* action' is poorly explained.[87] But at least it is insisted upon, and man's 'reason and freewill' are placed at the forefront of the discussion.[88]

[83] Hart, 'Blackstone's Use of the Law of Nature' at 170. A similar point is made in *CL* 187–8 [183–4].

[84] *CL* 88–9 [86–7].

[85] 'The only true and natural foundations of society are the wants and fears of individuals', I, 47. Cf. *CL* 193–200 [189–95].

[86] *CL* 193–200 [189–95].

[87] I, 39 (one of the weakest pages in the *Commentaries*).

[88] *Ibid.*

(2) Secondly, there is the definition of natural law as the rule of human action prescribed by the Creator and discoverable by reason. People often ask what relevance this notion has to the *Commentaries*, and conclude that it is a conventional ornament. But this notion is no more peripheral to Blackstone than a chapel was peripheral to the foundation of an English university college at any time between the thirteenth and nineteenth centuries. Whatever may be the case today, God's will for man was a subject of interest and concern, and the divine order of creation was reasonably seen as a pattern and precondition for man's ordering of his soul and thus of his society. The mere fact that municipal law could be given an autonomous definition was not regarded as a reason for ignoring questions of rational conscience.

Moreover, questions of conscience were integral to Blackstone's theoretical structure. For men's consciences, formed by the notion of natural rights conferred on them by the Creator, set up the trust upon which authority was conferred by peoples on governments.[89] And Blackstone, while insisting vigorously that *within constitutional and positive law* (for example, as a matter of judicial review, or of royal 'animadversion')[90] there was no restraint on parliamentary sovereignty, was cautiously willing to suppose that a basic violation by the government of its fundamental trust might amount to a dissolution of the constitution and a licence to the people to construct a new one.[91] Such a case, in Blackstone's view, would be one where 'though the positive laws are silent...nature and reason prevailed'.[92]

Furthermore, as promised, the 'primary rules and fundamental principles' of English law are indeed 'weighed and compared with the precepts of the law of nature'[93] as understood by Blackstone. The express references to particular implications of natural law and the 'state of nature' are so numerous that little more than a list of citations can here be offered,[94] with

[89] See I, 124, 127, 211. [90] I, 244. See also I, 91, 161–2.

[91] See I, 52, 161–2, 211, 213, 233, 244; IV, 440. [92] I, 245. [93] I, 36. See also I, 32.

[94] The following are some of the occasions for reference to natural law or the law of nature, roughly classified for convenience. I, 126–44 (individual rights); I, 211–13 (limitations on the Crown); I, 253 (ambassadors and *mala in se*); I, 365 (the poor laws); I, 423 (slavery); I, 447 (maintenance of children); I, 453 (maintenance of parents); I, 458 (maintenance of bastards); II, 2–3, 7–8, 293 (origins of property); II, 11 (succession by occupancy); II, 18 (property in water); II, 258–9 (occupation on death of tenant *pur autre vie*); II, 389, 392, 411 (animals *ferae naturae*); II, 438 (action popular); II, 455–7 (usury); III, 3 (self-defence); III, 31 (multiplicity of courts); III, 133 (need for certainty); III, 160–3 (*quantum meruit*, unjust enrichment, etc.); III, 168 (abatement of freehold); III, 208 (trespass); IV, 3 (basis of criminal law); IV, 7–11 (punishment); IV, 29 (*mala in se* and marital coercion); IV, 30 (*mala in se* and duress); IV, 42 (offences against private morality); IV, 66–71 (offences against law of nations); IV, 116 (self-defence); IV, 176–80 (homicide); IV, 199 (duelling); IV, 215–16 (sexual perversions); IV, 220 (arson); IV, 230 (larceny); IV, 242 (robbery); IV, 283 (*audi alteram partem*); IV, 320 (outlawry); IV, 416 (game laws). Contrast Barker, *Essays in Government*, at 138.

the warning that many 'reasons' advanced to explain features of English law might also count as natural law reasons though not advertised by Blackstone as such. Still, even a list should show why the first element in Blackstone's description of jurisprudence is that it is 'a science which distinguishes the criterions of right and wrong'.[95] Natural law is one criterion, and (as we have shown that Blackstone insisted) municipal law is quite another; a comparison is what seemed to Blackstone to be needed. Indeed, so interesting did such a comparison seem to Blackstone that he arranged the whole structure of the *Commentaries* to show how the rights and wrongs which were the *formal objects* of English law substantially (though not perfectly or inevitably)[96] corresponded to and protected the natural rights (but *not* natural duties)[97] which properly (that is, naturally) constituted its *material ends or objectives.* The first chapter of Book I explains this project in detail, and the introductory discourse is an indispensable preface.

(3) Thirdly, there is the notion of divine law, that part[98] of the natural law which God has revealed in the Holy Scriptures. Since it is merely the natural law in another mode, the divine law receives little separate discussion in the *Commentaries.* But its importance for Blackstone remains. It is, for him, of 'infinitely more authority' than any speculation on unrevealed natural law.[99] It is the basis of Christianity, and 'Christianity is part of the laws of England'.[100] Moreover:

> The belief of a future state of rewards and punishments, the entertaining just ideas of the moral attributes of the supreme being, and a firm persuasion that he superintends and will finally compensate every action in human life... these are the grand foundation of all judicial oaths....[101]

Above all, divine law (the basis of the established Church) was for Blackstone one of those available 'criterions of right and wrong' which in jurisprudence must be distinguished from municipal law with insistent care. He was loath to 'enter upon the detail of the several species of crimes and misdemeanours'[102] without having 'premised this caution':

> though part of the offences to be enumerated... are offences against the revealed law of God, others against the law of nature, and some are offences against

[95] I, 27. Note that Blackstone's first description of legal science is 'that science, which is to be the guardian of his natural rights and the rule of his civil conduct', I, 4.

[96] See e.g. I, 450–1, where children's natural right to education is said to be only defectively protected by English law. Also I, 365.

[97] See I, 124; IV, 41. [98] I, 42. [99] *Ibid.*

[100] IV, 59. Cf. Blackstone's speech in Parliament on 3 February 1769: 'When I see all religion made a mockery and jest of, it behoves me to vindicate my God and my King', Namier and Brooke, *The House of Commons 1754–1790*, 96.

[101] IV, 43–4. [102] IV, 41.

neither; yet in a treatise of municipal law we must consider them all as deriving their particular guilt, here punishable, from the law of man.[103]

This distinction was not a matter of merely analytical moment for Blackstone. It enabled him to insist upon the existence of private[104] moral duties 'which man is bound to perform considered only as an individual'[105] and hence of 'private vices' which in *foro conscientiae* are offences against divine law but which are (that is, ought to be) beyond the cognizance of human law because not 'attended with public inconvenience'.[106] This distinction between natural private duties and the natural private rights which the law of England providentially upholds was Blackstone's way of maintaining the classical tradition that crime and sin are not coextensive.

(4) The law of nations is the fourth notion prefaced to the discussion of municipal law. In Blackstone it occupies the same position in order of treatment as the *ius gentium* occupied in the scholastic treatise. But its meaning had shifted in Hooker from the law at once natural and positive, common to all societies, to a new meaning as the natural and contractual law governing relations between states.[107] Blackstone employs the newer meaning, though retaining formulae more appropriate to the old.[108]

The treatment of the law of nations is perfunctory, but not wholly so. It is not to be overlooked that the arrangement of Book IV follows that of the introductory discourse:

Crimes and Misdemeanors, cognizable by the Laws of ENGLAND, are such as more immediately offend, 1. The DIVINE Law [c. iv]. 2. The Law of NATIONS [c. v]. 3. The MUNICIPAL Law [cc. vi et seq.].[109]

It goes without saying that once again Blackstone insists on the formal distinction between offences against the law of nations, and offences against the law of nations 'as adopted by the law of England'[110]—despite his important doctrine that, *as a matter of fact*, the law of nations is 'a part of the law of the land' and 'adopted in its full extent by the common law'.[111]

[103] IV, 42.

[104] In Blackstone's terminology, 'absolute' as opposed to 'relative or social', I, 123.

[105] IV, 41. Also I, 123–4.

[106] IV, 42.

[107] *ST* I–II q.95 a.4; II–II q.57 a.3. Richard Hooker, *Of the Laws of Ecclesiastical Polity*, bk I, c. 10, §§ 12–13.

[108] I, 43. Traces of the old conception of *ius gentium* may be found in the citations on I, 43, and at II, 10: 'the universal law of almost every nation (which is a kind of secondary law of nature)'; II, 44, 258; III, 145.

[109] *Analysis* bk IV, c. iii, § 1. See I, 43; IV, 66.

[110] IV, 67. See also IV, 66, 68.

[111] IV, 67.

If further examples of the substantive relation between the introductory discourse and the contents of the *Commentaries* are desired, one might point to Blackstone's exposition and justification of the rule that foreign ambassadors lose their diplomatic immunity if they commit offences against natural law.[112]

(5) Sufficient has been said to show the organic yet differentiated relations between the definition of municipal law and the remainder of both introductory discourse and *Commentaries* as a whole.

(6) The last section of Blackstone's analysis of the introductory discourse that calls for any discussion here is the sixth: 'Society is formed for the protection of individuals, and States or governments for the preservation of society.' This statement is based on the orthodox contemporary theory of a double original contract;[113] but to say this does not exhaust the significance of Blackstone's theorem.

In the first place, it enabled Blackstone to cut through the debates of political theorists about the original contract to what he regarded as the essential principle of legal consequence:

> And this is what we mean by the original contract of society . . . : namely, that the whole should protect all its parts, and that every part should pay obedience to the will of the whole; or, in other words, that the community should guard the rights of each individual member, and that (in return for this protection) each individual should submit to the laws of the community; without which submission of all it was impossible that protection could be certainly extended to any.[114]

This principle of reciprocity is employed by Blackstone for the explanation and justification of many laws and institutions besides the state itself. In fact, since it is a principle which 'in *nature and reason* must always be understood and implied, in the very act of associating together',[115] it should be regarded as one of the most important elements of natural law thinking in the *Commentaries*. It expressly grounds a whole chapter on the king's duties;[116] the discussion of allegiance and citizenship;[117] the general theory of the merely civil rights of property and the various dependent doctrines of forfeitures;[118] the doctrine of action of debt upon judgment;[119] and by explicit analogy the notions of implied assumpsit on a *quantum meruit*, on a *quantum valebat*, and for money had and received, as well as the rules of

[112] I, 254; IV, 8.

[113] See Gierke, *Natural Law and the Theory of Society*, 107 n. 68 (ed. Barker, 1950).

[114] I, 47–8.

[115] I, 47–8 (emphasis added). See also I, 233, 366. Cf. II, 8.

[116] I, c. 6 (I, 233–7). See also IV, 139, where this notion of the duties of the superior to the inferior is accounted a central 'true principle' of government, radically distinguishing the genius of English law from the spirit of despotism.

[117] I, 366, 369–71; IV, 74, 77.

[118] I, 299; III, 161–2.

[119] III, 160.

account stated;[120] the doctrines of warranty of performance and fitness which have become the modern law of negligence and sale of goods;[121] the general theory of punishment of *mala* merely *prohibita*,[122] and the interesting and liberal discussion of capital punishment;[123] as well as the discussions of the constitutional implications of the Glorious Revolution,[124] of civil disobedience,[125] of papal usurpations and *praemunire*,[126] of parliamentary omnipotence,[127] of the principles of poor law reform,[128] and of recaption or reprisal.[129]

Next, this sixth heading of the introductory discourse provides the link (so important to Blackstone) between the formal juridical 'rights and wrongs' referred to in the definition of municipal law (sec. 5) and the natural and rational rights which English law successfully upheld. 'Society is formed for the protection of individuals', and English law (unlike some other systems) performed its trust.

Finally, the distinction drawn between the implied contract of society and the implied contract of government was employed by Blackstone to structure Book IV. For the theory produces the series: individual–society–government, and this is the series explicitly[130] employed to arrange all crimes after those against divine law and the law of nations: crimes against the king and government (IV, cc. vi–ix), against the commonwealth (IV, cc. x–xiii), and against individuals (IV, cc. xiv–xvii).

Thus, in sum, the concerns which Blackstone identified as central to his introductory discourse are shown to be central to the *Commentaries* themselves. And while the autonomy and the positivity of municipal law are strictly insisted upon, natural law is freely admitted as a source of law and jurisprudential explanation.

IV

None of the foregoing is intended as a defence of the content of Blackstone's theory of law. But by diverting attention from the superficial, a sound exegesis can reveal more fundamental objections to Blackstone's thought on the relations between natural and positive law. This is not the place to develop these objections, but the central problem should briefly be indicated.

[120] III, 161–3. [121] III, 165–6. [122] IV, 8. [123] IV, 9–11.
[124] I, 210–13, 245. [125] I, 250–1; IV, 82. [126] IV,110, 371. [127] I, 160–2.
[128] I, 365. [129] III, 4.
[130] IV, 42–3, 176, 250. See also the last contents page of the *Analysis*.

For Blackstone the 'state of nature' means not a historical state of affairs, but the condition of man considered as an individual, in abstraction from all social (or at least all civil) relations.[131] Reflection on this state of nature is the source of most of the rules of natural law identified by Blackstone. The state of nature is one of equality, liberty, and community of property (subject only to qualified individual rights of occupation and use), where every man has the right to punish infringements of these natural rights.[132] For example, since occupancy is a natural right, robbery and arson are natural offences; but larceny is only partially so, since most property rights are merely civil.[133]

At the same time, this state of nature is one attended by so many evils that a system of positive law is primitive and contemptible the more closely it approximates to it.[134] Moreover, the boundaries of the state of nature are ambiguous: when man is considered as an individual, is it permissible to consider him as husband of a wife and father of a family? And if, as Blackstone admits,[135] the family is a *natural* society, why are not also larger communities answering to other 'wants and fears of individuals'? If the rights and duties between parent and child and husband and wife are natural and extend, beyond mere respect for liberty, to duties of care and maintenance,[136] why should civil rights and duties be more limited or less natural?

Furthermore, the notion of a state of nature as the source of natural rights seems unable to account for the data. Blackstone lists reputation and good name among the natural individual rights upheld by English law,[137] and the classification seems appropriate until one reflects that reputation and good name are inconceivable in abstraction from society. Blackstone's explanation of his classification is interesting: 'without these it is impossible to have the perfect enjoyment of any other advantage or right'.[138] The explanation attempts, but fails, to disguise the fact that what is being discussed is a natural and social want: a desire to be well regarded by one's fellows.

So at this point the question becomes urgent: What is the relation between the state of nature and that pursuit of man's 'true and substantial happiness' which Blackstone described in his introductory discourse[139] as the single foundation of natural law? This question may prompt another: What is the relation between the 'self-love' that for Blackstone is the

[131] I, 123. [132] IV, 7. [133] IV, 220, 230, 242; II, 3, 258; I, 138.
[134] III, 327, Cf. III, 4. See also III, 168; I, 193, 213. [135] I, 47, 422.
[136] I, 422, 447, 453. [137] I, 134; III, 123–7. [138] I, 134.
[139] I, 41.

'universal principle of action' and guide to the content of natural law,[140] and the self-love that for Aristotle is the root of friendship, which in turn is the motive[141] and greatest good[142] of social life and the *polis*? These Aristotelian notions are explicitly the heart of the notion that the state is an association or community whose object is the full actualization of its members in the good, noble, independent, and happy life.[143]

In Blackstone's explicit theory, society and law *add* little or nothing to human life; their role is preservative.[144] Correspondingly, natural law looks back to the naked individual in his state of nature as a standard. Again, since natural law can be completely stated in abstraction from society, there is little relation of derivation between natural and positive law.

As against St German's thesis that

> in every law positive well made is somewhat of the law of reason and of the law of God; and to discern the law of God and the law of reason from the law positive is very hard...[145]

one finds Blackstone's disconcerting but express thesis that the bulk of human laws has no foundation in nature.[146] The various theories of derivation in Aquinas, Hooker, and St German[147] have all disappeared and have not been replaced. It is this impoverishment that lends substance to Hart's theory discussed above.[148]

Similarly, the concept of the common good, the component values of which might ground the varying manifold of positive laws, has virtually disappeared.[149] The only natural good is individual and pre-social, and the great ends of the law are the protection of pre-existing individual rights.[150] Of course, not even the law of the eighteenth century could adequately be accounted for, in the way Blackstone desired, with this limited theoretical apparatus. Ends deriving from the positive programme of western civilization have occasionally to be admitted: to explain laws on sexual matters, Blackstone has to allow that 'one end of society and government'

[140] I, 40–1. [141] *Pol.* 1280b39.

[142] *Ibid.* at 1262b7. Also *NE* 1167b5–16. [143] *Pol.* 1280a7–1281a9.

[144] Cf. Gierke's description of Locke's 'insurance' theory of society: *Natural Law and the Theory of Society*, 113 n. 110. Aristotle ridiculed the theory: *Pol.* 1280b5–1281a4.

[145] St German, *Doctor and Student*, bk I, c. 4. St German continues: 'And though it be hard, yet it is much necessary in every moral doctrine, and in all laws made for the commonwealth.' This is the challenge to which Blackstone responds, but unsuccessfully.

[146] I, 55.

[147] *ST* I–II q.95 a.2. Hooker, *Laws of Ecclesiastical Polity*, bk I, c. 10, § 10. St German, *Doctor and Student*, bk 1, cc. 5–7.

[148] See text at n. 63 above.

[149] It makes faint and skeletal appearances in passages such as I, 45 ('subsistence and peace of the society'); I, 125 ('general advantage of the public'); I, 126 ('common utility'); I, 129 ('public convenience'); I, 139 ('common good').

[150] I, 48, 124; II, 15.

is to prohibit promiscuity.[151] But in general, the category of end—so essential to Blackstone's whole explanatory and apologetical purpose—is eliminated from his *ex professo* theory of law.

The immediate consequence of these theoretical inadequacies is the confusion and terminological inexactitudes which have so muddled the interpretation of Blackstone. We have already tabulated some of the unadvertised shifts in the meaning of 'matters indifferent in themselves'.[152] For Blackstone to have adverted to these shifts would have raised the problem—for him unanswerable—of the differing modes of derivation of positive laws from natural values. For the same reason, Blackstone cannot explain the status of the 'principles of society' to which he often appeals, but which are neither natural nor merely positive.[153]

As a further consequence, because the state of nature is an ambiguous and impoverished explanatory category, because natural and positive law lack intelligible modes of interconnection, and because superior will rather than reasonable connection between end and means is made the basis of obligation,[154] Blackstone's theory is not only unable to account for his data or even his terminology but also in danger of collapsing into a positivism that will regard explanation as extraneous to the exposition of law.

The finest fruits of Blackstone's method were almost the last; they may be seen in Sir William Jones's *Essay on the Law of Bailments* (1781).[155] The essay has three parts, denominated *analytical*, *historical*, and *synthetical*. For Jones, to treat a set of rules analytically is to trace 'every part of it up to the first principles of natural reason';[156] to treat it historically is to show the extent to which various legal systems conform to these first principles; and to treat it synthetically is to restate the law by way of (a) definitions, (b) rules, (c) propositions derived from the combination of (b) with (a), and (d) exceptions to the propositions.[157] The definitions will derive principally from the experience and complexity of English law, while the rules 'may be considered as axioms flowing from natural reason, good morals and sound policy'[158] as verified against the vast comparative learning of the 'historical' survey.[159] How different from the programme announced by

[151] I, 438. [152] See n. 64 above.

[153] See e.g. I, 131; III, 168. See also citations in n. 108 above.

[154] See also Rinck, 'Blackstone and the Law of Nature' at 163, 166, 168, 173–4.

[155] For Jones, Blackstone's *Commentaries* were 'the most correct and beautiful outline, that ever was exhibited of any human science', *An Essay on the Law of Bailments*, 3.

[156] Jones (1781) 4. [157] *Ibid.*, 127. [158] *Ibid.*, 119.

[159] *Ibid.*, 11–116. Jones was the greatest comparative legal scholar of his age, and died in the midst of an immense study of Hindu and Islamic law.

Bentham in his *Fragment on Government* (1776) and thereafter followed by analytical jurisprudence:

To the province of the *Expositor* it belongs to explain to us what, as he supposes, the Law *is*: to that of the *Censor*, to observe to us what he thinks it *ought to be*. The former, therefore, is principally occupied in stating, or in enquiring after *facts*: the latter, in discussing *reasons*. The *Expositor*, keeping within his sphere, has no concern with any other faculties of the mind than the *apprehension*, the *memory*, and the *judgment*: the latter, in virtue of those sentiments of pleasure or displeasure which he finds occasion to annex to the objects under his review, holds some intercourse with the *affections*.[160]

This epistemology prevailed, and the notion was lost that any useful exposition of law will require an imaginative and sympathetic insight into the intelligible values which ground all human effort, which issue in general principles and which ramify into the manifold of particular rules variously derived according to convenience and circumstance.

After the spread of the Benthamite positivism, the sense of the natural law enterprise was forgotten and (despite the eclipse of Bentham's epistemology) it has remained usual to believe that the heart of any theory of natural law is not the problem of the varying derivation of positive from natural law, but the thesis that positive law is 'for all purposes' void if it contradicts natural law.[161] Thus Blackstone's introductory discourse and definition of municipal law have standardly been interpreted on the assumption that any discussion of the relation between natural and positive law must be headed for an assertion or denial of that crude slogan, *lex iniusta non est lex*. The foregoing remarks should help to show that the *content* of Blackstone's theory made such misunderstandings plausible, but that Blackstone's theoretical *intentions* were far more interesting and complex.

[160] Bentham, *A Fragment on Government*, 98–9 (Montague ed.). It was this analysis that, broadly speaking, prevailed in analytical jurisprudence, and not the notion which Bentham somewhat inconsistently introduced (at 117–22) that an expositor could not properly (i.e. 'naturally') arrange his work without first establishing a complete 'synopsis' or 'map' of the legal system (all legal systems) in terms of the tendency of actions to produce pain or pleasure.

[161] Cf. *CL* 207–12 [203–7].

9

WEBER, OBJECTIVITY, AND LEGAL-RATIONAL AUTHORITY*

I

Of the hidden streams nourishing jurisprudence in Oxford during the past thirty years, the work of Max Weber is among the most significant. Tracing out that influence will not be simple. Anthony Kronman's *Max Weber*[1] may well arouse an interest in this project of cultural history. But the book is not concerned at all with Weber's influence,[2] and this essay, too, is concerned only with the issues of jurisprudential method raised by Kronman.

Kronman's powerful and suggestive book offers a tightly integrated interpretation of Weber's theory of law (and of authority, economy, and religion). It is an interpretation intended to show that Weber's social theory not only is concerned with a single subject—the development of the institutions and forms of thought characteristic of modernity—but also has 'an overarching conceptual unity' (2). That unity derives, according to Kronman, from Weber's 'theory of value and the distinctive conception of personhood associated with it' (4). Kronman's own most striking thesis

* 1985b ('On "Positivism" and "Legal-Rational Authority"').

[1] In the series *Jurists: Profiles in Legal Theory* (Edward Arnold and Stanford University Press, 1983). Parenthetical references to page numbers in the text are to this book. The present essay does not attempt a full description or assessment of the book's many qualities.

[2] Kronman, *Max Weber* 194 remarks that Winch, *The Idea of a Social Science*,

> establishes an intellectual link (though not an historical one) between Weber and those social and legal philosophers, such as Hart, who have been influenced by the Wittgensteinian notion of rule-governed behaviour (anticipated by Weber's own treatment of the same concept in his *Critique of Stammler*).

It is not quite clear why Kronman wishes to contrast intellectual with historical links, in this context. As MacCormick says (very cautiously),

> Hart's adoption of a variant on [one of the most important elements in Weber's sociological thought] appears to have been filtered wholly or in part through his reading of Winch, op. cit., 57–65. (MacCormick, *H.L.A. Hart*, 166 (cf. 30).)

I would say 'in part' rather than 'wholly' (for reasons quite apart from the fact that Weber's work was mediated to Oxford jurisprudence not only by Winch but also by e.g. Kelsen, *GTLS* 171–2, 175–8, 188). [On the reasons I had in mind in 1985, see endnote †.]

goes beyond the interpretation of Weber's theory of society, and even beyond the views of Weber concerning the proper methodology of such a theory. Kronman's thesis concerns the fact that in Weber's typology of authority relations, one type—legal-rational authority—has a 'conceptual' or 'logical' primacy, a 'privileged position in the sense that it is taken to provide the standpoint from which the other two types [traditional and charismatic] are to be understood' (50, 55). This fact deserves, but has not often received, the prominence Kronman gives it. But his thesis is more arresting. It is that Weber 'was bound', by reason of 'certain logical or conceptual considerations', to 'accord this form of authority a privileged place in his classification of the various pure types of domination', 'because legal-rational authority is the one form of domination whose fundamental principle of legitimation expresses what Weber considered to be the truth about values' (52, 55).

For 'the truth about values', according to Weber, is that 'all norms, regardless of their content' 'must be created by men', a truth or opinion labelled by Kronman the principle of the *positivity of values*, or *principle of positivity* (55). And 'among the various types of domination, only legal-rational authority is based upon an explicit endorsement of this same [positivistic] conception of normativity':

> Every form of authority exemplifies this principle (in the sense that all authority relationships rest upon humanly created norms) but only legal-rational authority employs the principle of positivity as the basis of legitimation. (55)

'[I]t is this feature of legal-rational authority', he adds, 'which gives it its peculiarly self-conscious character', 'a self-consciousness which traditional authority lacks' and which 'explains the priority Weber assigns [to legal-rational authority] in his classificatory scheme' (55).

Kronman's thesis thus has four components:

(1) To understand the pure types of authority (each of which 'is based upon a distinct conception of legitimacy' (43)), 'and, indeed, [to understand] the structure of authority relationships in general', one must first understand that pure type of authority which appeals to a principle or method of legitimation or justification which is or rests upon a *true* theory of value, that is, upon a true or warranted 'epistemological assumption' about the way (the only way) that values can be established (52, 53).

(2) The legal-rational pure type of authority, as identified by Weber, explicitly and with self-consciousness 'embraces the principle that [all] norms must be created by men' (55), and that 'binding social

norms have no existence apart from those purposeful human acts of human legislation that bring them into being' (53).

(3) Weber believed that it is a truth of epistemology that all norms must be created by men; all principles or methods of legitimating authority, other than the legal-rational method, lack self-consciousness in that they deny or fail to acknowledge a truth about human value, about 'is' and 'ought', about the 'conceptual distinction' and 'separation of facts and values' (66–7).

From these three premises, it follows that:

(4) Weber was bound to give explanatory and conceptual priority to the accurately self-conscious legal-rational pure type of authority.

I shall consider the three premises in turn.

II

The first premise or component in Kronman's thesis is, broadly, that in descriptive and explanatory social theory, the concepts one uses to describe, classify, and explain existing and past human institutions, attitudes, and practices had better be concepts one would oneself use in a philosophically critical account of the power and limitations of human knowledge. Suppose, for example, that philosophical argument shows that particular actions can be justified only by first *choosing* (without any justifying reason) to treat something as a value and then (all the time treating the chosen value as valuable just because chosen) assessing the actions in question in terms of their conformity to the chosen value. On this supposition, the concepts to be employed in describing the human affairs studied in sociology or history had better be concepts used, or at least usable, in the self-conscious practices of persons whose beliefs include or are at least consistent with this philosophically warranted position.

The sense of this thesis will be clearer if we look at what is involved in selecting concepts for use in descriptive and explanatory social theory. Here, and throughout, I use Weber's sociology as the exemplar, because of its fundamental good sense and realism in seeking to understand social action, social relationships, and social order by understanding those actions and dispositions of human individuals which constitute those social actions, relationships, and forms of order. On opening Weber, we sense immediately that we have left behind the fog of abstraction that renders so much social theory barely intelligible and certainly untestable. We sense, too, that we have rejoined the great cooperative effort to understand human society without illusions, which Aristotle launches with the opening sentence of his *Politics*:

Observation shows us, first, that every *polis* is a species of association, and, secondly, that all associations are instituted for the purpose of attaining some good—for all men do all their acts with a view to achieving something which is, in their view, a good.[3]

Weber, no doubt, will refine and complexify our conception of what it is to act 'with a view to…', and will expand our knowledge of the things men have believed worth doing. But the Weberian programme is part of Aristotle's, a programme which Aquinas, in his reflective introduction to the *Politics*, defines as seeking knowledge of social wholes by careful consideration of their parts and their *principia*, their intelligible originating factors, particularly the (more or less) intelligent human *doings* (as distinct from *makings*) that actually constitute those social wholes,[4] doings which are to be understood by understanding their motivating *objectives*.

So: the empirical existence of that form of social relationship which we call authority (or 'domination') is understood when we distinguish the regularities of behaviour involved in authority-compliance relationships from those involved in such relationships as robbery, monopolistic or cartel control of a market, dominance in a discussion group, and so forth. The distinction is made by adverting to the beliefs of the persons involved in the relationship, in particular their beliefs as to the obligatoriness or peculiar propriety (in short, the legitimacy) of behaving as they do. As Weber puts it, there is authoritative domination when the manifested will or directive of the ruler(s) is meant to influence the conduct of the ruled and actually does influence it as if the ruled had made the content of the directive the maxim of their conduct for its very own sake.[5] This the ruled will do just insofar as they ascribe to the directive, and to its issuance from that author, some sort of legitimacy. Such ascriptions are made for many reasons; but these reasons or motivations tend to cluster into three or four characteristic types ('ideal' or, better put, 'pure' types):

(1) belief in the legality of enacted rules and in the right of those exercising authority under such rules to issue the directives in question;

[3] *Pol.* I.1: 1252a1. [4] Aquinas, *In Pol.*, proem.

[5] Weber, *Economy and Society*, 946, 941–5, 212–15, 31–2. It may be helpful to add the equivalent page references in widely used editions of portions of Weber's treatise, editions which, moreover, supply the English translations used (with emendations) by Roth and Wittich: viz., Weber, *Max Weber: The Theory of Social and Economic Organisation*, 324–8, 124–5; Weber, *Max Weber on Law in Economy and Society*, 328, 322–7.

(2) belief in the sanctity of immemorial traditions, and in the personal authority of the chief who issues directives from within a traditionally sanctioned sphere of authority binding even upon him;

(3) belief and trust in the revelatory, heroic, saintly, or exemplary qualities of an exceptional individual and in the novel directives revealed or ordained by him.[6]

Here, then, are three types of authority. Only very exceptionally is any one of them to be found instantiated in history in a pure form, unmixed with elements of the other.[7] For the *beliefs* on the basis of which authority is ascribed to those who actually exercise it are rarely simple. Indeed, Weber says, 'In the case of *legal authority*, it is never purely legal. The belief in legality comes to be established and habitual, and this means that it is partly traditional....'[8] Similarly, purely traditional authorities

> have never been stable indefinitely and, as is also true of bureaucratic authority [the specific instrument of legal rational authority], have seldom been without a head who had a personally charismatic status by heredity or office.[9]

But none of this suggests that it is useless to try to understand the history of many communities, including our own, in terms of the meaningful clusters of features picked out by concepts such as legal-rational, traditional, and charismatic authority.

The significance of the clustering together of the features picked out by any one of these concepts is carefully illustrated by Weber. He begins with legal authority 'in order to make it possible later to contrast the others with it'.[10] That is to say, as he remarks at the outset of the corresponding chapters of explanation, 'we shall proceed from the type that is the most rational and the one most familiar to us....'[11] (Note the easy conjunction of 'most rational' with 'most familiar to us', of rationality and modernity.) This, then, is the 'conceptual primacy' which Kronman noted and seeks to account for: what we might call an explanatory priority.

What does explanatory priority amount to? Well, look at Weber explaining a pure type to which he does not ascribe such priority, for

[6] Weber, *Economy and Society*, 215–16 (= *Max Weber: The Theory of Social and Economic Organisation*, 328–9).

[7] *Ibid.*, 216, 262 (= 329, 382). [8] *Ibid.*, 263 (= 382). [9] *Ibid.*

[10] *Ibid.*, 217 (= 329 n. 5).

[11] Weber, *Economy and Society*, 954 (omitted from *Max Weber on Law in Economy and Society*, 337).

example traditional authority: he does it largely by a series of privations, that is, of negations of the features of legal-rational rule:

The person exercising authority is *not* a 'superior', but a personal master, his administrative staff does *not* consist mainly of officials but of personal retainers, and the ruled are *not* 'members' of an association but are either his traditional 'comrades' or his 'subjects'. Personal loyalty, *not* the official's impersonal duty, determines the relations of the administrative staff to the master. Obedience is owed *not* to enacted rules but to the person who occupies a position of authority by tradition... In the pure type case of traditional authority it is *impossible* for law or administrative rule to be deliberately created by legislation... In the pure type of traditional rule, the following features of a bureaucratic administrative staff are *absent*: (a) a clearly defined sphere of competence 'subject to impersonal administrative rules, (b) a rationally established hierarchy, (c) a regular system of appointment on the basis of free contract, and orderly promotion, (d) technical training as a regular requirement, (e) (frequently) fixed salaries, in the type case paid in money... *In place of* a well-defined functional jurisdiction, there is a conflicting series of tasks and powers which at first are assigned at the master's discretion.[12]

And traditional rule tends to negate the distinction between private right and public authority; wherever traditional rule develops an administrative staff, there will be an assimilation of the ruler's authority to the status of an economic good, which can be sold, pledged as security, or divided by inheritance; where this assimilation is extended to the administrative staff itself, we have a very widespread type of patrimonial rule in which, Weber says, 'the decisive fact is that, regardless of content, governing powers and the related emoluments are treated as private rights'.[13]

The explanatory description of charismatic forms of authority follows the same strategy of contrast with the features of legal-rational authority.

Could the order of these accounts have been reversed? Could the forms of authority have been as well explained by treating first the charismatic pure type, and describing the traditional and the legal-rational by a series of negations? This is not a question of formal logic, which can readily generate an affirmative proposition out of a series of negations. The question rather concerns the formation and selection of the concepts to be used in the account. The proposed account is to be an account of *authority*, as distinct from other forms of motivation whereby one person 'follows' the directives of another. We hope to differentiate authority from terrorism or highway robbery, and from coordinations of action by constellations

[12] *Ibid.*, 227, 229 (= *Max Weber: The Theory of Social and Economic Organisation*, 341, 343) (emphasis added).

[13] *Ibid.*, 237; also 232 (= *Max Weber: The Theory of Social and Economic Organisation*, 353, 347).

of interest such as the relations between the monopolist and the others in his market.[14] But if we treated, say, charismatic rule as primary, main elements of authority would not come into view (except as apparently arbitrary importations into the accounts of the secondary forms): for example, the elementary distinction between exercises of authority by the ruler and mere expressions of his personal wishes. Similarly, if we treated traditional rule as primary, we would have no account (save by subsequent importation) of that elementary feature of authoritative rule, *legislative enactment*, the introduction, on the ruler's authority, of a *new* 'standing order' or general rule. Moreover, as we have seen from Weber's account of traditional patrimonial rule, we would lose sight of such elementary distinctions as that between public and private powers of control, or between acting as representative of the community, in some common interest, and acting as curator of one's private or family fortunes.

I have been suggesting an explanation of Weber's decision to give an expository and, in that sense at least, an explanatory priority to the legal-rational form of authority and legitimation. I have not appealed, and neither does Weber, to Kronman's principle that priority in social theory should be given to concepts justifiable in a philosophically critical epistemology.

Still, that principle has some attractions. A philosophically critical epistemology is attained by asking intelligent questions, and to the extent that it is a warranted or true epistemology is relatively invulnerable to further questions. A social order, or method of legitimation, which makes unwarranted assumptions about the source or status of its aims and methods is vulnerable to questions. No social order can suppress human questioning (though some can sometimes suppress, for a very long time, many of the results of such questioning); so one can discern a kind of instability in social orders resting on untrue assumptions about human good and the principles of social order. But what is at stake in determining method in social theory is not 'What is the wave of the future?' or 'What is the long-term successful social order?' We do not know how the human mix of good and evil, truth and error, will work out in the long term. What is at stake for us is explanatory power. A social order, actual or conceivable, resting on mistakes about human good is relatively opaque or unintelligible (because to some extent unintelligent).

One may, however, hesitate to affirm Kronman's first premise in all its universality. For it asserts that authority is to be understood primarily in

[14] Cf. *ibid.*, 214, 942–6 (= *Max Weber: The Theory of Social and Economic Organisation*, 326; *Max Weber on Law in Economy and Society*, 323–8).

terms of that pure type of authority which rests on an epistemologically warranted theory of value. But what if epistemology warrants no authority, but rather demonstrates that all forms of authority are illegitimate, unjustifiable claims by one human being upon another? What is it about legal-rational authority that makes it invulnerable to critical questions about its justifiability as directive of human action? Should we not be cautious, and accept Kronman's first premise just to this extent: that if there is a form of authority and corresponding principle of legitimation which is critically justified, then that form has an explanatory priority relative to forms of authority and principles of legitimation which are vulnerable to the critical questions of epistemology.

It is clearly time to look at Kronman's treatment of legal-rational authority and legitimation.

III

Kronman's second premise is that legal-rational authority rests upon an assumption which corresponds to the epistemological claim that 'binding social norms have no existence apart from those purposeful acts of human legislation that bring them into being' (53).

Now it is clear that legal-rational authority, as explained by Weber, is differentiated from traditional authority precisely by its assumption or postulate that binding social norms can be created by acts of legislation; indeed, it is differentiated also from charismatic authority by its postulate that such norms can become binding without the authority of inspiration or at least can, once made, remain binding without the continued sponsorship of an inspired author.

But Kronman slides from 'some' to 'all'. It does not follow that legal-rational systems of domination appeal for their legitimacy *exclusively* to acts of legislation. And in fact, the great teachers of western lawyers, say, Aristotle, Cicero, Gaius, Ulpian, Augustine, Justinian, Aquinas, St Germain, and Blackstone, all without exception deny that a system of legal-rational authority rests exclusively on acts of legislation. They all flatly deny the epistemological thesis which Kronman makes characteristic of rational-legal thought: that 'binding social norms have no existence apart from… purposeful acts of human legislation'. Yet these, especially Aristotle and Aquinas,[15] are the very theorists who most vigorously affirm the capacity of a human act of legislation to make binding what was, before that act, in no way binding. All take care to show that this significance

[15] *NE* V.7: 1134b19–24; *ST* I–II q.95 a.2c.

of the purely positive, of sheer legislation, must be explained by appeal to pre-existing, non-posited principles, binding (on legislator and subject alike) independently of any act of legislation.

Nor is this a freak of western intellectual history. Consider what Kronman says:

> … only legal-rational authority acknowledges the basic distinction between facts and values that is central to Weber's own theory of value. Traditional authority conflates 'is' with 'ought': from a traditionalist point of view, it is the age-old existence of a practice or institution which gives it legitimacy and normative force…Any argument intended to establish the legitimacy of a particular rule from a legal-rational point of view must…appeal to the fact that it, or some other rule, has been enacted in the proper way. (53)

Have we not here some conflating of fact with value, of 'is' with 'ought'? Kronman continues with a trace of unease:

> But this 'fact', unlike those invoked by all traditionalist justifications of power, has normative significance only because it is itself the product of, or more precisely, because it *consists in*, a deliberate and wilful act of norm-creation, an act of legislation. Legal-rational authority rests on the epistemological assumption that values can only be established in this way…(53)

I have observed that the last proposition is simply not true of the last two and a half millennia of legal-rational authority. But look at the preceding proposition: an act of legislation has normative significance only because it consists in a deliberate and wilful act of…legislation! What do we have here? *Reason*, the intelligent and rational, the epistemologically justified…? Or rather, dogmatism pure and simple, if not a belief in magic…? Someone's directive has normative significance, binding me to act or not act, *just* because he issued his directive deliberately and wilfully as a directive…To say the least, such a principle of legitimation is not invulnerable to questions.

Nor have such questions been lacking in the history of legal-rational orders. It is just such obvious questions that created the constant market for explanations such as those offered by Aristotle, Cicero, and Aquinas.

It is time to point out that Weber rejects Kronman's second premise. Kronman, for all his familiarity with Weber's works, has simply overlooked Weber's principal observations on the problem of legitimacy, particularly legal-rational legitimacy. We can begin with a fact that Kronman does notice (44n): although Weber usually speaks of three pure types of method or principle of legitimation, there is one place (prominent because it is precisely Weber's first mention of legitimation) where he lists *four*—tradition, affectual faith in the revealed or exemplary, positive enactment believed to be legal, and 'value-rational faith: valid is that which has been deduced as an absolute'.[16] Weber's explanation here is brief:

The purest type of legitimacy based on value-rationality is *natural law*...its logically deduced propositions...must be distinguished from those of revealed, enacted, and traditional law.[17]

One notices the uneasiness in an account which focuses on logical deduction without inquiring into the premises for the deductions. Kronman makes nothing of this. He simply observes (44n) that what Weber means by 'natural law' is not clear, and says not a word more. But Weber himself offers his profoundest reflections on legal legitimacy in the pages overlooked by Kronman.

The most important discussion is headed by Weber 'Natural Law as the Normative Standard of Positive Law'. It begins by remarking that conceptions of the rightness of law are sociologically relevant within a rational, positive, legal order only insofar as they give rise to practical consequences for the behaviour of legislators, legal practitioners, and other persons interested in the law, in other words

when practical legal life is materially affected by the conviction of the particular 'legitimacy' of certain legal maxims, and of the directly binding force of certain principles which are not to be disrupted by any concessions to positive law imposed by mere power.[18]

So Weber's discussion is going to describe, not endorse, the claims made by those with natural law conceptions. And what is such a conception?

Natural law is the sum total of all those norms which are valid independently of, and superior to, any positive law and which owe their dignity not to arbitrary enactment but, on the contrary, provide the very legitimation for the binding force of positive law. Natural law has thus been the collective term for those norms which owe their legitimacy not to their origin from a legitimate lawgiver, but to their immanent and teleological qualities.[19]

And now Weber adds what seems to be his own assessment of the whole problem of legitimating authority:

It [natural law] is *the specific and only consistent type of legitimacy of a legal order* which can remain once religious revelation and the authoritarian sacredness of a tradition and its bearers have lost their force.[20]

[16] Weber, *Economy and Society*, 36 (= *Max Weber: The Theory of Social and Economic Organisation*, 130).

[17] *Ibid.*, 37 (= 131).

[18] *Ibid.*, 866 (= *Max Weber on Law in Economy and Society*, 287).

[19] Weber, *Economy and Society*, 867 (= 287–8).

[20] *Ibid.* (emphasis added).

That is: when charismatic and traditional forms of authority have given way to the legal-rational, nothing but principles of natural law could provide a consistent type of legitimacy specifically for the legal order.‡

Weber's truthfulness is the cause of his lasting value. The predicament of modernity is spelled out in full (only to be overlooked by so competent a modern man as Kronman). In the past,

> natural law dogmas have influenced more or less considerably both lawmaking and lawfinding.... Formally, they have strengthened the tendency towards logically abstract law, especially the power of logic in legal thinking.[21]

But now things are different:

> All metajuristic axioms in general have been subject to ever continuing disintegration and relativization. In consequence of both juridical rationalism and modern intellectual scepticism in general, the axioms of natural law have lost all capacity to provide the fundamental basis of the legal system.... Consequently, legal positivism has, at least for the time being, advanced irresistibly.... In the great majority of its most important provisions, [the law] has been unmasked all too visibly, indeed, as the product or the technical means of a compromise between conflicting interests.
>
> But this extinction of the metajuristic implications of the law is one of those ideological developments which, while they have increased scepticism towards the dignity of the particular rules of a concrete legal order, have also effectively promoted the actual obedience to the power, now viewed solely from an instrumentalist standpoint, of the authorities who claim legitimacy at the moment. Among the practitioners of the law this attitude has been particularly pronounced.[22]

(This was written, one will recall, in Germany and not long before 1920. The claim made in the last sentence quoted was to be confirmed by Weber's philosophical friend, Gustav Radbruch, who after close acquaintance with the matter accused 'legal positivism' of encouraging supine acceptance of Hitler's legally authorized regime.[23])

The moral is not far below the surface of Weber's text. Insofar as contemporary legal and social thought denies that there are any principles valid by reason just of their intrinsic point and content, it rejects the only consistent justification of legal authority.

Two things follow. First, in continuing to accept such authority as legitimate, (these) modern men think and act without consistent reason,

[21] *Ibid.*, 873 (= *Max Weber on Law in Economy and Society*, 296). [22] *Ibid.*, 874–5 (= 298).

[23] See Friedmann, 'Gustav Radbruch' at 205; and the sources cited by Hart, 'Positivism and the Separation of Law and Morals' reprinted with additions in Hart, *Essays in Jurisprudence and Philosophy*, 50, 73–5. If Radbruch thus showed, as Hart says (*ibid.*, 74), 'extraordinary naivety', it was a naïvety which (as the passage just quoted shows) he shared with Max Weber, whom most will judge hard-headed and perceptive.

that is, irrationally. Weber brings himself to admit this. In a section entitled 'Natural Law and Vocational Ethics', he again offers a portrait of the modern state, prefaced by the remark that in

the medieval... traditionalistic ethics of vocation... relationships of domination have a character to which one may apply ethical requirements in the same way that one applies them to every personal relationship... Today, however, the *homo politicus*, as well as the *homo economicus*, performs his duty best when he acts... sheerly in accordance with the impersonal duty imposed by his calling... All politics is oriented [today] to *raison d'état*, to realism, and to the autonomous end of maintaining the external and internal distribution of power. These goals... must necessarily seem completely senseless from the religious point of view. Yet only in this way does the realm of politics acquire a peculiarly rational mystique of its own.[24]

Secondly, as the assimilation of *homo politicus* to *homo economicus* confirms, the differentiation between authority and constellations of interest is fundamentally obscured in such an attitude.

On both these counts, the very reasons which Weber himself had for giving legal-rational authority expository and explanatory priority in the sociology of authority—reasons concerning both superior rationality and increased differentiation from other ways of orientating social action, for example from constellations of interests—indicate that legal-rational authority can fully merit that priority only on condition that it itself (precisely as a source of purely positive laws as well as of laws *jure gentium*) is legitimated in the substantively- or value-rational mode, that is, by belief in some principles of the type traditionally labelled 'natural law'.

IV

Yet Weber himself, as Kronman's third premise says, did assert that belief in natural law is unreasonable or unwarranted faith. That is easy to understand, given his account of natural law theory:

'Nature' and 'Reason' are the substantive criteria of what is legitimate from the standpoint of natural law. Both are regarded as the same, and so are the rules derived from them, so that general propositions about regularities of factual occurrences and general norms of conduct are held to coincide.... The 'ought' is identical with the 'is', i.e., that which exists in the universal average....[25]

Thus some other characteristics of modernity begin to come into view: for example, that one of the most learned, and most representative of really

[24] Weber, *Economy and Society*, 600–1.
[25] *Ibid.*, 869 (= *Max Weber on Law in Economy and Society*, 290–1).

learned men of the modern age, himself not ignorant of Greek or Latin, can thus be simply unaware, or blankly uncomprehending, of the main lines of the classic philosophical and theological account(s) of practical reason, an account in which 'regularities of factual occurrences' and 'general norms of conduct' (let alone 'the universal average'), so far from being considered to 'coincide', are quite sharply and self-consciously distinguished.[26]

But, of course, the problem goes deeper than mere, grotesque misunderstandings of (some possible uses of) the (in any case not too happy) term 'natural law'. Here we are in the principal domain of that epistemological principle called by Kronman the positivity of values. As Kronman says:

> In Weber's view, the meaning of the world is something that can only be established by an act of will, by the deliberate imposition of some meaning-giving value on the world (which considered by itself, constitutes a meaningless series of amoral occurrences devoid of normative significance). (54)

Hilary Putnam has credited Weber with introducing 'the modern fact-value distinction', by which he means the modern denial of 'the objectivity of value judgments'[27]. Putnam treats Weber as having had one argument for that denial, and a bad argument at that: that people, or educated people, in fact disagree about values. The argument is indeed as weak as Putnam says, but Weber had others which Putnam and Kronman tacitly ignore.

There was, for example, the neo-Kantian argument that all judgments must rest upon presuppositions, and that selection amongst competing presuppositions must be a matter, not of rational judgment (which would itself require further presuppositions), but of the non-rational, ungrounded adoption of basic presuppositions. Weber, of course, like most neo-Kantians, strove to avoid the conclusion that logical and scientific (for example, causal), not to mention philosophical, judgments are rationally baseless. He sought to limit the sting of his argument to questions of value. But the argument in itself is perfectly general (and thus self-refuting). So Weber's effort involves an arbitrary limitation, and shows the way out of its grip. For human intelligence has the capacity to *understand* data, whether the data be found in the realm of nature, or of logic, or of cultural artefacts including

[26] Consider e.g. Aristotle's explicit contrast between the best (and thus the natural: *NE* V.7: 1135a5) with the average, in his fundamental methodological reflections on the study of societies and their constitutions: *Pol.* IV.I: 1288b10–40. Or Aquinas's view that most people and their deeds are foolish and corrupt: *ST* I q.113 a.1; I–II q.9 a.5 ad 3; q.14 a.1 ad 3; q.58 a.5; q.94 a.4; q.99 a.2 ad 2. Once again, the curious fact emerges that modernity, in the person of Weber (and Kronman), is not only unaware of the mistakes of antiquity, but actually repeats them. But since modernity also comprises those who are more or less aware of these mistakes and take some care to avoid them, it becomes apparent that appeal to the category of 'modernity' is a more than usually confused attempt to derive a normative conclusion from a bare statement of historical fact—in this case an insufficiently clarified fact, too.

[27] Putnam, *Reason, Truth and History*, 174–5.

language, or of the meaningful action of other human beings. And such insights are not the less intelligent and reasonable for being 'underived' from any higher or more basic principles. Their intelligibility and warrantedness is confirmed, moreover, by their satisfactoriness as answers to further questions about their subject-matter and by their coherence with other insights and judgments. The neo-Kantian foundations of Weber's denial of the objectivity of 'value-judgments' go unmentioned today[28] because they are as clearly self-refutatory and arbitrary as the verificationist principle of the logical positivists, a principle which Weber did not know or hold, but which some have used to support conclusions which sound like his. During its brief reign, logical positivism was bolstered by the claim that the correct linguistic analysis of statements about human good and evil is that they report or, in another version, *express* the attitudes of the speaker and thus have either no truth value or truth value only concerning the state of the speaker's own attitudes. That claim had no plausibility as an account of the logic of human speech about good and evil.

So today the denial of the objectivity of evaluative or moral propositions is once again framed in ontological terms. Such propositions do not figure in causal explanations of observations, so they do not affirm facts of nature which are the only sort of facts, truths, or knowledge.[29] But none of these arguments give any clear account of what it is to be a fact, or a fact of nature, or part of the world; nor are they able to show that entities or qualities or relationships such as the belonging of propositional meaning to concatenations of symbols, or of truth to propositions, or of validity to inferences, are not 'queer'[30] compared to the relation of billiard ball to billiard ball. These denials of the objectivity of evaluative and ethical judgments all depend upon an illusion: the illusion that that to which true judgments have their truth by corresponding ('the facts', 'the world', 'nature', 'reality') somehow lies open to an inspection conducted otherwise than by a truth-seeking process of rationally inquiring, understanding, considering, and judging, a process in which (as the debate about the proper analysis of evaluative and ethical discourse showed) evaluation and moral judging clearly intend to participate, in their own ways.

Reasonably enough, Kronman's exposition omits the shifting struggles of those who have tried to support Weber's conclusions about the 'subjectivity' of all values. However, Kronman also omits to mention the arguments that Weber himself used: (a) the argument from the irrationality

[28] They are not, I think, alluded to by Kronman. They are rightly given a central place in the account offered by Turner and Factor, *Max Weber and the Dispute over Reason and Value* esp. 34 et seq. For Weber's own use of the notion of presuppositions, see esp. his 'Science as a Vocation' in Gerth and Mills, *From Max Weber: Essays in Sociology*, 143–5.

[29] Harman, *The Nature of Morality*, chs 1–2.

[30] Cf. Mackie, *Ethics*, 38–43. For an assessment, see *FoE* 57–66.

of basic presuppositions, an argument which was rapidly abandoned by Weber's colleagues and immediate disciples for reasons already noted; (b) the argument from certain supposed political and/or ethical antinomies or dilemmas, before which reason is supposed to fall silent and call upon sheer decision, but which in fact, on careful analysis, prove to be no more than a stimulus to a more nuanced and resourceful practical reasoning which can identify good reasons for preferring one horn of the dilemma, or for settling upon some other course of action, or for narrowing the choice to a small range of reasonable alternatives to be contrasted with the indefinitely vast range of irrational or unreasonable alternatives;[31] and (c) the argument that there are distinct and incommensurable 'spheres' of practical judgment, such as the political, the erotic, and the ethical, each with its own ultimate values between which reason cannot adjudicate because reason operates only within spheres (a claim never worked out or defended by Weber, and contradicted by his own acknowledgement that these spheres interpenetrate one another).[32]

In place of all these, Kronman offers a new argument: a positivistic epistemology, denying that values can be known prior to their creation by non-rational human acts of will, is a prerequisite of any descriptive sociology. For

> the sociologist enters into the value-orientations of his subjects; only by doing so can he understand their behaviour in a meaningful way. At the same time, however, he abstains from making their values his own.... In order for this kind of detached empathy (and hence for the discipline of sociology) to be possible at all, normative evaluation and judgment must be distinct from understanding. This distinction in turn requires us to assume that a person's values are established through the exercise of a creative faculty (the will) distinct from the power of rational insight. (28)

Consider the decisive step in this argument: 'If evaluation and understanding were the same, no one could understand another person's values without having made them his own' (18).[33]

[31] See Strauss, *Natural Right and History*, 67–74; *NLNR* 51; Turner and Factor, *Max Weber and the Dispute over Reason and Value*, 31–8.

[32] See Turner and Factor, *Max Weber and the Dispute over Reason and Value*, 45–6; Brubaker, *The Limits of Rationality*, 69 et seq.

[33] Kronman says (20) that the assumption that understanding and evaluation are 'fundamentally different' may seem uncontroversial, but that not all philosophers have accepted it:

> One philosopher who denied the distinction was Socrates, judging from his views as they are presented in certain of Plato's early and middle dialogues. In these dialogues, Socrates defends the position that knowledge or understanding is a necessary and sufficient condition for virtue and hence for right conduct, a view that implies the impossibility of detached understanding of the sort that Weber claims is characteristic of all sociological inquiry. (18)

Or again:

Whether or not Kronman's argument is Weber's, there is a simple fallacy in it. For the sake of a word, let us call the alternative to detachment 'attachment'—as in 'I am deeply attached to sport, or scholarship...'—or 'commitment'. Then Kronman's argument amounts to this: the fact that there can be detached understanding, that is, understanding without attachment (or commitment), entails that attachment must be without understanding. Equally fallacious would be the weaker version of the same argument, viz.: the fact that there can be understanding without attachment entails that there *can* be attachment without understanding.

Such fallacies are evident enough. But behind them is a more interesting equivocation on the notion of 'understanding values', an equivocation between understanding that someone values X, and understanding that X is a value, that is, is a human good.

Take the first-person case first. I can observe and report that I myself regard some possibility as a good, and that I have a desiring or committed disposition towards the possibility thus regarded. Such a detached act of understanding (intelligent) observation and description is not an expression of desire or commitment. When I do express or pursue my desire or attachment, or act on my commitment, I do so with understanding—not, indeed, an understanding of the same 'theoretical' sort as is involved in the descriptive report of my own desires and attitudes, but an understanding of the value of the relevant possibility in terms of its human goodness or badness, that is, its *desirability*, what the classics called practical understanding, which (*pace* Socrates, Weber, and Kronman) can be of ends, even ends-in-themselves, as well as means. At least when we are acting humanly (and not merely in some quasi-reflex, automatic, or 'animal'

> Unlike Socrates' theory, which assigns the central role in moral life to our capacity for knowledge or understanding, Weber's positivistic theory of value assigns this same role to an entirely distinct power, to the will, the power of creative choice. (21)

One would not guess from Kronman's book that the rejection of Socrates' views began with Plato and was a foundation of the entire tradition of non-positivistic ethical thought in Aristole, Aquinas, and their successors. Nor would one guess that one of the great mistakes in the arguments by which Socrates is said to have defended his view that knowledge is sufficient for virtue was precisely an assumption shared with Hume and Weber: that 'reason moves us only because it depends on some previous desire for an end'. As Irwin has put it:

> In Socrates' view a rational desire is formed by deliberation about instrumental means to the final good; and therefore no desire for components of the final good can be rational. Plato rejects this view, and tries to show how the desire for something as an end in itself can be a rational desire formed by reference to intelligible and intelligent considerations (deliberation). (Irwin, *Plato's Moral Theory*, 80, 170, 173, 253.)

For Plato, like Aristotle, also rejected Socrates' essential assumptions that the end of human life is determinate, like the end of a craft, and that it is antecedently fixed for all by a determinate natural wanting to which reason or intelligence does not contribute: *ibid.*, 85–6, 166–7, 170. Thus the upshot of the classical critique of Socrates is that understanding is necessary but not *sufficient* for right dispositions and right action. The content of this understanding is explored in *NLNR* chs III–V, and *FoE* chs II–III.

fashion), we desire things because they seem desirable, good, worthwhile; it's not that we think things good because we desire them.

Analysis of what is involved in *choosing* certainly shows that any account of it must include reference to that active interest, that bestirring of oneself in pursuit of something, that attachment, and equally that positive aversion from other possibilities, all of which we can call 'will', willingness, decision (act of will)... But equally the account will be quite inaccurate unless it fully adverts to the fact that this attachment, this interest, this bestirring, this willingness to act and to reject, is motivated and directed by one's understanding (reasonable or unreasonable) that there is some good at stake, that one's interest and efforts have some point.

The process of deriving 'purely positive' schemes of legislation or common law from general principles deemed requirements of reason is not (usually) a deductive process, but it is a rational process. The classics, hazardously but accurately, thought of it as an interaction between reason and will.[34] 'Hazardously', because human willing (even when unreasonable or wicked) is never intelligible otherwise than as pursuit of understood good—a fact which the ancients (providing the essential but nowadays neglected corrective for their vocabulary) sought to convey by the definition of *will* as '*appetitus rationalis*', and the slogan '*voluntas est in ratione*'.[35]

Where does this leave our understanding of *other people's* desires and principles of action? We are now in a position to consider this question on its merits, without pressure from the fallacy that if detached understanding is possible, understanding (intelligent) commitment must be impossible. And the merits of the question are, I think, settled by what I have just said: human choices are for intelligible ends, for understood goods. So, just as we can understand another's assertion without sharing in or reproducing his performance of asserting it, or another's question without ourselves being puzzled, so too we can understand the point of another's choice or longing without ourselves choosing or longing for it.

Similarly, we can understand a muddle (such as Kronman's about detached understanding) by sorting it out into its clear components, to each of which we do or could assent but the combination of which is invalid and unworthy of assent. And, in descriptive jurisprudence, like anthropology, sociology, or history, we understand intentions, attitudes, practices, conventions, and institutions by sorting them out as attempts to pursue and participate in one or more of the basic human goods under the guidance of all, or all too few, of the basic requirements of practical reasonableness.[36] This

[34] See *NLNR* 281–90, 295, 337–42.

[35] *Ibid.*, 338. On 'understood good', see *FoE* 30–53.

[36] *NLNR* 29–33, 81–5, 127.

need not degenerate into 'rationalism', a complacently limited range of concepts uncritically claiming rational necessity and thus exclusiveness as categories for understanding human action. The critique of rationalism can, and can only, proceed from within the same project, that is, by making intelligible those aspects of human good which escape the rationalist's net of categories. And one can always make a human action or practice intelligible without showing that it is reasonable; for practical reasonableness is only one of the basic human goods, and its own requirements are manifold, so that an action can be reasonable in some respects while unreasonable in others. Finally, it is not to be overlooked that the effort of understanding, in which the descriptive and explanatory theorist draws upon his own understanding of human opportunities and of practical reasonableness, proceeds towards a kind of reflective equilibrium, in which his own prior beliefs about human good may have been expanded and corrected in the very process of descriptive sorting and explaining.[37]

V

My conclusions about the three stages of Kronman's general thesis are evident enough.

Explanatory priority in social theory should indeed be given to those action-guiding and institution-forming concepts which can be integrated into an epistemologically justified view of the goods for the sake of which human persons act and form institutions. But this explanatory priority is possible only if the epistemologically justified view of human goods is the view denied by Weber, namely, that human goods can be recognized and affirmed in acts of understanding, identifying (a) desirable objects-for-desire and worthwhile point-for-striving, and (b) requirements which guide critical assessments of desires in situations of choice, and which direct choices, just on the basis that such-and-such truly is the reasonable (rational) mode of participation in true human goods. For if the epistemologically justified view were that affirmed by Weber, all human acts and institutions would be afflicted with radical arbitrariness, and to attribute to one type of act, practice, or institution an explanatory priority over others would be without reasonable justification. In particular, the ascription of explanatory priority to legal-rational authority would be unjustified. For if the positive rules of a legal-rational order rest on nothing more than other rules likewise posited by sheer acts of will, the uncritical arbitrariness of ascribing authority to all or any of those rules

[37] *Ibid.*, 16–19.

is undisguised, and the distinction between recognition of authority and mere (perhaps coerced) convergence of interests completely collapses.

Of course, more remains to be said about *whether* or *why* authority *should* be distinguished from mere constellations of interest or from other forms of order.[38] Here it suffices that no good reason has been produced for accepting Weber's 'positivist' theory of value, and the new reasons produced by Kronman are no reason at all. Indeed, their weakness once again tells us something about modernity, something that will remove all temptation to give explanatory priority to a concept just on the score that it is the accepted modern concept.

NOTES

† *Hart, Weber and Winch*...(at n. 2). Subsequent to Lacey, *H.L.A. Hart*, 230–1, which sets out the facts I had in mind in writing n. 2, MacCormick recounted facts which indicate that Hart may well not have read Weber on law until long after the writing of *CL*.

‡ *Natural law as the specific and only consistent type of legitimacy of a legal order*...(at n. 20). Kennedy, 'The Disenchantment of Logically Formal Legal Rationality, or Max Weber's Sociology in the Genealogy of the Contemporary Mode of Western Legal Thought' is a helpful contextualization and application of many important aspects of Weber's thought that are relevant to his concept of legal rationality, but the exegesis at 1046–7, 1059 is certainly mistaken (as even passages quoted by Kennedy make reasonably clear) in limiting Weber's proposition to 'revolutionary natural law (the Rights of Man)'.

[38] *Ibid.*, ch. IX.

10

ON HART'S WAYS: LAW AS REASON AND AS FACT*

I

I remember Hart saying to two or three of his colleagues, over tea and biscuits in the Senior Common Room, that every ten years or so, going back a long way, he read the whole of Proust's *À la recherche du temps perdu*. I don't think he said why—Why should he have?—but central to what led him, repeatedly, through all seven of these novels, on the long way from *Du côté de chez Swann* to *Le Temps retrouvé*, will surely have been their reflexive, self-referential deployment and exploration of interiority, of the first person singular. As Neil MacCormick justly says in the first edition of his *H.L.A. Hart*, the 'fulcrum' and 'central methodological insight' of Hart's 'analytical jurisprudence' is that, as a 'descriptive legal or social theorist', one can and must '[hold] apart one's own commitments, critical morality, group membership or non-membership', and 'portray the rules for what they are in the eyes of those whose rules they are'.[1] One's account of law, as Hart himself puts it in *The Concept of Law*, must 'refer to the internal aspect of rules seen from their [the members of the group's] internal point of view' and 'reproduce the way in which the rules function in the lives' of those members, that is, in their 'claims, demands, admissions, criticism...all the familiar transactions of life according to rules', life as led by those for whom the rules count as reasons for action, and violations of those rules count as a reason for hostility.[2]

Somewhat less well known than Hart's prioritizing of the internal attitude or attitudes to law are his works on self-reference (especially self-referring laws[3]), and on intention (especially in relation to criminal liability, and to human causation). But these aspects of interiority are as central to his thought. In response to a remark of mine about, I think, how

* 2007b.

[1] MacCormick, *H.L.A. Hart*, 37–8

[2] *CL* 90 [88] (bracketed numbers give the pagination in the first edition, 1961).

[3] On self-referring laws, see Hart, *Essays in Jurisprudence and Philosophy*, 15–16, 170–8.

significant self-referential consistency is to the testing of philosophical positions,[4] he told me that what started his interest in philosophy, as a boy, was the breakfast cereal packet. From the 1890s, I have subsequently discovered,[5] packets of Quaker oats have depicted a substantial Quaker man holding a Quaker oats packet depicting a substantial Quaker man holding a packet of Quaker oats... (and so on 'to infinity', claims someone talking about these packets in Aldous Huxley's 1928 novel *Point Counter Point*[6]). In relation to crime and punishment, causation, and self-referring laws, Hart's attentiveness to our inner lives of thought, judgment, and decision was a motive for, and supplied arguments to advance, his resistance to more or less behaviourist currents of (as he often put it)[7] 'scepticism' about central aspects and institutions of law, a resistance which has been generally decisive for subsequent legal theory: a great legacy. In summing up his vindication of responsibility against the sceptic Barbara Wootton, he articulates what he calls 'an important general principle':

> Human society is a society of persons, and persons do not view themselves or each other merely as so many bodies moving in ways which are sometimes harmful and have to be prevented or altered. Instead persons interpret each other's movements as manifestations of intention and choices, and these subjective factors are often more important to their social relations than the movements by which they are manifested or their effects.[8]

This talk of intention and choice complements and corresponds to what *The Concept of Law*, published in the same year, says about the

> whole dimension of the social life of those [who]...look upon [the red traffic light] [not merely as a sign that others will stop, but] as a *signal for* them to stop, and so a reason for stopping in conformity to rules which make stopping when the light is red a standard of behaviour and an obligation.[9]

Here Hart italicizes *signal for*, and later on the same page he italicizes its equivalent: '*reason* for'. 'Reason' is italicized more than any other noun in the book;[10] it signifies practical reasons, the propositional element in thoughts of the form appropriate to guiding deliberation and eventual (possible) action. The first and fourth of the book's five italicizings of 'reason' are to make the argument that Hart was so eager, indeed impatient, to put

[4] See, latterly, essay I.4 (2005b).

[5] I knew what he meant, because an Australian cereal packet in the 1950s had the same feature, but with a frog not a Quaker.

[6] *Point Counter Point* (London: Chatto and Windus, 1928), 294.

[7] See my review of his *Punishment & Responsibility* in essay III.10 (1968a); the word 'scepticism' appears in virtually every one of these essays.

[8] Hart, *Punishment & Responsibility*, 182 (lecture delivered in 1961).

[9] *CL* 89 [87–8].

[10] See *CL* 11 [10], 55 [54], 90 [88], 105 [102], 194 [189].

forward even while he was setting up the three 'recurrent issues' about law—the argument that is his answer to the 'realist' scepticisms which reduce law to prediction. Sceptical 'realism' is poor as legal theory because it shuts one's eyes to the fact that 'the judge, in punishing, takes the rule as his *guide* and the breach of the rule as his *reason* and *justification* for punishing the offender';[11] a 'judge's statement that a rule is valid is an internal statement..., and constitutes not a prophecy of but part of the *reason* for his decision'.[12] By the time of *Essays on Bentham*, twenty years later, Hart had recast his theory of authority and law so as to emphasize yet further the centrality to it of reasons for action (peremptory and content-independent reasons).

> ...an authoritative legal reason...is a consideration (which in simple systems of law may include the giving of a command) which is recognized at least in the practice of the Courts, in what I term their rule or rules of recognition, as constituting a reason for action and decision [, a reason] of a special kind. Reasons of this kind...constitute legal guides to action and legal standards of evaluation.[13]

Now reasons of this kind, *as* articulated in commands or *as* manifested verbally or non-verbally in the practice of the courts, are historical facts. Like other historical facts about thoughts, decisions, and actions, they can, and often must, be understood, thoroughly, without being endorsed or approved, condemned or disapproved—just understood and faithfully described. Adulterating one's understanding of other people's valuations (or of one's own past evaluations) with one's own present valuations is sheer folly for the general, the advocate, the detective, the assessor (judge of fact), the historian. There should be no question here of 'interpretative charity' or 'making it the best of its genre', let alone morally best.[14] As Hart puts it in the posthumous *Postscript*, 'Description may still be description, even when what is described is evaluation.'[15] True, to bother investigating and describing *this* evaluation by *this* person or group, from among all the welter of other facts available for investigation and description, presupposes an evaluation by the investigator, not to mention the audience.[16] But that presupposed evaluation remains external to the evaluative thought—the concept, action or practice—described. So description can and, for many

[11] *CL* 11 [10]. [12] *CL* 105 [102].

[13] Hart, *Essays on Bentham*, 18. Here Hart uses 'evaluation' much more broadly than 'statements of value' in his contrast of the latter with 'statements of validity' at *CL*, 108 [104–5] (see text and note at n. 56 below).

[14] All this has been clear to me since I read R.G. Collingwood's 1939 *Autobiography* in the early or mid-1950s. See Twining, 'R.G. Collingwood's Autobiography' at 603.

[15] *CL* 244.

[16] 'It is the historian's judgments of value that select from the infinite welter of things that have happened the things that are worth thinking about.' Collingwood, *The Principles of History and Other Writings*, 217. Weber's version of this thought is better known.

purposes, should be value-free even when it describes the values and consequent actions of persons—of others or of oneself giving an account of one's own beliefs and conduct.

But Hart went further, both in the *Postscript* and earlier. As he puts it in the *Postscript*:

> ...the descriptive legal theorist must *understand* what it is to adopt the internal point of view and in that limited sense he must be able to put himself in the place of an insider; but this is not to accept the law or share or endorse the insider's internal point of view or in any other way to surrender his descriptive stance.[17]

Here there has been a shift which Hart never seems to have attended to, and perhaps would simply deny is a shift, from the description that is the stock in trade of the detective, the assessor, the translator, or the historian to what Hart calls 'descriptive general theory'.[18] This shift is both real and important. I am not going to dwell upon it in this essay; it is the burden of Chapter I of *Natural Law and Natural Rights* and of a number of recent writings of mine.[19] One's aspiration as a *theorist* about law and legal systems is to identify and affirm *general* and warranted propositions about a human practice or institution thoroughly shaped by thought. Developing a general theory requires one to select among all the particular and very various vocabularies and concepts that have been employed in social life both to shape and to describe the various practices or institutions which, as a theorist, one judges it accurate, illuminating, and theoretically fruitful to call and treat as instances of, say, law or legal system. This theoretic judgment is not settled by the concepts or criteria articulated and/or used by those whose thought and practice is being named and treated in this way—taking those one by one, or taking the whole disorderly series of them. It is a judgment that requires one as a theorist to select and adopt one's own concept and criteria, and to do so for reasons, as Hart does in working up his theory of law in *The Concept of Law*.[20] What he offers us in that book is a *new and improved concept* of law, corresponding closely to

[17] *CL* 242. [18] See *CL* 239–40.

[19] See essay 1, sec. II; 2007c, sec. 5.

[20] In his Introduction to *Essays in Jurisprudence and Philosophy*, Hart accepts, as part of his correction of what he had come to consider errors involved in his 'early invocation in jurisprudence of linguistic philosophy' (p. 5), that 'the methods of linguistic philosophy, which are neutral between moral and political principles and silent about different points of view which might endow one feature rather than another of legal phenomena with significance' were, precisely by reason of that neutrality and indifference to non-neutrality,

> not suitable for resolving or clarifying those controversies which arise, as many of the central problems of legal philosophy do, from the divergence between partly overlapping concepts reflecting a divergence of basic points of view or values or background theory.... For such cases what is needed is first, the identification of the latent conflicting points of view which led to the choice or formation of divergent concepts, and secondly, reasoned argument directed to understanding the merits of conflicting theories, [or] divergent concepts or sets of rules...(p. 6)

the concept of law already employed in societies he thought reasonably organized and reasonably and critically self-aware. But even in relation to the concepts widely employed in such societies, Hart's concept of law did 'add value', that is, provided an improved understanding of the cluster of features he identifies as the central idea and reality of law, and of why those features can well cluster together—an understanding of the social functions which that kind of clustering serves and promotes, in remedying defects and affording facilities for advancing human purposes.

The extent to which Hart's descriptive explanation of law depends for its explanatory power on presuppositions about good and bad in human affairs was hidden from Hart in some measure by, it seems to me, some assumption he made or thesis he held about *concepts*. In the notebook which seems to record the genesis of key parts of *The Concept of Law* the word 'Concept' appears a number of times in large capitalized form.[21] It was as if, in these preparatory thoughts, the investigation or identification of a Concept somehow lifted one's understanding, one's account, one's theory, above an investigation of what particular people or groups (or any merely statistical-frequency-based selection of them) have meant, or have intended, above their conceptions of what it is important to promote as desirable (good) and avoid as undesirable (bad), and above the theorist's own 'pre-theoretical' judgments about importance and desirability (good and bad), into a realm of timeless—truly *general*—essences or forms somehow available for adoption on inspection, a neutral, value-free, and 'theoretical' perception. This, I believe, is nowhere affirmed in *The Concept of Law*; if it is implied, as I think it is (and not only by the notebook and the book's title), it can and should be regarded as a philosophical myth, an illusion. In this respect, I think Hart's ideas about method in legal theory regressed from the position he had affirmed in 1953: that 'the fundamental issues of legal philosophy' are those 'discussed and reflected upon' by intelligent students of (and surely because they are issues raised and discussed in) Plato's *Republic* and Aristotle's *Nicomachean Ethics*.[22] Hart knew what he meant: he lectured in 1951 on Plato's ethical and political theory, where, as in Aristotle too, whatever is said or implied about the concepts, nature, or

Though it is not entirely clear how far this passage refers to concepts of law itself (the nature of law), the passage fairly clearly accepts the reality of and need for selection of concepts for use in a general theory of a subject-matter instantiated in varying forms because of the varying concepts (ideas) of those persons and groups in whose life that (range of) subject-matter(s) is instantiated.

[21] For one instance ('the *Concept* of law') see the transcription of an important passage from the 1950s notebook in Lacey, *H.L.A. Hart*, 222. With that passage's account of how to identify 'a *standard* legal system...without *prejudiced* description' compare the late 1985 manuscript note at *ibid.*, 351, and the similar passage published in 1983 and quoted in n. 20 above.

[22] Hart, 'Philosophy of Law and Jurisprudence in Britain (1945–1952)' at 357.

essence of government, constitutionality, law, and so forth is controlled by the respective philosophical author's *normative* moral and political theory. As Plato and Aristotle make clear, a theorist's judgments that certain conceptions of political community, government, constitutionality, and law should have primacy in the theoretical description, and the strongly evaluative (morally evaluative) grounds that Plato and Aristotle adduce for those judgments, in no way block the theorist's descriptions of other conceptions of polity, government, and law. In particular, those philosophers of human affairs can, and did, provide careful and illuminating accounts of the defective and inferior kinds and conceptions of polity, government, and law that are so frequently articulated or manifested, despite their normative inferiority (sometimes gross immorality), in the life and history of the human groups available for empirical study in their day.

II

Instead of pursuing further that well-trodden path, I want to turn in this essay to another question arising out of Hart's interest in the internal point of view and consequently in law's character as one kind or family of reason(s) for action. The question is this: Even when his account in *The Concept of Law* is enhanced by his adoption of something tantamount to Raz's concept of the detached professional perspective, neither external nor internal, in the central senses of those terms, *how well do Hart's accounts enable us to understand that kind of point of view* and that kind of reason for action? The issues I want to explore are not precisely those taken up by Neil MacCormick in the appendix to his *Legal Reasoning and Legal Theory*, where he disambiguates what he calls cognitive and volitional elements run together in Hart's relatively undifferentiated 'internal attitude'. But, while nervous lest there be a Humeian implicature to his distinction between cognition and volition, I take for granted, and accept, the many clarifications with which MacCormick there and in Chapter 3 of his *H.L.A. Hart* (1981) equips us for understanding what Hart was trying to articulate in his over-simple distinction between 'the internal' and 'the external' points of view.[23]

In January 1958, Stuart Hampshire and Hart published in *Mind* 'Decision, Intention and Certainty'. Though Hampshire's name comes first, perhaps as alphabetically prior, it is certain that Hart fully owned the paper's argument: while in Harvard the previous academic year, he had not only

[23] For my own, overlapping clarifications, drawing like MacCormick's on work by Raz, see *NLNR* 233–7.

worked on the article[24] but spoken at a philosophy seminar on 'Knowing what you are doing',[25] which is the article's theme and thesis. That thesis is: one has a knowledge of, and certainty about, what one is doing, one's own voluntary actions, which is not an observer's knowledge, and is not based like the observer/spectator's on empirical evidence or on the observation of one's own (the acting person's) movements; it is *practical* knowledge.[26] First-person statements about an action have the same meaning as third-person statements, but as with 'many concepts involving reference to states of consciousness' there is an 'asymmetry between first-person and third-person statements' about actions, corresponding to the radical difference between the 'means of verification' of the respective statements, the kind of knowledge they articulate.[27] For the same reason, the article contends, there is a 'necessary connexion'[28] between intending to do something and certainty about what one will do—certainty based not on reflection upon and induction from the evidence of one's experience (as might be the case with one's more or less *in*voluntary behaviour), but instead on one's having reasons for doing what one has decided to do: 'practical certainty about what to do'.[29]

Although neither 'internal' nor any cognate appears in the article, it is plainly a portrayal and exploration of what *The Concept of Law* will call the internal attitude or point of view as it bears, not on rules or rule-guided action, but on any sort of voluntary action. It explores other truths important to *The Concept of Law*: the importance of distinguishing that first-person perspective from the perspective or viewpoint or 'attitude'[30] of any observer or spectator, and the parallel difference between stating an intention—thereby evidencing one's acceptance of reasons for action—and making a prediction that one will act. The article is illuminating and sound, furthermore, in much that it stresses about the empirical reality of practical knowledge and 'free-will', and about the connection between freedom of decision and having reasons for decision.[31] But it has deep and pervasive mistakes, which shed much light on some principal features of contemporary legal philosophy, features manifested in and partly shaped by *The Concept of Law*.

At the very point where Hart and Hampshire bring us face to face with the reality and distinctness of one's practical knowledge of what one intends to do, or is doing, they mix up that practical knowledge with certainty;

[24] Lacey, *H.L.A. Hart*, 190. [25] *Ibid.*, 187.

[26] Hampshire and Hart, 'Decision, Intention and Certainty' at 1, 5, 6, 8–9. The thesis can also be found prominently in Anscombe, *Intention*, but unlike Hampshire and Hart she proceeds to a robust examination of practical reasoning and its upshot, intention. [27] Hampshire and Hart at 10.

[28] *Ibid.* at 1. [29] *Ibid.* at 4, 5, 12. [30] *Ibid.* at 5. [31] See *ibid.* at 4–5.

worse, the certainty they speak of is predictive. Moreover: since *will*, which culminates in choice (what they call decision), is really part and parcel of *reason* (for willing is one's responsiveness to what one believes to be reasons), it is unsurprising that, having conflated practical knowledge and predictive certainty, they make X's choosing consist in (be 'constituted' by) 'becoming certain'[32] about 'what he will do'.[33] Just when they are announcing that reason can be practical as well as descriptive/predictive, they dissolve its practicality into the descriptive/predictive. One's decision, like one's consequent intention (and thus, of course, one's disposition to act and one's action), is unhinged from the reasons that precede, and in an unexplored sense result in,[34] the deciding/choosing.

Though it is true that, as the authors underline,[35] someone who has not yet decided between two or more courses of action must be uncertain about what he will do, it is fallacious to conclude, as they do, that deciding is constituted by becoming certain about what one will do. Indeed, it is not even true that my deciding to do X entails, as they assert, that I am 'certain that I will do this, unless I am in some way prevented'. For I know that I may change my mind, reverse my decision, make a contrary choice. Hart and Hampshire, without signalling their shift, later acknowledge this, saying that once I have made my decision, which occurs when

> all uncertainty about what [I am going to do] has been removed from [my] mind, I will be said to intend to do whatever [I have] decided to do, unless either [I fall] into uncertainty again, as a result of further reasons suggesting themselves, *or until* [*I*] *definitely* [*change my*] *mind.*[36]

But neither the conditionality of conditional intentions[37] nor the standing significant possibility of change of mind (reversal of decision) is elucidated or even discussed by Hart and Hampshire.[38] The authors are left both asserting and denying that to decide and intend is to make a prediction (become certain) about what one will do.

[32] *Ibid.* at 3. [33] *Ibid.* at 2.

[34] *Ibid.* at 3:

> The [agent's] certainty [about what he will do] comes at the moment of decision, and indeed constitutes the decision, when the certainty is arrived at... as a result of considering reasons, and not as a result of considering evidence.... When he has made his decision, *that is*, when, after considering reasons, all uncertainty about what he is going to do has been removed from his mind, he will be said to intend to do whatever he has decided to do....

[35] *Ibid.* at 2. [36] *Ibid.* at 3. [37] See essay II.12 (1994a).

[38] They pertinently put to themselves the objection that, because 'deciding' and 'changing my mind' represent an act, something that I *do*, 'deciding cannot be adequately characterized as simply becoming certain about one's future voluntary action after considering reasons, and not considering evidence'. But their response restricts itself to asserting that it is unclear what is meant here by 'do', and never confronts the core objection.

The truth is that choosing, forming a definite intention, is settling not the indicative-future question 'What will I do?', but the gerundive-optative, *practical* question 'What am I to do?', 'What, in these or more or less specific future circumstances, *should* I do?', 'What is-to-be done [*faciendum, agendum*]?' It is compatible with uncertainty about the merits of the option chosen, and in that sense, compatible with uncertainty about *what to do*. For choice between alternative options, in the focal sense of 'choice' (*electio*, selection, and resolve), is really only necessary when (so far as the chooser can see) the reasons in favour of one option are not all satisfied, or as well satisfied in all dimensions of intelligible good, by the other option(s).[39] Choosing is also compatible with uncertainty about what one will do; for, especially when the carrying out of one's intention is conditional on contingent future circumstances, one can reasonably be alive to the possibility that one will sometime before then find reason to reverse one's choice (perhaps even reasons that one had considered when making one's original decision). Hart and Hampshire were right to point out the certainty one can and normally does have about what one is doing, but wrong to extrapolate to certainty about the future fulfilling of one's intentions; their error leads them to substantial self-contradiction about the allegedly predictive character of statements of intention, and to belated and unintegrated acknowledgement of changes of heart/mind.

Nor do they adequately explicate one's certainty about what one is doing. One knows what one is doing, I would say, because one's doing (in the case of fully voluntary actions) is the *carrying out of* the proposal/plan that one adopted in one's decision/choice. A plan is a rational structure, in thought, of ends and means. As Aristotle and Aquinas have brilliantly illuminated, each end except the one most ultimate (relative to some particular behaviour) is also a means to some more ultimate end, and each means, except the exertion involved in the very behaviour itself, also stands as an end relative to the means next more proximate to that exertion.[40] Moreover, in the deliberation that shapes alternative proposals for choice, ends and means figure propositionally, as reasons for the respective courses of action envisaged in the rival proposals. Each reason articulates a supposed benefit, a supposed intelligible good, promised (not guaranteed!) by the proposed course of action supported by that reason. Within each proposal that one shapes for oneself in deliberation, every means (and thus virtually every end) is transparent for the end which gives point to that means. So, too, when one has chosen one proposal in

[39] See further essay I.14 at 224–5 (1992a at 146–7); essay I.15 at 238–9 (1997b at 219–20).

[40] On their understanding of means as nested ends, see e.g. essay II.9 (1991a); *Aquinas* 58–71, esp. 64 n. 20.

preference to the other(s), the reasons favouring that proposal and course of action remain in play, giving one reason to exert oneself to carry out the chosen action, whether now or when appropriate circumstances arise. The propositional expression of this is not Hart-Hampshire's 'I am certain that *this* is what I will do', but Aquinas's *imperium*, '*This* is the thing for me to be doing—what I should be doing' (not necessarily a moral 'should')—the directive (*imperium*, command), from oneself as rational self-determining chooser to oneself as rational agent,[41] to do what it takes to achieve the intelligible benefits with an eye to which one chose (adopted the proposal one did), benefits one believed and believes attainable by or in such conduct (attainable if one's means prove to have the efficacy one envisaged for them in one's plan/proposal).

Under pressure of Hobbesian, Humeian, and Kantian misunderstandings of practical reasoning, choice, and (consequently) action, all this was much neglected in the period when Hart was turning his philosophical attention to the relation between reason and action, and correspondingly to the way in which behaviour becomes intelligible when understood as it is understood by the acting person, that is, 'from the internal point of view'. But as the role of reasons, though constantly pointed out, remains essentially unanalysed and incompletely integrated in the Hart-Hampshire treatment of intention and practical knowledge, so their role, though again constantly signalled, remains incompletely analysed and integrated in *The Concept of Law* and even, I think, in the later work explicitly focused on peremptory content-independent reasons for action.

III

Consider Hart's canonical account or definition of the internal attitude. As it bears on rules, it is the attitude of those who 'accept and voluntarily co-operate in maintaining the rules, and so see their own and other persons' behaviour in terms of the rules'.[42] And, says Hart, 'the acceptance of the rules as common standards for the group may be split off from the *relatively passive* matter of the ordinary individual acquiescing in the rules by obeying them for his part alone'.[43]

[41] On the important and neglected reality of *imperium* in personal choice and action, see *NLNR* 338–40. Hart, in conversation with me (again in the tea room), once lightly mocked my account as replacing 'push' theories of motivation (and obligation) with a 'pull' theory. But in understanding practical reason, and willing (which is *in* it, *in ratione*), we must in the last analysis treat as misleading all metaphors borrowed from sub-rational motivation, let alone those from subhuman forms of motion. Reason's directiveness, in practical as in theoretical reason, is *sui generis*, and so, accordingly, is willing, one's responsiveness to reasons (intelligible goods).

[42] *CL* 91 [88]; see also 90 [87–8], 98 [96], 102 [99]; 109–10 [106–7], 115 [112], 116 [113], 201 [197].

[43] *Ibid.*, 117 [114] (emphasis added).

What should strike us, however, is the relatively passive character of even the officials' internal attitude as characterized by Hart. True, they accept the rules not simply as commonly accepted standards but as common standards *for* themselves *and others*;[44] they use the rules to appraise their own and others' conduct. But in Hart's account they at most cooperate in *maintaining* rules that Hart's account treats as out there, available for acceptance and maintenance. What is striking is the contrast between this and the classical theory of law which treats as central and primary the *positing* of legal rules, and—rightly, I believe—takes their epistemologically and ontologically primary mode of existence to be their existing as a proposal adopted by the choice/decision of their maker; adopted, that is to say, as a plan of conduct for the community and its members and officials. Once made, promulgated, the rules will of course have to be maintained. But this very maintaining is to be understood as a kind of (re)novation of the making. That understanding is in line with Aristotle's definition of the citizen as one who is entitled to share and does share in governing the political community. Hart's notion of accepting rules *as common* standards for oneself *and others* is the nearest his core legal theory gets to the classical notion of law's existence: as a kind of extending of the law-making activities of the rulers, an extending by a kind of interior personal re-enactment, person by person, of the ruler's or rulers' legally decisive adoption of their own legislative or other law-positing proposals.[45]

[44] MacCormick, *H.L.A. Hart*, 34–5, begins his explanation of the 'stronger case' of acceptance of a rule, 'willing acceptance':

> Not merely has one a preference for observance of the 'pattern', but one prefers it as constituting a rule *which one supposes to be sustained by a shared or common preference* among those to whom it is deemed applicable (emphasis added).

Later, p. 41, he adjusts this to make the more important point:

> the element of 'preference' involved in the 'internal point of view' tends to be conditional: one's preference *that a given pattern of action be adhered to by all* may be conditional upon the pattern's being and continuing to be supported by common or convergent preferences among all or nearly all the parties to the activity contemplated (emphasis added).

This justified adjustment is carried forward on p. 43:

> Where there is common acceptance of certain standards envisaged as being shared or conventional standards, those who accept them belong to a 'group' but so 'from the internal point of view' *of these accepters* do all those to whose conduct they deem the standards applicable, and commonly that in turn depends on the possession by human beings of some characteristic which is not necessarily a voluntarily acquired characteristic. Hence Hart's crucial conception of a 'group' appears not to be prior to or definable independently of his conception of a rule.

This is illuminating, though the final 'hence' is not altogether clear to me, since members of a group of the kind in which the central case of law is instantiated are characteristically able to identify their group (nation) even when a good many rules, including at least some of the group's former rules of recognition have broken down.

[45] *Aquinas* 254–6:

> Aquinas proposes and argues for a definition of law: an ordinance of reason for the common good of a [complete] community, promulgated by the person or body responsible for looking after that

A law may, of course, as the classics constantly remind us, be a barely articulate belch of malevolence against a minority (or indeed a perhaps sheep-like majority), a decree mouthed by the terrorist ruler or rulers to a group of henchmen officials and 'people's' judges, and communicated by these officials only fragmentarily and in deliberately confusing form to the subjects, perhaps to induce some self-herding towards the slaughterhouse. But it would advance no theoretical purpose to take *such* decrees and such forms of governance as representative laws and legal governance when asking why it makes sense to transit from Hart's 'pre-legal' form of governance to what he calls the central case of law and legal system, or when reflecting on what would be lost in transiting from law to Marxian post-legal society, or when considering the point and worth of the principles 'which lawyers term principles of legality',[46] or joining the millennial debate about the respective advantages of the rule of law and the rule of legally unfettered rulers.

But leave that aside. After all, everyone knows that there have been and are—it's a matter of fact—rules laid down as laws, and described by makers and subjects alike as law, which were and are deeply unreasonable, unjust, immoral; it can happen that some of them do not even profess to be reasonable, just, or morally decent. That fact has nothing like the theoretical significance Hart thought it did. As a matter of *fact*, there is no necessary connection between arguments and logic or validity as argumentation; arguments worthless as argument—as *reasons* for a conclusion—can be found all over the place. As a matter of *reason*, an invalid argument is no argument. Again: as a matter of *fact*, there is no necessary connection

community. But in supplementing and explicating that definition, Aquinas immediately stresses that law—a law—is 'simply a sort of prescription {dictamen} of practical reason *in the ruler* governing a complete community', and that 'prescriptions' are simply universal propositions of practical reason which prescribe and direct to action. His explications also add that government (governing, governance) by law means, equally concretely, that these practical propositions conceived in the minds of those responsible for ruling must be assented to by the ruled, and adopted into their own minds as reasons for action. The assent may have been induced only by fear of sanctions, though such unwilling (reluctant) assent cannot be the central case of cooperation in government by law.... the present point is simply that law needs to be present in the minds not only of those who make it but also of those to whom it is addressed—present if not actually, at least habitually—as the traffic laws are in the minds of careful drivers who conform to them without actually thinking about them. The subjects of the law share (willingly or unwillingly) in at least the conclusions of the rulers' practical thinking and in the plan which the rulers propose (reasonably and truthfully or unreasonably and falsely) as a plan for promoting and/or protecting common good. For just as an individual's choice is followed and put into effect by the directive {imperium} of that individual's reason, so a legislature's or other ruler's choice of a plan for common good is put into effect by way of citizens taking the law's directive {imperium; ordinatio} *as if* it were putting into effect their own choice. The central case of government is the rule of a free people, and the central case of law is coordination of willing subjects by law which, by its fully public character (promulgation), its clarity, generality, stability, and practicability, treats them as partners in public reason (notes, citations, and cross-references omitted).

[46] *CL* 207 [202].

between medicines and healing; countless medicines do not heal and many of them in fact do nothing but damage health. As a matter of reason, such deleterious medicines are not medicines and are not referred to in discussions of whether there is good reason to devise medicaments and make them available. So too: as a matter of *fact*, there is no necessary connection between law and reasonableness, justice or morality; irrational and unjust laws abound, as natural law theory insists from earliest time until today. As a matter of practical reason, unreasonable (and therefore unjust and immoral) laws and legal systems are not what we are seeking to understand when we inquire into the reasons there are to make and maintain law and legal systems, and what features are essential if law and legal systems are to be acceptable—worthy of acceptance—and entitled to the obedience or conformity of reasonable people. (Of course, the study of arguments as reasons will include a study of fallacious arguments, the study of pharmacology will include the study of bad medicines, and a study of law, legality, and the rule of law will include a subordinate study of the ways in which bad laws and official abuse of legality and legal institutions corrupt law, legality, and the rule of law and need to be guarded against by laws and legal institutions designed for the purpose.)

In that light, we can see that laws and law-makers systematically offer their subjects *at least* four different kinds of reason for compliance.[47] (It goes without saying that, as Hart constantly said, laws like every other social fact provide the occasion for many other kinds of motivation for doing the same thing as the law requires to be done: conformism and conventionalism, careerism and cowardice, to name some of the motives, which Hart gave other names.[48]) Where the posited law attaches definitions and either penalties or other negative consequences to *mala in se* (say, rape), it invites its subjects to treat abstaining from these forbidden kinds of act as something required by the very same practical reason that the law-maker judged inherently sound and sought to refine and reinforce, *as well as* by the next three kinds of reason. Secondly, when we are in the zone of, broadly speaking, *mala prohibita*, the posited law offers to promote common good (including, as common good always does, what justice demands as proper respect for rights) by forbidding or requiring some kind of act which is not already, as such, or always and everywhere, excluded or required by well-judging practical reason. In this zone the law offers its subjects the

[47] I discuss here only obligation-imposing norms/rules, and leave aside both (a) power-conferring norms/rules and (b) the question of the collateral moral obligation (not to be seen to defy the positive law) that may subsist *in some of the instances* of laws so unjust that their legal validity is deprived of the moral entailment that, presumptively and defeasibly, it would otherwise have (*NLNR* 361).

[48] See *CL* 231 [226], 203 [198], 114 [111].

opportunity to accept and comply with it both (a) for the same sufficient though often *not* rationally conclusive, dominant, or compelling reason(s) as the law-maker(s) *decided* to give effect to in preference to the competing reasons for some competing alternative legislative scheme, and (b) for the next two kinds of reason.

Thirdly, then, in the same zone of *mala prohibita* or 'purely positive' laws, the rules in the second of these four categories are also held out to subjects who consider the reasons in favour of the rule insufficient to warrant the law-maker's adoption of it; for such subjects there remains, nonetheless, a kind of reason, often sufficient, to accept the rule as a common standard for themselves and others in the same country, the reason afforded by the fact that the rule is a valid part of the country's legal system.[49]

Fourthly, in respect of *mala in se* and *mala prohibita* alike, the law usually though not invariably offers its subjects, public or private, the kind of reason afforded by the prospect (and undesirability) of undergoing punishment or other penalties or authorized kinds of negative consequence. That kind of reason differs markedly from the reasons which the law-maker has for threatening and (usually different reasons) for imposing such penalties, and the reasons that people amenable to the first three kinds of reason have for complying with the rule to which the penalty is attached. For as Hart points out in the clearest of his rather slender explorations of law's place in the flow or network of practical reason(s),

> 'Sanctions' are...required not as the normal motive for obedience, but as a *guarantee* that those who would voluntarily obey shall not be sacrificed to those who would not. To obey, without this, would be to risk going to the wall. Given this standing danger, what reason demands is *voluntary* co-operation in a *coercive* system.[50]

This passage, illuminating though it is, is not very clear, for it shifts to and fro, without signalling, from viewpoint to viewpoint. Its first and third sentences address the perspective of the law-maker, and of the subject (citizen or friendly alien resident) who shares the law-makers' perspective; the first sentence also *alludes to* the perspective of those (who may even be the 'normal' majority) for whom the normal motive for obedience *is* fear of sanction. The passage's second sentence addresses the perspective of the subject as subject, contemplating obedience or disobedience. The passage's conclusion, about what 'reason demands', presupposes, strikingly but ineluctably, that the designer of the legal system, and anyone willing

[49] This is explored in some depth in essay 2; in essay 3, the analysis is defended against Raz's critique.

[50] *CL* 198 [193].

to adopt the designer's viewpoint and purposes, envisages (has as an end or objective) a system with a content (including forms and procedures) worthy of the *voluntary* cooperation of a *reasonable* subject. Hart here takes for granted that law, the central case legal system that is the real subject-matter of *The Concept of Law*, is an arrangement rationally prescribed, by those responsible for the community, for the common good of its members: *ordinatio rationis ad bonum commune, ab eo qui curam communitatis habet promulgata.*[51]

Notice that Hart does not specify what is bad in the 'danger' that those who voluntarily cooperate would 'go to the wall'; the passage gets much of its force from the plausible implication that it is, in some large part, the evil of unfairness to them (for the disobedience of the scofflaws would, by hypothesis, be going unpenalized). It is like the passage earlier in the book,[52] stating the 'defect' for which the 'remedy' is courts and 'secondary' rules of adjudication. For though Hart labels it inefficiency, what makes the absence of *judicial* means of resolving disputes about rule-violation a defect is surely, in some large measure if not predominantly, the unfairness to the party whose wronging causes the dispute and/or who, being the weaker, would probably be wronged if the dispute were ended by some non-judicial means. In each of these cases, the fairness being appealed to just beneath the surface of Hart's text is essentially the justice that he elucidates in his account of the justice of compensation for injury: the injury upsets the 'artificial equality' or 'equilibrium' established by moral (and, Hart should have added, legal) rules which put the weak and simple on a (normative) level with the strong and cunning; the upset is itself unfair/unjust, and it would be unfair/unjust to leave it unrectified by compensation.[53]

To understand Hart's legacy, however, one needs to notice that he never invites his readers to reflect on the relation—within the one book *The Concept of Law*, let alone within his writings as a whole—between what he says there about justice, what he says about reason, and what he says about the central case of law and the 'defects' it 'remedies' and the 'amenities' it provides. This neglect of pertinent questions parallels other refusals to raise questions. When judges around the English-speaking world needed the help of legal theory to respond to the juridical challenge of *coups d'état* and revolutions, they could find nothing illuminating in Hart's theory of the rule(s) of recognition.[54] For though that 'ultimate' rule is

[51] *ST* I–II q.90 a.4c; see *Aquinas* 255–6. [52] *CL* 93–4 [91].

[53] *CL* 164–5 [160–1]. Hart should have recalled all this when considering the justice of retribution as a general justifying aim of punishment, but seems never to have done so: *NLNR* 262–4; *Aquinas* 210–15. [Essay III.10 at 158–9; III.11 at 163; III.12 at 176–7.]

[54] So they turned, albeit inappropriately and fruitlessly, to Kelsen, whose general theory at least attempted to give a juridical account of the source of the validity of an existing constitution, i.e.

explained by Hart as the answer to a question, namely the question—which follows fittingly the lawyer's sequence of inquiries seeking the reason for the validity of by-laws and ministerial legislation—why a parliamentary enactment is valid, the answer, namely that the courts and officials (if not also private persons) *have the practice* of *using* the rule that what Parliament enacts is to be recognized as law, is treated by Hart as 'a stop in inquiries'.[55] What he has in mind is *not only*, as he reasonably says, a stop in inquiries seeking further, more ultimate posited rules, *but also*, as he disappointingly takes for granted, inquiries seeking other *juridically relevant* reasons for continuing, discontinuing, or modifying the practice in which the rule of recognition consists. When we entertain, for reasonable affirmation or denial, the proposition that the rule (and the system based on it) is 'worthy of support', we have simply moved, according to Hart, 'from a statement of validity to a statement of value'.[56]

In the idiom of the book, that is a way of saying we have moved outside legal theory, outside the law, outside the juridical, and have nothing to offer the judge who is asking, as judge, whether and when and how a successful *coup d'état* alters the law of the land. Nor anything, indeed, to say to judges who, in altogether ordinary times, ask themselves why they should continue their practice of using the rule(s) of recognition and the criteria of legal validity and juridical argumentation embodied therein or pointed to thereby. For the book's legal theory, its account of law and the juridical, includes no systematic engagement with 'value'—only episodic forays into disintegrated topics such as a justice, and later a minimum natural law for 'survival', which have no articulated connection with each other or with the explication of what makes law law.

In short: *The Concept of Law*, the *Essays on Bentham*, and Parts I–III and V of *Essays in Jurisprudence and Philosophy* display a legal theory or general jurisprudence that, having identified its own descriptive dependence on the internal point of view and attitude (in which rules are reasons for

of the relation between a 'momentary' legal system and the diachronic legal system in which each momentary system takes its place. See essay 21; Eekelaar, 'Principles of Revolutionary Legality'.

[55] *CL* 107 [104].

[56] *CL* 108 [104–5]. After delivering this paper, I read Simmonds, *Law as a Moral Idea*, which at 126–36 develops a valuable complementary critique of Hart's truncation of 'the domain of the juridical' (126). There is much illuminating argument and reflection in the book; it is mistaken, however, in saying (56 n. 28) that, in the theory of law developed in the central chapters of my *NLNR*, the treating of the common good as central to the understanding of law is 'a consequence of' the methodological claims I advanced in Chapter I about descriptive general theory. Though Chapter I of my book treats general legal theory which is descriptive in purpose as a legitimate enterprise (provided it acknowledges its dependence on evaluations internal to its method of concept-selection), the later chapters on law do not have a descriptive purpose, but (for reasons underlined in essay 1) are normative/evaluative in purpose as well as method, and are not at all dependent on the argument of Chapter I. [And see 2010b.]

action), leaves those reasons largely unexplored, and rests largely content with reporting the fact that people have an attitude which is the internal aspect of their practice. Having so fruitfully gone beyond the observer's or spectator's perspective on bodily movements and behaviour, it rests officially content with a *report* that the participants have reasons for their behaviour and their practice. It does not seek to understand those reasons as reasons all demand to be understood—in the dimension of soundness or unsoundness, adequacy or inadequacy, truth or error. To have been consistent in its abstinence from engagement with that dimension—from 'statements of value'—Hart's method should have restricted him to the observation that people often think they have reasons, that many people think or have thought that a pre-legal set of social rules is defective, think that secondary rules are the remedy, and so forth. But his book's engagement with its readers would then have been very different. And, since by no means everyone everywhere has the same beliefs about reasons, the question why select for report *these* supposed reasons rather than others would have become deafening; it would have broken up the party.

IV

Before turning, finally, to the question why Hart so truncated his inquiry into legal reasons, I should say a word about what Hart's successors, in their reflections on the nature of law, have made of his legacy. (Perhaps the word 'legacy' in this conference's title was intended, not in the lawyer's sense of what the testator chose to give, maybe with latent defects of which he was unaware—the sense on which I've been relying—but in the loose sense of what his successors made of it all.) Some have maintained (LP1) that

> in any legal system, whether a given norm is legally valid, and hence whether it forms part of the law of that system, depends on its sources, not its merits (where its merits, in the relevant sense, include the merits of its sources).[57]

Others have maintained (LP2) that

> determining what the law [in a given time and place] is does not necessarily, or conceptually, depend on moral or other evaluative considerations about what the law ought to be in the relevant circumstances.[58]

[57] Gardner, 'Legal Positivism: 5½ Myths' at 201. This seems to be practically equivalent to Raz's 'sources thesis', often called by others 'exclusive positivism'.

[58] Marmor, *Positive Law and Objective Values*, 71.

The first thesis (LP1) seems the more strenuous: 'never by reference to merits' is a stronger claim than 'not necessarily by reference to merits', and that helps to explain why John Gardner, sponsor of (LP1), ascribes to the thesis, and to its approach to law, 'comprehensive normative inertness'.[59] It corresponds to Hart's sharp distinction between 'statements of validity' and 'statements of value'. But in Hart that distinction seemed to have the purpose, and more clearly had the effect, of restricting the theory of law to accounting for social-fact-source-based validity without proposing any statement of value.[60] In Gardner, however, as in Leslie Green's similar account of legal theory, and Joseph Raz's, in his own way,[61] too, the affirmation of this sources thesis, (LP1), is said to be in no way 'a whole theory of law's nature'. (LP1) is compatible, they affirm, 'with any number of further theses about law's nature, including the thesis that all valid law is *by its nature* subject to special moral objectives and imperatives *of its own*',[62] and compatible with the thesis that 'in some contexts "legality"...names a moral value, such that laws may be more or less valid depending on...their merits', and with the thesis that 'one must capture this moral value of legality...in order to tell the whole story of law's nature'.[63] It thus becomes clear that (LP1) can and should be formulated more precisely, converting its universal quantifier to an existential one: (LP′). There is a 'technically confined'[64] and 'intra-systemic' sense of 'legal validity' such that validity in this sense can be predicated of a supposed rule by reference only to social-fact sources, without reference to what ought to be the law (or the sources of law) according to some standard not 'based on' social-fact sources.

[59] Gardner, 'Legal Positivism: 5½ Myths' at 203; cf. my comparison of his and Brian Leiter's uses of this phrase in essay 1 at 32–44 (2003b at 115–28).

[60] The *Postscript's* embrace (250–4) of soft or inclusive positivism does not significantly qualify this restriction, since it is a social-fact source that, in such a view, licenses the jurist to look beyond such sources to moral standards, and the legal *theory* of the kind that Hart undertook is restricted, by the descriptive purpose so emphasized in the *Postscript*, to reporting the social fact that jurists in the societies under study bring to bear, at this point in their legal reasoning, the relevant moral beliefs their society has and to which they are licensed to refer.

[61] See his distinction between applying the law (restricted to social-fact sources) and judicial argument *according to law* (which properly embraces moral reasons and reasoning about maintaining, developing, or amending the law): e.g. Raz, 'The Autonomy of Legal Reasoning'. [And p. 9 above.]

[62] Gardner, 'Legal Positivism: 5½ Myths' at 210 (emphases added).

[63] *Ibid.* at 226. Green, 'Legal Positivism', in the final paragraph, similarly affirms:

> Evaluative argument is, of course, central to the philosophy of law more generally. No legal philosopher can be *only* a legal positivist. A complete theory of law requires also an account of what kinds of things could possibly count as merits of law (must law be efficient or elegant as well as just?); of what role law should play in adjudication (should valid law always be applied?); of what claim law has on our obedience (is there a duty to obey?); and also of the pivotal questions of what laws we should have and whether we should have law at all. Legal positivism does not aspire to answer these questions, though its claim that the existence and content of law depends only on social facts does give them shape.

[64] See text at n. 69 below.

(LP′) is entitled, it seems to me, to the assent of everyone everywhere.[65] Certainly it is what was taken for granted by those who said *lex injusta non est lex*, which, understood as its authors understood it,[66] asserts that if a rule which is legally valid in the (LP′) sense is sufficiently unmeritorious it lacks the entitlement to be counted as personally decisive for them by judges, officials, and citizens, an entitlement to directive decisiveness that is central to the reasons we have for establishing and maintaining legal systems.

V

I return to the rule of recognition, which exists—and is the answer, ultimate for Hart's legal theory, to the question 'What is the reason for the validity of the highest rule of change, if not of all the rules, of this legal system?'—by being used as such in the practice of courts and other officials.

Like any other fact about what happens or is or has been done, *practice*, whether idiosyncratic, widespread, or universal, provides by itself no reason for its own continuation. From such an *Is* no *Ought* (or other gerundive-optative) can be inferred without the aid of another *Ought* or gerundive-optative *Is-to-be-pursued-or-done.* The fact that it is raining is in itself no reason to carry an umbrella, no reason at all, even in conjunction with the fact that without an umbrella I'll get wet. But facts like these can play their part in the reason, the warranted conclusion (that I should [had better] carry an umbrella) which gets its directive or normative element from some practical, evaluative premise such as: it's bad for one's health to get wet, or it's bad for one's ability to think and function to get uncomfortably wet and cold. *By virtue only of that* or some similar truth (as one supposes) about good and bad, the plain fact that an umbrella can prevent these evils by keeping me dry can contribute to the normative conclusion that

[65] See *NLNR* 290; essay 5 secs III–IV; essay 1 at 43–4; and more precisely 2007b sec. 3.1.

[66] Nothing could be stranger than Hart's decision to treat the saying as an invitation to treat all positive law as morally binding: *CL* 210–11 [205–6]; for my critique, see *NLNR* 364–6; for Hart's reply, *Essays in Jurisprudence and Philosophy*, 11–12. Yet MacCormick, *H.L.A. Hart*, 24–5 is right to give prominence to the thought that motivates Hart in his attempted critique of the tradition, the thought that we must '[hold] all laws as always open to moral criticism since there is no *conceptual* ground for supposing that the law which *is* and the law which *ought* to be coincide', with the result that 'the ultimate basis for adhering to the positivist thesis of the conceptual differentiation of law and morals is itself a moral reason... to make sure that it is always open to the theorist and the ordinary person to retain a critical moral stance in face of the law which is.' Since that moral concern was fully shared by the tradition assaulted by so many theorists calling themselves legal positivists, much of the history of jurisprudence over the past two hundred years or more is a tale of wasted zeal.

I have reason to, or ought to, carry an umbrella. Though David Hume himself thoroughly misunderstood and frequently ignored or violated it,[67] the inaptly named 'Hume's Law' remains valid and indispensable for an understanding of reason and normativity, ethical or otherwise.

In his last writings, Hart identified accurately enough the way in which his legal theory is enmeshed in something much more truly Humeian: Humeian psychology, Humeian conceptions of practical reason, and Humeian scepticism. His essay 'Commands and Authoritative Legal Reasons', the last (no. 10) of the *Essays on Bentham* (1983), concludes that 'judicial statements of the subject's legal duties need have nothing directly to do with the subject's reasons for action', a conclusion he rightly anticipates will seem paradoxical, confused, and open to the objection that it 'whittle[s] down the notion of [say, the judge's] *acceptance* of the legislator's enactments as reasons for action' to something very different from the essay's own explanation of what it is to accept some directive as a content-independent peremptory reason for doing what the directive directs—an objection which Hart virtually concedes, professing a lack of 'sufficient grasp of the complexities which I suspect surround this issue'.[68] The objection can be reformulated: as against the thesis of *The Concept of Law*, that at least officials (including presumably judges) must accept the rules as common standards for their own *and others'* conduct, this final essay holds that judges (and presumably other officials) need not do more than speak (and think!) in 'a technically confined way', that is 'as judges, from within an institution which they are *committed* as judges to maintain', stating not what the subject has reason to do but only 'what... may legally be demanded or exacted from him'.[69] But commitment, and appointment and practice as a judge, are all just facts, which of themselves afford no reason to act, no reason to stay committed or practise as a judge. So the account strips away not only (as Hart admits) the subject's reasons for compliance with law but also (as Hart does not signal) the judge's reasons.

Admittedly, this paradox or confusion *partly* arises from something distinct from the issues of reason and fact that concern me here, something only methodologically significant: namely, Hart's disorderly neglect of central-case analysis, his resort, pervasive in these late essays, to the question whether judges, officials, or anyone else *need* do or think or say such-and-such. To this question the answer will usually and all too easily be 'No, that way of acting, thinking or speaking is not necessary.' After all, countless kinds of less than fully reasonable ways of acting, thinking,

[67] See the detailed but evidently much ignored sec. II.5 in *NLNR* 36–42, along with 33–6 and 47–8.

[68] Hart, *Essays on Bentham*, 267 (emphasis added).

[69] *Ibid.*, 266 (emphasis added).

and speaking can and sometimes or even often do occur. But insistence that nothing save the logically or ontologically necessary can be given any descriptive-explanatory priority would devastate descriptive social theory, leaving it babbling about what is possible and silent about the important, central, and fully rational, and the main ways of diverging from that.

However, undiscussed retreat from central-case analysis is only one of the causes of Hart's final position about the internal attitude on which he had built his legal theory. That position can be reformulated as the claim that the central case of law, as also of adjudication, involves no proposing, not even a pretended proposing, of reasons for the subject's deliberation and action. But that more focused formulation still leaves it indeed a paradoxical position, and one that *misdescribes* what it is for judges to *accept* a rule in their practice of adjudication. Of course, Hart formulated it as a thesis not about judicial acceptance or attitudes, but about judicial speech. However, before judges can speak, in a technically confined way or otherwise, to litigants, witnesses, counsel, and spectators, they must resolve, in deliberation, in the presence, so to speak, of their own consciences, whether and how to speak. 'They are committed as judges', as Hart observes right here, to maintain the legal institution within which they work, and in the last analysis their work is not mere speech but interpersonal action which harms some and helps others in very palpable ways. What are they to *say to themselves*, one may ask, about their commitment?[70] The plain fact that they made that commitment, publicly and no doubt privately, by itself settles nothing, nothing at all, about what they have sufficient *reason* to do, that is, about what is to be done, had better be done, and in any relevant sense ought to be done by them. No *Ought* from a mere *Is*.

[70] It might seem as if Hart himself, on the previous page, had raised or identified this very question, when he says (*ibid.*, 265)

> ...it would be extraordinary if judges could give no answer to the question why in their operations as judges they *are disposed to* accept enactments by the legislature as determining the standards of correct judicial behaviour and so as reasons for applying and enforcing particular enactments (emphasis added).

But their question, if it is pertinent, should and will rather be of the form—or at least should rather have the meaning—'*Should* I be disposed to accept, apply and/or enforce particular enactments...? Are there sufficient reasons for my doing so, and if so what are they?' [Simmonds, *Law as a Moral Idea*, 129–35, takes the decisive question to be, not what reason judges have for applying the law, but what justification they can offer others, notably the litigants before them, for applying it. I agree that the latter question is of high importance, and very pertinent to the assessment of Hart's position. But the judge's own first-person singular question is *at least* equally important in itself and at least equally relevant to the theoretical debate. Simmonds is (134–5) as relaxed as Hart about the fact that judges' reasons for adhering to the law 'may be non-moral reasons grounded in self-interest'. Of course they 'may' and doubtless often are. But self-interest can never require more of judges than that they *appear* to be applying the law, and the opportunities for plausibly and 'deniably' corrupting the law's application are so great that here the first-person question—the question that is conscience—is also of high public importance and decisive for understanding the 'archetype' or central case of law and legal system.]

At this point, just before his admission of the appearance of paradox (which he cannot resolve), Hart suggests that his position would be quite different if legal reasons for acting (often action contrary to one's interests and inclinations) were 'objective, in the sense that they exist independently of [one's] subjective motivations'.[71] The implication of this and the whole paragraph, that Hart did not believe in objective practical reasons, legal or moral, was to be thoroughly confirmed by the last-written piece of work he published, his hard-working review of Bernard Williams, *Ethics and the Limits of Philosophy* for the New York Review of Books in July 1986. The review firmly endorses Williams's ethical subjectivism, while emphasizing its controversial character. I quote just one passage in relation to which the points I have been making about practices, commitments and the first-person perspective may again seem pertinent:

> ...the question, 'What should I do in these circumstances' is essentially 'first-personal' and not a mere derivative of and replaceable by 'What should anyone do in these circumstances?' For the 'I' of practical deliberation that stands back from my desires and reflects upon them is still the 'I' that has those desires, and, *unless I am already committed to the motivations of an impartial morality, reflective deliberation will not lead me to it.* To hold otherwise is to confuse reflection with detachment; and that confusion has encouraged the mistaken idea that if our moral beliefs are to be more than mere prejudices they must be regulated by some general ethical theory *au dessus de la mêlée* of our ethical practices.[72]

The French phrase perhaps recalls the title of a once famous pacifist tract by Romain Rolland, published in 1915 and alluded to directly in the last volume of Proust's great book. Be that as it may, the passage shows again how inadequately Hart's work represents the first-person perspective, in particular the form that reasons take in that perspective (when I am concentrating on reasons in the search for a right answer), and the way in which reasons can lead me to change my mind and, if they are practical reasons, acquire new motivations. The claim that 'unless I am already committed to the motivations of an impartial morality, reflective deliberation will not lead me to it' is simply wrong. Could it be plausible

[71] Hart, *Essays on Bentham*, 266–7:

> Of course, if it were the case, as a cognitive account of duty would hold it to be, that the statement that the subject has a legal duty to act in a way contrary to his interests and inclinations entails the statement that there exist reasons which are 'external' or objective, in the sense that they exist independently of his subjective motivation, it would be difficult to deny that legal duty is a form of moral duty. At least this would be so if it is assumed that ordinary non-legal moral judgments of duty are also statements of such objective reasons for action. For in that case, to hold that legal and moral duties were conceptually independent would involve the extravagant hypothesis that there were two independent 'worlds' or sets of objective reasons, one legal and the other moral.

[72] Hart, 'Who Can Tell Right From Wrong?' at 50 (emphasis added).

to anyone who does not accept the Humeian dogma that reasons cannot motivate?

As a general thesis about reason and will, that dogma is made to seem tolerable, if not credible, by the assumption that the impossibility of rational and rationally motivating *ends* leaves intact motivation by 'instrumental reasons', reasons which identify suitable and efficient means to sub-rationally desired (and therefore 'subjectively motivating') ends. But that assumption is illusory. If I have no reason for my ends, I have no *reason* for adopting or being interested in instrumental means to them, clever though the techniques embodied in some of those means may be. As I put it recently, adopting an argument of Christine Korsgaard:

> ... 'unless something attaches normativity to our ends, there can be no requirement to take the means to them.'[73] Such ends, moreover, have to be '*good*, in some sense that goes beyond the locally desirable.'[74] For 'I must have something to *say to myself* about why I am [willing an end, and am committed and remain committed to it, even in the face of desires that would distract and weaknesses that would dissuade me]—something better [to say to myself], moreover, than the fact that this is what I wanted yesterday'[75] (or indeed a moment ago or even, in the struggle of feelings, want now).[76]

What am I to say to myself? That question comes to mind when reading the final section of Hart's review of Williams. Having endorsed the author's main arguments for denying that ethical/moral beliefs have rational foundations, Hart asks 'What bearing on practice will and should these arguments have?' His answer begins by noting one of the fears that

> have been excited by such skeptical thought... [the fear] that if it becomes widespread we shall have nothing—or not enough—to say to the immoralist, whether he is the coldly selfish egoist of private life, or the brutal advocate of oppression in public life. But there is surely something laughable in the idea that anything we could draw from philosophy could weigh with such characters bent on having their way at others' expense. Why should it matter to them that there is a philosopher's proof that, in acting as they do, they are irrational, inconsistent, or flying in the face of some moral truths? As Williams says, 'What will the

[73] Korsgaard, 'The Normativity of Instrumental Reason' 251.

[74] *Ibid.*, 250–1. Korsgaard at 251, 252, is tempted to resile from this to allow for a 'heroic existentialist act' of 'just tak[ing] one's will at a certain moment to be normative, and commit[ting] oneself forever to the end selected at that moment', 'for no other reason than that [one] wills it so'. But she should concede that unless such a person considers that there is something worthwhile in doing so, some good in or reason for doing so, such an 'act of commitment' and of subsequent 'taking [it] as normative' is not rational but irrational.

[75] *Ibid.*, 250.

[76] Essay I.1 at 23–4 (2005a at 113–14). For my criticism of Korsgaard's attempts to develop a non-Humeian conception of practical reason, see *ibid.* at 24–8 (2005a at 114–18).

professor's justification do when they break down the door, smash his spectacles, take him away?'[77]

But the interesting question is not: What have I to say to the barbarians to persuade them that they should desist? It is: What have I to say to myself when I ask myself whether I shouldn't perhaps be on the winning side and team up with them?[78]

Williams and, more hesitantly, Hart attribute to certain ethical beliefs some measure of immunity from their scepticism: what they call 'substantive' or 'thick' ethical concepts, as used unreflectively and uncritically in 'a simple traditional society': concepts such as 'cruelty, lying, brutality, treachery, and gratitude', as distinct from 'abstract all-purpose evaluative concepts of "ought" and "right" and "good"'. But in this marshalling by Hart and Williams of practical predicates for classification between thick and thin we find omitted yet again, as in Hume and Kant and Chapter IX.1–2 of *The Concept of Law*, the intelligible goods of knowledge, life and health, friendship, reasonableness in one's inner life and one's outer actions, and the other fundamental reasons we all have for choosing and doing anything worthwhile we do or should do. These ends, taken in their fundamental intelligibility as good not only for me but anyone, and all the more when taken in their reflective implications as the elements of human flourishing and so[79] the key to understanding adequately our nature as persons, are so substantive, 'thick', and so far from being merely 'abstract', that they are the 'deep inside' of all that we can and should 'say to ourselves' to warrant our decisions as law-makers, law-appliers (executive or judicial), and citizens. The pursuit of these basic goods needs and can be given rational integration by the Golden Rule and other principles of

[77] Hart, 'Who Can Tell Right From Wrong?' at 52.

[78] Hart's next paragraph speculates about the reactions not of the immoralist or the egoist but of 'more ordinary people who with various degrees of conviction, difficulty, and backsliding manage to live up to the moral standards they have acquired and developed in their social life and to transmit them to their children', and gradually he locates 'us', the first-person plural, among them: when they/we discover the truth of ethical scepticism,

> the sense of necessity (the moral 'I must') in which the recognition of moral obligation often terminates, will have to be seen as coming not from outside, but from what is most deeply inside us even though it is normally also supported by others who share our practices and beliefs. The fear is that this will not be enough and that when we come to think of our moral standards as resting on no further foundation, we shall disregard them whenever they stand in the way of our getting or doing what we want.

Hart's response to this fear begins: 'How likely this is, is a question of moral psychology about which we know little enough ...', and never gets round to considering what one *should* think about the directive force of one's 'moral standards' once one discovers, through philosophical argumentation, that they merely 'come from what is most deeply inside us' and reflect motivations and 'concerns' which one just happens to have but which plenty of other people do not have, and which collide with other motivations and lively interests one has deep inside one.

[79] See *Aquinas* 29–34, 53, 90–2.

that reasonableness we call ethical/moral, and by the call of reason to be attentive to architectonic facts such as the possibility of free choice, and the subsisting of personal, familial, and (in different ways) national identity (partly given and partly constituted as the intransitive implications of free choices).[80] Such integration reinforces and makes more pointed the rational directiveness of the initial normativity entailed by the intelligible desirability of the basic human goods, that is, from their priority as reasons both for action and for abstention from what by entailment from them are basic forms of harm by conduct or neglect. These basic reasons for action are the rational ground for the Hartian primary rules restricting violence, theft, and fraud, and in their implications are the ground also for the Hartian remedies called secondary rules.[81]

Was the moral scepticism to which Hart gives restrained but clear voice in his last work a change of direction for him, something extrinsic to the architecture of his main work in the philosophy of law? I feel sure it was not.[82] In the notebook from which *The Concept of Law* emerges, on the page facing the key paragraph beginning 'I have the dim... outline of this book in my mind', are two sentences, on separate lines:

One side saying: you are blind
The other: you are seeing ghosts.

Midway between those years and the final years, his way of articulating the issue, on the one occasion when our conversation touched explicitly on ethical objectivity, was the same: It's a matter of 'You're blind' versus 'You're seeing things'. The ghosts he had in mind as *The Concept of Law* began to take shape surely included[83] the 'complex' and 'debatable' conceptions of 'the human end or good', conceptions entertained by philosophers before

[80] See essay II.2 (2005c).

[81] Hart's position in the *Postscript*, 249, that it is 'quite vain to seek any more specific purpose which law as such serves beyond providing guides to human conduct and standards of criticism of such conduct', is simply incompatible with the theory of law set out in *CL*: see *NLNR* 6–7. It is part and parcel of the disorderly retreat from central-case analysis that we see in *Essays on Bentham* (see pp. 249–50 above).

[82] His official position remained, to the end, that

> legal theory should avoid commitment to controversial philosophical theories of the general status of moral judgments and should leave open, as I do in this book ([*CL* 168 [164]]), the general question of whether they have what Dworkin calls 'objective standing'. (*CL* 253–4.)

But this was always an implicitly partisan neutrality. For, as the review of Williams I think concedes, to withhold the affirmation of such standing is to depart from the internal point of view of those who accept moral standards as binding—depart in a way they would consider fundamental. Joseph Raz, who knew Hart far better, I believe, than I did, speaks less cautiously about Hart's subjectivist and (not unlike Williams) naturalist (I would say scientistic) view on these fundamental matters and about their implications for his jurisprudence, in Raz, 'Two Views of the Nature of the Theory of Law' at 4–6.

[83] To be sure, the sentences in the notebook (which I quote from Lacey, *H.L.A. Hart*, 222) doubtless also refer to the Realists' view (mistaken, as Hart says) that obligation and associated reasons even for official (e.g. judicial) action are illusory projections of feelings, psychological compulsions, etc.

'other thinkers, Hobbes and Hume among them,... [were] willing to lower their sights'.[84] And as we know, what Hobbes, not to mention his disciple Bentham, found when the sights were right down and he looked inside was the brute fact of desires, will as no more than the desire that last precedes action, and, to make possible some unified theory, some desire by postulation dominant, such as (in early Hobbes) the desire to surpass others for the sake of surpassing them, or (in later Hobbes) to avoid death.

Trying to understand the internal point of view makes, I would say, no sense as a method in social theory unless it is conceived as trying to understand the intelligible goods, the reasons for action, that were, are and will be available to any acting person, anyone capable of deliberation or of spontaneously intelligent response to opportunities. Once these reasons are understood, along with the accompanying, potentially reinforcing, potentially disruptive, sub-rational inclinations (passions, emotions), theorists are equipped to understand the myriad ways in which the practices of individuals and groups can, do and doubtless will respond, reasonably and more or less unreasonably, in the ever-variable but far from random circumstances of human existence. Social theory may be fundamentally contemplative ('descriptive') in purpose, or it may be fundamentally practical, intending to guide action—the theorist's as much as anyone else's—by identifying at least some outlines and principles of right and wrong, better and worse. But descriptive social theory will be unable to get beyond an endless video of local histories—or a merely statistical ordering of them—unless it makes the judgments about reasonableness that are fundamental to practical social theory. (Hart's theory makes and relies on some.) And practical, morally oriented social theory will be a half-blind guide unless it profits from the practical insights, and the transmissible experience of inner and outer causes and effects, that are made available by history and social theory, perhaps distilled and by imagination and intelligence enhanced in great works of literary art.

The asymmetry between the first-person and third-person viewpoints[85] goes deeper than Hart and Hampshire identified. In the last analysis, it is this: the third-person view terminates in facts, including facts about the beliefs and attitudes, intentions and commitments of other persons; but in the first-person view 'I believe that *p*' is transparent for '*p*'.[86] The 'I believe' drops out, leaving '*p*', usually not just one proposition but a network of propositions some of which are reasons for believing others. One is looking not at oneself, one's attitudes and beliefs, as facts about oneself, but at the

[84] *CL* 191 [187]. [85] See text at n. 27 above.
[86] On this transparency, see *FoE* 70–4.

proposition(s) under consideration, the reasons there are for affirming it and the reason(s) it gives for making it one's belief, one's attitude, and one's action, whether the theoretical-practical action of judging it true or the practical-practical action of following and putting into effect the intelligent and reasonable guidance it gives, the good (benefits and goals) towards which it directs one. And because the first-person (practical) viewpoint is concerned not, in the end, with facts about oneself but with reasons (for action) that are both available to and bear on the good of anyone like me (generically, all human beings), it is the domain of *common* good and so the engine room, the most proximate efficient cause,[87] of law.

In that perspective there is no reason to be found for stopping at the supposedly 'minimum' set of reasons to which Hart appeals, not simply in his reflections on the 'minimum content of natural law', but much more importantly in his account of primary rules, private and public secondary rules, and the union of them that constitutes law in its central instantiation and concept(ion). I argued earlier in this essay that that account gets its persuasiveness partly from its suppressed appeal to reasons which, though largely unarticulated or, where articulated, unintegrated in the legal theory proposed in *The Concept of Law*, are reasons (good and not so good) pervasive in Hart's other writings and indeed in his own life. His work is a standing invitation to develop legal theory's critical account and promotion of those considerations of justice, of concern for common good, which include the general principles of legality and law common[88] to *civilized*[89] peoples and make law salient[90] as a means of governance and a reasonable exercise and acceptance[91] of authority.

[87] In respect of the law's positivity, it is also the formal (shaping) cause. Even wicked law will almost invariably purport to be for common good, and should be juridically and morally assessed by reference to the standing requirements of the common good that yield the principles of legality or the Rule of Law, and the general principles of law common to civilized peoples.

[88] In *NLNR* 286–9 I articulated some of those principles, and did so by reference to public international law. But their primary domain is, and will in justice remain, the legal system of what Hart called *countries*, i.e. the nation-state, the political community of persons who regard themselves as one people and organize their law and legal system to be theirs as distinct from other peoples'.

[89] Failure today to take seriously this qualifier makes freshly resonant the memoir contributed by Lord Wilberforce to the privately printed record of the memorial meeting for Hart in the University Examination Schools, Oxford, in 1993, recalling their friendship in the 1930s:

> We shared...a sense of coming disaster which we knew would destroy our way of life.... In 1938 we were together, with some lawyers and clerks, when the news came that Mr. Chamberlain was returning with 'Peace for our time'. There was applause, there was talk of going to the airport to cheer him home. We just looked at each other with tears in our eyes—it was unnecessary to speak.

[90] On this salience, see essay 2 (1984b) and essay 3 (1989b).

[91] On the not merely 'conceptual' reasons why authority entails obligation, and an earlier reflection on Hart's stopping short in the identification of reasons, see essay 4 (1987d).

11

HART AS A POLITICAL PHILOSOPHER*

I

Herbert Hart was born in 1907, a son of prosperous tailors in the north of England. From the age of 11 he was boarding-schooled in the south, but after some years was schooled close to home, at an excellent grammar school where he finished as Head Prefect, regarded by the headmaster as a head boy of unsurpassed loyalty and capacity. By competitive scholarship examination he proceeded to New College, one of the University of Oxford's oldest and best colleges, where he studied Greek, Latin, ancient history, and philosophy, with brilliant success. Before, during, and after his Oxford studies, he travelled widely throughout Europe; he had a gift for languages and throughout his life an immense enthusiasm for places, people, and literature.

Passing the Bar exams in late 1930, Hart joined commercial chambers in Lincoln's Inn where he practised with notable success, especially in tax matters. Though he had joined the Inns of Court Regiment early in his career at the Bar, and participated enthusiastically in stag-hunting and like pursuits, his political views, always liberal, moved decisively left during the mid-1930s even before he became associated in 1936 with Jenifer Williams, who had been a member of the Communist Party since 1934 and in her early years as a civil servant—which coincided with their beginning to live together—even had a Soviet controller. But, as she later wrote of Hart (whom she married in late 1941), 'he was strongly opposed to communism both as theory and practice'.[1]

In June 1940, Hart joined MI5, the intelligence organization dedicated to counter-espionage in Britain. There he worked until the end of the war on counter-espionage, the dissemination of disinformation to the enemy,

* 2009b ('H.L.A. Hart: A Twentieth Century Oxford Political Philosopher').

[1] Jenifer Hart, *Ask Me No More*, 72.

and the processing of results of MI6's ultra secret deciphering of the German codes; he was regarded within MI5 as outstandingly able, reliable, and acute, and patriotically maintained the mandated secrecy about these activities down to the end of his life.

At war's end, Hart returned not to the Bar but to New College, as fellow and tutor in Philosophy. It was hoped and expected that he would maintain the anti-empiricist tradition of his Platonist tutor H.W.B. Joseph, but he soon gravitated to the modern-minded opposition, the circle of philosophers who under J.L. Austin's leadership pursued a way of thinking philosophically that Hart like others was content to call linguistic, or sometimes analytical. Still, in 1952, immediately before his election to the chair of Jurisprudence, he was lecturing on Legal & Political Theories in Plato.

Hart's inaugural lecture in 1953 laid out and exemplified an agenda for an analytical jurisprudence informed by linguistic philosophy, which Hart presented as practised if not inaugurated by Jeremy Bentham. Nevertheless, as we shall see, his master work *The Concept of Law* (1961) is not in its deep structure either linguistic or analytical. Nor does Hart's best-known book, *Law, Liberty & Morality* (1963), owe anything to fashions in philosophical methodology.

In 1968, the year his *Essays on Punishment & Responsibility* appeared and six years before retirement age, Hart left the chair of Jurisprudence and the university (though not the family house in central Oxford), feeling he had said all he had to say.[2] He worked for the next five years on editing and commenting in essay form on Bentham's accounts of law, rights, powers, and legal language; and continued the quasi-governmental work he had begun in 1966 as a member of the Monopolies Commission. He returned formally to the university as Principal of Brasenose College, 1973–8, and thereafter until his death in December 1992 was granted a room for work in University College, where he had taught and written as professor of Jurisprudence. A principal scholarly concern of his in these late years was preparing a response to some main critics of *The Concept of Law*; the fruits of this, a response to his successor in the chair, Ronald Dworkin, appeared posthumously in 1994, edited by Hart's closest jurisprudential successor, Joseph Raz, as Postscript to that book's second edition.

Not long after his seventieth birthday, Hart wrote:

> loss of the belief that [moral judgment and argument] are backed by something more than human attitudes or policies is, and will continue to be, for many as profound as the loss of belief in God.[3]

[2] Lacey, *H.L.A. Hart*, 289. [3] Hart, 'Morality and Reality' at 35.

That he had undergone the latter loss, at some early stage of his life, is clear from the exceedingly intimate (and philosophically informed) biography published in 2004.[4] In retrospect, at least, everything suggests that—at least from the time he began to publish philosophical work—he also lacked the other belief, that moral judgments can be really true. But his activities as a philosopher, teacher, mentor, colleague, and friend, like his performance of wartime duties in defence of his country, his fidelity to his family, and his devoted care for their disabled youngest child, amply display a morally demanding range of virtues.

II

Hart's significance can be understood only when his work is measured against conceptions of political philosophy that were dominant in Oxford in the years between Hart's post-war return and the publication of his *The Concept of Law.* Though these conceptions might be divided, like Hart's own philosophical formation, between the pre-'linguistic' and the 'linguistic', they had much in common. As Eric Voegelin emphasizes in his mordant survey 'The Oxford Political Philosophers',[5] written in the summer of 1952, a contemporary pre-linguistic Oxford political philosopher as methodologically informed and representative as A.D. Lindsay held that political theory transcends the description of institutions by being a study of the 'operative ideals' which, as beliefs of citizens, sustain their respective states in existence. This makes political theory essentially a history of ideas, with some sorting, arranging, and axiomatizing in the mode (as Voegelin observes) of theology (which takes its principles not from philosophical considerations but as givens, *dogmata*). Lindsay's concession that there remains a question about the 'absolute worth' of operative ideals is fleeting: 'the primary business of the political theorist' remains the understanding of *actually operative* ideals; 'political theory, then, is concerned with fact'.[6]

What then of the linguistic-philosophical approach becoming dominant in Oxford around 1950? It was approvingly summarized, towards the end of its dominance, by Anthony Quinton, introducing a book of *Oxford Readings in Political Philosophy.* The great works in political philosophy (or, synonymously, political thought or theory), from Plato and Aristotle to Marx and Mill, consist, said Quinton, (a) of 'factual or descriptive

[4] Lacey, *H.L.A. Hart.* [5] Voegelin, 'The Oxford Political Philosophers' at 108.
[6] Lindsay, *The Modern Democratic State*, 45; cf. 37–8; also 47:

It is a philosophical discipline, not because it tries to base our conduct in politics on metaphysics, but because it demands that we should reflect on what we actually do and will, make explicit to ourselves what we do implicitly, think out the assumptions on which we as a matter of fact act.

accounts of political institutions and activities' (political science), (b) of 'recommendations about the ideal ends that political activity should pursue and about the way political institutions should be designed in order to serve those ends' (ideology), and (c) only to 'a small, though commonly crucial extent', of 'conceptual reasonings', the kind of reasonings now known, according to Quinton, to be the only properly philosophical activity, namely 'classifying and analyzing the terms, statements and arguments of the substantive, first-order disciplines' or modes of thought, disciplines or modes of thought which are 'concerned with some aspect or region of the world'—unlike philosophy, which is 'conceptual and critical, concerned with *them* [sc. those substantive, first-order modes of thought] rather than with the reality they investigate'.[7]

What makes reasoning 'conceptual' and/or 'analytical'? How might such reasoning add anything to descriptions of the institutions found in historically given societies and 'recommendations' (or indeed Lindsay-like historical accounts) of 'ideals'? These questions are left in shadow by Quinton and indeed by the whole school of philosophers whose self-understanding Quinton was articulating. Hart, too, while framing much of *The Concept of Law* in terms of 'analysis' of 'concepts', says little to make explicit what counts as conceptual or analytical, or what counts as success in such analysis.[8] But what he proposed as the fruits of his philosophical work in that book, and the arguments deployed to yield them, together made clear—showed in action—that political philosophy could and can still be pursued in a way that is simply not envisaged in Quinton's triad (institutional description, ideological recommendation, conceptual analysis). That way, moreover, is continuous with main parts of the tradition of political philosophizing which that triad so mischaracterizes.

Hart's preface to *The Concept of Law* speaks of 'the political philosophy of this book'. This seems to point to two of the book's theses or themes. The first is *articulated* firmly in terms of 'analysis' of 'concepts'. By 'referring', Hart says, to 'manifestations' of 'the internal point of view: the view of those who do not merely record and predict behaviour conforming to rules, but *use* the rules as standards for the appraisal of their own and others' behaviour,' we can provide an 'analysis' that dissipates 'the

[7] Quinton, *Political Philosophy*, 1. Quinton reports (*ibid.*, 2), without disavowing, the 'widely held' view that 'there really is no such subject as political philosophy apart from the negative business of revealing the conceptual errors and methodological misunderstandings of those who have addressed themselves in a very general way to political issues'.

[8] He quotes approvingly (*CL*, preface) from J.L. Austin, leader of the Oxford school of 'ordinary language', 'analytical' philosophy: 'a sharpened awareness of words [can be used] to sharpen our perception of the phenomena'. Here 'perception' is an evasive word for understanding, and 'phenomena' for reality, or truths.

obscurity which still lingers about [the concepts (which bestride both law and political theory) of the state, of authority, and of an official ...].' For while some manifestations of the internal point of view—those under 'the simple regime of primary rules'—are 'most elementary', the 'range of what is said and done from the internal point of view is much extended and diversified' with 'the addition ... of secondary rules', an addition that brings with it 'a whole set of new concepts ... legislation, jurisdiction, validity, and, generally, of legal powers, private and public'. Thus, 'the combination of primary rules of obligation with the secondary rules of recognition, change and adjudication' is not only the heart of a legal system but also 'a most powerful tool for the analysis of much that has puzzled both the jurist and the political theorist'.[9]

What matters here is not the various technical problems that commentators have identified in details of this analysis.[10] Rather, it is the argumentation employed by Hart to show that the distinctions marked by his new technical terms—internal and external points of view; primary and secondary rules—are distinctions not just in 'legal thought' or 'political theory' but in the social reality that he often prefers to call 'social phenomena', reality that if it does not exist (as it does in our here and now) can in favourable circumstances be deliberately and reasonably brought into being, as state, law, legal system, courts, legislatures, and so forth. For Hart's argumentation asserts that alternative 'general' accounts of law failed to recognize both the variety of ways on which rules of law *function* and, more fundamentally, the variety of *functions* which are served, or possessed, by social rules and legal systems, and by the main components of legal systems.

So the two fundamental ways in which rules function as guides to behaviour are by imposing obligations and conferring powers. But if a theorist, like Kelsen, denies that this duality of normative functioning is fundamental, Hart refutes him by pointing to the different functions served by the two types of rule. *Obligation-imposing* rules guide both the uncooperative (by threatening them with sanctions) and those who are willing to cooperate if only they are told what is required of them.[11]

[9] All the quotations in this paragraph are from *CL* 98–9. (In the 1961 edition the identical passages are, at this point in the volume, four or five pages earlier.)

[10] Thus, as Joseph Raz showed, not all secondary rules are power-conferring, and not all power-conferring rules are secondary: 'The Functions of Law', in Raz, *The Authority of Law*, 163–79 at 178–9. There is in fact a good deal of terminological inconsistency and substantive flux in *The Concept of Law*, in relation to the distinctions and relations between kinds of rule, as also about the precise characteristics and content of 'internal' and 'external' points of view.

[11] *CL* 39–40. Strictly speaking, the threat of sanction is created by a distinct or distinguishable ancillary rule empowering and to some extent obligating officials to impose penalties on those who violate the obligation-imposing rule.

Power-conferring rules, understood 'from the point of view of those [private persons] who exercise them', confer on private citizens the 'huge and distinctive amenity' of being 'private legislator[s]', 'made competent to determine the course of the law within the sphere of [their] contracts, trusts, wills, and other structures of rights and duties which [they are thereby] enabled to build'; and the introduction into society of rules conferring *public* powers such as legislative or judicial powers to make authoritative enactments and orders 'is a *step forward* as important to society as the invention of the wheel'.[12] The difference in normative types (ways of functioning) is grounded on the differences in social function, that is, on the different *reasons for valuing them*, which make exercise of powers 'a form of *purposive activity* utterly different from performance of duty or submission to coercive control'.[13]

Although Hart loyally continues to speak of this argumentation as 'giv[ing] some... analysis of what is involved in the assertion that rules of these two types exist',[14] it is clear that what is going on in his explanation of 'the features of law', and in his claim that his explanation has superior 'explanatory power', is not merely linguistic or conceptual.[15] Rather, it is an acknowledgement, or reminder, or disclosure, of certain aspects of the human condition as it really is. His later reflections on the grounding of the concept(s) of 'need and function' enable us to be more precise: in Hart's own self-understanding, appeals to function are 'ways of *simultaneously describing and appraising* things by reference to the contribution they make'[16] to a 'proper end of human activity'.[17]

Those later reflections are articulated by Hart in relation to the second of the two theses or themes he thought made a contribution to political philosophy: his discussion, in *The Concept of Law*'s chapter 'Law and Morals', of what he calls 'The Minimum Content of Natural Law'.[18] The section bearing this title—which might equally well have been 'The Minimum Content of Positive Law'[19]—argues vigorously, though with many signs of anxiety, that we should reject 'the positivist thesis that "law may have any content"'. Besides definitions of words and 'ordinary statements of fact', there is 'a third category of statements: those the truth of which is contingent on human beings and the world they live

[12] *Ibid.*, 41–2 (emphasis added). [13] *Ibid.*, 41 (emphases added). [14] *Ibid.*, 81.
[15] *Ibid.* [16] *Ibid.*, 192. [17] *Ibid.*, 191 (emphasis added). [18] *Ibid.*, 193.
[19] For the conclusions it reaches on p. 199 concern the 'indispensable features of municipal law' and reject 'the positivist thesis that "law may have any content"'. See also the phrase 'what content a legal system must have' in the 1957/8 essay quoted at n. 26 below. But Hart's attention wavers between features indispensable in any subsisting society (e.g. one living by primary, pre-legal rules alone) and features indispensable for a legal system (in which primary rules exist in union with secondary rules and institutions). This last point has been clarified for me by comments to me by Cristóbal Orrego, whose understanding of Hart is unrivalled: see Orrego, *H.L.A. Hart*.

in retaining the salient characteristics which they have'.[20] More precisely, such contingently *universal* truths include statements about what Hart calls 'natural necessity', by which, in this precise context, he means the *rational* necessity yielded by the conjunction of a universal human 'aim' and various natural facts or 'truisms' such as that human beings are approximately equal to each other in strength and vulnerability, are limited in their 'altruism', understanding, and strength of will, and are subject to scarcity of resources and the need for a division of labour to exploit them.[21] Given the common or universal wish to continue in existence ('survive'), and the truisms about vulnerability, 'what reason demands is *voluntary* co-operation in a *coercive* system'.[22]

Hart's anxiety about this head-on challenge, not only to Kelsenian legal positivism but to the reigning assumptions (such as Quinton's or Lindsay's) about method in political philosophy, is manifested in the immediately preceding, preparatory pages. On the one hand, he shows here that even after Aristotelian principles of cosmology and physics have been expelled, we cannot sensibly talk about, or adequately understand, human beings without having a 'teleological view'. He instances our talk of natural 'human *needs* which it is *good* to satisfy',[23] and of 'the *functions* of bodily organs'[24]—all the talk that makes possible our talk of harm and injury. He sketches, albeit without unambiguously endorsing or repudiating, a more developed version of this teleology of human existence and nature: 'a condition of biological maturity and developed physical powers' which 'also includes, as its distinctively human element, a development and excellence of mind and character manifested in thought and conduct'.[25]

But, on the other hand, just at this point he shrinks back, declaring that

> what makes sense of this mode of thought and expression is ... the tacit assumption that the proper end of human activity is survival, and this rests on the simple contingent fact that most men most of the time wish to continue in existence.[26]

[20] *CL* 199–200. [21] *Ibid.*, 194–7. [22] *Ibid.*, 198.
[23] *Ibid.*, 190 (Hart's emphases). [24] *Ibid.*, 191 (Hart's emphasis). [25] *Ibid.*, 190.
[26] *Ibid.*, 191. He continues:

> The actions which we speak of as those which are naturally good to do, are those which are required for survival; the notions of a human need, of harm, and of the *function* of bodily organs or changes rests on the same simple fact.

See also the slightly earlier version in 'Positivism and the Separation of Law and Morals' [1958], in Hart, *Essays in Jurisprudence and Philosophy*, 81:

> ... in asking what content a legal system must have we take this question to be worth asking only if *we who consider it cherish* the humble aim of survival in close proximity to our fellows. (Emphasis added.)

This drastically limited—and deeply ambiguous[27]—conception of 'the proper end of human activity' he ascribes to Hobbes and Hume, whose 'modest' or 'humble' conception of human ends should be preferred to the 'more complex and debatable' conceptions of Aristotle or Aquinas. Hart gives no sign, in this book, of noticing that survival, even when we ignore its ambiguities, is quite inadequate, as an aim or end, to account for the developed 'excellences of mind and character'. The inadequacy goes further, for concern to survive does not begin to account for the fundamental elements in his concept of law, the secondary rules introduced (as his first theme or thesis made clear) to remedy the defects—the social problems—which plague a society governed only by 'social morality's' pre-legal 'primary rules'.

Hart soon tacitly acknowledged this inadequacy. Writing the following year about 'social morality', not as temporally pre-legal but as the standards acknowledged, over and above the law, even in legally ordered societies, he articulated universal values, virtues, and standards, still on a purportedly Hobbesian basis but now with an adjusted rationale:

> ...all social moralities...make provision in some degree for such universal values as individual freedom, safety of life, and protection from deliberately inflicted harm.... Secondly,...the spirit or attitude which characterizes the practice of a social morality is something of very great value and indeed quite vital for men to foster and preserve in any society. For in the practice of any social morality there are necessarily involved what may be called *formal* values as distinct from the *material* values of its particular rules or content. In moral relationships with others the individual sees questions of conduct from an impersonal point of view and applies general rules impartially to himself and to others; he is made aware of and takes account of the wants, expectations, and reactions of others; he exerts self-discipline and control in adapting his conduct to a system of reciprocal claims. These are universal virtues and indeed constitute the specifically moral attitude to conduct....We have only to conduct the Hobbesian experiment of imagining these virtues totally absent to see that they are vital for the conduct of any cooperative form of human life and any successful personal life.[28]

So cooperation and social rules have a rationale going well beyond survival: a successful personal life. John Rawls in *A Theory of Justice* (1971) elaborates that kind of rationale in the 'thin theory of the good'—the range of 'primary goods' which are good for each one of us because needed '*whatever else one*

[27] Whose survival is my end? Mine at all costs? My children's, or friend's, at some risk or even certain cost to my own? My city's or country's?...

[28] Hart, *Law, Liberty & Morality*, 70–1. The passage continues:

> No principles of critical morality which paid the least attention to the most elementary facts of human nature and the conditions in which human life has to be led could propose to dispense with them.

wants'.[29] Hart himself had said a little more about his adjusted rationale in 1967: if law

> is to be of any value as an instrument for the realization of human purposes, it must contain rules concerning the basic conditions of social life.... without the protections and advantages that such rules supply, men would be grossly hampered in the pursuit of any aims.[30]

Such rules are provided for by social morality, but only in ways that 'leave open to dispute too many questions concerning the precise scope and form of its restraints'. Hence the human need for law, for a legal system which has a content—that is, which performs functions—of the type indicated in the first theme of Hart's account: the union of primary (mostly duty-imposing) and secondary (mostly power-conferring) rules.[31]

Both Hart and Rawls thus broke the bounds of political philosophy as it was conceived by many in their philosophical circle. They went beyond describing institutions, and beyond generalizations about historically given institutions, to offer—not recommendations of ideals—but sober accounts of what human persons and groups *need* and *rationally* desire, and of states of affairs and arrangements that are *universally* valuable (good) for beings with the nature we have. To that extent they rejoined the enterprise launched by Plato and Aristotle, though professing to admit only what would be admitted by a Hobbes who openly derided the 'old moral philosophers'[32] for their talk of what is intrinsically and most completely and constitutively good for human persons.

[29] Rawls, *A Theory of Justice*, 396–407, 433–4. Accordingly, Rawls's 'primary goods' ('liberty and opportunity, income and wealth, and above all self-respect') are goods that 'it is rational to want... whatever else is wanted, since they are in general necessary for the framing and the execution of a rational plan of life': *ibid.*, 433; also 253, 260, 328. Rawls expressly does *not* contend that 'criteria of excellence lack a rational basis from the standpoint of everyday life', and he grants that 'the freedom and wellbeing of individuals, when measured by the excellence of their activities and works, is vastly different in value' and that comparisons of intrinsic value can obviously be made': *ibid.*, 328, 329. But he will not allow such differentiations to enter at all into the rational determination of the basic principles of justice (*ibid.*, 327–32); to do so would be out of line with his 'rejection of the principle of perfection and the acceptance of democracy in the assessment of another's excellences': 527; also 419.

[30] 'Problems of the Philosophy of Law' [1967] reprinted in Hart, *Essays in Jurisprudence and Philosophy*, 112. See also 113:

> The empirical [not teleological] version of [natural law] theory assumes only that, whatever other purposes laws may serve, they must, to be acceptable to any rational person, enable men to live and organize their lives for the more efficient pursuit of their aims.

And 115:

> ...all men who have aims to pursue need the various protections and benefits which only laws...can effectively confer. For any rational man, laws conferring these protections and benefits must be valuable, and the price to be paid for them in the form of limitations imposed by the law on his own freedom will usually be worth paying.

[31] *Ibid.*, 114. [32] Hobbes, *Leviathan*, c. xi (ed. Oakeshott) (Blackwell, 1960), 63.

There is truth in John Gardner's remark that Hart and Rawls (with some others unnamed) 'together revived political philosophy (and helped to shape as well as capture the distinctive liberalism of the 1960s) by asserting political philosophy's relative autonomy from the rest of moral philosophy'.[33] Insofar as Hart's political philosophy was embedded in a philosophy of law, one might say more precisely that his attempt was to do political philosophy even if either there is *no* moral philosophy or moral philosophy yields a normative content as minimal as Hobbes professes (alternatives between which Hart's writings waver or, at best, suspend judgment). And his late-period work in philosophy of law shows, even more clearly than before, that the attempt could be sustained only by setting aside his own principal methodological device—the focus of reflection on the *central* case of the reality, 'phenomenon', or concept in issue—and looking instead to the marginal and incompletely reasonable, for example adjudicating, understood as it is by judges who adjudicate without sense of moral responsibility or justification but perhaps as cynical careerists or Machiavellian promoters of projects foreign or antithetical to the law's (and to the common good).[34] On the other hand, Hart's late-period work also shows the extent to which he was willing to admit, at least by implication, that the asserted autonomy of political from moral philosophy was unsustainable. For against Rawls, Mill, Nozick, and Dworkin, he objected that attempts to ground *basic individual rights or liberties*—rights such as he himself purported to endorse—on arguments of utility, or on the separateness of persons or their claims to equal respect, or on hypothesized choices by self-interested but partially ignorant parties in an original position, are all foredoomed:

> ...a theory of basic individual rights must rest on a specific conception of the human person and of what is needed for the exercise and development of distinctive human powers.[35]

[33] 'Introduction by John Gardner,' Hart, *Punishment & Responsibility* (2nd edn), xlviii–xlix. Gardner's phrase 'the rest of' hints at the fundamentally questionable character of this project. He also gives a valuable critical account, at xix–xxiii, of the relationship between Rawls, 'Two Concepts of Rules' and Hart, 'Prolegomenon to the Principles of Punishment', 1 (essay 1 in *Punishment & Responsibility*).

[34] In Hart, *Essays on Bentham*, 265–8 the questions of (a) the meaning of the judge's statements of the subject's legal duties, and (b) the judge's own grounds for so stating and enforcing the law, are each treated as a matter of what 'may' be the case, as a matter of logical and psychological possibility, rather than of what makes good and reasonable sense for people seeking really good reasons for action. At p. 267, at the end of the last substantive legal theory that he published, Hart half admits that in arguing 'that judicial statements of the subject's legal duties need have nothing directly to do with the subject's reasons for action', he is paradoxically denying the insight on which his legal theory was founded, that rules are reasons for action for subjects as well as officials.

[35] Hart, *Essays in Jurisprudence and Philosophy*, 17. Hart adds, *ibid.*:

> I am confirmed in this belief by the fact that when Professor Rawls came to reply to my arguments..., the modifications which he made in his original statement [in *A Theory of Justice*] of his

And such a theory of rights 'is urgently called for'.[36]

III

Hart's biographer says, credibly, that *Law, Liberty & Morality* (1963)

> stands, over 40 years after its publication, as the resounding late twentieth-century statement of principled liberal social policy. Its ideas continue to echo in both political and intellectual debates...[37]

Its key thesis she identifies accurately enough: 'democratic states are not entitled to enforce moral standards for their own sake: the mere belief that, say, certain kinds of sexual activity are immoral is not enough to justify their prohibition'.[38] She remains as innocent as Hart of the profound ambiguities which make his book's resounding success in shaping debate and policy a dismaying triumph of confusion and error.

The book opens with a misstatement of English law, an error which points directly to the whole book's misidentification of the political-philosophical issues at stake:

> The Suicide Act 1961, though it may directly affect the lives of few people, is something of a landmark in our legal history. It is the first Act of Parliament for at least a century to *remove altogether* the penalties of the criminal law from a *practice* both clearly condemned by conventional Christian morality and punishable by law.[39]

But though the individual, private *act* of committing or attempting to commit suicide ceased to be a crime, the 1961 statute rigorously confirmed, indeed strengthened, the criminal law's penalties and prohibitions against any social *practice* of suicide—against any and every kind of assistance, advice, promotion, or facilitation of it.[40]

Hart went on:

> Many hope that the Suicide Act may be followed by further measures of reform, and that certain forms of abortion, homosexual behaviour between consenting

own theory to meet my objections appear both to identify the basic liberties for which he argues and their priority over other values by reference to a conception of the human person and of what is necessary for the exercise and development of what he calls the moral powers.

[36] Hart, *ibid.*, 196 (essay first published 1979). This double-edged formula hints at Hart's deep scepticism about our capacity to make rational judgments (or 'theories') about such matters.

[37] Lacey, *H.L.A. Hart*, 7 (sc. debates 'about a range of social and legal issues such as criminal justice policy, euthanasia, abortion, and human rights'); 2 ('still read by practically all students of law, politics and sociology...the nearest thing to a manifesto for the homosexual law reform movement').

[38] *Ibid.*, 6–7. [39] *Law, Liberty & Morality*, Preface, opening sentences (emphases added).

[40] Suicide Act 1961, s. 2, imposes imprisonment for up to fourteen years for any counselling (advising), procuring, or assisting in advance of or in the act of suicide; and any attempt to provide such advice or assistance is a serious offence under the general law of criminal attempts.

adults in private, and certain forms of euthanasia will cease to be criminal offences; for they think that here, as in the case of suicide, the misery caused directly and indirectly by legal punishment outweighs any conceivable harm these practices may do.[41]

In all these matters, the structure of the issue at stake was fundamentally the same and was wholly overlooked by Hart. The issue was, and is: supposing that the truly *private acts* of an adult individual, or set of consenting adults, should and/or did cease to be criminal offences, what should be the policy of the law, and of society's other governing institutions (for example public education), in relation to the *public promotion or facilitating* of such acts?[42] After all, in many states outside the Anglo-American world a sharp distinction of principle was and is drawn between *private* and *public*, a distinction well grounded in the philosophical-theological tradition represented by Aquinas.[43] A classic articulation of this tradition is in Article 19 of the Argentine constitution, a provision unchanged since 1853 and with antecedents in earlier nineteenth-century constitutions:

19. The private actions of men which in no way offend [public] order or public morality, nor injure a third party, are reserved exclusively to God and exempted from the authority of judges.[44]

In states within this tradition, homosexual sex acts in private were not criminalized, but—speaking of the mid-twentieth century and earlier—homosexual practice was severely discouraged by prohibitions on homosexual prostitution, propaganda, places of public resort, solicitation in public spaces, adoption of children, pornography, and so forth. The tradition finds expression, implicitly, in the provisions of the European Convention on Human Rights (1950) which make 'morals', implicitly public

[41] *Ibid.* He went on, unrealistically, to express doubt that such reforms were likely in the near future. Homosexual acts of adults in private were de-criminalized in 1967, as were most abortions (effective 1968), not to mention the no-fault, all-on-paper divorce authorized by a statute of 1969. This was already readily predictable in 1963, from e.g. the enactment of the Obscene Publications Act 1959, and the unsuccessful prosecution of the publishers of *Lady Chatterley's Lover* in 1960; and in relation to homosexual acts it was indeed predicted to occur 'perhaps at an early date' by Lord Simonds in the passage from *Shaw v Director of Public Prosecutions* [1962] AC 223 at 268, quoted by Hart, *Law, Liberty & Morality*, 9.

[42] In the case of euthanasia, most who have reflected seriously on it, even those who think it morally unobjectionable in itself, conclude that it cannot be regarded as private, since death always has consequences (often highly beneficial) for others and must always be investigated by public authority to ensure that what seemed voluntary was truly so; and that the society-wide consequences of allowing some people to choose to kill others are so unjustly adverse for the vulnerable that even Hart's projected 'some forms of euthanasia' would be a grave public evil. See esp. *When Death is Sought* (New York: New York State Task Force on Life and the Law, 1993); essay III.16 (1998b).

[43] *ST* I–II q.100 a.2c; q.96 a.3c; q.98 a.1c; and see *Aquinas* 223–6 and ch. VII passim.

[44] 'Las acciones privadas de los hombres que de ningún modo ofendan al orden y la moral pública ni perjudiquen a un tercero, están solo reservadas a Dios, y exentas de la autoridad de los magistrados.' Constitution of the Argentine Nation, Art. 19, first part.

morals, a permitted ground of restriction on five of the protected rights and liberties.[45] Hart's *Law, Liberty & Morality* shows no sign, at any point, that its author was aware of this tradition. Indeed, his two references[46] to the countries where homosexual 'acts' were not criminal but homosexuality remained in general disfavour ignore those countries' legal provisions *enforcing public morality* on this matter.

And even when he quotes Lord Simonds articulating the key distinction with precision, Hart misses it entirely. The law lord said:

> Let it be supposed that at some future, perhaps early, date homosexual practices between adult consenting males are no longer a crime. Would it not be an offence [at common law] if even without obscenity such practices were publicly advocated and encouraged by pamphlet and advertisement?[47]

Hart simply ignores this issue,[48] dismissing the relevant paragraph as 'judicial rhetoric in the baroque manner'.[49]

Yet these serious deficiencies in Hart's handling of the legal issues are overshadowed by his mishandling of his principal theoretical topic, the idea of *enforcing morality as such.*

> Is the fact that certain conduct is by common standards immoral sufficient to justify making that conduct punishable by law? Is it morally permissible to enforce morality as such? Ought immorality as such to be a crime? To this question...[50]

[45] European Convention on Human Rights (1950), Arts 6(1), 8(2), 9(2), 10(2), 11(2).

[46] *Law, Liberty & Morality*, 52, 68:

> The notion that the overwhelming moral majority would or even could change heart morally and shed these deep instinctive feelings, if the State did not reflect in legal punishment their moral views on homosexuality, seems fantastic and is quite at variance with the experience of those countries where homosexuality between consenting adults in private is not legally punished.

[47] *Shaw v Director of Public Prosecutions* [1962] AC 223 at 268, quoted by Hart, *Law, Liberty & Morality*, 9.

[48] In the event, English law followed this course: during the thirty-five years after the de-criminalization of private adult homosexual acts in 1967, the publication of advertisements by private individuals of their availability for (even non-commercial) private homosexual acts remained an offence at common law (*Knuller (Publishing, Printing and Promotions) Ltd v Director of Public Prosecutions* [1973] AC 435, following Lord Simonds in *Shaw*); and the statutory prohibition of 'importun[ing] in a public place for an immoral purpose' was repeatedly held to extend to public importuning of adult males by adult males (e.g. *Regina v Goddard* (1990) 92 Crim App Rep 185). For evidence of Hart's later attitude to these ways of upholding public morality, and to the supportive but short-lived attempt to exclude from state schools the promoting among children of favour for homosexual parenting, adoption, and ways of life, see n. 66 below.

[49] He proceeds to distract himself (*ibid.*, 10–11) with two thoughts: (1) that the Law Lords' approval of the trial judge's direction about 'conspiring to corrupt public morals' implies that 'there need...be no approach to the "public" nor need the morality in question be "public" in any sense other than being the generally accepted morality'; and (2) that the authorities might circumvent precise statutory de-criminalization by charging the de-criminalized act itself under the common law concept of 'corruption of public morals'—something that in fact was never done, and if attempted would have been unsuccessful on a number of legal grounds.

[50] *Ibid.*, 4.

But here we should interject. The tradition of political philosophy flowing from Plato and Aristotle would have answered: 'This question' is not one, but at least two. For the fact that conduct is 'by common standards immoral' is never sufficient justification for punishing it; common moral standards notoriously may be more or less immoral. And if 'morality as such' means, as Hart presumes, the same as common moral standards *qua* common, the same reply applies. But if '(im)morality as such' refers (as it should) to what critical morality rightly judges (im)moral, then the tradition divides between (a) the Platonist-Aristotelian stream which 'paternalistically' authorizes penalizing immoral acts for the sake of the character of those who do or would otherwise engage in them, and (b) the Thomist tradition which we have seen articulated in the Argentinian constitution, authorizing penalization only when the act has a public character and jeopardizes public order or public morality or the rights of others.

Hart, alas, did not envisage either or any of those responses,[51] but plunged off in another direction, suggested to him by the ruminations of an English judge of no philosophic formation, Patrick Devlin. Having pointed to the pertinent distinction between critical and positive morality, Hart summarized the question his book tackles: 'our question is one of critical morality about the legal enforcement of positive morality'.[52] That was indeed Devlin's artless question. But it was a question that no one ought to take very seriously.[53] For when one is deliberating about the moral and the immoral, 'positive morality' is never determinative. Of course, customs can earn normative force in a critical morality; and one cannot reach a critical morality without working through the morality in which de facto one was brought up. But positive morality, as such, is nothing other than the set of opinions held, in fact, by a group of persons, concerning right and wrong actions, dispositions, etc. Such opinions, as facts about that group's beliefs, can never settle, for the deliberating person, what that person *should* judge to be right or wrong.

[51] In 1967, revisiting the debate, he begins by reporting (at last) what he calls 'the classical position', corresponding to the Platonist-Aristotelian as sketched above; he ignores the Thomist position, and says he will have nothing to say about the classical. (The same paragraph confirms his unawareness of the mainstream Christian (and Thomist) position that the strict requirements of revealed morality are *also* natural, that is accessible, under favourable epistemic conditions, by reason unaided by revelation.) See 'Social Solidarity & the Enforcement of Morality', in *Essays in Jurisprudence and Philosophy* at 248.

[52] *Law, Liberty & Morality*, 20.

[53] I am setting aside, as secondary, unfruitfully vague, and lacking in generalizable evidence, the question (one of fact) debated by Hart and Devlin: Will the non-criminalization of strongly held moral opinions lead people who hold them to crumble in their allegiance to society and/or their own morality?

In Hart's own terminology—employing the fruits of his main analysis in *The Concept of Law*[54]—the central case of morality understood from *the internal point of view* is (what the deliberating person takes to be) *critical*, that is, justified, morality. Conscientiously deliberating persons are deliberating about what they should count as *reasons* for action, and the bare fact that others count something a reason does not constitute something a reason (though it may be persuasive as ground for some evidentiary presumption that those other persons have some good reason for their belief). Indeed, one is scarcely thinking morally unless one considers that one's deliberated judgment could be morally right even if no one else now agrees with it. If we are interested in what 'morality as such' requires, references to positive morality are beside the point: morality as such just is *critical* (which is not to say that the deliberating person will succeed in critically judging aright, or that everyone or indeed anyone will agree with that person's judgment).

Hart's exclusive focus on positive morality cut the debate off from the main political-philosophic tradition, and from reason. It generated a casual presumption that those who uphold a group's morality have no moral reasons for doing so, or that no one need inquire what those moral reasons might be.[55] This pernicious presumption has a first manifestation in Hart's never examined assumptions that 'deviations from conventional sexual morality such as homosexuality afford the clearest examples of offences which do not harm others',[56] and that 'sexual morals [are obviously] determined... by variable tastes and conventions'.[57] But—to take up the issue on which Hart chose to focus—those who actually judge homosexual acts, *like other non-marital sex acts*, immoral, while they might grant that the private homosexual sex acts of two already morally corrupt adults in private do no harm, can argue with force that predisposing children to

[54] Note that in *CL*'s set-piece discussion (*CL* 168–84) of morality, Hart was clearly failing to grasp that even the adherents to a widely or universally accepted morality will each, at least in the central case, be adhering to it not because the others do but because they each consider it right, i.e., consider it justified by its successful articulation of the requirements of the well-being, dignity, honour, excellence, etc., of persons and groups. This serious failure in Hart's analysis was pointed out by Ronald Dworkin in 1972, who described what I have called the critical internal point of view in such a case as a 'consensus of *independent conviction*' (as opposed to a consensus of convention, in which the general conformity of the group is counted by the individual members as the, or a, reason for their acceptance of it): 'The Model of Rules II' (originally 'Social Rules and Legal Theory', Yale LJ 81 (1972) 855) in *TRS*, at 53. In the posthumously published Postscript to *The Concept of Law*, Hart conceded all this (255–6), admitting that the book had not provided 'a sound explanation of morality, either individual or social'. He had in fact been aware of this error, which he recognized as 'large', since at latest 1980: see Lacey, *H.L.A. Hart*, 335–6.

[55] The recent counterpart to this resultant of Hart's mistake is Dworkin's: Dworkin, *A Matter of Principle*, 67–8, 368. Analysis and critique: essay III.1 (1985a) at nn. 17–31; essay II.6 (2008b) at pp. 110-11.

[56] *Law, Liberty & Morality*, preface. [57] *Ibid.*, 73.

approve of adult homosexual sex acts, and to be disposed to engage in them when of age, is gravely and unjustly harmful to the child and to society, since it involves the child, and eventually perhaps the society, in a gross misunderstanding of the contribution sex acts have to make—and of the act-descriptive conditions without which such acts cannot make it—to marriage as the indubitably most favourable and fairest milieu for the procreation and upbringing of children and for the lifelong fulfilment of the married persons themselves.[58] Sexual morals, when upheld not only as justified but in a critical reflective manner, or in a community or tradition that has given really critical attention to justifying its judgments, are obviously not determined merely or primarily by variable tastes and conventions, but by living judgments about fundamental features of human nature—that is, of the conditions for human well-being and fulfilment—features philosophically explored, essentially without deference to taste or convention,[59] by Plato and Aristotle and more fully and adequately by Aquinas.

The issues at stake in sexual morality are such that sensible argument and deliberation about it will be no mere juxtaposition of 'recommendations of ideals'. It will involve attention to human needs, opportunities, and makeup (both individual and social[60]), to biological, physical, psychological realities and to such spiritual possibilities as commitment, in friendship, to paternity and maternity. If the Bloomsbury Set—to speak only of the ideas with which Hart's closest circle in the 1930s and after were imbued—propose a critical sexual ethic in which little is forbidden save sexual jealousy, and friendship even between spouses is supposed to be unaffected by sexual acts with others, a critical moral response can uphold the traditional position—not *as* traditional, Christian, or conventional—but as far superior in realism about human character, opportunity, and fulfilment. Such a response cannot be elaborated here. Enough to say two things.

First, the critical moral response to the Bloomsbury Set's now widely accepted and practised assumptions about sexual intimacies is fundamental not only to individual ethics but also to political philosophy. Plato's thought experiments about sharing of sexual partners in his *Republic* were what

[58] See essay 5 at 137–8.

[59] See Plato's telling remarks about the counter-cultural character of his own judgments about homosexual acts, and about the opposition they meet from people who are led by their unintegrated desires: *Laws* VIII, 835c, 839b.

[60] Social needs include, above all, an adequate and voluntary response to the fact recalled in Shakespeare's Erasmian *Sonnet* XI: 'If all were minded so', that is, not to procreate, 'the times should cease, / And threescore year would make the world away.'

Aristotle chose as a first priority for critical demolition in his *Politics*.[61] But Plato himself had pre-emptively adopted the essential results of that critique in his own last work, the *Laws*, where sex acts of a behaviourally non-procreative kind are treated as immoral, and their promotion a threat to the political community, because of their incompatibility with stable, loyal, and procreative friendship between man and wife.[62] That the nuclear family (with its grandparents and grandchildren) is 'the natural and fundamental group unit of society' was as evident to the founders of political philosophy as to the culturally diverse authors, sponsors, and signatories of Art. 16(3) of the Universal Declaration of Human Rights—evident, that is, not as a mere assumption but as a thesis warranted by careful attention to persons, world, and society, and by dialectical argument against objections. In the philosophy of practical reason (in which individual ethics, political philosophy, and legal theory have a primary place), that warranted thesis can be seen to be among practical thinking's first principles, picking out *marriage* as one of the basic aspects of human well-being.[63]

Secondly, direct ethical engagement with the Bloomsbury ethic can with critical justification unfold an understanding[64] of sex acts: that they have full intelligibility as, and only as, marital, that is, as expressing, actualizing, and enabling the spouses to experience commitment to marriage's uniquely appropriate context for procreative friendship and responsibility; and that that intelligibility is lost insofar as spouses hold themselves conditionally ready to engage (or be complicit in others engaging) in non-marital sex acts, as they do if they even approve of non-marital sex acts. On such a view—implicit in the commonsense of millennia—the sexual 'jealousy' (better: resentment) tabooed by the Bloomsbury ethic is both predictable and natural because the sex act's unique appropriateness for expressing exclusive commitment, *fides*, is natural (that is, fully intelligible); and the ethic of sexual liberation is a recipe for—to use Hart's favourite word in *Law, Liberty & Morality*—misery. Its malign results include the misery induced by the side effects of efforts, even successful efforts, to suppress and contemn one's own or others' reactions to want of *fides*. But the miseries to be counted extend also to the wider effects of sexual 'liberation' on children in their years of radical dependency, vulnerability, and need; and on those killed or damaged by damaged children; and quite generally on the vulnerable.[65]

[61] *Pol.* II, 1–2: 1260b37–1264b3; *NLNR*, 144–6, 58–9.

[62] *Laws* VIII, 835b–842a.

[63] On Aquinas's presentation of marriage as the subject of a first principle of practical reason, see *Aquinas* 82, 97–8, 143–54.

[64] See essay 5 at 135–8; essay III.20 (2008c) and works there cited.

[65] Jenifer Hart, *Ask Me No More*, 38, defends the Bloomsbury Set's sex ethic as natural; remarks that the Set's founder members 'themselves seem not to have felt sexual jealousy' (here both the

The 'distinctive liberalism of the 1960s' was distinguished by concern that its challenges to the social enforcement of moral condemnations of types of conduct should not seem to challenge those moral condemnations themselves.[66] This concern doubtless contributed to Hart's resolute non-engagement with any part of the real case for those condemnations and their direct or indirect enforcement. If the misconceived and sterile 'Hart-Devlin debate', and Hart's plausible success in it, had a large and long-lasting social impact, that suggests a decay going wider than just in the practice of political philosophy.[67]

IV

European states in the early twenty-first century move ever more clearly out of the social and political conditions of the 1960s into a trajectory of demographic and cultural decay; circumscription of political, religious, and educational speech and associated freedoms; pervasive untruthfulness about equality and diversity; population transfer and replacement

word 'themselves' and the word 'seem' are significant); and appeals to lines 149–63 of Shelley's *Epipsychidion*, contemning fidelity to 'one chained friend' and claiming that 'to divide is not to take away'. The year after composing and publishing it, the poet repudiated it as misbegotten, misconceived:

> the Epipsychidion I cannot look at; the person whom it celebrates was a cloud instead of a Juno, and poor Ixion starts from the centaur that was the offspring of his own embrace.... (Letter to John Gisborne, 22 June 1822.)

No need to dwell upon his wife's suicide and other miseries Shelley's 'dividing' of his sexual attentions actually brought about for women and children.

[66] When, by the 1980s, that liberalism had extensively succeeded in changing laws and public policies, but still had further to go, these restrictions fell away. Thus *H.L.A. Hart*, 356, reports:

> His reaction [in the 1980s] to Thatcherite social policies, particularly in the areas of education and sexual morality, reached the level of outrage. The enactment of 'clause 28', which prohibited local government from 'promoting' or using funds to 'support' propagation [in schools administered by local government] of the message that homosexual relationships ['as a pretended family relationship'] were of equal moral value to heterosexual ones, drew his particular wrath. 'I loathe it...', he told David Sugarman, who interviewed him in 1988.

[67] The climax of the lectures on knowledge and the good in Plato's *Republic* given in Hart's first years as a student by his tutor and friend H.W.B. Joseph and published, without comment or commentary, by Hart in 1948, is Joseph's conclusion about the point of the allegory of the Cave (*Rep.* 514a–517a): that what we need is not just intellectual formation from inevitable ignorance, but conversion 'from a plight into which we ought not to have come' but have come through the 'evil training' of social institutions; for though leaving people free to develop 'naturally', without such institutions, would only allow other pressures to distort and block sound judgment, it is in fact

> the pressure of lies that acts on us in States as they now are; and only by a hard struggle can a man reach, and only in the face of obloquy and opposition from those whom it disturbs can he teach, the truth. (H.W.B. Joseph, *Knowledge & the Good in Plato's* Republic (ed. H.L.A. Hart) (OUP, 1948), 43–4.)

It was not Hart's fate to have to face much obloquy on account of his teaching about critical morality's exclusions and requirements in politics and law, teaching which found prompt favour and recognition (*H.L.A. Hart*, 274) from the mid-1960s Labour government which superintended the liberalization of laws on pornography, abortion, homosexual acts, and divorce.

by a kind of reverse colonization; and resultant internal fissiparation foreshadowing, it seems, ethnic and religious inter-communal miseries of hatred, bloodshed, and political paralysis reminiscent of late twentieth-century Yugoslavia's or the Levant's. So the time seems ripe for a wider reflection on late twentieth-century political philosophies so characteristic, so suasive, so victorious, as Hart's.

That Hart had a political philosophy at all was an act of conscious resistance to scepticism. This resistance extended beyond the setting aside of methodological scepticism such as Quinton representatively articulated. It was particularly evident in Hart's repudiation of twentieth-century behaviourist reductionism, whether that took the form of Scandinavian or American legal 'realism', reducing the normative to the predictive or magical or diagnostic, or of Hobbesian or Austinian accounts of choice and action as mere predominant desire and muscular contraction, or of mid-twentieth-century criminological/penological theories denying responsibility by treating human behaviour as merely a more or less predictable cause of preventable harm.[68]

But the resistance was itself shaped and limited in its extent and content by Hart's own scepticism about something more foundational, the truth-value, and truth, of moral judgments (that is, as we have seen, of moral judgments intended as critical because asserted as true, sound, really justified). Only very late in his career did Hart allow himself to affirm in print this deep-going doubt, or rather denial.[69] But a determining consideration, throughout *The Concept of Law*, was that neither author nor reader, in taking a stand on issues in political or legal philosophy, need make any judgment about whether there are any 'true principles of right conduct rationally discoverable',[70] or whether instead moral judgments are but 'expressions of changing human attitudes, choices, demands, or feelings'.[71] In that book, the explicit attempt to 'evade these philosophical difficulties'[72] drives the reduction of law's rationale to survival, the later

[68] So 'scepticism' or its cognates appears as an antagonist in almost all the nine essays in *Punishment & Responsibility*.

[69] See n. 3 above, and the later review of Bernard Williams discussed in essay 10 at 251–4.

[70] *CL* 186. Right here the book employs a version of the simile that Hart's notebooks from the book's earliest gestation mark out as the (or at the very least, a primary) problematic in the book's conception: 'the disputants on one side seem to say to those on the other, "You are blind if you cannot see this" only to receive in reply, "You have been dreaming".' See Lacey, *H.L.A. Hart*, 222; and essay 10 at nn. 82–3.

[71] *CL* 168.

[72] *Ibid.*, explicitly reaffirmed in the posthumous Postscript, *ibid.*, 253–4. Orrego argues plausibly that Hart's motivation in postulating and holding to this agnosticism of legal philosophy about the objectivity or truth of moral judgments (even while, in his late work, casting doubt on the objectivity of legal rules and judgments as reasons for action!) was, in large measure, to protect legal positivism against the charge—damaging in the post-war years when the critique and punishment of Nazi wickedness made ethical scepticism unattractive—that it was a theory committed to ethical

repudiated assimilation of moral judgment to articulation of positive ('consensus of convention') morality, and the pervasive refusal to identify a central case of the internal point of view.

And in the discourse about the proper limits of the criminal law, the scepticism about morality is surely one primary motivation for the falling away from the level of Plato, Aristotle, and Mill to the essentially unphilosophical and irrelevant dialectic with Devlin. The popular success of that dialectic is a measure of the widespread loss of philosophical culture in the 104 years between *On Liberty* and *Law, Liberty & Morality*. For the first chapter of Mill's book makes the truly foundational issues explicit. It does so by its combined contentions (a) that state coercion may well be justifiable in the interests of the improvement of immature individuals or societies, or to protect a state where relaxation of 'the mental discipline' of any citizens might result in the overthrow of the state by 'foreign attack or internal commotion', and (b) that the 'salutary... effects of freedom' in accomplishing the necessary minimum of improvement in or of modern societies are 'permanent' effects, so that the qualifications on the 'principle of liberty' that were articulated in the first of those contentions can now, with us, be simply set aside. Hart criticized *On Liberty* for relying on a presumption of 'middle-aged' psychological caution and stability to justify rejecting paternalism in relation even to uncontroversial harms.[73] But he, and with him the whole extensive academic and popular discourse he inspired, left unexamined the much more deep-going and far-reaching issues raised by each of those Millian contentions.

That failure was symptomatic of a wider failure to examine a question extensively studied by Plato and Aristotle: What elements of individual and societal makeup are presupposed by political institutions capable of upholding justice and freedom and the practice of political philosophy itself? Primary and indispensable in such an examination will be two inter-linked questions, (a) the preconditions of shared sympathies, memories, temperaments, beliefs, and aspirations necessary to uphold the polity's existence against external enemies and internal subversion or want of civic spirit, of allegiance, of give and take, and of willingness to make personal and familial sacrifices for the common good, and (b) the ways of educating children and the structure of procreative and familial

scepticism and/or relativism: Orrego, 'Hart's Last Legal Positivism' at 77–8. Orrego also shows, at 75, that in essay 1 n. 4, I was misunderstanding Hart's tortured discussion in his *Essays on Bentham*, 266–7 as insinuating moral scepticism, when in fact Hart (though, as *other* evidence shows, a moral sceptic) was there implying scepticism about the objectivity of *legal* reasons for action.

[73] *Law, Liberty & Morality*, 33. Hart accordingly accepted a limited measure of paternalism in relation to more or less physical or psycho-somatic harms. [On Mill on Liberty, see essay I.18, sec. III.]

relationships (and related socio-economic and political practices) needed to maintain a population and its necessary civic spirit, not least its will to uphold a liberty neglected by Hart and his followers, the collective liberty of national self-determination. But, though Hart sketches a kind of analogue to Aristotle's ascent to the political via families and neighbourhoods—in *The Concept of Law*'s ascent to the legal, up from the pre-legal social order of 'social morality's' 'primary rules' sustainable or tolerable only in 'a small community closely knit by ties of kinship, common sentiment, and belief, and placed in a stable environment'[74]—his consideration of these rules never asks whether they include such rules as might be needed to order procreation and education within such a community.[75] And his repeated consideration of the disunity between officials and others in a legally ordered state focuses on the threat of internal oppression, not on the preconditions for the society's sustainability.[76]

As for *Law, Liberty & Morality*, its evasion or oversight of all questions of activities affecting public morality, as distinct from the truly private acts of consenting adults, results in thoroughgoing neglect of the question what conditions of procreation and education and self-understanding are needed to sustain political culture, and philosophy, and indeed the political community itself in face of threats external or internal. A liberalism that consciously evades 'material' moral issues,[77] as controversial or non-neutral, is prone indeed to evade essential facts, causalities, inter-dependencies, and the like, even when these tend to determine outcomes fundamentally. And prone to neglect the rational force of valid slippery slope arguments,[78] which point to the significance of adopting principles which justify not

[74] *CL* 92, 169, 198.

[75] Contrast *NE* VIII.12: 1162a16–29.

> Between husband and wife friendship seems to exist by nature; for man is naturally inclined to form couples even more than to form polities, inasmuch as the household is earlier and more necessary than the polity... human beings live together not only for the sake of reproduction but also for the various purposes of life; for from the start their functions are divided, and those of man and woman are different; so they help each other by throwing their peculiar gifts into the common stock. It is for these reasons that both utility and pleasure seem to be found in this kind of friendship. But this friendship may be based also on virtue, if the parties are good; for each has his or her own virtue and they will delight in that fact. And children seem to be a bond of union (which is the reason why childless people part more easily); for children are a good common to both and what is common holds them together.

[76] See e.g. *CL* 117 ('the sheep [members of the disaffected majority] might end in the slaughterhouse').

[77] See the passage quoted at n. 28 above. In *Law, Liberty & Morality* at 24, Hart casually presumes that the (unimportant and unclarified) issue of political morality he was debating with Devlin is 'surely, more interesting' than any question about 'the content of the morality to be enforced'.

[78] See Douglas Walton, *Slippery Slope Arguments*. Hart's published reflections on abortion display no interest in the implications or consequences of introducing into law and public policy approved killing of vulnerable innocent human beings, whether at the beginning or the end of a lifespan or in other conditions of vulnerability or of inconvenience or risk to others.

only actions and effects now desired but also actions and effects which others may well desire in some future time, perhaps imminent.[79]

Thus Hart's normative political philosophy has little indeed to say about the interrelations of common good, justice, and liberty in a nation whose liberty-minded citizens have largely given up procreating—or rather, bearing—children at a rate consistent with their community's medium-term survival, and whose law, considered in its much-obscured implications, marks out for them a path towards, first the loss of national self-determination;[80] and then their own replacement, as a people, by other peoples, more or less regardless of the incomers' compatibility of psychology, culture, religion, or political ideas and ambitions, or the worth or viciousness of those ideas and ambitions; and finally to the ruinous loss of most or much that Hart worked for, or took for granted, as precious. So there arises an interesting question for reflective speculation. How far were the deficiencies of political philosophies such as Hart's encouraged by—even as they, perhaps unwillingly (or at least reluctantly),[81] encouraged—the 'inclination' or 'mood' depicted by Voegelin in 1952: the inclination to take one's society's existence, especially when it has had 'a long and glorious history', for granted 'as part of the order of things', 'an inclination to disregard the structure of reality, of relaxing into the sweetness of existence, of a decline of civic morality, of a blindness to obvious dangers, and a reluctance to meet them with all seriousness', the mood of late, disintegrating societies no longer willing to fight for their existence[82] (an existence which is also a precondition for their serving the

[79] Hart was aware, as he told me on his return from Australia in 1971, that in his advocacy of abortion law reform in the 1960s he had failed to anticipate the scale of the institutional and social changes that would—with what he now saw to be quasi-inevitability—follow the removal of the criminal prohibition of certain specified classes of interventions by doctors on their patients. For the general point, without the admission of personal non-anticipation, see Hart, 'Abortion Law Reform: The English Experience,' Melbourne University L Rev 8 (1971–2) 388 at 408–9. Of the benefits of the liberalization, Hart put first (*ibid.*, 400–2, 411) the reduction in illegitimate births, which since he wrote have multiplied (as a proportion of all births in England and Wales) over fivefold. He was (402) unwilling to believe that the change in the law had led or would lead many women to change their sexual habits or attitudes to contraception.

[80] See my discussion, building on Raz's, in essay II.6 at 112–19.

[81] See e.g. Lacey, *H.L.A. Hart*, 268–71, esp. the 1987 interview quoted at 270, in which Hart says 'I think I am torn between my theories and my emotions here'. He was speaking of his support for an open borders policy ('a country to which anybody is entitled to come') and his opinion that

> what is valuable is an inherited culture, and any sharp discarding of that is objectionable, and indeed monstrous.... I suspect that it's too much to demand that people should disregard the ties of kith and kin absolutely—it's an ethic of fantasy that these could be put aside.

[82] Voegelin, *The New Science of Politics*, 168. Not long after Hart had asked me to contribute a book to his series, and to call it *Natural Law and Natural Rights*, I read this book and the contemporaneous article on Oxford political philosophers. My book articulates a philosophical theory offering to supply the element missing, as Voegelin's article observes, in virtually all the Oxford political philosophers, the element he named ('The Oxford Political Philosophers' at 103, 109), I think obscurely, 'a science of principles' and 'philosophical anthropology'.

common good of peoples and territories beyond their own)? Or were those political-philosophical deficiencies encouraged instead by the *contrasting* predispositions mentioned by Voegelin in the same passage: predispositions to an *activism* shaped by a kind of faith, such as liberal or Marxist or National Socialist beliefs in essentially inevitable cultural progress? After all, Mill's activist 'doctrine of liberty', as Hart called it, confessedly rested on just such a faith, in 'the salutary *permanent* effects of freedom'[83]—that is, we should now say, on sub-rational, spiritually disordered faith in a course of history that had brought societies such as ours up to a plateau of progress from which there *would not be* a falling off. Or was it neither of those predispositions, but instead no more than Oxford philosophers' standard bad practice of discussing, say, Plato's or Mill's 'theories' and 'doctrines' with a kind of detachment from their deepest truth-conditions? For these 'truth-conditions', taken broadly and adequately, include not only those great authors' reasonable will to get beyond theories and doctrines to the realities (actual and realizable) which, along with coherence, are the measure of the conceptual, but also careful attention by both authors and readers to the realities and goods[84] without which it would be impossible or senseless to engage in philosophical inquiry of any kind.[85]

Perhaps, rather, all three predispositions to error contributed to the philosophical deficiencies I have indicated. All are encouraged by aversion to acknowledging reality's full range and partly transcendent structure, the deep aversion which I mentioned in the first sentences of sec. I's last paragraph.

[83] Mill, *On Liberty*, ch. 1 (emphasis added).

[84] On the fundamental importance of conceiving the study of ethics (including political theory) as a *practical* undertaking, see *FoE* 1–6.

[85] See essay I.2 (1999a). Obviously, Plato's reflections (taken up in that article) on the will to seek truth and friendship, and the opposing will to domination, need to be extended to accommodate such historically and politically important realities as the sub-theological, sub-philosophical will (such as Mill's—or perhaps at least his wife Harriet Taylor's) to believe in ineluctable progress and avert the eyes from the fragile preconditions for a sustainable civil order (and social practice of philosophy).

12

REASON AND AUTHORITY IN *LAW'S EMPIRE**

Law's Empire will shape jurisprudence by its admirably resourceful attention to understanding a community's law 'internally'. It promotes reflective understanding of the practical argumentation constitutive of the attitude(s) in which that law subsists. But the book neglects some of practical understanding's resources of political and moral theory, and overestimates practical reasoning's power to identify options as the best and the right.[1]

I

The book 'takes up the internal, participants' point of view; it tries to grasp the argumentative character of our legal practice by joining that practice and struggling with the issues of soundness and truth participants face' (14).

Of course, this 'joining' is, at least for the most part, an 'only "virtual"' (422) participation; jurisprudence, as such, is only a propaedeutic to, or reflection upon, choosing; it is not itself a choice such as the participants themselves must make, to authorize or withhold, or to risk or accept, coercion—and take the consequences. But Dworkin rightly insists that jurisprudential work, insofar as it bears on the situation of some contemporary community, is genuinely continuous, indeed homogeneous, with the practical reasoning which characteristically precedes actual legal choices (legislative, judicial, or private) in that community: 'no firm

* 1987e.

[1] All parenthetical and/or otherwise unattributed numbers are references to pages of *Law's Empire*. I shall pass over many good things in the book: its neo-classical identification (413) of the ontological basis of law in an attitude (*voluntas, habitus*) rather than in propositions, processes, or persons as such; its identification, alongside its healthy individualism in ontology and epistemology, of the practical and moral reality of corporate responsibility ('personification') (167, 172, 296); its critique of two-level utilitarianism (290) and its comments on 'academic' and 'practical' elaboration of moral/political theory (285–7); its elaboration of community in terms of fraternity; its link between the theory of law, the theory of evil law, and the force of good law (110–11).

line divides jurisprudence from adjudication or any other aspect of legal practice.... Jurisprudence is... silent prologue to any decision at law' (90; see also 380). The *theory* rather confusingly labelled 'law as integrity', but proposed as an alternative to the theories labelled conventional*ism* and pragmat*ism*, 'offers itself as continuous with—the initial part of—the more detailed interpretations it recommends' (226). And since the opportunity (or lack of opportunity) to make a choice—literally to join a practice and take the consequences—does not affect the argumentative content of practical reasoning, the jurisprudential method envisaged is equally available, in principle, to guide the study of communities and laws foreign to us, or past.

Dworkin thus identifies argumentation (the argumentativeness of legal practice: 14) as centrally constitutive of the social phenomenon of law. Taking my cue from that, I have spoken here of practical reasoning.[2] But that is not a term which Dworkin promotes. Instead, he prefers to speak of *interpretation*. Now 'interpretation' is usually understood as, in a sense, passive or at least derivative, whereas practical reasoning, reasoning towards choice and action, is understood as active and creative. And indeed, Dworkin sometimes finds in the passivity or derivativeness implicit in the terminology of his master-concepts (amongst which *interpretation* has perhaps pride of place) a tacit and, I think, illicit support for his court-focused concept of law. Consider, for example, his brief *obiter dictum* about legislation: it is 'the practice of *recognizing as* law the explicit decisions of special bodies widely assumed to have that power [sc. of legislating]' (99, emphasis added). Shuffled out of view is the law-creating role and practice of legislatures; their responsibilities to engage in practical reasoning with an eye to the common good and the Rule of Law as Fuller outlined it thus never come into focus.

But I am running ahead, and pointing to a weakness when, for the present, I want to dwell upon the illuminating strength of certain of the book's guiding conceptions. Notable amongst these is certainly its author's willingness to endow his term or concept, *interpretation*, with much of the richness of practical reasoning's creative engagement with *goods* (including of course their privation: harms) and *ends* or *purposes*. Of the three terms I have just italicized, Dworkin really promotes only the term 'purpose'; but above all he emphasizes, massively, their functional equivalent: the role of *point* in interpretation.

[2] Of course, Dworkin often speaks, as we have seen, of law as a *practice*. But it is clear that he uses the term 'practice' to include any way of thinking or arguing, any 'methods [a social scientist's] subjects use in forming their own opinions...' (64).

The interpretative[3] attitude towards a practice assumes, he says, that the practice 'has value, that it serves some interest or purpose or enforces some principle—in short that it has some point' (47). Indeed, in the case of some practices (such as the law) but not others (such as tennis), the interpretative attitude makes another assumption: that the requirements of the practice are 'sensitive to its point', that is, are to be 'understood or applied or extended or modified . . . by that point' (47).

But at this juncture (which, as he says, is foundational for the whole book: 50), Dworkin shifts gear. The point or, synonymously here, the meaning of the social practice in question (courtesy, or law) is he says, to be 'imposed' (47).

> Interpretation of . . . social practices . . . is indeed essentially concerned with purpose not cause. But the purposes in play are not (fundamentally) those of some author but of the interpreter. Roughly, constructive interpretation is a matter of imposing purpose on an object or practice in order to make of it the best possible example of the form or genre to which it is taken to belong. (52)

This last assertion leaves much unclear. Is the interpreter supposed to have some other purpose than the formal purpose of making the object as good an instance of a genre as it can be? If genres provide the basis or framework of this formal purpose of interpretation, whose and what purposes inform and make the genre what it is? Dworkin does not stay to consider these issues. Indeed, what carries him towards his rather puzzling affirmation of the constructiveness of interpretation seems partly to be an equivocation on the word 'creative'. Interpretation of art and social practice is to be called 'creative' because it aims 'to interpret something created by people as an entity distinct from them, rather than what people say, as in conversational interpretation, or events not created by people, as in scientific interpretation' (50). The syntax of our language makes this use of 'creative' hazardously equivocal between the thus announced meaning ('pertaining to the created') and the meaning ('creative of . . .') which is suggested by the metaphors of 'imposing' and 'constructing' meaning and purpose.[4]

[3] Using a 'relaxed' and therefore (358) 'liberal' conception of the requirements of fit, I shall take as normative the usage established by the repeated use of 'interpretative' on p. 107, and, seeking to put the book in 'the best light' by a constructive interpretation, shall treat the appearance elsewhere of 'interpretive' as a mere *lapsus calami*, a 'mistake'.

[4] Dworkin is clear that the official meaning of 'creative' in his use of 'creative interpretation' is simply 'of a created object', and that, accordingly,

> interpretation is by nature the report of a purpose; it proposes a way of seeing what is interpreted . . . as if this were the product of a decision to pursue one set of themes or visions or purposes, one 'point', rather than another. (58–9)

The difficulties here are by no means all of Dworkin's own making. We can, as I have suggested elsewhere, usefully bear in mind four orders of intelligibility: the order (of nature) which is in no way established by human understanding; the order (studied by logic, methodology, and epistemology) which one can bring into one's own understanding; the order which one can bring into objects (boats, phonemes, poems, constitutions) by making them according to an intelligible plan or purpose; and the order which one can bring into one's dispositions, choices, and actions. By calling the interpretation which bears on law 'creative', Dworkin seems to place it in the third order (of making, *poeisis*, *factio*) rather than the fourth (doing, *praxis*, *actio*). Aristotle, Aquinas, and the classic western tradition down to Bentham's uncomprehending attack upon it chose to envisage law (like the other main aspects of political reality) in the fourth order: law has its principal intelligibility as a guide to choice, proposed to a community of choosers by the choice of that community's law-makers.[5] Still, one of law's usually characteristic features is that it has part of its reality as symbols or formulations, which are created objects in the third order, brought into being by legislation (including judicial fiat) and thereafter imbued with a reality independent of the intentions and choices of their maker(s)—a reality which thus creates a problem for interpretation distinct from the problem of interpreting those intentions and choices as *acts*. Moreover, we cannot say that when Dworkin calls legal interpretation 'creative' he thereby locates it in the third order as opposed to the fourth, for he does not seem to have any such distinction in mind. But we can say that it would have been helpful if he had. For there is something distracting about his appeal to the interpretation of artistic creations as the paradigm of the activity (let us allow, for the present, that it is interpretative) involved in the practice of law and legal argumentation, a practice which at bottom seeks to bring order into human choices and actions, present and future.

Of course, law in its central instantiations seeks to regulate present decisions and future conduct (*acta*, *agibilia*, *agenda*) primarily by attending to entities (rules, orders, precedents...) already existing because somehow brought into being in the past (*facta*). Dworkin acknowledges this explicitly by embracing 'the assumption that the most general point of law, if it has one at all, is to establish a justifying connection between past political decisions and present coercion' (98).[6] But the acknowledgement leaves something to be desired, because this statement of 'the most general point of law' revives or continues the puzzle about *whose* purposes or point are the

[5] See e.g. *In Eth.* I, 1; *ST* I–II q.90 aa.1–4. On the four orders, see *NLNR* 136–9, 157.

[6] 'The heart of any positive conception of law... is its answer to the question why past politics is decisive of present rights' (117).

primary or fundamental subject-matter of jurisprudential reflection upon law. Here, particularly, who is supposed to be doing the 'establishing'? The judge or jurist, now deliberating about the coercion which might now be ordered and, if so, justified by relation to the past decisions? Or the past decision-makers, who made their decision(s) with a view to *establishing* a justification—subsisting until terminated by preordained expiry or a new decision—for future (including now present) coercion (and, as Hart would wish to remind us, other present and future social law-regarding conduct)?

If, as the paradigm of interpretation suggests, the establishing of the justifying connection with the past is the work (and purpose) of the judge or jurist, still it is done as a moment in a process of justifying present choice and future conduct. It is done, in other words, in the course of a process of practical reasoning—indeed, reasoning towards choice and action, *praxis*—in which the justifying relevance of the past decisions (enactments, precedents, customs, etc.) must compete with countervailing considerations of expedience and principle. *In that respect*, this judicial or juridical process of reasoning or argumentation resembles—and has *pro tanto* the same point as—the reasoning which must precede any justified act of legislative decision-making.

And if we take the other alternative, and suppose that the justifying connection is established primarily in the legislative decision and act, the *point* of legislating is, even more obviously, in need of further identification. Classically, that point was identified as promoting the common good of the community for which the legislature is responsible. But that must be elaborated so as to articulate a more specific point, going to the legal form in which authority is thus exercised. This more specific point is summarized by the phrase 'The Rule of Law', a multiform point analysed by Fuller, Raz, and others in terms of the *desiderata* of formally or structurally good law-making. But this is scarcely attended to by Dworkin.[7]

In short, interpretation according to Dworkin is to be understood on the model of purpose, practical reasoning, and intention. This understanding lends power and illumination to his account of the interpretative attitude and its role in and in relation to law. But there is an irreducible passivity or derivativeness about the concept of interpretation, even after it has been transmuted by Dworkin from 'of created reality' to 'a creating and imposing

[7] 'General theories of law, for us, are general interpretations of our own judicial practice' (410). Why be so narrow?

of the interpreter's purpose' (and after 'construction' has likewise slid from 'construing' to 'creation').[8] Interpretation resists being taken for the whole of practical reasoning; or, perhaps more clearly, practical reasoning—for example, political *praxis*—resists being rendered as 'interpretation of a practice'. Adjudication and juristic interpretation resist being taken for the constitutive and legislative moments in the life of the law; those moments resist being understood, through and through, as interpretative. These resistances show up as missing or underdeveloped elements in the book's depiction of law's empire—an empire which is thus treated as if it were *acquired* in the way the British (some say) once acquired theirs: in a fit of absence of mind.

In short: even if Dworkin succeeded in showing that his account of interpretation and the interpretative attitude in legal practice is the best account, he would not thereby have shown (nor does he otherwise show) that law and legal practice and its point are adequately described and explained by that account.

II

There is more to be said about the book's epistemology before I turn to a more orderly treatment of its political and jurisprudential theory. The 'internality' of fruitful jurisprudence has a dimension or implication which goes beyond simply the resolve to understand legal phenomena as they are understood by those whose understanding and intending of them make them what they are. This further dimension or implication is in play in the book's discussion of 'internal' and 'external' scepticism (76–86). This discussion restates points made, perhaps more crisply and tellingly, in several recent articles by Dworkin. The correctness or otherwise of a legal answer to a legal question, or of a moral answer to a moral question, can be determined only by one who enters into the legal, or moral, arguments and uses legal, or moral, criteria to judge one answer better than another. From within the practices of legal and moral argument, the disagreements noted by the external sceptic are simply irrelevant—no argument at all. Arguments against the objectivity or truth of a particular legal or moral claim are worthless unless they

[8] Of course, the transmutation or slide does not go the whole way, but remains in the tension established by the requirements of 'fit' and 'soundness', the former tending to hold the interpreter to the pre-interpretative reality established by other people's purposes, practical reasoning and intention(s).

are legal or moral arguments. The external sceptic's denials that such claims can or do correspond to 'transcendental reality' or 'the fabric of the universe' trade on unexplained, indeed 'incomprehensible'[9] metaphors, and are empty and futile.

Law's Empire concludes that 'the only skepticism worth anything is skepticism of the internal kind' (86; see also 82). Internal scepticism accepts that some social practices (or other objects of interpretation) are better than others but denies that a particular object of interpretation has any of the worth attributed to it by its participants and those who share their interpretative attitude. But this conclusion is stated without the éclat of Chapter 7 of *A Matter of Principle.* Indeed, *Law's Empire's* official position (80, 266) is that neither the general significance nor the rightness of external scepticism need be considered in the book or, it seems, in any other jurisprudential (or political or moral) reflections.

The truth that even widespread disagreement is no argument against a moral or legal assertion has an equally important counterpart: the fact of one's agreement with an assertion is no ground for agreeing. In the logic of argumentation, only the *content* of my knowledge or beliefs is relevant, not the fact that I possess them. Albeit in a rather specialized context (331–2), Dworkin very clearly adverts to this 'transparency' of 'I believe that *p*' for 'It is true that *p*' and '*p*'. He also states the implication of this transparency, viz., that in making any affirmation, reaching any conclusion, answering any question, one is 'relying at the deepest level on what [one oneself] believes' (314). Dworkin's writings taken together make it clear that he rejects any subjectivist reading of this; in relying (say, for the premises of an argument) on what one believes, one relies on it under the description *what is* [or: *seems to be*] *the case,* not under the description *what I believe about* what is the case.

But I doubt whether Dworkin has focused sufficiently on the implications of these positions. In my Maccabaean Lecture,[10] I noted that his arguments against enforcement of 'majority preferences' fail to observe the transparency of many beliefs held and acted upon, *by* majorities, but not *because* they are so held. *Law's Empire* does not take up those arguments, so I need not restate that point. But it is worth noting here how often the book speaks in a way which, by syntactically overlooking transparency, gives needless (and, I believe, unintended) comfort to a subjectivist reading of the book and a subjectivist understanding of ethical, political,

[9] Dworkin, *A Matter of Principle* 172; for the arguments paraphrased in the present paragraph, see *ibid.*, 137–42, 171–7; *TRS* 123–4; Cohen, *Ronald Dworkin and Contemporary Jurisprudence*, 277–80.

[10] Essay III.1 (1985a), sec. II.

and legal theory. Consider the italicized redundancies in the following key statements:

(1) 'the exercise in hand is...: discovering which view of the sovereign matters we discuss sorts best with *the convictions we each, together or severally, have and retain about* the *best account of* our common practices' (86).

(2) 'Justice is a matter of the correct or best theory of moral and political rights, and anyone's conception of justice is his theory, *imposed by his own personal convictions*, of what these rights actually are' (97).

(3) 'Hercules is not trying to reach *what he believes is* the best substantive result, but to find the best justification he can of a past legislative event' (338).

Or again: Perhaps Dworkin needed to say that the good judge decides a hard case 'by employing his own moral convictions' (120), for he needed to make clear that the criteria of soundness ultimately used by the judge are of soundness as assessed by him, and not, in the last analysis, as assessed by (other members of) society. But he would have done well to add, immediately, that the judge does not employ his moral convictions *as* his but *as sound* criteria, principles, rules, or other factors relevant as premises in an argument.[11]

Finally, Dworkin seems to give relativists—legion amongst law students—needless (and again, I think, unintended) comfort by extending his denials much wider than was called for by the metaphorical metaphysics of the external sceptic. For Dworkin says that 'the practices of interpretation and morality give these claims [about *Hamlet* and about the wrongness of slavery] *all* the meaning they need *or could* have' (83, emphases added); and 'the "objective" beliefs most of us have [about such matters] are moral, not metaphysical, beliefs' (82). True, those practices and beliefs do not include the external sceptics' bugaboos, 'transcendental reality', 'the fabric of the universe', the 'out there', etc. But they do, commonly, include or presuppose conceptions of what counts as human flourishing, and these conceptions not only presuppose some beliefs about the nature of things (for example, freedom of choice, continuity of personal identity),[12] but also contribute to (the rational justification of) other beliefs about the nature of that (human) type of being whose flourishing could involve the opportunities and responsibilities

[11] Similarly, it is a pity Dworkin uses 'conviction', rather than 'consideration', 'factor', 'argument', or 'principle', in passages such as:

> The constraint fit imposes on substance...is therefore the constraint of one type of political *conviction* on another in the overall judgment [by?] which interpretation makes a political record the best it can be overall. (257, emphasis added).

[12] As Dworkin himself says, one's view about the point of law must rest on 'large questions of personality, life, and community' (101).

which moral judgments assert it does. The truth that practical knowledge cannot be deduced from theoretical does not entail that there is no ontology of morals, or that ethics has nothing to learn from and nothing to contribute to the metaphysical understanding of our nature and our world.

III

Epistemological or methodological issues closer to the central concerns of jurisprudence are raised by Dworkin's account of the 'semantic sting' and his rendering of legal positivism, legal Realism, and natural law theory into 'semantic theories of law'. Here the book seems to me confused and seriously misleading.

The 'semantic sting' is Dworkin's name for 'the argument that unless lawyers and judges share factual criteria about the grounds of law there can be no significant thought or debate about what the law is' (44). 'Semantic theories suppose that lawyers and judges use mainly the same criteria... in deciding when propositions of law are true or false...' (33).

One notices at once the lack of quantification of 'share factual criteria': share some, share many, share all? The second passage says: 'mainly'. But if *this* belief is fallacious—a poisonous sting to be drawn—it seems indistinguishable from Dworkin's own belief that 'the lawyers of any culture where the interpretive attitude succeeds must largely agree at any one time'—agree, that is, 'about what practices are legal practices', and about 'legal paradigms, proposition[s] of law like the traffic code that we take to be true if any are' (91). When stating his view that such 'pre-interpretive' agreement is a necessary precondition of any flourishing interpretative, critical, or juristic enterprise, Dworkin claims that his view differs from the semantic sting in not supposing 'that we identify these institutions [and paradigms] through some shared and intellectually satisfying definition of what a legal system necessarily is and what institutions necessarily make it up' (91).

But the latter supposition seems quite distinct from the suppositions earlier said to constitute the semantic sting and the semanticism of semantic theories of law—suppositions which, as we saw, made no assertions about 'what a legal system necessarily is', but were identified by Dworkin as claiming that the criteria of '*the* law' which are used by judges and lawyers—presumably, of a given, particular legal system—are 'mainly shared'. At this point I am not considering whether anyone has ever held any of the semantic theories, or been the victim of the semantic sting. I am concerned only with Dworkin's failure, both when defining vicious semanticism, and when speaking in his own voice, to distinguish between 'the law' (of a particular community, the topic of thought by that community's lawyers and judges) and 'law' (a topic of thought of anthropologists, sociologists, other historians, moralists, and jurisprudents such as Hart, Kelsen, and Dworkin). Dworkin treats 'the law' and 'law' as synonymous,[13] and I fail to see how he can be so indifferent to the manifest difference between the two terms, corresponding to the difference between the two sorts of intellectual enterprise which I have just indicated.

Positivist and natural law theories in jurisprudence are not, and do not even look like, theories about *the law* of any particular community (in the sense of offering to identify propositions of law which are true for that legal system), or about the criteria for identifying the law which are used by the lawyers and judges of any particular community. They look like theories about what *law*—a(ny) legal system—'necessarily is' (at least in its paradigmatic instantiations, its central cases).

Moreover, such theories are not, and do not even look, 'semantic', whether in the sense stipulated by Dworkin or in any other. Austin's 'main idea', Dworkin says, was 'that law is a matter of historical decisions by people in positions of political power' (36). Hart's, he says, is 'that the truth of propositions of law is in some important way dependent upon conventional patterns of recognizing law' (35). Neither 'main idea' is semantic.[14]

Similarly, Dworkin's semantic rendering of natural law theory produces a thesis which natural law theorists have not treated as integral to their theories: 'that lawyers follow criteria that are not entirely factual, but at least to some extent moral, for deciding which propositions of law are true' (35).

The truth is that neither positivism nor natural law theory is any more concerned about 'how all lawyers use the word "law"' (36) than Dworkin is.[15] The book's concern about the semantic sting and semantic theories

[13] e.g. in describing semanticism, he moves—without comment, and in consecutive sentences—from (the assumption that) 'we all use the same criteria in framing... statements about what the law is' to (the assumption that) 'we do share some set of standards about how "law" is used' (32).

[14] The account of Hart is quite inaccurate, too. Dworkin asserts that, according to Hart, the rule of recognition, in whose acceptance lie 'the true grounds of law', 'assigns to particular people or groups the authority to make law' (34). Consequently, anyone who obeyed Hitler's commands simply out of fear, and who thus did not accept a rule of recognition entitling Hitler to make law, would be committed, according to Dworkin's Hart, to say that 'no propositions of law were true' in Nazi Germany (35). This overlooks that Hartian rules of recognition are usually multiple, and contain rules which are in no way derived from (even when they are subject to) the supreme rule of change which identifies the people or group with supreme authority to make laws.

[15] As Dworkin quietly concedes in the notes to another chapter, Hart's theory was not controlled by semantic considerations, but by judgments about 'what would cure defects in the organization of political coercion that would be inevitable without [special legal] conventions [broadly accepted throughout the community]' (429), and by a view of which concept of law would 'facilitate moral reflection' (430). Dworkin's discussion of Raz's positivism is inaccurate. He claims that it 'explicitly denies any reliance on political convictions of any sort', and that it 'fall[s] back on linguistic rules, to say that this is just what "law" or "authoritative" means under any criteria for its application educated lawyers and laymen all accept' (429–30). In the article cited, 'Authority, Law and Morality', Raz in fact denies that he assumes any such conscious unanimity (304) or conceptual clarity (321),

of law seems to me a muddle and a distraction, save in one respect: the discussion of the pseudo-question whether immoral legal systems really count as law. It is the case that some legal philosophers, for example Hart, have thought that jurisprudence must make, 'once and for all', a choice between a 'wide' sense of 'law' (such that the Nazis had law) and a 'narrow' (such that they did not). Dworkin's discussion brings out well the context- and audience-relativity of statements such as 'the Nazis had law' (103–4).[16] Contemporary jurisprudence, in some of its arguments and positions, has indeed suffered somewhat from what I have called 'conceptual dogmatism', and Dworkin's protest against that is well taken.[17] But he errs in claiming that the framework self-interpretation of recent jurisprudence is, has been, or can be usefully represented as concerned with or founded upon linguistic agreement, or being in any other way 'semantic'.[18]

IV

It is time to attend to Dworkin's theory of law. But there is a bridge between his theory of interpretation and one of the main features of his theory of law 'as integrity'. The bridge: those pervasive Dworkinian categories, 'the best' and 'the right'.

The task of interpretation, remember, is to make its object *the best* it can be (within its genre), to show it 'in the best light possible' (243). The goal of law as integrity, that is, of the interpretative attitude constitutive of the practice we call law, is to find in every situation of civil dispute *the right* answer which the given civil society's law makes available 'in most hard cases' (viii), and which is identified by *the best* interpretation or theory of that legal system. So:

> Judges who accept the interpretive ideal of integrity decide hard cases by trying to find, in some coherent set of principles about people's rights and duties, *the best*

and founds his argument on claims about what practices are 'service[a]ble' and beneficial (304) and (evaluatively) 'important' (320).

[16] See also *NLNR* 234–7, 365–6; contrast Hart, *CL* 207, 210–12; *Essays on Bentham* 146.

[17] There has been a good deal of loose thinking, or talk, about 'conceptual analysis', explaining 'the concept of law', and the like. See e.g. *NLNR* 278–9. But the malady is not well diagnosed in terms of 'semantic theories', *a fortiori* when 'semantic' is itself used imprecisely (in the ways mentioned above, and so as to extend even to proposals about how words *should* be used: e.g. *Law's Empire*, 135).

[18] So Dworkin in the end misstates his legitimate point. He says that it is a mistake to ask whether wicked legal systems are law, because the question assumes that its answer turns on whether the linguistic rules we share for applying 'law' include or exclude such systems—whereas in fact 'we do not share any rules of the kind it assumes' (108). It would have been more accurate to say that while we do share linguistic rules which bear on the question, we can and do use or adapt or discard those rules, intelligibly, when certain contexts make our understanding and our communicative intentions sufficiently clear.

constructive interpretation of the political structure and legal doctrine of their community. (255; also 262).

Law, or 'law's attitude', 'aims, in the interpretive spirit, to lay principle over practice to show *the best route* to a better future, keeping *the right* faith with the past' (413).

We accept integrity as a distinct political ideal, and we accept the adjudicative principle of integrity as sovereign over law, because we want to treat ourselves as an association of principle, as a community governed by a single and coherent vision of justice and fairness and procedural due process in *the right* relation. (404; also 219, 398).[19]

Now it is true that injustice is done only when *wrong* choice is made in distributions of goods or in other dealings between persons. So, when no wrong is done in such dealings, *a right* answer has been found to a practical problem. But that in no way entails that justice has anything to do with searching for 'the right' distribution, or 'the right' answer.

Dworkin's efforts to show that a *uniquely* correct ('the right') answer is normally available in a hard case provide an impressive dialectical argument for the contrary and classical view that while there are many ways of going and doing wrong, there are also in most situations of personal and social life a variety of incompatible *right* options—that we should seek good answers, and eschew bad ones, but not dream of *best* ones. Indeed, Dworkin's account of the relations between 'fit' and 'soundness' in interpretation helps to make clear *why*, in any realistic context, no uniquely correct answer could be available in any case where there is identifiable a set of two or more options/answers which do not violate any rule binding on the judge or other chooser or interpreter.

It is important to note that my denial that uniquely correct, or best, answers are available to practical questions has nothing to do with scepticism, internal or external. Nor has it anything to do with the popular argument which Dworkin, as we have seen, is rightly concerned to scorn and demolish, viz., that disagreement is endemic. (The existence of disagreement is a mere fact about people, irrelevant to the merits of any practical or other interpretative claim.) As Dworkin says, 'the wise-sounding judgement that no one interpretation could be best must be

[19] And justice 'is a matter of *the right* outcome of the political system: *the right* distribution of goods, opportunities and resources' (404), while fairness 'is a matter of finding political procedures... that distribute political power in *the right* way' (164; also 404), and procedural due process 'is a matter of *the right* procedures... that promise *the right* level of accuracy...' (165; also 405).

earned and defended like any other interpretive claim' (237–8).[20] Dworkin himself provides the labour and materials for such a defence.

Nor does my denial rest on the observation that none of us has the 'superhuman' powers of Dworkin's Hercules. Hercules himself, no matter how superhuman, could not justifiably claim unique correctness for his answer to a hard case (as lawyers in sophisticated legal systems use that term). For, in such a case, a claim to have found the right answer is senseless, in much the same way as it is senseless to claim to have identified the English novel which meets the two criteria 'shortest and most romantic' (or 'funniest and best', or 'most English and most profound').[21] Two incommensurable criteria of judgment are proposed—in Dworkin's theory, 'fit' (with past political decisions) and 'justifiability' (inherent substantive moral soundness). A hard case is hard (not merely novel) when not only is there more than one answer which violates no applicable rule, but the answers thus available are ranked in different orders along each of the available criteria of evaluation: brevity, humour, Englishness, fit (integrity),[22] romance, inherent 'quality', profundity, inherent 'justifiability',[23] and so forth.

In earlier works, Dworkin tried to head off the problem of incommensurability of criteria by proposing a kind of lexical ordering: candidates (theories of law) must fit *adequately*, and of those which satisfy this 'threshold' criterion, that which ranks highest in soundness is '*the best*' even though it fits less well than (an)other(s).[24] This solution was empty,

[20] In the context, however, Dworkin seems to treat 'no interpretation could be best' as equivalent to: no interpretation is worthwhile because none can be identified as bad. I endorse the sentence quoted only in its literal meaning.

[21] Of course, it is conceivable that a novel might happen to be both the most romantic and the funniest. In any realistically rich field, such as the English novel, this cannot be expected and the injunction to look for such a novel is practically senseless.

[22] Cf.: 'questions of *fit* surface again, because an interpretation is *pro tanto* more satisfactory if it shows less damage to *integrity* than its rival' (246–7). Is it not surprising to find 'integrity' denoting both the overall virtue of the whole interpretative/legal enterprise and one of the 'dimensions' of that enterprise? Dworkin's reply seems to say that because commitment to integrity makes no sense without commitment to fairness and justice, every legal effort to be fair and just 'flows from [an] initial commitment to integrity' (263). *Non sequitur.*

[23] Is it not fishy to find 'justifiability', an inherently framework concept, denoting *one* of the dimensions or criteria, when the other criterion, 'fit', is itself inherently evaluative, that is, justificatory? 'Best and shortest' is similarly dubious, insofar as brevity is commonly accounted a virtue in novels. Of course, even when brevity is treated as a mere neutral fact, the quest for the best and shortest will still be chimerical in any realistically rich and complex field of candidates.

[24] See *TRS* 340–1 (where Dworkin expressly envisages the only really interesting and genuine form of hard case or contest between theories or interpretations of the law as a case where the rank order in terms of fit of alternatives which all fit 'adequately' is different from the rank order in terms of soundness), 342, 360, also 122; Cohen, *Ronald Dworkin and Contemporary Jurisprudence*, 272. In the third of these passages, Dworkin refers also, as if it were equivalent, to the account given in Dworkin, 'Is There Really No Right Answer in Hard Cases?', now *Matter of Principle*, 143; but there the story is that political/moral soundness comes into play if and, it seems, only if 'two justifications [sc. theories of law, interpretations, answers] provide an *equally* good fit with the legal materials' (emphasis added).

for he identified no criteria, however sketchy or 'in principle', for specifying when fit is 'adequate', that is, for locating the threshold of fit beyond which the criterion of soundness would prevail. Presumably, candidates for 'the right answer' to the question 'When is fit adequate?' would themselves be ranked in terms both of fit and of soundness. An infinite regress, of the vicious sort which nullify purported explanations, was well under way.

In *Law's Empire*, Dworkin abandons the simple picture of a lexical ordering between the dimensions of fit and soundness. He stresses that within the second dimension 'questions of fit surface again, because an interpretation is *pro tanto* more satisfactory if it shows less damage to integrity than its rival' (246–7); 'even when an interpretation survives the threshold requirement, any infelicities of fit will count against it... in the general balance of political virtues' (256; see also 257). This is a gain in moral realism. But it strips away the last veil hiding the problem of the incommensurability of the criteria proposed for identifying a best or uniquely right interpretation, theory, or answer. We are left with the metaphor: 'balance'—as in 'the general balance of political virtues' embodied in competing interpretations. But in the absence of any metric which could commensurate the different criteria (the dimensions of fit and inherent moral merit), the instruction to 'balance' (or, earlier, to 'weigh') can legitimately mean no more than bear in mind, conscientiously, all the relevant factors, and *choose*.

It is a feature of the phenomenology of choice that after one has chosen, the factors favouring the chosen alternative will usually seem to outweigh or overbalance those favouring the rejected alternative(s).[25] The chosen alternative will seem to have a supremacy, a unique rightness. But the truth is that the choice was not *guided by* 'the right answer', but rather *established* it in the sentiments, the dispositions, of the chooser. When the choice is that of the majority in the highest relevant appeal court (a mere brute fact), the unique rightness of the answer is established not only for the attitude of those who have chosen it, but also for the legal system or community for which it has thus been authoritatively chosen and laid down as or in a *rule*.

In the real world, of course, the problem of commensurability is much more intense than I have portrayed it; for there is not just one dimension of soundness or substantive political justifiability, but many incommensurable dimensions. Their incommensurability is profoundly important for ethics and political, not merely for legal, adjudication. It has not been sufficiently noted, in debate on Dworkin's work, how thoroughly he shares

[25] See Grisez, 'Against Consequentialism' at 46–7.

utilitarianism's deepest and most flawed assumption: the assumption of the commensurability of basic goods and thus of the states of affairs which instantiate them. And this assumption is not marginal to his theory of law, as his denial of absolute rights,[26] though important, can perhaps be said to be marginal; it is of its essence.

In sum: there are countless ways of going wrong in a hard case; the judgment that Mrs McLoughlin and her legal advisers should be summarily executed and their property distributed to the defendant can head a list of possible but erroneous judgments which has no end. A case is hard, in the sense which interests lawyers, when there is more than one right, that is, not wrong, answer. Dworkin's discussion of the two dimensions has made this clearer than ever.

The objection I have made in this section is not, I think, confronted in the book. Instead, Dworkin imagines and responds to some related objections which are easy to handle because exaggerated and ill-focused. 'There can be no best interpretation when more than one survives [the] test [of fit]'; therefore Hercules' claim to be enforcing *the law* is fraudulent, or grammatically wrong, or confusing (261, 262). Dworkin's reply? First, Hercules' claim could be grammatically wrong only if the semantic sting were truth rather than error. That we should accept. Secondly, Hercules' claim would be fraudulent only if he did not share Dworkin's view that the judgments made by each judge in a hard case are intended to state what the law is, not merely what it should now become. That, too, we should accept; deception is not an issue in jurisprudence.

But to the charge that Hercules' claim is confusing, Dworkin makes no reply. And the claim *is* confusing (and confused), precisely because (for the reasons I have been setting out, and not for the bad, sceptical, or external reasons which Dworkin envisages as objections), in a hard case, in legal systems like ours, there will be no one answer which, because uniquely right, should be described as '*the law* governing the case'. Moreover (though the descriptive sociology of all this is a secondary issue), Hercules' claim obscures the reality that conscientious judges do acknowledge that they are making new law, breaking new ground—interstitially, no doubt, and usually by a 'development' which respects and makes use of existing legal concepts and normative resources with an exclusiveness foreign to the legislature's ventures in law-making—but for all that, by choice, a new commitment, not mere discovery and application. To describe a conscientious judgment in a hard case as legal rather than moral is not

[26] *TRS* 354. On incommensurability, see Raz, *Morality of Freedom*, ch. 13; *NLNR* 112–18 (and see pp. 223–6 on absolute rights); *FoE* 86–93; *NDMR* 241–54, 267–70, 286–7 (and see 286–7 on moral absolutes).

wrong, for such a judgment will be both constrained and shaped by existing law in a way quite unlike any other moral judgment.[27] But to deny the difference between application and development, easy cases and hard cases in the sense I have specified, is indeed misleading.

Dworkin is right to insist that the answers to easy cases, too, presuppose conceptions of fairness and justice (354), and in *that* sense he is right to consider easy cases 'only special cases of hard ones' (266). But he has no valid argument against the commonsense of lawyers and others who think that in some cases there is only one answer which is not wrong, while in other (not infrequent) cases there is more than one such answer, and reason itself (whether legal or even moral) lacks the resources to identify one as best.

V

A primary and perennial source of the need for authority (including what Dworkin calls 'convention') is the rich variety of eligible—that is, not wrong—but incompatible answers to issues of choice[28] in social life.[29] I have already observed, in sec. I above, how Dworkin's attention is diverted from the constituent and legislative moments of law's 'practice'. Similarly, it is diverted from the question of political and legal authority's ultimate justification and legitimacy. We come upon law halfway through the story; the 'most abstract and fundamental point of legal practice is to guide and constrain the power of government in the following way...' (93).[30] But why acknowledge the 'power' of 'government' at all? *For what* should a ruler be exercising his power?

The book does offer a defence of the legitimacy of political authority. But it is very thin. It consists centrally of the claim that denying political legitimacy (Dworkin's term for what I would call justified authority) entails denying, implausibly, the legitimacy of all other associative obligations, that is, the obligations which arise from family, friendship, and other fraternal relationships (see 207). A principal weakness of this argument, as developed

[27] But, unlike Raz and Dworkin, I don't care whether these judgments are called judgments of law or not: see *NLNR* 290. [And see now essay 20.]

[28] It is hazardous to call such issues 'problems', a phrase which seems to suggest that the major issues of personal or social choice should be understood on the analogy of mathematical or technical problems which commonly do have a uniquely correct or best solution; the tendency to see life as a series of *problems* is doing major damage to western morality and civilization.

[29] See *NLNR* 231–3. Of course, there are other primary sources of the need for authority: the transaction costs of negotiation and deliberation; selfishness, malice, etc.

[30] Sometimes Dworkin speaks as if 'if law exists it provides a *justification for* the use of collective power against individual citizens or groups' (109, emphasis added) and says that 'the ultimate point of law is to license *and justify* state coercion...' (127, emphasis added). But the initial statement (at 93) is truer to his account, which is of law as a *constraint upon* the exercise of authority.

in the book, is that these other fraternal associations are characteristically founded upon shared interest in substantive human goods, whereas the political community, so far as Dworkin invites us to envisage it, eschews any official concern—certainly any imposition of obligations on the basis of such concern—for substantive human goods such as health, knowledge, beauty, the transmission of human life and culture, and so forth. In this respect, the book, while it differs from Dworkin's earlier books by abstaining from explicitly (but cf. 274) describing itself as 'liberal', retains the salient characteristic of Dworkinian liberalism: it portrays justified politics, and thus law, as neutral about what is truly worthwhile and what worthless in human life.[31] It lacks any articulated concept of the common good, an ensemble of conditions which favour the human flourishing (including rights) of all members of the community, and which ought to be promoted as well as respected by those in authority, and for the sake of which others acknowledge that authority.

The other principal weakness in Dworkin's account of legitimacy or authority is that his discussion of the problem of securing any desirable degree of *coordination* of human action in community is buried in his polemic against 'conventionalism' (see 144–50). Now I have no brief for (or against) conventionalism, an imaginary doctrine[32] which Dworkin envisages as the substantive political/jurisprudential counterpart (432) to the semantic theory he calls 'positivism'.[33] I will, however, observe in passing that his critique of conventionalism (147–50) is very weak. For he simply enrols 'pragmatism' to make the response, and purports to endorse a pragmatist claim that pragmatism is more 'efficient' at coordinating citizens' actions because 'it is so much more adaptive' (149). He himself will rightly later argue, in effect, that pragmatism is unwarranted in taking efficiency as the criterion or model of political justification.

But my present point is simply this: Dworkin's theory of law, and of law's authority or legitimacy, is weakened by his failure frankly to acknowledge the case, not merely for making 'past politics decisive of present rights'

[31] The unwillingness to speak of goods or harms is remarkably far-reaching. Thus, in the discussion of negligence, where we would expect a reference to harms we find only a reference to rights: see 293; cf. 307, 309, where, at last, the categories 'fundamental interests' and 'damage—e.g. threats to life' are acknowledged.

[32] Conventionalism, though imaginary, is presented in loaded terms: see 95, 135.

[33] Dworkin admits that perhaps no one has ever subscribed to conventionalism precisely as he describes it (94). But I doubt whether anyone significant subscribes to anything even resembling Dworkin's conventionalism, the key tenet of which is that 'the past yields no rights tenable in court, except as these are made uncontroversial by what everyone knows and expects' (118). To claim that 'if convention is silent there is no law' (118) is a far cry from asserting that the past has no justificatory 'power over the present' of a kind highly relevant to the judge's proper exercise of his judicial power and in that sense 'tenable in court'—an assertion few indeed have made, even those who have unwisely spoken of judicial 'discretion' when the law runs out.

in accordance with an ideal and virtue of 'integrity', but for creating and applying *rules* whose legal and moral authority is directly and simply ascribed to their *source*, authoritative enactment, or judicial adoption or some other form of 'convention'.[34] In attending to the fact of consensus—so fundamental to the existence and worth[35] of legal systems, and of a community's judiciary—Dworkin tries to make us choose between basing that consensus on convention—which means treating legal propositions as true 'just because everyone else accepts them' (136)—or on 'consensus of independent conviction', 'the way we all accept that it is wrong to torture babies or to convict people we know are innocent' (136). This disjunction between convention and consensus of conviction, so defined, is entirely inadequate to explain and justify legal authority, institutions, and obligation. We should refuse to make this choice. But if we were forced to choose, a sound natural law theory would have no hesitation in tracing the legal and thus the moral authority of most of the law's rules and institutions (the establishment, though not the content, of which is urgently required for the sake of fairness and the other components of the common good) not to consensus of independent conviction but to *convention*.[36]

NOTES

(1) In essay 17 (1990d), in the text after n. 29, towards the end of an extensive discussion of incommensurability, I add:

> I regret two things about my discussion of incommensurability in 'Natural Law and Legal Reasoning' (1990c)....I should have made it clearer that the incommensurability between Dworkin's two dimensions is not an instantiation of, but only a kind of analogy to, the

[34] Dworkin's text leaves me in doubt about whether he takes the conventions with which 'conventionalism' is concerned to be quasi-constitutional conventions defining broad institutions such as legislation, Congress, precedent, etc., or whether he takes them to include also particular institutions and rules established under those constitutional conventions. Much in the text suggests the former, but other passages are consistent with the latter, and at least one seems to require it: 'Suppose there is a convention in some legal community that judges must give both sides an equal opportunity to state their case' (123).

[35] Many will think that Dworkin's emphasis on consistency with the past (*passim*), and on demanding that a principle given effect to in one part of law should 'flow throughout the scheme' of the law (436), should have been balanced by a clear recognition (clearer and earlier than 401) of the worth of having clear rules (and loyal adherence to them) for securing that litigants are treated uniformly at a given time, and so do not suffer more than is inevitable from the excruciating sense that if their case had been tried *on the same day* by the judge next door it would probably have been determined differently (e.g. because each judge is attempting the impossible and all too creative interpretative task envisaged for him by Dworkin, instead of applying the rules). Is it symptomatic that the book contains some big mistakes in reporting precedents to which it refers, (notably (2) *Attorney-General v Jonathan Cape Ltd* [1976] QB 752; and (185) *Roe v Wade* 410 US 113); and some implausibly dismissive opinions about the *integrity* (as distinct from the justifiability in principle) of certain rules, such as the one giving immunity in tort to barristers in court (cf. 220, 401), or forbidding the *importation* of slaves only after a twenty-year run-off period (184)? The horizon is ordinarily not the best focus for the judicial gaze.

[36] See *NLNR* 281–90; 1984b.

> incommensurability between the human goods involved in morally significant, rationally motivated choices. And I should have made it explicit that I was only granting *arguendo* the intelligibility of Dworkin's talk (a) about measuring degrees of moral soundness and (b) about trading off moral soundness against fit; in fact, I cannot reconcile either of these crucial features of Dworkin's analysis... with any acceptable concept of morality.

These criticisms of 1990c apply also to the present (earlier) paper. See also essay I.15 (1997b), sec. IV.

(2) For an appreciation and application of what I think is valuable in Dworkin's suggestion that legal reasoning attends to 'fit' and 'moral soundness' in order to judge what is law, see essay 20. In the endnote to that essay (403 below), and in several paragraphs towards the end of sec. III of the Introduction (13–15 above), I point to an important though limited sense in which the 'only one right answer' thesis is correct.

13

CRITICAL LEGAL STUDIES*

Roberto Unger's *The Critical Legal Studies Movement* (1983) has been acknowledged as a seminal guide to the ideas of the 'Movement'. The present study critically examines the account of legal thought there developed by Unger, and tests it against Unger's own account of certain 'exemplary' difficulties in the Anglo-American law of Contract. These scrutinies reveal that Unger's account fundamentally misunderstands the ways of legal thought, and disguises its misunderstanding behind equivocations on '(in)determinate' and '(un)justified'. The complexities of the problems of fairness with which Contract law must grapple are not captured by Unger's triadic schemas, which are at once too complex and too simple. Behind all this is a poverty-stricken conception of the forms of human good and the requirements of practical reasonableness, and a scepticism which rests on unsound arguments.

I

The Critical Legal Studies Movement is perhaps no more than a passing fashion. But one ought not to assess arguments by guessing whether they portend the wave of the future or a mere footnote for historians. And attention to the arguments of the Movement can help in a reflection on two of the permanent questions of legal theory: (1) Why should law be treated as a social form or type that warrants a place in the grand explanatory typology of social forms that makes up social theory? (2) What is the relation between the positivity of law, its ability to make obligatory now what was optional only a moment ago, and the principles or critically grounded requirements of plain practical reasonableness ('background principles')?

* 1985c ('On "The Critical Legal Studies Movement"'). See also essay 14.

One preliminary remark about names. The term 'The Critical Legal Studies Movement' is one which, like the terms 'liberalism', 'conservatism', 'socialism', 'fascism', and the like, has no place in a critical social theory or legal study. It is a label chosen, in this case by supporters, as an instrument of persuasion in the rhetoric of political action within the academy. To point to the rationale of this act of choice is not to make an adverse judgment; the act in question is substantially concerned with both the content and the method of legal education and thus also of much of the practical public life of our communities; and the marshalling of supporters for programmes of action does indeed require labels to identify the programmes with sufficient brevity for purposes of debate and resolutions for action. Still, no one will simply take for granted that those who use the label with self-identificatory intent are actually sufficiently critical in method, or have a clear conception of legal studies, or constitute a movement fit to accomplish coherent goals by persuasion or other action. An assessment of those matters is not my purpose here.

Rather, the purpose of this essay is to pursue the two standing questions already mentioned, by way of a critical reflection on a recent work of the most influential, philosophically adept, and historically and sociologically learned exponent of the Movement. Roberto Mangabeira Unger's 'The Critical Legal Studies Movement'[1] is an essay which, like his earlier books *Knowledge and Politics* (1975) and *Law in Modern Society* (1976), is rich in insight into the predicament of social theory and of those (including himself) whose intellectual stance and principle of self-interpretation includes the concern to be modern men.

II

Unger introduces the Critical Legal Studies Movement as a movement critical of objectivism and formalism in legal thought, that is, in the thinking of those who have to interpret the law and to remake it by the judicial techniques familiar in American and other common law constitutional orders.

By 'objectivism' he means 'the belief that the authoritative legal materials—the system of statutes, cases and accepted legal ideas—embody and sustain a defensible scheme of human association'.[2]

[1] Unger, 'The Critical Legal Studies Movement'. [Subsequently published as Unger, *The Critical Legal Studies Movement*.] Among the many themes of Unger's engaging article which are not touched on in my discussion are the organization of government, the organization of the economy, and the theory of equal protection.

[2] *Ibid.* at 556.

The critique of objectivism is said to be

> essentially the critique of the idea of types of social organisation with a built-in legal structure and of the more subtle but still powerful successors of this idea in current conceptions of substantive law and doctrine.[3]

He identifies an 'insight required to launch the attack against objectivism—the discovery of the indeterminate content of abstract institutional categories like... the market'.[4]

One of the reasons for attending to Unger's work is to find ready material for a reflection on the contemporary incomprehension of the master thesis of classical legal theory, the thesis that in positive law we can find a mode of derivation of specific norms of action, that is, of practical reasonableness, by an intellectual process which is not deductive and does involve free choice (human will) and yet is intelligent and directed by reason. This process Aquinas labelled *determinatio*: we might translate this by 'specification', 'concretization', or 'implementation', but the point is not securely made by any one word.[5] A simple example, to indicate his point, would be the process by which an architect gives specificity or determinateness to a building plan in accordance with his commission to build a maternity hospital for South Bend. Much can be understood by reflection on such an example. But the process of *determinatio* in law has additional complexities which need to be identified, complexities derived from the fact that law works not in the order of making things (though it of course affects that order) but in the order of the self-constitution of human persons by choosing and doing in community with other *persons*.[6]

In the passage just quoted from Unger, we see a first example of an ambiguity which is going to recur. When he says that certain abstract institutional categories, such as 'the market', have an 'indeterminate content', what does he mean by 'indeterminate'? Does he mean formless, empty, and useless as a guide to practical reasoning and decision? Or does he mean orientative and decision-guiding by calling for and suggesting further specifications the content of which, however, is neither required by 'logic' nor rationally unconnected with the (partially) indeterminate idea with which we began? Not seeing this ambiguity and possibility, Unger fails to see that one might reasonably defend a set of rules and doctrines authoritatively established in the 'legal materials' (say, the current rules and doctrines of an American law of Contract), and defend them as 'embodying' and 'sustaining' a 'defensible' conception (say, of fair 'market'

[3] *Ibid.* at 568. [4] *Ibid.* at 570. [5] See *ST* I–II q.95 a.2; *NLNR* 284–6, 294–5, 380.

[6] On the four 'orders' in which human life is lived, see *NLNR* 136–8; on the significance of choice as self-constitutive, see *FoE* 139–42.

relationships), without claiming that, in all or even most respects, they are the *uniquely* reasonable rules and doctrines available for such embodiment and sustenance, or that such a conception is the *only* 'defensible' conception of a fair market.

To see, in principle, how this might be so (before seeing how it is so in a fragment of the law of Contract), consider the other target of the Movement's critique: 'formalism'. Formalism is said to be the belief that there is

> a method of legal justification that can be clearly contrasted to open-ended disputes about the basic terms of social life.... The formalism I have in mind characteristically involves impersonal purposes, policies, and principles as an indispensable component of legal reasoning.[7]

'An indispensable component': the other indispensable component(s) of legal reasoning, and the only component that could begin to 'contrast' legal with any other form of practical reasoning about social life, is carefully omitted by Unger here and virtually throughout: authority, the *fiat* of legislation, precedent, or custom, binding (though not absolutely) and determinative for legal reasoning (though not absolutely determinative) precisely because (though not only because) it has been *made* by relevant persons in relevant circumstances and because we need such exercises of authority to terminate disputes and resolve coordination problems both now and for the future, in a consistent and fair fashion.[8] As has been seen, Unger does observe the existence of 'authoritative legal materials',[9] or 'the constraints of institutional context'.[10] But he never stops to ask what the authority of these 'materials' is, and what could explain it.

This failure to consider the source of positive authority is a weakness shared, we may note, with the jurisprudence of Ronald Dworkin, a jurisprudence scornfully and not too scrupulously attacked by Unger as the 'hocus pocus' of the 'rights and principles school'.[11] Dworkin's failure, to use his own terms, is a failure to do the relevant parts of political philosophy, in which, as he rightly says, jurisprudence is embedded.[†] Unger's failure, in *his* own terms, is a failure to pursue thoroughly the typological analysis of social forms which he thinks is the legitimate successor to the largely discredited methods of classical political philosophy.[12]

Back to 'formalism'. Its vice, Unger says, is to regard the purposes, policies, and principles of 'the law' as 'indispensable' to resolve 'what would

[7] Unger, 'The Critical Legal Studies Movement' at 564.

[8] See essay 2.

[9] Unger, 'The Critical Legal Studies Movement' at 564, 577.

[10] *Ibid.* at 572.

[11] *Ibid.* at 575.

[12] Unger, *Law in Modern Society*, 43–5. On some relations between the problem of authority and the problem of the typology of social forms, see essay 9.

otherwise be incorrigible indeterminacy in the law'.[13] Note 'indeterminacy' again, and observe in passing that, being resolvable, it cannot be *sheer* indeterminacy. Observe also: the formalist is supposed to think that the indeterminacy is 'corrigible' by reasoning; but Unger does not stay to explore how formalists suppose (as, by the definition of formalism, they must) that legal reasoning differs from 'open-ended' reasoning about 'the basic terms of social life'. (Whatever Unger may think, we can make our own guess that the difference has something to do with the authoritativeness, for *legal* reasoning, of the *determinationes* of enactments and judicial precedents.)

The link between objectivism and formalism, in Unger's account, is this. Formalist legal doctrines 'often included' a third level beyond the levels of (1) authoritative rules and precedents and (2) ideal purposes, policies, and principles. This third level is the one with which objectivists, by definition, are concerned, the level of 'conceptions of possible and desirable human association to be enacted in different areas of social practice'.[14] For:

> just as the ambiguities of rules and precedents require recourse to imputed purposes or underlying policies and principles, so the ambiguities of these policies and principles can be avoided only by appealing to some background scheme of association....[15]

Thus, such third-level conceptions 'help make the entire body of law look intelligible and even justifiable'[16] by

> offer[ing] guidance about the relative reach and the specific content of the opposing principles and counterprinciples which, as we shall see, are supposed to settle provisionally what would otherwise be pervasive ambiguities in the more concrete legal materials.[17]

Notice the claim: third-level ideas 'make the law look intelligible and justifiable'. But 'justifiable' hovers between 'not unjustified, not unreasonable, not wrongful' and 'required by reason, rationally necessary'. By overlooking the ambiguity, Unger insinuates what he never clearly affirms, that dominant (that is, pre-'critical', 'objectivist', and 'formalist') legal doctrine proceeds on the unwarranted belief that the third-level conceptions of possible and desirable association both (a) necessitate or require the pursuit of *this* rather than *that* particular second-level purpose, policy, or principle, and *these* particular first-level rules, and (b) are themselves necessary, that is, are conceptions of what forms of association are *uniquely* desirable.[18]

[13] Unger, 'The Critical Legal Studies Movement' at 579. [14] *Ibid.* [15] *Ibid.*
[16] *Ibid.* at 578–9. [17] *Ibid.* at 619. [18] See e.g. *ibid.* at 579, 633.

Unger's own conception of Critical legal doctrine retains the three levels. In plainly affirming this, he also affirms that the revised third level will still 'assign distinct models of human association to different sectors of social practice', on the basis that different 'kinds of human association... can and should prevail in different areas of social life'.[19] It remains simply unclear how the methodological relationships between the levels of Critical legal doctrine will differ from those between the supposed three levels of existing doctrines; Unger says little more than that in the Critical view, 'no one scheme of association has conclusive authority' and there is a process of 'mutual correction of abstract ideals and their institutional embodiments'.[20] Pre-critical scholars will discern no novelty here. Unger, however, believes that they (wrongly) suppose the set of models of human association to be 'given' and 'rigidly defined' and 'natural'.[21] It is time to see how he tries to show this by an examination of Contract doctrine.

III

Unger's showpiece of Critical legal doctrine is, in fact, his lengthy study of certain rules and principles of current Anglo-American law of Contract. It aims to show two things. First: that current legal doctrine hides the relationship between its second-level principles and the controlling third-level conceptions of desirable forms of human association, and that those third-level conceptions remain uncriticized, uncorrected, and falsely supposed to be 'given' and 'rigidly defined' (prior to their embodiment in legal principles, rules, and institutions). Secondly: that in current doctrine, the second level consists of principles and counterprinciples, the latter being only grudgingly admitted, and marginalized by the principles which tend to extend, 'imperialistically', to all social life.[22]

So:

> The structure of reigning ideas about contract...can be stated with the greatest possible simplicity, in the form of two pairs of principles and counter-principles.[23]

The first principle is 'that of the freedom to enter or to refuse to enter into contracts. More specifically, it is the faculty of choosing your contract partner'.[24] And its counterprinciple is 'the freedom to choose the contract partner will not be allowed to work in ways that subvert the communal aspects of social life'.[25]

[19] *Ibid.* at 619, 649. [20] *Ibid.* at 580. [21] *Ibid.* at 633. [22] *Ibid.* at 619.
[23] *Ibid.* [24] *Ibid.* [25] *Ibid.* at 620.

One should be uneasy about these formulations. The counterprinciple is stated in a predictive or descriptive, not a normative form. Worse, the principle is never stated by Unger in other than a broken-backed form: 'the principle of freedom to enter...; the faculty of choosing your partner....' I suppose that what is intended is something like:

> each person is to be free of obligations purportedly imposed upon him by the agreements of other persons between themselves; correspondingly, no one has the power to impose, by agreement with another, obligations on one who does not agree to them.

Unger's carelessness about the formulation of a principle is a small sign of his deep misunderstanding of the role of principle in practical thinking.

You would also be right to suspect that a principle as negative in form and content as the principle of freedom to contract is rather unlikely to extend imperialistically to all social life. And, in the event, Unger takes the principle, its proper formulation, and its intended range of application entirely for granted, and focuses instead on 'manifestations'[26] of the *counter*principle that freedom to choose the contract partner will not be allowed to work in ways that subvert the communal aspects of social life.

The first manifestation is said to be the rules of law which, he says, 'operate to prevent the principle of freedom to contract from tracing the limits of liability so rigidly and narrowly that the fine texture of reciprocities is left entirely unprotected'.[27] These rules include rules imposing liability 'whether contractual or delictual'[28] based on occupancy of a status or exercise of a profession, rules or supposed rules of promissory estoppel, and the rules of quasi-contract for restitution on unjust enrichment. Now, to treat these rules as manifestations of a counterprinciple at work within the law of Contract makes sense only on the extraordinary assumption that the 'principle' of freedom to contract is taken as asserting that one has no legal liabilities at all other than contractual (that is, those one has freely agreed to)—an assertion very remote from the legal systems Unger is discussing, even if not altogether remote from some nineteenth- and twentieth-century theories of *Contract*.

Still, Unger's treatment of those rules was intended to be no more than fleeting, and he passes on to 'the most instructive application of the counterprinciple...the rules of contract law that discourage contractmaking in noncommercial settings'.[29] His example of such rules is 'the norms that govern the interpretation of the intent to contract'.[30] These norms he presents as three levels of rules (analogous in structure, but not to be confused with, the three levels of legal doctrine).

[26] *Ibid.* [27] *Ibid.* at 620–1. [28] *Ibid.* at 620. [29] *Ibid.* at 621. [30] *Ibid.*

On the first level is the rule that a declaration of intent to be (legally) bound may be unnecessary (and is unnecessary where the parties are 'devoting themselves to self-interest in the harsh business world'),[31] and that a declaration of intent not to be bound at law may be effective. On the second level is a rule which 'guides and qualifies the interpretation of the first-level one': that 'whenever possible', intention is to be construed 'in a manner that protects justified reliance and leads the parties out of a situation in which they stand at each other's mercy'.[32] The exclusion of liability will in such situations be interpreted as narrowly as possible. And on the third level is a rule which 'limits the scope of both the first-level and second-level ones'.[33] It qualifies the second-level rule by determining that, 'in noncommercial contexts', an intent to exclude liability is *not* to be construed as narrowly as possible. And it qualifies the first-level rule by determining that 'in family life or friendship the presumption of intent to be legally bound [is reversed]'.[34]

This grand structure of three levels of rules is illusory. The so-called third-level qualification of the first-level rule is no more than a component of that (in any case complex) rule, a component required to state it fully, by some such formula as: 'Business deals are presumed to be intended to have legal effect; family or friendship arrangements are presumed not to be intended to have legal effect.' The separation of this fairly straightforward rule into two different levels has a rhetorical function: to elevate to attention the relevant (alleged) manifestation of the counterprinciple, so that 'the principle' is depicted as the principle of a business or commercial realm of contract, while the counterprinciple is depicted as 'defend[ing] private community against the disruptive intervention of the law', that is, the law that flows (on Unger's loose assumptions) from the principle of freedom to contract. As he says:

> classical contract theory claims to describe and seeks to define [a form of life]—an existence separated into a sphere of trade supervised by the state and an area of private family and friendship largely though not wholly beyond the reach of contract.[35]

Now this important thesis about a distinction between spheres of social life, such that one sphere (family and friendship) is treated as largely beyond the reach of legal contract, is hardly reconcilable with Unger's general thesis that in current, pre-critical doctrine the principles are 'dominant' over the counterprinciples, which are 'pressed to the corner' and treated as 'mere ad hoc qualifications to the dominant principles'.[36] Nor is the spheres-of-social-life thesis easily reconcilable with the most striking fact about nineteenth- and twentieth-century Contract theory: that its rules

[31] *Ibid.* [32] *Ibid.* [33] *Ibid.* [34] *Ibid.* [35] *Ibid.* at 623. [36] *Ibid.* at 569.

and principles are expressed with great generality, no distinction being made between types of party (such as trader, consumer, friend, relative) or of transaction (in corresponding terms); and that many of its leading cases concern agreements between relatives or friends, of a sort that can only extravagantly be described as 'trade', let alone 'the pitiless world of deals'.[37]

Still, we should look more closely at the working-out of the thesis that the law distinguishes sharply between spheres of social life. For the central claim of the Critical Legal Studies Movement, on Unger's account of it, is that conceptions of desirable human association can retain their controlling 'third-level' status in legal thinking without being conceived, as at present they supposedly are, as 'given', 'natural', or 'rigidly defined'. So: classical theory, according to Unger, involves a 'polemical opposition of contract to community',[38] 'stark opposition of community as selfless devotion and contract as unsentimental money-making',[39] between 'a conception of community as an idyllic haven of harmony, and contract, as a realm of unadulterated self-interest and pure calculation',[40] with 'the practical result... [of leaving] inadequately supported the subtle interdependencies of social life that flourish outside the narrow zone of recognized community'.[41]

Thus: what is wrong with pre-critical doctrine, according to Unger, is its rigid, polemical opposition, at the third level, between two forms of human association, the world of commerce conceived as devoid (in fact, in conception, and thus in law) of mutual responsibility, and the world of private community, the 'prime instance' of which is 'the nineteenth century bourgeois family or its diluted successor'.[42]

To make his contrast plausible, Unger must introduce the family as 'subordinat[ing] the jealous defence of individualistic prerogative to the promotion of shared purpose and the reinforcement of mutual involvement'[43] in a 'flexible give-and-take that contract law... would disrupt'.[44] But the family unbalances Unger's typing. Within a page his depiction of this social type has taken a contradictory form:

> the whole view of family beyond contract depends upon the interaction between an impoverished conception of community and a narrow view of law in general and contract in particular. The conception of community defines communal life largely negatively, as the absence of conflict.[45]

[37] *Ibid.* at 635. [38] *Ibid.* at 625. [39] *Ibid.* at 641. [40] *Ibid.* at 644.
[41] *Ibid.* at 625. [42] *Ibid.* at 623. [43] *Ibid.* at 624. [44] *Ibid.* at 623.
[45] *Ibid.* at 625. Of course, Unger, *Law in Modern Society*, 144 claimed that, in 'liberal society', 'familial relationships are abandoned to the exploitation of power advantages within the family under the guise of respect for the integrity of the family group', so that 'the impersonality of the public realm and the communal character of the private one are always changing positions'. That has

'Absence of conflict?' Or 'promotion of shared purpose... mutual involvement... and flexible give-and-take?'

And what about the other social form, the market, a 'devolution of practical life to the harshest self-interest',[46] excluding even a 'partial reconciliation between the competing claims of self-interest and attachment to other people',[47] a realm of 'equality of distrust', and so forth? This depiction depends upon putting out of mind vast tracts of law. We have already observed Unger's oversight of the bodies of law outside Contract, such as Tort and Restitution, which though not treated as contractual are treated by the law as applicable and even primarily applicable to the world of commerce. It is now time to take into account the rules of law considered by Unger as subsumed under the second pair of principle/counterprinciple.

IV

The second of the two principles governing the law of Contract is freedom *of* contract, stated by Unger in, at last, a proper form:

> the parties must be free to choose the terms of their agreement. Save in special cases, they will not be second-guessed by a court, not at least as long as they stay within the ground rules that define a regime of free contract.[48]

And the second counterprinciple, supposedly marginalized in pre-critical law and doctrine, is 'that unfair bargains should not be enforced'. As Unger says:

> Fairness means not treating the parties, and not allowing them to treat each other, as pure gamblers unless they really see themselves this way and have the measure of equality that enables each to look out for himself.[49]

Thus, for example, a contract made by one party under the economic duress of a party possessing significantly superior bargaining power can be treated as voidable by the weaker party. Or again, where a contract is frustrated by unforeseen circumstances, the modern law provides for a mutual adjustment of losses which Unger somewhat grandly describes as each party insuring the other against mistakes and misfortunes falling outside the limited and discriminate risks defined by the contract (including its unspoken presuppositions).[50] Such a 'mutual insurance' amounts, as Unger says, to treating the contracting parties as if they were in a kind

some plausibility as an observation on the *effect* of liberal legal doctrines. What has no plausibility is that those legal doctrines are flagrantly self-contradictory, as they would be if they were what Unger, 'The Critical Legal Studies Movement', claims.

[46] *Ibid.* at 622. [47] *Ibid.* at 623. [48] *Ibid.* at 625. [49] *Ibid.* at 632. [50] *Ibid.*

of partnership, or joint enterprise—a kind of community. To this extent, as Unger rightly says, the second counterprinciple, requiring fairness, intersects with (that is, reinforces) the first counterprinciple.

Unger's point, now, is that in pre-critical law and doctrine, operating in a society where gross inequalities of bargaining power exist, the counterprinciple of fairness is restrained from 'running wild' and correcting almost every contract[51] by drawing 'unstable, unjustified and unjustifiable lines....'[52] But do we not find here the perennial sophistic complaint that wherever any line is drawn by law, 'for every situation corrected, there seems to exist another similar to it that is left untouched',[53] so that the line itself is arbitrary and thus unjustifiable and thus unjustified, that is, ripe for subversion? Someone who accepts this refuses to acknowledge the rationality of *determinatio* (illustrated in sec. II above). He cannot fix a speed limit, or a scale of progressively rated taxation, or divide examinees into first, second, and third class....

And the further question, in relation to Unger's own enterprise, is whether he shows that in drawing its lines, the law is guided by some ideal of the market, an ideal statable at a third level, that is, prior to and independent of the (counter)principles of fairness and equality which work at the second level. To answer this question, we can look at Unger's claim that the Critical Legal Studies Movement has a countervision of Contract based on a countervision of the market, yielding not a competing concern within a shared conceptual framework of Contract law but rather a new conceptual framework. Unger offers to illustrate his notion of a 'struggle between conceptual frameworks' by examining the progress of such a struggle in areas of 'exemplary difficulty' in existing legal doctrine: his chosen examples are some problems concerned with mistakes made in the process of forming a contract.

Suppose that a contract is being negotiated not face to face or by telex but by correspondence, and one party changes his mind about the offer or counteroffer he has made, or about the acceptance he has sent off to the offeror, and so tries to revoke his offer or counteroffer or acceptance. A contract, once formed, cannot (of course) be simply revoked by one party. So the question is: Precisely when is the contract irrevocably formed? And precisely when does the purported revocation take effect if it can take effect? Unger says that the classic and current Anglo-American Contract doctrine refuses to distinguish, for these purposes, between innocent and wrongful (purported) revocations. The explanation for this, he says, is that such problems arise in a 'fully commercial context', in which the parties are engaging in 'pure gambles beyond the reach of the counterprinciples

[51] *Ibid.* at 629. [52] *Ibid.* [53] *Ibid.* at 633.

of community and fairness'.[54] Alternatively, he acknowledges that the current doctrine considers the relevant distinctions in the moral quality of the conduct of the revoking party to be 'too fine and fragile to serve as useful bases'[55] for rules about formation and revocation. Critical legal doctrine proposes, on the other hand, to reverse the relations between principle and counterprinciple, under the guidance of a countervision of human association. It therefore proposes to distinguish between wrongful revocations, which will be treated as ineffective, and innocent revocations, which may be effective even after the contract itself has come into existence. And what is the proposed distinction? Wrongful revocations are those attempted 'because of afterthoughts about the profitability of the deal or changes in market conditions supervening upon the dispatch of the acceptance'. Innocent revocations are those made 'to correct a mistake that does not concern business judgment', for example 'faulty calculations or... a misapprehension of what [one] has agreed to do' *including* 'negligent' miscalculations and misapprehensions, and an 'ordinary' measure of imprudence.[56] And then, where the revocation is in that sense 'innocent',

> the losses ought to be divided between the offeror and the offeree according to the degree of the [revoking party's] negligence and even the comparative ability of the parties to bear the loss.[57]

Comparative ability when? And which losses? Objections to Unger's proposal will spring to mind.

Unger's proposal asks A to 'insure' B in relation to the very matter over which B has exclusive control, that is, over B's own conduct in making his calculations about the content of the obligations, costs, and benefits he is proposing to contract for. But as to external market conditions, affecting price, profit, feasibility of performance, etc., each 'party' is treated as a self-insurer, a high-risk gambler, simply because these are, according to Unger, 'business judgments'. Here is a distinction which *does* seem arbitrary, not because it draws a line between 'similar situations', but because it is groundless or wrong in principle.

And if one makes this objection, one is surely not participating in the advertised 'struggle between conceptual frameworks'. Rather one is pointing out that Unger is just using, ineptly, an existing conceptual framework—a framework which does, in various contexts, take account of negligent and wrongful conduct, and in others of that sort of autonomous responsibility for one's own affairs which Unger calls high-risk gambling; and that he is doing so without regard to the costs of unpredictability and

[54] *Ibid.* at 643. [55] *Ibid.* at 634. [56] *Ibid.* at 634–5, 638. [57] *Ibid.* at 636.

of the extensive litigation required to settle, ad hoc, the relation between such incommensurables as 'degrees of negligence' and 'ability to bear the loss'.

Contract law has to grapple, in any case, with complex situations. Consider, for example, another of Unger's 'exemplary instances', a variant on the preceding case. A careless subcontractor discovers his carelessness, and seeks to revoke his bid before it has been accepted but after the general contractor has become bound to the client on terms which presupposed the subcontractor's original bid. No need to go into the details of Unger's discussion and proposal, which share the weaknesses of his earlier discussions. Notice only the fact, which he records but glides past: pre-critical Contract doctrine makes the legal solution turn on the question whether the general contractor knew or had reason to know or suspect that the subcontractor's bid was predicated on a miscalculation; for if he did have this knowledge, suspicion, or ground for suspicion, he cannot hold the subcontractor to the bid, despite his own costly reliance on the bid.[58] Unger is bound to glide past this, because it illustrates the principle of fairness already embodied in a body of law which he wrongly treats as sponsoring 'harshest self-interest', 'high-risk gambling', etc.

The fact is that existing Contract law and doctrine is rich in concern for moral principles of fairness and can expand or contract its *determinatio* of those principles without engaging in any struggle between conceptual frameworks. The competition, which no one thinks can be resolved by deduction, is between such considerations as excluding the unfairness of taking advantage of another's mistake; the unfairness of defeating actual reliance; the unfairness of submitting the relations between parties with many diverse interests to the indefinite delay and unpredictability and incidental waste of litigation necessitated by rules which are indefinite because formulated in *terms* of 'fairness'; and so on. Unger is aware of the latter problem. He confronts the objection that there is a

> need to choose between a ready but crude generality [in the legal rules] and a subtle but painstaking and uncertain particularism, with its potentially invasive probing of the springs of conduct and the nuances of moral discrimination.[59]

This formulation of the objection to his countervision rather overdoes the concern about invasiveness and underplays the concern about certainty, predictability, consistency, and finality. Anyway, he parries it in two ways.

[58] *Ibid.* at 637. [59] *Ibid.* at 642.

First, he says it is 'often' advanced as a cover for an 'ideological' attempt to 'confine to a narrow range of situations the idea of contract as a common enterprise animated by mutual loyalty'.[60] Maybe. But the problems of early certainty about the rights and liabilities of the 'parties' remain real problems, quite apart from ideology. And it also remains that the question in issue was precisely whether there is yet a contract to which the parties ought to be loyal, or only an uncompleted negotiation.

His second parry points out that his own countervision itself accommodates some 'brightline' rules of contract of 'the classical form' in 'special cases'. He does not stay to consider whether, and how, there can be a (in his sense) non-arbitrary and 'justifiable' 'bright line' between 'special cases' of this sort and other situations where the critical legal doctrine is going to authorize courts to impose obligations and create entitlements in ill-defined ways unrecognized by pre-critical Contract law.

V

The key move in Unger's Critical strategy is a fallacy. For it is a fallacy to assert that 'bright lines', that is, definite rules—such as those in Contract which refer only to events, times, states of mind, etc., and not at all (in their formulation) to reasonableness or fairness or *ex post facto* ability to pay—could be justified only if there were a bright line, a 'stark contrast',[61] between ideals of human association, say between community and commerce, between family (or friendship) and the market.

On the contrary, the case for bright lines at the first level of rules is best made on the basis that the ideals of human association are related one to another in the way indicated by Aristotle's analogy of *philia*, friendship, which extends, in differing but related forms, from the central case of friendship to play-friendship, communal good neighbourliness (*philia politikē*), and business friendship.[62] And what is the substance of these lines of analogy or relationship between forms of association as different as 'real' friendship and business friendship? It consists surely in the fact that each of these forms of association exemplifies the basic human good of community, and that each is structured, though in differing ways, by common principles of fairness, honesty, and responsibility.

Indeed, the realm of commerce as envisaged in the law of Contract is a realm in which the mutual obligations are not only controlled by the side-constraints of fairness but are actually grounded on fairness and on the

[60] *Ibid.* at 642–3. [61] *Ibid.* at 644.

[62] See *NE* VIII. 2: 1155b17–20; 3–4: 1156a6–1157b6; *NLNR* 139–44, 157–8.

common benefits made available by respect for undertakings; and these principles of fairness and common good are not different from the principles of fairness and common good which structure forms of interdependence and loyalty *not* involving the deliberate undertaking of mutual obligations by mutual promises.[63] They are principles which have a claim and a bite more or less independent of any descriptive or ideal typology of forms of human association.

Unger does not understand the moral underpinnings of existing, pre-Critical Contract. According to him, it is only his countervision that

> treats the counterprinciples of community and fairness as possible generative sources of the entire body of law and doctrine, [and] finds the standard source of obligations in the only partly deliberate ties of mutual dependence....[64]

According to him, pre-critical doctrine sees the counterprinciples of community and fairness 'as mere ad hoc qualifications to the dominant principles, [and] identifies the fully articulated act of will and the unilateral imposition of a duty by the state as the two exhaustive sources of obligations'.[65] In other words, before the Critical Legal Studies Movement, everyone was a voluntarist or a positivist.

A glance at the pre-critical discussions of the obligation of promises in Charles Fried's work[66] or mine[67] will correct that impression. And a fair assessment of the existing law will show what I have already indicated, first, that pre-critical doctrine treats Contract as only a fraction of the legal universe, a universe in which duties of compensation, of restitution, of fiduciary obligation and trust abound; and secondly that the law of Contract itself is shot through with conceptions of honesty and fair dealing, and with public policies supported but not merely invented by the state.

The case for having a brightline rule, such as that preventing revocation of a contract once formed but allowing free revocation of offer, counteroffer, or acceptance until the moment of formation, is a case which does not at all rest on the superstition that an act of will has some normative significance on its own or when linked with another, contemporaneous act of will. Nor does the case rest on the absurd thesis that contract, being commerce, is part of a distinct form of human association in which harshest self-interest must be allowed to flourish without the restraints of community or fairness. It is a case which points partly to the advantages to all of a 'business efficacy' enhanced by clarity

63 *NLNR* 298–307.
64 Unger, 'The Critical Legal Studies Movement' at 569.
65 *Ibid.*; cf. 597, 639.
66 Fried, *Contract as Promise*, 13–17.
67 *NLNR* 299, 303–8, 320–5, 344–6.

and stability of expectations at each stage of conceiving and conducting a business venture; partly to the unfairness typically occasioned to third parties whenever a contract is revoked or invalidated; partly to the risks of unfairness occasioned by rules which encourage perjury; and partly to the waste, misery, and unfairness, of having to leave disputes to the hazards of litigation and palm-tree justice, instead of solving them with brisk efficiency, months or years earlier, by pointing to the relevant brightline rule in the 'rule book'.

To say this is not to say that this case is so overwhelming that reform of the law in the directions suggested by Unger and others would be irrational or unreasonable. The existing brightline rules, even where reasonable, are not *deductions* from the principles of fairness and community of which they are *determinationes*. It is Unger who is the absolutist, that is to say the disappointed methodological absolutist, who if he cannot find deduction proclaims that the movement of legal thought from his two higher levels (which I have been arguing are really but one, complex, higher level) to the first-level rules is a movement 'flawed',[68] 'confused',[69] 'arbitrary',[70] 'unjustifiable', and even 'unjustified' in (he hints) the strongly negative sense of demonstrably wrong. Most of the time—and, when criticizing others, always[71]—he (like, with opposite motivations, Ronald Dworkin) overlooks the distinctive reasonableness of *determinatio*. By *determinatio* there can be a particularization of general ideals, commitments, and principles by architects, musicians, legislators, and jurists, by steps none of which are themselves necessary, and all of which could reasonably have been in some respect different—so that there is, in these myriads of instances, no uniquely correct solution—but all of which are reasonable and none of which could without risk of *error* have been taken randomly or without regard to coherence with the larger whole constituted both by the initial general idea or ideas of value, commitment, or principle and by the steps already taken.

It is this requirement of coherence—of the integrity of the system both as a set of rules and principles extending analogously over many different but comparable forms of relationship and transaction, and as a set of interrelated institutions (for example a hierarchy of courts,

[68] Unger, 'The Critical Legal Studies Movement' at 580, 615, 647. [69] *Ibid.* at 570.

[70] *Ibid.* at 633; cf. also 577.

[71] Cf. 615, where, in relation to his own proposed doctrine he acknowledges that 'at each crucial juncture' in the steps from higher to lower levels 'different conclusions might reasonably be drawn'; his normal assumptions, however, are displayed at 571: 'it would be strange if the results of a coherent, richly developed normative theory were to coincide with a major portion of any extended branch of law'.

themselves more or less subject to legislatures)—that distinguishes legal thought from 'open-ended' practical reasoning: 'formalism', if you will; fairness, 'due process and equal protection of law', and systematic integrity, if one wants more accurate labels. This is a form of that loyalty of officials—say, judges and even legislatures—to their own previously settled and announced standards, that fidelity, which Lon Fuller rightly made the feature which distinguishes law from managerial direction, that is, from the bureaucratic rule to which Weber had more or less assimilated it.

VI

Determinatio is practical reasoning, the principles of which are provided by the understood basic forms of human goods, and the normative requirements of one of those goods, practical reasonableness. Like Kronman's positivist,[72] though with a different animus, Unger's Critical Legal Studies Movement uncritically supposes that norms and obligations can be justified or explained simply by pointing to facts about the present or the past. Obligations, he says in his set-piece account of the 'premises' of his countervision, 'arise primarily from relationships of mutual dependence that have been only incompletely shaped by state-imposed duties or explicit and perfected bargains'.[73]

But when is interdependence a good to be maintained, and when had it better be moderated or superseded by relative autonomy or by other forms of interrelationship? When is interdependence no more than parasitism, and what distinguishes parasitism from the honourable dependence of the infant, the unborn, the insane, the infirm? Unger does not seem to ask.

Indeed, the content of the countervision, of the forms or ideals of human association to be encouraged by the Movement, remains almost wholly negative. The individual is to be 'freed from the tyranny of abstract social categories'...

> The search for the less conditional and confining forms of social life is the search for a social world that can better do justice to a being whose most remarkable quality is precisely the power to overcome and revise, with time, every social structure in which he moves.[74]

[72] Kronman, *Max Weber*, 55 and passim; see essay 9 at 218–22.
[73] Unger, 'The Critical Legal Studies Movement' at 639.
[74] *Ibid.* at 584–5.

A genuinely critical student will have two reflections on this. First, he will reflect that the truly dependent had better look fearfully to their future when they hear these proposals to overcome every abstract social category and every social structure. For what is the aspiration and reality that Aristotle named the Rule of Law, and what are the legal structures of fair trial, or of the 'welfare' rights to food and water, or of the right not to be deliberately killed, but abstract social categories and structures to be 'overcome'? The world envisaged (or at least spoken of) by the Movement is not a world for children.

Secondly, one will reflect that the fundamental programme of the Movement—of introducing a society in which 'social life makes available in the course of ordinary politics and existence the instruments of its own revision'[75]—is at war with Unger's own proposed revision of Contract law on the basis of the 'counterprinciples' of fairness and community. For fairness and community are conceived by him precisely as extending (not revising, breaking down, remaking, or overcoming) the interdependencies and mutual obligations of persons—obligations which, indeed, he subsumes under the name of loyalty (for example loyalty between parties to a supposedly pre-contractual negotiation). But is not *loyalty* a strange name on the lips of those dedicated to the permanent revision of all confining social structures, all schemes of division and hierarchy? For what is Contract but a device for deliberately creating obligations backed by the coercively confiscatory power of the state, for creating restrictions (on the freedom of the parties thereafter), for creating divisions (between those subject and those not subject to the obligations thus created), and for creating a kind of hierarchy (between the party who—at least legally—is dominant, because he has the unsatisfied right, and the party with the unperformed obligation . . .)?

As Unger seems to admit, his Movement has no 'proposal about how to reconcile freedom with other ends'.[76] It rests uncritically content to ignore that problem of reconciliation, or at least to put off indefinitely the task of identifying and living out those 'other ends'. I say 'uncritically' because the value of freedom, which the Movement affirms, is arbitrarily exempted from its denial of objective human goods. The exemption is disguised by careful choice of words:

> if the central tradition of modernism is to be believed, nothing lies on the further side of blind constraint . . . but a confrontation with the real and anguishing sense of freedom itself. . . . [But] freedom, to be real, must exist in lasting forms of life; it cannot merely exhaust itself in temporary acts of context smashing.[77]

[75] *Ibid.* at 662. [76] *Ibid.* [77] *Ibid.* at 660, 661.

Here the words 'real', 'must', and 'cannot' conceal the affirmation of a good and the proposal to avoid an evil: a life of context smashing is not a good life... is worthless.

Note the assumption Unger has laid bare: '... if the central tradition of modernism is to be believed....' Genuinely critical social theorists will ask a few questions before believing the central tradition of anything. They might begin by asking whether Unger has offered good reasons for denying that there are any objective human goods. And they will find that Unger has offered four reasons; two of them are contradicted by him, and the other two rest on the characteristic modern failure to examine the possibility that the requirements of practical reasonableness, while ruling out a few classes of action and thus making possible an acknowledgement of a few fully specific human rights not to be treated in certain ways, for the rest have a directive quality, far short of specifying a unique set of individual or social commitments, yet far richer than emptiness.

> To affirm objective human goods [says Unger] is to affirm that the mind can grasp and establish moral essences.... But this has never been shown, and the conception of reason on which it rests has been discredited in nonmoral areas of thought.[78]

But this talk of the 'essences' bogey is merely conjuring with a forgotten word. What is at stake is no more and no less than the question whether the mind can understand anything and hold and communicate some definite meaning to define and express what it understands; and the 'what it understands' is no more and no less an 'essence' in thought about human good than it is in thought about geometry, biology, chemistry, or particle physics. Unger's denial of essence is contradicted by many of his own affirmations, not least his acknowledgement that there is a human nature.

Equally self-contradictory is Unger's claim that 'the doctrine of objective value falsely teaches us to forget the connection between what is good for us and what we are'.[79] For he had himself, in the same book, acknowledged that

> the conception of objective value [proposes that we think] of... norms of conduct as ends whose fulfillment would bring our worthiest capacities to their richest development....[80]

As Aquinas does not tire of saying (but is often not *heard* to say), we come to know our nature (what we are) by coming to know what are our capacities, and these we come to know by understanding what we do (our actions), and

[78] Unger, *Knowledge and Politics*, 77. [79] *Ibid.* at 239. [80] *Ibid.* at 77.

these we understand by understanding their point, their ends, the goods that they realize and participate in.[81]

Unger's third charge is that a theory of objective goods 'degenerates into either meaningless abstraction or unwarranted parochialism'.[82] With this one can and should be brisk. The charge could only be established by someone who participates in specific discussions of particular goods, particular requirements of practical reasonableness, and particular *determinationes* of those goods and requirements in the commitments of an individual life-plan or the institutional structures and practices and legal rules and principles of a given community. Unger, for the most part, omits to engage in such discussions; his discussion of the current rules and principles of Contract does not encourage confidence in his claim that there is no middle ground between meaningless abstraction and unwarranted parochialism.

Finally, and I think most near to his own heart, is the contention that the 'doctrine' of objective human goods

> denies any significance to choice other than the passive acceptance or rejection of independent truths. Our experience of moral judgment, however, seems to be one of at least contributing to shape the ends we pursue. A conception that puts this fact aside disregards the significance of choice as an expression of personality.[83]

Unger, in other words, treats the claim that there are objective human goods and moral requirements as the claim that we can 'kn[o]w the moral good with certainty, and underst[an]d all its implications and requirements perfectly',[84] to the extent that we do not need any individual choice of obligation-creating commitments or vocations, or any social mechanism of 'impartial adjudication', of authoritative *determinatio*.

I have tried in this essay to show how far this distorts our human situation as that situation is understood in the social theory of Aristotle and, say, Aquinas. That social theory remains still to be refined and elaborated, but methodologically it is far sounder than the criticisms which Unger and his fellows have brought against it. And its explicitly moral and political normative theory is sounder by far than the criticisms they have brought against social practices that are still best accounted for by its principles of theoretical method and of practical reasoning and choice.

[81] See citations and commentary in *FoE* 20–5. [Now also *Aquinas* 29–34.]

[82] Unger, *Knowledge and Politics*, 239; also 77. [83] *Ibid.* at 77. [84] *Ibid.* at 93.

NOTE

† *Dworkin's failure to do the parts of political philosophy that consider authority's source and justification*... (at n. 11). Subsequently, in *Law's Empire* (1986), Dworkin offered, albeit briefly, an account of the justification of the authority of the state. See the assessment of this in essay 12, sec. V (295–7).

14

'LEGAL LIBERALISM' OR *LIBER ET LEGALIS*?*

Despite the powerful criticisms it rightly advances against Critical Legal Studies (CLS), David Price's review remains, in two respects, under the influence of the movement's flawed theses. First, he has accepted that the alternative to CLS is 'legal liberalism', a category, or term, much promoted, if not invented, by the CLS movement: see secs I–III below. Secondly, he has accepted too much of the CLS claim about 'contradictions' within the law and legal doctrine: see sec. IV below.

I

Now it is clear enough that his adoption of legal liberalism as a primary structuring element of his paper has implications which David Price himself finds embarrassing. Several times he feels obliged to note that positions central to what he calls 'liberalism' are shared by 'conservatives'.[1] It is to underline this problem that I have recalled, in an antique language, a twelfth-century label for the normal citizen of England: '*liber et legalis homo*', the free person[2] who lives in accordance with the law, enjoys the freedom it recognizes and protects, and participates in the life of the law not as official but precisely as citizen.[3] If individual rights and the rule of law are the defining features of legal liberalism, as Price maintains, and if the representative founding fathers of liberalism are Locke and Blackstone, as he also says, then the presence of such ideas (indeed, of such a conjunction of ideas) many centuries before Locke should make us reluctant to accept the CLS claim that the alternative to CLS ideals is legal liberalism.

* Unpublished comment (for a conference in the University of Cambridge) on a draft of David Price, 'Review of Critical Legal Studies', subsequently published in revised form as 'Taking Rights Cynically: Review of Critical Legal Studies'. My original page references to his draft have been eliminated and replaced where possible by footnoted references to the printed version.

[1] Price, 'Taking Rights Cynically' at 272 n. 3, 273, 275, 293.

[2] The Latin for 'man' as opposed to 'woman' is 'vir', not 'homo'.

[3] The phrase is used in the royal writ for holding a view of disputed lands; the king bids the sheriff send 'liberos et legales homines' from the neighbourhood to view the lands: see *Glanvill* , Book II para. 3; Pollock and Maitland, *The History of English Law*, 407, make much of the phrase.

I could, of course, have chosen other labels or slogans or phrases to suggest that 'liberalism', understood as engendered in the seventeenth century, is not a safe description of the rights and rule of law which Price wishes to defend against CLS antipathy and subversion. I could have recalled the passage from James Harrington's *Commonwealth of Oceana* (1656) which, I suppose, provides the remote but direct origins of the title of Ronald Dworkin's book:

> ... if the liberty of a man consists in the empire of his reason... then the liberty of a commonwealth consists in the empire of her laws...; and these I conceive to be the principles upon which Aristotle and Livy... have grounded their assertion that 'a commonwealth is an empire of laws and not of men'.[4]

Harrington here recalls the extent to which Greek philosophy and Roman republican law have contributed to the edifice which CLS contemns. (And I take the opportunity to note, in passing, that in *Law's Empire*, Dworkin no longer uses the term 'liberal' as a framework category, as he had in *Taking Rights Seriously*.[5])

My point is not that we should treat legal liberalism as ante-dating the seventeenth century (which, as a matter of fact, knew the term 'liberalism' no more than Aristotle did—the term in its application to politics emerges in the nineteenth century).[6] My point is that we should conduct our conversations about rights and the rule of law *without using the term 'liberalism', or any other relativizing term, at all.*[7]

Rather, we should be prepared to say that CLS is a threat, not to liberalism, but to human rights (particularly the rights of the vulnerable[8]) and to the Rule of Law—that it neglects or contemns or undermines, not an opinion or doctrine, however popular and fundamental to our polity, but some important truths about human dignity and justice. Of course, we will then have to argue for the truth of our assertion. But that is not a burden to be rejected.

II

Let me make the point another way. Legal liberalism is defined by David Price in terms of individual rights and the rule of law. As understood in CLS, legal liberalism includes those items, but as elements, parts, of a social-theoretical construct called 'liberalism', the theory of which has

[4] Harrington, *Political Works* (ed. Pocock, 1977), 170.

[5] 'The various chapters define and defend a liberal theory of law': *TRS* vii.

[6] See Voegelin, 'On Liberalism and Its History'.

[7] [That is to say, we should not use 'liberal' as a framework category, as it was used by Dworkin in *TRS* and by Raz (with some precautions) in *AL*, e.g. Essays 14 and 15, i.e. in the same way as political discourse must use terms such as 'just', 'fair', 'free', 'tyrannical', etc.]

[8] See Price, 'Taking Rights Cynically' at e.g. 278, 298.

been most amply developed, and with some real historical learning and philosophical penetration, by Roberto Unger.

Liberalism, according to Unger, is one of a set of 'forms of life', each 'a meaningful whole of the most comprehensive kind' which 'embodies an entire mode of human existence',[9] and each of which has 'a unity of sense rather than of logic or causation'.[10] Unger attends, in his *Law in Modern Society* (1976), to six such types: tribal society, aristocratic society, liberal society, and then traditionalist, revolutionary-socialist, and post-liberal (social-democratic) societies.

Each form of social life is distinguished by the way in which it deals with three basic problems of human association: the distribution of individuals among significant groups, the character of their relations to each other as insiders or strangers, and the way people understand the relationship between what is and what ought to be.[11] Unger's summary of the defining features of the liberal form of life is, accordingly:

> ... the central theme of consciousness and existence in liberal society is a peculiar set of interdependencies among three factors. The first element is the multiplication of significant groups with the diminishment of the area of individual life dominated by each group. Roles are specialized, but every person occupies a variety of them. The second basic feature of liberal society is the disappearance of a sharp distinction between strangers and outsiders. The social order becomes an association of interests that plays on men's need for each other's approval [rather than on their participation in an identical vision of the truth and the good]. Third, ideals are opposed to actuality [; social arrangements are no longer seen as expressions of the good, the beautiful or the holy].[12]

Against this background, Unger advances the thesis which most immediately concerns us now: 'the legal order emerged with modern European liberal society'.[13] By 'legal order', he means the type of law which is responsive to the ideal of the rule of law, law 'committed to being general and autonomous as well as public and positive'.[14] Law is 'autonomous' when (a) 'the rules formulated and enforced by a government cannot be persuasively analyzed as a mere restatement of any identifiable set of nonlegal beliefs on norms, be they economic, political, or religious', (b) 'its rules are applied by specialized institutions whose main task is

[9] Unger, *Law in Modern Society*, 252. [10] *Ibid.*, 261. [11] *Ibid.*, 137–40.

[12] *Ibid.*, 167, with additions from 145, 146. This account of liberalism needs to be supplemented by Unger's claims about the 'liberal psychology', according to which (a) desire, not reason, is the moving, active or primary part of the self, (b) desires are arbitrary, and (c) knowledge is no more than the combination or aggregation of sensations and ideas; and by his claims about 'liberal political theory', particularly the principle that all values are subjective: Unger, *Knowledge and Politics*, 29–103.

[13] Unger, *Law in Modern Society*, 54. [14] *Ibid.*, 52, 54.

adjudication' and (c) whose ways of justifying their acts differ from the ways used in other disciplines and practices, and (d) there is a special group, the legal profession, manipulating the rules, staffing these institutions, and engaging in legal argumentation.[15]

Now it is true, I think, that only in modern times, and in Europe, do we find states which fully embody legal order so understood, with the relevant specialized institutions and practices constitutive of legal autonomy as Unger uses that term. Similarly, it is only in relatively modern times that we find societies in which Glanvill's conception of the status of the *liber et legalis homo* actually extends, in social reality, to all adults not disqualified by their own default or personal incapacity. But the real question raised by CLS is not whether the societies in which individual rights and the rule of law were first fully embodied were also 'liberal' in the ways identified by Unger (or, for that matter, in the different ways identified by, say, Ronald Dworkin). Rather, the question is whether the assertion that individuals have rights against the law, and that justice requires the rule of law, can be held as justifiable and true by someone who does *not* share the beliefs, the 'consciousness', which Unger calls 'liberal'.

And the answer to that question is clear. Aristotle clearly identifies and affirms the case for the rule of law and not of men. Thomas Aquinas, well before the emergence of 'modern' European society, identifies and affirms all the features of Ungerian legal autonomy (except perhaps the last, the existence of a legal profession, which we perhaps see him taking for granted in his many references to 'jurists'). He has a particularly clear and firm conception that positive law, which must be general (non-discriminatory) and autonomous, is no mere restatement of morality,[16] that the role of the judge is entirely distinct from any other social role and is intrinsic to a well-ordered society, and that legal argument is thoroughly distinguishable from ethical and political argument. Yet Aristotle and Aquinas are not Ungerian liberals. They utterly deny that civil or political society is merely an association of interests; they equally deny that social arrangements, including justice and law, cannot in the real world participate, in varying ways, in the true, the good, the beautiful, and even the holy.[17] And it is open

[15] *Ibid.*, 52–3.

[16] A version of Aquinas's masterly argument for this aspect of legal autonomy is to be found, summarily stated, in essay 13, not least in the passage quoted by Price, 'Taking Rights Cynically' at 287 (viz. essay 13 at 301–2). It seems to me a mistake to regard that passage, as he does, as a reply to CLS's loose thinking about 'contradictions'. Instead, it is a part of my reply to CLS's loose talk of 'indeterminacy'. My own reply to CLS talk of contradictions is found elsewhere in essay 13 at 306, 309–15, esp. 310 and 314.

[17] Thus they would regard as fallacious and erroneous the following central Ungerian claim:

> If objective values were available to us, if we knew the true good with certainty, and understood all its implications and requirements perfectly, we would not need a method of impartial

to us today to make and defend, in our own way, the same affirmations and denials.

That is why I proposed that we say, not that CLS threatens liberalism (legal or otherwise), but that CLS threatens justice and certain fundamental truths about human good and human relationships.

III

Some marginal remarks about David Price's conceptions of the rule of law and individual rights.

As to the rule of law, which he identifies in terms of the actions of government being constrained by legal sources, and of the political preferences of officials being separated from the laws they administer: I think this account needs to be supplemented by the other features of the rule of law identified by Lon Fuller, Joseph Raz, and indeed by Unger.[18]

As to individual rights: I think it is misleading, or in danger of being misleading, to use the spatial metaphors of a 'zone', 'sphere', or 'realm', whether of privacy[19] or autonomy,[20] particularly if one reinforces the spatial character of the metaphor by saying that the individual has rights '*within* his or her private zone'.[21] There is no zone or sphere or realm beyond the rightful claims of other people and the rightful authority of the law, no zone which could be identified prior to identifying *one's rights.*

There are, of course, attempts to identify such a zone or set of zones. They all seem to me to fail. The US Supreme Court, in *Griswold v Connecticut* (1965)[22] and *Roe v Wade* (1973),[23] tried to identify zones of privacy: the marital bedroom, the doctor-patient relationship, the use of one's own body. But no one can defend the proposition that whatever is done within these zones is a matter of individual right beyond the reach of rightful legal prohibition. The husband who perforates his condom with the intention of infecting his wife with HIV so that she will die of AIDS, and succeeds, commits the offence of murder; the wife who discloses the trade secrets of her employer in pillow-talk with her husband, a business

> adjudication.... The problem of adjudication, as presented in modern jurisprudence, is therefore inextricably linked with the conception that values are subjective and individual. (Unger, *Knowledge and Politics*, 93.)

Aristotle and Aquinas think that there are many and basic objective values, really sharable, but that these do not have just one 'perfect' and perfectly knowable set of implications and requirements, knowledge of which could, even in principle, eliminate the need for authoritative legislative and judicial determinations of positive law.

[18] [See now Price, 'Taking Rights Cynically' at 275 esp. n. 15.] For a synthesis, see *NLNR* 270–6.

[19] Price, 'Taking Rights Cynically' at 273. [20] *Ibid.* at 300. [21] *Ibid.* at 273.

[22] 381 US 479. [23] 410 US 113.

rival of her employer, can rightly be liable for breach of her employer's right of confidentiality. A mother who watches her child drown in a puddle cannot resist a charge of manslaughter with the plea that what she does with her own body is outside the realm of legal regulation.

Of course, there are many and important moral entitlements which can be broadly indicated with the terms 'individual liberty' and 'autonomy' and which should be protected and promoted by the law. But they cannot be defined in terms of spheres of the individual's activity, or without reference to the moral requirements imposed by the entitlements of other persons—entitlements which include, as I think, the rights of children to grow up in a milieu which preserves them from inducements to engage in worthless forms of life which will threaten their ultimate self-mastery (integration of emotions with intelligent grasp of real human goods), *autonomia*, autonomy.[24]

IV

The second way in which David Price's review seems to me to concede too much to the CLS is this: he says that 'legal rules embrace contradictory aims and assumptions, and thus do not perfectly serve any one of them'.[25] His only example, I think, of 'contradictory' principles (or aims or assumptions) is in the quoted passage where Unger says that alongside the freedom to choose the partner and freedom to choose the terms are the 'counterprinciples' that 'freedom to contract would not be allowed to undermine the communal aspects of social life and that grossly unfair bargains would not be enforced'.[26] But these are not examples of genuine contradiction, or anything approaching contradiction. As I show in my own essay on this work of Unger's, there simply is no statable principle of law that one has no legal obligations to others except those which one has freely chosen to adopt by contract: contract law exists within a legal matrix of obligations and liabilities to others incurred more or less independently of one's specific choice to incur them—obligations in tort, in restitution, in estoppel, as constructive trustee, and so forth.[27] One cannot apply the concept of 'contradiction' to the principles of contract mentioned by Unger except in the quixotic sense of 'contradiction', according to which the defence of self-defence 'contradicts' the definition of murder, or the

[24] Cf. *NLNR* 215–18; on autonomy, see *ibid.*, 169, 192, 261, 308.

[25] Price, 'Taking Rights Cynically' at 286; also 285. [But my comments may be based on a crabbed reading of Price's nuanced remarks about the significance of contradiction, *ibid.* at 285–8.]

[26] *Ibid.* at 285, quoting Unger, *Law in Modern Society*, 7 (= Unger, 'The Critical Legal Studies Movement' at 569 (see essay 13 at n. 36)).

[27] Essay 13 at 305, 308, and 313.

requirement that one feed one's children is 'contradicted' by the requirement that one not murder one's neighbour's child in order to feed the body to one's starving children. The whole law, on virtually every topic, consists of norms with inbuilt limitations, qualifications, conditions, and the like. There is no good reason to treat these limitations as contradictions or as signs or forms of incoherence.

Nor should we imagine that, but for the horse-trading of interest groups and legislators, we could 'perfectly' serve any one human 'aim' in abstraction from other aspects of human well-being and from the other entitlements of other human beings to share in the multi-faceted, multi-person common good. No aspect of that human good which is the proper concern of politics and law can rightly be understood as a 'goal' which, like the goals of specific *techniques*, can be perfectly accomplished by the artful disposition of measurably effective means.

15

INDIVIDUALS, COMMUNITIES, AND POSTMODERNISM: SOME NOTES*

I

Daniel Ortiz's interesting 'work-in-progress' tackles some of the most important issues in the domain of our conference or workshop. My main doubt is whether the paper keeps those issues as distinct as I think they properly are.

As introduced on Ortiz's first page, the issue is whether 'the individual is the basic, given unit of political and social analysis'. That question is quite understandably called 'ontological'. For ontology is disciplined reflection on the being of things, what makes them what they are; and the question what sort of thing human societies are, and the question whether *that* question can be answered without first considering what human individuals *are*, are questions reasonably called ontological. So, Ortiz says, some traditional defences of liberalism metaphysicalize the individual as a transculturally and transhistorically stable and basic entity; or again, they (like Robert Bork)[1] 'metaphysicalize autonomy' by holding that 'the individual necessarily stands prior to everything else, including his beliefs and desires'.[2] Some communitarians, on the other hand, hold like Duncan Kennedy that (in Ortiz's quotation and paraphrase)

> 'when an individual sets out to produce...what gets made is a product of... group...experiences' [and] [i]ndividuality exists in this view...only in the sense of a community performance located in a single human mind or body.[3]... It is as if communities are larger versions of the...individuals of metaphysical liberalism.[4]

* Unpublished comment (for a conference in 1995 in the University of Oxford) on a draft paper by Daniel R. Ortiz, then entitled 'Disaggregating Identity', subsequently published with revisions and a new title, 'Categorical Community'. Published here with the kind permission of Daniel Ortiz.

1 [References to Bork are to Bork, 'Neutral Principles and Some First Amendment Problems'.]

2 [Ortiz, 'Categorical Community' at 774.]

3 [*Ibid.* at 777–8, quoting Kennedy, *Sexy Dressing Etc.* 67–9.]

4 [Ortiz, 'Categorical Community' at 780.]

Other theorists, on the other hand, such as Ronald Dworkin, insist that (in Ortiz's paraphrase) 'despite what some vulgar communitarians may say, the state does not necessarily have a sex life'.[5] And these claims and counter-claims are all ontological and indeed metaphysical, claims and counterclaims about what sorts of things human individuals, human communities, and states, really are; they are claims about that the first sentence calls the 'metaphysical underpinnings of liberalism'.

The trouble begins in the second sentence, in which these underpinnings are redescribed as 'the philosophical foundations of individual sovereignty'. 'Sovereignty' is perhaps the paper's key term, as in 'individual sovereignty' or 'sovereignty of the individual', 'the vision of people as sovereign individuals' and 'society primarily as a collection of sovereign individuals' versus the vision of 'the community...as sovereign and individuals as expressions of it';[6] and then again as the 'radical subjectiv[e]' notion of 'plac[ing] sovereignty in the only value-giver we have: the individual';[7] and so on. Why do I think this is troublesome?

Well, in the first place, this late thirteenth-century word is particularly elusive. Not only twentieth-century English lawyers but also, for example, the late eighteenth-century liberal Kant hear it as connoting a supremacy which is somehow without limit, beyond restriction (which is why Kant repudiated as mere 'self-conceit' the idea that in the moral realm we are or ever could be sovereigns—for in truth, although we have legislative power in that domain, we are 'subjects in it, *not sovereigns*' (*Critique of Practical Reason*, 82–3), since none of us is godlike, 'a completely independent being, without needs and with an unlimited power adequate to one's will' (*Groundwork* 433–4)).[8] In another inflection, however, Queen Elizabeth II is sovereign; and each of the fifty states of the Unites States is constitutionally sovereign *within its sphere*; and the Pacific island state of Tuvalu, with all of 10,000 inhabitants, is (like the United States of America) a sovereign state. So, if we want to affirm the 'ontological priority of the individual' or the individual's 'fundamental independence', we would speak more clearly if we used terms other than 'sovereign'. The late thirteenth-century postmodern[9] Parisian intellectual, Thomas Aquinas, affirms the human person's fundamental freedom (one's ontological capacity to make at least some free choices between options each of which has its attraction to one's reason) by speaking about one's 'power over oneself', of one's

[5] [*Ibid.* at 783.] [6] [*Ibid.* at 770.] [7] [*Ibid.*]

[8] [For citations and comment, see essay III.2 (1987c) at nn. 32–3.]

[9] In the sequence *classical/traditional* (Augustine; Bernard), *modern* (Abelard), *postmodern* (Aquinas). But Aquinas would not thank me for attaching to him a label so afflicted with built-in obsolescence.

'mastery [or dominion: *dominium*] over [or ownership of: *dominium*] one's own acts', about one's will as mistress over its choices, and so forth[10]—the implicit metaphors are, like 'sovereignty', drawn from the legal-political domain, but make a claim which is more modest and precise. The same thinker defends the ontological primacy or priority of individuals over their societies by arguing that societies are not organisms, but rather are no more than orders—arrangements—of the actions and dispositions of individual human persons, who each perform many acts which are not the acts of any society or community.[11]

But there is no case for pursuing that line of thought here. For a second and, it seems to me, more serious problem with the talk of sovereignty is that it systematically obscures the distinction between 'is' and 'ought', between the ontological or metaphysical (propositions about *what things are* independently of our thinking) and the normative (propositions about what order *to bring* into our deliberating and choosing as individuals acting on our own behalf or as members or agents or leaders of our societies). And this is not a mere matter of terminology. The fact is that the bulk of Ortiz's paper is concerned not with questions of ontology or metaphysics but with engaging certain theses about what the relation between individuals and their political communities should be, what individuals or communities are entitled to, what *authority* the latter *properly* or *rightly* have over the former, and what justifies or fails to justify certain social 'demands' on and 'claims over' individuals; and so forth. In this dimension of the paper, the contrast is not between individual and society as alternative basic or primary 'units of political and social analysis'; it is between, for example, 'individualism *and altruism*'—normative not ontological positions. The charge which Ortiz brings against Kennedy and, it seems, Dworkin—of 'anthropomorphizing' society by considering it as 'totalitizing'[12]—turns out to have the same ambiguity: the anthropomorphizers' mistake is of saying 'that a community *determines* all the important aspects of its members' identity'—a mistake of fact, if anything—and of denying or overlooking that a society (such as an orchestra) 'exerts strong but limited claims over its members'[13]—a mistake about justified and justifying normativity, if anything. Some sentences in the paper shift with unsettling facility between 'is' and 'ought': for example (offering to report Dworkin), 'The extent of [the state's] communal life and the reach of its claims depend upon the social practices that constitute

[10] [See *Aquinas* 20–1.] [11] See essay II.5 at 95–6 (1989a at 270–1); *Aquinas* 24–9.

[12] [See Ortiz, 'Categorical Community' at 788: 'Dworkin's interpretation of our political community also exhibits the other unhappy feature of Kennedy's community: monolithicness. Monolithicness has two components: uniformity and totalization.']

[13] [*Ibid.* at 783.]

it'.[14] To me, the two questions—of the extent to which communal life absorbs and determines individual existence and action, and of the morally justifiable reach of the political community's claims upon us—are entirely distinct. Indeed, so far from there being a coherent 'communitarian' position in which the community both determines and exerts wide claims over individual action, such a position is incoherent and absurd. If B's action is *determined* by entity or factor A, it is impossible for A to make any meaningful *claims upon* B; for there is no sense in addressing claims, or in offering any normative guidance whatever, to someone whose actions are in any case determined by some other entity or factor.

II

As I suggested a moment ago, Ortiz's primary interest is in the normative, not the ontological issue(s). He makes this manifest by taking as motto Walt Whitman's complacent-seeming claim to be large enough to contain multitudes including contradictions.[15] For the contradiction which Ortiz wishes to bring to light, the 'contradiction *within us*', is, I think, the 'contradiction' between 'the claims of individualism' and 'the claims of altruism'—and these claims are not assertions about facts but rather appeals for 'commitment' (the context is a paraphrasing of Kennedy but I read it as articulating a position which Ortiz approves at least as a statement of position even if not as the conclusion of an argument).[16] Ortiz wants to contend, against the simple-mindedly anthropomorphic and totalitizing Kennedy, that the conflict or contradiction hereabouts is more subtle, since each of us is a member of many communities, not just one, and 'people can even find themselves members of two conflicting communities at once, as lesbians and gay men within the Catholic church can attest'.[17] Against Dworkin's equally 'simple-minded' anthropomorphism, Ortiz wishes, like Kennedy, to 'envision[ ] the possibility of real conflict between communities', and so he speaks sardonically of 'Dworkin's confidence in resolving our great public controversies, like abortion....'[18]

But I fear I may be misunderstanding Ortiz's views about contradiction. Perhaps he does not mean to be as tolerant of it as he often seems to profess to be. At one point he envisages some normative considerations that in

[14] [*Ibid.*]

[15] Do I contradict myself?
Very well then I contradict myself,
(I am large, I contain multitudes.)
(Walt Whitman, 'Song of Myself', sec. 51.)
[Ortiz, 'Categorical Community' does not mention Whitman or have any motto.]

[16] [Ortiz, 'Categorical Community' at 776–7.] [17] [*Ibid.* at 781.] [18] [*Ibid.* at 789.]

a sense transcend, and enable us to transcend, the competing standards of the different communities to which we belong. For of those competing standards we can ask 'Which set is more useful for whatever purposes we hope to achieve through scholarship'[19] (scholarship and 'the academic enterprise'[20] being the domain relevant to the standards which he happens at that point to be envisaging). Here we at least glimpse a criterion that would enable us to go beyond contradiction 'towards positions in which whatever confidence we have will not be misplaced'.[21] And our confidence would certainly be misplaced if it were accompanied by tolerance of genuine contradiction. 'The academic enterprise' in which Ortiz invests some hope is utterly frustrated by such tolerance; self-contradiction—more particularly the acceptance of what one knows to be contradictory beliefs—makes thought not 'useful' but futile. The eminently contradictable thought that contradiction is sometimes tolerable would be as futile as any other.

Still, I am unsure whether Ortiz accepts this. He is 'a postmodern kind of guy',[22] though with unspecified reservations about postmodernism; so far as I can see he is not dissenting from Kennedy when he says that

> following postmodernism, Kennedy notes that there is no position outside of community from which to judge particular communities' beliefs and practices... we cannot escape our own communities to find an Archimedean point or unsituated perspective from which to judge others. 'There is [accordingly,] no intellectual space outside ideology'... all knowledge... reflects power, not truth.... knowledge contains no truth....[23]

It would not be out of place for Ortiz's paper to note at this point that the statements 'all knowledge reflects power, not truth' and 'knowledge contains no truth' are as absurd a pair of statements as can be imagined, each being both self-contradictory (in as much as 'knowledge' means *true* belief) and self-refuting (because purporting to state a truth and to communicate *knowledge* which Kennedy has attained by—as they say—critical study).

The paper might also seize the opportunity to venture a little critique of Kennedy's uncritical, Rortyesque talk about there being no 'Archimedean point' or 'unsituated perspective' from which to judge, 'no intellectual space outside of ideology' and so forth. This sort of talk assumes, along with the naïvest empiricisms, that knowledge is all a matter of taking a look. (It is a sibling of the early Bork's gross and indefensible assumption that all one's intending is seeking 'gratification' for oneself.) But doing philosophy, like

19 [*Ibid.* at 781.] 20 [*Ibid.* at 782.] 21 [*Ibid* at 782.]
22 [Ortiz, 'Categorical Community' at 771.]
23 [*Ibid.* at 778, where the last four words are absent.]

doing mathematics or history, is for the most important part not a matter of taking a look, but of understanding and reasoning, processes which have some foundation in the visible and imaginable but rapidly, effortlessly, and validly go far beyond anything that could be captured with the lame, spatially dominated metaphors of 'perspective', 'Archimedean points', and so forth. As for the claim that there is no intellectual space outside ideology, it naïvely invokes the contempt it deserves; it invites dismissal as one more piece of ideology, or refutes itself by asserting a proposition capable of being truly—non-ideologically—affirmed or denied. The 'heavy artillery of "postmodernism"'[24] is aimed (if at all) at itself, and in the ears of scholars will, I think, silence itself soon enough.

III

I called Whitman's statement complacent-seeming. But that, like much else in these rough comments of mine, was much too simple. To be sure, there is some complacency in Whitman's more or less pantheistic celebrations of his self. But Whitman is willing to admit (though again with a touch of complacency?) that the 'Song of Myself' which he 'sounds...over the roofs of the world' is in some respects 'a barbaric yawp' (sec. 52, seven lines after Ortiz's quotation from sec. 51). He is no philosopher, and uses the word 'contradict' with about as much precision (though not in the same ways) as his contemporary Karl Marx or our contemporaries the Critical Legal Scholars. Whitman's homespun epistemology falls promptly into self-refutation:

Only what proves itself to every man and woman is so,
Only what nobody denies is so. (sec. 30.)

But for all his declamatory confusion Whitman is no fool; his celebration of himself is as soul (soul of course united with body, indeed with a highly sexual bodiliness), like every other human self an image (if not an instance!) of the divine and *therefore* 'large' and 'contain[ing] multitudes'. And the 'contradict[ing]' of himself which Whitman is aware of, in the passage taken by Ortiz for a motto, is precisely the contrast between, on the one hand, his calling on the divine (as he does *in the preceding three lines*) to disclose itself ('Listener up there! what have you to confide to me?'), and on the other hand, his telling his own listeners, a couple of pages earlier, not to be curious about divinity:

And I say to mankind, Be not curious about God,...

[24] [*Ibid.* at 777.]

> Why should I wish to see God better than this day?
> I see something of God each hour of the twenty-four, and each moment then...
> I find letters from God dropt in the street, and every one is sign'd by God's name,
> And I leave them where they are ...' (sec. 48.)

So Whitman is a transitional figure. He is a great celebrant of spirit's (mind's, intelligent soul's) matter-transcending reach ('large[ness]'), and of the good order, peace, and justice that are possible *on an assumption* which he articulates with remarkable power in the 1855 Preface to the volume in which 'Song of Myself' first appeared—the assumption that every morally, humanly good, and decent action, and for that matter every immoral and sordid action, 'is duly realized and returned' and affects the acting man or woman not only in his or her lifetime or the hour of death but also 'affects him or her onward afterward through the indirect lifetime' which is a kind of present, of infinite duration. And it is precisely here and on the basis of this assumption that he affirms that 'the push of charity [genuine love] or personal force [can n]ever be anything else than the profoundest *reason*'.[25] But we can clearly see, even if Whitman did not, that this assumption (like Kant's analogous assumption of the rationality of human history)[26] was sufficiently warranted only by the 'letters from God' delivered by certain priests..., and that Whitman's real, self-undermining complacency was his belief that 'There will soon be no more priests',[27] that is, that there is no need for letters of *that* sort, and no need to interest oneself in the question whether there has been a true public disclosure (revelation) of divine providence, goodness, and justice. In the interval between Whitman and us, his belief that 'there will soon be no more priests' has in one important sense been verified: the priests and their letters from God have ceased to be of even the slightest public interest or concern to such as Kennedy, or Dworkin, or the early Bork. So it is not too surprising that Whitman's confidence in reason and spirit has disappeared from public discourse (and education), too.

Postmodernism has the great merit of drawing out the most relevant conclusion, the conclusion which is the real content of Kennedy's otherwise incoherent declamations about 'knowledge' or ideology as power: that since 'reason' and 'spirit' (the understanding mind) correspond to nothing in the fabric and order of things, there remains nothing of genuine interest save *power* (and its handmaiden, fraud) deployed in the service of arbitrarily

[25] 'Preface to "Leaves of Grass"', in Whitman, *Selected Poems & Prose*, 227–9 (emphasis added).
[26] See *NLNR* 374. [27] Whitman, *Selected Poems & Prose*, 231.

adopted individual or group purposes. In the 'academic enterprise' of education and scholarship and debate, Ortiz wishes to find and affirm what is *common*—what can be *shared* by people in different communities—and goes beyond mere power. I am sure he is right to make a reflection on the ontological and normative preconditions of education, scholarship, and debate the pivot of an attempt to move us towards positions whatever confidence in which we have will not be misplaced. This move forward will, I think, need to reach all the way down and back to positions held not only by Whitman but also, and with better reason, by the earlier liberal philosopher I jokingly called 'postmodern'.

Part Three

Legal Reasoning

16

ALLOCATING RISKS AND SUFFERING: SOME HIDDEN TRAPS*

I

In his first lectures on jurisprudence, Adam Smith told his students that the imperfect rights which are the subject of distributive justice do not properly belong to jurisprudence. For they fall not under the jurisdiction of the laws but rather under 'a system of morals'. 'We are therefore in what follows to confine ourselves entirely to the perfect rights, and what is called commutative justice.'[1] Of course, he did not in fact confine himself to commutative justice, but discoursed broadly on the foundations of government, on family and slavery, and on the wealth of nations ('national opulence' as he then called it) which can meet the natural wants of mankind by a division of labour based on the industry of the people and proportioned to an appropriately regulated system of commerce. All this as Jurisprudence (and for students aged from 14 to 16)!

His *The Theory of Moral Sentiments*, published three years earlier in 1759, convincingly demonstrates Adam Smith's real familiarity with the classics. Yet when he speaks of 'distributive justice', to dismiss it from Jurisprudence, he uses the term quite differently from Aristotle.[2] For Aristotle, distributive justice concerns the problem of allocating the community's *common stock* of resources, opportunities, profits and advantages, roles and offices, responsibilities, taxes, and other burdens. In Adam Smith's formal treatments of justice, this whole problem has disappeared, along with the corresponding virtue of Aristotelian distributive justice. Smith's 'distributive justice'—and hereabouts he wishes to be relying on Grotius, Pufendorf, and his own Scottish philosophical mentor Hutcheson, as well as his admired friend David Hume—concerns only such matters as the weak, imperfect, and metaphorical 'right' of brilliant or learned people to

* 1990b.

[1] Smith, *Lectures on Jurisprudence*.

[2] Smith, *The Theory of Moral Sentiments*, Pt VII, § ii, ch. 1, 436.

be praised, or the right of beggars to seek other people's charity (which is not a right to be given anything, nor indeed an *enforceable* right even to beg).

Adam Smith's jurisprudence is crippled by inattention to distributive justice, to the allocation of the common stock of goods and roles (with the risks incident to them). But in our day jurisprudence not only risks forgetting commutative justice, but also risks misunderstanding (and mislocating the rationality of) the principles for resolving the problems of distributive justice.

II

The economic analysis of which Adam Smith is a principal founder is helpful in practical reasoning about problems of justice precisely insofar as it systematically calls attention to the side effects of individual choices and actions and behaviour. Adam Smith's interest in side effects is intense and pointed even in his *Theory of the Moral Sentiments*, published seventeen years before his *The Wealth of Nations*. In a brilliant chapter of the earlier treatise he identifies the way in which admiration for technical accomplishment and potential utility overwhelms reasonableness in human action—the way in which people, in my jargon, confuse capabilities and attainments in the fourth order with reasonable goals and fulfilments in the third.[3] Anticipating the age of mail-order electronic gadgetry, gentlemen of his time could be found with 'their pockets stuffed with little conveniences'.

> How many people ruin themselves by laying out money on trinkets of frivolous utility? What pleases these lovers of toys, is not so much the utility as the aptness of the machines which are fitted to promote it.[4]

And in this sort of confusion and misdirection of sentiment and of purpose, Adam Smith sees something which is 'often the secret motive of the most serious and important pursuits of both private and public life'[5]—seen without the distorting influence of this confusion, power and riches are nothing but 'enormous and operose machines contrived to produce a few trifling conveniences to the body…'[6] But it is good that nature induces in us this sort of confusion. For 'It is this deception which arouses and keeps

[3] On the four orders of reality in which human life is lived, see essay 5 at n. 3; essay I.14 at pp. 217–18.

[4] Smith, *The Theory of Moral Sentiments*, Pt IV, ch. 1, 299.

[5] *Ibid.* This use of 'motive' is not to be confused with reasons which motivate by entering into conscious deliberation and choice.

[6] *Ibid.* at 302.

in continual motion the industry of mankind.'[7] For, from the heap of wealth produced by this industry in the deluded pursuit of riches and power,

> the rich only select... what is most precious and agreeable. They consume little more than the poor; and in spite of their natural selfishness and rapacity, though they mean only their own conveniency, though the sole end which they propose from the labors of all the thousands whom they employ be the gratification of their own vain and insatiable desires, they divide with the poor the produce of all their improvements. They are *led by an invisible hand* to make nearly the same distribution of the necessaries of life which would have been made had the earth been divided into equal portions among all its inhabitants; and thus, *without intending it, without knowing it*, advance the interest of the society... When providence divided the earth among a few lordly masters, it neither forgot nor abandoned those who had been left out of the partition. These, too, enjoy their share of all that it produces. In what constitutes the real happiness of human life, they are in no respect inferior to those who would seem so much above them.[8]

Here the invisible hand accomplishes what might have been the work of the missing distributive justice. In *The Wealth of Nations*, the same or a similar 'hand' accomplishes rather the initial productive work of enhancing (domestic, national) wealth: the individual engaging in or, rather, directing production 'intends only his own gain', but 'he is in this, as in many other cases, led by an invisible hand to promote an end which was no part of his intention'.[9] In this later, more famous passage, Adam Smith has qualified the reference to unawareness of the side effects ('without knowing it' is replaced by: not knowing 'how much he is promoting it'); he now focuses rather on what is essential: the contrast with intention. A side effect, as I use the term, simply is an effect not intended—not chosen either as end or as means—however much it may have been foreseen by the one who intends, chooses, and acts.

But you will have noticed Adam Smith's optimistic partiality in attending to the side effects of production. Not only is he sublimely optimistic about the automaticity of the trickle-down benefits to the poor. He is also entirely inattentive to the question of *harmful* side effects of the processes of production, distribution, and consumption by the 'vain and insatiable' wealthy. Doubtless this inattention is little more than one aspect of Adam Smith's failure to anticipate certain important aspects of the impending industrial revolution. Still, it is notable. If providence, without human attention or intention, is allocating to the poor a share in the wealth produced at the direction of the rich, it is also allocating to them an abundant share in the environmental degradation and risk

[7] *Ibid.* at 303. [8] *Ibid.* at 304–5 (emphasis added).
[9] Smith, *An Inquiry into the Nature and Causes of the Wealth of Nations*, Pt IV, § ii, ch. 10, 476.

of environmental catastrophe engendered by the economic and security policies of the rich(er).

The brilliance of Adam Smith's first account of the invisible hand consists in his transformation of the classical reasons for denying that wealth and power are the point of human existence. Without rejecting the classical critique of confusing mere means with intrinsic ends, Smith deepens it by identifying the attraction of these means as an admiration for excellence—'aptness'—but excellence in an order (I call it the technical) which is not to be confused with the existential order of human choices oriented by intrinsic human goods. But the irony is this: Adam Smith's own account, at least in this work, falls prey to the very fascination with the technical which it denounces. Captivated by his genuine and fruitful mastery of a new technique—let us call it economic(s)—the technique of identifying causal systems created and constituted by the side effects of human choices whose intentions lie quite elsewhere, Smith neglects to subordinate the technique to the ends and principles of reasonable human existence, ends and principles which would have directed him to an impartial survey of the risks and suffering engendered by the same invisible hand of the economic system he misleadingly styles 'providence'.

Of course, the developed analytical art of economics is well able and used to make such an even-handed survey. And that, I repeat, is its true utility as a help-mate for ethics and political theory and thus for jurisprudence. Still, it would be a mistake to conclude that we need only a more adequate account of the benefits and burdens up for distribution or allocation by those responsible for the common good or general fate. We need also to bear in mind what Smith did not forget and what economics does not comprehend, the requirements of commutative justice. To see this, we may look at one of the economic and security policies of the rich which was developed in England in the half-century after Adam Smith's flourishing: the policy of laying hidden traps.

III

These mantraps were, typically, spring-guns: heavily loaded shotguns, with triggers attached to springs and wires arranged in hidden lines along which the blast of shot would travel when anybody tripped them. They were set in woods and gardens to deter, disable, and punish poachers, who under the law of the day were no more than trespassers.

The ground of principle on which such lethal outdoor mantraps were eventually prohibited by law is clearly stated by Holmes giving the majority judgment of the Supreme Court in 1921 in *United Zinc & Chemical Co. v Britt*:

> The liability for spring guns and mantraps arises from the fact that the defendant has not rested in [the] assumption [that trespassers would obey the law and not trespass], but on the contrary has expected the trespasser and *prepared an injury* which is no more justified than if he had held the gun and fired it.[10]

In other words, shooting a trespasser, who is engaged in no act of violence against oneself or another, is simply killing *with intent to kill*, that is, murder, or at least with *intent* to do serious bodily harm; and setting a spring-gun is just arranging to do the same 'without personally firing the shot'.[11] What one lawfully cannot, with intent, accomplish 'directly' (in person) one cannot, with the same intent, accomplish 'indirectly' (mechanically).

It is embarrassing to have to say that when this argument was squarely put before a strong Court of King's Bench in 1820 it was unanimously rejected.[12] The arguments employed by the English judges to distinguish shooting by machine from shooting in person are weak and of little interest. Of greater interest is the preliminary argument employed in the first two of the four judgments, an argument to which Holmes is responding when he says that the defendant landowner has not been content to assume that trespassers will not trespass but has expected the trespasser and 'prepared for him an injury'. The argument is one you sometimes hear today when Christians try to defend the public policy of nuclear deterrence against the well-grounded charge that it involves, willy-nilly, an intent to kill non-combatants.[13]

Abbott CJ puts it thus:

> I believe that many persons who cause engines of this description to be placed on their grounds do not do so with the intention of injuring any one, but really believe that the notices they give of such engines being there, will prevent any injury from occurring, and that no person who sees the notice will be weak and foolish enough to expose himself to the perilous consequence likely to ensue from his trespass.[14]

Unless he is supposing a high degree of ignorance or self-deception about the frequent[15] 'accidents' involving spring-guns (such as the accident to the nut-gatherer in *Ilott v Wilkes*), Abbott CJ is clearly confusing hope with

[10] 258 US 268 (1922) at 275 (emphasis added). [11] *Addie v Dumbreck* [1929] AC 358, 376.

[12] *Ilott v Wilkes* (1820) 3 B & Ald 304, 311, 106 Eng Rep 674. See the opening sentences of the argument of counsel for the plaintiff-respondent. *Id.* at 307, 106 Eng Rep at 676.

[13] See *NDMR* 124 regarding an argument of Gerard Hughes SJ.

[14] *Ilott v Wilkes* at 309, 106 Eng Rep at 676.

[15] See Parl. Deb., HC, cols 19, 26 (23 March 1827) (the Home Secretary, Robert Peel, here speaks of the 'daily accidents and misfortunes arising from the use of them').

intention. Bayley J's confusions are between ends and means ('motive' and 'intention', in a common legal jargon; 'further' and 'proximate' intention), and between intention and emotions such as enthusiasm or vindictiveness, or *ex ante* reluctance and *ex post* regret:

Such instruments may be undoubtedly placed without any intention of doing injury, and for the mere purpose of protecting property by means of terror; and it is extremely probable that the defendant in this case will feel as much regret as any man for the injury which the plaintiff has sustained....[16]

These confusions about that central legal and jurisprudential concept, intention, were mercilessly exposed in two great articles in the *Edinburgh Review* in 1821 by the famous publicist Sydney Smith. About Abbott's argument, for example, Smith said:

But if this be the real belief of the engineer—if he think that mere notice will keep people away—then he must think it a mere inutility that guns should be placed at all: if he think that many will be deterred, and few come, then he must mean to shoot those few.[17]

And then Smith pressed home the argument which had failed in the hands of counsel in *Ilott* but was to prevail in Parliament in 1827 and in the eventual American position summarized by Holmes in 1921 and by the Supreme Court of Ohio in 1938.[18]

Why were the King's Bench judges of 1820 so anxious to find that setting spring-guns need involve no intention to hurt or kill? They wanted to get into a position to dispose of the issue (precisely: liability to one injured by a spring-gun with notice of the hidden presence of spring-guns) on the twin bases of assumption of risk (*volenti non fit injuria*) and the general utility of protecting property, encouraging residence by landowners, suppressing crime, and so forth. So, likewise, even Lord Ellenborough (the rising young politician son of the late Lord Chief Justice Ellenborough), making the very last and most brutally frank, or frankly brutal, of the parliamentary speeches in defence of spring-guns, felt the need to veil the immediate intention by confusing it with motive (further intention):

The object of setting Spring-guns [is] not personal injury to any one, but to deter from the commission of theft; and that object [is] as completely obtained by hitting

[16] *Ilott v Wilkes* at 310, 106 Eng Rep at 677.

[17] S. Smith, 'Spring Guns' (1821) in *Works* I, 325; see Evatt, 'The Judges and the Teachers of Public Law' at 1151–2.

[18] *State v Childers* 133 Ohio St 508, 514–15, 14 NE2d 767, 770 (1938).

[B]y the overwhelming weight of authority, a person is not justified in taking human life or inflicting bodily harm upon the person of another by means of traps... unless, as a matter of law, he would have been justified had he been personally present and had taken the life or inflicted the bodily harm with his own hands.

an innocent man as a guilty one. [T]he bill [is] contrary to that principle of the English law, which [gives] a man protection for his property, in proportion to the difficulty with which it would be protected by the ordinary means....[19]

The veil is here truly diaphanous—see-through—for the argument tacitly concedes that the deterrent object will be attained only by an at least occasional injury or death to a trespasser, innocent or culpable; such injury or death is thus intended as a means to achieving the deterrent object. In the fundamental structure of the common law, as of sound jurisprudence, one private person's killing or injuring another with intent to kill or injure is simply a commutative injustice, whatever the killer's further purposes, objects, or motives. It is the sort of conduct, of transaction between persons, which is simply excluded from justification whether by assumption of risk, fear of future greater harm, or any considerations of distributive or allocative justice as between landowners, game consumers, poachers, and nut-gatherers like the unlucky Ilott.

But what about self-defence? Well, when defending oneself or another against immediate personal violence, one's real intent need not be to do harm to the assailant for the sake of some further object such as deterrence, or disablement from some future revenge attack, or satisfying one's desire to get one's own back. One's intent can and should be simply to *stop this attack* by whatever means of stopping it are at hand. Thus, all the harm to the assailant can be a side effect, unintended. But are not the side effects of one's actions within one's responsibility? Certainly. And are they not subject to moral assessment and possible condemnation? Certainly; the very point of this essay is to reflect on some possible jurisprudential implications of our moral responsibility for our actions' side effects. So, if it can be fair and in all other ways reasonable to take measures to stop an assailant, knowing that those measures may or will be death-dealing, might it not also be fair and reasonable to take death-dealing measures against mere trespassers and poachers, intending not their death or injury as such, but simply to stop them in their current unlawful entry? No. To do so, or think so, would be to confuse the intrinsic personal good of human life with the merely instrumental good of property. And it would be to depart from the Golden (and rational) Rule of impartiality; for though a gentleman who found himself being homicidally attacked by one of his own family or house guests might defend himself with even a shotgun if nothing else lay to hand, no gentleman, nobody, would use a shotgun and blow away one of his own family or house guests whom he spotted making off with one of his pheasants. That one should do nothing to others, and

[19] Parl. Deb., HL, col. 296 (9 April 1827) (substituting direct for indirect speech).

impose on them no harmful side effects, which one would not be willing to do to or impose upon oneself and one's nearest and dearest is the most significant of those norms of reasonableness, and thus of morality, which govern the creation of risk and suffering as the unintended effects of one's choices and actions.

But, as young Lord Ellenborough's frankness made plain, the purpose of laying spring-guns was, often enough, precisely to *do harm*, as a deterrent *means* of stopping poaching, not merely to impose the risk of harm as a side effect of stopping poaching. Take the facts in *Bird v Holbrook*,[20] in which, a year after Parliament had outlawed outdoor spring-guns, the Court of Common Pleas—its chief justice doubtless ruefully mindful of the public denunciation which, as junior justice in the Court of King's Bench in *Ilott v Wilkes*, he himself had received in 1821 at the hands of Sydney Smith—ingloriously announced that what Parliament had just enacted had all along been the common law in relation to spring-guns laid *without notice*. In this case, concerned with events before the Act of 1827, the defendant tulip gardener's reason for not posting notices was that he wanted to catch the tulip thieves, *by injuring them*. (Instead, of course, he mutilated only young Bird, who was trying, in broad daylight, to help a neighbour by recapturing a peahen which had strayed into Holbrook's booby trapped garden.)

IV

Richard Posner made *Bird v Holbrook* the centrepiece of his earliest published exposition of the implications of economic analysis for the common law.[21] Indeed, this is the one case which Posner cites in his textbook treatment of the category of intentional torts.[22] Disclaiming (at that point) any normative purpose, and offering only to 'explain' the law's 'pattern', Posner says that the issue in the case 'involved two legitimate activities, raising tulips and keeping peahens'.[23] Spring-guns may be the most cost-effective means of protecting tulips in an era of negligible police protection; but they discourage the owners of domestic animals from pursuing them onto other people's property and so increase the costs (enclosure costs or straying costs) of keeping animals.[24] The challenge was 'to design a rule of liability

[20] (1828) 4 Bing 628, 130 ER 911.
[21] Posner, 'Killing or Wounding to Protect a Property Interest' at 209.
[22] Posner, *Economic Analysis of Law*, 119–22.
[23] Posner, 'Killing or Wounding to Protect a Property Interest' at 209.
[24] *Ibid.* at 209–11.

that maximized the (joint) value of both activities, net of any protective or other costs (including personal injuries)'.[25]

With a stroke, the whole question of intention to injure is swept from view; not only are the 'personal injuries' homogenized into the other costs of keeping peacocks, but the fact that *these* injuries were done by one who *intended* to injure a human being (albeit not anticipated to be a mere peacock-pursuer) is treated as wholly irrelevant. The argument which had prevailed in Parliament is treated as of no consequence. And explicitly so: 'intentionality is neither here nor there', says Posner.[26] Why not? The answer is a paradigm of the *non sequitur*.

> It is surely not correct to say that society never permits the sacrifice of human lives on behalf of substantial economic values. Automobile driving is an example of the many deadly activities that cannot be justified as saving more lives than they take. Nor can the motoring example be distinguished from the spring-gun case on the ground that the one who sets a spring-gun intends to kill or wound. In both cases, a risk of death is created that could be avoided by substituting other methods of achieving one's ends (walking instead of driving); in both cases the actor normally hopes the risk will not materialize.[27]

In short, for Posner, intending death and carelessly risking causing death are equivalent because both involve creating the risk of death; A is equivalent to B if A includes what is important about B. There is no need to dwell on this fallacy. It is more profitable to notice some of the other equivocations in this passage.

First, the equivocation on 'sacrifice'. Posner's use of the phrase 'sacrifice of human lives' treats as equivalent the decision to build a skyscraper, expecting that about three construction workers will fall off and be killed, and the decision to kill three construction workers to encourage the others to meet their performance targets.

Secondly, the equivocation on 'hopes'. Posner's claim that both in carelessly and in intentionally killing, 'the actor normally hopes the risk will not materialize' involves a double confusion: (a) the careless driver hopes there will be no collision *and* that if there is, no one will be killed; the man-trapper hopes that no one will invade his property but that anyone who does *will* be shot; (b) many murders, perhaps most, are done with great emotional reluctance and repugnance (if only for fear of detection and punishment). Like Bayley J in *Ilott v Wilkes*, Posner has confused emotion with will and willingness—that is, with intention.

[25] *Ibid.* at 210. [26] *Ibid.* at 206. [27] *Ibid.*

Posner's writings on intention are, indeed, a feast of fallacies. To prove that the distinction between intentional and unintentional torts is 'confusing and unnecessary', his textbook, for example, begins:

> Most accidental injuries are intentional in the sense that the injurer knew that he could have reduced the probability of the accident by taking additional precautions. The element of intention is unmistakable when the tortfeasor is an enterprise that can predict from past experience that it will inflict a certain number of accidental injuries every year.[28]

This argument is even less acceptable than the earlier proof that 'intentionality is neither here nor there'. For now we have, not the claim that intention is irrelevant to economic and legal analysis, but a claim that intention is actually the same as foresight, and that the intentional is just a version of the accidental. This is tantamount to saying that those who fly the Atlantic, foreseeing jetlag, intend to get jetlag, that those who walk intend to wear out their shoes—what one may call the 'pseudo-masochistic' theory of intention.

It is tempting to dwell on the corrupting potential of this conception of intention. Since, for example, one can foresee that lecturing and writing on difficult topics is certain to confuse some of one's audience, one may as well (I don't suggest that Posner himself does) throw in a few deliberate falsehoods when convenient for attaining one's goals—providing one sets out with the *hope* that one will not 'have to' resort to those measures, and resorts to them with feelings of reluctance and regret.

But for present purposes it is enough to insist, against Posner, that those who intend a result, whether for its own sake or as a means to something else, are not merely creating a risk of that result. Rather, in their own self-understanding, they are trying (however reluctantly) to bring it about; they are not trying to create a risk of a result but trying to create that result. They are not content to leave things to chance, that is, to hazard or to risk, but are intervening to achieve what they intend. The only risk they will acknowledge is—not the risk of that result happening—but: the risk of that result *not* happening. That risk is just an inevitable side effect of their intention, choice, and action, since none of us have the divine capacity of making things be the case simply by willing them to be the case.

V

Someone will object: Posner and the whole school of Economic Analysis of Law who follow him in this[29] are not concerned with the point of view,

[28] *Economic Analysis* at 119.

[29] See e.g. the discussion of spring-guns in Calabresi and Melamed, 'Property Rules, Liability Rules, and Inalienability' at 1126 n. 71.

the self-understanding, of agents, but with states of affairs in the world, particularly states of affairs to which monetizable value can be attributed. And, whatever one's school, one may say that it is far from clear why an essay on allocating risks should be dwelling for so long on intention—particularly an essay which insists that the intending in torts and crimes of intention is a case neither of *allocating* (distributing a common stock) nor, properly speaking, of creating a *risk* of harm. Let me address both these objections together.

People say they are interested in states of affairs, not in the content of the state of mind of the one who, whether deliberately or accidentally, brings those states of affairs about. Very well. But they overlook the fact that *choices last.* To intend something is to choose it, either for its own sake or as a means; and to choose is to adopt a proposal (a proposal generated by and in one's own deliberation). Once adopted, the proposal, together with the reasoning which in one's deliberation made that proposal intelligently attractive, *remains*, persists, in one's will, one's disposition to act. The proposal is, so to speak, synthesized into one's will, one's practical orientation and stance in the world. This is a real, empirical (though 'spiritual') effect—side effect—of one's adopting a proposal.

Now, whatever consequences lie outside one's proposal, whatever results of one's choice are not included in the proposal because neither wanted for their own sake nor needed as a means, are not synthesized into one's will. Though one may foresee these results, and accept that one will be causing them, or the risk of them, one is not adopting them. They are side effects, incidental risks. One may be culpable in accepting them. But the ground of culpability will not be that one intended them, but that one wrongly, for example unfairly, accepted them as incidents of what one did intend. And just as one is never trying to achieve them—not even reluctantly trying—so one's character is not changed or shaped by one's acceptance of them, in the manner it is shaped by forming and pursuing an intention.

Next we must notice that when one intends some harm to (an)other human person or persons—when one's proposal includes, however reluctantly, some destruction of or damage to some basic aspect of their personhood, for example their bodily integrity, or their participation in knowledge of reality—whether one intends that harm for its own sake, as in revenge, or as a means, as in killing or maiming *pour encourager les autres* or in deception for the sake of fraud or in perjury for the sake of justice, one is shaping oneself as one who, in the most radical way, exploits others. The reality and the fulfilment of those others is radically subjected to one's own reality and fulfilment, or to the reality and fulfilment of some other group of persons. In *intending* harm, one precisely makes their loss one's gain, or the gain of some others; one to that extent uses them up, treats them as material, as a resource for a good that no longer includes their own.

In Economic Analysis of Law, this exploitativeness is especially drastic and especially unreasonable. For, as Lewis Kornhauser points out, the Economic Analysis of Law 'applies neoclassical microeconomic theory to the analysis of...legal systems' (rather than applying the classical theory of, for example, Adam Smith), and 'neoclassical microeconomics assumes that individuals always act in their own, fixed, immutable self-interest' and precisely by doing so are 'completely rational'.[30] Kornhauser will not, I think, object if I say that this use of the term 'rationality'—however widespread it may be in economics, game theory, public choice theory, and the like—is profoundly misleading.[31] And the theories of human behaviour which employ it, if taken as *sufficient* guides to real choices and actions, are exemplary instances of the folly denounced (as we saw) by Adam Smith, the folly of thinking that an ingenious gadget which might at some time be useful for something is therefore a good thing to have, to work for, to be concerned with.

For, in reality, the very first insight of human practical understanding is that human goods and harms, as intelligible objects of intelligent wanting or avoidance, *have no proper names attached to them.* Intelligent human motivation is not egoistic. It responds to the value of human flourishing, in its diverse aspects and diverse personal subjects, whoever they may be. One can *choose* to be an egoist. But then one is following, not reason, but *feelings* of self-preference. (The way one then pursues one's self-interest may be cunning or in some other way intelligent, but this will not make one's egoistic self-preference an intelligent motivation.) And one is also overlooking or mislocating and mutilating the intelligible human good of community, of harmony between persons in a mutual sharing in fulfilment—a harmony which is a basic human good, intelligibly valuable for its own sake.

In short, what neoclassical economics calls 'rational' is rational only within the project (and resulting technique) of being a successful egoist. But the project of being an egoist is a paradigmatic form of irrationality, or practical unreasonableness.[32]

In its execution, of course, Economic Analysis of Law always looks to some community wider than the ego. (It would have no audience if it did not.) But its identification of the community whose self-interest is to be advanced, whose wealth is to be maximized, is always as little the work of

[30] Kornhauser, 'Economic Analysis of Law' at 234.
[31] See essay 2 at 54–61. [32] See 1987f at 101, 114–15.

a maximizing reason as is Posner's arbitrary declaration that the issue in *Bird v Holbrook* was not whether one subject of the law can intentionally kill or maim another subject of the law, but whether laying spring-guns increases the costs of peacock-rearing more than it diminishes the costs of tulip-growing. If one really cares for one's own interests, or if one's community and its government and law attend only to the interests of its current members, one will, of course, attend not at all to the interests of future generations. (And thus the very intelligibility of 'a community' will be lost, somewhat as the intelligibility of motion is lost (as Zeno observed) if one tries to reduce it to a sequence of points; for people are being born into and dying out of the community at every moment: Which momentary community, then, is to count in assessing efficiency, whether productive or allocative?)

The inability of Economic Analysis of Law to handle, with its own conceptual resources, the problem of future generations—generations which, or rather who, start right now—is obvious enough.[33] Similarly, economistically minded governments, such as the United Kingdom's, recommend a discount rate to be used in cost-benefit analyses of social projects; the rate reflects the time preferences of British adults today, for jam today as opposed to a little more jam tomorrow.[34] But the whole approach overlooks the fact that 'the people today are not the same as the people tomorrow. Discounting wealth accrued tomorrow therefore disadvantages later generations.'[35] And the UK government's discount rate renders negligible the costs of latent deaths from current risk-producing activities if those deaths are delayed for as little as thirty years.[36] Our judgment that this is unreasonable cannot be supported, or undermined, by any *economic* principle.

What might support such a judgment? I return to the apparently different topic of intention and intentional harm. The principle that one must never choose (intend) harm to the person of any human individual both expresses and preserves the judgment that each human individual is more than just a locus of utility or wealth (to be measured at some arbitrarily *chosen* future moment), or a channel or conduit for maximizing that wealth or utility (again, a maximum as measured at some chosen future moment). It expresses and preserves each individual person's *density*, so to speak, or *dignity*, if you will, as an equal of *everyone* else in basic rights. To

[33] It is patiently and helpfully explored in Kornhauser, 'A Guide to the Perplexed Claims of Efficiency in Law' at 614–16.

[34] Health and Safety Executive, *The Tolerability of Risk from Nuclear Power Stations*, 34.

[35] Kornhauser, 'A Guide to the Perplexed Claims of Efficiency in Law' at 615.

[36] Health and Safety Executive, loc. cit.

choose harm is the paradigmatic wrong, the exemplary instance of denial of right.

When the techniques of neoclassical economics are allied to the doctrines of legal positivism, one gets Economic Analysis of Law as it is practiced by Posner, Calabresi, and others. The function of law is then conceived as: to allocate entitlements with a view to future maximizing of wealth. The fact that one person has in the past—just a moment ago—been intentionally harmed and thus wronged by another is 'neither here nor there', except insofar as a law may have been *made* to bestow on the injured party, or on someone else, a remedy in the interests of maximizing social wealth by deterring and thus minimizing waste in transactions and dealings between persons.

In another jurisprudential perspective, however, a primordial and always primary (though not the only primary) function of government and law is to rectify this commutative injustice by ensuring that the injurer does the injured the commutative justice of reparation. (There was reason for the Roman jurists to treat Delict under the heading of Obligations.) No doubt there is a distributive, allocative aspect to this activity of government and legal system. From a common stock of possible activities to be undertaken, costs incurred, and individual responsibilities to be drawn upon and distributed, the government and the law assign some part to this task of underwriting and guaranteeing commutative justice. Doing so is an act of distributive justice, but is ancillary to the prior, identifiable relationship of commutative injustice and potential commutative, reparative justice between the individuals. In this perspective, again, the dignity of the individuals, each ends in themselves (and in each basic aspect of their reality and potentiality as persons), is again expressed and preserved. A judge who tried to decide *Bird v Holbrook* by the method commended by Posner—comparing costs of tulip-growing with costs of peacock-rearing—would be gravely violating his duty.

And government and law, in that act of reparative justice, can be seen to have a role quite distinct from achieving any future 'end-state' state of affairs. The political community, unlike a one-project firm which must account to its shareholders at the end of the project, has no *goal.* Its success in fulfilling its responsibilities cannot be measured by any technique comparable to accounting. Success and failure are measured by quite other norms. Is everyone protected from intentional harm and every (other) form of exploitation by anyone else? Is the whole stock of natural resources made available to all—not by a naïve communistic distribution and continual redistribution to ensure steady equal shares for all current members of the community, but by a system of appropriation and husbandry which will preserve the interests of future members of the community by encouraging fair distribution between 'life tenant', heirs, employees, and other present dependants, and future remaindermen and reversioners, in a sustainable economy in a sustainable world?

VI

This is not the place to continue sketching the requirements of justice in political community. But I should say a little more about how intention and intentional wrong are related to the vast problem of harmful side effects (including latent and long-term side effects in environmental degradation of every kind).

Moral responsibility and consequent legal liability for intentional infliction of harm are paradigmatic, exemplary. Avoiding such wrongs is only a necessary, not a sufficient, condition of acting justly. But the same respect for each individual whom one might have harmed as a means to an end carries over into, and informs, the quite different principle of fairness. Here one encounters the quite different type of commutative injustice involved in imposing harmful side effects without complying with rational principles such as the Golden Rule, and without attending to truths such as that no one has an a priori superior claim on the earth's resources and no one, therefore, has unqualified dominion over any part of them.

The Golden Rule in its application involves a discernment of feelings and then a dispassionate rational adherence to the standard of care established by one's feelings. To what I have said in my other essay,[37] let me add that, without denying the peculiar and strategic importance of intention, legal thought can and does reasonably find criteria of fairness and unfairness in *analogies to the intentional.*

So the prohibition on spring-guns (or at least on unnotified spring-guns) laid with intent to wound extends to identify as unjust the omissions of those who inherit already-laid spring-guns and retain them without such intent to wound; or who allow similarly lethal and concealed conditions to persist on their land when they know that what disguises the lethality also exercises a fatal attraction or allurement to innocent strangers, including trespassers. But the range of the analogy must be controlled not by verbal or 'conceptual' considerations—puns on 'trap', 'entrapment', etc.—but by considerations of fairness: how one wishes others to behave towards oneself and one's friends; how one would behave when one's friends or children strayed from the straight and narrow. If one would not, even for a

[37] See 1990c at 11–12 [and essay I.14 at 227–8].

substantial reward, bury bombs accessibly under the surface of one's land with warning notices likely to disappear (without replacement) in one's children's lifetime, then one should not, I suggest, regard it as right to accumulate and bury lethal wastes the lethality of which will far outlast any likely duration of one's warning notices.

This conception of the fairness which informs commutative justice is not, to use Adam Smith's title, a theory of *moral* sentiments. But it is a theory of the proper role of sentiments in giving content and application to a moral principle which itself is simply rational. The normal form in which these sentiments make their presence felt in jurisprudence and legal reasoning, of course, is in the form of conventions,[38] customs, the far from bloodless life of the reasonable person—a life fit for use as a jurisprudential and judicial reference point only if purified, however, of those self-deceptions, dishonesties, evasions, and pragmatic Machiavellianisms which give us the idiomatic pejorative sense of 'practical': 'let's be practical about this'—a thinly veiled invitation to unfairness or some other form of injustice.[39]

[38] See Kelley, 'Who Decides? Community Safety Conventions at the Heart of Tort Liability'.
[39] See Tushnet, 'A Critical Legal Studies Perspective', sec. II.

17

PRACTICAL REASONING IN LAW: SOME CLARIFICATIONS*

I. METHOD IN NATURAL LAW THEORY

Jeremy Shearmur's problems with my work arise from a misunderstanding of the *practical* character of natural law theory (as I conceive it). He both overstates and understates it.

As his title 'Natural Law Without Metaphysics' suggests, Shearmur thinks that a theory which, like mine, aspires to be 'purely practical' cannot respond to a *theoretical*, metaphysical challenge such as might be based on a Dawkins-like theory of the teleology of genes. He thinks that an 'internalist' theory like mine aspires, as Dworkin's apparently does, to be purely internal, unwilling and unable to engage in metaphysical and scientific argument. He supposes that I agree with Dworkin that 'external' sceptics need no answer.

In fact, however, my *Natural Law and Natural Rights* and *Fundamentals of Ethics* presuppose (though in varying senses of 'presuppose') a number of strongly metaphysical positions, and indeed explicitly propose and in certain cases carefully argue for them: for example, the four types of order, the reality and lastingness of free choice, the distinctness of the human species, the nature of human bodily life as distinct from the other basic aspects of human flourishing,[1] the existence of an uncaused creator, the principles of sound empirical judgment, and so forth.

I don't share Dworkin's unwillingness to challenge external scepticism about morality and practical reason and truth. Classic modern forms of such scepticism are vigorously argued against in both the above-mentioned books.[2] If someone were to seriously propose (as Shearmur eventually

* 1990d. The papers of the other symposiasts, in the discussion of essay 16 (1990b) and 1990c, were published along with these three papers of mine in Cleveland State Law Review 38. A revised version of 1990c is essay I.14 (1992a); and see n. 11 below.

[1] Carefully explicated in *NDMR* 304–9.

[2] See *NLNR* 73–5; *FoE* 26–53. Shearmur complains that I have offered no argument that all knowledge is a value, and questions whether the world is a better place for someone's knowing how many letters there are in a dictionary. He does not say whether or not he thinks my argument that

shrinks from doing) that we are but instruments of our genes, and that the only true good is the survival of genes, I should gladly extend my already published arguments to take account of this new folly, for I agree with Shearmur that such a theory puts mine in question. I would argue what I now merely summarize: such a Dawkins-like proposal (a) is grossly guilty of the naturalistic fallacy, (b) is quite implausible in restricting objective teleology to only one level, (c) is radically unscientific in its generalization from data about genes without attending to the data about greater wholes such as human persons and their societies, (d) has no plausibility in its articulation of a basic ethical principle, (e) is self-refuting in proposing that naturalistic explanations have the non-naturalistic property of overriding and excluding the affirmation of 'non-naturalistic properties', and (f) is self-refuting in its claim that the genes, in order to maximize their own survival, have set up human life, including human intelligence which (in Richard Dawkins and co.) discovers that purpose and so (as Shearmur admits) frustrates it.[3]

I have been discussing Shearmur's overstatement of my theory's exclusively internal or practical character. I now turn to his understatement of that character. He fails to see that, in the parts of the theory which are strictly practical (a reflective, meditative restatement of practical understanding and reasoning), I am not seeking to *describe* the 'phenomenology of moral action'. I am not offering a 'picture of our moral experience'; still less am I trying to read off my theory from such a picture, or from the experience itself. I agree with Shearmur that appeals to the phenomena of our moral experience are quite insufficient to show the objectivity of moral principles. It is a characteristic confusion and inadequacy of 'phenomenological' modes of philosophizing that they do not, frankly, attend to the *objects* of our experience and our motivation so as to display and clarify their worth as objects, but instead focus upon the fact that those objects are present to our experience and motivation—a fact from which nothing follows. My theorizing is in another mode. Since Shearmur overlooks its strategy, he sees it as an argument-free attempt to read off ideas from the fabric of the universe, a performance dogmatic in content as well as tone.

scepticism about the good of knowledge is self-refuting is valid. I say that knowledge is valuable 'in itself' just in the sense that it is an aspect of human flourishing; without it one cannot be flourishing. The subjects (objects) of knowledge have, I observe, internal hierarchies of worth. Normally, one can be flourishing without knowledge of propositions such as 'There are x letters in the dictionary.' But sometimes even such normally trivial knowledge is an essential component of the important, worthwhile knowledge (knowledge about the origins, nature, and destiny of our world, our societies, ourselves). In a society which superstitiously believes that the number of letters in the *Oxford English Dictionary* is a key to predicting the future because it mystically corresponds to the outer dimensions of the Great Pyramid in millimetres, it is good to know the sober truth about that number: it doesn't.

[3] This last instance of self-refutation is comparable to the instance sponsored by David Barnhizer in his quotation from Ernest Becker, in which we are *publicly* urged to preserve at all times the *fiction* that we have freedom and/or valid aspirations.

I cannot restate my strategy here. I may give a flavour of it by quoting one key passage from *Natural Law and Natural Rights*; it begins the section entitled 'The Basic Forms of Human Good: A Practical Reflection':

> It is now time to revert, from the descriptive or 'speculative' findings of anthropology and psychology, to the critical and essentially practical discipline in which each reader must ask himself: What *are* the basic aspects of my well-being? Here each one of us, however extensive his knowledge of the interests of other people and other cultures, is alone with his own intelligent grasp of the indemonstrable (because self-evident) first principles of his own practical reasoning. From one's capacity to grasp intelligently the basic forms of good as 'to-be-pursued' one gets one's ability, in the descriptive disciplines of history and anthropology, to sympathetically (though not uncritically) see the point of actions, life-styles, characters, and cultures that one would not choose for oneself. And one's speculative knowledge of other people's interests and achievements does not leave unaffected one's practical understanding of the forms of good that lie open to one's choice. But there is no inference from fact to value. At this point in our discourse (or private meditation), inference and proof are left behind (or left until later), and the proper form of discourse is: '...is a good, in itself, don't you think?'.[4]

Of course, any effort to propose and defend a non-sceptical, non-relativist view of the basic principles and concepts of ethics and politics (and thus of law) will meet with the classic sceptical epithet, 'dogmatic'.[5]

Shearmur complains that I 'lay down' a number of principles of sound empirical judgment (norms of theoretical rationality) without discussing possible objections to them or alternative views of their status. True, I identify a number of such principles, for two purposes ancillary to the main argument about *practical* principles: to help explicate the concept of self-evidence,[6] and to exemplify the sort of rational (not logical) necessity

[4] *NLNR* 85–6.

[5] Thus Sextus Empiricus begins the classical manual of scepticism:

> The natural result of any investigation is that the investigators either discover the object of search or deny that it is discoverable and confess it to be inapprehensible, or persist in their search. So, too, with regard to the objects investigated by philosophy, this is probably why some have claimed to have discovered the truth, others have asserted that it cannot be apprehended, while others again go on inquiring. Those who believe they have discovered it are the 'Dogmatists,' specially so called—Aristotle, for example, and Epicurus and the Stoics... (*Outlines of Pyrrhonism* 1.1 (c. 200 AD).)

This is a nice example of persuasive or rhetorical definition. The dogmatism of many sceptical arguments is obvious enough; it shows through, too, in Shearmur's incidental remark: 'it [the question about an uncaused cause] hardly seems a question to which someone must think there has to be an answer at all (for example, if they hold a theory that explanation is inescapably relative...)....' The question is whether a theory that *all* explanations must be relative can possibly be shown to be something 'one must think'; without such a proof, this way of brushing off the series of *arguments* involved in the 'cosmological argument' to an uncaused cause must seem at once dogmatic and evasive. If Shearmur points to the inescapable limitations of a symposium article, I accept the plea, and only ask the same sort of indulgence for my already over-lengthy *NLNR*.

[6] *NLNR* 68.

involved in arguing to the existence of an uncaused cause.[7] I introduce them with the warning that the self-evidence of any such principle or norm of rationality is consistent with the fact that a formulation of it may be in some respect inaccurate or not 'acceptably refined and sufficiently qualified'.[8] But the more pertinent warning, which I think Shearmur's criticisms about dogmatism rather overlook, is my general warning on the first page of *Natural Law and Natural Rights*:

> The book is no more than introductory. Countless relevant matters are merely touched upon or are passed over altogether. Innumerable objections receive no more than the silent tribute of an effort to draft statements that would prove defensible if a defense against objections were explicitly undertaken.[9]

If it is 'false' that 'an account or explanation of phenomena is not to be accepted if it requires or postulates something inconsistent with the data for which it is supposed to account', it is true that an account or explanation of phenomena is not to be accepted if it *both* requires or postulates something inconsistent with the data for which it is supposed to account *and* gives no reason to judge that the inconsistent phenomena are apparent rather than real. But in making this addition in order to meet Shearmur's objection, I make no change in my account of the norms of rationality. For I am doing no more than import into my statement of *this* principle the further principle which I had already stated—indeed, in the preceding sentence of my book. For I listed seven (out of 'many') principles, and the sense of each is not independent of the sense of the others.

II. 'RATIONAL CHOICE' AND INCOMMENSURABILITY

A sound natural law theory grounds morality in what is good for human persons. The question immediately arises, therefore, whether reasonable and right choice is a matter of choosing the available option which offers *more good* (or less bad) than other available options. The simple—indeed simple-minded—thought that moral choice should be guided by the search for the greater good and/or lesser evil informs utilitarianism, Economic Analysis of Law, and other forms of aggregative, consequentialist, or in general (as I shall here call it) *proportionalist* moral reasoning. A sound natural law theory accepts that there are many appropriate comparisons between goods, and accordingly many appropriate uses for the terms 'better' and 'best' in the context of human choices.[10] But it goes on to

[7] *Ibid.*, 385. [8] *Ibid.*, 68. [9] *Ibid.*, v. [10] See *NDMR* 261–7.

point out that none of the comparisons which reason can make amount to the form of comparison—the form of commensuration—proposed by supporters of proportionalist moral theories. When morally significant *options* are in question, it turns out that an option better in one (or more) respect(s) is worse in another (or other) respect(s).

In making this critique of proportionalist moral theory, we do not trade on any general scepticism about commensuration. Luban thinks 'it makes no sense to say that Kant is twenty-six times as famous as Mahan'.[11] I am not so sure that this makes no sense. I am willing to entertain a high degree of (mathematically structured) commensurability—quantitative ordering—amongst very many types of objects. I only observe that, whatever proportionalist moral theorists mean by 'greater' and 'lesser' when they offer to guide morally significant, rationally motivated choice by identifying the option promising greater good or lesser evil, *that* form of commensuration cannot be made by reason. Our argument does not proceed from any a priori theory of commensurability, but from a dialectical consideration of the nature of human options and the conditions of human freedom of choice.

In early statements of the natural law theory developed by Germain Grisez, Joseph Boyle, myself, and others, the source of the incommensurability of options for morally significant choice was located in the diversity of categories of basic human good (life, knowledge, etc.).[12] This might be called 'inter-categorial incommensurability'. But while it is an important source of the incommensurability in issue, it is by no means necessary for such incommensurability, or its only source.[13] There is incommensurability also between choosable instantiations of one and the same basic good. For instance, what makes vacationing at the beach appealing and what makes vacationing in the mountains appealing—such alternatives are incommensurable in the sense that each possibility has some intelligible appeal not found in what makes the other appealing.

So David Luban's statement that 'Finnis believes that interdimensional comparisons are impossible because the basic goods are incommensurable'[14] needs important qualification.

[11] Luban, 'Incommensurable Values, Rational Choice, and Moral Absolutes' at 66. [Luban's critique, discussed throughout this section, is of 1990c, and significantly shaped the revisions that resulted in my essay with the same title ('Natural Law and Legal Reasoning'), essay I.14 (1992a); see esp. sec. II and the last para. of sec. III of that essay.]

[12] See e.g. *NLNR* 115.

[13] This is already indicated in *FoE* 89 and more explicitly in 1987f at 110.

[14] Luban, 'Incommensurable Values, Rational Choice, and Moral Absolutes' at 69.

A more basic misunderstanding underlies Luban's main critique. He asks: 'What is the connection between commensurability and rational choice that Finnis is exploring?' And he answers:

> Finnis appears to be arguing... that if rational choice among goods is possible, they must be commensurable. For though he does not state this latter point in so many words, he does offer the logically equivalent claim that incommensurability of goods implies that rational choice among them is impossible. Indeed, this claim is the central point of his argument....[15]

Well, if the words are being used in the sense in which I use them, Luban has got things upside down. My claim is not that commensurability makes rational choice possible. It is that commensurability makes rational *choice* impossible.[16] My claim is not that incommensurability implies the impossibility of rational choice. It is that incommensurability implies the *possibility* of rational *choice*. These are indeed the central claims of my essay.

Behind this apparently catastrophic misunderstanding lies a less dramatic, verbal explanation. The term 'rational choice' has three important, distinct senses:

(1) choice which is fully reasonable, complies with all the requirements of practical reasonableness, and is thus morally upright;

(2) choice which is rationally motivated in the sense that its object has been shaped by practical intelligence and has rational appeal, even if it is in some respect(s) motivated by feeling rather than reason, feelings which have to some extent fettered and instrumentalized reason, and is therefore unreasonable and immoral, though rational;

(3) decision and action motivated by a dominant reason, that is, a reason which can be commensurated with the reasons for alternative options and which includes all that these offer and some more.

Sense (3) is the sense in which Luban uses the phrase 'rational choice'. I use it in sense (2) (or senses (1) and (2)) but never in sense (3), except in one incautiously phrased sentence where I am explicitly reporting the views, and implicitly the self-description, of the 'game' and 'decision' theorists (who are interested only in sense (3)). For the whole point of my argument about the relation between incommensurability of options and rationally motivated, morally significant free choice is that if one option dominates the others (that is, offers *unqualifiedly* greater good or lesser evil), the others cease to

[15] *Ibid.* at 67–8.

[16] Subject only to a qualification about resisting the temptation to purely emotionally motivated choice, a matter irrelevant to proportionalism's methodological concerns. See my comments on Part III of Luban's paper, below.

have rational appeal; but morally significant, rationally motivated *choice* is *between alternative options* each of which has rational appeal; therefore where one option is dominant, deliberation ends not in choice but in *insight* (into the unqualified rational superiority of that option) and *action*.[17]

Virtually the only realistic context in which an option can rationally be regarded as dominant is within the confines of 'third order', 'technical' reasoning and action, for example, competitive games. 'Game theory' is the name of a vast and sophisticated body of reasoning about situations of ordinary life (for example, 'bargaining') conceived *as if* they had the simple, unitary-goal, and typically self-interested structure of a competitive game, where there is no ambiguity about what counts as winning and losing and the only problem is the individual player's problem how to win (or avoid defeat, or minimize one's defeat). The very first axiom of game theory is the axiom of transitivity: if a is better than b and b is better than c, then a must be better than c; if x is worse than y and y than z, then x is worse than z; etc.[18] Clear-headed masters of game theory acknowledge that in real life, *intransitivities* abound: a is better than b in one respect (for example, proximity to school), and b is better than c in another respect (for example, physical amenities), but since the two bases of comparison (proximity and amenities) are not commensurable with each other, it does not follow that a is better than c in any respect, let alone unqualifiedly better.[19]

In short, Luban reserves the term 'rational choice' for the peculiar situation of games and other technical operations considered technically. He does not notice that in my usage of terms, there is no choice in such situations, only calculation and judgment.[20] (The word 'decision' is particularly liable to confuse, here, since in common idiom it is equivocal between *judgment*—that is, rationally compelled conclusion to calculation—and *choice*.)[21]

[17] This, again, is subject to the qualification mentioned in the preceding footnote.

[18] See Luce and Raiffa, *Games and Decisions*, ch. 1.

[19] So Luce and Raiffa are reduced to saying: 'We may say that we are only concerned with behavior which is transitive, adding hopefully that we believe this need not always be a vacuous study.' *Id.* at 25. On the same page they acknowledge the typical cause and effect of intransitivities: a topic or situation forces 'choices between inherently incomparable alternatives. The idea is that each alternative invokes "responses" on several different "attribute" scales and that, although each scale may itself be transitive, their amalgamation need not be.' *Ibid.*

[20] In his n. 32, Luban (after asserting the substantial identity of two substantially different theses) expresses the view that my understanding of free choice is 'existentialist', and associates himself with the view that the good person's actions are *determined*. The latter view is either rhetoric or a grave misunderstanding of the conditions of moral goodness, praiseworthiness, and in general responsibility. The former view labels 'existentialist' a basic insight of Judaeo-Christian anthropology which is a permanent, philosophically warranted acquisition of natural law theory: see e.g. Boyle, Grisez, and Tollefsen, *Free Choice*.

[21] Notice that the second, third, and fifth sentences of sec. IC of Luban, 'Incommensurable Values, Rational Choice, and Moral Absolutes', actually equate 'choice' with 'rational choice' with 'rational *solution* to [a] *decision* problem'.

Thus Luban, asserting that for me 'incommensurability of goods implies that rational choice among them is impossible', and that this is indeed my central claim, adds:

> Finnis insists that if states of affairs are truly incommensurable then no rational grounds exist to criticize someone who instead chooses the road not taken.[22]

Not so. I in no way reserve the term 'rational' for game theoretical or other technical contexts. Choice between incommensurable options is often rational in two ways: (a) in as much as it opts for the chosen option for the reasons which make that option rationally appealing (even though those grounds do not make that option unqualifiedly more appealing than alternative options); and (b) in as much as it conforms to all the requirements of practical reasonableness which we call moral, for example fairness, consistency, exclusion of any choice to destroy, damage or impede any basic human good, etc. Both (a) and (b) provide rich grounds for rational criticism of choices.[23] There is only one sense in which the last quotation from Luban is true: the *mere fact* that A chooses x while B chooses y does not entail that there is rational ground for A to criticize B or for B to criticize A.[24]

All this leaves, however, a number of interesting observations by Luban on the question of commensurability. Some of these, while interesting in themselves, are of peripheral relevance here, because they are based on his erroneous assumption that I grant, if only *arguendo*, the '*intra*-dimensional commensurability of the basic goods'—and he wishes to dissuade me from conceding this. No dissuasion is necessary. In the senses relevant to Luban's critique, I never grant such commensurability, even *arguendo*. I do analogize the incommensurability of options in morally significant choices to the incommensurability of weight and area prior to the *adoption* of measures. But one should not press the analogy into a granting of something irrelevant to my point (which was not that weight *is* commensurable with weight after the adoption of a measure, but that, prior to adoption of measures, weight is *in*commensurable with size). And in my critique of Dworkin, I do grant, *arguendo*, the intradimensional commensurability of 'fit' and 'soundness'. I ought to have made much clearer than I did that this incommensurability

[22] *Ibid.* at 68.

[23] Lynn Henderson's fear that the incommensurability thesis paralyses deliberation and decision is quite groundless. Henderson, 'Whose Nature?' at 181.

[24] Notice that, in the proportionalist model of moral reasoning, in which the task of deliberation is to identify the unqualifiedly greater good or lesser evil, the mere fact that A decides for x and B (in the same situation) decides for y entails that either A has rational ground for criticizing B, or B has rational ground for criticizing A.

is only analogous to, not an instantiation of, the incommensurability of rationally choosable, morally significant options.[25]

So I need not attend to the details of Luban's 'Nash-style' argument, designed to dislodge a 'background assumption' which I do not make. But one observation may be helpful here, as an introduction to the much more important and interesting question of 'large-small tradeoffs'.

The observation is this. The availability of a unique 'Nash solution' depends on 'rationality assumptions', 'constraints', or 'axioms'. But the arguments of sound natural law theory against proportionalist ethics have never denied that unique solutions (commensurability; 'decidability') are available *if enough assumptions are made*. Moreover, if some of the assumptions on which the unique solution depends are, as Luban seems to admit, assumptions alternatives to which can be rationally envisaged, then the solution is not truly (rationally) unique. Making such 'assumptions' is *making a choice* (in my sense of choice, between rationally appealing alternative options). And natural law theory's thesis about incommensurability has never denied that commensuration is possible *after* certain strategic choices have been made.[26]

This point can be clarified by considering the examples Luban discusses in perhaps the most interesting part of his interesting paper, concerning the 'large-small tradeoffs' which 'we press into service against moral absolutists' (like me). Luban's engagingly frank phrase 'press into service' already suggests a willed, prior determination to exclude the 'absolute' moral judgments for which the field lies open if proportionalist commensurations can be shown to be irrational. But his willingness to argue for proportionalist commensuration is more important than any such resolution to beg the question. So I shall attend to the arguments, which develop largely by way of examples.[27]

Case 1, the college athlete. Luban suggests (a) that it is irrational for him to devastate his studies by undertaking a rigorous training programme, and (b) that this irrationality exemplifies a commensurability between the basic goods of health, knowledge, and excellence in work/play—a

[25] See bracketed n. 18 [added after the symposium] in 1990c at 9 [=essay I.14, n.17 and sec. VI].

[26] Some of the other 'assumptions' in game/bargaining theory are designed, as Luban observes, to preserve 'fairness'. But again, natural law theory's incommensurability thesis has never denied that *moral* standards of judgment can identify certain options as 'irrational', i.e. unreasonable, morally bad. The fact remains that immoral choice is possible precisely because immoral options can remain rationally appealing in a way which proportionalist ethics leaves incomprehensible. I may add that natural law theory, which acknowledges the rationality of choices made in the absence of 'unique solutions', will scarcely be concerned to deny the existence of 'unique solutions' that depend upon a *lottery* between alternative options (the fourth of Luban's Nash-assumptions).

[27] In attending to Luban's arguments, I shall not repeat what I have already observed, particularly that he is mistaken in his assumption that the incommensurability thesis *depends* upon establishing cross-categorial incommensurability between categories of basic human good.

commensurability in the case where the gain (or loss) in one basic good is very great and the loss (or gain) in another basic good is very small: 'large-small tradeoff'. I do not question (a). But (b) is mistaken. The commensuration we make or presuppose when we judge it irrational for this athlete to undertake the programme is made possible not by the size of the respective gains and losses in different basic goods, but by the plan of life which this athlete has *already adopted* (chosen)—by his commitment to whatever he needs his college studies for (medical practice..., classical scholarship...). We could judge the *very same* gain in athletic proficiency and loss in scholastic performance *rational* if we were told that this young man is in college in order to get into the pro's.

Case 2, the trial lawyer. As in Case 1, the options (prepare cross-examination; sleep to avoid feeling tired) are easily ranked *by her commitment* to legal practice. It is of some importance to notice that Luban is mistaken in assuming that tiredness involves damage to a basic human good. In fact it does not, unless it significantly damages health. Tiredness which does not threaten health is repugnant; like pain it is an emotional *bad* but is often an *intelligible* good, being the bodily sign of the need (for health's sake) to cease activity, and a stimulus to doing so. When health is not at stake, it is irresponsible for a professional to skimp on preparation 'urgently required' for fulfilling the responsibilities established by the usual norms of that profession and thus by the reasonable[28] expectations of the client.[29] Once again, one who has made a prior choice can often, and easily, make a rational commensuration between options, including options involving different basic goods.

So Luban's 'Finnis to the contrary' was misdirected: I have no difficulty in accepting that, in each of these two cases, one of the options is irrational, that is, unreasonable for that person.

Luban's other examples in his section on 'large-small tradeoffs' are of less interest, because they concern comparisons, not between morally significant options in the third order but cultural-technical objects in the fourth order. For the book designer, a gain in page size of 50 per cent outweighs, *ceteris paribus*, a 2 per cent increase in weight. But the *ceteris paribus* clause is important. As soon as one brings the object out of the purely technical sphere into a relationship with relevant human goods, the assumption that

[28] What is reasonable is established not by some pre-moral aggregation of goods but by customs and conventions established by the choices characteristic of a certain culture, choices which will be upright if fair.

[29] But when health is at stake, the options once more appear incommensurable. Still, even when her health is at stake, *this* professional *may* find the options rationally commensurable, *if she* has made a prior commitment to fight this case 'at all costs', i.e. self-sacrificially. Accepting severe personal loss as a side effect of devotion to a good cause need not be either irrational or unreasonable.

other things are 'equal', that is, irrelevant, comes into question. A 2 per cent increase in weight can be intolerable to mail-order purchasers, and a 50 per cent increase in size unacceptable to librarians, war-time paper rationers, and so on. As for Luban's comparison of judgments which differ slightly on 'fit' but greatly in 'moral attractiveness', or vice versa, I simply deny that the postulated great disparity in the differences makes it per se rational to prefer the judgment which is better on the criterion where the difference is very great. I note that Luban is uneasy here; he says only that 'many of us would think...' Dworkin, for one, has disagreed: below the 'threshold of fit', moral soundness is irrelevant; above the threshold of fit, only moral soundness counts.

I may add that I regret two things about my discussion of incommensurability in 'Natural Law and Legal Reasoning' [1990c]. As I have already remarked, I should have made it clearer that the incommensurability between Dworkin's two dimensions is not an instantiation of, but only a kind of analogy to, the incommensurability between the human goods involved in morally significant, rationally motivated choices. And I should have made it explicit that I was only granting *arguendo* the intelligibility of Dworkin's talk (a) about measuring degrees of moral soundness and (b) about trading off moral soundness against fit; in fact, I cannot reconcile either of these crucial features of Dworkin's analysis (and Luban's example) with any acceptable concept of morality.

What should be said about Luban's other example of cross-categorial comparison, the decathlon score chart? First, that the moral he wants to draw from it is irrelevant to sound natural law theory; for this theory does not seek to dismiss the possibility of rational cross-categorial comparisons; it merely observes that where such commensuration between options is possible, there is no free choice of the sort that proportionalist ethical theories offer to guide. Secondly, Luban entirely misstates the source of the rationality of the decathlon score table. Its rationality is the rationality of a *fair* comparison between different types of track and field athletic performance: the problem is to determine the best overall track and field athlete, and the challenge is to devise a scoring system which (a) will not *give* any one type of performance a priority which it doesn't have relative to overall track/field athletic superiority, and (b) will not include criteria (for example, memory) which are irrelevant to track/field athletic prowess. Luban's talk of 'accuracy' is misdirected. Moreover, the score table does not allow us to say that an athlete who scores 1,100 in one event is a better athlete than one who scores 1,050 in another event; it only allows us to say that one who scores more in the ten events is better overall *as a track and field athlete*—a culturally determined category. *This* sort of cross-categorial commensuration has—as Luban perhaps concedes—only scant analogy with the problem involved in morally significant choices outside the frameworks of comparison established by prior commitments.

Luban's Part III makes, very shortly, two points. The confusions involved in the first I have already dealt with. But the second obliges me to clarify my use of the shorthand phrase 'morally significant choice'. As is made clear in the parallel discussion in *Nuclear Deterrence, Morality and Realism*, but not in 'Natural Law and Legal Reasoning', this use is not intended to deny the moral significance of successfully overcoming temptations to choose, for emotional motivations, options known to be rationally (for example, morally, or 'prudentially') inferior. If it were possible to do the proportionalist commensuration and to identify the option promising unqualifiedly greater good (or lesser evil), there would still remain a 'choice' of a 'morally significant' sort, namely, to succumb to or resist emotional motivations such as fear or lust. *But that is not the problem which proportionalist ethics offers to solve.* My discussion of 'morally significant choice' was not an attempt to say everything which can appropriately be said about what is and is not morally significant in human deliberation and action; my discussion was focused entirely on the proportionalist claim to be able to guide morally significant, *rationally motivated* choice, that is, choice between options each of which is *rationally* appealing.

Although (or because?) it involves a series of mistakes and misunderstandings, Luban's discussion of moral absolutes is well worth careful attention. For here as elsewhere the mistakes are by no means peculiar to him, but are signs, causes, and effects of the ramifying grip of proportionalist thinking.

A first large mistake is, once more, about my meaning. Throughout this section, Luban says and supposes that, according to me, 'we cannot identify reasons *for* an option' and 'cannot identify reasons for promoting basic good'. He even attributes to me the pure incoherence of holding in one and the same breath that where there are reasons for O_1 and reasons for O_2 there is no reason for either O_1 or O_2! This is all quite groundless, and flat contrary to the text he quotes from me at note 31 of his paper.[30] Unless there are reasons for an option, *and* for alternative options, rationally motivated choice of either option is impossible; and my primary concern is with rationally motivated, morally significant choice. Luban has simply

[30] ['If there were a reason (for doing X) which some rational method of comparison... identified as preferable... [t]here would remain no choice in the morally significant sense of choice, between the alternative options.' See now the similar sentence in essay I.14, i.e. the sentence after n. 23 of that essay.] However, the last part of that passage, as I note in a new footnote to [1990c] [see now essay I.14 n. 23], needs qualification; when basic human goods are at stake and provide the reasons against an option, there can be reasons *for* the option but they *cannot* be rationally preferable.

confused 'The reasons for O_n are not rationally preferable to the reasons against O_p' with 'There are no reasons for O_n'. More briefly, he has confused 'a reason' with 'a reason sufficient to override a contrary reason'.

Fortunately, the other mistakes in his discussion are more interesting and fruitful. Particularly interesting is his denial that there is an asymmetry between reasons for and reasons against. But his discussion remains at the level of a purely verbal logic of convertibility, and overlooks the fundamental context of all human choosing. Options which there are reasons *for* my choosing are infinite in number. Being finite, I simply cannot do everything, cannot choose every option for which there are reasons. But I can refrain from doing anything; I can respect every reason *against* choosing options. A further ground of the asymmetry is that many human goods (for example, the lives of others) are gifts, givens, which we can destroy but cannot create.

Luban goes on to ascribe to me the view that 'Forbearance from damaging basic goods is the default position.'[31] This repeated summary is hazardously equivocal. As much of my essay was concerned to stress, the distinction between intended harm and harm done as a side effect is fundamental to my argument, and to the whole conception of specific moral absolutes. So my view had better be summarized as: 'Forbearance from choosing to damage basic goods is the default position' or, equivalently, 'Forbearance from intentional damage to basic goods is the default position'. And again, this morally vital distinction between intention and side effect is rooted in the fundamental context of all human choosing and acting: we *cannot* avoid damaging human goods as a side effect of our choices, but we *can* always refrain from choosing to damage them, that is, from intending to damage them, that is, from damaging them intentionally.

Later still, Luban shifts to the more precise formulation: 'Forbearance from intentionally injuring basic goods is the default position.' But immediately he makes it clear that, for him[32] 'intentionally' means no more than 'knowingly' and does not make the vital distinction between intended results and side effects. So, he says, 'When I tell a panhandler to get lost I am intentionally failing to promote a basic good', and he calls this an 'intentional lapse' and 'intentional bad Samaritanism'. All this utterly confuses two quite different types of willing: in telling a panhandler to get lost, I certainly act intentionally, and I certainly intend that he should get no money from me; what is not certain is that I intend him to starve. I may be intending him to starve; I may want him to suffer because I resent

[31] Luban, 'Incommensurable Values, Rational Choice, and Moral Absolutes' at 81.
[32] As for Henderson, 'Whose Nature?', too.

him (that is, as an end in itself), or to deter him and others from future begging (that is, as a means). In these cases, his starving is intended by me because it is chosen by me *as an end or as a means*. If this is what Luban had in mind when he spoke of 'intentionally failing to promote a basic good', then I agree that this is morally equivalent to 'actively injuring'. Quite different is the case—equally covered by Luban's vague phraseology and loose conception of intention—where I intend that this panhandler should get no money from me because I am on my way to give the available money to somebody else in need; here I may know that the panhandler will starve, but I in no way intend that side effect of my choice.[33]

Luban assumes that my 'default position' is not meant to cover intentional omissions as well as intentional actions. But it is! My only proviso is that 'intentional' must here be understood as signifying, not merely 'knowingly causing', but choosing as an end or as a means. A sound theory of natural law does not sponsor Luban's 'homely intuition' that 'sins of commission are worse than sins of omission'.[34] Leaving one's baby behind on a lonely mountain top and omitting to tell rescue services, because one intends the baby to die, is as bad as drowning it. Luban's phraseology hereabouts is shot through with ambiguities foreign to a sound ethics. 'Killing you is morally worse than letting you die' is true if 'letting you die' refers to a side effect fairly accepted, but is false if the ambiguous phrase refers to an intended putting to death by a policy of omissions—a form, in fact, of killing.

Ethics judges actions as *shaped by the will*, that is, *as motivated*. Luban's willingness to analyse an action such as pushing a button independently of what he vaguely calls 'motive' removes his discussion from the proper sphere of the ethical. Although his description of Lichtenberg's artificial predicament is far too ambiguous to warrant the conclusion that 'it is clear that [pushing and not pushing the button] are morally equivalent', a sound natural law theory can easily accept—indeed, has always proclaimed—that considered independently of the motives (reasons) which shape choices, the distinction between actions, that is, chunks of physical behaviour, and omissions carries no moral weight. For chunks of physical behaviour, as such, carry no moral weight. Natural law theory's vital distinction between affirmative and negative responsibilities is not to be confused with the

[33] Note: this analysis of intention and side effect does not settle the morality of the second choice; my rejection of the panhandler's plea in favour of somebody else's *might* be unfair; this panhandler might be my own son, and/or I may be favouring the other person in order to win future illicit favours in return. Side effects can be unfairly, immorally imposed. But, they can also be fairly imposed, whether by 'act' or 'omission'.

[34] Luban, 'Incommensurable Values, Rational Choice, and Moral Absolutes' at 82.

conventional, physical-behaviour oriented and ethically indeterminate distinction between actions and omissions.

There remains one last shot in Luban's critique of my sketch of the case for moral absolutes. Once again, it is an example, rather than an argument: 'by lying to a Gestapo spy you are able to save hundreds of innocent lives'.[35] But, now the example must stand on its own since Luban failed (I have argued) in his earlier attempt to show that large-small tradeoffs are an exception to the incommensurability (prior to moral judgment and choice) of morally significant options.

Luban thinks it indubitable that the lie is 'rationally preferable to truth-telling'. Already his discussion has derailed, for the question is not whether lying is rationally preferable to truth-telling but whether it is rationally preferable (independently of moral judgments and standards) to the alternatives to lying—and these alternatives include silence, inviting the spy to have a cigarette or to join in a hymn, suicide, attacking the spy, and so forth. Proportionalist 'calculations' of the greater good or lesser evil (and thus of the 'rationally preferable') characteristically proceed by arbitrarily restricting the range and content of the comparisons, and this is Luban's first arbitrary restriction.

His next is equally characteristic of proportionalist method; to eliminate the calculation of comparative risks one simply helps oneself to a 'knowledge' of the alternative outcomes. So here, Luban tells us that, on the one hand, this lie will 'only slightly damage' human goods while, on the other hand, it *will* (he implies) save hundreds of lives. But, ethics concerns options, that is, future actions and their consequences, and these consequences are not known to us. The choice to lie to this spy here and now is a choice to lie 'when it seems necessary, or very advantageous' and the consequences of this choice spread out far beyond the situation under consideration. It is a choice to adopt a certain stance in the world, a certain character, and the consequences of *this*, for good and ill, are indefinitely and unpredictably wide, lasting, and serious. Equally, the hoped-for good effects of the lie are not yet facts but are possibilities, the probability of which, like all probabilities of one-off events, is a matter of speculation, and the further consequences of which are even more speculative.

None of the points I have just made suggest that it is unreasonable to want to save the hundreds of lives and to want the spy to remain in an ignorance, or act under a delusion, which will tend to save those lives. My argument is simply that *reason* does not authorize the conclusion that the harm to human good indubitably done *in*, and potentially resulting *from*,

[35] *Ibid.* at 80.

the act of deliberately asserting a false proposition with intent to deceive is objectively *less than* the gain to human good from the hoped-for effects of subsequent choices expected to be made by the person so deceived and those whom he himself unwittingly deceives. The *feeling* that one course of action is rationally preferable to the other comes from a failure to assess the alternatives even-handedly, including in the assessment all the relevant reflexive effects on character and the differential but hardly calculable levels of probability or risk.

Our seventy-two-page analysis in *Nuclear Deterrence, Morality and Realism* of (a) the attempts of pro-deterrent proportionalists to identify nuclear deterrence as the lesser evil, and (b) the equally futile attempts of anti-deterrent proportionalists to identify it as a greater evil, shows clearly enough that aggregative, pre-moral reasoning is impotent to make the assessments which proportionalist ethical theory demands, and that what does the work in these 'calculations' is *feelings*—the (justified) fear of tyranny, the (justified) fear of nuclear holocaust, the (partly justified and partly unjustified) concern for self and friends in preference to future generations, etc. And feelings are characteristically able to do this (self-deceptive) work because the comparison of alternative options is not rigorous and even-handed. Luban's loaded account of his lying-to-the-Gestapo case exemplifies well enough these rational deficiencies of proportionalist moral methodology.

Finally, Luban makes another closing shot, at the asymmetry between affirmative and negative responsibilities: 'there is no more reason to enact a law prohibiting murder than to enact a law positively requiring state intervention to fight famine'.[36] I think he is mistaken here, too. There can be no state without some law against killing of human beings, and the requirement of fairness demands that this law be generalized. But the state *need* not get into the business of famine relief. There will be many situations in which it is appropriate, and an implication of fairness, for the state to organize and supply famine relief. But equally, there will be many situations where it is just and altogether reasonable to leave this up to families and other non-state networks.

Indeed, natural law principles, which universally require everyone to refrain from killing the innocent, do not *universally* require the establishment of a state and, therefore, do not universally require the enacting of a positive (state) law against murder: consider the situation of Eskimos for many centuries.[37] So the final sentence of Luban's paper needs qualification,

[36] *Ibid.* at 84.

[37] A brief comment on Luban's footnote 11 concerning (a) work and (b) political participation. *Work* was mistakenly omitted from the summary lists of basic human goods in *NLNR* and *FoE*. But I

too: given a lot of contingent (in the sense of non-universal) factors, we should say that natural law requires the formation and maintenance of a state and thus of a law against murder; given *further* contingent factors, natural law requires also the politically organized redistribution of wealth to satisfy 'welfare rights'.

III. 'CONSEQUENTIALISM'

Randy Barnett hopes to replace 'conflict between modes of analysis' with a relationship of 'redundancy' between them, such that one backs up another and takes over when the other runs out. The principal modes of analysis he identifies are the 'consequentialist' and the 'deontological or rights-based'.[38]

I fear his hopes are misplaced. Redundancy in aircraft design relates not to conflicts between systems, but to the availability of a backup system when the primary system has been defeated by other circumstances or by its own internal failure. But between consequentialist and non-consequentialist[39] ethical theories or systems there is a genuine conflict. Each entails that the other is false and unacceptable, whether as a primary system, a backup method, or at all. Between these systems or methods or modes of analysis there can be no coexistence. They stand to each other as a propellant system stands to an auto-destruct system primed to detonate as the aircraft reaches take-off speed.

never blankly claimed that 'the list is exhaustive'; rather I expressed both the intention to provide an exhaustive list and a clear acknowledgement of 'the scope that exists for modification of the details of the list,' a list which 'there is no need for the reader to accept...just as it stands': *NLNR* 92. My own modification of the list, replacing 'play' with 'excellence in play and work for its own sake' is made explicit in 1987f at 107. I do not consider that this requires any significant modification of the quite complex discussion of private ownership of the means of production in *NLNR* 169–73. As for the 'good of political participation,' Luban's arguments that it is a basic good are clearly fallacious. The fact that sociability extends to beings who have no political life (brute animals) in no way entails that political participation is not a form of the sociability peculiar to beings who can and need to associate in a deliberative way (human persons). And to say that political action lifts us out of our social station is not to say that it lifts us out of society. But there is no need to speculate that I assimilate political participation to sociability. In *NLNR* 149, I offer a complex analysis of political participation, suggesting that it involves a number of goods over and above the basic good of sociability, including the basic good of play and other goods and rationales. I think Arendt spoke in some respects sentimentally and loosely about political participation, just as she exaggerated the distinction between *homo ludens* and *homo faber*.

[38] He also treats '(substantive) justice' and '(formal) rule of law' considerations as different modes of analysis. This seems to me mistaken; these are different topics of analysis, not different modes of analysing the same topic. Oddly, his conception of 'justice' includes non-consequentialist norms such as 'the guilty should be punished', while his conception of the 'rule of law' includes 'forward-looking', if not downright consequentialist norms such as 'police irregularities should be deterred'. I am inclined to think that a rule excluding illegally obtained evidence is opposed both to justice and the rule of law. But these un-American thoughts of mine need not be pursued here.

[39] Not safely called 'deontological': see *FoE* 84.

The important thing to notice is that a decent ethics—a sound natural law theory—is *concerned through and through with consequences* (and so, in a weak sense, might be called 'consequentialist'). But since the overall net best consequences (the greatest good, the lesser evil), relative to the options available in situations of morally significant choice, cannot be identified prior to moral judgment and choice, consequences are not to be pursued according to the incoherent, futile (and thus ethically false) consequentialist method, but in conformity with all relevant moral norms.

For example, feeding one's children has the good consequence that they stay alive and capable of participating in all the other basic human goods, can support one in one's old age, can become productive members of society, and so forth. Principles of fairness, fidelity to commitments, etc., generate the strong moral norm, the affirmative moral responsibility: 'Feed your children!' But if the only food available is the flesh of the children living next door, you must not feed your children—for there is another moral norm which excludes *choosing* to damage the good of life and health *as a means* to any end however worthy. The relationship between the affirmative moral norm prescribing feeding one's children and the negative moral absolute[40] proscribing intentional harm is only superficially one of 'conflict'. The tension between them is intra-systemic. The two norms are capable of being accurately stated in a single coherent rule-with-exceptions.

An example closer to the lawyer's concerns is the firm tradition of natural law theory concerning judicial duty. 'Never convict the innocent' is an important moral norm of judicial responsibility. But it is consistent with another important moral norm: 'If the only evidence of innocence is inadmissible, you may rightly, and often should, convict.'[41]†

IV. FAIRNESS

The moral question underlying the constitutional issue in *Croson* was whether the Richmond Plan was fair. David Barnhizer is convinced that it was. His reason seems to me to focus on 'the need to create basic life opportunities for racial minorities who have been deliberately prevented from participating in the economic and political system', the need for a 'rectification of known conditions of injustice'.

[40] Note: all the specific moral absolutes proposed in natural law theory are negative; there is not and cannot be an absolute duty to preserve human life as David Barnhizer supposes in 'Natural Law as Practical Methodology' at 24 n. 29. Conversely, these moral absolutes, which are entailed by the first principles of practical reasonableness, *do* (*pace* Barnhizer) dictate *some* specific answers for the judge (though they leave many questions unanswered).

[41] See *ST* II–II q.64 a.6 ad 3; q.67 a.2c; *NLNR* 345. [See now the endnote.]

I in no way question these needs when I suggest that some further questions call for answers before one can be sure the plan was fair. Suppose the effect of the racial quota is that 30 per cent of construction contracts go to members of the defined racial minorities, and the remaining 70 per cent go to large, wealthy corporations; and suppose that in the absence of the racial quota, 20 per cent of the contracts would go to businesses owned by and/or employing poor members of the majority race—who as the result of the quota are put out of business and/or employment. These facts would not entail, inexorably, that the Plan is unfair. But equally, the needs of the designated racial minorities do not entail that the Plan is fair.

The question is whether those who decided upon the Plan really had the needs of all relevant needy parties in mind, and were not deflected by irrelevant considerations such as that they desired the votes of one group more than the other, or wanted the votes of those who, on racial grounds, sympathize with one group more than the other.

This impartiality is a primary component in what is meant by saying that the legislator must act for the *common* good. This has very little to do with aggregation, or 'the greatest good of the greatest number'. It has very much to do with a real, unfeigned willingness on the part of each legislator to do to or for *all* members of the community what he or she is willing to be done to or for himself, herself, and those he or she holds near and dear.

It seems to me to be often the case that the legislators in our western communities, being well-off themselves, impose schemes of redistribution which (are designed to) benefit the very poor *at the expense of the not-quite-so poor rather than at the proportionate expense of the well-off.* I would like to be sure that the Richmond Plan was not tainted by this sort of injustice. I am inclined to think that Barnhizer's critique of Justice O'Connor's opinion fails to respond to a number of points made in the judgments of the six majority Justices, not least the point put thus by Justice Stevens concurring:

> instead of carefully identifying the characteristics of the classes of contractors that are respectively favored and disfavored by its ordinance, the Richmond City Council has merely engaged in the type of stereotypical analysis that is the hallmark of violations of the Equal Protection Clause.[42]

V. EASY CASES

Mark Tushnet comes round to acknowledging that my concept of practical reasoning is not tied to the class-conceptions of a legal profession subservient to the interests of corporations. More interesting is the idea he

[42] *City of Richmond v J.A. Croson Company* 488 US 469, 515 (1989).

attributes to Alasdair MacIntyre, that practical reasoning comes into play only when there is a difficult decision to be made. This idea is, I think, a mistake.[43] There is need for practical reasoning even in an easy case, just as there is practical reasoning in the game-theoretical situations where, on my conception of (rationally motivated) choice, there is no choice because one option can be shown (perhaps quite easily) to be dominant for the potential chooser in question.

I think easy cases and highly determinate rules (the existence of which Tushnet concedes) are a very important part of the law and of legal practice. And 'easy legal reasoning' is a very important element in the structure of almost all hard cases; the 'hard' issue in such cases is usually quite distinguishable from many other, more or less easy issues which are present in the case (and are perhaps disputed at the trial and even, to some extent, at the first appellate stage). The easiness of easy cases may be of less interest to lawyers (though in fact they should and do welcome the manageability it brings to the identification of distinct 'hard' issues). But it is of the highest interest and importance to ordinary folk (not to mention corporations). And it is very important to the justification of law's claims to be just, and thus to its claims on our rational, morally motivated obedience as free subjects of the rule of law.

VI. THE OBLIGATION TO OBEY THE LAW

There is much to agree with in David Forte's paper. But in the end, I remain unconvinced that his term 'Pharisaism' denotes a clear and helpful concept rather than a bundling-together of vices better analysed separately. And I remain unclear about how the legal system is supposed to 'incorporate' and 'provide for' a range of 'justifiable non-compliance' or 'legitimate opportunities for non-compliance'.

In the classic moral reflection on law and the moral obligation to obey it, non-compliance with a legal rule interpreted according to its tenor is considered morally justifiable and legitimate on one or other of three types of ground: (1) 'equity' (*epieikeia*)—the author of the rule would have agreed to this exception if he had considered the situation; (2) desuetude—contrary custom is tolerated by the authorities to an extent which makes it unfair to demand compliance of any individual; (3) injustice—for example, the unfairness or inequity of the burdens imposed by the rule. It seems to me that one or more of these considerations may well apply to some or all

[43] See the bracketed n. 1 in 1990c [in particular: 'not all practical reasoning issues in choice'].

of the rules which Forte complains of, for example the rule about second kitchens. Of course, our legal system does not generally permit the judges to apply these moral considerations as such in the application of the law in findings of guilt or liability. But they are considerations which are highly relevant at the sentencing stage, and English courts make fairly wide use of the absolute discharge after conviction.

If non-compliance cannot be brought within one or more of the classic grounds, it seems to me to be more of an 'affront to the legal system' than is civil disobedience of the type familiar in the English-speaking nations in modern times. The non-compliance which Forte has in mind seems to be covert and (if not on one or other of those three grounds) self-serving. But civil disobedience is a public manifestation of allegiance to the law:

> Civil disobedience involves essentially (i) overt violation of a law, (ii) to express one's protest against that law, or against something public closely connected with some application of that law, together with (iii) ready submission to the law's sanctions. The violation must not involve doing anything otherwise immoral, and its manner and circumstances must make it clear to observers, not only that it *symbolizes* opposition to some important and clearly identified matter of law or policy, but also that this opposition seeks justice not advantage.[44]

If it is true that since 1980 my insistence on the presumptive moral obligation to obey the law has 'become even more pronounced', it is also true that that insistence remains coherent with my acknowledgement, indeed insistence, that that moral obligation, being presumptive and affirmative, can give way to other moral responsibilities. The generic moral obligation to obey the law, despite its presumptive character and its defeasance by competing moral responsibilities, is not empty of significance for the morally upright citizen.[45] For it is never overridden by considerations of convenience or desire or preference, as such.

NOTE

† *Convicting where evidence of innocence is inadmissible*... (at n. 41). As Paul Brady has remarked to me, this sentence needs much qualification. For a start, it assumes that the applicable rule making the exculpatory evidence inadmissible is itself a substantively reasonable rule—as n. 38 already says, some existing rules against admissibility are probably not. Moreover, the sentence omits to consider whether the judge in this situation should not rather recuse himself; Aquinas's famous (and always controversial) discussion of this case (a) implicitly assumes that recusal is not possible (or not possible without serious disruption to the administration of justice), and (b) explicitly requires the judge to take all lawful measures to admit exculpatory evidence. For although it is

[44] *NDMR* 355. For my exploration of the conditions on which such civil disobedience is morally justified, see *ibid.*, 354–7.

[45] This is not the place to restate the *grounds* for affirming that obligation. For a fairly recent treatment, see essay 3 (1989b) and works of mine cited there.

clear that a judge who in this kind of situation convicts the probably innocent person on the basis of lawful and sufficient evidence does not intend injustice, nonetheless the grievous harm of being falsely convicted (in a loose sense, a grave injustice) is certainly a side effect foreseen as at least probable—an effect the causing of which, as with all foreseen side effects, is subject to the moral requirements of fairness. So, e.g. in applying the norms of fairness to this anticipated side effect, the judge will have to take into account the difference between likely consequences such as a small fine for a regulatory offence and, on the other hand, likely consequences such as capital or other irreparable punishment.

18

RIGHTS: THEIR LOGIC RESTATED*

Why do students usually get into a muddle when analysing legal situations in Hohfeldian terms?

What is the use of trying to straighten out the muddles, and of teaching Hohfeldian analysis at all?

This little essay concerns solely these two pedagogical questions; it says nothing new or formally rigorous about the problems of legal analysis and structure.

The short answer to the first question is that Hohfeld was clear-headed in applying his scheme, but because of his writing style and his odd views about definition was regrettably gnomic about the meaning and interrelations of the terms of that scheme—while the professors who have expounded him in students' textbooks are often quite muddled both in explaining and in applying the scheme.

The short answer to the second question is that clear-headed familiarity with Hohfeld's scheme can bring with it an awareness of the questions regularly begged when 'claims of right' are raised in law, politics, and moral debate, and thus some awareness of the ambiguity, evasion, and overkill afflicting the western debate since 'rights' became the basic counter in discourse.

Note on terminology: by 'Hohfeld's schema' shall be meant the first of his two squares of opposition:

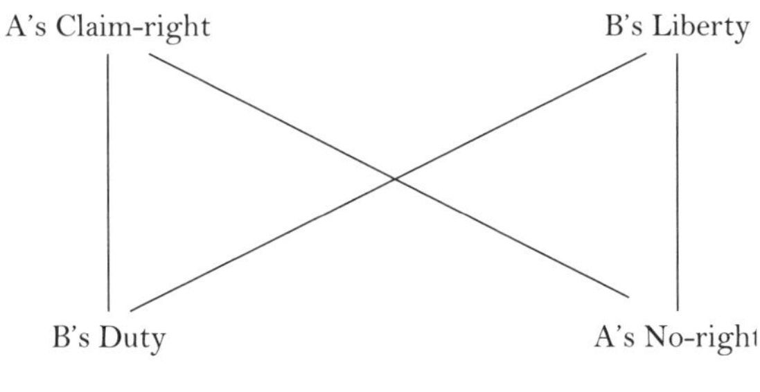

* 1972b ('Some Professorial Fallacies about Rights'). The essay's author held the academic rank of lecturer, and the essay develops the conceit that authors making mistakes about Hohfeld's analysis all hold the higher academic rank of professor, whereas the authors of sound treatments are all of sub-professorial rank. One or two exceptions to this light-hearted 'rule' are quietly conceded.

Thus, if A has a claim-right that B do (or not do) X, a correlative duty to A to do (or not do) X must inhere in B. If the rule (or inference) providing for the foregoing relation is negated (or the inference denied), the new (or asserted) situation will be such that B, not now having that duty to A, has a liberty not to do (or to do) X, while A now has no right ('a no-right') that B do (or not do) X. I use 'privilege' and 'liberty' synonymously and indifferently throughout.[1]

I

Students of Hohfeld who look into Professor Stone's *Legal System and Lawyers' Reasonings* (1964), or into his *The Province and Function of Law* (1946), will read that

> in Hohfeld's sense...it is improper to speak of A having a privilege *vis-à-vis* B unless it can be shown that B has a no-right to prevent its exercise. (*LSLR* 140; *PFL* 117.)

And further on:

> For the ambiguously wide term 'a liberty', [Hohfeld] substituted the notion of 'a privilege' limited to those situations in which the law permits A to act as he wishes, but imposes no duty on B to permit him to do so, or in other words, leaves B also free to act as he wishes. B in this case has, in Hohfeld's sense, 'a no-right' to prevent A, but he does also have a privilege (Salmond's 'liberty') of preventing him, if he wishes. The correlative of this 'privilege' of A is B's 'no-right' to legal redress when A exercises this terminating privilege. *(LSLR* 143.)[2]

And again:

> The 'privilege' of Hohfeld is...that kind of 'liberty' which the law tolerates but does not support by imposing a duty on anyone else. (*LSLR* 143; *PFL*, 121.)

Now students will remain with Hohfeld on the straight and narrow path only if they realize that Stone's exegesis (a) is incompatible with Hohfeld's

[1] I remain throughout within the Hohfeldian framework, treating legal relations as three-term relations between two persons and one *activity*. Thus I ignore rights to or in respect of *things*, as to which see Honoré's important critique of Hohfeld: Honoré, 'Rights of Exclusion and Immunities against Divesting'. I also ignore the problems of Hohfeld's analysis of [the second of his two squares of opposition:] powers, liabilities, immunities, and disabilities.

[2] Sic. But what is 'this terminating privilege'? I can make sense of the sentence (which appears, without the last nine words, in *PFL* 120) only if 'A' is substituted for 'B', and vice versa, throughout the sentence. I forbear to ask whether Stone, by characterizing B's privilege (but not A's) as 'Salmond's "liberty"' intended to distinguish between two types of 'privilege'...

text, and (b) ignores and defies three axioms essential to the comprehension of Hohfeld's work.

(a) First, Hohfeld's text, which is clear on the point in issue:

If X has a right against Y that he shall stay off the former's land, the correlative (and equivalent) is that Y is under a duty toward X to stay off the place… [W]hereas X has a *right* or *claim* that Y, the other man, should stay off the land, he himself has the *privilege* of entering on the land; or, in equivalent words, X does not have a duty to stay off… [T]he correlative of X's privilege of entering himself is manifestly Y's 'no-right' that X shall not enter. (Hohfeld, *Fundamental Legal Conceptions* (1923) 38–9.)

This is Hohfeld's introductory and principal illustration of his leading terms. It leaves rather little room for Stone's exegetical claim that a Hohfeldian privilege exists only when the law allows others ('anyone else': all others!) the privilege to frustrate the exercise of the first-mentioned privilege.[3] For Hohfeld's privilege is paradigmatically the privilege of the landowner to walk on his own land; and, in all the legal systems familiar to Hohfeld's readers, this is not a merely 'tolerated' liberty, but is rather a liberty surrounded by a perimeter of supporting claim-rights[†] of the landowner against attempted interference with him in the exercise of his liberty. The existence of such supporting claim-rights is not, of course, a condition of the existence of the liberty: Salmond and Hohfeld are both clear about this. But still less is the *absence* of such supporting claim-rights a condition (as Stone seems to claim) of the existence of the liberty.[4]

[3] Hohfeld, *Fundamental Legal Conceptions as Applied in Judicial Reasoning*, 48 n. 59 is clear evidence that he recognized that Salmond's 'liberty' was, like his own 'privilege', 'the mere negation of duty' (cf. 44). *Pace* Stone, Hohfeld was not substituting a narrower or more closely defined term ('privilege') for an 'ambiguously wide' Salmond-'liberty'. He simply preferred one word to the other.

[4] Hohfeld, *Fundamental Legal Conceptions*, 41 gives two analyses of Gray's shrimp salad affair. The primary analysis notes that the subject will 'primarily' have 'two classes of relations', viz. a privilege of eating the salad and a claim-right that others shall not interfere with this activity of eating. Hohfeld notes that 'these two groups of relations seem perfectly distinct; and the privileges could, in a given case, exist even though the rights mentioned did not'. The last-mentioned *secondary* possibility is reproduced by Stone (*LSLR* 143; *PFL* 121) as if it were *the* Hohfeldian analysis of a privilege and *the* Hohfeldian analysis of the shrimp salad imbroglio. Stone then feels free to say (*LSLR* 144 n. 22; *PFL* 121 n. 19) that in a case where there was a binding contract to allow the subject to eat the salad [i.e. Hohfeld's primary case], the subject would have a claim-right [!] to eat the salad. Stone's confusion of two 'perfectly distinct' relations could not be more complete. Stone's criticism of Salmond (*LSLR* 142 n. 15; *PFL* 119 n. 13) is based on the same absurd notion that there can be a claim-right ('a "right" in the strict sense') to *do* something. Salmond (*Jurisprudence* (1902) 232) sees quite clearly (like Hohfeld) that where a liberty to act is protected by a claim-right 'not to be hindered in so acting', then 'in such a case there are in reality two rights and not merely one: and there are instances in which liberties are not thus accompanied by protecting rights'. The parallelism with Hohfeld, in emphasis as well as in conceptual structure, is complete.

(b) The misreading of Hohfeld is only possible, and only significant, because of a neglect of basic principles. These principles overlap, but can be treated under three heads or axioms.

(1) *Each Hohfeldian relation* (for example of claim-right: duty, or of privilege: no-right) *concerns only one activity of one person.*

There is one complete Hohfeldian relation between X and Y (in Hohfeld's example) with respect to the topic of Y's going (or not going) on X's land. There is another complete and logically independent relationship between X and Y with respect to the topic of X's walking on his own land. There is yet another and again logically independent relationship between X and Y with respect to the topic of Y interfering with X's walking on his (X's) own land. And so on.

To sharpen the point, let it be particularly noted that, while somebody's activity is one topic for Hohfeldian relationships between that person and other persons, interference with that person's activity is always another topic for other Hohfeldian relationships.

Thus the correlative of X's privilege is Y's no-right that X shall not exercise that privilege; and that is all that can be said about this relationship. The matter of Y's possible privilege (or even duty) to interfere with X's exercise of his (X's) privilege is always a further problem requiring a distinct solution by positive law; nothing can be asserted about it by inference from the first-mentioned relationship. Stone's attempt to link X's privilege, not merely with Y's no-right, but also (conceptually) with Y's privilege of interfering, is inconsistent with this first axiom of Hohfeldian method.[5]

(2) *A Hohfeldian claim-right can never be to do or omit something: it always is a claim that somebody else* do or omit something: A's claim-right is always to B's action or omission, never to A's.

All Hohfeld's statements and examples take this for granted: would that he had somewhere said it explicitly! In any event, the axiom can readily be verified by asking oneself what could (logically) be the content of B's

[5] Professor Paton makes the same mistake, but chooses the opposite conceptual link:

> liberty represents what I can do for myself, free of the possibility of legal interference by others...Here no precise relationship to others is in question, save that the law will protect my liberty if others interfere with its exercise. (Paton, *Jurisprudence*, 255.)

Mr Dias gets the whole matter right with the terse formulation: 'X's privilege to wear the bowler hat and his right not to be prevented from so doing are two different ideas' (*Jurisprudence* (2nd edn, 1964) 232). A nuanced account, clear-headed on the logic of the Hohfeldian schema but sensitive to the practical pressures to support privileges with claim-rights, is given by Lucas in *The Principles of Politics*, 157–8.

correlative duty if A had [*per impossibile*] a claim-right to do (or omit) something...[6]

It follows that a Hohfeldian 'no-right' is equally incapable (logically) of being predicated of the actions (or omissions) of the bearer (subject) of the no-right. So it is strict nonsense to speak (as Stone does above) of B having both a privilege and a no-right to 'prevent A' (or to do anything else). For B's 'preventing' is an action, and thus can be for B the object only (within the Hohfeldian schema) of duties or privileges.

It is conceivable[7] that Stone's error at this point was not so much a failure to respect this axiom, but rather an equivocation on the notion of 'preventing' or 'interfering': such that, when thinking of B's privilege he was thinking of some action of B directly and personally interfering with A, while when thinking of B's no-right he was thinking of B's (not) having a 'legal remedy' for A's action (as B would have had if A had been under a duty to him...). If so, the third axiom becomes relevant.

(3) The relevance of 'legal remedies' to the defining terms of his schema is left entirely undetermined by Hohfeld.

Further stipulative definitions (which he never provided) are required before the schema can be applied to the analysis of any concrete legal situations; in particular, answers must first be stipulated for the following requests for clarification:

(i) If B has a duty (say) not to walk on Whiteacre, does A have the correlative claim-right
   — if and because he (A) has an interest in Whiteacre; or
   — if and only if he (A) has a 'legal remedy' to 'enforce' B's duty?

(ii) If the latter, has A got the claim-right if he is not entitled to an injunction to restrain B, and/or if he is under a duty not to use force against B by way of self-help, but can in any case get damages? In short, if having a remedy is a condition of having a claim-right, what counts as a remedy for these purposes, and in particular need it amount to an ability (even if only *de jure*) to *prevent* B from acting contrary to his duty?

[6] Stone's n. 22 in *LSLR* 144 (*PFL* 121 n. 19) seems to suggest that 'the duty not to interfere' is the correlative of a claim-right to act. More clearly still, he says (*LSLR* 144; *PFL* 121) that 'the correlative' burdens on A, B, C, and D to X's privilege, are their 'no-rights' to keep him off. All this defies the elementary logic of Hohfeld's schema, by introducing a fourth term into what is (and can only be) a three-term relationship between two persons and one action (or omission).

[7] But not likely, since (as noted at n. 4 above) Stone elsewhere speaks of a claim-right to eat a salad.

It is clear enough that Stone has not pressed any of these questions. His failure in this respect is more complete, but not perhaps more spectacular, than that of Professor Lord Lloyd, whose *The Idea of Law* (1970) offers to analyse two hypothetical examples to show how Hohfeldian terminology 'assists in clarifying legal analysis and avoids confusion between different legal situations which may have different legal consequences'. It is not necessary to follow his analysis very far:

In the first example Smith buys a theatre ticket for a reserved seat at a performance at Brown's theatre. If, as a matter of law, Brown is not able to exclude Smith from taking his seat, this would amount to the grant of what is called in law an 'irrevocable licence'. Smith in this case has a liberty to enter and take his seat and Brown has 'no-right' to interfere with this freedom of Smith. (Lloyd, *The Idea of Law*, 315.)

Let us interrupt to note that the analysis has already miscarried. The correlative of Smith's liberty to enter and take his seat is Brown's no-right *that Smith shall not do so.* A correct analysis of the vaguely described 'irrevocable licence' is presumably that Brown has a duty (contractual, no doubt) to allow Smith to enter (that is, not to exclude Smith), and Smith has a correlative claim-right that Brown shall not exclude him from entering. This claim-right adds to and supports (in a practical sense) Smith's privilege of entering. But Lloyd goes on:

Suppose, however, that before the performance is due Brown wrongfully purports to withdraw Smith's permission to enter. The law may well say in this case that though Brown has acted wrongfully, Smith cannot legally compel Brown to let him in, so that Smith's only remedy is to sue for damages for breach of contract. This means therefore that Smith has no liberty to enter but only a right to sue for damages. (*Ibid.*)

Students will want to know how this state of affairs is consistent with the hypothesis that 'Brown is not able to exclude Smith from taking his seat'—it seems that indeed, in many senses, he 'can'! Much more important, however, is Lloyd's muddle about the liberty to enter; on the law as stated by Lloyd,[8] there is no reason to suppose that Smith has lost his liberty of entering, for there is no reason to suppose that he has a duty not to enter (as he might well have had but for the purchase of the ticket). What he has lost is not the liberty, but (if anything) the claim-right to be allowed to enter (that is, not to be excluded). But has he lost even that? Is Brown to be regarded as free from a duty not to exclude Smith just because he is not (? any longer) liable to a mandatory injunction or some other such

[8] My comments are restricted to this hypothetical law, and are not to be taken as a commentary on the much more involved legal position in English and Australian law.

specific remedy? After all, he presumably remains liable in damages. Are we to say that one never has a claim-right to the performance of a contract unless one can get specific performance? Hohfeld never formally pursues such questions, though he seems definitely to have assumed that claim-rights exist (for example, at law) even in the absence of secondary rights to specific reparation (for example, in equity).[9] Lloyd, without warning or discussion, simply assumes a particular and none-too-attractive solution-by-stipulation, singling out one special type of remedy (specific) as decisive of the problem of stipulating the truth-conditional analysis of a Hohfeldian claim-right.

But this range of problems can now be left to appear more forcibly in the second part of the paper. One could extend the unravelling of the misconceptions in the textbook accounts of Hohfeld. But readers who are armed with the three axioms can safely be left to do it themselves.

II

What is the use of understanding Hohfeld's scheme of analysis? As we have seen, a superficial familiarity with the terms of the scheme spreads darkness rather widely. But a secure grasp of Hohfeld opens the way to a ready penetration of some common sophistries. Certainly, no one is going to be secured against the moral and political confusion of the age merely by technical logical facility and clarity. But an awareness of technical derailments in the arguments of intelligent men is the basis for any inquiry into the deeper causes of the confusion. One or two illustrative analyses may perhaps suffice to make the point.

In his well-known article, 'Taking Rights Seriously',[10] Professor Ronald Dworkin raises once again the question, 'Does an American ever have the moral right to break a law?' (186). His answer is based on the assumption that Americans 'have certain fundamental rights against their government, certain moral rights made into legal rights by the Constitution' (190). I shall not be questioning this assumption or its formulation, but only the argument used to get from this premise to the conclusion that

> [i]n our society a man does sometimes have the right, in the strong sense, to disobey a law. He has the right whenever that law wrongly invades his rights against the government (192).

[9] See e.g. Hohfeld, *Fundamental Legal Conceptions as Applied in Judicial Reasoning*, 132, 101–14, 150–1.

[10] Dworkin, 'Taking Rights Seriously'. [Parenthetical numbers in the present text are page references to the version, essentially unchanged, in Dworkin, *TRS*.]

The argument is based on the analysis of 'rights in the strong sense':

In most cases when we say that someone has a 'right' to do something, we imply that it would be wrong to interfere with his doing it, or at least that some special grounds are needed for justifying any interference.... There is a clear difference between saying that someone has a right to do something in this [strong] sense and saying that it is the 'right' thing for him to do or that he does no 'wrong' in doing it. Someone may have the right to do something that is the wrong thing for him to do... Conversely, something may be the right thing for him to do and yet he may have no right to do it, in the sense that it would not be wrong for someone to interfere with his trying... Thus we say that the captured [enemy] soldier has a 'right' to try to escape when we mean, not that we do wrong to stop him, but that he has no duty not to make the attempt (188–9).

Dworkin provides further cogent illustrations of the pattern of terms and relations thus defined, and again I shall not question the set of definitions. It is clear enough that Dworkin's 'strong-right' is essentially a (moral and thus American legal) Hohfeldian claim-right (against everybody else: a multital or general claim-right) not to be interfered with in doing an act, X; normally each such claim-right will be conjoined with a Hohfeldian liberty to do X; but the claim-right is not forfeited by the fact that on occasion the subject may have a (moral...) duty not to do X (that is, no liberty to do X[11])—in which case X is not 'the right thing for him to do' but he has the 'strong-right' to do it. And this is all perfectly intelligible.

The next stage in Dworkin's argument is to assert that if Americans' rights are to be significant and worth bragging about

then these rights must be rights in the strong sense I just described. The claim that citizens have a right to free speech must imply that it would be wrong for the government to stop them from speaking, even when the government believes that what they will say will cause more harm than good...(190).

Let this be conceded. The nub of the argument follows (192):

But then the answers to our two questions about disobedience seem plain, if unorthodox... If [a man] has a moral right to free speech... then he has a moral right to break any law that the government, by virtue of his right, had no right to adopt...

[Careful! By virtue of the man's right, the government *was wrong* (by definition) to adopt the law. But remember: one can (by definition) have the (strong) right to do what is wrong.]

[11] We are assuming that Dworkin would really wish to defend his equation of 'wrong' with that which one has a 'duty' not to do. But it would not affect the general argument if, as might be more plausible, he abandoned this equation and retained 'wrong' in some sense independent of duties.

My right against the government means that it is wrong for the government to stop me from speaking;

[Yes.]

the government cannot make it right to stop me just by taking the first step…

[Well, let this pass; but remember Lloyd's Mr Brown, who makes it right for himself to exclude Smith just by wrongfully taking the first step… And the common law sides with Brown on this point,[12] being unaware of the impossibility (moral or logical?) alleged by Dworkin. But let it pass.]

…passing a law cannot affect such rights as men do have, and that is of crucial importance… If a man believes he has a right to demonstrate, then he must believe that it would be wrong for the government to stop him, with or without benefit of a law. If he is entitled to believe that, then it is silly to speak of a duty to obey the law as such, or of a duty to accept the punishment that the state has no right to give (192–3).

If readers treat this as the conclusion of a valid argument their derailment will now be complete; the repeated equivocation on the phrase 'has no right' will have done its rhetorical work. What the premises and assumptions warrant is the conclusion that the state or government *is wrong* to legislate against or interfere with or punish the speech or demonstration. What the premises and assumptions do *not* warrant is the conclusion that the state 'has no right' to do so, if by 'no right' is meant no 'strong right'. In fact, as I interjected earlier, the premises explicitly allow for the possibility that a subject of rights and duties (and why not the state?) can have the strong right to do what it is wrong for that subject to do (and Dworkin stresses the point again at the end of his argument; see 196).

In short, Dworkin's apparent argument omits to consider and exclude the possibility that while the citizen has the strong right to (wrongfully) speak or demonstrate (so that the state is wrong to interfere with him), the state has the strong right to (wrongfully) interfere, in which case *the citizen would be wrong to interfere with the state's interference.* But to refuse to 'accept the punishment' would be one way of interfering with the state's interference. So the omission is precisely a failure to prove what Dworkin sets out to prove, viz. that the subject of strong rights has no duty to accept punishment for breaking a (wrongful) law.

If it were necessary, we could go further. Consideration of the possibility that the state has a strong right alerts us to the topic overlooked by Dworkin: interference with interferences. And our second axiom for Hohfeldian studies will remind us that interference with an action (even

[12] *Cowell v Rosehill Racecourse Co. Ltd* (1936) 56 CLR 605 [High Ct of Aust.].

if the action be itself an interference...) is always a conceptually distinct topic for Hohfeldian relations. This train of reflections will bring to our attention a more subtle but still important further weakness in Dworkin's argument: 'speaking/demonstrating' is one thing, one topic for moral deliberation; but 'breaking a law against speaking/demonstrating' is formally another thing, another topic for moral deliberation, with different aspects and consequences to be weighed and with a conceptually distinct set of Hohfeldian relations to be predicated of it. This difference is ignored as Dworkin's argument proceeds, *via* what looks like a piece of purely conceptual analysis (free from additional moral or political premises), from the strong right to speak/demonstrate to the strong right to break a law against speech/demonstration.

Meanwhile, the topic of interferences with interferences will have stirred some memories of the real problems of political philosophy. For has not Kant based the liberal conception of the state and of public law on the need to hinder those hindrances to individual freedom which arise from the actions of other individuals (*Science of Right*, Introduction, sec. D)? This dimension of the problem is missing from the core of Dworkin's argument; it makes elsewhere a belated appearance, when it forces some rather arbitrary stipulations about the proper limits of claims of right (194–5). It deserves more reflection, not only because the need to hinder hindrances to freedom might well be a basis for a possible 'strong right' of the state, but also because we have not yet confronted the real complexities of the problem of 'rights' in society.

Let these reflections be limited to a single proposition that would presumably be entailed by the more grandiose proposition that 'There is a right to freedom of speech'. Let us assume a society consisting of three citizens, A, B, and C, with a government or state authority, S. Now let us ask: What could be meant by the modest proposition, 'A has a right to say X to B'? Let us suppose that B has no duty to listen to A. Then our reflections simply ring the changes on the elements provided by the three axioms...

One might be asserting (a) that C has (or ought to have) no right of action in tort or contract against A for saying X to B; and/or one might be asserting (b) that A will not be criminally liable for saying X to B. There are many situations in contemporary legal systems where the first assertion is true while the second is false, and vice versa, and many where both are true.[13]

[13] It may not be out of place to recall some of the many types of speech and expression which are prohibited or otherwise legally discouraged in the modern law: perjury; libel and slander; seditious libel, conspiracy to commit crime or any unlawful or indecent act; threatening, abusive, or insulting language whereby a breach of the peace or incitement to racial hatred is likely to be

Alternatively, one might mean that A's communicating X to B is or should be free from prior censorship by S, but not from *ex post facto* suit by C or prosecution by S. As Milton says in the *Areopagitica*, 'it is of greatest concernment to the... commonwealth to have a vigilant eye how books demean themselves as well as men; and thereafter', that is, after publication 'to confine, imprison and do sharpest justice to them as malefactors'.

Alternatively, or additionally, one might be asserting that C has a duty not to interfere with A's communicating X to B. And to say this may mean that if C does interfere he will be penalized by S, and/or it may mean that A can get damages against C for C's interference, and/or that A can get an injunction against C's interfering, and/or that A can resort to self-help against C's interference without thereby incurring criminal liability to S or liability in damages to C or to an injunction by C or to counter-self-help by C—or any combination of these combinations...

Alternatively, or additionally, one might be asserting that A has the liberty to communicate X to B without being snooped on by C or S. And this may mean that snooping by C is an offence penalized by S, and/or actionable in damages and/or by way of injunction by A, and/or a trespass against A giving a right to self-help... and so on as before.

Alternatively, or additionally, we might be asserting that C and S are under a duty to A not to deny him access to B and/or the means of communicating with B; and again, what it is to assert that C and S have a duty and A a corresponding claim-right varies along the range of A's interests and of types of enforcement action, self-help, non-interference, etc.

Thus, long before one examines the content (X) of the act of communication, it is evident that the assertion, 'A has a right to say X to B', has hundreds if not thousands of possible legal meanings. Correspondingly, it has hundreds if not thousands of possible moral meanings within the

occasioned; obtaining property or credit by false pretences or fraud; many sorts of false declarations in connection with public documents; inducing breach of contract; shocking public decency; using obscene language; glorifying the use of drugs; using words with intent to deprave or corrupt, or likely to deprave and corrupt, persons likely to hear or read them; making false reports tending to show that a crime has been committed; communication of official secrets; interrupting public meetings with intent to prevent the business; contempt of court; cheating the revenue; advertising rewards for return of stolen goods on a no-questions-asked basis; inciting disaffection amongst the police and armed forces; causing panic by shouting 'fire!' in a theatre (though perhaps the law does not take so strict a view as John Stuart Mill, who said, in ch. III of *On Liberty*, that 'An opinion that corn-dealers are starvers of the poor, or that private property is robbery... may justly incur punishment when delivered orally to an excited mob assembled before the house of a corn-dealer, or when handed about among the same mob in the form of a placard').

Some people would like to see the foregoing list of legal prohibitions and discouragements extended: e.g. to make it an offence to record or communicate certain types of true and objective information (record as a student, bad debts, ...).

moral discourse about what the morally just legal system should stipulate concerning acts of communicating X. No one of all these possible meanings is self-evidently the right moral claim. So the only way to specify the meaning of 'right' in some claim of right—and then the only way to justify the restriction of the claim to this specified sense of 'right'—will be to appeal to some principles which are pertinent in moral discourse but which are not expressed in terms of 'rights'.

To this ambiguity and the problems of its resolution must be added the ambiguity veiled by the symbol 'X'. Unless one takes the heroic (not to say corrupt) view that A has the right to say anything to B, however treasonable, damaging, or gratuitously vile it may be when uttered to B, one is faced with the problem of specifying what is to count as X for the purposes of making reasonable the assertion that A has the right to say X to B. Here again, the postulate that human beings have rights is of no help. The justifiable specification of X will vary according to time, place, and circumstance and everything else that affects the good of B, of C and of the whole community for which S is immediately responsible and for which we (as imagined architectonic legislators and/or as good lawyers, judges, and citizens) are ultimately responsible.

So most claims of right in the modern western debate are, as they stand, indefensible stumbling-blocks in the path of clear discussion between people of good will. A convenient and representative concrete example is afforded by the Vatican Council's Declaration 'On the Right of the Person and of Communities to Social and Civil Freedom in Matters Religious' (1965).[14] The Declaration begins with a flourish:

> the human person has a right to religious freedom. This freedom means that all men are to be immune from coercion on the part of individuals or of social groups and of any human power, in such ways that in matters religious no-one is to be forced to act in a manner contrary to his own beliefs. Nor is anyone to be restrained from acting in accordance with his own beliefs, whether privately or publicly, whether alone or in association with others, within due limits (s. 2).

'Within due limits'! Does this mean that the Hohfeldian claim-right being asserted (not to be restrained in one's religious practices) only exists when the religious practices are the right ones? No. But it does mean that the right *exists* only to the extent that 'the just requirements of public order

[14] The Declaration simply makes explicit one way of explaining the juridical order established by e.g. the Universal Declaration of Human Rights (1948), Arts 18 and 29, the European Convention for the Protection of Human Rights and Fundamental Freedoms (1950), Art. 9, and thus the human rights provisions of many new Commonwealth constitutions: see e.g. the Fiji Independence Order 1970, SI 1970, p. 6630, Sch. ch. 1. The drafting of the Vatican Council's Declaration is probably to be ascribed mainly to Professor J.C. Murray SJ.‡

are observed' (s. 7).[15] These requirements, in turn, are specified by certain moral norms:

> these norms arise out of the need for effective safeguard of the rights of all citizens and for peaceful settlement of conflicts of rights. They flow from the need for an adequate care of genuine public peace, which comes about when men live together in good order and in true justice. They come, finally, out of the need for the proper guardianship of public morality (s. 7).

When religious practices conflict with these norms of public order, they are said by the Council to be (*not*, as I said above, outside the scope of the right, so that the right does not *exist* with respect to such practices, but rather) 'abuses of right', against which abuses the government has a 'special duty' to protect public order. (And such special duties are no doubt to be conjoined with governmental Hohfeldian claim-rights/Dworkinian strong rights against interference.)

'Abuse of right' is a juridically improper concept. If it means anything juridically relevant it means *absence* of right, that is, 'no-right' and/or 'duty not...'. The introduction of the phrase 'abuse of rights' is a sign that the speaker is covertly deflating an inflated claim of right. What justification can there be for making claims, knowing that one cannot and will not defend them when questioned about their implications?

The Vatican Council is not, in sum, defending a right to unhindered religious practice. Nobody who is aware of the range and variety of religious practices is likely to want to defend such a claim of right. The Council is asserting that the pursuit of truth about divine things, and the expressions of beliefs about divine things, are important values, important aspects of an individual's worth and dignity, even when the pursuit miscarries, the beliefs are wrong, and the expressions offensive to more reasonable, sensitive, or well-informed men. And as values and as aspects of a citizen's worth, such beliefs and expressions ought at least to be permitted (and at most to be encouraged) unless they threaten public morality, public peace, or the welfare of fellow citizens.[16] All this could have been said without

[15] What the Council actually says is that the right may only 'be exercised' to this extent and subject to these requirements. It is very odd to speak of exercising an immunity; and this oddity is closely related to the juridically improper notion of 'abuse of rights'—on which see my text below.

[16] [Cf. Universal Declaration of Human Rights 1948, Art. 29(2):

> (2) In the exercise of his rights and freedoms, everyone shall be subject only to such limitations as are determined by law solely for the purpose of securing due recognition and respect for the rights and freedoms of others and of meeting the just requirements of morality, public order and the general welfare in a democratic society.

But, for (it seems) reasons like those suggested in *NLNR* 213–15, the Vatican Council's Declaration avoids referring to 'general welfare' or 'common good' as a ground of limitation, and instead justifies limitations of the right to be free from coercion in religious matters on the narrower concept of 'public order', explained as public peace, public morality, and respect for others' rights. Art. 9(2) of the

resorting to overkill about a non-existent 'inviolable right to religious freedom'.

The evils of overkill are considerable. First, nonsense: for example, the talk about 'abuse of rights'. Secondly, evasion: thus the Declaration, uneasily aware of the nonsensicality of 'abuse of rights', pretends that what it is allowing the government to interfere with is 'possible abuses committed *on pretext* of freedom of religion'—thus introducing an irrelevant (and much more tractable) issue about *mala fide* claims of right. Thirdly, devaluation of moral currency: thus genuine and genuinely inviolable rights, such as the right of an innocent person not to be intentionally or negligently killed, are put on the same level as spurious (because inflated) claims of right, and are in danger of being watered down (by people whose common sense exceeds their moral sensitivity) by a compendious exception clause to the effect that *all* human rights are subject to the exigencies of public order... §

NOTES

The analysis set out in this essay is synthesised in *NLNR* 199–205, and was earlier given a thorough workout, in a moral context, in essay III.18 (1973b), sec. I.

† *A perimeter of supporting claim-rights*... a metaphor and conception that I owe to Hart's lectures on Hohfeld, which I heard in the Schools in Oxford in October 1963.

‡ *Drafting of Vatican II's Declaration on Religious Liberty*... n. 14's attribution of this 'probably' to John Courtney Murray SJ goes too far. For a more balanced and exact account of the Declaration, see essay V.4 (2006a).

§ *Is 'abuse of rights' a spurious or juridically improper concept/way of speaking?*... The strenuous position taken in the last three paragraphs of this essay needs some qualification. There is an intelligible doctrine of abuse of right(s) in civil law systems, restricted for the most part to any exercise of rights of owners over their own property which is motivated by spite, malice, or unfair purposes, especially in relation to a neighbour. See now essay II.11 (1995a) and its final endnote.

European Convention on Human Rights avoids general welfare and common good by a somewhat different set of grounds of justified limitation: 'public safety,... protection of public order, health or morals, or... of the rights and freedoms of others'.]

19

ANALOGICAL REASONING IN LAW*

Scott Brewer's paper portrays its thesis as 'the voice of one crying in the wilderness'—or rather 'in this paper'. But of course the paper is the antithesis of a wilderness. It's rich, clear, engaging, and thoroughly illuminating, and will markedly raise the level at which we lawyers and legal theorists commonly understand our intellectual operations. I have learned a great deal from it, and very much hope my few comments will not distract discussion away from it.

Brewer's biblical allusion to the prophetic *vox clamantis* is nicely poised. We cannot tell whether it is from Isaiah 40:3 or Matthew 3:3, and thus are delicately reminded of the radical difference in form between rabbinical practical reasoning (or casuistry), which proceeds characteristically by elaboration of analogies with a dearth (one can think) of appeal to norms, and western scholastic practical reasoning (or casuistry), which proceeds characteristically by elaboration of principles and norms with a dearth (one may think) of appeal to concrete analogies. In Islam (straddled between its Judaic and its Christian sources), the philosophical exposé of the logical deficiencies of reasoning from analogy resulted (I gather) in a contest which in the early middle ages was authoritatively settled by an expulsion of Greek philosophy and a virtual ban on non-analogical forms of practical reasoning.

The express point of Brewer's self-description as a voice crying in the wilderness is, of course, this: in contemporary Anglo-American discourse there are no dissenters from the view that analogical argument is not reducible to deduction. The paper, it says, is the one voice raised in dissent.[1]

* Unpublished commentary (for a conference in Oxford in July 1994) on a draft of Brewer, 'Exemplary Reasoning: Semantics, Pragmatics, and the Rational Force of Legal Argument by Analogy', then entitled 'Interpreting Analogical Legal Interpretive Reasoning Analogically'. My essay (reproduced here with kind permission of Scott Brewer) includes comments on a number of statements, and some argumentation, to be found in Brewer's draft but not in his greatly amplified published paper. Page references to the draft have been eliminated.

[1] [The modified position which Brewer arrives at is articulated at 961:

one striking feature that all of these accounts share is *nondeductivism*: the view that, whatever else the analogical argument may be reduced to, it is *not* reducible to *deduction*. On this judgment,

This thought, that he is the solitary exponent of a deductivist account of analogical reasoning, is illustrated in the footnote which identifies Hospers and MacCormick as examples of opposition to such an account, just because they deny that analogical reasoning has the conclusiveness or compelling force which deduction from a rule would have. Thus Brewer seems to claim, by implication, that in showing its deductive form he will be able to establish the conclusiveness or compelling force of analogical reasoning. Does he make good that implied claim?

Let me raise a doubt, first at a rather low level by raising some questions about the two exemplary cases which Brewer selects to illustrate respectively argument by analogy and argument by disanalogy. Argument by analogy is illustrated by *Adams v New Jersey Steamboat* (1896).[2] My first observation about this is that the argument there adopted and presented by the New York Court of Appeals seems not to have persuaded other state courts; a judgment of the Massachusetts Supreme Judicial Court in 1900, selected as representative by the 1908 editors of the New York State Reports (111 NYS App at 171), remarks: 'In New York... a steamboat is a regarded as a floating inn [*Adams v* [*NJ*] *Steamboat*] but we believe this view is peculiar to that state'.[3] The Massachusetts court, apparently in line with many other state courts, considered it well settled that the strict liability cast on common carriers and innkeepers does not extend to steamboats any more than it extends to railroads, sleeping cars, or 'palace-cars' (whatever they were).

My second observation is that it is difficult to judge the rational force of the argument from analogy in *Adams* (staterooms on riverboats are like, or more like, rooms in inns) without being exposed to and considering the argument from disanalogy which, in order to make room for *Mills v Wyman*,[4] Brewer has left out (staterooms on riverboats are not like, or are less like, sleeping cars on railroads).[5] When one does read that argument, one has the uneasy impression that the considerations adduced to establish the disanalogy with sleeping cars are not convincing, indeed are in most if not all instances completely question-begging:

(1) 'Sleeping-car companies are neither innkeepers nor [common] carriers'—but with what justification are they not treated as carriers?

there are no dissenters. While agreeing that analogical argument is not *reducible* to deduction, I contend that, in some contexts, including the context of argument within legal institutions, deduction plays a far more important role in argument than other theorists have recognized.]

[2] (1896) 151 NY 16. [In Brewer the case is discussed principally at 1003–6, 1013–17.]

[3] *Whicher v Boston & Albany Railroad Co.* 57 NE 601.

[4] (1825) 20 Mass (3 Pick) 207 [see Brewer at 1009–17].

[5] [See now Brewer at 965–6, 1004, 1006–12, 1015–20 for a substantial discussion of the argument to, from or by disanalogy, not least in relation to *Adams*.]

(2) 'A berth in a sleeping car is a convenience of modern origin, and the rules of the common law in regard to carriers or innkeepers have not been extended to this new relation'—but with what justification is the common law so closed to treating like cases alike, whether they happen to be recent or ancient in origin?
(3) Sleeping cars are for 'furnishing extra accommodations, not to the public at large nor to all the passengers, but to that limited number who wish to pay for them'—but cannot exactly the same be justifiably said of cabins on a steamer?
(4) '[T]he passenger [on a train] has no right to expect, and does not expect, the same degree of security from thieves while in an open berth... as in a stateroom of a steamboat, securely locked in and otherwise guarded from intrusion'—but surely the question of analogy or disanalogy concerns not open berths but sleeping cars?
(5) 'The use of sleeping cars by passengers in modern times created relations between the parties to the contract that were unknown at common law, and to which the rule of absolute responsibility could not be applied without great injustice in many cases'—but what is this injustice and why does it not obtain also as between cabin passengers and deck passengers on a steamboat?

The more one looks at the opinion of the court the more it seems clear that the real question was whether the ancient rule of strict liability for common carriers *of goods* and for innkeepers should be extended to relatively new forms of conveyance of passengers in private temporary accommodations, or should be frozen at the technological stage reached in the previous generation (at steamboats) if not restricted altogether to the ancient forms of transport, rather than applied or extended to any and every form of transportation of persons in private temporary accommodation. The deliberations of the court, so far as one can discern them, concern the merits of alternative *rules*, rather than the comparison of particular types of case (inn, steamboat, sleeping car) for their likeness or dissimilarity.

And here I may say a word about *Mills v Wyman* (1836), the case selected by Brewer to illustrate argument by disanalogy. Unlike the judgment in *Adams*, the judgment of Chief Justice Parker in *Mills* makes absolutely no appeal to the concept of analogy. The argumentative structure of the opinion is this:

There is an unquestioned general rule of law ('established for the protection and security of honest and fair-minded men') that verbal promises without consideration are not binding; in some decided cases courts have asserted a universal 'rule' that moral obligation is a sufficient consideration for an express promise; but the 'rule' thus stated is too wide, for 'if moral obligation…is a good substratum for an express promise, it is not easy to perceive why it is not equally good to support an implied promise' such as of parents and children to lend each other support in time of need; but we know that the law withholds its coercive support from such moral obligations, just as it notoriously withholds its support from the moral obligations which arise from express promises admitted to be without consideration. Why then should it lend its support to such a moral obligation by the device of calling the moral obligation good consideration? And in fact the cases which pronounced the 'rule' to that effect are all distinguishable, because in these cases the moral obligation arose in circumstances where there was also good consideration at law and thus a legally binding contract which later was overridden by some legally implemented public policy (for public convenience, rather than the benefit of the party obliged) such as time bar or discharge in bankruptcy. So the 'rule' is not a universal rule that moral obligation is a sufficient consideration for an express promise, but is rather the rule that moral obligation is a sufficient consideration for an express promise 'where at some time or other a good or valuable consideration has existed' to support the relationship between the parties.

Parker CJ's underlying argument, it seems to me, is that if the 'rule' that moral obligation is consideration were accepted, the more fundamental legal rule requiring consideration in contract would be undermined and left incoherent if not empty. He declares that the principles he is announcing 'are deduced from the general current of decided cases upon the subject, as well as from the known maxims of the common law'.

The question in each of these two exemplar cases, then, is whether an ancient rule or principle should be upheld or whether, rather, a competing rule or principle (no liability without fault; morally binding promissory obligations should be legally enforceable) should be extended at the cost either of gutting and effectively abandoning the ancient rule/principle or of maintaining it by the substantively arbitrary device of drawing the line between *old* (steamboats and inns) and *modern* (railroad sleeping cars) types of subject-matter.

Against this background, then, we can express my basic doubt at a somewhat higher level, by pressing the objection which Brewer puts to himself in the part entitled 'Challenging Deductive Analogy'. Argument from analogy is said to have the five-step schema:[6]

(1) x has F and G

(2) y has F and G

[6] [Cf. the modified version of this five-step schema in Brewer at 966 and 1007.]

(3) x also has H
(4) all things that have F and G also have H (or: F and G are sufficient conditions for H)
(5) therefore y has H

What, then, is the point of the *analogy*, the comparison of x with y? Aren't steps (1) and (3) completely redundant, and isn't all the argumentative work done by the simple deduction constituted by (4) (the so-called analogy-warranting rule) as major, (2) as minor, and (5) as conclusion?

And here I may interject a further objection, one which I think Brewer does not put to himself. The schema of argument in five steps fails to display the connection between H and the conjunction of F and G, the connection which Brewer hints at, immediately above the five-step schema, by calling H an 'inferred characteristic', that is, inferred even in the 'source' case x. In the case he is analysing at that point, *Adams*, H means 'has strict liability', and this is indeed inferable from F and G, in the weak but not insignificant sense that the shared characteristics F ('has a client who procures a room for privacy' and G ('has [especially] tempting opportunities for fraud and plunder of client') provide *grounds*, at least defeasible reasons, for H (strict liability).

What is Brewer's reply to the first of these two objections, the objection which he himself forcefully puts? It is that analogy-warranting rules are discovered by an abductive process which proceeds, at least 'in part, by consulting the analogy-warranting principles that organize analogized particular items into a sensible pattern'.[7] But that, it seems to me, is clearly no answer to the objection. For the objection was that reference to the source case, let alone comparison of the source case with the target case, is redundant—unless the analogy-warranting *principles* are discoverable (or usable, consultable) only by and in the course of considering and comparing the source and target cases, x and y respectively. Brewer, surprisingly, does not clearly affirm the necessity for such a consideration and comparison of the source and target cases in his treatment of the example which he selects to illustrate this process; the triangle example. What he *needs* to say is something like: to discover the rule 'all polygons of three straight lines (F) each intersecting the two others at different points (G) are triangles (H)', one needs to inspect a source case (some non-isosceles triangle) and compare it with the target case (some isosceles triangle). But all he

[7] [See Brewer at 1021:

In order for those [analogy-warranting rules] to be compelling, they must be *explained* and *justified* by rationales that are independent of the [analogy-warranting rules] themselves and that organize analogized particular items into a sensible pattern.]

in fact says is: the child may 'sort through characteristics, make use of other things he may have learned about triangles to discern the definitive, deductively applicable rules for triangularity'. And that, it seems to me, is too unfocused a description to make the point his general argument needs: that abduction of the analogy-warranting rule is a process which proceeds by comparison of source and target cases, that is, *by analogical reasoning* if not by analogical (and thus deductive) argument.

Brewer adopts Norwood Hanson's schema of abductive argument, but Hanson's schema[8] in turn was lifted almost word for word from Peirce (whom Brewer also cites in the footnote). Peirce, significantly, used the terms 'abductive' and 'hypothetical' interchangeably, and that was fitting because the conclusion of an abductive inference as described by him[9] (and as described by Hanson) is no stronger than 'Hence there is reason to suspect [Brewer's quotation has Hanson saying "to think"] that H [an explanatory hypothesis] is true'.[10] To Hanson's remarks about perceiving or grasping the pattern in phenomena, which Brewer quotes and subsequently relies upon, one might add the following corroborative but also corrective remark by Hanson's mentor, Peirce:

> The abductive suggestion comes to us like a flash. It is an act of *insight*, although of extremely fallible insight. It is true that the different elements of the hypothesis were in our minds before; but it is the idea of putting together what we had never before dreamed of putting together which flashes the new suggestion before our contemplation.[11]

Brewer of course recognizes all this by noting that 'From the epistemic [as distinct from the logical] point of view, the result of an abduction is an explanatory hypothesis...'.[12] But then I do not see how he can fail to accept that the analogical *part* of his five-step schema of argument has the character of inconclusiveness which was the reason given (as he reports) by Hospers and MacCormick for denying that it is deductive. Since he admits that 'from a logical point of view, the [abductive] inference is a familiar invalid pattern of affirming the consequent...',[13] I don't see, in the end, how he counts his position as being in disagreement with Joseph Raz's claim

[8] Hanson, *Patterns of Discovery* 85–7 [quoted in Brewer at 948].

[9] See Peirce in Buchler, *Philosophy of Peirce*, 151. Peirce in Hartshorne and Weiss, *Collected Papers of Charles Sanders Peirce*, sec. 733 has a very interesting presentation of argument from analogy as involving an abductive or hypothetical inference, an inductive inference, and a final deduction by conjunction of the (fragile) conclusions of the two prior inferences.

[10] Hanson, *Patterns of Discovery*, 86 [quoted in Brewer at 948].

[11] Buchler, *Philosophy of Peirce*, 304 (Peirce's emphasis) [quoted now in Brewer at 979 n. 171]. [On Peirce, see essay 5, sec. 12.]

[12] [See Brewer at 948.]

[13] [See *ibid.* at 949.]

(as Brewer has it) that 'all instances of analogical applications of legal rules are not deductive'.

In short: it seems to me that Brewer's message is not really that analogical argument, *qua* analogical, is truly deductive. Rather it is that analogical reasoning (or, better, insight or understanding) is an intellectually respectable (albeit non-deductive) antecedent[14] to the deductive reasoning from rule to application which is demanded by that regulative ideal which we call the Rule of Law (the ideal rejected, if the story I told earlier is true, in mediaeval Islam).[15]

Peirce worked out his account of abductive or hypothetical reasoning in relation to the natural world (we know that four major planets rotate on their axes and we infer—see reason to hypothesise—that the remaining four probably do likewise). He applied it also, without much explanatory detail, to perception that an object is one of 'a well-recognized kind of object'[16] and to historical inference (there's all this evidence...so there probably was a man Napoleon who...). We should not expect that his accounts, or Hanson's, will apply without adjustment to practical reasoning whether towards free choice in the open domain of an individual's or society's whole life (the moral domain) or towards some confined and postulated goal (the domain of art, *technē* of every kind). Though I think his paper needs a longer final section to work out and exemplify this adjustment, Brewer certainly warns us of the need for such an adjustment by his title and his final words: he is interpreting analogical legal reasoning and (mutatis mutandis) argument *analogically*, that is, I take it, by analogy with, say, scientific reasoning and argument. The terms *analogical reasoning* and *abductive reasoning* are, one may say, analogical: their meaning shifts systematically (that is, according to some principle or rationale) as one shifts from one context to another.

Now that proposition is not, I think, the conclusion of a piece of inferential reasoning, though it is certainly a proposition which one understands and entertains 'in the light of data' (in this case the data one gathers by engaging in and reflecting upon one's various reasonings), and one which one can defend dialectically (as Aristoteleans would say). So it seems to me that the statement which Brewer quotes from me, in which I say (following

[14] [The unfriendly account of Brewer's position by Lloyd Weinreb, e.g. in Weinreb, 'Legal Reason Redux' at 604, is quite inaccurate in representing it as the position that 'analogy functions in legal reasoning as a fuse that has no further function once the fire of reason is lit' and is 'dispensable'. The citations offered by Weinreb do not support the representation.]

[15] [Brewer at 990–7 has a rich discussion of Rule of Law norms and values as the context (also in the Gricean sense) of legal analogies and the pressure towards deductive form in legal argument and judicial judgment.]

[16] Buchler, *Philosophy of Peirce*, 304–5.

Hart, Lonergan, and the Aristotelean tradition) that 'a term is analogical when its meaning shifts systematically (i.e. according to some principle or rationale) as one shifts from one context to another'[17] does not deserve a place in his assemblage of jurists' accounts of analogical argument. 'Accounts of analogy' are not necessarily accounts of analogical reasoning or argument.

[17] *NLNR* 20 [quoted in Brewer at 958].

20

ADJUDICATION AND LEGAL CHANGE*

Law has a double life. It is in force as a matter of fact; historians and contemporary observers can describe—and make predictions about—its content and effect by attending to the opinions and practices prevalent among certain persons and groups, especially courts and their officers. But it has its force by directing the practical reasoning of those persons and groups. And since one engages in practical reasoning to reach normative conclusions (such-and-such ought to be done, or ought not, or is desirable, or permissible, etc.), facts count in practical reasoning only by virtue of some further, normative premise(s), the source of the reasoning's directiveness for decision and action. Law stated *in* such reasoning, not least in judicial reasoning, is stated as a norm, and exists *as* directing one towards or away from decisions and actions, validating or invalidating one's transactions, and so forth, precisely by being itself justified as part of a set of such standards. Law's existence, force, and effect—its life—can always thus be understood as sheer fact (historical or predictable) or alternatively as directive standard. Our law's double life is at the root of the problems, partly substantive, partly illusory, which divided the Lords in *Kleinwort Benson Ltd v Lincoln City Council*,[1] a case important for the law of restitution, but here considered for its jurisprudential interest.

Between 1982 and 1985, payments due under interest rate swap transactions had been made by the appellant plaintiff bank to the respondent councils, in the belief, shared by the parties and other participants in the capital markets, that such transactions were within the council's authority. That belief's correctness was questioned by the Audit Commission in 1987 and denied by the Divisional Court in 1989; by early 1991 the House of Lords had declared[2] that such transactions were at all times *ultra vires* and void. There followed many proceedings in which councils and banks

* 1999c ('The Fairy Tale's Moral').

[1] [1998] UKHL 38, [1999] 2 AC 349.

[2] *Hazell v Hammersmith and Fulham London Borough Council* [1992] AC 1.

recovered from each other the net payments they had made under such transactions; the mechanisms for compelling recovery were orders for rectification of the councils' accounts, and for restitution of payments made without consideration. The present appeal involved transactions in which restitutionary recovery would be time-barred unless founded, not on want of consideration, but on mistake.

In holding that the Local Government Acts did not authorize such transactions, the court in *Hazell* and subsequent proceedings was holding that the rights of the parties were profoundly different from what they had believed them to be when they entered upon the relevant transactions. It was measuring the legal effects of those transactions, and of the payments made under them, against the law which, in and after 1989, it judged to have been applicable to those parties at an earlier time, the time of the transactions and payments.

So the majority of the House in *Kleinwort Benson* were plainly right in holding that the plaintiff had acted under a mistake. The mistake was one of law. Such a mistake is identified by measuring the party's *belief about* the transaction ('this local authority has power to enter this transaction, which thus is binding') against the law applicable to the *transaction*. The law for assessing the validity of the parties' transaction is the law declared in *Hazell*. It would have been indeed surprising had *Kleinwort Benson* concluded that the law for assessing the correctness of the parties' belief about that validity could be other than that same law.

However, Lord Browne-Wilkinson and Lord Lloyd of Berwick dissented, arguing that the question whether the parties had been mistaken in believing their transactions valid and their payments due was not settled by *Hazell*'s declaration that no such transaction was ever valid. Though the transactions were indeed to be assessed by the Local Government Acts as interpreted by the courts in *Hazell*, the parties' belief about their transactions' validity should even now be considered to have been correct if, at the time of the transactions, it was in line with a settled opinion among all lawyers skilled in the field. For such a settled practice and understanding would amount to settled law, or at least to settled 'law'. This proposal to assess beliefs about transactions' validity by a 'rule' contrary to the rule being used to assess that validity seems doubly implausible in relation to the transactions in issue, which few 'skilled lawyers' seem to have considered at all until shortly before the judiciary (as soon as approached) held them inconsistent with statute and underlying constitutional principle. What seems to have made the proposal plausible to the minority was a different, 'paradigm' situation imagined by counsel for the respondents. Postulate a Court of Appeal decision of 1930, unchallenged until 1995 and overruled by the Lords in 1997. Could payments made in 1990, and due if but only if the 1930 decision were good law, be said in 1998 to have been made under a mistake? Surely not (the minority argued); the 1997 decision changed the law established in 1930, and though it was retrospective and retroactive as regards the *rights* of parties affected by the abrogated rule, that 1997 decision could not change the *historical fact* that in 1990 the *belief* that payments were due was correct not mistaken. To hold that belief to have been mistaken would be, they said, to 'falsify history' and to accept 'a fairy tale in which no one any longer believes', the myth that judicial decisions (such as the postulated decision of 1997) do not make or change the law.

The 'paradigm case' gained some immediacy from the fact that *Kleinwort Benson* itself happened to be overruling a line of authority which, though never affirmed by the Lords, went back to some years before 1802. According to those authorities, no restitutionary action could be founded only on a mistake *of law*. The whole House in *Kleinwort Benson* agreed that this restriction was unsound because it corresponded to no principle of justice, was discordant with the unifying restitutionary principle of unjust enrichment, involved a distinction (mistakes of fact v mistakes of law) the enforcement of which yields capricious results, had inevitably been subjected to exceptions and qualifications of similarly capricious effect, and had been abandoned elsewhere in the common law world. So the rule followed in the English courts since 1802 should be set aside. Even the majority in *Kleinwort Benson* described their decision to do so as a decision to 'abrogate' (Lord Goff of Chieveley and Lord Hoffmann) or to 'end' (Lord Hope of Craighead) that rule. So they would have to apply the same analysis to the 'paradigm case': the (postulated) 1997 decision changed the law (postulated to have been) established in 1930. Why, then, were the majority clear and firm that, even in the paradigm case, parties who in 1990 acted on the basis of the 1930 ruling should now, as from the 1997 ruling, be held to have acted on a mistake? A mistaken *prediction* cannot ground a restitutionary action. Should not the imaginary parties in 1990 be said to have made no mistake as to existing facts, and no mistake as to existing law, but only a 'mistake' as to what the Lords would decide at some future date, say 1997?

The answer is that adjudication is not the telling of some story which if accurate might be called history—or prescient prediction—and if inaccurate a myth or fairy tale. Adjudication is the effort to identify the rights of the contending parties *now* by identifying what were, in law, the rights and wrongs, or validity or invalidity, of their actions and transactions *when entered upon and done.* If those rested on a view of the law then widely settled, the judge may nonetheless have the duty now to take and act upon a contrary view of the law if (a) adhering to that former view would conflict with other elements of our law—notably with principles of law and other judicially cognizable policies and standards—applicable then and now to the parties, (b) departing from that former view would not collide with duties specific to the judge (for example the duty to follow a recent decision of the court immediately superior in the hierarchy), and (c) departing from the formerly settled view would not be an injustice to the parties before the court. The facts about precedent and about currently or predictably prevalent opinion enter into judicial reasoning, but even when decisive (as is usual) they have their directiveness only by virtue of legally normative standards—a set of legal standards which, just as they are the source of the authoritativeness of opinion and precedent, can on occasion give reason to reject and depart from even a well-settled and judicially approved understanding of the law.

The 'declaratory theory of law' was mocked by Austin and dismissed by Lord Reid as a 'fairy tale'[3]—as the dissentients in *Kleinwort Benson* recalled with approval. And if it is taken as a 'historical', descriptive assertion, it is of course falsified by the fact that the common law's rules have changed over the centuries. But it is better taken as a way of stating an important element in judicial duty, an element emphasized in Lord Reid's article and well explained here by Lord Goff in approving a 'reinterpreted' declaratory theory: the duty of judges to differentiate their authority and responsibility, and thus their practical reasoning, from that of legislatures. Overlooking the law's double life, the declaratory theory's despisers have not attended to its essential, normative claim.

True, the *Kleinwort Benson* majority may seem to have been, and perhaps were, speaking in the descriptive (historical) mode when they talked of 'abrogating' the old rule about restitution for mistake of law. But when being more precise about their decision, at least two of them spoke differently, articulating their adjudicative action normatively, as being a judicial *application* of long-standing if not permanent legal standards. So Lord Goff:

> When a judge decides a case which comes before him, he does so on the basis of what he understands the law to be.... In the course of deciding the case before him he may, on occasion, develop the common law in the perceived interests of justice...This means not only that he must act within the confines of the doctrine of precedent, but that the change must be seen as a development...of existing principle and so can take its place as a congruent part of the common law as a whole.

[3] Reid, 'The Judge as Law Maker' at 22.

And Lord Hoffmann:

> The [mistake of law] rule is... not founded upon any defensible logic or principle. It is the proper business of your Lordships in a judicial capacity to clarify and develop the common law by restating rules in accordance with principle, even when this may require the correction of ancient heresies.

In this way, he adds (reinforcing the echoes of Dworkin), a properly judicial change in the 'settled view of the law' is to be distinguished from a new rule's adoption 'founded purely upon policy; upon a utilitarian assessment' that the new rule 'would, on balance, do less harm than good'—an adoption which would be improper even for the House of Lords because it 'would be a legislative act in a sense in which the abrogation of the mistake of law rule would not'. (Of course, in saying that the Lords can properly reaffirm principles against even ancient heresies, Lord Hoffmann was not saying that every 'heresy' can properly be corrected by the supreme judicial tribunal. In a case decided six weeks after *Kleinwort Benson*, he said that recent Lords' decisions restricting recoverability in tort for psychiatric injury are a departure from principle, a wrong turning, but one that 'it is too late to go back on'; 'until there is legislative change, the courts must live with them...'.[4]) Lord Hope, while not affirming the declaratory theory of adjudication expressed by Lord Goff and implied by Lord Hoffmann, did join them in holding it inappropriate for judges, as distinct from legislatures, to introduce a rule, of the kind proposed by the minority, denying restitutionary recovery for mistake where the payments were made in accordance with 'a settled view of the law'.

Whether compelling restitution for mistake of law will work injustice in the absence of some such restricting rule, or a newly formulated time bar for actions founded on mistake, is a substantive issue. The majority reasonably decided to wait and see, and to leave any remedy to suitably nuanced legislation, justifiably fearing that the minority's proposed rule would itself work injustice by its inherent uncertainty and lack of nuance. But in any event, it was primarily the illusory philosophical argument against 'falsifying history' that moved the minority, having swallowed the camel of 'retrospective' application of law to past transactions, to strain at the gnat of applying the same law to the accompanying past beliefs about those transactions.

Mistakes of law, because identifiable only by using a legal rule to assess the correctness of beliefs, need not and should not be understood as simply another kind of mistake of fact. Correctly identifying a belief as having been mistaken in law need involve no denial or neglect of any historical

[4] *White* [or *Frost*] *v Chief Constable of South Yorkshire Police* [1999] 2 AC 455 at 500.

fact. The law, in our metaphor, has a double life. One can switch between the descriptive (historical or predictive) and the normative ways of thinking and talking about it, and everyone regularly does. Shifting between these warranted, complementary perspectives, one can without contradiction make statements which, if made from one and the same perspective, would be contradictory. One can say both that a settled rule of common law existed from 1930 to 1997 (or even from 1802 to 1998), *and* that all those years the settled view that the supposed rule is part of our law was an error awaiting correction by better legal reasoning and sound adjudication.

The latter statement can be qualified and amplified. The institutional duty of the Court of Appeal and lower courts to apply the supposed rule until the House of Lords declared the newly clarified law does provide good reason—even within a strictly normative perspective—to speak of the declaration as a 'change', an 'abrogation', and a 'development', with 'retrospective effect', and to treat the superseded rule as having thus been more than merely 'supposed'. (There was surely no such duty or reason in relation to the capital market's legal assumptions set aside in *Hazell* and thus in *Kleinwort Benson* itself; the present reflections concern the different, and rare 'paradigm'.) A higher tribunal, looking beyond prevalent opinions and the purely institutional duties of, say, lower courts, and considering our law as a principled and lasting whole, could with equally good reason declare a contrary rule, and apply it to the parties, their transactions, and their supporting beliefs, as having been at all relevant times legally correct and an authentic legal rule. From this highest-level view of our law as a justifying because justified whole, the newly declared rule would not, in the last analysis, be retroactive—would, in the last analysis, abrogate no part of our law's substantive content. The judicial reasoning towards, and act of declaring, the rule would be fundamentally different from the enactment of new statutory provisions; only in result would it coincide even with that rare form of legislative action which, sometimes reasonably, makes new statutory provisions retroactive.

Indeed—and this is really the point—adjudication involves the duty not to declare and apply a rule unless it can fairly be said to have been all along a legally appropriate standard, more appropriate than alternatives, for assessing the validity and propriety of the parties' transactions. When that can fairly be said, the same rule, having been declared and applied, is clearly the only legally appropriate standard for assessing the *correctness* of the parties' belief in the legal validity and propriety of their transactions. And it will equally be the appropriate standard for judging correct or mistaken the similar belief of parties to legally similar transactions during the period stretching *at least* as far back as it would be reasonable to allow the results of completed but invalid or improper transactions to be disturbed.

Of course, to show that parties made and received payments under such a mistaken belief is, as with any kind of mistake, only one step towards showing that retention of the payment would be *unjust*, by the standards of fairness enforced in the law of restitution. This further question of fairness further divided the minority from the majority in *Kleinwort Benson*, but cannot be taken up here.

NOTE

The main opposing view comes down to the position that the law at a given date is simply what most (competent) lawyers at that date think that the courts would at that date (or very soon afterwards) hold it to be. This raw legal Realism is articulated in Birks and Swadling, 'Restitution' at 397. For a critique of that view, parallel to this essay's, see Sheehan, 'What is a Mistake?'. But it is one thing to say that both the question what the law is at that date, and the question what the law was on that date, are questions of law (not predictions of what the courts would then have held or, indeed, would now hold); it is quite another thing to say, with Sheehan (at 564, adopting 'the Dworkinian approach'), that there is 'always a right answer to any question of law'. If the latter statement is given its Dworkinian interpretation as the jurisprudential proposition that there is (rare cases of ties aside) always a single right answer to questions of law, it goes further than is needed to reject the Realist confusion of prediction or judicial say-so with law. It is enough that there is a sound legal critique of (in the context of the issues debated in this essay) the earlier judicial decision or settled professional opinion, a critique holding that that earlier decision was or is out of line with the law. Judges in a supreme court, at least, can adopt that critique, and apply it to reverse or overrule the earlier decision (and accordingly to hold mistaken-in-law all the professional opinions that were given in line with it), without being rationally required to believe that their deciding that it was legally wrong (i.e. mistaken) and should be overruled is just like enacting a retroactive statute, or to believe that any fellow judge dissenting is—at the moment of judging!—judging contrary to the law (i.e. simply mistakenly). The dogmatic, *res judicata* content of the prevailing decision of the court is, admittedly, 'this is the one right answer' and contrary judgments and opinions are mistakes of law. But just as that is not the whole story for legal doctrine and argumentation outside that adjudication and beyond that 'moment', so it is not the whole or best story jurisprudentially. See the penultimate paragraphs of sec. III of the Introduction, at 13–15.

Part Four

The Two Senses of 'Legal System'

21

REVOLUTIONS AND CONTINUITY OF LAW*

...the State and its legal order remain the same only as long as the constitution is intact or changed according to its own provisions.[1]

INTRODUCTION

Devolution of authority from the Imperial Crown in Parliament has been followed, rather regularly, by revolution within the new states of the Commonwealth. Judicial and academic accounts of both devolution and revolution have been largely dominated by a theory of legal discontinuity. In its simple form, this theory asserts that every illegal change in the constitution of a state is a revolution, and that a revolution overturns the entire legal order, replacing it with a new system.[2]

* 1971a ('Revolutions and Continuity of Law').

[1] Kelsen, *GTLS* 368. See also Kelsen, *The Pure Theory of Law*, 209. Below, nn. 2, 14.

[2] Hans Kelsen is the principal exponent of this view, and has been relied upon in the judicial decisions mentioned below, nn. 22 and 62. There are, however, problems in interpreting his texts. Thus *GTLS* 117 appears to be defining 'revolution' as that which 'occurs whenever the legal order of a community is nullified and replaced by a new order in...a way not prescribed by the first order itself'. But other passages show that Kelsen's argument is not simply *ex definitione*. For example, *GTLS* 368 says:

> To assume that the continuity of national law, or—what amounts to the same—the identity of the State, is not affected by revolution or *coup d'état*, as long as the territory and the population remain by and large the same, is possible only if a norm of international law is presupposed recognizing victorious revolution and successful *coup d'état* as legal methods of changing the constitution. No jurist doubts, for instance, that it is legally the same Russian State that existed under the tsarist constitution and that now exists under the bolshevist constitution and under the new name of U.S.S.R. But this interpretation is not possible if we, ignoring international law, do not go beyond the Russian constitution as it exists at a given moment. Then the continuity of the legal order and the identity of the Russian State become incomprehensible. If the situation is judged from this point of view, the State and its legal order remain the same only as long as the constitution is intact or changed according to its own provisions.

See also *ibid.*, 117–19, 220–1; Kelsen, *The Pure Theory of Law*, 209–10. For expositions of similar views, see Cattaneo, *Il concetto di rivoluzione nella scienza del diritto*, 96–8, and the works cited in O'Connell, *State Succession in Municipal Law and International Law*, i, 101, n. 2.

Exponents of this theory of discontinuity are well aware that in almost all cases the content of the post-revolutionary legal system is similar, if not identical, to that of the pre-revolutionary system.[3] Both the general rules of law (especially private law) and the particular rights (contractual, real, remedial, etc.) actually acquired under those rules are likely to survive, in the sense that 'the same' rules and rights will be enforced after as before the revolution. Still, the fact that the law of property is 'the same' in one country as in another does not imply that one and the same rule is in force in both countries. Likewise, the fact that the law of property in a certain country is 'the same' at one time as at another does not entail that one and the same rule is in force at both times. If the two times are separated by a revolution, then on the theory of discontinuity the law will not be one and the same, since the basis or reason for the validity of the rules will be different. Every rule has its particular identity as part of a particular system, and the identity of a system changes (it is said) when its constitution, its basic norm, its rule of recognition, is changed in a manner not legally permitted or provided for.

The theory, so stated, has an engaging elegance and simplicity. Closer examination reveals, however, that it is ambiguous and arbitrary, and that these defects are the shortcomings of a central tradition of modern legal philosophy. So before raising questions about the truth of the theory, it will be as well to clarify its meaning. Two questions immediately arise, the first concerning the *sufficient* conditions of a change in the identity of a legal system, the second concerning the *necessary* conditions of such change:

(1) Does every illegal or 'unconstitutional' act, of the sort that would usually be called a *coup d'état*, amount to a change in the constitution and thus in the identity of the legal order? Or is there a class of *coups d'état* that, while illegally supplanting legal officials, nevertheless leave the constitution, in Kelsen's sense, intact?

(2) Can there be a change in the identity of a legal system otherwise than by violation of some rule of the system existing at the time of the supposed change?

I. THE PROBLEM OF THE *COUP D'ÉTAT*

In his exposition of the theory of discontinuity, Kelsen says that he includes *coups d'état* among the revolutions that effect the destruction and creation

[3] Usually, the new men whom a revolution brings to power annul only the constitution and certain laws of paramount political significance... A great part of the old legal order 'remains' valid also within the frame of the new order... The laws which, in the ordinary inaccurate parlance, continue to be valid are, from a juristic standpoint, new laws whose import coincides with that of the old laws. (*GTLS* 117–18; cf. *The Pure Theory of Law*, 209–10.)

of legal systems.[4] But other exponents have been hesitantly willing to recognize a category of unconstitutional acts which involve a modification of the law in force without bringing to birth a new legal system, because these acts do not affect the supreme source or criterion of validity of the system.[5] It will be convenient stipulatively to name this category the 'mere *coup d'état*', without assuming either that this is what Kelsen means when he uses the term *coup d'état*, or that the distinction thus drawn will still be viable at the end of a jurisprudential analysis.

A modern lawyer, contemplating the accession of a usurper to the throne, is likely to say:

> The answer, which Kelsen has taught us to analyse correctly, is that the old legal order [gives] way to a new, which [may] happen to coincide largely in content with the old…it [is] the rules of the new, not the old order, which require his subjects to bear him allegiance.[6]

The Year Books thought otherwise. When, for example, the Yorkist Edward IV seized the throne in 1461, the Lancastrian kings from Henry IV to Henry VI were officially regarded as usurpers who had overthrown the true line of succession. So when a question arose about the validity of the acts of the Lancastrians, counsel argued, apparently with success:

> It is necessary that the Realm should have a king under whose authority laws will be held and upheld, and though [Henry VI] was in power by usurpation, any judicial act done by him and touching Royal jurisdiction would be valid, and will bind the rightful king when the latter returns to power.[7]

The language of this successful argument of counsel brings out the issue. There is a 'realm' in which 'authority' is exercised by the 'king' by way of 'judicial acts' of 'Royal jurisdiction'. Into this structure of offices or jurisdictions the usurper inserts himself; he disturbs the monarch but not the monarchy. Of course, usurpations were not without legal consequence; for example, all royal commissions had to be renewed and all suits in the royal courts recommenced. But this in any event occurred, in English law,

[4] *GTLS* 117; Kelsen, *The Pure Theory of Law*, 209; cf. below, text at n. 14.

[5] See e.g. Cattaneo, *Il concetto di rivoluzione nella scienza del diritto*, 70.

[6] Honoré, 'Allegiance and the Usurper' at 233; but cf. the later article, Honoré, 'Reflections on Revolution'.

[7] Pluis d'assis Bagot, ore fuit le matter reherce et touche, que non obstante cel act les patentes de legitimation sont bones, car le roy H. fuist roy en possession, et il covient que le roialme eit un roy south que les leyes serront tenus et maintenus, donque par ce que il ne fuist eins forsque par usurpation, uncore chescun act judicial fait par luy que touche jurisdiction roial serra bon, et liera le roy de droit quant il fait regresse, etc. (*Bagot's Case* (1469) YB 9 Edw IV, Pasch, pl. 2.)

See Chrimes, *English Constitutional Ideas in the Fifteenth Century*, 55–6, 369; Vinogradoff, *Collected Papers* (1928), i, 199. On *Bagot's Case* and subsequent authorities, see *State v Carroll* 38 Connecticut 449 (1871); *In re Aldridge* (1894) 15 NZLR 361 at 369 et seq.; *Adams v Adams* [1971] P 188 at 210.

on the death of the monarch. Significantly, constitutional law in the age of usurpations dealt with usurpation and the death of the king alike as 'demise of the Crown'.[8] There was no question of glossing over or minimizing the illegality of usurpation; the constitutional lawyers did not deal kindly with the attempts sometimes made to justify treason by alleging that allegiance is due to the Crown rather than to the king.[9] But the self-interpretation of English law has been clear and definite in its assertion that the law, even the constitutional law, of the kingdom is affected neither in content nor in identity by *coups* and counter-*coups*.

This interpretation, moreover, seems eminently reasonable. So it is not surprising that some exponents of the theory of discontinuity are unwilling to include *coups d'état* among law-destroying revolutions. But their hesitations are also understandable, for if an exception is to be made in favour of mere *coups d'état*, where is the line to be drawn? May not the exception in favour of continuity swallow up the rule of discontinuity?

It is tempting to suggest that a line between law-destroying revolutions and mere *coups d'état* can be fixed as follows: in a mere *coup d'état* only the rules governing the succession of persons to legal office are affected; the rules concerning the powers and hierarchy of the offices themselves are unaffected. This suggestion seems to correspond to a suggestion made by Hart, that there is a category of acts which entail only the legally unauthorized substitution of a new set of individuals as officials;[10] the suggested distinction would, moreover, explain the attitude of English lawyers to usurpations of the Crown. But before the suggestion could be adopted, it would be necessary to show that it is consistent with the premises of the theory of discontinuity which it is designed to make more palatable. So it is necessary to examine those premises more closely.

[8] Kantorowicz, *The King's Two Bodies*, 371 and works there cited. See also the argument of counsel (following the opinion of the judges in the *Case of the Duchy of Lancaster* (1561) I Plowden 212 at 213) in *Willion v Berkley* (1561) Plowden 225 at 234 (75 ER 339 at 355):

> ...the King has two capacities, for he has two bodies, the one whereof is a body natural, consisting of natural members as every other man has...; the other is a body politic, and the members thereof are his subjects...; and this body is not subject to passions as the other is, nor to death, for as to this body the King never dies, and his natural death is not called in our law (as Harper said) the death of the King, but the demise of the King, not signifying by the word (*demise*) that the body politic of the King is dead, but that there is a separation of the two bodies, and that the body politic is transferred and conveyed over from the body natural now dead, or now removed from the dignity royal to another body natural. So that it signifies a removal of the body politic of the King of this realm from one body natural to another.

See also Blackstone, *Commentaries* I, 249.

[9] See Kantorowicz, *The King's Two Bodies*, 364–6; Blackstone, *Commentaries* I, 249.

[10] *CL* 118 [1961 ed. 115].

In any constitution distributing authority among officials or estates there will be, inter alia, three categories of rules:[11]

A. *rules of succession to office*, including rules governing both accession to and succession in office or estate;

B. *rules of competence*; rules governing the distribution of powers as between offices or estates;

C. *rules of succession of rules*, including all rules (whether or not included also in category *A* or category *B* or both) governing the amendment, suspension, or replacement of rules of each of these three categories.

Even in the simplest absolute monarchy, the *rules of succession to office* governing succession to the Crown may be liable to lawful alteration, and such alteration will be regulated by a *rule of succession of rules* which happens to coincide with the simple *rule of competence* governing legislative authority, viz. 'What Rex enacts, and only what Rex enacts, is law.'[12]

Granted the clear and distinct conception of *rules of succession of rules*, it is open to the jurist to explain the validity of the existing constitution by reference to the rules of the preceding constitution, and in particular by reference to that rule of the preceding constitution which governed the amendment or replacement of that constitution. Thus, with Kelsen, the jurist can proceed back, via a succession of *rules of succession of rules*, to a 'historically first constitution'. This constitution, by definition, emerged without legal authority, and can be regarded as the ultimate and highest posited source of validity of the existing constitution and thence of the whole existing legal system. On Kelsen's recent analysis, the *Grundnorm* is an injunction (not posited but 'fictively' postulated 'as if' it were the content of an act of will) to obey the will of the founders of this 'historically first constitution'.[13]

But although *rules of succession to office* are distinct from *rules of succession of rules*, rules of the former category cannot be violated by an overt usurper without violating some rule of the latter category. For because overt usurpation is not a once-for-all act accomplished at some *punctum temporis* like a murder, but involves a claim to *hold* office, it is more than merely the violation of some rule or rules. To usurp the Crown in an absolute monarchy is to insist that the particular *rule of succession to office*

[11] The analysis which differentiates these three categories is adapted ad hoc to the problem of the *coup d'état*, and is not intended to supplement or supplant more fundamental analyses of types of rule or norm.

[12] Cf. Hart, 'Review of Fuller's *The Morality of Law*' at 1295.

[13] Kelsen, *The Pure Theory of Law*, 200; 'On the Pure Theory of Law' at 6; *GTLS* 115–16.

identifying the lawful holder of royal office shall be *changed*, at least so that it becomes a rule identifying the usurper as the present lawful holder (even if the usurper has no dynastic ambitions and is content that, after him, the succession to office shall be determined as if there had been no usurpation). Now *ex hypothesi*, this change or amendment or abrogation or suspension of some *rule of succession to office* is accomplished in violation of some *rule of succession of rules* which governs the change, amendment, abrogation, or suspension of constitutional rules: otherwise an overt usurpation would not be identifiable as such.

Therefore, even if Kelsen were to accept the suggestion that there is a distinguishable category of mere *coups d'état* in which the *rules of succession to office* are affected while leaving the *rules of competence* governing the powers of the offices unaffected, he would have to point out that the effect of a *coup* on rules of the former category entails a violation of some *rule of succession of rules*. Because of this violation, rules generated and legal acts done after the *coup* cannot be traced back to the same sources of validity as rules and acts before the *coup*; the unity of the system is broken; there are two systems, and only the system interpreted as including the post-*coup* constitutional rules (of each category) is effective and, consequently, existent as an object of legal cognition (that is, valid). Thus Kelsen is bound in consistency to reject the distinction between law-destroying revolutions and mere *coups d'état*. And this, on the whole, he does (although he accepts, perhaps inconsistently, that a usurpation of *supreme judicial* office effects only a 'revolutionary partial change', not a 'revolutionary total change' of the constitution).[14]

But if the notion that the unity of a legal system is constituted by derivation, via rules of succession of rules, from a historically first constitution demands a clear and unequivocal rejection of the mere *coup d'état* as a jurisprudential category, it is the occasion of doubt and equivocation in answering our second question, to which we now turn.

II. THE PROBLEM OF LAWFUL DEVOLUTION

On the theory of discontinuity, all revolutions effect a change in the identity of a legal system. But can such a change be effected otherwise than by a 'revolution'?

[14] Kelsen, *The Pure Theory of Law*, 276. Note that it is possible to imagine circumstances which might be styled a *coup d'état* but which might involve no violation of constitutional law and would thus constitute an exception to our demonstration that all *coups d'état* are revolutions in the Kelsenian sense: e.g. if the Vice-President were to assassinate the President of a state whose constitution provided that the Vice-President should succeed the President on his death from whatever cause (provided that the legal system did not contain the rule that no man may profit from his own wrong).

At one level, this question raises no more than a terminological difficulty, visible in Kelsen's expositions,[15] in the use of the term 'revolution'. For, on the one hand, the term can be used to indicate simply an effective seizure and exercise of rule-making power or authority in violation of, at least, some rule of succession of rules. On the other hand, the term can be used to indicate any situation in which the speaker considers that a change in the identity of a legal system has been effected, whether by division of one system into two, or by absorption of several into one, or for some other reason. When, in the theory of discontinuity, it is affirmed that 'all revolutions effect a change in the identity of a legal system', the term 'revolution' is used in the former sense; and this is its sense throughout this essay.

However, at another level, the present question—Can the identity of a legal system be changed without violating some existing rule?—exposes important difficulties in the Kelsenian model of a legal system. According to that model, all the rules of a system are linked to each other by common derivation from the rules of competence in a 'historically first constitution', the derivation being governed and verified by reference to rules of succession of rules. Now, given these rules of succession of rules, it is clear that the *original* rules of competence in the historically first constitution need no longer be 'in force'; they may have been replaced by other rules of competence in accordance with the relevant rule of succession of rules; and this rule may have itself replaced an earlier rule of succession of rules in accordance with the earlier rule's reflexive provisions for its own replacement. As Kelsen puts it:

> If we ask for the reason of the validity of the constitution... we may, perhaps, discover an older constitution; that means the validity of the existing constitution is justified by the fact that it was created according to the rules of an earlier constitution by way of a constitutional amendment. In this way we eventually arrive at a historically first constitution that cannot have been created in this way and whose validity, therefore, cannot be traced back to a positive norm created by a legal authority; we arrive, instead, at a constitution that became valid in a revolutionary way, that is, either by breach of a former constitution *or for a territory that formerly was not the sphere of validity of a constitution and of a national legal order based on it.*[16]

The passage italicized is ambiguous: it may refer simply to formerly 'uncivilized' regions; or it may refer to territories that once were merely *part* of a larger territorial sphere of validity, as, say, Pakistan was once, in law, a part (and not even a sub-unit identifiable as such) of the British

[15] Above, n. 2. [16] Kelsen, *The Pure Theory of Law*, 200 (emphasis added).

Empire and constitutionally subject to the general imperial rule that 'what the Queen in the Imperial Parliament enacts is law'. But in the latter case, the problem becomes evident: save by way of a *breach* of a former constitution, how can the Pakistani legal system have managed to separate from the Imperial (British) legal system? After all, ultimate rule-making authority over Pakistan was transferred to the Constituent Assembly of Pakistan by the Indian Independence Act 1947, an Imperial statute enacted in accordance with British constitutional rules of succession of rules. No breach or violation of law occurred.

Indeed, the Kelsenian analysis is often felt to derogate from the genuine independence of former imperial territories. The demand has been raised for a 'local root' of sovereignty or constitutional authority, for a 'shift in the *Grundnorm*', for 'autochthony'. Great care has, on occasion, been taken to perform some unauthorized act in the course of transfer of authority, so that it may be claimed that, *because* there has been a revolution, *therefore* the validity of the new constitution legal order *cannot* be traced back to the British imperial constitution.[17] The problem has been familiar to continental jurists, too: when an absolute monarch grants a constitution purporting to limit his rule-making authority (an *octroi* constitution), one can dispute endlessly whether the new rule perhaps gets its validity from the old, or whether the old rule has been completely superseded and eliminated.[18]

These disputes get their heat from the practical question whether or not the new rule and constitution could be repealed by an exercise of authority under the old rule and constitution. Could the Imperial Parliament reassert its authority over Pakistan? Perhaps one will be inclined to say, with Hart, that according to British law it can, but according to Pakistani law it cannot.[19] This answer, however, evades rather than settles the theoretical problem, which arises from the fact that, on the Kelsenian analysis back to a historically first constitution, the 'Pakistani legal system' seems to be no more than a sub-unit in the British legal system, from which it cannot be freed save by way of some violation of British law. Nor will it suffice to say that the Indian Independence Act was *intended* to transfer rule-making authority over Pakistan irrevocably away from the Imperial Parliament.

[17] See Wheare, *The Constitutional Structure of the Commonwealth* ch. IV. Cf. also Latham, *The Law and the Commonwealth* esp. 534–40; Roberts-Wray, *Commonwealth and Colonial Law*, 289–301.

[18] The discussion in Raz, *CLS* 102–3, of a case of 'peaceful transfer of powers' (cf. 107), while making a valid point against Kelsen (along lines similar to those developed in this essay), rather minimizes the need for a fully developed legal theory of independence by relying on a supposed 'general consensus of both lay and professional opinion', which consensus is in fact often lacking. 'This opinion is completely justified' says Raz; but this he assumes rather than explains (and cf. *CLS* 34, 188). See also n. 49 below.

[19] *CL* 121 [118].

For, on the one hand, one can reply that the British rule of succession of rules, as it existed in 1947, did not itself authorize the Imperial Parliament to transfer parliamentary authority irrevocably away ('Parliament cannot bind its successors'). And on the other hand, one can reply, more radically, that if, as the Kelsenian analysis entails, an earlier constitution is the source of the validity of later constitutions, there seems no reason why it should not validate a rule purporting to repeal a later constitution, whether or not the later constitution authorizes such repeal. To this radical suggestion, it would be no sufficient rejoinder to say that the old constitution (or rule of succession of rules) and the new 'relate to different periods of time';[20] for the whole problem, on the Kelsenian analysis, is *how* they relate to different periods of time, granted that the earlier constitution is as much the *present* source of the validity of the remotest and latest of its lawful successors as it was (is?) the source of the validity of all the intermediate, lawfully repealed constitutions in the historical succession of constitutions.

Various attempts have been made to escape from the obviously unsatisfactory analytical state of affairs indicated in the preceding paragraph. The most common escape is by arguing that a constitution, or at least an ultimate rule of succession of rules, *cannot* be wholly replaced in accordance with its own stipulations; purported replacements are really 'legal camouflage' for a 'peaceful revolution' in which the replacement is a *break* with the past, accomplished by 'universal consent', or transfer of allegiance,[21] or by a 'factual social psychological change in the political ideology', accomplished by a 'magical act which alone can loose the bond forged by' the pre-existing rule of succession of rules.[22] In this argument we discern the theoretical pressures underlying the ambiguity, mentioned at the beginning of this section, in the legal use of the term 'revolution'. To minimize the ambiguity Alf Ross named the relevant 'social-psychological change' not 'peaceful revolution' but 'evolution'[23] (to be contrasted, no doubt, with lawful 'devolution').

In favour of this view, Ross offered a number of arguments. One was that it is logically impossible for a proposition to refer to itself; thus a rule

[20] Cf. Hart, 'Self-Referring Laws', in *Festskrift till Karl Olivecrona* at 314.

[21] Wade, 'The Basis of Legal Sovereignty' at 196.

[22] Ross, *On Law and Justice*, 83; cf. n. 48 below. Similarly, on a practical level, Beadle CJ reasoned (in the case on the status of the revolutionary Rhodesian government) that after a complete change from one constitution to another, the position of a judge who was appointed under and accepted the earlier constitution is the same when the change was effected in defiance of the rules of change in the earlier constitution as when it was in accordance with them. In either case, the earlier constitution is 'completely gone' and 'non-existent' 'for all purposes'; so the judge must simply make a free option to accept or not to accept the new constitution: *Madzimbamuto v Lardner-Burke* 1968 (2) SA 284, 328–9.

[23] Ross, *On Law and Justice*, 81.

of succession of rules cannot provide reflexively for its own supercession.[24] The alleged logical impossibility, however, has not impressed all logicians,[25] let alone the many British draftsmen who nowadays resort to double (that is, reflexive) entrenchment of constitutional provisions; so we propose to ignore the argument here. More pertinent was Ross's argument that where a constitutional clause governing constitutional amendment is amended in accordance with its own rules, the new amending clause cannot be regarded as derived from the old, or as valid because derived from it.

> Any such derivation presupposes the validity of the superior norm and thereby the continued existence of the same, and by derivation cannot be established a new norm which conflicts with the source of the derivation.[26]

Hart replied that there is no conflict if a rule of amendment is amended in accordance with its own provisions, for the original rule and the amended rule relate to different periods of time.[27] This reply is correct as far as it goes; but, as we have already remarked, it fails to recognize that for Ross the source of the difficulty was that (on any view other than his own) the original rule *remains* in some way 'in force' as a source of the validity of the amended rule—so that, as Ross insisted, it is hard to see why an amendment of the amended rule should not rely for *its* validity, too, on the original rule rather than on the former amended rule,[28] in which case there would indeed be a conflict, though perhaps not precisely the conflict indicated by Ross.

A consideration of Hart's *Concept of Law* reveals why he displayed little sympathy for Ross's difficulty, and why he summarily dismissed as 'questionable' Ross's 'statement that a derivation of a new norm presupposes not only the validity of the superior norm but its continued existence after the creation of the new norm'.[29] For in Hart's analysis of legal system the transtemporal validation of basic rules, relied on by Kelsen and recognized as troublesome by Ross, is simply and silently omitted.

> Is this purported by-law of the Oxfordshire County Council valid? Yes: because it *was* made in exercise of the powers conferred, and in accordance with the procedure specified, by a statutory order made by the Minister of Health.... Finally, when the validity of the statute has been queried and assessed by reference to the rule that what the Queen in Parliament enacts is law, *we are brought to a stop in inquiries concerning validity*: for we have reached a rule which...is...unlike

[24] *Ibid.*, 81; see also Ross, 'On Self-Reference and a Puzzle in Constitutional Law' at 7–17, and n. 48 below.

[25] See Hart, 'Self-Referring Laws', in *Festskrift till Karl Olivecrona* at 316.

[26] Ross, *On Law and Justice*, 82.

[27] Above, n. 20.

[28] Ross, *On Law and Justice*, 83.

[29] Above, n. 20.

[the intermediate statutory order and statute] in that there is no rule providing criteria for the assessment of its own legal validity.[30]

For Hart, the existence of a rule of recognition is simply a present matter of fact. Likewise, the question whether a legal system retains its identity or has become two legal systems is simply a question of fact (though it *can* also be regarded as a question of law within a given system of law),[31] and the answer to the question is in no way affected by the way in which this matter of fact came about. The result is the same, whether the parent legislature 'retire[d] from the scene by removing legislative power over the former colony', or whether there was a revolutionary 'break' by violence: in either case 'the ultimate rule of recognition now accepted and used [no longer includes], among the criteria of validity, any reference to the operations of legislatures of other territories'.[32]

But can we accept Hart's escape from the problem of the temporal dimension of legal rules and systems? We can, only if we stifle legitimate questions. I shall devote the rest of this section of this essay to raising and evaluating two particular lines of questioning.

(1) In the first place, can we accept that, after a change of rule of recognition, the new rule of recognition 'no longer includes *any* reference to the operation of legislatures of other territories'? Suppose that in Australia the rule of recognition changed, in 1942, from 'What the Westminster Parliament enacts is law' to 'What the Canberra Parliament enacts is law',[33] and suppose (for the time being) that no questions are raised about the basis of the latter rule; there remain urgent questions about the basis of the *present* validity of the whole set of legal rules in force in Australia immediately *before* the change. It seems that the new rule of recognition must indeed contain a clause identifying as law all those rules, not since repealed, that were valid immediately before the change; and such rules can only be identified compendiously as those valid by virtue of enactment by the Westminster Parliament before 1942 or 1939. Thus the new rule of recognition must indeed include a clause referring to the operations of a foreign legislature, albeit to operations in the past. In a later work, Hart has said:

In any full description of the criteria used by the courts after [a] revolutionary break in ascertaining the law, the old legislation would have to be specifically mentioned *eo nomine*. Had there been no revolution, it would have been identified

[30] *CL* 107 [103–4] (emphasis added). [31] *Ibid.*, 121 [118]. [32] *Ibid.*, 121 [117–18].

[33] Cf. Statute of Westminster Adoption Act 1942 (Comm. of Aust.), bringing the Statute of Westminster 1931 (Imp.) into force in Australia as from 3 September 1939. Of course, the real rule of recognition in Australia may be thought of as changing in 1942, 1939, 1931, or even earlier or even later.

by reference to the general provision qualifying the unbroken succession of legislators. After the revolution, therefore, the validity of the old legislation comes to rest on a different rule of recognition from before.[34]

Hart is not here considering the problem of colonial independence. But how would his remarks apply to that problem? After Australian independence, *however attained*, the Australian courts will accept a rule specifically mentioning the old legislation '*eo nomine*'. True, and can we not go on to say that, if independence was attained by virtue (at least indirectly) of an Act of the Westminster Parliament the old legislation can still be identified 'by reference to the general provision qualifying the unbroken succession of legislators'? What is 'broken' about the succession from the Westminster to the Canberra Parliament, if that succession was regulated by a rule of succession of rules, in force at the time of the succession? Hart could reply, perhaps, that if the succession of legislators is not broken, nevertheless the succession of rules of succession of rules is broken because the rule of succession of rules in 1940 was 'Whatever rule of succession of rules the Westminster Parliament enacts is law', whereas after 1940 it is 'Whatever rule of succession of rules the Canberra Parliament enacts, with the approval of a referendum[35] is law'. But this reply would not suffice, since there seems no reason to call this change from one rule of succession of rules to another 'a break', except the assertion that rules of succession of rules cannot be regarded as reflexive. This assertion would indeed save Hart's opinion, in the *Concept of Law*, that the rule of recognition in a newly independent territory is not affected, in nature, content, or jurisprudentially recognizable *raison d'être*, by its mode of creation.[36] But, of course, it would not cohere with his insistence, as against Ross, that the ultimate rules of succession of rules in a system can indeed be reflexive. For what would be the point of insisting on the reflexive capacity of a rule of succession of rules (rule *A*) if one at the same time insisted that the legal validity of any successor (rule *B*) to rule *A* would be legally unquestionable *whether or not* rule *B* had been created in accordance with the reflexive provisions of rule *A*? Yet Hart does insist that no question can be raised about the legal basis of the rule of recognition, that here 'we are brought to a stop in inquiries concerning validity'.[37] And this provokes our second line of questions.

[34] Hart, 'Review of Fuller's *The Morality of Law*' at 1295.

[35] Cf. Constitution of the Commonwealth of Australia 1900, s. 128. Note, incidentally, that this constitution was promulgated as a Schedule to an Imperial Act, 63 and 64 Vict. c. 12.

[36] *CL* 121 [117–18].

[37] *CL* 107 [104]. Cf. also Kelsen, *The Pure Theory of Law*, 195: 'This final norm's validity cannot be derived from a higher norm, the reason for its validity *cannot be questioned*' (emphasis added).

(2) Is not the outlawing of further questions always an occasion of suspicion in theoretical study? And in this context, is it not particularly dubious? Hart's 'rule of recognition' is a complex of disparate elements. One of these elements is a power-conferring rule (that is, rule of competence) qualifying, here and now, a rule-making body to create rules.[38] But we have seen that there is another element, viz. a rule of identification, which is not a rule of competence since it confers no powers on any existing body, but which identifies, and validates, *eo nomine* and for the present, the rules created in the past by a rule-making body that then was, but now perhaps is not, qualified (by a rule of competence) to create those rules. And this present rule of identification does not itself rest on, nor is it identified by reference to, any existing rule of competence. Hart wishes to say that, as with the existing basic rules of competence, its existence is a matter of fact, viz. the fact of 'the rule of recognition', which is to be counted as one rule because, notwithstanding their multiplicity, the rules of competence and identification within it are 'unified by their hierarchical arrangement'.[39] But, to repeat, this hierarchical arrangement is one of 'relative subordination' *not* of derivation.[40] This is to say, the rule of identification supporting the pre-revolutionary or pre-independence law is not itself supported by or derived from the rules of competence (although it is subordinate to them insofar as the present rule-making body is authorized to repeal the pre-existing law). It exists by virtue of the fact of 'official acceptance'.

Now if there is, in a system, a rule that does not depend for its existence on present rules of competence, one can raise the question whether perhaps there are other rules similarly independent, existing simply by virtue of the fact of their official acceptance. And one can raise the more radical question whether *any* rule need be regarded as dependent on present rules of competence. Perhaps all rules exist simply by virtue of the fact of their official acceptance?

It might be replied that the function of Hart's rule of recognition is to explicate the word 'official' in the phrase 'official acceptance'. But this reply would overlook the fact that, on Hart's own account, the rule of recognition

[38] There are problems about this. Hart says that 'rules of the second type confer powers' (*CL* 81 [79]), and the rule of recognition is of this second type. Moreover, a standard formulation of the rule of recognition is 'What the Queen in Parliament enacts is law' (*CL* 107 [104], 120 [117] etc.); in this formulation the ambulatory present tense of 'enacts' suggests that the rule includes (a) a 'rule of change' qualifying the acts (including speech acts) of certain persons at time T_1 as authentic 'acts in the law' (i.e. valid *acts* of legislation), as well as (b) a rule of identification enabling the products of those acts of legislation to be recognized as valid *rules* at all times subsequent to T_1. On the other hand, Raz (*CLS* 199) is confident that 'this [sc. that the rule of recognition is a power-conferring rule] is not Hart's intention, as he himself confirmed to me', but is rather a duty-imposing rule. In short, the rule of identification also imposes a duty on officials to apply the rules it identifies.

[39] Hart, 'Review of Fuller's *The Morality of Law*' at 1293.

[40] *CL* 101 [98].

may contain at least one element which is not a rule of competence indicating who is 'official': for it may contain a rule of identification indicating as valid all those existing rules that cannot be regarded as supported by existing rules of competence. And the radical question can be pressed by another route. If there is a set of rules which depend, not on any 'existing' rule of competence, but on a rule of identification incorporating 'past' rules of competence, why should this set be privileged and peculiar? Why should we not say of all the other rules of the system that, once created according to the then existing rules of competence, they no longer depend for their validity on those rules *qua* 'present' rules of competence, but rather depend on a 'present' rule of identification incorporating those rules of competence *qua* 'past' (that is, *qua* 'present' at the relevant times, 'past', of their creation)? The drift of these questions is obvious: may it not be the case that revolutions of all sorts, disturbing only rules of competence, need not be regarded as disturbing any other rules of the system, since all these other rules can be regarded as based on rules of identification which the revolution may leave quite unaffected?

The questions just raised call for exploration even if one accepts, as I do not, that it is obvious that no questions can be raised about the legal basis of the rule of recognition insofar as it is a present rule of competence.

To recapitulate; we set about our examination of the theory of discontinuity by asking about the sufficient and necessary conditions for a change in the identity of a legal system. Analysis of the *coup d'état* showed that, if any revolution accomplishes, *eo ipso*, a change in the identity of a legal system, a *coup d'état* must do likewise. But the second question, whether there are methods of changing the identity of a legal system otherwise than by revolution, proved more resistant to analysis. Standard discussions of the problem differ widely. At the root of the differences lies a disturbing obscurity about the very object of legal theory, the legal system. Kelsen considered that 'past' constitutions, if they have been replaced in accordance with their own reflexive provisions, are in some way a present part of the legal system which, as a whole, is validated by the present basic norm. Ross considered that past constitutions are wholly irrelevant to the present legal system since they cannot provide reflexively for their own replacement, and must therefore have been suppressed by the magic of a perhaps peaceful revolution, that is, by evolution as opposed to lawful devolution. Hart saw no difficulty in reflexive provisions for constitutional replacement, but refused to grant that 'past' rules of recognition have any systematic relationship to the existence of 'present' rules of recognition. But this amputation of the past of the rule of recognition opened the way for embarrassing problems about the relevance of the present rule of recognition (*qua* rule of competence) to the admitted present existence of rules which, after all, were created in the past.

In short, Hart and Ross freed the 'present' legal system from the incubus of a mass of superseded constitutional rules, but at the price of suppressing relevant questions about the relevance of the upper levels of their hierarchical models of 'legal system'. Kelsen tackled these questions, and answered them in a lawyer-like fashion by accepting lawful devolution of ultimate constitutional rules. But this left Kelsen incapable of explaining how a legal system might divide into two independent systems by process of law. And, much more serious, Kelsen's analysis employed a concept of 'validity' (that is, 'existence') incapable of distinguishing between the existence of a 'present' rule of competence and the existence of a 'past' rule of competence, lawfully superseded, but still somehow 'valid' and present as a source of the validity of the 'present' rules.

The question of the necessary conditions of change of identity of a legal system cannot, therefore, be answered until an attempt has been made to clear the analytical logjam that has developed.

III. WHEN DOES A RULE CEASE TO EXIST?

It will first be useful, in resolving the analytical confusion, to attain some caution and self-consciousness in using, for theoretical purposes, the practically serviceable lawyer's terms, 'valid', 'in force', and 'existence'. Very often, theorists use such terms as these as if they were univocal, clear in meaning, and self-explanatory. But in the law, their meaning is often a matter for debate and decision—and the decisions will vary according to context and purpose.

Consider the notion of repeal. Joseph Raz, with the confidence of the analytical jurist, offers three propositions about repeal and the existence of repealed and repealing laws:

(1) P1 'It is doubtful whether there is much point in regarding a repealing law...as existing after the laws it repealed ceased to exist.'[41]

(2) P2 'There are good grounds to argue that...norms are repealed not by repealing-norms but by repealing-acts.'[42]

(3) P3 'No termination of a norm legalizes offences committed while the norm was in force: offences committed while the norm existed can, of course, be punished later.'[43]

[41] *CLS* 58. [42] *Ibid.*, 64 n. 2.
[43] *Ibid.*, 64. I have inverted the order of sentences here.

Now it happens that in England, prior to 1850, the common law notion of repeal included the rule that the repeal of a repealing Act† revived the Act originally repealed. There is nothing conceptually odd about this notion of repeal; its practical inconveniences led to its supersession (see now the Interpretation Act 1889, s. 11(1) and s. 38(2)(a)), but it is obvious that, where such a notion prevails (as it did for centuries in England and still does, perhaps, in other legal systems) propositions P1 and P2 would not be as intuitively persuasive as here and now they are. Proposition P3 represents English law, subject to the important proviso that section 38(2)(c) of the Interpretation Act 1889, while adopting (in effect) proposition P3, does so only 'unless the contrary intention appears'. Since a 'contrary intention' does sometimes appear, and since section 38(2)(c) in any case replaces a common law rule of precisely opposite effect[44] the 'of course' in Raz's formulation P3 must be rejected as suggesting an unwarranted claim to analytical necessity: indeed, the universality of proposition P3 ('No termination...') is unfounded.

As with 'repeal', so with 'existence' and 'force'. Both the theorist (Raz) and the English rule (Interpretation Act 1889, s. 38(2)(a)) speak of repealed rules being 'not in force or existing'. But, as we have just seen, the effect of repealing a rule need not be to obliterate it completely as if it had never been passed and had never existed. English law since 1889 agrees with P3: persons for instance who aided escaping felons before 1 January 1968 can, and perhaps will, be punished years after the rules about misprision of felony and accessories after the fact were repealed from that date.[45] From the point of view of such persons, and of their legal advisers, the police, and the courts who must judge them, it is in many senses just not true that the repealed rules do not exist and are not in force. They do exist and they are in force! They are present guides to decision.

With this in mind, let us examine a related passage in Raz, where he takes up the more general issues discussed in the preceding section of this essay:

> By representing [laws conferring legislative powers] as conditions for sanctions enacted on their basis, Kelsen assumes that their effect is merely to establish the validity of laws already in existence. He overlooks the fact that they confer legislative powers which have not yet been exhausted, that new laws can yet be created on their basis. But this forward-looking aspect of these laws is their *real legal meaning*: by repealing a law conferring legislative powers the laws which

[44] On 'contrary intention' here, see e.g. *Hosie v Kildare CC* [1928] Ir R 47. For the old common law rule contradicting P3, see *R v Swan* (1849) 4 Cox CC 108; *Bennett v Tatton* (1918) 88 LJKB 313.

[45] Cf. *R v Fisher* [1969] 2 QB 114.

have already been created on its basis are unaffected; the only change is that it [sc. the power-conferring law] cannot be used for creating new laws.[46]

Now, the notion of repeal used in the last sentence is only one among several legal meanings of the term 'repeal':[47] if we find it the most attractive meaning, we ought to ask ourselves whether this is not precisely because it would be (usually) pointless and inconvenient if repeal were to entail consequences with respect to things already done and laws already enacted on the basis of the law repealed. And when thinking in terms of 'point' and 'pointless', we are thinking of what Raz calls the 'real legal meaning' of the laws in question (though he is speaking, not of repealing laws, but of power-conferring laws).

In any event, what Raz has said seems acceptable (if too rigidly expressed). Its consequences should now be explored. He has not argued from a denial of the Kelsenian premise that power-conferring laws 'establish the validity' of laws created in the exercise of those powers. But he denies that the validity of the laws so created must, at every moment, rest on the continuing 'existence' of the appropriate power-conferring law. On what, then, does the validity of a law rest once its authorizing law has been repealed? Does it rest on the repealing law? Raz thinks not; indeed, there seems something extravagant in supposing that a repealing law is the basis of the validity of all laws created by virtue of the power-conferring law it repeals. And the supposition is not necessary. For it seems reasonable to suppose (and here we go beyond Raz) that there is a general principle of the practical and theoretical understanding of law which can be formulated as follows: a law once validly brought into being, in accordance with criteria of validity *then in force*, remains valid until *either* it expires according to its own terms or terms implied at its creation, *or* it is repealed in accordance with conditions of repeal in force *at the time of its repeal*.[48]

[46] *CLS* 117 (emphasis added).

[47] Indeed the English doctrine is that repeal of an enactment empowering rule-making *abrogates* rules already made thereunder, unless the repealing law expressly saves them (*Watson v Winch* [1916] 1 KB 688). This case shows the doctrine to be a mere relic of the common law principle (not without exceptions in favour of completed transactions and vested rights) of obliterating repeal, a principle itself largely abrogated by the Interpretation Act 1889, s. 38(2) [now Interpretation Act 1978, ss. 15 and 16, which replace the common law principle even more completely, but without affecting the doctrine in *Watson v Winch*]. Saving clauses are common, and some legislatures (e.g. Ontario) have now adopted the policy of the Act of 1889, introducing the rule Raz takes for granted. [See further first endnote below, and endnote to essay 22 on implied repeal.]

[48] Cf. Ross's newly invented 'basic norm' designed to resolve the puzzle of constitutional amendments without resort to 'magical acts'—'Obey the authority instituted by [the ultimate rule of amendment] until this authority itself points out a successor: then obey this authority, until it itself points out a successor, and so on indefinitely' (Ross, 'On Self-Reference and a Puzzle in Constitutional Law' at 24). The 'general principle' above generalizes Ross's 'legally unchangeable' basic norm.

If this general principle is accepted, it is easy to see that the repeal of the power-conferring law (rule of competence) by virtue of which a given rule was created *need* have no effect on the rule so created: the continuing and present validity of the rule, after its creation, rests on the general principle—and while the general principle refers to the power-conferring law as existing, this reference is to the existence of the power-conferring law *at the time* (past) of the creation of the rule in question. The general principle, by thus referring to the power-conferring law, makes it ever-presently relevant to the continuing existence of the rules once created on the basis of the power-conferring rule: in this sense, the power-conferring law can be said to be 'existing' and 'in force' even if it is no longer 'existing' or 'in force' in its 'forward-looking aspect', its 'real legal meaning' as a law conferring power to create *new* rules. It will be seen, too, that the 'rule of identification' which we identified earlier in this essay as a post-independence component of the 'rule of recognition', is only an instance of the general principle at present under discussion. And it is clear that if the general principle is recognized as the basis of the validity of present rules, one can accede to the lawyer-like demand for a root of title without imperilling the independence and autochthony of a new state or the stability of an *octroi* constitution: there can be no legally plausible appeal to this root of title *against* the present rules of succession of rules. Finally the effects of successful revolutionary assaults on certain rules of the legal system, even on the most basic power-conferring law, need not be regarded as entailing any effect on the rest of the system: for even the rules now valid 'by reason of' power-conferring laws which the revolutionaries have successfully eliminated are valid really 'by reason of' the general principle, which identifies and supports them by a reference to those power-conferring laws as being in force at the time of the creation of the rules; and this reference back need not be the object of revolutionary attack. A revolution, unless it deliberately seeks the total subversion of the order of society, does not challenge, even temporarily, the general principle. All that a revolution normally seeks to do is to modify the application of the general principle in one special respect, viz. insofar as this general principle is the present basis of *the rules of succession of rules*: the revolutionaries postulate new conditions of repeal, and on the basis of this postulate, they repeal (or modify) first the pre-existing rules of repeal and then (in accordance with the new rules of repeal) such other rules (if any) as they may wish to.

But why should we accept this general principle? Why does it 'seem reasonable to suppose' it? One might defend it simply as a purely 'analytical' explication of 'the ordinary man's point of view' or of a 'general consensus of lay and professional opinion'.[49] Certainly, it makes sense of the history and practice of legal systems and lawyers. But it seems to me that to rely on this defence of the principle would be evasive and incomplete. If we are prepared to discuss the *point* of power-conferring rules, or of repeals, in general and in particular forms, we ought to be prepared to say that the general principle presupposes, expresses, and realizes (or secures) the most general and basic *function* of 'the law'—namely, to relate the past to the present, by providing a present guide to actions which take place and have effect in the future (when this present will be in the past). Always what is wanted of 'the law' is a present guide, and always the action and decisions so guided will be in the future; but what is wanted is a guided response to a situation which *has been* brought about, often by men who were then relying on 'the law' to guide them; to shut one's eyes to their reliance would be a paradigmatic form of unfairness as well as a sowing of the whirlwind. This tension of 'the law' between past, present, and future is expressed in the very formulation of the general principle we have been discussing.

But the relation of 'the law' (the legal system) of 'now' with 'the law' of 'then' or 'then' presents further problems. In the present section I have been discussing the legal meanings of terms such as 'the law in force', in relation to legally prescribed shifts between one meaning and another, and the justification and point of adopting such meanings for practical and thence for descriptive and analytical purposes. But the problems of the existence of 'the law', the legal system, are not exhausted by an explanation of the senses in which particular laws do and do not, *as a matter of law*, exist.

IV. IS 'THE LEGAL SYSTEM' A SET OF RULES?

In modern jurisprudence, the legal system is commonly assumed to be a set of rules or principles. But it is further assumed that this set of rules has a duration, that is, an identity through time. On this basis, finally, it is assumed that revolution, at least, can *put an end* to one legal system and *initiate* another.

Sometimes, indeed, it is asserted, as by Hart, that a legal system

> like a human being, may at one stage be unborn, at a second not yet wholly independent of its mother, then enjoy a healthy independent existence, later decay and finally die.[50]

[49] Cf. *CLS* 200 n. 2; also 201 ('an explication of common-sense and professional opinion'); 103.
[50] *CL* 112 [109].

Now such an appeal to organic analogy could never be made by Kelsen, though Hart (like Kelsen) offers to analyse the legal system as a set of rules ('union of primary and secondary rules'). But Hart's remark may focus the question which underlay the analytical 'to and fro' of the preceding sections: How can *a set of rules* be regarded as coming into being, lasting, and passing away?

No lawyer will deny that every rule in a legal system is equally valid. There are no grades of validity. No doubt the legal rule that contracts are not valid without consideration is more interesting and fecund than the legal rule that cars may not be parked outside the Oxford Town Hall on Fridays; but the latter is no less valid than the former. This being so it cannot be denied that 'English law' is *changing every moment* by the addition and subtraction of rules which, however trivial, particular, and concrete, are just as valid—that is, just as much members of the set—as the most long-standing and hallowed general rule. Thus, not only every time a local authority makes a by-law, but also every time a judge grants probate of a will, every time a contract is made, every time a judgment is entered, new rules are created, and one set of rules called 'English law' is replaced by a new set with different components.

Thus, there is no escaping the conclusion that the set of rules called English law and loosely spoken of as subsisting with the same identity in 1970 as in 1900 is really a *sequence of sets*.[51] Thus, our question about the duration of a set of rules resolves into the question: What is it about a sequence of sets of rules that entitles us to interpret it as an existing or subsisting system of rules with a lasting identity or duration?

Modern jurisprudence will incline us to reply to this question (which, however, is not usually raised in its present form) by asserting that what gives the sequence of sets continuity is the lasting constitution, or basic norm, or rule of recognition.[52] But can this form of reply bear critical scrutiny?

Bare reference to 'the constitution' will evidently not suffice. For 'the constitution', too, is a set of rules which range from the general and abstract to the concrete and particular. Every time one of these rules changes, we are obliged (since all rules are equally valid) to say that there is a new set of rules. Thus 'the constitution', like 'the legal system' as a whole, is a sequence of sets of rules, and the basis of the continuity of the sequence is what is in question.

To refer to 'the basic norm' will not suffice either. Kelsen's basic norm is an overtly fictitious construction designed to suppress theoretical questions rather than to answer them. In reality, one can know the rules

[51] See also *CLS* 35, 170. [52] Cf. *CL* 116 [113].

which the basic norm is said to validate, only when one has already answered all the questions which matter in jurisprudence, viz. all questions about the existence and *raison d'être* of those rules. Moreover, as we have already noticed, the basic norm is as much the basis of the validity of 'the historically first constitution' as of the 'present' constitution; there thus arise the embarrassing questions raised in sec. II of this essay and never answered by Kelsen, about whether a lawfully 'superseded' 'historically first constitution' is or is not still 'valid'.[53] Finally, it must be further noticed that the basic norm can give an appearance of unity to a sequence of sets of rules only because, in itself, it refers to an apparently unitary set, viz. 'the historically first constitution'. But one is entitled to assume that there is a single, identifiable 'historically first constitution' only if one already assumes the theory of discontinuity—that is, if one assumes that a revolution necessarily makes a *tabula rasa* of the law of the constitution. For, unless this is one's assumption, it is clear that 'the historically first constitution' is, like the rest of the legal system, a 'set of rules', rules which originate at different moments of time and which therefore constitute, in reality, a sequence of sets—the basis of whose continuity is what is in question.

To refer to 'the rule of recognition' will not solve the problem. In the first place, 'the rule', even considered synchronically as Hart usually considers it, is really a set of rules, some of them power-conferring and others mainly identificatory, some superior, and some subordinate. Even synchronically, these rules seem to have rather little in common with one another, other than that they are not derived from one another and that legal questions indeed 'cannot' be raised about their derivation. Even synchronically, then, the basis of the unity of the set is problematical. Diachronically, the problems are much greater. Hart has discussed the ways in which, standardly, a court has power, or assumes the power, to determine authoritatively and finally disputed questions about the content of the 'rule of recognition' (including questions about the powers of the courts, not excluding the power just mentioned).[54] Thus, from time to time, rules (whether general or particular) are added to and subtracted from 'the rule', and so the problem once more appears of the basis of the unity of the sequence of sets thus produced.

[53] Note that for Kelsen, the 'temporal sphere of validity' of a norm is an element of its *content* and does not represent or account for the existence and duration of the norm-with-that-content: see Kelsen, *The Pure Theory of Law*, 13. Kelsen's wide-ranging attempt to replace the concept of *existence* with that of *validity*, throughout his legal theory, leads to many well-known problems.

[54] *CL* 152–4 [148–50].

Is there *any* component of 'the rule of recognition' which is privileged in the sense that it lasts unchanged and thus unifies the sequence of sets of criteria of validity, and such that when it changes one is obliged to recognize that a new rule of recognition (and thus a new legal system) has come into being? It seems not. The only plausible candidate seems to be that offered by Alf Ross: the rule authorizing the amendment of the constitution, that is, the ultimate rule of succession of rules.[55] The candidacy of this rule is dependent on Ross's very dubious assumption that this rule cannot be reflexive or self-referring and thus is immune from legal change.[56] Moreover, the proposal to base the unity of the legal system on a rule from which perhaps no other rules in the system are derived, and which is often (as in the United Kingdom) of the most ambiguous and disputable character (at least to the extent that virtually every concrete use of it must count as the determination or concretization of a new particular rule and thus as the creation of a new set in a sequence of sets...)—this proposal is so bizarre that one may suspect that its origins are ideological rather than purely theoretical.

This suspicion may, however, need qualification. For the theoretical implication of the arguments we have pursued in this section is certainly radical, and there need be no surprise at finding rather desperate measures adopted, on occasion, to avoid it. The implication is this: *the legal system, considered simply as a set of 'valid rules', does not exist*, since, considered simply as a set of rules, of inter-dependent normative meanings, there is *nothing* to give it continuity, duration, identity through time. As Eric Voegelin has pointed out, the existence in continuity of a legal system can no more be explained by reference simply to sequences of sets of valid rules than can motion, as Zeno discovered, be explained by reference to sequences of points.[57]

Still, if it is a basic phenomenon of legal experience that all valid rules are equally valid (and that was the starting point in this analysis), it also is a basic phenomenon of such experience that legal systems do indeed exist and last. And if their existence cannot be grounded on any 'basic' rule or set of rules, there seems only one conclusion: the continuity and identity of a legal system is a function of the continuity and identity of the society in whose ordered existence in time the legal system participates. Hart has said that it is a defect of the pre-legal social rules that they had

[55] Ross, *On Law and Justice*, 80. [56] Above, nn. 22–6.

[57] Eric Voegelin, *The Nature of the Law*, an unpublished paper [of 1957] to which I am much indebted in this section of the essay. [Now Voegelin, *The Nature of the Law and Related Legal Writings* in *The Collected Works of Eric Voegelin*.]

no common identity save that of the group of human beings which accepts them.[58] He offers the 'rule of recognition' as a remedy for this 'defect', but when the identity through time of this rule, *qua* rule, is critically analysed it becomes clear, as we have seen, that recognition of a 'rule of recognition' presupposes recognition of a continuing society whose lasting order can be interpreted as including that 'rule', as a matter of fact. This no doubt is why Hart and Ross embed their ultimate 'rules' in a matrix which provides those 'rules' with the substance and duration that the 'rules' alone fail to provide for 'the legal system' as a whole. For Ross, the lasting substance underpinning the legal system is 'a dominant ideology';[59] for Hart it is a 'shared official viewpoint' accompanying a 'complex congruent practice' amounting to 'acceptance' from an 'internal viewpoint' of common standards of action.[60]

Legal, like pre-legal, social rules have no common identity or basis of existence in time save that of the group of human beings which accepts them. In times of crisis, the lawyer is obliged to admit that his judgments rest on a critical assessment of the identity of an object which normally he regards as 'artificial and anomalous' and legally barely intelligible—viz. the great 'unincorporated society' in which he lives.[61] As soon as the Rhodesian judges had decided that Rhodesia was, as a matter of 'fact', a distinct society with its own accepted power structure and intelligible commonweal, not merely a fragment of imperial power and commonweal, their decision (if not their reasoning) became almost inevitable.[62] The reason for this inevitability was expressed, as we saw, by lawyers of Edward IV: 'it is necessary that the realm should have a king under whose authority laws should be held and upheld'.[63]

It is indeed possible to speak of a legal system growing, flourishing, and withering away—but only if one considers it as something importantly more than a set of rules, however profoundly analysed.

[58] *CL* 92 [90]. [59] Ross, *On Law and Justice*, 83. [60] *CL* 118 [114].

[61] Cf. *Leahy v A-G for New South Wales* [1959] AC 457, 477, per Viscount Simonds:

> ... the artificial and anomalous conception of an unincorporated society which, though it is not a separate entity in law, is yet for many purposes regarded as a continuing entity and, however inaccurately, as something other than an aggregate of its members.

[62] I have discussed these cases at greater length in [1968b at 89–95; 1969a at 108–13; 1970d at 71–8.][‡] Discussion of other Commonwealth judicial decisions in which appeal was made to the theory of discontinuity will be found in 1968b at 82–4 (Uganda); 1969a at 73–5 (Pakistan). See also *Sallah v A-G for Ghana* (unreported), Judgement no. Const SC 8/70; comments by Tsikata and Tsikata, 'Sallah v. AG, Kelsen and Other in the Court of Appeal'; in this case two of the judges were unwilling to accept the theory of discontinuity, one considered it irrelevant to the issue, and one accepted it; and see Elias in (1971) 5 Nigerian LJ 129.

[63] Above, at n. 7.

V. REFLECTIONS ON METHOD IN JURISPRUDENCE

By a route similar but not identical to that followed in this essay, Joseph Raz has reached like conclusions. He has distinguished between momentary and non-momentary legal systems, and has remarked that the crux of the problem of the continuity of non-momentary legal systems is the question of continuity, viz. the problem of deciding whether two given momentary systems belong to the same legal system.[64] Like me he holds that:

> ... neither the 'constitutional continuity' of the new laws nor their content are necessary or sufficient conditions for establishing the continuity or lack of continuity of legal systems. Legal systems are always legal systems of complex forms of social life, such as religions, states, regions, tribes, etc.... The identity of legal systems depends on the identity of the social forms to which they belong. The criterion of identity of legal systems is therefore determined not only by jurisprudential or legal considerations, but by other considerations as well, considerations belonging to other social sciences.[65]

He adds that, since he does not wish to 'trespass on other fields', he will confine himself to the problem of the identity of momentary systems, but he stresses that it should *not* be assumed that momentary systems can be analysed independently of the (non-momentary) legal systems to which they belong—for the identity of a momentary system can be determined only by reference to other momentary systems *of the same legal system*[66] (in our terminology, by reference to rules of competence and rules of succession of rules in force at some earlier time).

But if the analysis even of momentary systems depends on an understanding of non-momentary systems, and if this understanding is not to be had without reference to 'other social sciences' than law and jurisprudence, it seems worthwhile to ask what these other 'social sciences' may be.

The original master of the philosophy of human affairs, Aristotle, has carried out an analysis of our problem from the other end—starting not with the identity of the legal system or constitution but with the identity of the society which has the system. Embarrassingly enough, he reached the opposite conclusion: that the identity of the *polis* changed every time the constitution (*politeia*) was changed by revolution.[67] This conclusion was forced on Aristotle by his procedure in carrying over to the analysis of human society the theoretical apparatus ('matter' and 'form') which

[64] *CLS* 187. [65] *Ibid.*, 188–9. [66] *Ibid.*, 189.

[67] *Pol.* III.1: 1275b34–1276b15; a convenient translation and paraphrase is Barker, *The Politics of Aristotle*, 97–100.

he had devised for the analysis of organisms, artefacts, and purposive actions.[68] Thus, he considered the citizens of a *polis* to be its matter, and its constitution to be its form; and change of form entails change of identity. This is plainly unsatisfactory (though we cannot here unravel the reasons for the 'obvious technical derailment'),[69] and Aristotle recognizes this. For as soon as he has reached his conclusion that there is a new *polis* with every revolutionary change of *politeia*, he adds: 'Whether a *polis* is bound in justice to fulfil its engagements when it changes its *politeia* is another question.'[70] In this sentence, the *polis* is a subject that retains its identity through the changes of constitution and 'legal systems'—it is a subject that has a *history* which embraces, and is not ended by, revolutions; and it is a subject that has or may have *ethical* obligations unaffected by revolutions.[71]

'History' and 'ethics' (the latter subsuming much of political philosophy) are the 'social sciences' concerned with the identity of the societies and legal systems with which jurisprudence is concerned. It is not possible here to undertake any full discussion of the theoretical situation which unfolds when any jurisprudential analysis is pushed to its limits, and which can be indicated in the proposition: analytical jurisprudence is intrinsically subalternated either to history or to ethics or to both, and cannot be an independent discipline, with a viewpoint of its own. A few summary remarks must here suffice.

On the problem for history—What is the relevant unit which has an identity and thus a history?—we can say very little. The nature of the problem with which Hegel grappled (not least in his *Philosophy of Right*), can be indicated by Eric Voegelin's remarks on the impasse into which Aristotle, as we have seen, was led in his analysis of the *polis*:

> ... the society in the whole extension of its historical course, with its cycle of constitutional sub-forms, was well established [for Plato and Aristotle] as a unit of inquiry. Moreover, since it was recognized that the cycle of forms applied not only to one particular polis, e.g. Athens, but was typical within a range of variations for all Hellenic poleis, even the single polis was already superseded as the ontological unit and had given way to the Hellenic society, organized as a manifold of poleis, as the unit of empirical inquiry ... the process was well under way in which the object of inquiry expands from the order of the concrete societies to civilizations which belong to the same type of order, and ultimately to the order of history of a mankind which is no finite unit of observation at all as it extends indefinitely into the future.[72]

[68] See the outstanding analysis and commentary in Voegelin, *Order and History*, 325–6, 331–6.
[69] *Ibid.*, 332. [70] *Pol.* III.1: 1276b14. [71] Voegelin, *Order and History*, 326.
[72] *Ibid.*, 334.

The problem for ethics—What is the relevant society to which I owe allegiance and with whose collective debts I am concerned?—is more immediately germane to jurisprudence. For as Hart has shown, a 'view' of a 'legal system' as a 'social phenomenon'[73] is 'realistic'[74] only if it *reproduces* 'the way in which the rules function as rules'[75] in the lives of those members of society who voluntarily accept the rules as common standards of behaviour, who have an 'internal' attitude to the rules.

Now this 'internal attitude' calls for further analysis before it can be used with precision as a criterion of relevance in jurisprudence. On Hart's account, the man with an internal attitude to the law is willing to do what is legally required; he wishes to arrange his affairs predictably;[76] he could see no reason for allegiance to a set of laws that provided no restrictions on the free use of violence, theft, and fraud or that did not back its restrictions with sanctions.[77] Indeed, Hart does not allow that the internal viewpoint is consistent with every sort of motivation whatever; for example, to regard the law as a reason for acting simply out of one's short-term self-interest in avoiding sanctions is precisely *not* to have the internal attitude.[78] But, despite all this, it seems that Hart would deny that the internal attitude must standardly be based on the communal or civil friendship (*philia politikē*) that Plato, Aristotle, and Aquinas were inclined to identify as the standard motivation of law-making and law-maintenance in its central forms.[79] Hart does indeed list 'disinterested interest in others' as one of the possible motives for allegiance to the law; but he insists that 'mere wish to do as others do' or 'an unreflecting inherited or traditional attitude' or 'calculations of long-term self-interest' will suffice.[80]

Doubtless these motives do all suffice. But is there any reason not to apply to the philosophical concept of the 'internal viewpoint' those philosophical techniques applied by Hart in his philosophical analysis of 'law'—viz. the identification of a central or standard instance among other recognizable but secondary instances?[81] And in fact the listed types of reason for accepting law as a reason for action do not seem all equally appropriate as standards of relevance in philosophically determining the criteria of law as a specific type of reason for action. Both 'traditional attitudes' and 'desire to conform' seem derivative from, and thus secondary to, the attitudes of others (forebears and fellows) who have adopted the internal viewpoint for other reasons. Moreover, to accept law simply out of respect for tradition

[73] *CL* 201 [197]; cf. vi [v], 209 [205]. [74] *Ibid.*, 201 [197]. [75] *Ibid.*, 90 [88].
[76] *Ibid.*, 40 [39]. [77] *Ibid.*, 91, 193, 198 [89, 189, 193].
[78] *Ibid.*, 90, 114–17, 201 [88, 111–13, 197].
[79] See e.g. Plato, *Rep.* 462; *Statesman* 311; *Laws* 627–8, 693, 701, 743, 757. Also *NE* IX, 6: 1167b3–4; IX, 1: 1155a23; *ST* I–II q.99 a.2c.
[80] *CL* 203, 232 [198, 226]. [81] Cf. *ibid.*, 16, 81, 280 [15, 79, 234].

or, especially, out of long-term self-interest (in the narrow and colloquial sense of that term) would be to have no reason for obeying or applying it in a strictly legal fashion—for tradition and self-interest do not provide any sufficient reason for 'taking seriously'[82] the policy—so central to the 'internal viewpoint' and allegiance to law—of applying in different cases, and against competing pressures and attractions, 'the same general rule, without prejudice, interest, or caprice'.[83]

In short (though the matter cannot be fully argued here),[84] we are led to adopt the position Hart was concerned to reject when he advanced his list of possible sufficient motivations for allegiance to law: the position that law can only be fully understood as it is understood by those who accept it in the way that gives it its most specific mode of operation as a type of reason for acting, viz. those who accept it as a specific type of moral reason for acting. Once one abandons, with Hart,[85] the bad man's concerns as the criterion of relevance in legal philosophy, there proves to be little reason for stopping short of accepting the morally concerned man's concerns as that criterion. In this way we can bring together those disparate figures whose apparently varying standards of relevance haunt the works of analytical jurists—for example, Kelsen's 'jurist' who sometimes seems to be within and sometimes outwith society; or Raz's 'ordinary man' and his 'judge faced with the question "which law ought to be recognized?"'[86] Analytical jurisprudence rejoins the programme of philosophizing about human affairs, the programme whose conditions have been identified by Aristotle: 'We hold that in all such cases the thing really is what it appears to be to the mature man [the *spoudaios*].'[87] If Aristotle is asked for what purposes he draws a theoretical distinction or elaborates a theoretical concept, he will answer that he is seeking to show forth the concerns and self-understanding of the *spoudaios* and the categories relevant to the *spoudaia polis*.[88] There is no distinct 'theoretical purpose' of the 'scientific observer' which could be set over against the 'practical purposes' that the *spoudaios* has in drawing the boundaries of concepts by using them in his life in society. The concepts thus differentiated for analytical use are the relevant 'standard cases' (for example of repeal, of power-conferring rule, of law, of legal system); secondary or deviant cases are not banished to other disciplines, but are recognized and dealt with by this discipline as secondary (that is, as being best understood in the light of the analysis of the primary, standard cases).

[82] Cf. *ibid.*, 161 [156]. [83] *Ibid.*, 161 [157].
[84] I have argued it a little more fully in essay I.6 (1970a). [85] *CL* 40 [39].
[86] *CLS* 200, n. 2. [87] *NE* X.5: 1176a17. [88] *Pol.* VII.2: 1332a33.

To say this is not to provide an answer to any concrete problem about the identity of any society or legal system. It is simply to say that the problem for the jurist is the same as the problem for the historian or for the good man wondering where his allegiance and his duty lie. From neither perspective is the thesis of discontinuity, as expressed by Kelsen, persuasive or acceptable. A revolution is neither a necessary nor a sufficient condition for anything that should be described as a change in the identity of the state or the legal system.

The historian will be inclined to say that rules exist because of a continuing willingness to recognize them as standards for action in the present. This willingness is more fundamental than the act(s) of will which originally put forward the rule, in its determinate form, for acceptance by officials and citizens as a standard for action. And with respect to the vast bulk of rules in a system, the historian finds that revolutions rarely affect that continuing willingness.

This is not surprising. For it is (ethically) reasonable to shape one's willingness to recognize posited rules as standards for one's action by referring to compendious rules or principles of identification, for the sake of maintaining coherence of action-in-society through time. (For everybody's life has to be lived as a project in time.) Hence, it is usually reasonable to accept the new rules of competence and of succession of rules proposed by the successful revolutionaries who have made themselves masters of society and thus responsible for meeting the contingencies of the future.§ And by the same token it is reasonable to adhere to the 'general principle' (put forward towards the end of the preceding section) as providing a reason, unaffected by the revolution, for the validity of the remaining bulk of the legal system. In both cases this 'reasonableness' is the reasonableness of justice and *philia politikē*, which demand legal coherence and continuity and respect for acquired rights.

Of course, justice has other demands. So sometimes the character of a revolution is such that allegiance to the revolutionary order of society is unreasonable. Citizen, judge, and jurist should, in such cases, say that the legal system is no longer the one they recognized previously (except in some secondary senses of 'same legal system'). But it is only in such extreme cases that the elements of discontinuity are more significant for analysis (moral, legal, jurisprudential) than the principle of continuity.

NOTES

† *Repeal of a repealing Act*... (at p. 422). Interpretation Act 1978, replacing the Act of 1889, provides more distinctly, by s. 15, for the effect of the repeal (including implied repeal) of repealing Acts, and then in s. 16(1)(a) makes ('without prejudice to s. 15') more general provision for the effect of repeal

on (viz. that the repeal does not revive) 'anything not in force or existing at the time at which the repeal takes effect'.

‡ *Decisions of the Rhodesian courts after the unlawful declaration of independence*...(at n. 62). The commentary in 1969a at 108–12, on the judgments in the Appellate Division of the High Court of Rhodesia in *Madzimbamuto v Lardner-Burke* 1968(2) SA 284, concludes (112):

> The jurisprudence available in standard books seems inadequate to the uses to which it was put. For that jurisprudence suggests that legal systems stand or fall as a whole,[89] so that if a judge recognises the unlawful dissolution of one constitutional rule he must recognise the dissolution of the rule empowering him to act judicially. But why should it not be the case that, during and after a revolution, judges have a genuinely lawful authority to determine, in a lawyerlike and principled fashion, what is, and what is to be, the principle or rule of recognition on which a sufficiently systematic body of rules of change (legislation) can be reconstructed to deal with the necessities of the common good? They have this authority because it was bestowed on them by law, and because nothing need have occurred which, in a sound jurisprudence, need be deemed to have divested them of it. To pick and choose among rules of recognition does not divest them of that authority; in common law jurisdictions a principled picking and choosing among substantive or primary rules of law—on the basis of equity, public policy, justice and the common good—is a recognised judicial function. As Lord Morris said in *Conway* v. *Rimmer*: 'Though precedent is an indispensable foundation on which to decide what is the law, there may be times when a departure from precedent is in the interests of justice and the proper development of the law.'[90] In *Madzimbamuto's* case all the judges felt the need for something more supple than the all-or-nothing offered by positivist constitutionalist jurisprudence. But they did not break with that jurisprudence cleanly enough to concentrate sufficiently on the difficult task of elaborating principles on which to proceed to a lawyerlike reconstruction of the legal system in the light of the existing circumstances.[91]

The commentary in 1970d at 71–4, on the judgments in the Judicial Committee of the Privy Council, sitting as the highest court of (Southern) Rhodesia, in *Madzimbamuto v Lardner-Burke* [1969] 1 AC 645, concludes:

> It will be seen that the difference between Lord Pearce and the majority is not as great as at first appears: Lord Pearce's appeal to necessity is strongly tempered by his requirement that the courts should do nothing contrary to the policy of the lawful but ousted sovereign. Had the Order in Council stood alone, without the context of the Governor's directive and of the British government's evident toleration of the dalliance of the Rhodesian courts with the regime, Lord Pearce like the majority would have put the Rhodesian courts to the stark all-or-nothing election: Do we sit as courts under the 1961 Constitution, as modified by the Order in Council of 1965, or do we shift our allegiance to the 1965 Constitution? As was argued in this *Survey* last year,[92] the general theory and nature of law does not require such an all-or-nothing election. Whether, on the other hand, it is practically desirable that courts should regard themselves as bound to that election by the nature of their judicial office, is another and more difficult question, complicated by the fact (not mentioned in the Privy Council) that to opt for the 1961 Constitution would be to court dismissal and replacement by revolutionary judges and justice.

§ *The new rules of competence and of succession of rules proposed by the successful revolutionaries*...(at p. 434). On the responsibility of making such rules, the conditional duty of accepting them, and their place in the general sequential account of the emergence of rules without authority, see 2008d sec. IV, esp. 336–7.

89 [The footnote referred to an earlier passage, 1969a at 109–10, the gist of which is in *NLNR* 275–6.]

90 [1968] AC 910 at 958.

91 To say this is not to say that it would have been wrong or muddled, from a jurisprudential point of view, to have decided either that the regime and its laws were entitled to no recognition whatsoever, *or* that the regime and its laws were entitled to full and unreserved recognition.

92 1969a at 109–12 [esp. para. just quoted].

22

JUST VOTES FOR UNJUST LAWS*

Summary. The form of enactments must be distinguished from their legal meaning (their 'juridical effect'), that is, from the propositions of law which those enactments, properly interpreted, *make* legally valid. This distinction makes it possible, and rationally necessary, to conclude that, in certain contexts, a certain statute which declares or textually implies that some abortions are legally permitted (but others prohibited) is not a *permissive law* within the meaning of the principle, assumed in this essay to be true, that permissive abortion laws are intrinsically unjust and may never be voted for. A permissive statute, in that sense, is one which has the legal meaning (juridical effect) of *reducing* the state's legal protection of the unborn.

I. THE OBJECTION

Legislators[1] typically take it as common sense that if you can help to enact a legislative proposal that would reduce the injustice of some existing law, you should regard it as morally permissible (and in some cases obligatory) to do so, notwithstanding that the restriction will leave intact some of the existing law's unjust elements. This commonsense position is entirely sound. But it faces an objection which also seems plausible. Call it the Objection: you should never vote for[2] a proposition or proposal that will insert into the law a morally wrong and unjust rule; so you must never vote

* 2004b ('Helping Enact Unjust Laws Without Complicity in Injustice').†

[1] By 'legislator' I will always mean a voting member of a legislative body. There is a morally significant difference between the legislative acts of a person who can change the law by his or her own individual legislative act and the acts of legislators in the sense I have just defined: see 456 below.

[2] It is accepted on all sides in this debate that 'vote for' refers to substantive votes, and not to votes that are 'procedural' in the sense that they might be cast 'in favour' of a bill in, say, committee in order to get the bill or the voting legislator into a position where a decisive, 'substantive' vote can be cast against it.

for a proposal which does the injustice of protecting some people from the existing law's injustice while openly leaving some other people still subject to that injustice; and this is particularly obviously impermissible when the proposal to be voted upon ratifies or restates part of existing law's unjust provisions. The present essay argues that, despite its plausibility, the Objection is mistaken.

This essay traverses ground I traversed in 1994/6[3] and 1997/9.[4] But it treats as primary a line of thought that was present in the earlier essays, but only in a rather unclear and unexplored form. The present essay treats as secondary the line of thought that in the earlier essays was primary. The proper exposition of what will here be called the Primary argument shows the utility of jurisprudential reflection and analysis. But it only makes explicit what is already part of the common sense of lawyers, from fairly early in their study of the law through the reading of cases, statutes, and other legal materials.

Some statements made by ecclesiastical authorities and sources appear in this essay, but only as illustrations. The line of thought pertains to natural law (natural reason), indeed to common sense articulated in a jurisprudential reflection on what laws really are. Many but not all the ecclesiastical statements concern laws relating to abortion, and this essay's focus on that matter is for its convenience as an example of issues that can and do arise in relation to many other matters.

II. THE PRINCIPLE

The Objection condemns voting for proposals (bills or laws) that aim to prohibit some but not all seriously unjust acts of a certain kind, and to eliminate some but not all unjust elements of the existing law relating to that kind of act. Call all such proposals, bills and resultant laws restrictive laws. One reasonable way of putting and arguing for the Objection is to point to the statement of principle in the encyclical *Evangelium Vitae* (1995) sec. 73.2:

> In the case of an intrinsically unjust law, such as a law permitting abortion or euthanasia, it is therefore never licit to obey it, or to 'take part in a propaganda campaign in favour of such a law, or vote for it'.[5]

[3] 1996d; earlier, 1994i. [4] Essay V.7 (1999d).

[5] The internal quotation is from sec. 22 of the Declaration on Procured Abortion, made by the Congregation for the Doctrine of the Faith [CDF] in November 1974: *Acta Apostolicae Sedis* 66 (1974) 730–47.

Call it the Principle: it is never licit to vote for an intrinsically unjust law.[6] To say that something is *intrinsically* unjust is to say that it is unjust under all circumstances. So, if it would not be morally acceptable[7] to vote for a proposed abortion[8] law that replaced a complete prohibition with some permission (say, of abortion up to 14 weeks of pregnancy), how can it be acceptable to vote for the very same proposal when it would replace a more permissive law (say, permitting abortion up to 24 weeks)? If voting for a law that leaves abortion permitted up to 14 weeks is *intrinsically* unjust, must not the circumstance that this law will be more restrictive than existing law be incapable of rendering the vote morally acceptable?

[6] 'Intrinsically unjust' replaces the term 'intrinsically immoral' predicated of such laws in the Declaration on Procured Abortion made by the Congregation for the Doctrine of the Faith in November 1974. Neither term, as predicated of a kind of law, is traditional, and there are problems with the notion which I shall ignore in this essay. As the encyclicals *Veritatis Splendor* (1993) and *Evangelium Vitae* (1995) each teach, *intrinsece mala* (intrinsically evil [acts]) are those kinds of acts which are picked out in the exceptionless *negative* moral norms of Christian teaching about the content of the natural moral law. (See generally 1991c.) The obligation legally to prohibit murder or abortion is the content, however, not of a negative moral norm, but an affirmative or positive one, prescribing that a certain kind of act (in this case, legislation or its equivalent) be done. Moreover, justice and injustice are predicated of laws only by an analogy (of attribution), for justice is 'the steady and undeflected will [*of a person*] to give to others what they are entitled to'. These facts create significant strains in extending the traditional and sound idea of intrinsically immoral acts to categories of *laws* and to the positive obligation to make laws against murder and abortion. But I shall ignore those problems in this essay, though they cannot be overlooked in real life. More positively, I suggest that the newly articulated category, properly understood, picks out three types of law: those that permit the violation of a fundamental human right (e.g. abortion), laws which establish a public policy violating such a right (e.g. licensing and funding human embryo production and or experimentation), and laws which institutionalize an intrinsically evil type of act (e.g. ratifying 'homosexual marriage').

[7] The question thus is whether such a vote is *intrinsically* wrong. Even if the answer to that question is that such a vote is not intrinsically wrong (i.e. that it is acceptable/permissible, i.e. can be licit), there is in all actual cases the further question whether it is right in all the circumstances to cast such a vote. The answer to that further, always relevant question is given by moral norms which are situation-relative in a way that the question of *intrinsic* wrongness is not.

[8] By 'abortion(s)' throughout this essay I shall mean all and only those terminations of pregnancy which, because they *intend* the death of the unborn baby, or *intend* the cessation of its development, are intrinsically wrong and have been judged wrong in the Christian tradition. It follows that the term as I use it does not include those kinds of termination of pregnancy (some or all of which may be conventionally described as types of 'therapeutic abortion') that cause the death of the child only as a side effect (some of which may, however, be unjust albeit not instances of *intrinsece malum*). (See e.g. essay II.13 (2001a).) The terms 'termination of pregnancy' and 'abortion' in state laws may in many cases not be so precise, and if used without explicit qualifications or exceptions would entail the legal condemnation of actions which Christian tradition and sound moral analysis would not condemn. This is a serious problem for Catholic and other pro-life efforts at restrictive reform, and needs much more attention than it received in *Evangelium Vitae* and other such documents. In this essay I take for granted that *all abortions should be legally prohibited*, even though this proposition is not true if 'abortion' is understood in a different sense, perhaps closer to legal and everyday usage. This essay is not the right context for going deeper into this important practical and theoretical issue. [See also essay II.19 (1993a), sec. I.].

An answer to those challenges can begin by noticing the tight parallel drawn in *EV* 73.2 between the question of obedience to a permissive abortion law and the question of voting for it: 'it is... never licit to obey it or... vote for it'. Suppose that a law[9] is *restrictive*, that is, is partly permissive and partly prohibitive.[10] It expressly or tacitly permits some abortions but prohibits others. It ought, I shall assume, to prohibit all abortions.[11] So we might be tempted to say: this whole law is simply intrinsically unjust. But the temptation should be resisted. For if the whole law is simply unjust, then it 'is never licit to obey it',[12] and so no police officer or judge could rightly obey the law's directive to prevent and punish the abortions it prohibits. *EV* 73.2 cannot have meant that. So, instead of saying that the restrictive law, taken as a whole, is permissive and therefore simply unjust, one should say that this restrictive law is unjust *insofar as* it is permissive but is just (and fit to be obeyed) *insofar as* it is prohibitive.

But the point can be put more precisely, and the primary argument of this essay given a first airing. What is commonly and acceptably called a 'law restricting abortion' must actually comprise two (or more) distinct *propositions of law*—indeed, two (or more) *laws* in a strict sense of the word. One is a proposition of law that certain abortions are prohibited. The other—which may be articulated in the same statute or judgment, or may be implied in the constitution, or in the general legal principle that what is not prohibited is permitted—is the proposition of law that other abortions are permitted. Only by keeping in mind this kind of distinction can we make sense of *EV* 73.2's reference to obedience. And since that reference is in strict parallel to its reference to voting, it follows that *EV* 73.2—even before we reach *EV* 73.3—opens up the possibility and indeed the necessity of distinguishing, and dealing separately with (a) rules or elements or propositions of

[9] At this stage of the argument, I am still speaking in the broad terms normally used (and used in *Evangelium Vitae*). So this 'a law' here could refer to a whole statute, a set of code provisions, or even a single code provision or one-clause statute or rule; and sometimes it will refer to a proposal or bill which would be law if enacted.

[10] Such a law could also be called 'incompletely restrictive' or 'incompletely prohibitive'. I shall use 'restrictive' to mean 'incompletely prohibitive'. I shall use 'prohibitive' and 'prohibition' to include both complete and incomplete prohibition, and let the context make clear whether the prohibition to which I am referring is complete or incomplete. So: restrictive laws are prohibitive, but only incompletely prohibitive. In virtually all instances, I use 'restrictive' as shorthand for 'prohibitive but less prohibitive than reason (justice) requires'.

[11] See n. 8 above.

[12] I am not here considering the complexities that arise in considering different kinds of injustice in law (as to which see *NLNR* 352–62), but only the interpretation and effect of *EV* 73.2.

a state's law which permit abortion (and are therefore[13] intrinsically unjust) and (b) rules, elements, or propositions of the state's law which prohibit abortion, and therefore can rightly (and should) be obeyed *and can rightly be voted for.*

It will turn out that the key to understanding the relation between *EV* 73.2 and 73.3, and thus to understanding 73.2 itself, and dissolving the Objection, is to recognize that the decisive phrase, '*a law permitting* abortion or euthanasia', needs interpretation, and is referring to a measure which either *introduces* a permission (where hitherto there was a prohibition), or continues in force a permission *which would otherwise have expired* (on its own terms, or by repeal or override).

III. HOW TO UNDERSTAND THE PRINCIPLE: *EV* 73.3

EV 73.2 ratified nearly two decades of episcopal teachings embracing comparative analyses of the circumstances and potential object of a legislator's vote in more or less concrete historical contingencies in Italy,[14] Britain,[15]

[13] See n. 8 above.

[14] On 28 March 1980, the Italian Radical Party began collecting signatures for a referendum in favour of the modification of Law 194/78 in order to make it more completely and openly favourable to abortion. Faced with the prospect of having to choose between the existing law 194/78 and one which would be worse, the Italian Pro-Life Movement began collecting signatures for two referenda: one giving maximum protection to human life by eliminating every possibility for abortion, except in the case of conflict with the life of the mother, and another which represented the minimal position: it condemned abortion in general terms, but allowed legal abortion in two cases: grave threat to the life of the mother and verified pathologies which constitute a grave risk to her physical health. As expected, on 4 February 1981, the Constitutional Court of Italy declared that the minimum referendum of the Pro-Life Movement was admissible, but the one giving maximum protection was not, since it contradicted an earlier decision of the Court of 18 February 1975 (n. 27). The question of conscience then arose regarding whether someone who was absolutely opposed to abortion could vote in favour of the minimal referendum as drafted by the Pro-Life Movement. The Italian Conference of Bishops offered an important clarification on 11 February 1981: 'The referendum proposed by the Pro-Life Movement is morally acceptable and binding for the consciences of Christians since it seeks, by *overturning some elements in the current abortion law, to restrict, as much as possible, its extent and to reduce its negative effects.* It does not follow, however, that the remaining elements in the civil law in favour of abortion may be seen as morally licit and may be followed. (Luño, 'Evangelium Vitae 73' at 3 (emphasis added).)

This article closely parallels Bertone, 'Catholics and Pluralist Society', an article by the prelate who was Secretary of the Congregation for the Doctrine of the Faith at the time when *EV* 73 was drafted. The Bishop of Rome is represented in the Italian Conference of Bishops; it is no surprise that this statement is echoed in *EV* 73.3's response by the Pope to the 'problem of conscience' of which the Italian issue of early 1981 was one kind of instance.

[15] In 1989 the Bishops' Conferences of Great Britain published a statement by the Catholic Bishops' [of England, Wales, Scotland, and Ireland] Joint Committee on Bio-Ethical Issues, addressed to the question 'How far may I support a bill which *inadequately* protects human rights or other important aspects of the common good', taking, 'for simplicity', the example of abortion. The

the United States,[16] and Ireland.[17] When *EV* 73.3 takes up a 'particular problem of conscience', it is alluding to a kind of problem that arose

statement declared that a legislator faced with 'a law or a bill for weakening restraints on abortion' could never vote for it on the ground that killing an unborn child or stopping its development is sometimes needed, or on tactical grounds such as to preserve one's career even for the sake of doing 'greater good in the future'. But in a society where securing for the unborn the equal protection of the law is or seems practically impossible for the foreseeable future,

> Catholics may support and vote for a bill or other proposal which would *strengthen the law's protection* for the unborn, even when the bill fails to extend such protection to the full extent that justice truly requires.... Catholics who are publicly lending their support to such imperfect legislation should not disguise their view that all procuring abortion is unacceptable.

Thus the statement treated as decisive the same criterion as the Italian Bishops: Does the amending proposal, bill, or law *change* the existing law by making it *more restrictive*? In the next paragraph this criterion was restated: 'a measure of protection which is less than complete but which is greater than that accorded by today's unjust law' and is judged to have 'a better prospect of being enacted and brought into force' than any proposal to extend to the unborn what they are entitled to—'fully equal protection' by the law. And this broad and commonsense criterion, statable in many different but equivalent forms of words, was to be the criterion adopted in *EV* 73.3.

[16] The British/Irish statement of 1989 was warmly endorsed by Cardinal O'Connor, then chairman of the Committee on Pro-Life Activities of the National Conference of Catholic Bishops: Cardinal John O'Connor, 'Abortion: Questions and Answers', Origins 20/7 (1990). In this statement, later included along with the British/Irish statement in the small CDF dossier running up to the CDF Conference preparatory to *EV* 73.3, the Cardinal offered his own version of the dynamic and comparative explanation later found in *EV* 73.3:

> The conflict over imperfect law has definitely been divisive to the pro-life movement. It seems to me that our goal must always be to advance protection for the unborn child to the maximum degree possible. It certainly seems to me, however, that in cases in which perfect legislation is clearly impossible, it is morally acceptable to support a pro-life bill, however reluctantly, that contains exceptions if the following conditions prevail:
>
> A) There is *no other feasible bill restricting* existing permissive abortion laws *to a greater degree* than the proposed bill.
>
> B) The proposed bill is *more restrictive than existing law*, that is, the bill *does not weaken the current law's restraints* on abortion. And,
>
> C) The proposed bill does not negate the responsibility [sic.: sc. possibility] of future, *more restrictive* laws.
>
> In addition, it would have to be made clear that we do not believe that a bill which contains exceptions is ideal and that we would continue to urge future legislation which would *more fully* protect human life.

[17] In November 1992 the Irish bishops themselves had to confront the very immediate and politically fraught problem of conscience which had arisen since in March 1992 a Supreme Court judgment had made abortion legal in what the bishops termed 'a potentially wide range of circumstances'. The Irish government and legislature, in response to that judgment, were promoting amendments to the constitution. In the opinion of the bishops the principal amendment, while it 'would improve the constitutional protection of the unborn as this now stands in the light of the Supreme Court judgment', would 'give constitutional support to a principle which is morally false and unjust...that it can be legitimate to deliberately destroy a human life'. They then outlined 'two contrary conclusions' which 'can be drawn by people, all of whom are equally opposed to abortion'. Some consider themselves bound to vote NO, 'whatever the legal and political consequences'. But others

> who view abortion with total abhorrence see the Amendment as a means of *curtailing* the worst features of the Supreme Court judgment. They have no confidence that any more satisfactory opportunity of doing so will be presented to them. They do not see a YES vote as bringing about the introduction of abortion. *Abortion, with potentially wide availability, has already been introduced by the Supreme Court judgment.* They consider that the passing of the Amendment would substantially mitigate that totally unacceptable legal position. Their desire is to *improve the situation as best they can*, but they do not intend to endorse the flaws in the Amendment. They believe that

constantly, and was extensively debated, during the two decades preceding the Encyclical. Making a key part of *EV* 73.2 a quotation from the Holy See's own statement of principle in 1974 is an indication, or hint, that in 73.3 judgment will be passed on a matter that by 1995 had been disputed for more than two decades among people opposed to abortion and permissive abortion laws. The judgment is, in purpose and effect, a clarification of the Principle stated in 73.2. In particular, 73.3 is a clarification of what 73.2 means by 'law permitting x'.

The most immediate historical precursor to *EV* 73 was the reform of the Polish law on abortion, introducing very extensive prohibitions of abortion but leaving intact the existing permission of abortion in a small number of cases specified by excepting from the new law's prohibitions certain cases involving serious threats to health or life of the mother, rape, or serious and permanent disability of the child. This legislation was adopted early in 1993. But before the end of 1992, the Holy See[18] began direct preparations for a conference to be focused entirely on the question what judgment might properly be made, at a level transcending the national, on 'the delicate problem of the collaboration of Catholics with imperfect laws (for example, laws which permit abortion in certain cases, but are *more restrictive* compared with existing laws)'.[19] This conference was held in the Vatican in early October 1994, and all the participants were invited to reflect on a sheet of paper articulating (in less than 150 words of Italian) a 'possible official position on the problem of imperfect laws'. What was articulated on that sheet of paper is what now, reordered and partially reworded but in substance identical, was to be found in March 1995 as *EV* 73.3, which reads:

[73.3] A particular problem of conscience can arise in cases where a legislative vote would be decisive for the passage of a more restrictive law, aimed at [It: *volta cioè a*] limiting the number of authorized abortions, in place of a more permissive law already passed or ready to be voted on. Such cases are not infrequent. It is

they are restoring, insofar as is open to them at present, the constitutional guarantee of the right to life of the unborn child.

The Bishops' Conference then gave its 'considered opinion that from a moral point of view both of these stances are tenable insofar as each is intended to reflect a total abhorrence of abortion and the determination to make that abhorrence clear'. 'The referenda: Statement by the Irish Bishops' Conference', 5 November 1992, para. 10 (emphasis added).

[18] The Congregation for the Doctrine of the Faith was doubtless acting within the framework of the preparations for the encyclical *Evangelium Vitae* which were launched by the special consistory of cardinals summoned by the Pope on 4–7 April 1991 and the papal letter to the episcopate '*De Evangelio vitae*' dated 19 May 1991 (see *EV* 5).

[19] From the Prefect of the Congregation's invitation of 1 July 1994 to the conference (emphasis added).

a fact that while in some parts of the world there continue to be campaigns to introduce laws favouring abortion, often supported by powerful international organizations, in other nations—particularly those which have already experienced the bitter fruits of such permissive legislation—there are growing signs of a rethinking in this matter. In a case like the one just mentioned, when it is not possible to overturn or completely abrogate a pro-abortion law, an elected official, whose absolute personal opposition to procured abortion was well known, could licitly support [Lat: *suffragari*][20] proposals aimed at [Lat: *velint*] *limiting the harm* done by such a law and at lessening its negative consequences at the level of general opinion and public morality. This does not in fact represent an illicit cooperation with an unjust law, but rather a legitimate and proper attempt to limit its evil aspects.

Like all the preceding episcopal statements, this paragraph expresses the judgment that casting a vote for a bill that will leave the state's laws inadequately restrictive of abortions and thus unjust can be acceptable and right because, and only because, the new law which the passing of the bill will enact will itself *make* the state's law *more restrictive*. Like each of its predecessors, the statement made in 73.3 focuses upon the new law's (the bill's or referendum proposal's) *object*, most essentially upon the *immediate legal effect* it is to have on the state's laws. If that object and juridical effect is in itself simply prohibitive, the bill or referendum proposal is just (so the statement implies), and voting for it can be an act of justice because the legislative proposal, and the amend*ing* law enacted if the bill is passed, is a just one.[21] It will be a just law because the difference it makes to the state's whole law regarding abortion is just. The new statute's *juridical* meaning and effect is simply prohibitive. The statute *does* nothing but prohibit abortions. Of course, the state's laws, even as amend*ed*, will remain unjust because incompletely prohibitive (= partly permissive). The analysis, in every case, looks to see what *change* is made by the bill or new statute, and *compares* the statute about to be made (and the state's law as altered by the new statute) with the existing law. The existing law is taken as a *baseline* for this essential comparison.[22] If the change made by the new statute is

[20] This word picks up the Latin *suffragiis sustinere* used to translate 'vote for' in *EV* 73.2. The Latin is official and normative, but it is a translation of a document conceived from beginning to end (and in all probability approved and signed off by the Pope) in Italian; the Italian version thus has an authority not shared by translations (such as the English).

[21] As always, this is an over-simplification. 'Just' here as almost everywhere in this paper, means 'not intrinsically unjust'. In reality, a law is not truly just unless it is not only not intrinsically unjust but also does not violate any of the situation-relative moral norms bearing upon the relation between persons which is under consideration. (See also n. 7 above.) This is another complexity which I usually ignore in order not to clutter up the discussion.

[22] It goes without saying that the *standard* of or *measure* for the comparison is not the baseline but the *moral norm* constantly upheld by the Church and reaffirmed in *Evangelium Vitae*, which

restrictive, the fact that the statute does not prohibit everything that might and should be prohibited does not entail that the partial prohibition—the new restriction(s) created by bill/statute—is an unjust act of legislating: the amending statute so enacted should not be regarded as an intrinsically unjust statute or, in itself, an unjust law.[23]

Baselines may differ while the wording of a proposal or bill or law remains the same. One and the same bill may have to be compared with a more permissive law (baseline A), or, in a different time and place, with a less permissive law (baseline B). Depending on the baseline, the necessary comparative analysis differs in result. Against baseline A, the bill can be judged supportable. Against baseline B it will necessarily be unjust and insupportable.[24] That was the gist of all the statements referred to above.

There seem to have been no episcopal or similarly significant ecclesiastical statements repudiating this kind of comparative or baseline analysis. However, it met with incomprehension and/or outright opposition from some people, who reasoned that any bill or new statute which leaves some abortions permitted is intrinsically (that is, by its nature)—whatever the good intentions and difficult circumstances of any who vote for it—an unjust proposal or law, and therefore incapable of being justly supported or voted for. After 1974 these people could point to the *Declaration on Procured Abortion* by the Congregation for the Doctrine of the Faith [CDF], sec. 22:

> man can never obey a law which is in itself (*intrinsece*) immoral, and such is the case of a law which would *admit in principle the liceity of abortion.* Nor can he take part in a propaganda campaign in favor of such a law, *or vote for it.*

These objectors could and did object that any bill or new statute which selects for prohibition some but not all classes of abortions is either tacitly or explicitly—but in either case objectionably—'admitting in principle the liceity of abortion' by failing to simply repeal the existing laws'

demands that the protection of the law of the state against homicide include the unborn with the born. That moral norm entails that a bill the effect of which is to permit abortion is unjust and cannot be supported. Whether a bill has that effect, however, can only be determined by comparing it with the baseline, the existing law. (Cf. n. 24 below.)

[23] Of course, a vote for it *can* be described as a vote for an unjust law—a vote, i.e. for the state's law remaining unjustly permissive after its amendment. But that description is too broad and undiscriminating to be a proper basis for an analysis of the justice or injustice of voting for the amending bill/law.

[24] There are other, more complex baselines, e.g. where the existing law is a dead letter, and is about to be replaced by one or other of two specific proposals, 'ready to be voted on'. In such a situation, as *EV* 73.3 plainly implies, it is possible that the real baseline is the more permissive of the two proposals.

permission(s).[25] A vote for such a proposal is therefore ruled out, according to the objectors, by the *Declaration* sec. 22. How can what is intrinsically wrong be made acceptable by the circumstances? Isn't any comparison between the proposed law and the existing baseline law a reference to the circumstances of the proposal? How can the circumstance that the proposal is 'more restrictive' make right what is intrinsically wrong?

As mentioned above, many episcopal statements made between 1974 and 1995 presuppose the error of this way of interpreting the *Declaration* and of this objection to the view that such amending bills and new laws need not be unjust and voting for them can be acceptable and indeed desirable. *EV* 73.3 was clearly intended to ratify the *comparative* analysis of an amending bill or law against the existing law (or some other relevant baseline). Phrase after phrase keeps that analysis in the foreground. Proposals of the kind in question are acceptable insofar as they propose 'a *more restrictive* law, *aimed* at *limiting* the number of authorized abortions, *in place of* a more permissive law'. Acceptable proposals are '*aimed* at *limiting* the harm done by' the state's permissive, pro-abortion law. They represent 'a legitimate and proper *attempt* to *limit* [the] evil aspects' of the law they (only partially) supplant. The attempt to enact a new law that will have such an (incomplete) effect can be legitimate and proper provided that 'it is not possible to overturn or *completely abrogate* [the] pro-abortion law' the place of which the new law will *incompletely* take. In such cases, therefore, so 73.3 plainly affirms, voting for such a bill or new law need not be regarded—and indeed, provided the intentions and circumstances indicated in 73.3 are present, should not be regarded—as an instance of the kind of act declared by 73.2 to be always impermissible: voting for a permissive and therefore intrinsically unjust law. In what they juridically *do*—immediately, as a matter of law—such proposals, and the bills and new laws (statutes) giving effect to them, are (precisely speaking) *not permissive but prohibitive.*

That is how 73.3 and 73.2 must be understood if they are to be regarded as consistent with each other.[26] While it is logically possible, it is interpretatively absurd to take 73.3 as intended to state an *exception* to the

[25] The fact is that 'would admit in principle the liceity of abortion [ammettesse, in linea di principio, la liceità dell'aborto]' is ambiguous between: (a) affirm the proposition that abortion is permissible; (b) not deny the proposition that abortion is permissible; (c) introduce a new permission of abortion; and (d) not repeal an existing permission.

[26] This reading also treats them as consistent with the straightforward dynamic and comparative analysis used by responsible episcopal teachers and pastors in all the cases mentioned on pp. 440–2 (and others). It is fanciful to think that the Pope would have left sec. 73 of his encyclical bare of any hint of a correction of that analysis (and its practical conclusion) if he had thought that such analyses, and the many acts of Catholic legislators done in reliance upon them—extending most recently to his own much loved homeland, under the guidance of Catholic statesmen very well known to him—were actually misguided attempts to justify the unjustifiable, the intrinsically immoral act of voting for a bill or law unjust by its very nature.

principle stated in 73.2 to be exceptionless.[27] Proportionalist theologians (situation ethicists) commonly imagine that the Church's specific moral teachings are wholly or largely a matter of ecclesiastical legislation ('rules', 'prohibitions', 'bans', which we are 'supposed to' follow) to which Church 'rulings' can make exceptions. But that is opposed to the moral doctrine reiterated vigorously two years before *Evangelium Vitae*.[28] It would be outlandish to think that *EV* 73.2, teaching that one may *never* support or vote for intrinsically unjust laws (including laws permitting abortion), might be immediately followed in 73.3 by an *exception* (= not never). So 73.3 must be taken to be, or to imply, an interpretation of 73.2's phrase 'law permitting abortion', such that laws (proposals/bills/enactments) of the kind delineated in 73.3 (restricting but not completely[29] prohibiting abortion) are precisely a subset of the class 'laws that do NOT permit abortion'.

IV. THE RESTRICTIVE VIEW OF *EV* 73.3

It is sometimes suggested (a) that *EV* 73.3 has a more limited meaning and application than it appears to have, and (b) that, in any event, the principle recognized and affirmed in *EV* 73.2 is incompatible with all but a few ways of reforming a permissive legal abortion regime.

(a) The readings of *EV* 73.3 that would restrict its application to non-substantive amendments—such as the introduction of a clause declaring that medical personnel with a conscientious objection to abortion are under no obligation to participate in it—rely on treating the ruling given in the last sentence of 73.3 as completely separate from the statement of the 'particular problem of conscience' in the first sentence. In this way, the

[27] That interpretation is, however, proposed by Griffin, '*Evangelium Vitae*: Abortion' at 170. The quality of Griffin's discussion can be seen from the following excerpts from her conclusions about *EV* 73 (*ibid.*, 171). Her exposition of the encyclical's teaching:

> *Evangelium Vitae* forsakes the natural law and asks Catholic politicians to enact a theological teaching into law...[and] impose the Church's teaching on non-Catholics. For pragmatic reasons, Catholics may vote for less restrictive abortion laws when their absolute ban on abortion cannot be passed. Catholics may vote only to restrict abortion rights or to ban abortion altogether.... Moral error has no rights.

Her own position:

> *Evangelium Vitae* imposes a theological doctrine upon the Church's faithful, but theological doctrine should not be imposed on non-Catholics by the state and politicians, not even by Catholic politicians.

And so forth.

[28] See John Paul II, Encyclical *Veritatis Splendor* (1993), condemning proportionalist moral theologies, and reaffirming the exceptionlessness of certain moral norms such as those against intentionally killing the innocent.

[29] Recall n. 8 above.

category of 'more restrictive law, aimed at limiting the number of abortions' is shuffled off the table, as if it were an idle, throat-clearing warm-up to the real business of the paragraph, which is to declare the legitimacy of proposals 'aimed at limiting the harm done by [pro-abortion] law' subject to a proviso not hinted at in 73.3 but read in from 73.2, viz. that these proposals cannot be legitimate if they in any way treat abortion as permitted.[30] As interpretations of 73.3, these seem improbable, or even perverse.

(b) Another implausibly restrictive reading of 73.3 is that it allows substantive changes to abortion law, provided that neither the bill nor statute making the change nor the law it changes, when read after the change, permits abortion. This proviso could not be satisfied except in relation to a codified set of abortion provisions in which each abortion-related article of the code is a complete law independently of any other abortion-related article.

On this restrictive reading of 73.3, which I shall call the Restrictive View, it is intrinsically unjust to support a bill which leaves an abortion-permitting clause less permissive. Even if the amending bill/statute does not mention permission, it is argued that it must be understood as *ratifying* and *continuing* some (though not all) of the permission that was previously included in the clause. On this view the Italian bishops, and implicitly the Holy See, were wrong to advise that voters could licitly support the 1981 pro-life referendum proposal to *amend* Art. 6 of Italy's abortion law by repealing some but not all of the permissive phrases in that article.[31] Similarly (so the argument goes), suppose the existing law (the Abortion Act) were in the following form:

Legislative Form A

1. Abortion is permitted up to the 24th week of pregnancy, and thereafter is prohibited—

Then it would never be acceptable (they say) to support a bill of the form:

Reform R1

Clause 1 of the Abortion Act is repealed and replaced by '1. Abortion is permitted up to the 14th weeks of pregnancy, and thereafter is prohibited'.

[30] So Harte, 'Challenging a Consensus' at 329.

[31] The pro-life referendum would have repealed Art. 4 which extensively permits abortion during the first 90 days, and then would have repealed in Art. 6 the phrases here italicized:

> 6. L'interruzione volontaria della gravidanza, *dopo i primi novanta giorni*, può essere praticata: (a) quando la gravidanza o il parto comportino un grave pericolo per la vita della donna; (b) quando siano accertati processi patologici, *tra cui quelli relativi e rilevanti anomalie o malformazioni del nascituro*, che determinano un grave pericolo per la salute fisica *o psichica* della donna.

Those 'remaining elements' of Italy's abortion law which are said by the Italian Bishops' Conference to be not morally licit can only be found in Art. 6 itself, as amended. (See n. 14 above.)

Nor would it be acceptable (they say) to support the following:

Reform R2
In clause 1 of the Abortion Act, substitute '14' for '24'.

But (they say) the same effect might be licitly achieved if, instead, the existing law relating to abortion comprised a series of independent articles, one or more of which could be simply repealed without referring to the other articles. Imagine a criminal code were in the following (improbable) form:

Legislative Form B
273. Abortion from 1 to 14 weeks is permitted if two doctors agree.
274. Abortion from 14 to 24 weeks is permitted if one doctor agrees.
275. Abortion for handicap is always permitted.
276. Abortion of a fetus of gipsy parentage is always permitted.
277. Subject to arts 275 and 276, abortion after 24 weeks is prohibited.

Then, according to supporters of the Restrictive View, a reform bill/statute of the form:

Reform R3: 'Art. 274 is repealed'

would not be unjust, and supporting it would be acceptable: for from that enactment, read by itself, you cannot tell whether any abortions remain permitted. Act R3, despite leaving arts 273 and 275 (not to mention 276) untouched, neither permits nor even tolerates abortion (they say). Indeed, they say, the legislature itself that approves R3 *and leaves arts 273, 275, and 276 untouched*, does not choose to tolerate abortion!

Test this a little further. Suppose that a (different) Criminal Code has the form:

Legislative Form C
354. Abortion is permitted—

(a) from 1 to 14 weeks if 2 doctors agree;
(b) from 14 to 24 weeks if one doctor agrees;

and otherwise is prohibited.

It is unclear what, on the Restrictive View, should be said about the justice or intrinsic injustice of:

Reform R4
'Art. 354 is amended by deleting (repealing) sub-clause (b)'

or

Reform R5
'In art. 354 sub-clause (b) is repealed.'

Neither of these reforming statutes *mentions* that clause (a) remains in force.[32] But nor does R2 *mention* that abortion is permitted—it mentions nothing but two numerals. But R2 is to be rejected (they say) because it has a 'juridical meaning' which refers to abortion being permitted up to 14 weeks, not 24. So by parity of analysis, the 'juridical meaning' of R4 or R5 presumably refers to abortion being permitted up to 14 weeks. It would follow that (on this theory) R4 and R5, like R1 and R2, are intrinsically unjust, but R3 is not.[33]

But that result is absurd. There is no significant difference, either in legal analysis or common sense, between R3 and R4 or R5. Indeed R3, too, could be analysed into its 'juridical meaning' as follows: the Code provisions on abortion are amended by repealing the article permitting abortion from 14 to 24 weeks, leaving abortion permitted up to 14 weeks under art 273, and in all cases of handicap or gipsy parentage under arts 275 and 276. The truth is that there is no legally significant distinction between these five enumerated reform provisions. There are differences between them that might have some relevance to their cultural side effects among a population in the grip of words. But a moral analysis that judges some but not others of them *intrinsically* unjust is deeply mistaken.

V. THE PRIMARY ARGUMENT

The confusions about the nature of a law that underpin both the Restrictive View and the Objection can now be seen at their core.

A law is a 'proposition of practical reason',[34] that is, a proposition that by being (legally) true/valid is ready to direct and change the course of a subject's practical reasoning and deliberation towards choice and action. The state's law is the whole set of such propositions. No enactment or other pronouncement has juridical relevance unless it *introduces* into that set some proposition(s) not formerly part of the set, or *prevents* the elimination

[32] Would it make a difference, on the Restrictive View, if the statute repealing sub-cl. (b) also stated that sub-cl. (a) is no longer numbered '(a)'?

[33] The examples are adapted from the papers in which the Restrictive View is pertinaciously articulated by Harte, 'Problems of Principle in Voting for Unjust Legislation' and 'The Opening Up of a Discussion'.

[34] Aquinas, on the first page of his classic discussion of *lex* (law), states that laws are essentially '*propositiones* universales rationis practicae ordinatae ad actiones', universal propositions of practical reason directed to actions: *ST* I–II q.90 a.1 ad 2. 'Universal' here is used in the logician's sense, to signify the picking out of a *kind* of action, however specific that kind (short of the pure particularity of e.g. a command directed to a single person to do or abstain from a particular act on a particular occasion). Hence, as he goes on to say, a law 'is simply a prescription of practical reason *in the ruler* governing a complete community' [and not, essentially, in statute books or other documents, even though promulgation is essential to its validity]: I–II q.91 a.1c; also q.92 a.1c; both passages looking back to q.90 a.1 ad 2.

of some proposition which would otherwise have ceased to be part of the set, or *eliminates* from the set some proposition(s) formerly part of it. The concept of 'ratification' has no juridical relevance except in special contexts where the very existence of a rule of law is in doubt (for example because of uncertainty about whether proper procedures were followed in enacting it). Except in such special contexts, a statute 'ratifying' another statute *does nothing* juridically. That is, it leaves the state's law exactly as it was; the set of propositions of law (legally) applicable in that community remains unaffected. Ratification's only meaning and significance (the special contexts aside) are 'political' effects, for example on public opinion, party morale, or such like. These are important, and are one concern of the kind of restrictive reforms approved by *EV* 73.3, but they are not the concern of the Principle in *EV* 73.2.

Equally misconceived is the notion that an amending provision such as R2—'In clause 1 of the Abortion Act, substitute "14" for "24"'—*continues* (while restricting) the existing statute's unjust permission. The truth is that the amending statute, in such a case, *does nothing* except prohibit abortion from the 14th week onwards. The amending statute introduces into the state's law the new proposition that abortion is prohibited between 14 and 24 weeks, to supplement the already (legally) true proposition that abortion is prohibited from 24 weeks to the end of pregnancy. The already existing proposition that abortion is permitted up to 14 weeks remains (legally) true. It continues to be true, but not because of the amending statute. Juridically, the amending statute does *not* continue the existing permission. 'Continue' has a juridical meaning and relevance if, and only if, some proposition of law *would cease* to be true *but for* the effect of the statute that continues it. And that is not the case in any of these examples.

The Restrictive View's deep confusion is this. It treats words and statements (for example in an amending statute) as identical with or equivalent to propositions. Supporters of the view might, for example, object to what I say in the previous paragraph along the following lines. Before the amending statute there was, they might object, no proposition of law, *no law*, that abortion is permitted up to 14 weeks; the only relevant proposition was in section 1 of the Abortion Act, namely that abortion is permitted up to 24 weeks. To which the relevant reply is: the *statements* in section 1 of the Abortion Act, and in the articles of the code are one thing, but the relevant propositions of law are another. The law on a subject-matter is not what is stated in some relevant statute or code but rather, what is stated in the relevant code or statute *interpreted* or understood in the light of all relevant legal principles, written and unwritten, and all other relevant provisions of codes and statutes and the opinions of judges and other learned authorities. There are as many true propositions of law as there are legally answerable questions that might be raised about the subject-matter. The following are at all relevant times (legally) true propositions of law in the imaginary state(s) we are considering: 'Abortion is lawful at ten days', 'Abortion is lawful at four weeks', and so on, indefinitely.

Lawyerly common sense, whether in a 'codified' system or a 'UK-type' (partially) uncodified system, understands the state's law as a vast sea of (legally) true propositions: 'Abortion is permitted at 10 days', 'Abortion is permitted at 12 days', 'Abortion is permitted at seven weeks', 'Abortion is permitted at eight weeks', 'Abortion is permitted at 13 weeks', 'Abortion is permitted at 14 weeks', 'Abortion is prohibited at 15 weeks', and so forth.[35] It is, legally/juridically, entirely irrelevant whether you amend this set (a) by assigning arbitrary numbers to the propositions permitting abortion between 14 and 24 weeks and then declaring that all the propositions so numbered are hereby repealed, or (b) by enacting that abortion is prohibited from 14 weeks on, or (c) by enacting that in the code provision or statutory clause permitting abortions, '24' shall be replaced by '14' . . . : there are many other ways of making one and the same change in the law.

The whole matter is too serious to turn on distinctions which are purely verbal or formalistic, in the worst sense—unhinged from reality and the relevant truths about a state's law. The Restrictive View focuses upon what bills and statutes *say*, rather than on whether those bills and statutes *make* (legally) true any (and if so which) proposition(s) of law not already true independently of them.[36] This focus results in a series of distinctions devoid of moral significance (and unknown to *EV* 73): for example, between codified and uncodified systems, between repealing a statute (but substituting an only partially changed alternative) and amending it (= partially repealing it)[‡], and between statutes that (supposedly) do and statutes that don't constitute 'the whole abortion law' of the state.

No statute, indeed no code, could constitute the whole of a state's law on abortion (or any other topic). The law on any issue is the proposition about that issue that is made legally true by the interaction of relevant statutory provisions with constitutional and other statutory provisions,

[35] Despite their relative specificity, these are all 'universal propositions' within the meaning of Aquinas's essential characterization of a law as a universal proposition of practical reason. So they are all rules. This is not to say that there is much of importance in the distinction between, on the one hand, relatively specific universals (= rules) and, on the other hand, propositions about particulars (= applications of rules in particular propositions such as that Jane's abortion of her baby this week is/was/would be lawful/unlawful).

[36] Or, of course, on whether the statute will *prevent* the ceasing to be true of some proposition of law which would otherwise cease to be true.

with judgments of superior courts, and with the general principles of law presupposed by all juristic thought. Among these general principles is that what is not prohibited is permitted, and that what is permitted is a legal right unless, though not criminally or civilly prohibited, it (as English lawyers would say) is 'contrary to [a judicially cognisable] public policy'.[37]

Permission is the default position. This is not a matter of logic[38] but of one of the 'general principles of law recognised by civilized nations'.[39] Trying to create a legal permission is redundant and futile (juridically, but perhaps not politically) unless the matter in issue is already prohibited or contrary to a legally recognized 'public policy'.[40] At least in the eyes of the law, prohibitions exist like artificial islands in a boundless ocean of permission. In any modern state the default to permission is greatly strengthened, in the case of abortion, by constitutional principles protecting and enforcing the right to bodily or personal security, the right to privacy, equal protection of women, and so forth. It is a mistake to think that a short code or statute could comprise 'the whole of a country's abortion law'.

So, whether in R2 in which a statutory provision is amended by replacing '24' with '14', or in R1 in which a statutory provision 'Abortion is permitted up to 24 weeks [and prohibited thereafter]' is amended (or repealed and substituted for) so as to read 'Abortion is permitted up to 14 weeks [and prohibited thereafter]', the effect of the change (repeal, partial repeal, amendment—draft it as you please and call it what you will) is the same. A set of propositions (indefinite in number but bounded in meaning and effect) affirming abortion's legal permissibility cease to be (legally) true, and a new set of propositions *become* (are *made to be*) legally true, prohibiting abortion. The words of the amending statute(s) speak of permitting abortions up to 14 weeks, but their legal effect on the permissibility of abortion is nil. So the restrictive line of argument entails that, except in the exotic and unheard of case of a statute or code which conveniently frames a set of

[37] As supporters of the Restrictive View contend, any distinction between legal permission and legal toleration can reasonably be assumed to be beside the point in relation to a matter of fundamental rights like abortion. The point is taken for granted in *EV* 73, and in all my papers on the subject; it may have been obscured somewhat in the CDF's Declaration of 1974, with deleterious effects on the decisions of the (West) German Constitutional Court thereafter.

[38] Logic is open to Aristotle's position that the default position is prohibition.

[39] This is the phrase used in the Statute of the International Court of Justice, Art. 38, to pick out one of the principal elements in law, alongside law established by those instruments that establish laws (in the international context conventions, in the sense of agreements or treaties; in the intra-state context statutes and other enactments) and law existing by virtue of custom.

[40] Properly interpreted, laws prohibiting murder, manslaughter, or, in general, homicide should be interpreted as extending their protection to the unborn. But to say that the law's default position is permission does not contradict that. In countries without explicit prohibitions on abortion, it is today universally true that the homicide laws are *not* interpreted as prohibiting abortion, and so such countries exemplify the default permission: what is not prohibited is permitted.

complete one-by-one permissions repealable one-by-one, all abortion statutes are intrinsically unjust—and no reforming abortion statute can ever under any circumstances be voted for in a decisive ballot—unless they are entirely prohibitive. *All or nothing* is the essence of this position.

EV 73's position is radically and rightly different. Abortion statutes creating prohibitions which otherwise would not exist are just (in the sense of: not intrinsically unjust) in all that they juridically do. What they juridically do or effect is make true a set of propositions of law, indefinite in number but bounded in meaning and effect. *Every* proposition of law that these amending or partially repealing statutes bring into being or make true is *nothing but prohibitive.* The state's law remains unjust to the extent that its permission of certain abortions remains in place and legally true. But that is not the result of anything in the amending statute. Appearances are misleading.

Still, someone may say it is 'self-evident' that legislators cannot rightly vote for a reforming bill which replaces a law permitting abortion up to 24 weeks with a law permitting it up to 14 weeks (or six weeks, or two weeks, or two days). For all such proposals '*specifically permit* abortion'! But, as Justinian's *Digest* observes at the outset (I.3.17), 'Knowing the law is not a matter of clinging to the wording [*verba*] of laws but of understanding their force and impact [*vim et potestatem*]'—what can be called their juridical meaning and juridical effect (logically prior to and distinct from any empirical effect they may have on the human behaviour they address). *The fact that a statute says that abortion is permitted does not entail that that is the statute's juridical effect.* And in fact—that is, in legal truth—the reforming bill or statute's only effect is prohibitive. So far from it being self-evident that the statute *permits*, that is, makes permitted, some abortions, it is juridically and strictly speaking not true that a reforming statute of the kind just described permits any abortion, even one. What the Objection takes to be self-evidently true is in legal reality false.

It is evident that such legal realities are the concern of *EV* 73. And, as it happens, there is an important element in *EV* 73.3 which makes doubly clear the document's indifference to all appearances and appearance-based distinctions of the kind that the Restrictive View relies upon. This element concerns the baseline against which any bill or amending statute is to be compared when assessing whether the amendment (or partial repeal) is permissive (and thus intrinsically unjust), or prohibitive and thus capable of being voted for by a Catholic or other pro-life legislator. In my own writings prior to *Evangelium Vitae*, I treated the baseline as the law in force at the time of the putting of the proposal (bill) to the decisive vote. But the encyclical takes the robustly commonsense approach that for the essential and crucial comparison there can also be another baseline, namely, the law that *will* be in force, not in some speculative future, but imminently—paradigmatically, 'tomorrow'—if the pro-life restrictive bill is not enacted. For, according to *EV* 73.3, the baseline may be 'a... law already passed' *or* '[a...law [technically a bill]] *ready to be voted on*'. If this baseline law (legal position), already in force *or* virtually certain to be in force unless defeated by a pro-life alternative, is more permissive than that pro-life alternative, then the latter should be regarded, not as introducing into the state's law permissions, but rather as making valid certain prohibitions which would otherwise have been absent from the law tomorrow. As prohibitive, it is essentially just. True, it is conspicuously permissive by comparison with the old law. But the old law is no longer a relevant baseline for comparison; in situations of the kind the document is here considering the old law is doomed and practically speaking defunct. If the pro-life bill under consideration is not enacted, the state's law will tomorrow be completely or highly permissive. So: enacting the pro-life bill/statute introduces into (or maintains in) the law certain propositions which tomorrow would have been excluded from the law, propositions which all prohibit what would otherwise, tomorrow, have ceased to be prohibited. Despite the incompleteness of its prohibitions, the pro-life bill/statute is thus not a 'permissive law' within the true meaning of *EV* 73.2's principle that one must never vote for a permissive law.

In short, not every statute that declares some abortions permitted is a permissive law in the sense intended by *EV* 73.2. For some such statutes *permit—make permitted*—nothing, but only prohibit. In these cases, the reforming statute's stipulation that abortion is permitted up to 14 weeks (or that it is prohibited only as from 14 weeks, or that '14' is substituted for '24'—the differences of formulation don't matter) is not the cause of the (legally) true proposition of law that abortion is permitted up to 14 weeks. Despite its wording, the reform permits nothing, but prohibits abortions from 14 to 24 weeks. It withdraws no part of the law's (= the state's laws') protection of unborn babies, but simply extends it. And this is apparent not only as a matter of legal technicality. It is the common sense of the matter.

VI. OTHER MISTAKES CONTRIBUTING TO THE OBJECTION

Prohibition and permission are not symmetrical, for (as recalled above) the law's default position is always permission, never prohibition. So it is a mistake to claim, with one supporter of the Objection and Restrictive

Position, that 'a proposal to repeal intrinsically unjust law can never be intrinsically unjust'.[41] This claim is false if the Objection is true, namely that a statute which states that some or all abortions are permitted is an intrinsically unjust law. For simple repeal of a statute prohibiting abortion after 24 weeks will leave the state with *no prohibition of any abortion at all*[42]—law intrinsically even more unjust. Such a repeal will be an intrinsically unjust measure. A real-life instance of such unjust action is the Canadian Supreme Court's invalidation of the Canadian abortion statute which had a few years earlier been unjustly amended so as to permit a wide range of abortions.[43] This invalidation—in substance though not in form a repeal—has left Canada with a law on abortion which is certainly intrinsically unjust but can be given alternative descriptions, each of them correct and, despite appearances, consistent with the other: 'no law at all', or: 'a completely permissive law'.[44]

But two other important mistakes at the root of the Objection have yet to be mentioned. The first is the assumption that 'intrinsically unjust' means unjust regardless of context and circumstances, and intentions of any acting person. In truth, however, when a certain kind of action is called 'intrinsically' wrongful, what is meant is that it is wrongful independently of context, circumstances, and intentions *other than those circumstances and intentions* which are part of the 'object' or 'matter' by reference to which this kind of action is identifiable (defined) as always wrong. So: as *EV* 74 recalls, theft is intrinsically unjust, but theft is highly contextual and intention-relative: it is only those takings of another's property that are carried out without urgent necessity, and without a claim to be entitled to this property, and without a belief that the owner would consent, and so forth. No definition of lying is sound unless it includes the speaker's intent to assert, not merely state, a proposition, and the speaker's belief that what is being asserted is false. And so forth. So, similarly, it is one of the evident purposes of *EV* 73.3 to make clear that a statute or other law-making statement does not fall within the class of 'intrinsically unjust' laws mentioned in *EV* 73.2 unless the context or circumstances are such that it *renders* (makes) non-prohibited what was or would otherwise tomorrow have been prohibited. These are matters of context and circumstance and intention ('aim') that enter into the very meaning of 'permissive' as that term is used in *EV* 73.2 to identify a class of intrinsically unjust laws.

[41] Cf. Harte, 'Problems of Principle in Voting for Unjust Legislation' at 205 (edited).

[42] See n. 40 above. [43] *R v Morgenthaler* [1988] 1 SCR 30.

[44] The fact that each of these *verbally* contradictory descriptions is correct should have warned Harte that simple theorems such as 'if a law is intrinsically unjust you can never vote for it' need very careful handling—as *EV* 73.3 in effect warns readers of 73.2.

The second important mistake sometimes made by defenders of the Objection is the assumption that it makes no difference whether the legislator whose action we are considering is a member of a group (a legislature, a court, a referendum electorate…) or is a *sole ruler* with authority to make whatever law(s) he or she chooses. But the difference is important in understanding the very meaning of a proposal to restrict abortion. In the case of a sole ruler who has the opportunity to choose[45] what propositions of law shall be (legally) true in relation to abortion, the ruler's proposal to restrict abortions but not completely prohibit them is a choice that here prohibition shall end and permission shall begin. It cannot fail to be the expression of the unjust judgment that unborn children of a certain immaturity, or race, or condition of handicap are not entitled to the protection of the law. But in the case of statutes enacted by a group legislature, the very same bill and statute need not, and in many circumstances does not, express any such judgment.

This can be understood by reference to an analogy. Suppose a group of twenty stalwarts travelling in a desert region come upon a fortified camp. Observing it from outside its fence they discover that inside are hundreds of children being tortured to death, one by one, by the camp's guards. The group outside have no competing responsibilities capable of affecting their obvious responsibility to rescue the children if they can. And (they judge) they can, provided that *all twenty* cooperate in a coordinated assault on the camp while the evil guards are mostly asleep. All but five of the group are determined to rescue every child. But those five insist that they are not willing to participate in the rescue, and indeed will positively block the rescue of any children at all, unless children of a race that (they say) persecuted the five's parents are left behind. There are three of these children, and they are the occupants of hut P. The fifteen protest at this unjust limitation on the rescue, but to no avail. The recalcitrant five veto all plans that include hut P. Reluctantly, but with all necessary vigour, the fifteen then carry out a rescue, together with the discriminatory five whose assistance proves, indeed, to be as vital as was anticipated. Hundreds of children are rescued, but the five discriminatory rescuers block every attempt to go beyond the plan and liberate hut P.

The willingness of the fifteen non-discriminatory rescuers to carry out the rescue in no way expresses a judgment that the three children in hut P were not as fully entitled as the others to be rescued. That unjust

[45] Here I leave aside considerations that would complicate such a ruler's deliberations, and responsibility and culpability, if the ruler's decisions on this matter were likely to be *rejected* and passively or actively *resisted* and rendered *ineffectual* or clearly *counter-productive* by popular opposition or corruption and indifference.

judgment is made by the small minority of rescuers, whose judgments and willingness overlap and converge with but partially differ radically from the just judgments and will of the majority. The resultant rescue itself can be described as a group act, and that group act can be described as unjust—indeed, intrinsically unjust—insofar as from the outset it excluded three rescuable children. But more accurately the event can be described as two converging and overlapping but partially diverging group acts. One is the act of the fifteen just rescuers. The other is the act of the five unjust rescuers (whose act includes manifesting readiness to block any attempt by the fifteen to rescue the last three children). The accurate description of the fifteen's group act is: 'an attempt to rescue *every child* that it is within our power to rescue'. That is a completely just kind of choice and act. The accurate description of the group act of the five is: 'an attempt to rescue all the children within our power except three whom we choose to leave to certain death and to prevent others from rescuing'. That is an unjust act.

The Objection's most tireless defender has said that when a restrictive abortion law is enacted there is just one group act, 'the act of the legislature'. That is a common way of talking which, though widely sensed to be something of a fiction, is accurate enough for many practical purposes—start with the name: statutes are appropriately called Acts of Congress, not Acts of a, say, 51:49 majority of each House. But talking in this way ceases to be accurate, or even reasonable, in the kind of context, and in relation to the kind of question, that we are considering. There should be no need to labour through a statement of the detailed applicability of the desert rescue analogy to situations of the kind dealt with in *EV* 73.2/3 and the present debate. Suffice it to say that if the fifteen were capable of carrying out the rescue without the cooperation of the five, their position would be like that of a single law-maker with sovereign powers (unshackled by any court or constitution), or like that of a *fully united controlling majority* in a legislature with authority to make what law 'it chooses' in relation to abortion. And that is simply not the kind of situation under discussion.

It is not irrelevant to bear in mind the effect of these various mistakes. With a few ungrounded exceptions (based on an unsound notion of codification), defenders of the Objection rule out all attempts to rescue the unborn through law unless all are to be rescued, even though the limitations on the rescue result entirely from the unjust will of a sub-group within the larger group willing and able to mount a rescue, a sub-group who block the efforts of the pro-life sub-group who are willing and ready and *otherwise* able to rescue all. The Objection meets a particular nemesis in situations, such as Canada (and in substantive respects, the United States), where the existing law on the permissibility of abortion is essentially, one may say, *no law*. For here there are, for all practical purposes, no statutory words validly declaring abortion sometimes prohibited and sometimes not.[46] The Restrictive View's candidate for acceptable restrictive abortion reform ('pure' repeal of neatly separate existing items of articulated permission)—a solution rarely if ever available in the real world—is out of the question in such a situation. Yet supporters of the Objection are content to think that the principle obviously means (and that the Catholic Church *obviously* teaches—just read the words of EV 73.2!) that in such countries nothing can be done, under any circumstances, to introduce any legal prohibition, however extensive and beneficial, unless it is a prohibition as fully complete as justice demands.

VII. INADEQUATE FORMULATIONS OF THE PRIMARY ARGUMENT

In my previous treatments of this whole issue I failed to analyse it with all the precision that it calls for. As a result, my earlier discussions gave too much prominence to the distinction between intention and side effect, and too little attention to the ambiguities in the phrase 'unjust law' and 'permissive law', ambiguities which the foregoing sections of the present essay try to bring to light.

My principal earlier treatment was written for the CDF's conference preparatory to *EV* 73.3; its main passage is perhaps this:

The question *what* one is choosing to support (or not support, or oppose) is also conditioned by context, namely by the existing legal situation. For example: a *law* of the form 'Abortion is lawful up to 16 weeks' is an unjust law. But a *bill* of the form 'Abortion is lawful up to 16 weeks' might either (a) be proposed precisely as introducing a permission of abortions hitherto prohibited, or (b) be proposed precisely as prohibiting abortions hitherto permitted between 16 and 24 weeks. The choice to support the bill in situation (a) is a substantially different choice from the choice to support the bill in situation (b). For what is being chosen—the object of the act of supporting the bill—is different in the two cases. In case (a) it is supporting the permission of abortion. In case (b) it is supporting the prohibition of abortions, indeed of all the abortions (let us suppose) that legislator at that moment has the opportunity of effectively helping to prohibit.

To say this is not to embrace 'situation ethics' or proportionalism or any other theory which denies that there are intrinsically evil acts incapable of being justified by circumstances and/or intentions or ends. On the contrary, I take for granted

[46] This is not to say that there are in these jurisdictions no laws at all regulating the practice and circumstances of abortion.

that *supporting the making of legal permission of abortion (at any stage of pregnancy) a part of the law* and *supporting the retaining of such permission as part of the law* are intrinsically evil acts incapable of being justified by circumstances and/or intentions or ends or 'proportionate reasons', even 'to reduce the total number of abortions'.[47] I have been addressing the prior questions: What is *support*? What is *making permission a part of the law (or retaining it as part of the law)*?[48]

My discussion in the essay unpacks the answer to that last question, which even as it stood made clear that a primary question—in the present context, the primary question—is: What is it for a law to be—'objectively', if you like—'permissive'? Is that question settled by looking to see what a document, the bill, or statute, *says*, regardless of the legal context or circumstances which may and usually will profoundly affect what *law* is brought into being or maintained in being by this bill or statute? But the rest of my discussion in that 1994/6 essay in fact focused upon the intentions of the voting legislator, and I loosely spoke, a couple of paragraphs later, of the restrictive reforming bill 'continu[ing]' the unjust existing law. That way of putting it failed to keep in view the distinction between what the statute says and what it juridically means and does, a distinction I have spelled out above. The same failure is to be found in a 1997 address of mine, where I spoke at one point of the restrictive reforming statute as 'a law which does in fact permit abortion',[49] even though the case I was discussing was of a statute which would neither create any permission nor keep in being any permission that would otherwise have ceased to be part of the state's laws.

The ambiguity that I was failing to keep steadily in mind is in substance the ambiguity (or one key aspect of the ambiguity) which has caused an

[47] Harte ('Problems of Principle in Voting for Unjust Legislation' and 'The Opening Up of a Discussion') says that voting for restrictive reforming legislation of the kind under debate is an unethical moral compromise. Harte provides no argument for this assertion save his general fallacious argument that every restrictive statute permits (= makes permissible) what it does not prohibit. And his distinction between the political and the moral is an unacceptable way of speaking. But he is right that the matter in debate excludes compromise. As I wrote to the Secretary of the CDF on 15 January 1995:

> Permissible *obiecta* [for choice] do *not* include 'compromising with evil' or participating in the promotion of unjust or wrongful legislation. The only relevant *obiectum* which is permissible is *eliminating, or preventing, a wrongful law as far as concretely possible*.... Support [for a restrictive reforming bill of the kind in debate] is not, in truth, a compromise with those seeking to maintain or introduce wrongful elements [of law]. There is a *material coincidence* between the upright Catholic legislator's or citizen's project and the wrongful project of those seeking to maintain or introduce wrongful elements. But this material coincidence is not appropriately describable as compromise, even if it is accompanied by certain agreements which the Catholic legislator may enter into in order to facilitate his project (e.g. the agreement to hold the vote at a specific time, or to 'pair' supporters and opponents who wish to be absent from the vote on legitimate business elsewhere). (Emphases in original.)

[48] 1996d at 599–600; 1994i at 106–8.

[49] Essay V.6 at 122 (1999d at 269).

interpretative problem for readers of Aquinas. Here is how I sketched that problem in 1991:

Aquinas sometimes says that God can dispense from the Decalogue and sometimes (in the same works [works from both his early and his late writings]) says that God cannot.

Interpretative methods like the restrictive approach to *EV* 73 and to the juridical meaning of statutes would here yield the confident conclusion that, self-evidently, one or other of these sets of texts should be abandoned, and that Aquinas was a bungler. But in fact, as I went on, the contradiction is only apparent, for:

Insofar as the Commandments consist of *formulations* which can be taken as dealing with behaviour which is *conventionally* defined as murder, adultery, and so on, or which is behaviourally (physically) the same as murder or adultery defined *ex objecto* (i.e. in terms of intentions and choices), they *can* be dispensed from by God, since his special mandate so changes the circumstances that the chooser's [proximate] intention, the *object* of the act, can be different from what it is in all other cases to which the behaviourally *or conventionally* specified norm applies: cf. *In Sent.* I d. 47 q. 1 a. 4; *In Sent.* 4 d. 33 q. 1 a. 2; *De Malo* q. 3 a. 1 ad 17. But when the Commandments are considered as they should be, as *propositions* bearing on human acts understood in terms of their precise [and proximate] intentionality (*ex objecto*), they are altogether exceptionless and cannot be dispensed from by God: *In Sent.* 3. d. 37 a. 4; *Summa Theol.* I-II q. 100 a. 8.[50]

The preceding sections of the present essay show how talk of a 'permissive' (and therefore unjust) abortion 'law' has a similar systematic ambiguity. This ambiguity must be identified and cleared up before the true principle that one must never vote for a permissive abortion law can be rightly understood and applied so as to do justice, rather than the injustices that the restrictive (mis)understanding of it (in all innocence) would often cause.

VIII. THE SECONDARY ARGUMENT

Even though the intention/side-effect distinction should not have had the prominence it did in my former discussions of this issue, it is relevant and necessary for a correct understanding of two points. One is an element in the enactment of all restrictive abortion laws. The other is a special issue that may arise from time to time.

[50] *MA* 39, emphases adjusted. I added: 'For this interpretation, see Lee, "Permanence of the Ten Commandments ..." See also *MA* 91.

The general point is this. A restrictive bill or statute does in a political and public-relations sense publicly 'ratify' and 'continue' some of the existing unjust permission of abortion. It *appears* to do what the Restrictive View mistakenly thinks it legally or juridically does, and this appearance conveys the false and corrupting message that some babies are not morally entitled to the protection of law. And, more fundamentally, it does leave some babies without the protection of law to which they have an urgent and overriding entitlement. Neither of these two broad classes of 'effects' makes the statute a permissive law in the sense of the Principle or *EV* 73.2. But both are very bad aspects of the enactment of the restrictive statute. Still, neither aspect is intended by a pro-life legislator. As *EV* 73.3 says, these legislators have a strict responsibility to make their 'absolute opposition'[51] to abortion 'well known'. If they can prevent or avoid the formulation of the restrictive statute in terms such as 'abortion is permitted up to…', they ought to.[52] But the bad effects of seeming to withdraw legal protection from some of the unborn are *praeter intentionem*, side effects, for pro-life legislators whose intention in voting for the bill/statute is simply to prohibit all the abortions they can. As for the 'leaving unprotected', this is not really an effect at all, but rather the absence of a desirable effect. It is like a fireman who can carry only two persons leaving behind a third in a burning building. It is true that the firemen have a strong obligation to rescue each and every person in the building. But they are not at fault, and are not 'choosing the lesser evil' or 'compromising', when they rescue everyone they can, leaving behind those they cannot. That leaving behind is an important part of the story. Like its sequel or outcome, it is deeply regrettable, albeit in no sense culpable. If it is an effect at all it is

[51] The encyclical uses the unfortunate phrase 'absolute personal opposition', unconscious of the way this sounds in the ear of English speakers who have heard politicians profess their 'personal opposition' to abortion while in word and deed articulating and acting upon the view that legal prohibition of abortion is more or less improper or at least not a moral responsibility.

[52] In my paper prepared for the CDF conference and republished as 1996d, I took as my stock example a bill of that form. I was dealing with the issue proposed to the symposium by its organizers—the very same 'problem of conscience' as is articulated in *EV* 73—and I was deliberately framing it in a form *unusually difficult* for the Catholic or other pro-life legislator. The same problem of conscience can arise in forms which have all the appearance of being easier, and I could have made my argument rhetorically easier by using one of these. For example: if the existing permissive legislation read 'Clause 1: Abortion is freely permissible up to 24 weeks of pregnancy', the reforming bill might simply read: 'In Section 1, replace the word 24 with the word 16.' Such a bill would *say* nothing about permitting abortion. Or the reforming bill might read: 'Notwithstanding section 1, abortion after the end of the 15th week is absolutely prohibited.' Such a bill would *say* nothing about permission and would articulate only a prohibition entirely appropriate and just in what it prohibited. But it was clear to me that the relevant problem of conscience does not turn on drafting formalities and differences. So, avoiding rhetorical advantages, I envisaged and discussed a bill whose *form(ulation)* was of the most unpromising and repellent kind: 'Abortion is lawful up to 16 weeks.' Even when those formalities and differences have a public impact which the draftsman ought to avoid if possible, failure to live up to this obligation is not an intrinsic wrong.

certainly a side effect, notwithstanding the certainty with which it can be foreseen. Common sense has little difficulty in reaching a right judgment about this.

The special point is this. Sometimes it will happen that pro-lifers who have initiated or supported a restrictive reforming bill whose only juridical effect would be prohibitive are confronted with an amendment to it which will make it in, say, one respect permissive. Imagine a one-clause pro-life bill to extend the prohibition of abortion from 24 weeks to three weeks[53]—thus saving 99 per cent of all who would otherwise be aborted—onto which is tacked at the last minute (over the total but unavailing opposition of the pro-life legislators) a new clause B cancelling the existing legal prohibition of abortion sought on the ground of forcible rape. The bill thus amended is put to a final vote, and if it is not carried there will be no reform of abortion law for many years if ever (so far as human foresight goes). The bill is now, in one part (clause B), permissive within the meaning of *EV* 73.2 and the true principle that paragraph of the encyclical articulates. When asked by the Speaker to vote Aye or Nay, can the pro-life legislators vote Aye? Surely.

But, the objector may say, legislators voting for proposals are willing and choosing to enact precisely what is contained within those proposals. What the legislature 'does' (in willing that certain permissions, tolerations, prohibitions, etc. be enacted as law) is indistinguishable from what an individual legislator 'does' (in willing that the proposal with those very permissions, tolerations, prohibitions, etc. be enacted). Voting for the whole of the proposal which is presented as the matter of the vote is *the act of the legislator* just as the enactment of the whole of the proposal is *the act of the legislature* (sec. 5.2). This objection sounds plausible, if one is in the grip of one's society's conventions, but as an action-description fit for moral analysis it is simply false. The pro-life legislators each say 'Aye' or walk through the 'Yes' lobby. An effect of that behaviour is that, if enough others do likewise, the whole bill, and each of its parts, will be enacted. But what these pro-life legislators intend, both the proximate intention that each of them have—the precise object of their voting acts—and any further intention(s) or motive they have, is settled not by what other people or social conventions make of their behaviour but by their own course of deliberation, their own authentic practical reasoning (not to be confused with some inauthentic inner or outer story they might tell themselves or others to rationalize their real purposes). And it is their object, 'the

[53] The pro-life legislators have floated a bill to extend the prohibition to 0 weeks (= from conception), but find that this has no support from those compromising legislators whose support is indispensable if there is to be any reform at all.

proximate end of a deliberate decision which determines the act of willing on the part of the acting person',[54] that settles the question *what they are doing*, the act(ion) which, thus accurately described, can then be subjected to moral analysis.[55] Their object in voting Aye is the enactment of clause A. By virtue of the conventions (rules) of the legislature and the morally bad will and actions of the pro-choice and centrist legislators who secured the addition of clause B, the effect of their *voting for clause A* will be that the whole bill, including clause B, will be enacted. This effect is certain and inevitable, but (like many other certain and inevitable effects of what we choose to do) it is not part of what they intend or choose or do, in the senses of those words which are necessary for a true analysis (and for a Catholic analysis). The enactment of clause B is for these legislators a side effect. (For others, of course, it is an important part of what these others intend and do.)

As argued in earlier sections, a law is essentially a proposition of law, and one bill/statute can thus, whatever its verbal structure, contain many distinct laws. It follows that, in a case like this, the legislator who votes for the law made (legally) true by clause A does not *vote for* the unjust law made (legally) true by clause B. In the true principle articulated in *EV* 73.2, not only the phrase 'permissive law', but also the phrase 'vote for' must be understood with precision. One does not, precisely speaking, vote for what one does not intend to vote for.

But it also remains true that, in the broader sense that counts for parliamentary procedure and its outcomes, one votes for the whole bill and all its parts. The enactment of the whole bill including its unjust part(s), here clause B, is a side effect for which the pro-life legislators are morally responsible, as one is always responsible for side effects that one can or should foresee and could avoid. But the norms that govern the moral assessment of their willingness to cause that side effect are not the strict and exceptionless negative moral norms which apply to what one intends, chooses, and in that strict sense does. They are norms of fairness, commitment, role responsibility, which are situation-relative,[56] and which allow for the judgment that *for these legislators*, who do not intend the enactment of clause B, the willingness to do what foreseeably and certainly has the effect of enacting clause B (and is conventionally *counted*

[54] Encyclical *Veritatis Splendor* (1993), 78.

[55] The morality of the human act depends primarily and fundamentally on the 'object' rationally chosen by the deliberate will, as is borne out by the insightful analysis, still valid today, made by Saint Thomas [fn. *ST* I–II q.18 a.6]. (*Ibid.*, 78.)

Harte has sometimes suggested that the citation of q.18 a.6 somehow qualifies the obvious sense of *Veritatis Splendor* 78. It does not. See n. 58 below, and *MA* 65–74.

[56] See n. 7 above.

as 'intentionally voting for' and enacting the whole bill including clause B) is not unjust to the babies who will unjustly perish because of clause B's enactment.

This is a special and perhaps rather unusual kind of case; the more usual case is the kind discussed above, in which the reforming bill is nothing but restrictive. But the truth that precisely what a voter is doing in voting is settled by his or her actual course of deliberation, not by what is deemed in law or convention to be the effect of so behaving, is a general truth. So too is the truth that, whatever its verbal structure or drafting formalities, a bill/statute has the logical structure of a list of distinct propositions of law, rather like the Restrictive View's imaginary code,[57] whose articles could each be eliminated without affecting the other articles—with the consequence that the object and intent of legislators in going through the 'Aye' lobby can rationally be to enact some of these propositions of law, accepting the enactment of the others as a side effect for which they are morally responsible but not in the uniquely stringent way that one is morally responsible for what one intends and chooses as an end or as a means. Thus the emphasis on the distinction between intention and side effect in my earlier analyses of the *general* problem of voting for restrictive abortion legislation was not so much mistaken as unnecessary and therefore misleading.

IX. CONCLUDING NOTE ON INTENTIONS (MOTIVES)

It follows from the Secondary Argument that though they are voting for the same legislation, at the same time, and within the same context, for some legislators the action is evil, and for others the action is good. And there should be no surprise. The real possibility of identical behaviour being different descriptive species and different moral species of human acts is an immediate implication of a sound act-analysis. One finds such an analysis, for example, in Aquinas—not least in, amongst many other passages, *Summa Theologiae* I–II q.18 a.6, recalled in *Veritatis Splendor* 78. As that passage puts it,[58] one's actually (interiorly) willed end or ends—purpose(s),

[57] Form B in sec. IV above.

[58] *ST* I–II q.18 a.6c:

So, just as one's external act gets its species or character from the object which it concerns, so one's internal act of will gets its species from one's end(s), as if that were its own object. But [or: And thus] *whatever pertains to one's will stands as shaping and characterising in relation to whatever pertains to one's external act.* For one's will employs one's members as its instrument in one's acting, and *one's external acts only have moral significance insofar as they are willed.* And so the species or *character of a human act is formally* [*essentially*] *analysed by reference to one's end(s)*, and is analysed in terms of its matter by reference to the object of one's external act. Thus as Aristotle says in

non-proximate intention(s)—stand(s) to the object (the proximate end) of one's exterior act as decisively characterising, *formale*, that is, as form stands to matter, namely as *making the thing what it is*. So, in the context of action, it is the ends and intentions of the acting person that make *the act*—what is *done*—what it is.[59] And they thus can make immoral what would otherwise be morally right. Two soldiers on a mission to rescue people from an extermination camp are alongside one another, returning the rifle fire of the camp guards. One soldier intends his potentially lethal return fire to disable the guards from blocking the rescue mission. The other soldier intends to satisfy his lust to see or hear and gloat over hated men dying in agony. The first's acts are acts of just defence of self and others, the second's identical *behaviour* is 'materially' the same but formally (that is, more really) and primarily (according to the teaching of Aquinas, following Aristotle) an act or set of acts of immoral lust or hatred.[60] At any rate, they are substantially different *acts*, as that term is used in moral reflection.

The same can and often holds true of two legislators going through the voting lobby together: their behaviour is identical, their acts different, and one is acting uprightly, the other immorally. In neither this case nor the extermination camp rescue need this make the cooperation between the rescuers or legislators morally unacceptable. Legislators whose intention is to do justice so far as is possible for them in the legislative situation are not complicit in the bad intentions or motives of those whose bad will prevents them doing all that justice requires.

NE V, if one steals in order to commit adultery, one is, strictly speaking, more an adulterer than a thief.

{Sicut igitur actus exterior accepit speciem ab obiecto circa quod est, ita actus interior voluntatis accepit speciem a fine sicut a proprio obiecto. *Id* [or: *Ita*] *autem quod est ex parte voluntatis se habet ut formale ad id quod est ex parte exterioris actus*, quia voluntas utitur membris ad agendum sicut instrumentis, *neque actus exteriores habent rationem moralitatis nisi inquantum sunt voluntarii*. Et ideo actus humani *species formaliter consideratur secundum finem*, materialiter autem secundum obiectum exterioris actus. Unde Philosophus dicit, in V Eth., ut ille qui furatur ut committit adulterium est, per se loquendo, magis adulter quam fur.}

In Aquinas's philosophy, 'form' and *formale* refer to what is most essential to something being what it is—almost the opposite meaning from the modern idiomatic English '(mere) formality' etc. On what Aquinas means by speaking of an act's 'matter', see *Aquinas* 142 nn. 43–4 with the citations especially to *De Malo*: in short, in this context 'matter' and 'object' and 'close-in intention' are interchangeable.

[59] Elsewhere, and pervasively, Aquinas will remind us that good and bad are not symmetrical: good (further) intentions cannot make good an act made bad by its matter = object = proximately intended behavioural characteristics, but bad intentions (and/or inappropriate circumstances) make bad an act despite its being in its matter/object a good or not-bad kind of behaviour such as almsgiving or walking. See *ST* I–II q.18 a.4 ad 3; *Aquinas* 148 at n. 73.

[60] See n. 58 above.

NOTES

† This essay belongs in this volume rather than Vol. V because it focuses on clarifying, philosophically, the logic of law-making and law-finding, as operations on and with propositions rather than statements, expressions, texts, and so forth. This clarification makes possible a significant improvement in the interpretation of the ecclesiastical texts it discusses as exemplars of the logical point in issue. My essays 1994i, 1996d, 2005f, and 2005g, and the criticisms of them in Harte ('Problems of Principle in Voting for Unjust Legislation' and 'The Opening Up of a Discussion', and *Changing Unjust Laws Justly*), all seven of which were written before the present essay, should be read in the light of the clarification.

‡ *Amendment as partial repeal*...(text after n. 36)

> [W]hen an Act of Parliament not using the word 'repealed' contains a provision which alters the provisions of a previous Act it repeals that provision. It is not necessary that the word 'repeal' should be used, or that the Act repealed should be in the schedule to the second Act. You may easily have a repeal which is not made by using the word 'repeal' and is not effected by putting the Act into shape. It seems to me that when 150l. was altered to 200l., when 10l. was altered to 15l., and when the provision was inserted that you might not deduct weekly payments so as to reduce the total sum payable to dependants below 200l., you [sc. the Workmen's Compensation Act 1923] were repealing three provisions of the [Workmen's Compensation Act] 1906...(*Moakes v Blackwell Colliery Co.* [1926] 2 KB 64 at 70 (CA).)

The judgment goes on to say that such implied repeal counts as repeal also for the purposes of the provisions of the Interpretation Act 1889 relating to the effect of repeals (as to which see essay 21 at n. 47).

BIBLIOGRAPHY OF THE WORKS OF JOHN FINNIS

1962	a		'Developments in Judicial Jurisprudence', Adelaide L Rev 1: 317–37
	b		'The Immorality of the Deterrent', Adelaide Univ Mag: 47–61
1963			'Doves and Serpents', The Old Palace 38: 438–41
1967	a	I.17	'Reason and Passion: The Constitutional Dialectic of Free Speech and Obscenity', University of Pennysylvania L Rev 116: 222–43
	b	IV.8	'Blackstone's Theoretical Intentions', Natural L Forum 12: 63–83
	c		'Punishment and Pedagogy', The Oxford Review 5: 83–93
	d		'Review of Zelman Cowen, *Sir John Latham and Other Papers*', LQR 83: 289–90
1968	a	III.10	'Old and New in Hart's Philosophy of Punishment', The Oxford Review 8: 73–80
	b		'Constitutional Law', *Annual Survey of Commonwealth Law 1967* (Butterworth), 20–33, 71–98
	c		'Separation of Powers in the Australian Constitution', Adelaide L Rev 3: 159–77
	d		Review of Neville March Hunnings, *Film Censors and the Law*, LQR 84: 430–2
	e		'Natural Law in *Humanae vitae*', LQR 84: 467–71
	f		Review of H. Phillip Levy, *The Press Council*, LQR 84: 582
	g		'Law, Morality and Mind Control', Zenith (University Museum, Oxford) 6: 7–8
1969	a		'Constitutional Law', *Annual Survey of Commonwealth Law 1968* (Butterworth), 2–15, 32–49, 53–75, 98–114
	b		Review of Herbert L. Packer, *The Limits of the Criminal Sanction*, Oxford Magazine, 86 no. 1 (new series), 10–11
1970	a	I.6	'Reason, Authority and Friendship in Law and Morals', in Khanbai, Katz, and Pineau (eds), *Jowett Papers 1968–1969* (Oxford: Blackwell), 101–24
	b		'Natural Law and Unnatural Acts', Heythrop J 11: 365–87
	c		i. 'Abortion and Legal Rationality', Adelaide L Rev 3: 431–67 ii. 'Three Schemes of Regulation', in Noonan (ed.), *The Morality of Abortion: Legal and Historical Perspectives* (HUP)
	d		'Constitutional Law', *Annual Survey of Commonwealth Law 1969* (Butterworth), 2–4, 27–34, 37–50, 65–81
	e		Review of H.B. Acton, *The Philosophy of Punishment*, Oxford Magazine, 87 (new series) (13 April)
	f		Review of Colin Howard, *Australian Constitutional Law*, LQR 86: 416–18

1971	a	**IV.21**	'Revolutions and Continuity of Law', in A.W.B. Simpson (ed.), *Oxford Essays in Jurisprudence: Second Series* (OUP), 44–76
	b		'The Abortion Act: What Has Changed?', Criminal L Rev: 3–12
	c		'Constitutional Law', *Annual Survey of Commonwealth Law 1970* (Butterworth), 2–4, 17–31, 33–42, 51–60
1972	a	**III.11**	'The Restoration of Retribution', Analysis 32: 131–5
	b	**IV.18**	'Some Professorial Fallacies about Rights', Adelaide L Rev 4: 377–88
	c		'The Value of the Human Person', Twentieth Century [Australia] 27: 126–37
	d		'Bentham et le droit naturel classique', Archives de Philosophie du Droit 17: 423–7
	e		'Constitutional Law', *Annual Survey of Commonwealth Law 1971* (Butterworth), 2–5, 11–25, 28–41
	f		'Meaning and Ambiguity in Punishment (and Penology)', Osgoode Hall LJ 10: 264–8
1973	a	**III.3**	Review of John Rawls, *A Theory of Justice* (1972), Oxford Magazine 90 no. 1 (new series) (26 January)
	b	**III.18**	'The Rights and Wrongs of Abortion: A Reply to Judith Jarvis Thomson', Philosophy & Public Affairs 2: 117–45
	c		'Constitutional Law', *Annual Survey of Commonwealth Law 1972* (Butterworth), 2–8, 23–56, 62–6
1974	a		'Constitutional Law', *Annual Survey of Commonwealth Law 1973* (Butterworth), 1–66
	b		'Commonwealth and Dependencies', in *Halsbury's Laws of England*, vol. 6 (4th edn, Butterworth), 315–601
	c		'Rights and Wrongs in Legal Responses to Population Growth', in J.N. Santamaria (ed.), *Man—How Will He Survive?* (Adelaide), 91–100
	d		Review of R.S. Gae, *The Bank Nationalisation Case and the Constitution*, Modern L Rev 37: 120
1975			'Constitutional Law', *Annual Survey of Commonwealth Law 1974* (Butterworth), 1–61
1976	a		'Constitutional Law', *Annual Survey of Commonwealth Law 1975* (Butterworth), 1–56
	b		Chapters 18–21 (with Germain Grisez), in R. Lawler, D.W. Wuerl, and T.C. Lawler (eds), *The Teaching of Christ* (Huntingdon, IN: OSV), 275–354
1977	a	**I.3**	'Scepticism, Self-refutation and the Good of Truth', in P.M. Hacker and J. Raz (eds), *Law, Morality and Society: Essays in Honour of H.L.A. Hart* (OUP), 247–67
	b		'Some Formal Remarks about "Custom"', in International Law Association, Report of the First Meeting [April 1977] on the Theory and Methodology of International Law, 14–21
1978	a		'Catholic Social Teaching: *Populorum Progressio* and After', Church Alert (SODEPAX Newsletter) 19: 2–9; also in James V. Schall (ed.), *Liberation Theology in Latin America* (San Francisco: Ignatius Press, 1982)

b ‘Conscience, Infallibility and Contraception’, The Month 239: 410–17

c ‘Abortion: Legal Aspects of’, in Warren T. Reich (ed.), *Encyclopedia of Bioethics* (New York: Free Press), 26–32

1979 V.18 ‘Catholic Faith and the World Order: Reflections on E.R. Norman’, Clergy Rev 64: 309–18

1980 a *Natural Law and Natural Rights* (OUP) (425 pp)

Legge Naturali e Diritti Naturali (trans. Di Blasi) (Milan: Giappichelli, 1996)

Ley Natural y Derechos Naturales (trans. C. Orrego) (Buenos Aires: Abeledo-Perrot, 2000)

Prawo naturalne i uprawnienia naturalne (trans. Karolina Lossman) Klasycy Filozofii Prawa (Warsaw: Dom Wydawniczy ABC, 2001)

自然法与自然权利 ([Mandarin] trans. Jiaojiao Dong, Yi Yang, Xiaohui Liang) (Beijing: 2004)

Lei Natural e Direitos Naturais (trans. Leila Mendes) (Sao Leopoldo, Brazil: Editora Unisinos, 2007)

b ‘Reflections on an Essay in Christian Ethics: Part I: Authority in Morals’, Clergy Rev 65: 51–7: ‘Part II: Morals and Method’, 87–93

c V.19 ‘The Natural Law, Objective Morality, and Vatican II’, in William E. May (ed), *Principles of Catholic Moral Life* (Chicago: Franciscan Herald Press), 113–49

1981 a [*British North America Acts: The Role of Parliament*: Report from the Foreign Affairs Committee, House of Commons Paper 1980–81 HC 42 (21 January) (87 pp)]

b ‘Observations de M J.M. Finnis’ [on Georges Kalinowski’s review of *Natural Law and Natural Rights*], Archives de Philosophie du Droit 26: 425–7

c [Foreign Affairs Committee, *Supplementary Report on the British North America Acts: The Role of Parliament*, House of Commons Paper 1980–81 HC 295 (15 April) (23 pp)]

d [Foreign Affairs Committee, *Third Report on the British North America Acts: The Role of Parliament*, House of Commons Paper 1981–82 HC 128 (22 December) (17 pp)]

e ‘Natural Law and the “Is”-“Ought” Question: An Invitation to Professor Veatch’, Cath Lawyer 26: 266–77

1982 a (with Germain Grisez) ‘The Basic Principles of Natural Law: A Reply to Ralph McInerny’, American J Juris 26: 21–31

b Review of Anthony Battaglia, *Towards a Reformulation of Natural Law*, Scottish J Theol 35: 555–6

1983 a ‘The Responsibilities of the United Kingdom Parliament and Government under the Australian Constitution’, Adelaide L Rev 9: 91–107

b *Fundamentals of Ethics* (OUP; Washington DC: Georgetown University Press) (163 pp)

c ‘Power to Enforce Treaties in Australia—The High Court goes Centralist?’, Oxford J Legal St 3: 126–30

	d		'The Fundamental Themes of *Laborem Exercens*', in Paul L. Williams (ed.), *Catholic Social Thought and the Social Teaching of John Paul II* (Scranton: Northeast Books), 19–31
	e		['In Vitro Fertilisation: Morality and Public Policy', Evidence submitted by the Catholic Bishops' Joint Committee on Bio-ethical Issues to the [Warnock] Committee of Inquiry into Human Fertilisation and Embryology, May, 5–18]
1984	a	I.10	i. 'Practical Reasoning, Human Goods and the End of Man', Proc Am Cath Phil Ass 58: 23–36; also in ii. New Blackfriars 66 (1985) 438–51
	b	IV.2	'The Authority of Law in the Predicament of Contemporary Social Theory', J Law, Ethics & Pub Policy 1: 115–37
	c		['Response to the Warnock Report', submission to Secretary of State for Social Services by the Catholic Bishops' Joint Bioethics Committee on Bio-ethical Issues, December, 3–17]
	d		'IVF and the Catholic Tradition', The Month 246: 55–8
	e		'Reforming the Expanded External Affairs Power', in Report of the External Affairs Subcommittee to the Standing Committee of the Australian Constitutional Convention (September), 43–51
1985	a	III.1	'A Bill of Rights for Britain? The Moral of Contemporary Jurisprudence' (Maccabaean Lecture in Jurisprudence), Proc Brit Acad 71: 303–31
	b	IV.9	'On "Positivism" and "Legal-Rational Authority"', Oxford J Leg St 3: 74–90
	c	IV.13	'On "The Critical Legal Studies Movement"', American J Juris 30: 21–42; also in J. Bell and J. Eekelaar (eds), *Oxford Essays in Jurisprudence: Third Series* (OUP, 1987), 145–65
	d		'Morality and the Ministry of Defence' (review), The Tablet, 3 August, 804–5
	e		'Personal Integrity, Sexual Morality and Responsible Parenthood', Anthropos [now Anthropotes] 1: 43–55
1986	a		'The "Natural Law Tradition"', J Legal Ed 36: 492–5
	b		'The Laws of God, the Laws of Man and Reverence for Human Life', in R. Hittinger (ed.), *Linking the Human Life Issues* (Chicago: Regnery Books), 59–98
1987	a	I.9	'Natural Inclinations and Natural Rights: Deriving "Ought" from "Is" according to Aquinas', in L. Elders and K. Hedwig (eds), *Lex et Libertas: Freedom and Law according to St Thomas Aquinas* (Studi Tomistici 30, Libreria Editrice Vaticana), 43–55
	b	II.8	'The Act of the Person' *Persona Verità e Morale*, atti del Congresso Internazionale di Teologia Morale, Rome 1986 (Rome: Città Nuova Editrice), 159–75
	c	III.2	'Legal Enforcement of Duties to Oneself: Kant v. Neo-Kantians', Columbia L Rev 87: 433–56
	d	IV.4	'On Positivism and the Foundations of Legal Authority: Comment', in Ruth Gavison (ed.), *Issues in Legal Philosophy: the Influence of H.L.A. Hart* (OUP), 62–75

e IV.12 'On Reason and Authority in Law's Empire', Law and Philosophy 6: 357–80

f Germain Grisez, Joseph Boyle, and John Finnis, 'Practical Principles, Moral Truth, and Ultimate Ends', American J Juris 32: 99–151 (also, with original table of contents restored, in 1991d)

g *Nuclear Deterrence, Morality and Realism* (with Joseph Boyle and Germain Grisez) (OUP) (429 pp)

h 'Answers [to questions about nuclear and non-nuclear defence options]', in Oliver Ramsbottom (ed.), *Choices: Nuclear and Non-Nuclear Defence Options* (London: Brasseys' Defence Publishers), 219–34

i 'The Claim of Absolutes', The Tablet 241: 364–6

j ['On Human Infertility Services and Bioethical Research', response by the Catholic Bishops' Joint Committee on Bioethical Issues to the Department of Health and Social Security, June, 3–12]

1988 a V.21 'The Consistent Ethic: A Philosophical Critique', in Thomas G. Fuechtmann (ed.), *Consistent Ethic of Life* (Kansas: Sheed & Ward), 140–81

b V.20 'Nuclear Deterrence, Christian Conscience, and the End of Christendom', New Oxford Rev [Berkeley, CA] July–August: 6–16

c 'Goods are Meant for Everyone: Reflection on Encyclical *Sollicitudo Rei Socialis*', L'Osservatore Romano, weekly edn, 21 March, 21

d '"Faith and Morals": A Note', The Month 21/2: 563–7

e Germain Grisez, Joseph Boyle, John Finnis, and William E. May, '"Every Marital Act Ought to be Open to New Life": Toward a Clearer Understanding', The Thomist 52: 365–426, also in Grisez, Boyle, Finnis, and May, *The Teaching of Humanae Vitae: A Defense* (San Francisco: Ignatius Press); Italian trans. in Anthropotes 1: 73–122

f 'Absolute Moral Norms: Their Ground, Force and Permanence', Anthropotes 2: 287–303

1989 a II.5 'Persons and their Associations', Proc Aristotelian Soc, Supp. vol. 63: 267–74

b IV.3 'Law as Coordination', Ratio Juris 2: 97–104

c V.11 'On Creation and Ethics', Anthropotes 2: 197–206

d 'La morale chrétienne et la guerre: entretien avec John Finnis', Catholica 13: 15–23

e 'Russell Hittinger's Straw Man', Fellowship of Catholic Scholars Newsletter 12/2: 6–8 (corrigenda in following issue)

f 'Nuclear Deterrence and Christian Vocation', New Blackfriars 70: 380–7

1990 a I.12 'Aristotle, Aquinas, and Moral Absolutes', Catholica: International Quarterly Selection 12: 7–15; Spanish trans. by Carlos I. Massini-Correas in Persona y Derecho 28 (1993), and in

A.G. Marques and J. Garcia-Huidobro (eds), *Razon y Praxis* (Valparaiso: Edeval, 1994), 319–36
b **IV.16** 'Allocating Risks and Suffering: Some Hidden Traps', Cleveland State L Rev 38: 193–207
c 'Natural Law and Legal Reasoning', Cleveland State L Rev 38: 1–13
d **IV.17** 'Concluding Reflections', Cleveland State L Rev 38: 231–50
e **V.16** 'Conscience in the Letter to the Duke of Norfolk', in Ian Ker and Alan G. Hill (eds), *Newman after a Hundred Years* (OUP), 401–18
f Joseph Boyle, Germain Grisez, and John Finnis, 'Incoherence and Consequentialism (or Proportionalism)—A Rejoinder' American Cath Phil Q 64: 271–7
g 'The Natural Moral Law and Faith', in Russell E. Smith (ed.), *The Twenty-Fifth Anniversary of Vatican II: A Look Back and a Look Ahead* (Braintree, MA: Pope John Center), 223–38; discussion (with Alasdair MacIntyre), 250–62

1991 a **II.9** 'Object and Intention in Moral Judgments according to St Thomas Aquinas', The Thomist 55: 1–27; rev. version in J. Follon and J. McEvoy (eds), *Finalité et Intentionnalité: Doctrine Thomiste et Perspectives Modernes*, Bibliothèque Philosophique de Louvain No. 35 (Paris: J. Vrin, 1992), 127–48
b **II.10** 'Intention and Side-effects', in R.G. Frey and Christopher W. Morris (eds), *Liability and Responsibility: Essays in Law and Morals* (CUP), 32–64
c *Moral Absolutes: Tradition, Revision and Truth* (Washington DC: Catholic University of America Press) (115 pp) *Absolutos Morales: Tradición, Revisión y Verdad* (trans. Juan José García Norro) (Barcelona: Ediciones Internacionales Universitarias, EUNSA SA) *Gli assoluti morali: Tradizione, revisione & verità* (trans. Andrea Maria Maccarini) (Milan: Edizioni Ares, 1993)
d 'Introduction', in John Finnis (ed.), *Natural Law*, vol. I (International Library of Essays in Law and Legal Theory, Schools 1.1) (Dartmouth: New York University Press), xi–xxiii
e 'Introduction', in John Finnis (ed.), *Natural Law*, vol. II (International Library of Essays in Law and Legal Theory, Schools 1.2) (Dartmouth: Aldershot, Sydney), xi–xvi
f 'A propos de la "valeur intrinsèque de la vie humaine"', Catholica 28: 15–21
g 'Commonwealth and Dependencies', in *Halsbury's Laws of England*, vol. 6 re-issue (4th edn, London: Butterworth), 345–559

1992 a **I.14** 'Natural Law and Legal Reasoning', in Robert P. George (ed.), *Natural Law Theory: Contemporary Essays* (OUP), 134–57
b **III.7** 'Commentary on Dummett and Weithman', in Brian Barry and Robert E. Goodin, *Free Movement: Ethical Issues in the Transnational Migration of People and of Money* (University Park, Pennsylvania: University of Pennsylvania Press), 203–10

	c	III.15	'Economics, Justice and the Value of Life: Concluding Remarks', in Luke Gormally (ed.), *Economics and the Dependent Elderly: Autonomy, Justice and Quality of Care* (CUP), 189–98
	d	V.9	*'Historical Consciousness' and Theological Foundations*, Etienne Gilson Lecture No. 15 (Toronto: Pontifical Institute of Mediaeval Studies) (32 pp)
	e	V.17	'On the Grace of Humility: A New Theological Reflection', The Allen Review 7: 4–7
1993	a	II.16/ III.19	'Abortion and Health Care Ethics', in Raanan Gillon (ed.), *Principles of Health Care Ethics* (Chichester: John Wiley), 547–57
	b		'The Legal Status of the Unborn Baby', Catholic Medical Quarterly 43: 5–11
	c	II.19	'*Bland*: Crossing the Rubicon?', LQR 109: 329–37
	d		'Theology and the Four Principles: A Roman Catholic View I' (with Anthony Fisher OP), in Raanon Gillon (ed.), *Principles of Health Care Ethics* (Chichester: John Wiley), 31–44
	e		'The "Value of Human Life" and "The Right to Death": Some Reflections on *Cruzan* and Ronald Dworkin', Southern Illinois University LJ 17: 559–71
1994	a	II.12	'On Conditional Intentions and Preparatory Intentions', in Luke Gormally (ed.), *Moral Truth and Moral Tradition: Essays in Honour of Peter Geach and Elizabeth Anscombe* (Dublin: Four Courts Press), 163–76
	b		'Law, Morality, and "Sexual Orientation"', Notre Dame L Rev 69: 1049–76; also, with additions, Notre Dame J Law, Ethics & Public Policy 9 (1995) 11–39
	c		'Liberalism and Natural Law Theory', Mercer L Rev 45: 687–704
	d		'"Shameless Acts" in Colorado: Abuse of Scholarship in Constitutional Cases', Academic Questions 7/4: 10–41
	e		Germain Grisez and John Finnis, 'Negative Moral Precepts Protect the Dignity of the Human Person', L'Osservatore Romano, English edn, 23 February
	f		'Beyond the Encyclical', The Tablet, 8 January, reprinted in John Wilkins (ed.), *Understanding* Veritatis Splendor (London: SPCK), 69–76
	g		Germain Grisez, John Finnis, and William E. May, 'Indissolubility, Divorce and Holy Communion', New Blackfriars 75 (June), 321–30
	h		'"Living Will" Legislation', in Luke Gormally (ed.), *Euthanasia, Clinical Practice and the Law* (London: Linacre Centre), 167–76
	i		'Unjust Laws in a Democratic Society: Some Philosophical and Theological Reflections', in Joseph Joblin and Réal Tremblay (eds), *I cattolici e la società pluralista: il caso delle leggi imperfette: atti del I Colloquio sui cattolici nella società pluralista: Roma, 9–12 Novembre 1994* (Bologna: ESP), 99–114
1995	a	II.11	'Intention in Tort Law', in David Owen (ed.), *Philosophical Foundations of Tort Law* (OUP), 229–48

b III.14 'A Philosophical Case against Euthanasia', 'The Fragile Case for Euthanasia: A Reply to John Harris', and 'Misunderstanding the Case against Euthanasia: Response to Harris's First Reply', in John Keown (ed.), *Euthanasia: Ethical, Legal and Clinical Perspectives* (CUP), 23–35, 46–55, 62–71

c 'History of Philosophy of Law' (465–8), 'Problems in the Philosophy of Law' (468–72), 'Austin' (67), 'Defeasible' (181), 'Dworkin' (209–10), 'Grotius' (328), 'Hart' (334), 'Legal Positivism' (476–7), 'Legal Realism' (477), 'Natural Law' (606–7), 'Natural Rights' (607), in Ted Honderich (ed.), *Oxford Companion to Philosophy* (OUP)

1996 a III.5 'Is Natural Law Theory Compatible with Limited Government?', in Robert P. George (ed.), *Natural Law, Liberalism, and Morality* (OUP), 1–26

b III.13 'The Ethics of War and Peace in the Catholic Natural Law Tradition', in Terry Nardin (ed.), *The Ethics of War and Peace* (Princeton University Press), 15–39

c IV.7 'The Truth in Legal Positivism', in Robert P. George (ed.), *The Autonomy of Law: Essays on Legal Positivism* (OUP), 195–214

d 'Unjust Laws in a Democratic Society: Some Philosophical and Theological Reflections', Notre Dame L Rev 71: 595–604 (a revised version of 1994i)

e I.13 'Loi naturelle', in Monique Canto-Sperber (ed.), *Dictionnaire de Philosophie Morale* (Paris: Presses Universitaires de France), 862–8

1997 a 'Natural Law—Positive Law', in A. Lopez Trujillo, I. Herranz, and E. Sgreccia (eds), *'Evangelium Vitae' and Law* (Libreria Editrice Vaticana), 199–209

b I.15 'Commensuration and Public Reason', in Ruth Chang (ed.), *Incommensurability, Comparability and Practical Reasoning* (HUP), 215–33, 285–9

c III.21 'Law, Morality and "Sexual Orientation"', in John Corvino (ed.), *Same Sex: Debating the Ethics, Science, and Culture of Homosexuality* (Lanham: Rowman & Littlefield), 31–43

d III.22 'The Good of Marriage and the Morality of Sexual Relations: Some Philosophical and Historical Observations', Am J Juris 42: 97–134

1998 a I.16 'Public Reason, Abortion and Cloning', Valparaiso Univ LR 32: 361–82

b III.16 'Euthanasia, Morality and Law', Loyola of Los Angeles L Rev 31: 1123–45

c V.3 'On the Practical Meaning of Secularism', Notre Dame L Rev 73: 491–515

d *Aquinas: Moral, Political, and Legal Theory* (OUP) (xxi + 385 pp)

e 'Public Good: The Specifically Political Common Good in Aquinas', in Robert P. George (ed.), *Natural Law and Moral Inquiry* (Washington DC: Georgetown University Press), 174–209

	f		'Natural Law', in Edward Craig (ed.), *Routledge Encyclopaedia of Philosophy*, vol. 6 (London: Routledge), 685–90
1999	a	I.2	'Natural Law and the Ethics of Discourse', American J Juris 43: 53–73; also in Ratio Juris 12: 354–73
	b	III.12	'Retribution: Punishment's Formative Aim', American J Juris 44: 91–103
	c	IV.20	'The Fairy Tale's Moral', LQR 115: 170–5
	d	V.6	'The Catholic Church and Public Policy Debates in Western Liberal Societies: The Basis and Limits of Intellectual Engagement', in Luke Gormally (ed.), *Issues for a Catholic Bioethic* (London: Linacre Centre), 261–73
	e		'What is the Common Good, and Why does it Concern the Client's Lawyer?', South Texas L Rev 40: 41–53
2000	a	II.1	'The Priority of Persons', in Jeremy Horder (ed.), *Oxford Essays in Jurisprudence, Fourth Series* (OUP), 1–15
	b	II.17	'Some Fundamental Evils of Generating Human Embryos by Cloning', in Cosimo Marco Mazzoni (ed.), *Etica della Ricerca Biologica* (Florence: Leo S. Olschki Editore), 115–23; also in C.M. Mazzoni (ed.), *Ethics and Law in Biological Research* (The Hague, London: Martinus Nijhoff; Boston: Kluwer, 2002), 99–106
	c		'Abortion, Natural Law and Public Reason', in Robert P. George and Christopher Wolfe (eds), *Natural Law and Public Reason* (Washington DC: Georgetown University Press), 71–105
	d		'On the Incoherence of Legal Positivism', Notre Dame L Rev 75: 1597–611
	e		'God the Father', in Peter Newby (ed.), *Occasional Papers from the Millennium Conferences at the Oxford University Catholic Chaplaincy* No. 1 (Oxford), 24–6
2001	a	II.13	'"Direct" and "Indirect": A Reply to Critics of Our Action Theory' (with Germain Grisez and Joseph Boyle), The Thomist 65: 1–44
	b	III.6	'Virtue and the Constitution of the United States', Fordham L Rev 69: 1595–602
	c		'Reason, Faith and Homosexual Acts', Catholic Social Science Review 6: 61–9
2002	a	IV.5	'Natural Law: The Classical Tradition', in Jules Coleman and Scott Shapiro (eds), *The Oxford Handbook of Jurisprudence and Philosophy of Law* (OUP), 1–60
	b	V.22	'Secularism, the Root of the Culture of Death', in Luke Gormally (ed.), *Culture of Life—Culture of Death* (London: Linacre Centre)
	c		'Aquinas on *jus* and Hart on Rights: A Response', Rev of Politics 64: 407–10
	d		Patrick H. Martin and John Finnis, 'The Identity of "Anthony Rivers"', Recusant History 26: 39–74
	e		—— and —— 'Tyrwhitt of Kettleby, Part I: Goddard Tyrwhitt, Martyr, 1580', Recusant History 26: 301–13

2003 a III.8 'Natural Law & the Re-making of Boundaries', in Allen Buchanan and Margaret Moore (eds), *States, Nations, and Boundaries: The Ethics of Making Boundaries* (CUP), 171–8

b IV.1 'Law and What I Truly Should Decide', American J Juris 48: 107–30

c V.10 'Saint Thomas More and the Crisis in Faith and Morals', The Priest 7/1: 10–15, 29–30

d 'Secularism, Morality and Politics', L'Osservatore Romano, English edn, 29 January, 9

e 'Shakespeare's Intercession for *Love's Martyr*' (with Patrick Martin), Times Literary Supplement, no. 5220, 18 April, 12–14

f 'An Intrinsically Disordered Attraction', in John F. Harvey and Gerard V. Bradley (eds), *Same-Sex Attraction: A Parents' Guide* (South Bend: St Augustine's Press), 89–99

g 'Nature and Natural Law in Contemporary Philosophical and Theological Debates: Some Observations', in Juan Correa and Elio Sgreccia (eds), *The Nature & Dignity of the Human Person as the Foundation of the Right to Life: The Challenges of Contemporary Culture* (Rome: Libreria Editrice Vaticana), 81–109

h Patrick H. Martin and John Finnis, 'Tyrwhitt of Kettleby, Part II: Robert Tyrwhitt, a Main Benefactor of John Gerard SJ, 1599–1605', Recusant History 27: 556–69

i —— and —— 'Thomas Thorpe, "W.S." and the Catholic Intelligencers', Elizabethan Literary Renaissance, 1–43

j —— and —— '*Caesar*, Succession, and the Chastisement of Rulers', Notre Dame L Rev 78: 1045–74

k 'Commonwealth and Dependencies', in *Halsbury's Laws of England*, vol. 6 re-issue (4th edn, London: Butterworth), 409–518

l 'Abortion for Cleft Palate: The Human Fertilisation and Embryology Act 1990', Sunday Telegraph, 7 December

m 'An Oxford Play Festival in 1582' (with Patrick Martin), Notes & Queries 50: 391–4

2004 a II.18 'Per un'etica dell'eguaglianza nel diritto alla vita: Un commento a Peter Singer', in Rosangela Barcaro and Paolo Becchi (eds), *Questioni Mortali: L'Attuale Dibattito sulla Morte Cerebrale e il Problema dei Trapianti* (Naples: Edizioni Scientifiche Italiane), 127–39

b IV.22 'Helping Enact Unjust Laws without Complicity in Injustice', American J Juris 49: 11–42

2005 a I.1 'Foundations of Practical Reason Revisited', American J Juris 50: 109–32

b I.4 'Self-referential (or Performative) Inconsistency: Its Significance for Truth', Proceedings of the Catholic Philosophical Association 78: 13–21

c II.2 '"The Thing I Am": Personal Identity in Aquinas and Shakespeare', Social Philosophy & Policy 22: 250–82; also in Ellen Frankel Paul, Fred. D. Miller, and Jeffrey Paul (eds), *Personal Identity* (CUP), 250–82

d IV.6 'Philosophy of Law' (Chinese trans.), in Ouyang Kang (ed.), *The Map of Contemporary British and American Philosophy* (Beijing: Dangdai Yingmei Zhexue Ditu), 388–413

e 'On "Public Reason"', in *O Racji Pulicznej* (Warsaw: Ius et Lex), 7–30 (Polish trans.), 33–56 (English original); <http://ssrn.com/abstract=955815>

f 'Restricting Legalised Abortion is not Intrinsically Unjust', in Helen Watt (ed.), *Cooperation, Complicity & Conscience* (London: Linacre Centre), 209–45

g 'A Vote Decisive for . . . a More Restrictive Law', in Helen Watt (ed.), *Cooperation, Complicity & Conscience* (London: Linacre Centre), 269–95

h 'Aquinas' Moral, Political and Legal Philosophy', Stanford Encyclopedia of Philosophy; <http://plato.stanford.edu/entries/aquinas-moral-political/>

i Patrick H. Martin and John Finnis, 'Benedicam Dominum: Ben Jonson's Strange 1605 Inscription', Times Literary Supplement, 4 November, 12–13

j —— and —— 'The Secret Sharers: "Anthony Rivers" and the Appellant Controversy, 1601–2', Huntingdon Library Q 69/2: 195–238

2006 a V.4 'Religion and State: Some Main Issues and Sources', American J Juris 51: 107–30

b 'Observations for the Austral Conference to mark the 25th Anniversary of *Natural Law and Natural Rights*', Cuadernos de Extensión Jurídica (Universidad de los Andes) no. 13: 27–30

2007 a III.9 'Nationality, Alienage and Constitutional Principle', LQR 123: 417–45

b IV.10 'On Hart's Ways: Law as Reason and as Fact', American J Juris 52: 25–53; also in Matthew Kramer and Claire Grant (eds), *The Legacy of H.L.A. Hart: Legal, Political & Moral Philosophy* (OUP, 2009), 1–27

c 'Natural Law Theories of Law', Stanford Encyclopedia of Philosophy; <http://plato.stanford.edu/entries/natural-law-theories/>

2008 a I.5/II.7/V.8 'Reason, Revelation, Universality and Particularity in Ethics', AJJ 53: 23–48

b II.6 'Universality, Personal and Social Identity, and Law', address, Congresso Sul-Americano de Filosofia do Direito, Porto Alegre, Brazil, 4 October 2007; Oxford Legal Studies Research Paper 5; <http://ssrn.com/abstract=1094277>

c III.20 'Marriage: A Basic and Exigent Good', The Monist 91: 396–414

d [V.13] 'Grounds of Law & Legal Theory: A Response', Legal Theory 13: 315–44

e 'Common Law Constraints: Whose Common Good Counts?', Oxford Legal Studies Research Paper 10; <http://ssrn.com/abstract_id=1100628>

f *Humanae Vitae*: A New Translation with Notes (London: Catholic Truth Society) (31 pp)

2009 a **II.3** 'Anscombe's Essays', National Catholic Bioethics Q 9/1: 199–207

b **IV.11** 'H.L.A. Hart: A Twentieth Century Oxford Political Philosopher', American J Juris 54: 161–85

c **V.1** 'Does Free Exercise of Religion Deserve Constitutional Mention?', American J Juris 54: 41–66

d **V.2** 'Telling the Truth about God and Man in a Pluralist Society: Economy or Explication?', in Christopher Wolfe (ed.), *The Naked Public Square Revisited: Religion & Politics in the Twenty-First Century* (Wilmington: ISI Books), 111–25, 204–9

e 'Endorsing Discrimination between Faiths: A Case of Extreme Speech?', in Ivan Hare and James Weinstein (eds), *Extreme Speech and Democracy* (OUP), 430–41

f 'Discrimination between Religions: Some Thoughts on Reading Greenawalt's *Religion and the Constitution*', Constitutional Commentary 25: 265–71

g 'Commonwealth', in *Halsbury's Laws of England*, vol. 13 (5th edn, London: LexisNexis), 471–589

h 'Why Religious Liberty is a Special, Important and Limited Right', Notre Dame Legal Studies Paper 09–11; <http://ssrn.com/abstract=1392278>

i 'The Lords' Eerie Swansong: A Note on *R (Purdy) v Director of Public Prosecutions*', Oxford Legal Studies Research Paper 31; <http://ssrn.com/abstract=1477281>

j 'The Mental Capacity Act 2005: Some Ethical and Legal Issues', in Helen Watt (ed.), *Incapacity & Care: Controversies in Healthcare and Research* (London: Linacre Centre), 95–105

k 'Debate over the Interpretation of *Dignitas personae*'s Teaching on Embryo Adoption', National Catholic Bioethics Q 9: 475–8

2010 a **II.14** 'Directly Discriminatory Decisions: A Missed Opportunity', LQR 126: 491–6

b 'Law as Idea, Ideal and Duty: A Comment on Simmonds, *Law as a Moral Idea*', Jurisprudence 1: 247–53

OTHER WORKS CITED

Abbott, Walter M. (ed.) (1966), *The Documents of Vatican II* (London: Geoffrey Chapman)
Anscombe, G.E.M. (1957), *Intention* (Oxford: Blackwell)
——(1976), 'On Frustration of the Majority by Fulfilment of the Majority's Will', Analysis 36: 161–8; also in Anscombe (1981) 123–9
——(1978), 'On the Source of the Authority of the State', Ratio 20: 1–29; also in Anscombe (1981) 130–55
——(1981), *The Collected Philosophical Papers of G.E.M. Anscombe*, vol. 3, *Ethics, Religion and Politics* (Oxford: Basil Blackwell)
Anson, William (1907), *Law and Custom of the Constitution* (3rd edn, OUP)
Arrow, Kenneth (1963), *Social Choice and Individual Values* (2nd edn, New Haven: Yale University Press)
Aubert, J.-M. (1955), *Le Droit romain dans l'oeuvre de saint Thomas* (Paris: J. Vrin)
Austin, John (1832), *The Province of Jurisprudence Determined* (ed. H.L.A. Hart) (London: Weidenfeld & Nicolson, 1954)
Barker, Ernest (1946), *The Politics of Aristotle* (OUP)
——(1951), *Essays in Government* (2nd edn, OUP)
Barnhizer, David (1990), 'Natural Law as Practical Methodology', Cleveland State L Rev 38: 15–63
Beck, L.W. (1969), *Foundations of the Metaphysics of Morals* (ed. R.P. Wolff) (Indianapolis: Bobbs Merrill)
Bentham, Jeremy (1776), *A Comment on the Commentaries* (ed. C.W. Everett) (OUP, 1928)
——(1776), *A Fragment on Government* (ed. Wilfrid Harrison) (Oxford: Blackwell, 1967)
——(1776), *A Fragment on Government* (ed. Montague) (OUP, 1891)
——(1780), *An Introduction to the Principles of Morals and Legislation* (ed. Wilfrid Harrison) (Oxford: Basil Blackwell, 1967)
——(1843), *Works* (ed. John Bowring)
——(1970), *Of Laws in General* [1789] (eds J.H. Burns and H.L.A. Hart) (London: Athlone Press)
Bertone, Tarcisio SDB (2001), 'Catholics and Pluralist Society: "Imperfect Laws" and the Responsibility of Legislators', in Juan de Dios Vial Correa and Elio Sgreccia (eds), *Evangelium Vitae: Five Years of Confrontation with the Society* [Proceedings of the Sixth Annual Assembly of the Pontifical Academy for Life, 11–14 February 2000] (Vatican City: Libreria Editrice Vaticana), 206–22
Birks, P.B.H. and W. Swadling, 'Restitution' [1998] All England Law Reports Annual Review 390
Blackstone, William ([1765–9] 1783), *Commentaries on the Laws of England* (9th edn, OUP)
Bodenheimer, Edgar (1962), *Jurisprudence: The Philosophy and Method of the Law* (HUP)
Boorstin, Daniel (1941), *The Mysterious Science of Law: An Essay on Blackstone's Commentaries* (HUP)

Bork, Robert H. (1971), 'Neutral Principles and Some First Amendment Problems', Indiana LJ 47: 1–35
Bourke, Vernon J. (1966), *Ethics: A Textbook in Moral Philosophy* (3rd edn, New York: Macmillan)
Boyle, Joseph M., Grisez, Germain, and Tollefsen, Olaf (1976), *Free Choice: A Self-Referential Argument* (Notre Dame: University of Notre Dame Press)
Brewer, Scott (1996), 'Exemplary Reasoning: Semantics, Pragmatics, and the Rational Force of Legal Argument by Analogy', Harv L Rev 109: 923–1028
Brubaker, Rogers (1984), *The Limits of Rationality: An Essay on the Social and Moral Thought of Max Weber* (London: Allen & Unwin)
Buchler, Justis (1940), *The Philosophy of Peirce: Selected Writings* (London: Routledge & Kegan Paul)
Bull, John W. (1884), *Early Experiences of Life in South Australia and an Extended Colonial History* (Adelaide and London)
Burlamaqui, Jean Jacques (1784), *The Principles of Natural and Political Law* (trans. Nugent) (3rd edn)
Calabresi, Guido and Melamed, Douglas (1972), 'Property Rules, Liability Rules, and Inalienability: One View of the Cathedral', Harv L Rev 85: 1089–128
Cattaneo, Mario A. (1960), *Il concetto di rivoluzione nella scienza del diritto* (Milan-Varese: Istituto Editoriale Cisalpino)
Chrimes, S.B. (1936), *English Constitutional Ideas in the Fifteenth Century* (CUP)
Cohen, F.S. (1935), 'Transcendental Nonsense and the Functional Approach', Columbia L Rev 35: 809
Cohen, Marshall (ed.) (1983), *Ronald Dworkin and Contemporary Jurisprudence* (London: Duckworth)
Coleman, Jules (2001), *The Practice of Principle: In Defence of a Pragmatist Approach to Legal Theory* (OUP)
—— and Leiter, Brian (1996), 'Legal Positivism', in Dennis Patterson (ed.), *A Companion to Philosophy of Law and Legal Theory* (Oxford and Cambridge, Mass.: Blackwell), 241–60
—— and Shapiro, Scott (2002), *The Oxford Handbook of Jurisprudence and Philosophy of Law* (OUP)
Collingwood, R.G. (1999), *The Principles of History and Other Writings in Philosophy of History* (eds W.H. Dray and W.J. Van der Dussen) (OUP)
Delhaye, Philippe (1949), 'L'Enseignement de la Philosophie morale au XIIe siècle', Medieval Studies 9: 77
De Lubac, Henri (1977), *The Mystery of the Supernatural* (London: Geoffrey Chapman)
Diels, Hermann (1922), *Die Fragmente der Vorsokratiker* (4th edn, Berlin)
Dixon, Owen (1935), 'The Law and the Constitution', LQR 51: 590
Dworkin, Ronald (1970), 'Taking Rights Seriously', New York Review of Books, 17 December, Special Supplement, 23–31
—— (1977, 1978), *Taking Rights Seriously* (rev. edn with Reply to Critics) (HUP; London: Duckworth)
—— (1978), 'Is There Really No Right Answer in Hard Cases?', New York Univ L Rev 53
—— (1985), *A Matter of Principle* (HUP)
—— (1986), *Law's Empire* (HUP; London: Fontana)
Eekelaar, J.M. (1971), 'Principles of Revolutionary Legality', in A.W.B. Simpson (ed.), *Oxford Essays in Jurisprudence: Second Series* (OUP), 22–43

Endicott, Timothy (2003), 'The Reason of the Law', AJJ 48: 83–106
Eser, Albin (1966), 'The Principle of "Harm" in the Concept of Crime: A Comparative Analysis of the Criminally Protected Legal Interests', Duquesne U L Rev 4: 345–437
Evatt, H.V. (1940), 'The Judges and the Teachers of Public Law', Harv L Rev 53: 1145–63
Eyre, Edward John (1845), *Journals of Expeditions of Discovery into Central Australia... including an Account of the Manners and Customs of the Aborigines and the State of their Relations with Europeans* (London)
Fredborg, K.M. (ed.) (1988), *The Latin Rhetorical Commentaries by Thierry of Chartres* (Toronto: Pontifical Institute of Mediaeval Studies)
Freund, Julien (1968), *The Sociology of Max Weber* (trans. Mary Ilford) (London: Allen Lane)
Fried, Charles (1981), *Contract as Promise: A Theory of Contractual Obligation* (HUP)
Friedmann, Wolfgang (1960), 'Gustav Radbruch', Vanderbilt L Rev 14: 191
—— (1960), *Legal Theory* (4th edn, London: Stevens)
Fuller, Lon L. ([1964] 1969), *The Morality of Law* (rev. edn, New Haven and London: Yale University Press)
Gans, Chaim (1981), 'The Normativity of Law and Its Coordinative Function', Israel Law Rev 16: 333
Gardner, John (2001), 'Legal Positivism: 5½ Myths', AJJ 46: 199–227
—— (2008), 'How Law Claims, What Law Claims', Oxford Legal Studies Research Paper No. 44/2008; <http://ssrn.com/abstract=1299017>
Gauthier, R.-A. (ed.) (1969), *Sententia Libri Ethicorum* in *Sancti Thomae de Aquino Opera Omnia* (ed. Leonine) xlvii, 1 (Books I–III) and 2 (Books IV–X) (Rome)
Gavison, Ruth (ed.) (1987), *Issues in Contemporary Legal Philosophy: The Influence of H.L.A. Hart* (OUP)
Geach, Peter (1977), *The Virtues* (CUP)
George, Robert P. (ed.) (1992), *Natural Law Theory: Contemporary Essays* (OUP)
—— (ed.) (1996), *The Autonomy of Law: Essays on Legal Positivism* (OUP)
—— (1999), *In Defense of Natural Law* (OUP)
Gerth, H.H. and Mills, C. Wright (eds) (1948), *From Max Weber: Essays in Sociology* (London: Routledge)
Glanvill, Ranulph de ([c. 1188] (1965)), *The Treatise on the Laws and Customs of the Realm of England, Commonly called Glanvill* (ed. G.D.G. Hall) (London: Nelson)
Gordley, James (1991), *The Philosophical Origins of Modern Contract Doctrine* (OUP)
Gough, John W. (1955), *Fundamental Law in English Constitutional History* (OUP)
Green, Leslie (1983), 'Law, Co-ordination and the Common Good', Oxford J Legal Studies 3: 299
—— (2003), 'Legal Positivism', *The Stanford Encyclopedia of Philosophy* (Spring 2003 edn); <http://plato.stanford.edu/archives/spr2003/entries/legal-positivism>
Griffin, Leslie C. (1997), '*Evangelium Vitae*: Abortion', in Kevin Wm Wildes SJ and Alan C. Mitchell, *Choosing Life: A Dialogue on* Evangelium Vitae (Georgetown University Press), 159–73
Grisez, Germain (1967), 'Man, the Natural End of', *New Catholic Encyclopedia*, vol. 9 (New York: McGraw-Hill)
—— (1978), 'Against Consequentialism', AJJ 23: 21–72
—— (1983), *Christian Moral Principles* (Chicago: Franciscan Herald Press)
—— (1993), *Living a Christian Life* (Quincy: Franciscan Press)

Grover, Robinson A. (1974), 'The Ranking Assumption', Theory and Decision 4: 277–99
Hampshire, Stuart and Hart, H.L.A. (1958), 'Decision, Intention and Certainty', Mind 67: 1–12
Hanson, Norwood R. (1961), *Patterns of Discovery: An Inquiry into the Conceptual Foundations of Science* (CUP)
Harman, Gilbert (1977), *The Nature of Morality: An Introduction to Ethics* (New York: OUP)
Hart, H.L.A. (1953), 'Philosophy of Law and Jurisprudence in Britain (1945–1952)' American Journal of Comparative Law 2: 355–64
——(1955), 'Are There Any Natural Rights?', Philosophical Review 64: 175–91
——(1956), 'Blackstone's Use of the Law of Nature', South African Law Review 169
——(1958), 'Positivism and the Separation of Law and Morals', Harv L Rev 71: 593
——(1959), 'Prolegomenon to the Principles of Punishment', Proc Aristotelian Soc 60: 1–26
——(1961), *The Concept of Law* (2nd edn, OUP, 1994)
——(1963), *Law, Liberty & Morality* (London: OUP)
——(1964), 'Self-Referring Laws', in *Festskrift till Karl Olivecrona* (Stockholm)
——(1965), 'Review of Fuller's *The Morality of Law*', Harv L Rev 78: 1281–96
——(1968) *Punishment & Responsibility: Essays in the Philosophy of Law* (OUP)
——(1971–2), "Abortion Law Reform: The English Experience', Melbourne University L Rev 8: 388–411
——(1978), 'Morality and Reality', New York Review of Books 25/3 (9 March)
——(1982), *Essays on Bentham* (OUP)
——(1983), *Essays in Jurisprudence and Philosophy* (OUP)
——(1986), 'Who Can Tell Right From Wrong?', New York Review of Books (17 July), 49–52
——([1968] 2008), *Punishment & Responsibility: Essays in the Philosophy of Law* (2nd edn, with Introduction by John Gardner, OUP)
——and Honoré, Tony ([1959] 1985), *Causation in the Law* (2nd edn with new Preface, OUP)
Hart, Jenifer (1998), *Ask Me No More: An Autobiography* (London: Peter Halban)
Harte, Colin (2002), 'Challenging a Consensus: Why *Evangelium Vitae* Does Not Permit Legislators to Vote for "Imperfect Legislation"', in Luke Gormally (ed.), *Culture of Life—Culture of Death* (London: Linacre Centre), 322–42
——(2005), *Changing Unjust Laws Justly* (Washington DC: CUA Press)
——(2005), 'Problems of Principle in Voting for Unjust Legislation', in H. Watt (ed.), *Cooperation, Complicity & Conscience: Problems in Healthcare, Science and Public Policy* (London: Linacre Centre), 179–231
——(2005), 'The Opening Up of a Discussion: A Response to John Finnis', in H. Watt (ed.), *Cooperation, Complicity & Conscience: Problems in Healthcare, Science and Public Policy* (London: Linacre Centre), 246–68
Hartshorne, Charles and Weiss, Paul (eds) (1932), *Collected Papers of Charles Sanders Peirce*, vol. II (HUP)
Hastie, W. (1887), *The Philosophy of Law: An Exposition of the Fundamental Principles of Jurisprudence and The Science of Right* by Immanuel Kant (Edinburgh: T. & T. Clark)
Health and Safety Executive (1988), *The Tolerability of Risk from Nuclear Power Stations* (London: HMSO)

Hekman, Susan J. (1983), *Max Weber and Contemporary Social Theory* (Indiana and Oxford: Robertson)
Henderson, Lynn (1990), 'Whose Nature? Practical Reason and Patriarchy', Cleveland State L Rev 38: 169
Hering, H. (1939), 'De Iure subiective sumpto apud S. Thomam', Angelicum 16: 295–7
Hobbes, Thomas (1650), *De Corpore Politico*
Hohfeld, Wesley N. (1923), *Fundamental Legal Conceptions as Applied in Judicial Reasoning* (ed. W.W. Cook) (New Haven: Yale University Press)
Holdsworth, William (1938), *History of English Law*, vol. XII (OUP)
Honoré, A.M. (1960), 'Rights of Exclusion and Immunities against Divesting', Tulane L Rev 34: 453
——(1967), 'Allegiance and the Usurper' [1967] CLJ 214–23
——(1967), 'Reflections on Revolution', The Irish Jurist 2: 268–78
Irwin, Terence (1977), *Plato's Moral Theory: The Early and Middle Dialogues* (OUP)
Jones, J. Walter (1940), *Historical Introduction to the Theory of Law* (OUP)
Jones, William (1781), *An Essay on the Law of Bailments* (London: Charles Dilly)
Kant, Immanuel ([1790] 1887), *The Science of Right* in W. Hastie, *The Philosophy of Law: An Exposition of the Fundamental Principles of Jurisprudence and The Science of Right* by Immanuel Kant (Edinburgh: T. & T. Clark)
Kantorowicz, Ernst H. (1957), *The King's Two Bodies: A Study in Medieval Political Theology* (Princeton: Princeton University Press)
Kelley, Patrick (1990), 'Who Decides? Community Safety Conventions at the Heart of Tort Liability', Cleveland State L Rev 38: 315
Kelsen, Hans (1945), *General Theory of Law and State* (HUP)
——(1966), 'On the Pure Theory of Law', Israel LR 1: 1–7
——(1967), *The Pure Theory of Law* (Berkeley and Los Angeles: University of California Press)
——(1991), *General Theory of Norms* (trans. Michael Hartney) (OUP)
——(1992), *Introduction to the Problems of Legal Theory* (trans. from 1st edn of Kelsen (1934), *Reine Rechtslehre* (*Pure Theory of Law*) by B.L. and S.L. Paulson) (OUP)
Kennedy, Duncan (1993), *Sexy Dressing Etc.: Essays on the Power and Politics of Cultural Identity* (HUP)
——(2004), 'The Disenchantment of Logically Formal Legal Rationality, or Max Weber's Sociology in the Genealogy of the Contemporary Mode of Western Legal Thought', Hastings LJ 55: 1031–76
Kornhauser, L.A. (1980), 'A Guide to the Perplexed Claims of Efficiency in Law', Hofstra L Rev 8: 591–639
——(1986), 'Economic Analysis of Law', Materiali per una Storia Della Cultura Juridica 16: 233
Korsgaard, Christine (1997), 'The Normativity of Instrumental Reason', in Garrett Cullity and Berys Gaut (eds), *Ethics and Practical Reason* (OUP) 215–54
Kronman, Anthony (1983), *Max Weber* (London: Edward Arnold)
Kuttner, Stephan (1936), 'Sur les origines du terme "droit positif"', Revue historique de droit français et étranger 15: 728–40
——(1937), *Repertorium der Kanonistik (1140–1234)* (Studi e Testi, Biblioteca Apostolica Vaticana)
Lacey, Nicola (2004), *H.L.A. Hart: The Nightmare and the Noble Dream* (OUP)

Ladenson, Robert (1980), 'In Defense of a Hobbesian Conception of Law', Philosophy & Public Affairs 9: 134–59

Latham, R.E. (ed.) (1965), *Revised Medieval Latin Word List from British and Irish Sources* (OUP)

Latham, R.T.E. (1949), *The Law and the Commonwealth* (OUP)

Lee, Patrick (1981), 'Permanence of the Ten Commandments: St Thomas and His Modern Commentators', Theological Studies 42: 422–43

Leiter, Brian (2003), 'Beyond the Hart/Dworkin Debate: The Methodology Problem in Jurisprudence', AJJ 48: 17–51

Lewis, David K. (1969), *Convention: A Philosophical Study* (HUP)

Lindsay, A.D. (1943), *The Modern Democratic State* (OUP)

Lloyd, Dennis (1970), *The Idea of Law* (Harmondsworth: Penguin)

Locke, John ([c.1660–64] 1990), in Robert Horwitz, Jenny Strauss Clay, and Diskin Clay (eds), *John Locke: Questions concerning the Law of Nature* (Ithaca: Cornell University Press); also published as von Leyden (ed.), *John Locke: Essays on the Law of Nature* (OUP, 1965)

—— (1693), *Some Thoughts Concerning Education* (London)

Lottin, Odon (1931), *Le Droit naturel chez Saint Thomas d'Aquin et ses predecesseurs* (Bruges)

Luban, David (1990), 'Incommensurable Values, Rational Choice, and Moral Absolutes', Cleveland State L Rev 38: 65–84

Lucas, John R. (1966) *The Principles of Politics* (OUP)

Lucas, Paul (1963), 'Ex parte Sir William Blackstone, "Plagiarist": A Note on Blackstone and the Natural Law', Am J Legal Hist 7: 142–58

Luce, D.H. and Raiffa, H. (1957), *Games and Decisions* (New York: Wiley)

Luño, Angel Rodriguez (2002), 'Evangelium Vitae 73: The Catholic Lawmaker and the Problem of a Seriously Unjust Law', *L'Osservatore Romano*, English edn, 18 September 2002, 3–5

Lyons, David (1981), 'Need, Necessity and Political Obligation', Virginia L Rev 67: 63–77

MacCormick, Neil (1978), *Legal Reasoning and Legal Theory* (OUP)

—— (1981), *H.L.A. Hart* (London: Edward Arnold)

Macedo, Stephen (1990), *Liberal Virtues* (OUP)

Mackie, John (1977), *Ethics: Inventing Right and Wrong* (Harmondsworth: Penguin)

Marmor, Andrei (2001), *Positive Law and Objective Value*s (OUP)

McKnight, Joseph W. (1959), 'Blackstone, Quasi-Jurisprudent', Southwestern LJ 13: 399

Miller, Fred D. (1995), *Nature, Justice, and Rights in Aristotle's Politics* (OUP)

Namier, Lewis and Brooke, John (eds) (1964), *The House of Commons 1754–1790* (London: HMSO)

Nozick, Robert (1974), *Anarchy, State and Utopia* (Oxford: Blackwell)

O'Connell, Daniel P. (1967), *State Succession in Municipal Law and International Law* (CUP)

—— and Riordan, Ann (1971), *Opinions on Imperial Constitutional Law* (Sydney: Law Book Co.)

Oldfather, William A. (trans.) (1931), Samuel Pufendorf, *Elementorum Jurisprudentiae Universalis Libri Duo* (OUP)

Orrego, Cristóbal (1997), *H.L.A. Hart: Abogado del Positivismo Juridíco* (Pamplona: Eunsa)

——(2004), 'Hart's Last Legal Positivism: Morality Might be Objective; Legality Certainly Is Not', in Kenneth Einar Himma (ed.), *Law, Morality and Legal Positivism* (Franz Steiner Verlag), 73–9
Ortiz, Daniel R. (1999), 'Categorical Community', Stanford L Rev 51: 769–806
Owen, Richard (ed.) (1995), *Philosophical Foundations of Tort Law* (OUP)
Parliamentary Papers (1841), *Correspondence Relative to Settlement of South Australia* (vol. xvii; HC Paper 129)
——(1843), *Papers Relative to South Australia* (vol. xxxii; Command Paper [505])
Parsons, Talcott (ed.) (1947), see Weber (1947)
Paton, G.W. (1964), *Jurisprudence* (ed. David Derham) (4th edn, OUP)
Peirce, Charles Sanders (1997), *Pragmatism as a Principle and Method of Right Thinking: The 1903 Harvard Lectures on Pragmatism* (ed. Patricia Ann Turrisi) (Albany: State University of New York Press)
Pocock, J.G.A. (ed.) (1977), *The Political Works of James Harrington* (CUP)
Pollock , Frederick and Maitland, F.W. (1898), *The History of English Law Before the Time of Edward I* (2nd edn, CUP)
Posner, Richard A. (1971), 'Killing or Wounding to Protect a Property Interest', J Law & Econ 14: 201
——(1977), *Economic Analysis of Law* (2nd edn, Boston and London: Little, Brown)
——(1981), *The Economics of Justice* (HUP)
——(1990), *The Problems of Jurisprudence* (HUP)
Postema, Gerald J. (1982), 'Coordination and Convention at the Foundations of Law', Journal of Legal Studies 11: 165–203
Pound, Roscoe (1959), *Jurisprudence* (St Paul: West Publishing)
Price, David Andrew (1989), 'Taking Rights Cynically: Review of Critical Legal Studies', Cambridge LJ 48: 271–301
Pufendorf, Samuel (1660), *Elementorum Jurisprudentiae Universalis Libri Duo*, vol. ii, *The Translation*, by W.A. Oldfather (OUP, 1931)
——(1672), *De Jure Naturae et Gentium Libri Octo* by Samuel Pufendorf, vol. ii, *The Translation*, by C.H. Oldfather and W.A. Oldfather (OUP, 1934)
Putnam, Hilary (1981), *Reason, Truth and History* (CUP)
Quine, W.V. (1963), *Ontological Relativity and Other Essays* (New York: Columbia University Press)
Quinton A.M. (ed.) (1967), *Political Philosophy*, Oxford Readings in Philosophy (London: OUP)
Rawls, John (1955), 'Two Concepts of Rules', Philosophical Rev 64: 4–13
——(1964), 'Legal Obligation and the Duty of Fair Play', in Sidney Hook (ed.), *Law and Philosophy: A Symposium* (New York: New York University Press), 1
——(1971), *A Theory of Justice* (HUP)
——(1993), *Political Liberalism* (New York: Columbia University Press)
Raz, Joseph ([1970], 1980), *The Concept of a Legal System* (2nd edn with a new Postscript, OUP)
——(1975), *Practical Reason and Norms* (London: Hutchinson)
——(1977), 'Promises and Obligations', in P.M.S. Hacker and Joseph Raz (eds), *Law, Morality and Society: Essays in Honour of H.L.A. Hart* (OUP)
——(1979), *The Authority of Law: Essays on Law and Morality* (2nd edn, 2009; OUP)
——(1984), 'The Obligation to Obey: Revision and Tradition', Notre Dame J Law, Ethics and Public Policy 1: 139–55

——(1985), 'Authority, Law and Morality', The Monist 68: 295–324
——(1986), *The Morality of Freedom* (OUP)
——(1986), 'The Purity of the Pure Theory', in Richard Tur and William Twining (eds), *Essays on Kelsen* (OUP)
——(1992), 'Formalism and the Rule of Law', in Robert P. George, *Natural Law Theory: Contemporary Essays* (OUP)
——(1993), 'The Autonomy of Legal Reasoning', Ratio Juris 6: 1–15
——(1994), *Ethics in the Public Domain* (OUP)
——(1998), 'Postema on Law's Autonomy and Public Practical Reasons: A Critical Comment', Legal Theory 4: 1–20 (also in Raz (2009))
——(1998), 'Two Views of the Nature of the Theory of Law: A Partial Comparison', Legal Theory 4: 249–82 (also in Raz (2009))
——(2001), 'Two Views of the Nature of the Theory of Law: A Partial Comparison', in Jules Coleman (ed.), *Hart's Postscript to the Concept of Law* (OUP) (also in Raz (2009))
——(2003), 'About Morality and the Nature of Law', AJJ 48: 1–15 (also in Raz (2009))
——(2003), 'Comments and Responses', in Lukas H. Meyer, Stanley L. Paulson, and Thomas W. Pogge (eds), *Rights, Culture and the Law: Themes from the Legal and Political Philosophy of Joseph Raz* (OUP)
——(2009), *Between Authority and Interpretation: On the Theory of Law and Practical Reason* (OUP)
Reid, Lord (1972), 'The Judge as Law Maker', J Soc Pub Teachers L (NS) 12: 22–9
Rheinstein, Max (ed.) (1954), *Max Weber on Law in Economy and Society* (HUP)
Rhonheimer, Martin (1994), *Praktische Vernunft und Vernunftigkeit der Praxis* (Berlin: Akademie Verlag)
Riker, William (1982), *Liberalism against Populism: A Confrontation Between the Theory of Democracy and the Theory of Social Choice* (San Francisco: W. Freeman)
Rinck, Hans-Justus (1960), 'Blackstone and the Law of Nature', Ratio 2: 162–80
Roberts-Wray, Kenneth (1966), *Commonwealth and Colonial Law* (London: Stevens)
Ross, Alf (1958), *On Law and Justice* (London: Stevens)
——(1969), 'On Self-Reference and a Puzzle in Constitutional Law', Mind 78: 1–24
Salmond, John (1902), *Jurisprudence or the Theory of Law* (2nd edn, London and Adelaide: Stevens & Haynes)
Sartorius, Rolf (1981), 'Political Authority and Political Obligation', Virginia LR 67: 3–17
——(1987), 'Positivism and the Foundations of Legal Authority', in R. Gavison (ed.), *Issues in Contemporary Legal Philosophy: The Influence of H.L.A. Hart* (OUP), 43–61
Schauer, Frederick (1991), *Playing by the Rules: A Philosophical Examination of Rule-Based Decision-Making in Law and in Life* (OUP)
Schelling, Thomas (1969), 'Some Thoughts on the Relevance of Game Theory to the Analysis of Ethical Systems', in Ira Buchler and Hugo Nutini (eds), *Game Theory in the Behavioral Sciences* (University of Pittsburgh Press)
Sen, Amartya (1977), 'Rational Fools: A Critique of the Behavioral Foundations of Economic Theory', Philosophy & Public Affairs 6: 317–44
Sheehan, Duncan (2006), 'What is a Mistake?', Legal Studies 20: 538–65
Shils, E.A. and Finch, H.A. (eds) (1949), *Max Weber on the Methodology of the Social Sciences* (Glencoe: Free Press)
Shuman, Samuel I. (1963), *Legal Positivism: Its Scope and Limitations* (Detroit: Wayne State University Press)
Simmonds, N.E. (2007), *Law as a Moral Idea* (OUP)

Simmons, A.J. (1979), *Moral Principles and Political Obligation* (Princeton: Princeton University Press)
Simon, Yves (1951), *The Philosophy of Democratic Government* (Chicago: University of Chicago Press)
—— (1962), *A General Theory of Authority* (Notre Dame: University of Notre Dame Press)
Smith, Adam ([1759] 1976), *The Theory of Moral Sentiments* (eds D.D. Raphael and A.L. Macfie) (OUP)
—— ([1776] 1976), *An Inquiry into the Nature and Causes of the Wealth of Nations* (eds R.S. Campbell and A.H. Skinner) (OUP)
—— (1978), *Lectures on Jurisprudence* (eds R. Meek, D.D. Raphael, and P. Stein) (OUP)
Smith, M.B.E. (1973), 'Is There a Prima Facie Obligation to Obey the Law?', Yale LJ 82: 950
Smith, Sydney ([1839] 1859), *The Works of the Rev. Sydney Smith* (London: Longman) vol. I
Stone, Julius (1946), *The Province and Function of Law: Law as Logic, Justice and Social Control* (Sydney: Associated General Publications)
—— (1964), *Legal System and Lawyers' Reasonings* (Stanford: Stanford University Press)
Story, Joseph (1891), *Commentaries on the Constitution of the United States* (5th edn, Boston: M.M. Bigelow)
Strauss, Leo (1953), *Natural Right and History* (Chicago: University of Chicago Press)
Taylor, J. (trans.) (1961), *The Didascalicon of Hugh of St Victor* with an introduction and notes by J. Taylor (New York: Columbia University Press)
Tsikata, Tsatsu and Tsikata, Fui (1970), 'Sallah v. AG, Kelsen and Other in the Court of Appeal', U Ghana LJ 7: 142
Tubbs, J.W. (2000), *The Common Law Mind: Medieval and Early Modern Conceptions* (Baltimore and London: Johns Hopkins University Press)
Tugwell, Simon (1988), *Albert and Thomas: Selected Writings* (New York: Paulist Press)
Turner, Stephen P. and Factor, Regis A. (1984), *Max Weber and the Dispute over Reason and Value* (London: Routledge and Kegan Paul)
Tushnet, Mark (1990), 'A Critical Legal Studies Perspective', Cleveland State L Rev 38: 137
Twining, William (1998), 'R.G. Collingwood's Autobiography: One Reader's Response', J Law & Soc 25: 603–20
Ullmann-Margalit, Edna (1977), *The Emergence of Norms* (OUP)
—— (1981), 'Is Law a Co-ordinative Authority?', Israel L Rev 16: 350–67
Unger, Roberto M. (1975), *Knowledge and Politics* (New York: Free Press)
—— (1976), *Law in Modern Society* (New York: Free Press)
—— (1983), 'The Critical Legal Studies Movement', HLR 96: 561–675
—— (1986), *The Critical Legal Studies Movement* (HUP)
Vinogradoff, Paul (1928), *The Collected Papers of Paul Vinogradoff* (OUP)
Voegelin, Eric (1952), *The New Science of Politics* (Chicago and London: University of Chicago Press)
—— (1953), 'The Oxford Political Philosophers', Philosophical Q 3: 97–114
—— (1957), *Order and History*, vol. 3, *Plato and Aristotle* (Chapel Hill: Louisiana State University Press)
—— ([1960] 1974), 'On Liberalism and Its History', Review of Politics 37: 504–20
—— (1991), *The Nature of the Law and Related Legal Writings* in *The Collected Works of Eric Voegelin*, vol. 27 (eds Robert A. Pascal, James L. Babin, and John W. Corrington)

(Baton Rouge and London: Louisiana State University Press)
von Leyden, W. (ed.) (1954), *John Locke: Essays on the Law of Nature* (OUP)
Wade, H.W.R. (1955), 'The Basis of Legal Sovereignty' [1955] CLJ 172
Walton, Douglas (1992), *Slippery Slope Arguments* (OUP)
Waluchow, W.J. (1994), *Inclusive Legal Positivism* (OUP)
Ward, Keith (1972), *The Development of Kant's View of Ethics* (Oxford: Blackwell)
Waszink, J.H. (ed.) (1962), *Timaeus a Calcidio Translatus Commentarique Instructus* (London: Brill)
Watt, Helen (ed.) (2005), *Cooperation, Complicity & Conscience: Problems in Healthcare, Science and Public Policy* (London: Linacre Centre)
Weber, Max (1947), *Max Weber: The Theory of Social and Economic Organisation* (ed. Talcott Parsons, from Weber, *Wirtschaft und Gesellschaft* (1922)) (New York: Free Press)
——(1954), *Max Weber on Law in Economy and Society* (ed. Max Rheinstein, from Weber, *Wirtschaft und Gesellschaft* (1922)) (HUP)
——(1968), *Economy and Society* (eds Roth and Wittich, from Weber, *Wirtschaft und Gesellschaft* (1922)) (Berkeley: University of California Press)
Weinreb, Lloyd L. (2007), 'Legal Reason Redux', J Legal Educ 57: 600–14
Weinrib, Ernest (1995), *The Idea of Private Law* (HUP)
Weisheipl, James A. (1975), *Friar Thomas D'Aquino: His Life, Thought and Works* (Oxford: Blackwell)
Wheare, K.C. (1960), *The Constitutional Structure of the Commonwealth* (OUP)
Whitman, Walt (1966), *Walt Whitman: Selected Poems & Prose* (ed. A. Norman Jeffares) (OUP)
Winch, Peter (1958), *The Idea of a Social Science and Its Relation to Philosophy* (London: Routledge and Kegan Paul)
Woozley, A.D. (1979), *Law and Obedience: The Arguments of Plato's Crito* (London: Duckworth)
Zammit, P.N. (1939), 'The Concept of Rights according to Aristotle and St Thomas', Angelicum 16: 245–66
Zipursky, Benjamin C. (1998), 'Legal Malpractice and the Structure of Negligence Law', Fordham L Rev 67: 649–90
——(1998), 'Rights, Wrongs and Recourse in the Law of Torts', Vanderbilt L Rev 51: 1–100

ACKNOWLEDGEMENTS

The following essays were originally published as indicated:

Essay 1: 'Law and What I Truly Should Decide', American Journal of Jurisprudence 48: 107–30

Essay 2: 'The Authority of Law in the Predicament of Contemporary Social Theory', Journal of Law, Ethics & Public Policy 1: 115–37

Essay 3: 'Law as Coordination', Ratio Iuris 2: 97–104

Essay 4: 'On Positivism and the Foundations of Legal Authority: Comment', in Ruth Gavison (ed.), *Issues in Legal Philosophy: the Influence of H.L.A. Hart* (OUP, 1987), 62–75

Essay 5: 'Natural Law: The Classical Tradition', in Jules Coleman and Scott Shapiro (eds), *The Oxford Handbook of Jurisprudence and Philosophy of Law* (OUP, 2002), 1–60

Essay 7: 'The Truth in Legal Positivism', in Robert P. George (ed.), *The Autonomy of Law: Essays on Legal Positivism* (OUP, 1996), 195–214

Essay 8: 'Blackstone's Theoretical Intentions', Natural Law Forum 12: 63–83

Essay 9: 'On "Positivism" and "Legal-Rational Authority"', Oxford Journal of Legal Studies 3: 74–90

Essay 10: 'On Hart's Ways: Law as Reason and as Fact', American Journal of Jurisprudence 52: 25–53

Essay 11: 'H.L.A. Hart: A Twentieth Century Oxford Political Philosopher', American Journal of Jurisprudence 54: 161–85

Essay 12: 'On Reason and Authority in Law's Empire', Law and Philosophy 6: 357–80

Essay 13: 'On "The Critical Legal Studies Movement"', American Journal of Jurisprudence 30: 21–42

Essay 16: 'Allocating Risks and Suffering: Some Hidden Traps', Cleveland State Law Review 38: 193–207

Essay 17: 'Concluding Reflections', Cleveland State Law Rev 38: 231–50

Essay 18: 'Some Professorial Fallacies about Rights', Adelaide Law Review 4: 377–88

Essay 20: 'The Fairy Tale's Moral', Law Quarterly Review (Sweet and Maxwell) 115: 170–5

Essay 21: 'Revolutions and Continuity of Law', in A.W.B. Simpson (ed.), *Oxford Essays in Jurisprudence: Second Series* (OUP, 1971), 44–76

Essay 22: 'Helping Enact Unjust Laws without Complicity in Injustice', American Journal of Jurisprudence 49: 11–42

INDEX